BAR/BAT MITZVAH EDUCATION

A SOURCEBOOK

Helen Leneman, Editor

With a Foreword by Harold M. Schulweis

A.R.E. Publishing, Inc.
Denver, Colorado

Published by:
A.R.E. Publishing, Inc.
Denver, Colorado

Library of Congress Catalog Card Number 93-70474
ISBN 0-76705-031-4

Printed in the United States of America
10 9 8 7 6 5 4 3 2 1

DEDICATION

This book is dedicated to B'nai Mitzvah everywhere, and to Sima and Maya.

ACKNOWLEDGEMENTS

To the following individuals, I am most grateful:

Audrey Friedman Marcus and Rabbi Raymond A. Zwerin of A.R.E. Publishing, Inc. for their initial interest in this project and their encouragement and support as it progressed.

The Coalition for the Advancement of Jewish Education (CAJE) for providing a mini-grant, which not only offered financial assistance, but far more important, validated my belief in this project as one whose time had come.

Dr. Stuart Schoenfeld for reading parts of my manuscript and for his very encouraging comments.

Dr. Sima Lieberman, computer maven and editor, whose vision and constant support enabled me to complete this manuscript.

The many educators who called and wrote with enthusiastic comments and suggestions.

Everyone who sent material, whether or not it finally appeared in this work. In the process of reading through and editing the rich variety of materials sent to me, I absorbed many refreshing new ideas. These ideas inspired and aided me in the writing of these chapters, and in my own teaching. My students have been the beneficiaries of this increased creativity. It is my hope that educators who read this volume will be similarly inspired.

The sense of a vast network of dedicated professionals is very heartening. Yet, many creative educators may read sections of this book and wonder why the network did not extend to them, why their own particular programs were not included. The initial survey, which launched this book, was sent only to members (in 1991) of the CAJE Bar/Bat Mitzvah Network. I assumed that these would be the most involved and interested educators in the field, and thus most likely to respond to the questionnaire. The high percentage of responses, and the additional comments and materials sent, supported my theory. However, there are surely dozens of educators with fine and creative programs which did not find their way into this volume. *This book is only a beginning.* As new programs and ideas continue to come my way, I plan to function as a central clearinghouse and to ensure that the best of these reach everyone who might benefit. Every educator should have access to the best programs that are available. Our Bar/Bat Mitzvah students will be the beneficiaries of improved educational tools, and this will guarantee the continued growth and enrichment of our Jewish community.

CONTENTS

FOREWORD
Harold M. Schulweis ix

PREFACE xi

INTRODUCTION: SURVEY RESULTS, IMPLICATIONS, AND EVALUATION 1

UNIT I: ON THE BAR/BAT MITZVAH PROCESS
Overview 25
1 Personal Insights on Bar/Bat Mitzvah 27
Sherry H. Blumberg
2 Reflections of a Hazzan 30
Marshall Portnoy
3 Bar/Bat Mitzvah: A Window of Opportunity 36
Saul Wachs
4 Bar/Bat Mitzvah: Policies and Programs 39
Carol K. Ingall
5 My Ideal Bar/Bat Mitzvah Program 45
Jeffrey Schein
6 Personalizing Bar/Bat Mitzvah in a Large Congregation 58
Robin Eisenberg
7 Solving Problems: The Religious Practices Committee 62
George Stern
8 Setting Standards: The Bar/Bat Mitzvah Committee 73
Shoshana Silberman
9 Folk Judaism, Elite Judaism, and the Role of Bar Mitzvah in the Development of the Synagogue and Jewish School in America 78
Stuart Schoenfeld

UNIT II: THE TUTOR'S VOICE
Overview 91
10 A Tutor Reflects 93
Helen Leneman
11 "Panel": Discussion of B'nai Mitzvah Tutors 109
12 A Methodology for B'nai Mitzvah Tutoring 116
Shira Belfer
13 The Job of Tutoring B'nai Mitzvah 123
Ellen Goldenberg
14 Children with Special Learning Needs 126
Sara Rubinow Simon
15 Three Special Children 130
Helen Leneman
16 "Panel": Discussion on Tutoring Special Needs Children 133

UNIT III: TEACHING TROPE

Overview 139

17 Teaching Trope: The Hows, Whys, and Whens 141
Helen Leneman

18 "Panel": Strategies for Teaching Trope 153

19 Cantillation 156
Marshall Portnoy

20 On Teaching Trope 158
Linda Hirschhorn

21 Strategies for Teaching Trope 160
Shira Belfer

22 Trope by Computer 162
Benjamin Levy and Shira Levy

23 Trope Teaching Sources 168
Helen Leneman

UNIT IV: MITZVAH PROGRAMS

Overview 175

24 Components of a Mitzvah Program 177
Helen Leneman

25 Putting the Mitzvah Back in Bar and Bat Mitzvah 181
Jeffrey K. Salkin

26 Enriching the Bar/Bat Mitzvah Experience with a Mitzvah Program 187
Carol K. Ingall

27 "B'Mitzvotav": A Learning-through-Doing Program 194
Janice Roger

28 Becoming a Bar/Bat Mitzvah through Mitzvot 198
Marlene Myerson

UNIT V: FAMILY EDUCATION

Overview 207

29 Family Education: A Synthesis 209
Helen Leneman

30 A Maiden Voyage into Family Education Programming 213
Emily Bank

31 B'nai Mitzvah Family Education 218
David Lieb

32 *Windows* by Vicky Kelman 221
Reviewed by Helen Leneman

33 A Bar and Bat Mitzvah Family Preparation Program 223
Barry Lutz

34 A Family Workshop Program 228
Ron Aigen

35 Facilitating the B'nai Mitzvah Experience through Family Education Programming 239
Roberta Louis Goodman and Lois J. Zachary

UNIT VI: CURRICULAR AND EXTRA-CURRICULAR MATERIAL

Overview 247

36 Designing a B'nai Mitzvah Curriculum 249
Helen Leneman

37 The Dorshei Emet Pre-Bar/Bat Mitzvah Curriculum 255
Ron Aigen

38 *Coming of Age as a Jew — Bar/Bat Mitzvah* by Shoshana Glatzer 261
Reviewed by Helen Leneman

39 "Living Mitzvot": An Experiential Approach to B'nai Mitzvah Instruction 263
Allan C. Tuffs and Helen Leneman

40 *Crossing the River: An Apprenticeship Program* by Burt Jacobson 268
Reviewed by Helen Leneman

41 A Bar/Bat Mitzvah Retreat Program 273
Julie Vanek

42 *Seven Weekends that Make a Difference* by Philip Warmflash and Craig Taubman 278
Reviewed by Helen Leneman

43 A Mini-course on Writing a Drash 281
Risa Gruberger

UNIT VII: POST-B'NAI MITZVAH PROGRAMS

Overview 289

44 Post-Bar/Bat Mitzvah Education 291
Susan Protter

45 Life After Bar/Bat Mitzvah: The "Chai" Program 302
Paul Sidlofsky

UNIT VIII: SOCIAL AND PSYCHOLOGICAL ASPECTS

Overview 307

46 The Psychosocial Tasks and Opportunities of Bar/Bat Mitzvah 309
Ian Russ

47 Growing Up: Expanding our Bar and Bat Mitzvah Horizons 316
Sandy Eisenberg Sasso

48 Celebration and Negotiation: How To Keep the Divorce Battle off the Bimah 318
Sally Weber

49 The Significance of the Social Aspects of Bar/Bat Mitzvah 325
Stuart Schoenfeld

50 Para-Rabbinic and B'nai Mitzvah Counseling Program 339
Sally Shafton

BIBLIOGRAPHY 349

CONTRIBUTORS 353

Foreword

The Bar/Bat Mitzvah has been the target of caustic criticism. It is to the credit of the educators contributing to this sourcebook that while quite aware of the inadequacies of the contemporary Bar and Bat Mitzvah, they offer positive, concrete proposals based on empirical experimentation to repair the broken ceremony. The contributors are all aware of the artificiality of many of the Bar and Bat Mitzvahs resulting from the detachment from the natural process of Jewish identity and growth. They recognize that the isolation of the ceremony is symptomatic of the erosion of Jewish wholeness. And they have put their minds and hearts to doing something about this widespread malaise.

Two phenomena disturb them: riteless passages and passageless rites. There is something sad about a Jewish child who has not had a Bar or Bat Mitzvah. They have heard it said so often by adults: "I am truly sorry that I have never had a Bar/Bat Mitzvah." And even at the poorest Bar/Bat Mitzvah ceremony, there is something unique and significant that is experienced by the child. Attention is being paid to the child. In an age of inattention, it is important that the child experience the excitement of special attention. Even the sometimes maudlin remarks of parents in their address to the child enables them to express their gratitude and love out loud to the child who has not heard that praise articulated. We have witnessed the blush of pride and appreciation on the face of the youngster. The contributors are sensitive to the travesty of passageless rites, the pro forma memorization of a text that is recited, but that seems unrelated to the inner life of the child. The child senses that he or she is a performer, applauded for voice, for memory.

In common, the contributors seek to overcome the insulary character of the ceremony, and that calls for the enlargement of the Bar and Bat Mitzvah that must embrace the entire family. The Bar and Bat Mitzvah is both an individual and a familial experience. It calls for an empathic understanding of both child and parent. What is happening to our son and daughter at this stage of their lives? What is the new role assigned us as their parents? How does the wisdom of our tradition prepare us to appreciate the metamorphosis of their lives and of our own?

Each rite, from birth to death, marks a passage, from one stage of identity to another. And in each rite there is an act of continuity and an act of separation, a holding on and a letting go. We are like aerialists on a swinging trapeze, letting go of one ring to catch on to another.

The duality of holding on and letting go is true for both parent and child who celebrate the Bar/Bat Mitzvah rite of passage. Both child and parent are called upon to let go of each other in order to find other attachments. Standing on the threshold of adulthood, the adolescent lets go a part of the security of dependence. To be a Bar/Bat Mitzvah is to become a person subject to new moral and legal imperatives. This is clear from the old custom that called upon the father to pronounce a public benediction before the child completed the benediction over the Torah. The father recited, "Praised be He who has released me from the responsibility of this one." The child is now accountable and henceforth is counted in the *minyan* that constitutes community.

According to a Rabbinic insight, the *"yetzer tov"* or good inclination is developed on the thirteenth year of a child's existence (*Abot D'rabbi Nathan* 16:3). Before the thirteenth year, the libido prevailed; on the thirteenth year, conscience is born. With that birth, the parents must let go. It is a release of courage and wisdom. The parent must step back a little so as to allow the adolescent to step forward. The Bar/Bat Mitzvah at the synagogue service stands on his/her two feet to lead the congregation in prayer and to read the Torah without parental support. The first of the blessings on the occasion of the child's birth — study of Torah, marital canopy, practices of good deeds, has been publicly fulfilled. The induction of the child into maturity is exhibited through the mastery of the biblical text.

The reins of the family circle are loosened, and that is good, because adolescents need the opportunity for aloneness. Parents, too, need distance. When parents live for or through their child, they violate not only their own growth, but that of their child.

A child is not ours. A child is not created in our image to be shaped and formed in accordance with our ambitions. A child is created in God's image and therein lies the child's reality, identity, and worth. This principle which underlies the *brit* (covenant) and *pidyon haben* (redemption) embraces the Bar/Bat Mitzvah rite. Parents must be reminded that they are not owners but custodians of a child's life. A child is not slave to our ambitions. There is no privately owned creation.

At the Bar/Bat Mitzvah ceremony, parents accompany their children to the threshold of adulthood. This life passage requires courage to hold on and let go . . . with wisdom. Nissin Ezekiel, a Jewish poet in India, spoke the prayers of loving parents:

> "Protect my children
> from my secret wish
> to make them over
> in my image and illusions.
> Let them move
> to the music that they love
> dissonant perhaps to me."

Harold M. Schulweis, Rabbi
Valley Beth Shalom
Encino, California

Preface

Bar/Bat Mitzvah education is a key concern of most synagogue Religious Schools. This is so for practical as well as philosophical reasons. The year of the Bar/Bat Mitzvah is seen as a crucial window of opportunity. Through this window, schools can take advantage of a "captive audience." It is a well-known fact that many families join synagogues primarily in order to have a place for their child's Bar/Bat Mitzvah ceremony.

The simple rationale behind this book is this: knowing we have this unique window of opportunity, we should find ways of opening it further. Many fine Bar/Bat Mitzvah programs have been created locally with no hope of reaching a national audience of educators. With the goal of establishing a "central clearinghouse," I began, through a national survey, to solicit ideas and programs. This book — the end result of that search — contains descriptions of a wide range of programs, viewpoints, practical and pedagogical approaches, from Reform, Conservative, and Reconstructionist educators. Solutions to many commonly cited problems in Bar/Bat Mitzvah education can be found in these pages. It is my hope that the high quality of the material presented here will inspire all of us to continue thinking creatively and seeking new solutions to our problems. This book was written by and for you, the Bar/Bat Mitzvah educators.

A wide variety of topics is covered, from the general to the extremely specific. The more general chapters are of interest and use to everyone involved directly or peripherally with B'nai Mitzvah education, as a source of information or to stimulate new thinking and increase understanding of the whole process. The more specific chapters are useful for those who work directly with B'nai Mitzvah students: Directors of Education (this term is used throughout to include all of those who run schools, whatever their titles), Cantors, Rabbis, tutors, and Family Education Directors. All chapters will be of use to a synagogue seeking to start, expand, or improve its Bar/Bat Mitzvah program.

The Introduction to this book which follows this Preface, "Survey Results, Implications, and Evaluation," is critical reading for an understanding of the issues and results of the national survey upon which this book is based. Here you will find an overview of what works and what everyone else is doing. Following is a brief summary of the contents of each Unit. More detailed descriptions of the chapters are outlined in the Overviews for each Unit.

Unit I, "The Educator's Viewpoint," contains personal reflections of several professionals with many years of experience in the field of B'nai Mitzvah education. These include three Professors of Jewish Education (one of whom is also a Rabbi), a sociologist, and a Cantor.

Unit II, "The Religious School Viewpoint," highlights solutions to common problems in B'nai Mitzvah programs that can be sought through committees, by the Director of Education alone, or by the Religious School working together with families. These different approaches are presented anecdotally.

The survey showed that about 75% of the training of all our B'nai Mitzvah students is entrusted to professional tutors. Unit III, "The Tutor's Voice," offers a broad cross-section of approaches described by tutors and by Cantors who tutor.

These chapters will give tutors — and the synagogue educational leaders for whom they work — an opportunity to compare and contrast a variety of tutoring methods. This Unit also includes several chapters on strategies for tutoring special needs children.

Unit IV is called "Teaching Trope." Trope is a multifaceted, challenging skill for B'nai Mitzvah students to master. While taught primarily in traditional synagogues, more and more liberal synagogues are now teaching trope as well. Methods of teaching trope vary greatly, and this Unit presents a wide spectrum of equally valid approaches. Those who teach trope will glean many new ideas from these chapters. Synagogues considering adding trope to their curriculum, or wanting to improve the way it is presently taught, will also benefit.

Unit V, "Mitzvah Programs," describes programs that add a *mitzvah* component to Bar/Bat Mitzvah training. Children learn the true meaning of *mitzvot* best by doing them; this is the rationale for Mitzvah Programs. The reader will find much practical information for creating such a program from scratch, or improving an existing one.

Family Education is a rapidly growing field in religious education. The chapters in Unit VI, "Family Education," contain descriptions of successful Family Education programs and describe some of the newest programs available. Here, too, the descriptions are detailed enough to help the reader start such a program from scratch or to inject new ideas into an already existing program.

Uniquely innovative curricula, largely unknown, are reviewed in Unit VII, "Curricular and Extra-Curricular Material." It is hoped that such programs will be widely emulated and that they will stimulate the creation of more such material in congregations.

Low retention after Bar and Bat Mitzvah is a common complaint from Religious Schools. The two chapters in Unit VIII, "Post B'nai Mitzvah Programs," call attention to the need to inspire students to continue their religious education after Bar/Bat Mitzvah. The authors argue for a radically different approach in these grades so that students feel they have undergone a rite of passage. These chapters should challenge the reader to begin building the foundation of a strong post-B'nai Mitzvah program.

Underlying all Bar/Bat Mitzvah education must be an understanding of adolescents. Unit IX, "Social and Psychological Aspects," reflects the diverse viewpoints of a Rabbi, sociologist, psychologist, and social worker and provides crucial information for anyone working with adolescents.

As the completion of this volume drew near, buds were appearing on the tree branches outside my study window. Those same buds had shown themselves a year ago, when I sat down to launch this project, never dreaming how enriching, fulfilling — and overwhelming — a task I was undertaking!

As I once again watched flowers appear, it occurred to me that a garden metaphor is perfect for our work of teaching B'nai Mitzvah students. We Jewish educators are all Johnny and Janie Appleseeds, planting seeds, visualizing wonderful future gardens filled with trees and flowers, but never really knowing which seeds will sprout and bloom. Many will lie dormant for years. Yet, we all know stories of the bored, rebellious student who never paid attention in Religious School, who then became a Rabbi or a Jewish scholar.

To carry the metaphor further, we are all trying to improve the quality of the seeds we plant, as well as the method of planting, watering, and nurturing our garden as it begins to grow. The garden of Jewish knowledge is an eternal and infinitely varied one. It needs constant care, and the continual planting of new seeds. Think of this book as one large "seed catalogue," and find new varieties to plant for *your* garden.

Introduction

Survey Results, Implications, and Evaluation

Helen Leneman

INTRODUCTION

In 1991, a questionnaire concerning Bar/Bat Mitzvah practices was sent to 320 Jewish educators (see Appendix). All of the recipients were part of the Coalition for the Advancement of Jewish Education (CAJE) Bar/Bat Mitzvah Network in the U.S., Canada, England, Australia, and Israel. Each of these individuals was, at that time, a member of CAJE who had enrolled in the Network in order to keep up with the latest developments in Bar/Bat Mitzvah education. Of the 320 questionnaires sent, 116 responses were received.

The over-arching goal in conducting this survey and in the subsequent compiling of this book has been the improvement of Bar/Bat Mitzvah programs. It was the intention to ascertain from the survey the programs that are currently in use, to determine the main reasons for satisfaction or dissatisfaction with present programs, to uncover solutions that have been found to pressing problems, and to share all of this information with others in the field. Hopefully, readers of this volume will be stimulated to evaluate and to enrich the Bar/Bat Mitzvah programs for which they are responsible.

In a letter attached to the questionnaire, six key concerns were delineated for respondents:

1. Deficient Hebrew skills for adequate Bar/Bat Mitzvah preparation.
2. Lack of sufficient exposure to Torah and Prophets prior to and in the seventh grade.
3. Lack of time, motivation, and teachers for trope skills.
4. Poor understanding of the concept of Bar/Bat Mitzvah.
5. Lack of parental involvement.
6. Lack of commitment to continuing religious education after Bar/Bat Mitzvah.

The results of the survey proved that these concerns represent very real problems, although the problem of "emphasis on the *bar* and not the *mitzvah*" was more predominant than others (see Table 17). In many instances, solutions to these problems have been sought through special synagogue programs. Many such programs are described in the different chapters of this book.

It was of interest to determine how dependent the answers to the questionnaire were on the following variables: congregation size, affiliation, and in some cases, the number of B'nai Mitzvah a year. The last variable affects the work load, while the congregation size influences the number of resources available. The tables were therefore constructed accordingly.

The questions asked in the survey were aimed at discovering the priorities of a given synagogue and its Religious School. The long-term goals of a Religious School, however, can differ from the more short-term goals and objectives of a Bar/Bat Mitzvah program, which is not necessarily linked to the Religious School. A Bar/Bat Mitzvah program may be run by the Cantor, Rabbi, and one or more professional tutors, none of whom work within the Religious School program. The course of study offered depends on these priorities and goals as much as on available time, staff, and budget. While priorities may be known or discerned from the survey results, the underlying reason or philosophy behind those priorities is not. It would have been helpful to sit down with each respondent and discuss these questions individually. Nonetheless, with the results obtained, certain patterns emerge.

Some of the findings in the following tables could be useful for those setting up a Bar/Bat Mitzvah program from scratch. And, educators ready for a change will also find these results of value. Additionally, these survey results will provide a clue as to "what works" in the area of Bar/Bat Mitzvah programming.

RESULTS AND IMPLICATIONS OF B'NAI MITZVAH SURVEY

Of the 116 responses to the survey, 61 were from Reform congregations, 47 from Conservative, and 8 from another movement or unaffiliated. The samples from this last group were too small to include in the results. It was not possible to know what percentage of each movement responded, because affiliation was not always known at the time of the mailing.

Geographically, the Northeast is disproportionately represented. A total of 51 responses came from the Northeast, 21 from the Midwest, 18 from the West, 16 from the Southeast, 5 from the South, 3 from Canada, and 1 from Brazil.

Each table will be introduced and its implications discussed. Following this, evaluations and recommendations will be offered. The "N" (number of respondents) varies in each Table, because not everyone answered every question. In this survey, I have grouped congregations into four size categories (A, B, C, and D). The smallest size congregation (under 250 family units) is called "A", the next size (250-500) is "B", the third (500-1000) is "C", and the largest size (over 1000) is "D". The number of B'nai Mitzvah in a year was not entirely dependent on the congregation size, although, of course, there is a correlation. Obviously, that number is most clearly linked to the average age of the congregants. What is clear from this table is that the average number of B'nai Mitzvah is related to congregation size, but the range (lowest number to highest number of B'nai Mitzvah) is quite variable. The responses were as follows:

TABLE 1

Size	*# of respondents*	*Average # of B'nai Mitzvah*	*Range*
		Reform	
A	15	10	3-20
B	19	28	12-85
C	17	40	12-90
D	10	65	32-125
		Conservative	
A	9	9	3-15
B	22	21	5-75
C	12	29	10-75
D	4	51	40-60

The possible number of B'nai Mitzvah for a given size congregation has a very wide range. This was taken into account in several of the questions, and responses were based on numbers of B'nai Mitzvah in addition to congregation size. It was assumed that larger congregations have greater resources and would therefore accomplish more. However, this does not take into account what dedication can accomplish, regardless of financial resources. In that regard, the results that follow are very instructional.

The most obvious conclusion one could draw from the above chart is that Conservative congregations are rarely as large as Reform (compare highest two numbers: 125 Reform vs. 60 Conservative). But that is not a fair conclusion based on a random sample. There is no way of knowing how many Conservative "D" size congregations did not respond, or if the CAJE network is a random or skewed sample of synagogues. Based on this sample, however, more B'nai Mitzvah do seem to be trained in Reform congregations, relative to size, which may only indicate that these are often younger congregations. It may also indicate that families in Conservative congregations tend to remain members long after their children become B'nai Mitzvah, whereas there may be more of a tendency to drop out of synagogue life in the Reform movement. These hypotheses would require further evaluation.

SECTION 1: GENERAL

Part I: Who is Responsible for Training the B'nai Mitzvah?

The matter of who trains B'nai Mitzvah is crucial, because the one-on-one experience with either a tutor, Cantor, Rabbi, or a combination of these, will ultimately determine if the whole experience for the Bar/Bat Mitzvah child is a positive or negative one. Who actually trains the B'nai Mitzvah students is probably dependent more on the number of B'nai Mitzvah per year than on congregation size, but results were tallied both ways.

The term "train," of course, is open to interpretation. For example, many respondents clarified that the Rabbi's role was limited to two sessions of hearing the student's speech; others wrote that the Cantor checked up on the student only in the last few weeks. But most did not specify what they meant by "training," so that this ambiguity should be kept in mind when reading these results. For the purposes of these results, training means skills mastery. However, Rabbis in larger congregations are rarely involved in this aspect. So when "Rabbi" is checked off, it is assumed that speech preparation and general discussions were put in the "training" category by that respondent. One thing to observe is a shift in the pattern of who does the training, as the congregation size increases. This is true for both movements. In Table 2, "Combined" means the Rabbi, Cantor, or professional tutor does the training in tandem with one or more other professionals. There were any number of combinations possible: Cantor and Rabbi, Cantor and professional tutor, Rabbi and lay person, or even three or four of these together.

As stated earlier, the variation in the "N" is due to the fact that not every respondent answered every question. For example, some failed to indicate either the size of their congregation or the number of B'nai Mitzvah.

The combinations, as stated above, could include all of the professionals in different combinations, along with occasionally a Hebrew School teacher or teenage tutors. The last two categories of individuals do not appear in the table, but are sometimes involved in training B'nai Mitzvah. It should be kept in mind that who does the training depends on what is taught in this "training," both in terms of quantity and subject matter.

The category of lay educators appeared only once, in 33% of the "A" size Conservative congregations. Many congregations indicated a need for more tutors, so it seems worth exploring the idea of utilizing resources already present in congregations. The Reform congregations represented in this survey, and possibly in general, are far more reliant on professional tutors, even in smaller congregations. This could imply less of a "family feeling" than might be achieved when lay members of a congregation are involved in the training of other congregants' children.

These results also show a striking difference between the two movements in the roles assigned to Rabbi and Cantor. In those congregations with few B'nai Mitzvah, the Reform Rabbi is almost exclusively in charge of the training. On the other hand, the Conservative Rabbi has a smaller role in this training than does the Cantor who has traditionally been seen as the clergy in charge of B'nai Mitzvah students. In the Reform movement, the Cantor takes on an increasingly larger role in the training as the congregation size grows. These differences are due partly to traditions in the movements, but also to the different training Cantors receive.

The trend toward increasing the Cantor's role is already visible in medium-size Reform congregations. The professional tutor plays a larger part there also, and the Rabbi assumes less responsibility. The Cantor in mid-size congregations is solely responsible for the training exactly twice as often as his/her Reform counterpart.

In mid-size congregations, the only significant difference between the figures based on congregation size, and those based on numbers of B'nai Mitzvah, is the larger presence of the Rabbi, though only in

Table 2

Who Trains the B'nai Mitzvah?

Size	*R1*	*R2*	*C1*	*C2*	*P1*	*P2*	*N*
Reform							
A	50%	50%	0	13%	0	26%	15
B	0	37%	20%	31%	20%	37%	19
C	0	59%	12%	35%	18%	59%	16
D	0	50%	0	70%	0	70%	10
Conservative							
A	33%	22%	0	0	0	0	9
B	0	10%	40%	35%	15%	25%	20
C	0	0	54%	41%	0	15%	13
D	0	0	25%	50%	0	75%	4
Reform							
Under 10	54%	38%	0	0	0	0	13
10-300	0	55%	15%	33%	18%	44%	27
30-500	0	5%	0	62%	25%	75%	8
Over 50	0	46%	23%	46%	0	61%	13
Conservative							
Under 10	19%	25%	37%	19%	0	0	16
10-300	0	10%	42%	31%	16%	16%	19
30-500	0	0	40%	60%	0	60%	5
Over 50	0	25%	25%	50%	0	50%	4

Key to Table 2:

R1: Rabbi only
R2: Rabbi in combination with others
C1: Cantor only
C2: Cantor in combination with others
P1: Professional tutor(s) only
P2: Professional tutor(s) in combination with others

combination with other professionals. Whenever these "combinations" are indicated, the precise roles are not clearly spelled out. In other words, the proportion and nature of work done by each professional involved is not described in any detail.

It is interesting that the proportion of use of professional tutors and the Cantor in combination with others is about the same in mid-size congregations of both movements. The only striking difference, again, is the vastly larger role of the Cantor in this area in Conservative congregations, and the smaller role of the Rabbi, compared to these two clergy in Reform congregations. Again, the reasons can probably be found in the training they receive and in denominational expectations.

In larger Reform congregations, the professional tutor and Rabbi are again seen in equal numbers, combined with other professionals (including one another). In the larger Conservative congregations, on the other hand, the Cantor is involved in virtually all the training, either alone or with other professionals (some teenage tutors are used at this level in addition to professional tutors). In these larger congregations, the Rabbi seems to have no role in specifically training B'nai Mitzvah.

In the larger congregations, professional tutors are utilized more. These tutors are involved 100% of the time in Reform congregations, either alone or with others, and 60% in Conservative congregations. The Cantor, who has a role in every size Conservative congregation, in larger congregations represented here is involved in literally 100% of the training. In the case of both the tutors and the Cantor, there is variability in what that 100% may entail, due to the nebulous nature of the term "train," and the standards and requirements which vary among congregations. For example, there might be differences in approach, in frequency of lessons, length of time of these lessons, as well as differences in the number of professionals involved in the training, and how that training is divided up among them. In most cases, when professional tutors are involved, they generally do at least 75% of the actual teaching of skills. In those cases, the Cantor and Rabbi do mostly "polishing" at the end, rehearsals, and work on the speech.

The largest congregations all depend on a team effort of one kind or another. The Rabbi in Reform congregations appears to be much more involved than his/her Conservative counterpart, but this could be partly due to the frequent presence of two or more Rabbis on the staff of the largest synagogues. Figures for the two movements are closer when compared based on numbers of B'nai Mitzvah than on congregation size.

It seems quite remarkable that a Cantor working alone would be able to train over 50 B'nai Mitzvah a year. The numbers of these samples are small: 13 Reform, and only 4 Conservative, so the results may be a bit skewed. It is still interesting that only in the largest congregations do the Conservative Rabbi and Reform Cantor play a greater role. Possibly there is a need to escape the sense of the impersonal in very large congregations that intensifies the need of a clerical presence in every area.

These results show a great reliance on professional tutors in most synagogues of average to large size. A thorough and large scale survey has yet to be done, and should be done, showing who these tutors are, what their qualifications are, where they received their training, and what methodology they use. (See Chapter 10 for a discussion of the Editor's experiences as a professional tutor. Chapters 11-16 offer the viewpoints and methodologies of several other full-time professional tutors.) The other obvious result is the variable role played by the Cantor and Rabbi, depending on congregation size, numbers of B'nai Mitzvah, and affiliation. Chapters 2 and 3 present perspectives on the level of clergy involvement in B'nai Mitzvah training. On the whole, there seems to be a feeling among both the clergy and laity that more contact between B'nai Mitzvah with Rabbi and Cantor is desirable. Based on these feelings, clergy may want to consider a reordering of their priorities.

Part 2: What Do B'nai Mitzvah Learn for their Ceremony?

This question of what B'nai Mitzvah learn for their ceremony refers to the amount of liturgy, Torah, and Haftarah learned by the students. The choice of what is taught involves the philosophies and priorities of the Religious School, congregation, and professional and lay leaders. In some cases, the choices are made based mainly on tradition: for example, in a majority of Conservative synagogues, the Bar/Bat Mitzvah chants the Haftarah portion in its entirety.

When reading these results, it must be kept in mind that there are major differences in the two movements, especially in the area of liturgy. If a child does "all" the liturgy of the Shabbat service in a Reform synagogue, the amount of Hebrew and *nusach* learned is a fraction of that of his/her Conservative counterpart. On the other hand, the priorities of the Reform movement are different, as is (usually) the amount of time spent in Religious School every week where there has been less stress on Hebrew and more on a study of the heritage.

The word "learn" itself has layers of meaning: understand, analyze, memorize, to name only a few. The quality is far more important than the quantity, but only the latter can be statistically measured. Bearing this in mind, for the question in Table 3, the number of Torah verses learned, the range of answers was enormous, and responses had to be categorized. When the answer was "3", it was assumed that that was the same as *Maftir,* which is usually 3 verses.

Results were initially tabulated according to congregation size, but the differences were not significant, so they are presented here based on affiliation only.

Table 3
Number of Torah Verses Learned

Responses:

# of verses	*% Reform doing*	*% Conservative doing*
3	6%	28%
3 minimum	0	44%
4-9	10%	0
6-12	18%	6%
12-21	50%	4%
21-30	10%	0
As much as possible	4%	12%
	N=61	N=47

In addition to these responses, one Reform respondent wrote "up to 40," one Conservative respondent wrote "all," and one wrote "none." In general, these results show a much greater variability in number of verses done in Reform congregations, as well as a larger number of verses. This reflects the value placed on individual choice in the Reform movement, as well as the stress on Torah. The Conservative movement has traditionally placed much greater emphasis on mastering a Haftarah portion than on chanting additional Torah verses. For this reason, the difference between the movements was far greater in the question about number of Haftarah verses learned (Table 4). The variability within the Reform movement was also greater, again reflecting the philosophy of freedom of choice.

One Reform respondent wrote "none." As will be shown in a later question (see Table 11), the fact that B'nai Mitzvah are expected to master a Haftarah portion does not necessarily imply they study the Prophets in any depth at any stage in their Religious School training. The Conservative movement views Haftarah chanting as a skill, one which can be used repeatedly throughout one's life as a synagogue going Jew. Chanting Torah is seen as a life skill only in those synagogues (mostly Conservative) that do not employ a professional Torah reader, but encourage their own congregants to be Torah readers. In such congregations, there is also more motivation for B'nai Mitzvah to master Torah trope and attain superior Hebrew skills, as there are lay role models to emulate. Many Reform congregations, on the other hand, do not hold Shabbat morning services when there is no Bar/Bat Mitzvah ceremony. Therefore, there would be no occasion for a congregant at such a synagogue to utilize the skill of either Torah or Haftarah chanting. Ideologically, also, the Reform movement tends to give more thought to the content and relevance of all aspects of the service, rather than to reusable skills. These different philosophies are quite visible in the responses to later questions (see Table 15).

Table 4
Number of Haftarah Verses Learned

# of verses	*% Reform*	*% Conservative*
3-5	12%	0
6-12	38%	0
12-20 (or ½)	20%	8%
As much as possible	6%	4%
All	10%	87%
All in English	12%	0
	N=60	N=47

In regard to the next question, how much of the liturgy the students learn (Table 5), remember that "all" for the Reform movement is seen as a substantial accomplishment, within the context of that movement, given the amount of hours of Religious School a week, even if the actual amount learned is a fraction of what the Conservative service would be. In addition, the fact that the Bar/Bat Mitzvah ceremony is often more central in a Reform synagogue, since it might be the reason a Shabbat service is being held, also accounts for the greater participation of the Bar or Bat Mitzvah in the service. A differentiation is made between the response "as much as possible" and "depends," because though in reality these may mean the same thing, there is a difference in *attitude* between those two responses. "Depends" implies a high degree of respect for individual differences in ability, while "as much as possible" implies a desire to push all students to achieve the maximum. This describes a more ambitious program.

Table 5

How Much of the Service?

Amount done	*% Reform*	*% Conservative*
None	13%	0
Some	23%	60%
Most	25%	13%
All	31%	2%
Depends	8%	8%
As much as possible	0	15%
	N=61	N=47

A very small number of respondents checked "other" as an additional part of the Bar/Bat Mitzvah's requirements. Many others may have such requirements, but respondents could have assumed that they were too standard to bear mentioning. In any case, of those that did answer the question in Table 6, all said the other requirement was "speech" or "*drash*." (A distinction is made between the two, since a speech may be a *drash* about the Torah portion, but may also be many other things.)

Table 6

What Else Do They Learn for the Service?

What they do%	*Reform*	*% Conservative*
Speech	63%	40%
Drash	37%	60%
	N=16	N=10

Part 3: Where is the Primary Stress?

The question of where the primary stress is (Table 7) may seem redundant after the above questions have been answered. But this was a check for consistency. In other words, are synagogues teaching more of those parts of the service they want to stress? One Cantor had a clever response to this question: "All are equally stressful!"

Table 7

Where Is the Primary Stress?

Subject & Ranking	*% Reform*	*% Conservative*
Torah #1	69%	4%
#2	23%	46%
#3	3%	35%
Haft. #1	11%	89%
#2	28%	6%
#3	38%	0
Prayer #1	38%	15%
#2	26%	38%
#3	18%	35%
	N=61	N=45

Because respondents often rated more than one subject as #1, the percentages do not total 100%. Between 6-8% of respondents, of both affiliations, listed a speech or *drash* as #3 or #4 in importance. The same percentage of Reform respondents listed these two, or a *mitzvah* project, as #1. In terms of stress placed on learning Haftarah or Torah, this chart is certainly consistent with Tables 3 and 4.

In terms of the importance of prayer, the question of which aspect of prayer is important to the respondent (understanding the words or general sense, or mastering the Hebrew, or both) was not addressed. The term "leading service" is also used, and this is not the same as learning the meanings of prayers. This has a certain connotation of a performance, and many synagogues reject this idea because they want a Bar or Bat Mitzvah ceremony to be part of a regular Shabbat service. On the other hand, nothing can stimulate a child to learn this service better than knowing he/she will actually be leading the congregation in the prayers. In any case, just over a third of the Reform responses indicated that leading the service was ranked first, and a quarter of them ranked it second. About a third of the Conservatives ranked it either second or third. It is interesting to compare these figures to those in Table 5, where it can be seen that about 75% of students in both movements do at least some, or most, of the service. This could show that synagogues are following certain traditions in what they train the

B'nai Mitzvah students to do, but philosophically they do not necessarily agree that this is where the stress should be. The policy makers and those asked to implement those policies are not often the same people. There are even cases in which the original policy maker retired years earlier, but the congregation has certain expectations that the newer staff members are expected to realize. It is also possible that those answering the questionnaire are not the policymakers in that synagogue, and are not very familiar with all the policies.

Part 4: Do They Read or chant Their Portions?

One of the motives in asking this question was to discover how much has changed in the Reform movement, which at one time rejected the idea of chanting Torah and Haftarah portions, as well as teaching the trope system (Table 8). The enormous variability of practice within the Reform movement that emerged in the survey was a surprise, as was the totally monolithic character of the Conservative movement, in which 100% of students chant. It was conceivable that the variability in Reform practice might depend on congregation size, so the responses were tabulated this way. But the results showed no dependence on size; therefore, these answers have been combined.

Table 8

Do They Read or Chant?

What they do	*% Reform doing this*	*% Conserv.*
Chant	28%	100%
Read	10%	0
More chant than read	11%	0
More read than chant	11%	0
Depends (on ability)	26%	0
Read Torah, Chant Haftarah	6%	0
Chant Torah, Read Haftarah	6%	0
	N=61	N=47

If all the possible combinations that include chanting are totalled, about 75% of B'nai Mitzvah in Reform congregations are chanting. This result may surprise some readers, but it does indicate a trend in the Reform movement back to more traditional practices. At the same time, the variability is indicative again of the Reform philosophy of free choice.

The question of choice comes up in the next question: "Do they get a choice between reading or chanting?" This elicited some emotional responses, in the frequent presence of an exclamation point after the "No!" And, in fact, 100% of the Conservative respondents answered this question in the negative, often emphatically. Several of the Reform answers were "Of course they do!" as if freedom of choice were an unquestioned right of all students. A total of 58% of Reform respondents answered yes to this question, while the remaining 42% answered no, which is a surprise and not in keeping with the emphasis on free choice. However, this may be a transition period; in some Reform congregations it may be felt that if they want the teaching of trope to become standard, they must initially impose this teaching on B'nai Mitzvah students *without* a choice.

The question of whether students learn the trope system, memorize the portion of the Torah from a tape, or both learn the system and get a tape (Table 9), is a very touchy issue in many congregations. Very briefly, the pros and cons of each are these: just learning the trope system is extremely challenging for students, and those gifted enough to master it enjoy the challenge. But many are not gifted or motivated enough to master it and to use the skill to learn a Haftarah and/or Torah portion without a tape. Just giving out tapes teaches no skill and does not even encourage the student to master the Hebrew of the portion. It is quick and easy, though, and a necessary method when no teacher is available to teach trope. Teaching trope *and* giving a tape is a method that simply makes the whole process less daunting for the less musically gifted, and provides a backup for students who do not see their tutors that often. As is seen in Chapter 17, the majority of students who have mastered trope refuse to listen to the tape, because they prefer the greater challenge.

Table 9

Do They Learn Trope, Get a Tape, or Both?

What they do	*% Reform*	*% Conservative*
Learn trope only	4%	21%
Get a tape only	45%	13%
Both	51%	66%
	N=57	N=47

Several respondents said students learn trope, but in a later question, indicated that trope is not taught at their synagogue. In checking back with some of these respondents, it was learned that trope is taught by professional tutors outside the Religious School. It is still the synagogue leadership making the decision that the students should learn the trope system.

There are more specific questions about teaching trope in the next section, Specific Subject Areas. The most surprising result in Table 9 above is that less than a fourth of Conservative congregations depend exclusively on students learning the system (no tape is given out). It is also somewhat surprising that 13% do not teach the system at all, but only give out tapes. The practice of doing a combination of these two is done by more Conservative than Reform congregations, but there is not as large a spread as might have been expected. There does not seem to be any size-based difference in these responses. The choices are probably based on philosophy and tradition, in addition to more practical concerns such as availability of tutors and time factors. This question is an example of measuring quality, not quantity alone. Even though there are congregations which, because of the dearth of tutors, cannot teach trope even if they want to, there can be no question that teaching the trope system is teaching mastery of a skill (quality teaching), whereas memorizing a portion from a tape is pure rote learning (teaching quantity of verses only — no quality).

The newest method for teaching and learning trope and portions is computer software. About a hundred congregations have begun using software, and chances are in another generation, cassette tapes will be as passé as records are now. The creators of Lev Software discuss this latest technological development in Chapter 22.

SECTION II: SPECIFIC SUBJECT AREAS

Part 1: Hebrew

Many respondents not connected to a synagogue Religious School could not answer the question about testing students at the end of the school year (Table 10). This problem was not foreseen prior to sending out the questionnaires. In other cases, especially responses from Canada, individual synagogues do not offer a Religious School; children attend one of several community afternoon schools. Also in Canada, many Conservative affiliated families send their children to one of the three branches of the United Synagogue Day Schools (the Conservative day schools) or to the nominally Orthodox Associated Hebrew Schools. Most Conservative congregations do have their own afternoon schools, at least in Toronto.

This question was asked to determine how common "tracking" is. If students are regularly checked and offered extra help when they fall behind, Hebrew deficiencies in B'nai Mitzvah students would be minimized.

Here are the results of this question (keeping in mind they are based on a smaller sample than other responses):

Table 10

Are Students Tested/
What are the Consequences?

Do you test students?	*% Reform*	*% Conservative*
Yes	77%	67%
No	23%	33%
	N=57	N=37
What do you do if they fail?		
Insist on extra tutoring	43%	48%
Offer remedial work	15%	16%
	N=39	N=26

Many respondents ignored the second part of the question regarding failing. That may either mean they do nothing, or they thought it was too obvious to answer. A few actually wrote that they do nothing. One answered that the tests are so easy, no one fails.

Other solutions proposed were: the parents tutor the failing students, Bar/Bat Mitzvah is delayed, the school or the teacher is notified, a complaint is lodged against the teacher, the Rabbi talks to the teacher. Among the less effective solutions proposed were to give the student a second chance, or to retest until he/she passes.

As seen in Table 17 below, Hebrew is perceived as an area fraught with difficulties. Many tutors have had to train students who did not yet know the complete *alef bet*, but they had no say in whether such a student should rightfully become Bar or Bat Mitzvah in a public ceremony. Yet, based on the responses in Table 13 below, not much creative energy has yet been expended on this problem. Of the many interesting and innovative programs received from respondents, only a handful dealt seriously with improving Hebrew skills prior to and during seventh grade. (Actually, many schools *drop* Hebrew in seventh grade, assuming the students have already had enough!)

Part 2: Torah/Haftarah

The question of in what grades Torah and Haftarah are taught (Table 11), and with what stress (see Appendix), had the same built-in problem as the previous question. Too many respondents were unfamiliar with the Religious School curriculum. It is particularly alarming how many Cantors and Rabbis could not answer this question for that reason.

The other difficulty with this question was in the meaning of "taught"; when Torah is "taught" in primary grades, that teaching is not the same as it would be in the seventh grade. Also, some respondents probably misunderstood the question, and assumed it meant when are B'nai Mitzvah students taught to read or chant Torah and Haftarah, not when are they taught about Torah and Haftarah in Religious School. This also suggests two different kinds of teaching, since *meaning* is more likely to be emphasized in classes, while teaching for the Bar/Bat Mitzvah ceremony itself is more likely teaching to read and/or chant a specific portion.

There was enormous variety in the responses to this question; in fact, practically no two were alike. In addition, several respondents used the Hebrew classifications for grades: *"Daled"*, *"Hey"*, etc., not realizing this was meaningless because these letters stand for different grades in different synagogues (it depends on what year the Religious School starts). Therefore, those responses could not be included. Since the focus here is on training for B'nai Mitzvah students, the responses were classified accordingly.

Table 11
In What Grades are Torah and Prophets Taught?

Grades	*% Reform*	*% Conservative*
Torah		
All grades	18%	32%
Sixth, along with others	52%	73%
Seventh, along with others	67%	62%
	N=48	N=37
Prophets		
Sixth, along with others	37%	40%
Seventh, along with others	33%	33%
	N=43	N=30

This table shows a slightly higher percentage of Conservative congregations teaching Torah throughout, except in the seventh grade, when the two movements place equal stress on this study. These results are not surprising, considering the fact that students at Conservative congregations must attend Hebrew School three days a week, while those in Reform attend once or twice, and for shorter hours. Yet, there is inconsistency when this table is compared to Table 7. If the greatest stress in 69% of Reform B'nai Mitzvah ceremonies is Torah, why is there not more Torah in the curriculum? This may again be a case of non-integration between the "program" and the school.

There is a similar inconsistency in Conservative congregations, in terms of Haftarah. There are very few areas where the responses of the two movements are so close! And yet, the greatest stress in 89% of Conservative congregations is chanting Haftarah (Table 7 above). It seems more than inconsistent to teach the subject matter contained in that Haftarah portion to fewer than half of the sixth and seventh grade classes. The mastery of a Haftarah portion would surely be more meaningful to a student who has some understanding of that prophet's historical context and the meaning of some of the key Hebrew words. Of course, the private tutor can cover this material with the student, but probably rarely does. And in any case, that cannot be a substitute for a fully integrated curriculum which includes some in-depth study of the prophets and the prophetic tradition.

The last part to this question, regarding the emphasis in these classes (see Appendix), was subject to the same problem as the other parts: lack of knowledge of the Religious School curriculum. Also, the stress changes throughout the curriculum, being totally different in seventh than in third grade. "Narrative" would obviously be the stress in an earlier grade, and "*midrashic* understanding" in a later grade. Virtually no one circled "translating," and several wrote in "concepts, values, relevance." The question was obviously too complex to be boiled down this way, and for that reason, the responses were not tabulated.

Part 3: Trope

When framing the question of whether or not trope is taught (Table 12), which trope (Torah or Haftarah) was not specified. It is clear from the Conservative respondents' answers that in most cases respondents are referring to Haftarah trope. The expression "for future use" was explained in an earlier section. Basically, if a synagogue has a tradition of teenage and adult congregants chanting Torah and/or Haftarah at Shabbat services, this creates a future use for the skill. Other respondents may feel this is a skill any Jew should master, for use in any congregation throughout his or her lifetime. About a third of the respondents, of both movements, left this question blank, as is reflected in the much smaller sample sizes (N). Teaching or not teaching trope may be synagogue policy, the reasons for which may be unknown to the respondent. In some cases, the reasons may predate the present policymakers, as mentioned earlier. Nonetheless, definite trends emerge.

Table 12

Do You Teach the Trope System? Why/Why Not?

Do you teach it?	*% Reform*	*% Conservative*
Yes	35%	82%
No	51%	13%
To some	13%	4%
	N=60	N=46
Why?		
It is authentic	14%	25%
For future use	50%	54%
It makes it easier	36%	21%
	N=14	N=24
Why not?		
No time	21%	25%
No staff	29%	75%
No interest or future use	25%	0
Combination of these	25%	0
	N=24	N=4

Some of the Conservative respondents made additional comments. For example, "It is very important to keep alive and use the skill" and "An educated Jew should know trope, not just for the purpose of becoming Bar/Bat Mitzvah." To reinforce the frequently cited motive of "future use," some congregations actually assign another Torah and/or Haftarah reading subsequent to the date of the Bar/Bat Mitzvah ceremony. This seems an excellent way of getting across the idea that the Bar/Bat Mitzvah ceremony is a beginning, not an end.

A comparison of this Table with Tables 8 and 9 above shows general agreement. Presumably, the 13% of Conservative congregations not teaching trope are the same 13% that only give out tapes. The same 51% of Reform congregations not teaching trope are the same ones not asking B'nai Mitzvah to chant.

Fewer than half of the Reform congregations responded to the next question regarding the grade in which trope is taught (Table 13), because obviously it is taught more often by the private tutor than in a classroom setting (which some of the respondents specified). This is probably due to staff shortages and limited classroom time. It is also more traditional in the Conservative movement to learn trope in the classroom.

Table 13

In What Grade Do You Start Teaching Trope?

Grade	*% Reform*	*% Conservative*
Sixth	25%	45%
Seventh	39%	16%
Privately, seventh grade	32%	16%
Dalet-Hay (fifth or sixth)	—	21%
	N=28	N=42

Differences between the two movements emerge very clearly in this area. The Conservative movement obviously favors starting earlier, and using the classroom setting, twice as often as the Reform. There are pros and cons to beginning this study in the sixth grade. On the plus side, students will be familiar with the terminology and what the system entails, even if they forget some of the tunes when they enter seventh grade and begin B'nai Mitzvah training. On the minus side, students may have trouble concentrating much energy on mastering a system that they will not use for a minimum of one year, possibly two. And by the time they enter seventh grade and begin studying trope again, much of it will have been forgotten — a discouraging realization.

The next question (see Appendix), whether or not there are sufficient trained tutors to meet the needs of the congregation, did not address the issue of trained teachers to teach trope to classes. A quarter of the Reform respondents did not answer this question, while most Conservative respondents did. Of those that responded, 75% of both Reform and Conservative respondents indicated that they have enough trained tutors.

Part 4: General

The question "Is there sufficient cooperation between your Religious School and Bar/Bat Mitzvah program?" (see Appendix) was answered by only a small percentage of respondents. Some actually wrote that it was too loaded a question. Some 86% of the Reform and 82% of the Conservative respondents felt there is sufficient cooperation between the Bar/Bat Mitzvah program and the Religious School. Certain reasons were repeatedly cited. This Table is based on those responses. (Because many respondents gave more than one reason in their answer, the percentages do not add up to 100%.)

Table 14

What Element is Responsible for this Cooperation?

Element	*% Reform*	*% Conserv.*
Smallness	8%	0
Communication	15%	7%
Personality, commitment of staff	12%	14%
Integration of Bar/Bat Mitzvah Program & Religious School curriculum	38%	36%
Same director for both	29%	42%
	N=35	N=14

The last two items represent integration — how much more integrated can two programs be than when run by one person? In fact, one Cantor who runs both programs wrote, "It's good to be king." One Rabbi of a "D" congregation gave as his reason, "I insist on it." Another wrote that long-range planning was the reason.

Surprisingly, "personality" was seldom given as a reason. This element seemed to be cited more in the negative responses. And yet, a good mix of personalities is crucial to the successful running of a synagogue. Possibly, when that mix exists, those involved don't see it as a factor. When there are conflicts, the importance of personality emerges. This table shows the importance of integration — when the two answers indicating integration are combined, close to 75% of the positive responses give this as the reason. And although the negative responses were impossible to classify, they frequently cite a lack of integration.

Some of the negative responses to this question were outpourings of frustration and anger. Since these were too lengthy and complex to classify, excerpts are quoted below from the most representative of these responses.

The question was, if there is not sufficient cooperation, what possible solutions can you propose? Some answers were very pithy and to the point: "Coordinate the curriculum," "Change the Religious School curriculum." These two responses were from Cantors. The following, obviously, were not: "Get a different Cantor! He does not relate well to anyone, therefore, the Bar/Bat Mitzvah program is in a vacuum." "Cantor needs to play a more active role in the school." "Our Cantor is such a perfectionist that he does not allow kids to participate beyond the absolute minimum because he accepts nothing less than perfection in reading and chanting. The lessons become singing lessons, and the educational value is at a minimum. It is frustrating . . . My goal is to create a positive experience for the child and not to demoralize them. I want kids to know that just because there is a Cantor doesn't mean they will never have an opportunity to lead or be part of a service somewhere down the road."

Problems with Cantors may be related to the integration issue, as well as to personality problems. Clashes also occur when goals and objectives differ.

Some respondents indicated they are on the road to improved relations between the school and the Bar/Bat Mitzvah program. One specified problems with the tutors, who "should be consulted by the Director of Education and school committee." One respondent, a Cantor, said:

> "Trope should be part of the curriculum, but of course the bottom line is finances. No one in Budget & Finance wants to pay a qualified person for the extra hours. The school response is that they would have to cut the history program."

When each area of the synagogue has a different set of priorities, this leads to a lack of integration, not only of programs, but of philosophies and goals. One Cantor, in response to the request at the end of the questionnaire for original programs, wrote, "Extra input is not encouraged." Other Cantors have created original curricular material (which is included in other chapters), but which their synagogues have shown no interest in implementing. It seems such a waste when one professional attempts to integrate all the programs, and others do not cooperate. Of course, personality issues could be involved in some of these cases.

The response "Getting better" shows a commitment on the part of several involved professionals to improving the total program. The Cantor who wrote "getting better" added: "My Education Director and I are discussing reworking the curriculum."

This indicates a very positive step, one which apparently many synagogue professionals could emulate. A seventh grade teacher who filled the back of two pages of the questionnaire seems overwhelmed with the problems she faces. She expressed that "the prayer curriculum is not integrated with the Bar/Bat Mitzvah program, though this is now being reviewed. I am working with the Cantor, a committed layperson, and together we are trying to coordinate a good program. (But we seem to get no support from the congregation.) The Hebrew program is abominable. I have been so discouraged by all of this, that I am taking a year off and hope to develop a good program."

The levels of commitment among educators are heartening, but the amount of apathy and resistance from congregants appears to be discouraging.

SECTION III: PHILOSOPHICAL ISSUES

Part 1: Rating Emphasis

The purpose in asking educators to rate concepts (Table 15), skills and values on a scale of 1-3 in terms of emphasis, was to stimulate thought about these issues. Two respondents refused to answer on principle, writing, "Bad question!" and "Disagree!" Others refused in another manner, simply giving a "1" to all three areas. This is an area where the discrepancy between the respondent's philosophy and the practice of the school or synagogue can be a source of strife. In answering "Rate these in terms of your emphasis," some readers probably gave their own personal emphasis. Others saw themselves as the agent for the synagogue school and answered accordingly. Either way, the responses were interpreted to be representative of affiliation. (Because of the many different possible combinations offered by respondents, the totals do not add up to 100%.)

Table 15
Rating Concepts, Values, and Skills by Emphasis

Rating		*% Reform*	*% Conservative*
Values	#1	43%	7%
	#2	23%	43%
	#3	16%	32%
Concepts	#1	9%	7%
	#2	42%	36%
	#3	31%	43%
Skills	#1	43%	77%
	#2	22%	7%
	#3	29%	7%
All equal		5%	11%
		N=55	N=44

Several respondents specified an "ideal" rating as distinct from the "real" rating. For example, some Reform respondents would like to see values as #1, while others would like concepts to be #1. For one respondent, the ideal is skills as the *only* emphasis, and for another the ideal would be that all be treated equally. Among Conservative respondents listing an ideal, 7% wrote that values-concepts-skills is the ideal order.

The most obvious problem with this question is the unavoidable vagueness of terminology. This is the shortcoming of any survey, which tries to boil ideas down to the minimum number of words. "Concepts" implies a sort of abstract thinking, both about the meaning of the Bar/Bat Mitzvah ceremony and about Jewish studies. This approach may be more appropriate for a Confirmation class. Several respondents, in fact, indicated that this emphasis begins in the higher grades. Yet, whatever respondents' understanding of the meaning of "concepts," a third or more rated it second or third in emphasis, though a very small percentage in both movements rated it first.

The teaching of values is generally done in the classroom, and several respondents even wrote that this is not part of the Bar/Bat Mitzvah training. Since it is obvious from earlier questions that many respondents are not familiar with the school curriculum, these respondents would not know how much values teaching is done in sixth and seventh grade in their own synagogue. But assuming respondents answered to the best of their knowledge, and have at least a *sense* of the emphasis at their synagogue, some interesting results emerge. Comparing the ratings for values and skills, 43% of the Reform respondents rated both of these #1; whereas the Conservatives rated skills as #1 exactly 11 times as often as values (77% vs. 7%). A very small percentage of Conservative respondents rated skills anything lower than #1, whereas about a quarter of the Reform respondents rated them #2 or #3. Conservative respondents rated values as #2 or #3 about twice as often as Reform respondents. Reform respondents actually rated concepts as #2 or #3 twice as often as they put values in those slots, whereas for the Conservatives, the ratings for values and concepts is virtually the same.

This is by no means an indictment of the Conservative ideology. Skills have traditionally been a major part of Bar/Bat Mitzvah preparation in the Conservative movement. More hours per week are spent in Religious School, and many of those hours are devoted to learning skills, of which Hebrew is primary. Therefore, it is realistic when Conservative respondents assert that skills are the main area of emphasis.

There are different expectations in a Reform synagogue. It has been stated that many Reform congregants were turned off by an Orthodox or ultra-Conservative upbringing. There is a gut reaction among these individuals to the study of trope and memorization of prayers. This lack of support can often discourage Directors of Education from including such studies in their curriculum. Conversely, parents joining a Conservative synagogue expect a large emphasis on skills, and demand a certain level of mastery from their children.

Here are quotes from several respondents, most of whom seem to be justifying their stress on skills:

> Skill is the focus of the private tutorial; in class our focus is on values and concepts, teaching Bar/Bat Mitzvah as a life cycle event.

> Our emphasis is on skills and values because our Bar/Bat Mitzvah teachers really aren't equipped to handle concepts, and our Rabbi isn't as active at teaching them in his hour a week with the kids as he should be.

> I believe strongly in *na'aseh v'nishma,* we will do and *then* we will understand. Effective Jewish education has always stressed learning through doing. We do our best to instill values and concepts.

> Skills are most easily learned at a younger age; values and concepts can be better grasped at an older age.

> Disagree! We teach the skills, values, and concepts because our goal is to create educated Jews, whether or not they intend to have a Bar/Bat Mitzvah ceremony. For example, we teach Haftarah trope because an educated Jew should know it, not for the purposes of Bar/Bat Mitzvah.

> In the context of our program, skills are what we can teach successfully. Concepts grow out of understanding skills; values grow out of analyzing concepts. The establishment of skills provides a foundation upon which we might build the other two.

> Skills are good access to values and concepts. And a good excuse to meet often!

These last two responses show a very pragmatic, practical approach. Accepting what can and cannot be done in a given time frame is one of the most important starting points for a successful program, and will also help avoid frustration.

Several respondents indicated that they teach all three of these at different grade levels: skills are taught to earlier grades, values are integrated throughout the curriculum, and concepts are incorporated in the seventh grade. Another common division is by staff: values and concepts are usually taught in the classroom and/or in special classes with the Rabbi, while skills are taught by the Cantor or tutor.

Part 2: Is the Bar/Bat Mitzvah Ceremony a Right or Privilege?

A one word response (see Table 16) and a reason for that response was requested, along with a description of how their program reflects this philosophy. Many interesting comments resulted, some of which are quoted below. Many respondents pointed out that becoming a Bar or Bat Mitzvah is automatic, so obviously it is a right; only the ceremony is a privilege. (That is why "ceremony" was included in the question.) But since so many respondents pointed out the distinction, a special category was made for that answer. There were respondents refusing to answer this question, too. One wrote, "Bad question!" Others answered, "Neither," and then explained their reasoning. Those responses are included in the comments following the Table.

Table 16
Is the Bar/Bat Mitzvah Ceremony a Right or a Privilege?

Response	*% Reform*	*% Conservative*
Right	21%	12%
Privilege	50%	45%
Both	15%	22%
Bar/Bat Mitzvah=right; Ceremony=privilege	9%	20%
	N=52	N=40

Almost twice as many Reform respondents see the ceremony as a right, but this may not be an accurate figure, since twice as many Conservative respondents distinguish between becoming Bar/Bat Mitzvah and having the ceremony. The Reform congregations responding indicate an awareness of the distinction, but do not tend to stress it. Those that answered "both" may have been essentially saying the same thing as those making that distinction. Many Conservative respondents indicated that a Shabbat morning ceremony is a privilege to be earned. Requirements generally include four or five years of attendance at Religious School, certain service attendance requirements, and a general level of competence in all skills. Since the Conservative movement sees all 13-year-olds as B'nai Mitzvah, those that do not meet the requirements may still have a ceremony, but on a Shabbat afternoon (Minchah/Ma'ariv/Havdalah), weekday (Monday or Thursday, when Torah is read) or a Sunday Rosh Chodesh. The Reform congregations rarely offer these last two options. Both movements sometimes offer the option of a Friday night ceremony for special cases.

More interesting than the actual responses were the comments that went with them. This seems to be another area of conflict, especially between Directors of Education and Rabbis. The first few quotes below expand on the viewpoint of Bar/Bat Mitzvah as a privilege. The first quote is representative of many, in which either the Cantor or Director of Education feels there should be more stringent requirements, and the Rabbi does not agree.

> I as Education Director see the ceremony as a privilege earned through study, whereas the Rabbi quotes *halachah* and says turning 13 is all that is really required, and thus sometimes excuses those who have not been attending Religious School sufficiently or at all, and makes little demands on anyone.

> Personally I view it as a privilege, but our program makes it look like a right . . . We are cracking down on overall school requirements which, if not fulfilled, would mean denying the Bar/Bat Mitzvah.

> I feel it is a privilege. The parents and students feel it is a right. I think children need to be thoroughly educated before they are ready to become B'nai Mitzvah. If they do not know and understand the *mitzvot,* how can they be full participants?

> Leading the congregation in prayer is a privilege. It has to be done so that those who are attending services (not the Bar/Bat Mitzvah ceremony) will be comfortable.

> It is a privilege to be a mature, active Jew, accepted as such by the community.

> Parents expect the ceremony often in place of "coming out" parties of other generations. The religious significance of B'nai Mitzvah is often lost in the social hoopla that surrounds these occasions. We state our position (local Board of Jewish Education), but it has little effect.

Here are some quotes explaining the "right" viewpoint:

> It is a right — in a small WASP town, we would not be able to exist otherwise.

> It is not only a right but a fact, and the ceremony does not change that. However, there should be standards for learning established prior to participation in a major service.

> In fact, it's a right — no one is ever denied this opportunity . . . perhaps it should be viewed more as a privilege, but we can't realistically expect thirteen-year-olds to make the right choices were we to reorient the program in this way.

Some see it as "both" or "neither":

> It is both. At our synagogue, a Bar/Bat Mitzvah becomes part of our regular service. Our service does not become part of a Bar/Bat Mitzvah!

> I see it as an *expectation,* shared by the community and congregation, the family, and the student. One takes one's place as a maturing individual.

> It is neither. I see it as a weighted and intense moment in education, which is a process.

Table 17

What is the Most Pressing Problem in Your/Other Synagogues?

	Reform:		Conservative:	
Problem	*Ours*	*Others*	*Ours*	*Others*
Continuing after	15%	28%	5%	22%
Poor Hebrew skills	26%	16%	27%	15%
Parent commitment	28%	25%	35%	37%
Wrong emphasis	11%	39%	13%	41%
Lack of time	13%	11%	24%	11%
Lack of staff	15%	8%	13%	7%
	N=46	N=36	N=37	N=27

It is neither; it is a ceremonial taking on of responsibility.

The classical Reform philosophy did not consider the Bar/Bat Mitzvah ceremony as an important phase in a person's life. Confirmation was one of the highlights of a Reform Jew's life. Today the Bar/Bat Mitzvah ceremony has become an important social function for the families; I do not feel that there is any philosophy behind the ceremony yet.

The common thread in these thoughtful comments is the need to put these ideas into action: to create educational programs leading up to the Bar/Bat Mitzvah ceremony that will contain within them the lofty concepts found in the above quotes. The degree to which this is being accomplished can be seen in the responses to the next question.

SECTION IV: PROBLEM SOLVING

Parts 1 and 2: What is the Most Pressing Problem in Your Own Bar/Bat Mitzvah Program? What Do You Perceive as the Most Pressing Problems in General?

The question of what is the most pressing problem (Table 17) sparked the lengthiest and most interesting comments. There was such an enormous variety in the responses that it was difficult to categorize them. Once again, therefore, following Table 17, some individual comments have been offered.

Other problems mentioned several times were: lack of understanding of the process, lack of interest, volume (the Bar/Bat Mitzvah factory syndrome), not enough tailoring to the individual, too much emphasis on skills, not enough skills incorporated into curriculum, too little time spent with clergy, too much separation between Religious School and Bar/Bat Mitzvah program, programs not demanding enough, conflict between parents' expectations (short-term objectives) and those of the school (long-term goals), and lack of relevance.

Table 17 above is possibly the most illuminating one in this chapter in the way it clarifies the problems that exist in programs now, and the perceptions that respondents have of what problems exist. The biggest spread between the respondents' own problems and the problems they perceive in other synagogues rested in the matters of "wrong emphasis" and in continuation after the Bar/Bat Mitzvah year. The now well-known quote "the bar is more important than the *mitzvah*" has come to stand for a misguided emphasis, generally on the part of parents. In both Reform and

Conservative responses, roughly four times as many respondents saw that problem as one that *others* have to deal with. Some of those "others" referred to, of course, were they themselves. Is this a matter of blindness to one's own shortcomings, or did that many more respondents truly feel this is a problem found more often elsewhere? It is also interesting that roughly the same percentage of Reform and Conservative respondents answered both questions the same way.

Keeping students in the school after the Bar/Bat Mitzvah year is perceived by roughly double the Reform, and over four times the Conservative, as more of a problem for others. (Would that all those who have truly solved the problem shared their solutions with those who are still groping for answers!)

The problems which respondents felt are not found as often in other synagogues as in their own are those of Hebrew deficiency, lack of time, and lack of staff. About a quarter of respondents of both affiliations listed Hebrew as a problem area, and both felt this was a problem they don't share with that many other synagogues. Similarly, lack of staff, though not cited by many as a major problem, was seen in similar numbers in both movements, and twice as many respondents felt it was uniquely their problem. Lack of time to accomplish their goals was cited by twice as many Conservative as Reform respondents, an interesting finding considering that their Hebrew School meets for more days and hours than the Reform schools. Obviously, they are setting standards they cannot meet.

The second most frequently cited problem was parent commitment. And, in fact, when respondents mention "wrong emphasis," they are probably referring more to mistaken priorities of parents, rather than of schools. More than a third of the Conservative respondents cited "parents" as a problem area, and slightly more than that cited this as a problem for others. A little over a quarter of the Reform respondents answered this same way. If we take the liberty of combining "parents" with "emphasis," close to half of all the respondents find this the biggest problem area, and close to three quarters of them believe it is a problem for other synagogues. Based on the numbers of Family Education programs that have proliferated over the last few years (see chapters in Unit V), educators are aware of this problem and are responding to it.

Issues like lack of time or staff are more specific to individual congregations, and apart from administrative changes, solutions are not generally available. Only small numbers of congregations seem to feel that continuing after seventh grade is a problem. This problem seems to have lessened during the past several years, perhaps because there are programs and curricula available that were created in response to it. The only problem area not yet adequately addressed seems to be Hebrew. Solving this by greater integration of the curriculum seems the ideal, but programs must still be created.

Here is the eloquent testimony of some respondents, presented in three categories: Problems Not Mentioned Above, Problems and Solutions That Have Been Tried, and Solutions and Innovative Ideas.

Problems Not Mentioned Above

> As a tutor, I feel disconnected from the seventh grade program. Not being considered a staff member has both advantages and disadvantages. (For more on this subject, see chapters in Unit II).

> *Equality* is a problem — wanting all students to feel good about their own Bar/Bat Mitzvah given their individual abilities. The most pressing problem? That there are "B'nai Mitzvah programs" apart from Religious School. What do you mean by B'nai Mitzvah programs?

> How to incorporate skills-learning into the central curriculum so as to avoid excess tutorial time (financial constraints). How to avoid trivializing the experience, with more parent consultation, more student counseling, a deemphasis on performance competition, more on skills for the sake of skills, and the spiritual content of the whole experience.

> Too little time spent with Cantor and Rabbi. Our clergy are not "tuned in" to adolescents, and the training is not enjoyable.

Peer pressure — both on children and parents.

Parent issues include: 1) parental pressures on kids, 2) lack of parental understanding of the requirements, 3) their desire to set dates years in advance. Relative to the school, I don't believe the Hebrew Schools in general or the Bar/Bat Mitzvah program make sufficient demands on our students.

Parents don't understand the massive commitment their children must make; they need to encourage them more every step along the way. Also, I see no standards among synagogues or between different segments of Judaism.

Our Cantor refuses to teach anything but the most rudimentary skills, and only 6-8 months before the Bar/Bat Mitzvah.

Problems and Solutions That Have Been Tried

Some of the problems outlined by respondents follow, along with some of the solutions they suggested.

Problem: The current system is designed in such a way that kids get "shoved through" without the necessary explanations or educational preparation. The process begins in seventh grade and should begin much earlier. The kids and parents are still way too party focused.

Solution: This year I visited every family in their home a few weeks prior to the Bar/Bat Mitzvah to facilitate a discussion with parents and child about the meaning of the ceremony. It was an exhausting effort and more effective in some cases than others. It felt like too little too late. Next year I'm considering conducting 'parlor meetings' of five or so families of fourth and fifth graders in their homes. There is a positive effect in moving the discussion into the home. Optimally, I would love to offer a parent/ student seventh grade learning program.

Problem: More attention needs to be paid to concepts and values, but the technical performance expected of our students makes it difficult to focus on anything beyond skills development.

Solution: What we do, though, is encourage tutors and family members of the B'nai Mitzvah to read Torah at the service. This makes it more of a family project and shows that learning continues. If students attend 11 Saturday morning sessions out of 18, they receive a *Chumash* (it's easy to attain the goal — naturally, we *want* them to have the *Chumash!*).

Problem: Our biggest problem is dealing with a hardheaded Cantor who has no professional education or expertise and is not interested in learning how to teach.

Solution: The Rabbi, on the other hand, meets with four or five seventh graders weekly to discuss the week's Haftarah. This has created a good relationship with the kids and he really makes them think and teaches more about the prophets.

Problem: Problems occur when the expectations of parents exceed the abilities of students.

Solution: One solution is constant contact with parents.

Problem: Parents are not well educated Jewishly and usually just drop the kids off on Shabbat without coming to services. However, more parents are expressing a willingness to be educated, so I'm hopeful. Also, the ceremony needs to be relevant to kids today. We tell the child, "Today you are an adult," but really, in this society, until they get their driver's license they don't feel like an adult. The chances of their joining a *minyan* are remote.

> Solution: One solution is parent groups for parents of students in fifth to tenth grades.

Solutions and Innovative Ideas

> I feel this is the first and, who knows, in some cases, the only time students have the opportunity to be cared for and nurtured by clergy and also to feel good about who they are and what they are doing. We need to make certain that the Rabbi and Cantor not only teach portions, but help them grow as young adults and listen carefully to what they say and do not say, ask and do not ask. This should be treated more as a sacred task.

> Since we initiated Saturday morning classes for grade 7, service attendance is not a problem. We also require a contract signed at the beginning of the year for both parent and student.

> Sixth and seventh graders who attend Shabbat services regularly are rewarded with an annual class trip. We have an annual school Shabbat service conducted by children, which includes dance, sign language, junior choir, drama, and puppetry. We also have an annual sixth-seventh grade service and luncheon with a special program geared to the needs of the B'nai Mitzvah families.

> We have a teacher/Director of Education/ Rabbi/ tutor committee to assess students' abilities, then a contract listing all expectations and their due date is drawn up and signed.

Several elements seem to be present in these ideas: the importance of truly *caring* for the students; effective use of positive reinforcement; and the importance of spelling out requirements very clearly, for example with the use of a contract. These ideas recur and are expanded upon in the many programs described throughout this volume.

EDITOR'S COMMENTS

The key word in my own philosophy of a successful Bar/Bat Mitzvah program, which has run like a thread throughout this chapter, is *integration.* I have worked for many synagogues, of different affiliations, and have rarely seen this concept work effectively. When it has not worked, it is always due to a lack of communication between the various segments of a synagogue: the Religious School, the clergy, and the congregation itself. Until more agreement can be reached about all areas of education in our synagogues, we are all working against one another, rather than together as one community.

One potential area of disagreement is that of *goals.* Frequently there is a conflict between the long-term goals of the Religious School or synagogue, and the short-term objectives of the Bar/Bat Mitzvah program and/or the parents and children involved in that program. The solution I propose here as elsewhere is *integration* . . . on many levels. There should be integration between the Religious School and the Bar/Bat Mitzvah program, as well as between different subject areas.

A factor that often prevents this integration is interpersonal conflicts. I have seen extreme cases where some of the professionals in a synagogue are not even on speaking terms. Often the office locations of the Director of Education, Rabbi, and Cantor are as distant from one another as are the philosophies and goals of those three people.

If the common goal becomes improving the whole program, personal agendas should take a back seat. When curriculum is planned, long-range goals should be kept in mind. All professional staff members should be participants in this planning. Some may have more expertise than others, but there is no reason to compartmentalize professionals totally. Unfortunately, such compartmentalization and resultant lack of integration are often the rule. When a new staff member is about to be hired, meetings should be held between all the professionals. If there are major philosophical or personal differences, these should be ironed out ahead of time or a different employee should be considered.

I recommend more involvement of clergy at all levels. Some Rabbis or Cantors are neither trained as educators or so motivated. Ironically, the same synagogue in the survey that complained of the lack of its Cantor's involvement in the Religious School also complained that the Cantor and Rabbi were out of touch with adolescents, whose contact with these clergy, therefore, was a negative experience. In cases like this, all the professionals should sit down together to discuss their roles. Each one should define what he/she does best and what his/her greatest involvement should be. Roles and boundaries could then be established, and the synagogue's resources used more wisely. There has to be flexibility, of course. I have worked with professional staffs that engaged in turf battles to the point that it felt like a gang war if one professional stepped over another's line. These attitudes are both the cause and result of a lack of mutual respect between staff members.

By opening the lines of communication, the professional staff will begin to see and understand each others' strong points. There should be no hidden agendas among staff people. Any one professional working alone is working against the whole synagogue. If that one person is the only effective one on the staff, he/she should make the effort to reach out and mediate between all other staff members. In that way, they can begin to share common goals and purposes. Nothing will be so effective as a professional staff working as a team, integrating their program, and maximizing what each one has to bring to that program.

The survey responses (see comments on Tables 10 and 11) revealed how synagogue educators (other than the Director of Education) often know little about the Religious School curriculum. The ideal of total integration between all areas of the synagogue can seem unattainable in the face of such gaps. To begin closing those gaps, I would like to propose solutions in specific subject areas. These solutions can either grow out of or lead to greater integration.

Hebrew

Solutions are needed for enhancing the study of Hebrew prior to and in the seventh grade. One solution is to integrate Hebrew study into other areas, such as Torah, Prophets, and values studies. This could be done through study of a text such as *Pirke Avot,* with some Hebrew terminology learned along the way. Such an integrated curriculum remains only an ideal in many places because of the lack of teachers capable of teaching it. As a result, Hebrew classes become separate entities from values teaching, and even from the study of Torah. Integrating the study of Hebrew with other study areas would make Hebrew more relevant and meaningful because it would be seen in a context. This implies, of course, a thorough grounding in Hebrew fundamentals in earlier grades.

Trope

I recommend also that there be a course called "Introduction to Trope" sessions during sixth grade. These would be short sessions, and their sole purpose would be to familiarize students with the system. It will be clear they are not required to master or retain what they learn. Sometimes putting forth more realistic expectations can lead to superior results. Such classes would also put trope in the context of Religious School classes, so that it is not seen as an study unconnected to other subjects.

Torah/Prophets

Based on the survey responses, lack of sufficient exposure to Torah and Prophets prior to and in the seventh grade is not perceived as a problem for many educators. This result surprised me, but perhaps the issue is too narrow and specific to be perceived as a pressing one. If there is already a lack of time and staff, schools will not be willing to add yet another subject. My prediction is that if the study of Torah and Prophets were integrated with Hebrew in an interesting curriculum, and this integrated program were taught in a more concentrated form to parents, then many of the problems we now have would diminish.

Curriculum: General

Hebrew School has to compete with sports and other extra-curricular activities. We must find a way to make it relevant and meaningful. We cannot expect students and their parents to remain interested unless we offer them something interesting. I believe that by integrating the various studies of Hebrew, Torah, Prophets, and trope, each one will be given a meaningful context, and one will enhance the study of the other. Subjects, like the educators who teach them, should not be kept in isolation.

I agree with those respondents in the survey who said that ideally skills, values, and concepts should all be of equal importance. An ideal curriculum would be one that integrates all three areas. I have seen seventh grade curricula that were nothing but values clarification exercises, with no Torah or Prophets study, and Hebrew a distant memory of earlier years. I have seen others exclusively focusing on Torah and Hebrew with no discussions of Jewish values or concepts. (Several curriculum recommendations may be found in Chapter 36.) There is no reason the two movements cannot share each others' best ideas. The study of values need not take away from that of skills, but rather can enhance it. Conservative and Reform synagogues should be eager to implement new curricula that integrate the whole.

Parent Education and Involvement

When I speak of the need for parent education, I do not mean education only in history and religious customs. Parents are entitled to be told far more about the whole B'nai Mitzvah process. For example, many parents might find the results of this survey enlightening. It could give them ideas of the differences in approach and ideology among synagogues, and this could guide them in what to look for in both a Religious School and a Bar/Bat Mitzvah program.

My experience has been that the Bar/Bat Mitzvah program is usually not integrated into the Religious School program. Parents may choose outside tutors from a list, and these tutors have no connection to the school or to the synagogue service. Such tutors might also utilize different methodologies and trope systems, and have different standards. Parents in certain areas seem used to this system and see nothing wrong with it, since they don't know anything else. I feel the lack of continuity and cohesiveness is a real negative for children, and a disincentive to continue participating in the congregation whose school has such a fractionalized system.

The only solution is to have the same person doing the tutoring, teaching part of the B'nai Mitzvah class (if not all of it), and being present at the ceremony. If this one person can be the Cantor, that is ideal. A qualified educator would also be acceptable. But this solution is not so easily implemented when parents are used to local tutors and to the whole system. This is another example of the clash between short-term objectives and long-term goals. Only when parents become more educated about the whole process, can synagogues using this system change to a more cohesive one.

CONCLUSION

The greatest shortcoming of a survey such as this is that measuring quality along with quantity, in all areas, is impossible. For example, the number of verses of Torah or Haftarah chanted at the Bar/Bat Mitzvah ceremony is a very small part of a larger picture. For how many years did the child study different parts of the Torah or Prophets? What was the approach in those classes? Was the curriculum stimulating enough that the student retained a large part of what was learned? Does that girl who is up there chanting so perfectly want to chant? Does she understand any of the Hebrew she is reciting? Is she aware of the long history and origins of the trope system so that she takes pride and shares a sense of history and continuity with her ancestors while she is chanting the text? Or, is she merely parroting verses learned by rote from a tape, just as the other students in her class have done?

The chapters that follow are the result of the search for solutions to the problems discussed in this survey. These solutions are innovative and exciting, reflecting a committed and thoughtful community of educators. It is hoped that these ideas will attain wide circulation and will in turn spark a universe of discourse that will revitalize and strengthen the field of Bar/Bat Mitzvah education.

APPENDIX

Questionnaire for B'nai Mitzvah Educators

Your synagogue's affiliation: (circle one)
Conservative Reform Reconstructionist
Orthodox Other

Size of congregation: (Family units; circle one)
Under 250 250-500 500-1000 Over 1000

Number of B'nai Mitzvah in a year, on average:

I. GENERAL

1. Who is responsible for training them?

   a. Rabbi
   b. Cantor
   c. Professional tutors
   d. Teenage tutors
   e. Other (explain):

2. What do they learn for their ceremony?

   a. Torah: how many verses?
   b. Haftarah: how many verses?
   c. Liturgy: how much of the service?
   d. Other (explain):

3. Where is the primary stress? Please rank in order of importance. (#1 is most important):

   Torah reading
   Haftarah reading
   Leading service
   Other (explain):

4. Do they read or do they chant their Torah/Haftarah portion?

   a. If they chant, do they:
      Learn the trope system
      Get a tape of the portion
      Both of the above
   b. Do they get a choice between reading or chanting?

II. SPECIFIC SUBJECT AREA

1. Hebrew:

   Do you regularly test students at the end of each school year, to track their progress?

   What do you do if the student does not pass the test?

2. Torah/Haftarah:

   In what grades is Torah taught?

   In what grades are Prophets taught?

   What is the stress in these classes? (i.e., translating, grasp of the narrative, midrashic understanding, or other)

3. Trope:

   Do you teach the trope system?

   Why/why not?

   If yes, in what grade do you start?

   Are there sufficient trained tutors to meet the needs of your congregation?
   (discuss)

4. General: Impacting on all of the above subject areas is the relationship between the B'nai Mitzvah program and the Religious School curriculum.

Is there sufficient cooperation and coordination between your B'nai Mitzvah program and your synagogue Religious School?

If yes, to what do you attribute this success?

If no, what possible solutions can you propose?

Please expand on your answer; feel free to use the back of this sheet.

PLEASE FEEL FREE TO WRITE AT ANY LENGTH IN RESPONSE TO THE FOLLOWING TWO SECTIONS. YOU MAY ATTACH ADDITIONAL SHEETS OR MATERIALS.

III. PHILOSOPHICAL ISSUES

1. Bar/Bat Mitzvah preparation is a combination of teaching concepts, values and skills. Rate these in terms of your emphasis (#1 is most important), and explain your outlook:

   The need to teach concepts
   The need to skills
   The need to values

2. Do you see the Bar/Bat Mitzvah ceremony as a right or a privilege, and why? In what way do you feel your program reflects this philosophy?

IV. PROBLEM SOLVING

1. What is the most pressing problem in your own B'nai Mitzvah program?

2. What do you perceive as the most pressing problem in B'nai Mitzvah programs in general?

3. What creative and innovative ideas have you implemented to address these problems? Please expand on these ideas. If you have created an original program, please describe it in terms of goals, objectives, procedure, and results. If you have created original curricular materials, please include these.

Additional comments:

Your name and synagogue (optional):

Unit I: On the Bar/Bat Mitzvah Process

Overview

The chapters in this Unit are both controversial and wise. They reflect observations about the Bar/Bat Mitzvah process by experienced and involved Jewish professionals. Their opinions will stimulate much discussion and possibly some changes in Bar/Bat Mitzvah education.

In Chapter 1, Dr. Sherry Blumberg discusses what she learned from her many years as a Director of Education. She describes her work today, training future Rabbis and Cantors and preparing them to work with the B'nai Mitzvah of the next century.

In Chapter 2, Cantor Marshall Portnoy offers the perspective of a Cantor with over 20 years experience in training B'nai Mitzvah students. He describes the educational process he has developed, including discussions of his Bar/Bat Mitzvah class, how he involves the family at every step, and his approach to individual instruction.

In Chapter 3, Dr. Saul Wachs describes the importance of the profound impact on him of his close relationship with his Cantor. He stresses that if our children are to embrace our tradition, a powerful role model can be very important.

In Chapter 4, Carol K. Ingall gives consideration to Bar/Bat Mitzvah policies, the scheduling nightmare, the involvement of congregants, and the initiation of an educational program specifically for this age group that is separate from Religious School.

In Chapter 5, Rabbi Jeffrey Schein poses a challenge to all educators to revise their thinking about the whole process of Bar/Bat Mitzvah education. His clarion call for reform should stimulate the reader to rethink many common assumptions.

In Chapter 6, Robin Eisenberg shares ways through which her very large congregation manages to keep Bar and Bat Mitzvah a personal and individualized experience.

In Chapter 7, Rabbi George Stern outlines the process of problem solving related to Bar/Bat Mitzvah that took place in his congregation. He and Cantor William S. Wood made recommendations to the Religious Practices Committee which, in turn, set standards and conveyed them to the congregation.

In Chapter 8, Dr. Shoshana Silberman provides an overview of a similar process at her congregation. In this case, a separate Bar/Bat Mitzvah Committee was convened to address problems and suggest solutions.

The experiences of these two congregations can serve as models for other synagogues seeking solutions to similar problems.

In Chapter 9, Dr. Stuart Schoenfeld offers an interesting historical analysis of the place of Bar/Bat Mitzvah in America.

Chapter 1
Reflections on Bar/Bat Mitzvah

Sherry H. Blumberg

I look back with mixed emotions to the time when I was a congregational Director of Education working with Bar/Bat Mitzvah students. In one congregation I was the sole trainer who taught the students to chant and then turned them over to the Rabbi when they were ready to begin their final month of preparation. As much as I loved working with the individual students, sometimes hearing the same prayers over and over became difficult and boring. I realized that it was the same for the students, so I did as much work as possible in a classroom situation: I had students teach each other, made the review process a challenge with games, provided tapes when needed, and often geared the learning to the individuals. Still, the process is repetitive and time consuming and requires a great deal of thought and work from both the trainer and the participant — to say nothing about the car pooling, nagging, and energy required of parents and family.

It all became worth the effort when the student stood on the *bimah* and read or chanted the service, Torah, and Haftarah portions. However, the process of getting the student to the point of readiness often required more time than was possible of a busy congregational Director of Education with a school and other synagogue responsibilities. I often wished for someone who could do the training exclusively, or that the congregation had a Cantor who would share the work.

During my next position, I got my wish. There was a person who did the training of the students, someone who loved the role and loved the students. The educator in me was delighted. I was with students only to perfect their voice and presentation and during the family educational components which we required. Yet, I greatly missed the personal relationship that had been developed during the training period. It is this personal contact that makes the experience special for the teacher.

Now, in my role as professor at Hebrew Union College-Jewish Institute of Religion in New York, I help train Cantorial and Rabbinical students. Many of these students, while holding student pulpits, create units and lessons on how to work with B'nai Mitzvah students. Some of them have created alternative training programs for B'nai Mitvah students based on the particular situations and needs of the congregation they were serving. I have observed them as they taught their Bar/Bat Mitzvah students individually and in classes and have been able to evaluate their programs.

The following thoughts are a combination of my reflections on practice, and my observations connected with educational scholarship and research.

Transcendence

Bar/Bat Mitzvah can be a moment of transcendence for the participant and for the whole family. It is often a moment when something special, something Jewishly significant, occurs. Transcendence can be defined as "moving beyond oneself at the cognitive, moral, and affective levels."[1] This moment can be a time when God enters the consciousness of the student, when an encounter with God is possible. It is a moment of celebration, of connection with our people, with generations of the family, and with the community of Israel.

Often this moment goes unrecognized until it is reflected upon. If pressed, a student may recall a special feeling at the end of the service that was more than relief, more than a pride at what they had accomplished. Sometimes the student remembers the passing of the Torah from grandparent to parent and to himself/herself as a symbol of the importance of Torah throughout the generations. Almost all remember the party and the family gathering.

Planting the seeds for receptivity to this special moment, helping the student to identify it and place it into a religious context, is a special responsibility of the Bar/Bat Mitzvah trainer, the Cantor, and Rabbi, and others who work with the family at this time. A moment of thought and silence before the ceremony begins, a family prayer together, a moment for personal blessings afterward, might help students be open to the transcendent significance of the event.

I would suggest that there be an educational team approach to the Bar/Bat Mitzvah training with the inclusion of Rabbi, Cantor, Director of Education, teacher, synagogue administrator, and if possible, a social worker or psychologist. I recommend the inclusion of the psychologist because (especially in recent times with divorces, blended families, and both Jewish and non-Jewish family members), family gatherings can be a time of great stress instead of a time of joy (see Chapter 48). Each of the team members brings a special relationship to the student and to the family. Each person will be able to add an expertise to the approach. This will enable the training, the ceremony, and the follow-up to become experiences that enrich the individual participant, the congregation, and the family.

Family Education

Family educational components can be very effective during this time (see Chapters 29-35). Some congregations require that families attend services and/or a number of special programs with their children. Occasionally, a congregation will hold a Bar/Bat Mitzvah retreat (see Chapters 41 and 42). Involving the families in ushering, in learning together, in sharing reflections about their experience after the ceremony with families who will soon be going through this event, are all part of what makes a complete experience.

There are already some good programs available,[2] but congregations can also develop their own to meet their specific needs (for guidelines, see Chapter 29). I would suggest that both family education and family life education are important. The areas that I have found to be most effective involve 1) issues of *Sh'lom Bayit;* 2) the makeup and meaning of the Shabbat service; 3) the meaning of the Torah portion; 4) the importance of *mitzvot;* and 5) the historical connections of Bar/Bat Mitzvah for *Am Yisrael,* our Jewish extended family.

Individual Differences

Individual students learn in different ways. These differences can be made use of effectively during the training and development process. I would suggest that we not standardize so much that we miss the opportunity provided for individuals to utilize their learning strengths.

Research on learning styles[3] shows that some students learn best aurally. These students need tapes and the chance to learn with others. Some students learn best visually and will thrive with visual methodologies. Some students are primarily kinesthetic or tactile learners and must write out the *parashah* in order to be able to do it well. Some students respond best when a peer is their teacher; others need authority figures. Some students excel with individual attention, while others learn best in groups. There are students who need to move in order to learn, and short study sessions with breaks are best for them. Others need longer, more sustained concentration times. Some students, no matter what we do, learn at the last minute and need the pressure of deadlines, and still others plod along and need more than the usual six months.

The Bar/Bat Mitzvah experience that is provided by the congregation should capitalize on the students' strengths and stretch the students' abilities while remaining flexible to meet the needs of the learner. A feeling of success in the process, as well as on the day of the ceremony, is of primary importance.

Post-Bar/Bat Mitzvah

My last reflections are on the time after the ceremony. I believe that follow-up is crucial and that *something should change in the student's relationship to the synagogue as a result of the ceremony.* Since we are trying to teach that one becomes religiously responsible for one's own Jewish life after the age of 13, this "coming of age" goes unnoticed if something does not change. Unfortunately, the most profound change is a lessening of the time commitment to Jewish study (which gives exactly the opposite message from what we say we want).

Some congregations enable post-Bar/Bat Mitzvah students to be assistants in the Religious School. Some encourage the students to lead portions of the service for the main congregation, or to read the Torah portion on the anniversary of their *sedra* (if the *sedra* is not taken by this year's Bar or Bat Mitzvah). Some congregations grant a limited membership to the student, maintained not by dues, but by further involvement in study and in the youth group. Whatever is the wish of the congregation, something needs to be done in order for this special moment to be recognized and for future commitment to be encouraged.

John Dewey defined the self as "something in continuous formation through choice of action."[4] My hope is that we can encourage our new B'nai Mitzvah students to be those responsible Jewish selves who choose Jewish actions, such as study, worship, and deeds of loving kindness. Opportunities to participate on a more adult level after the ceremony of Bar/Bat Mitzvah, both as individuals and in groups (toward the ceremony of Confirmation perhaps) is a vital consideration for the Bar/Bat Mitzvah program.

Conclusion

These reflections, based on my experience and learning, are offered with the knowledge that many great things are happening in this area of Jewish education, and that much more can be done. This book is a step in that sacred task, the work of Jewish education.

NOTES

[1]This specific definition is taken from Walter Conn in his book *Christian Conversion: A Developmental Interpretation of Autonomy and Self Surrender* (New York: Paulist Press, 1986), but it is similar to many others that speak of transcendence as rising above, passing beyond the self for a moment of time.

[2]See Janice Alper, ed., *Learning Together: A Family Education Source Book* (Denver, Colorado: A.R.E. Publishing, Inc., 1988), and the materials gathered in the CAJE Curriculum Bank, for examples.

[3]For more information about learning styles and learning factors, see *Learning a Matter of Style* by Rita Dunn, videotape and workbook (Alexandria, Virginia: Association for Supervision and Curriculum Development, 1979).

[4]John Dewey, *Democracy and Education* (New York: Macmillan, 1916), p. 408.

Chapter 2
Reflections of a Hazzan

Marshall Portnoy

My motivation is to foster in every Bar/Bat Mitzvah a renewing sense of pride in our Jewish heritage that will transcend this milestone event and sustain them for a lifetime. That Bar/Bat Mitzvah might ever represent the culmination of a person's religious education and the zenith of his/her participation in Jewish life is tragic. So, we who prepare our youngsters for B'nai Mitzvah have the sacred responsibility of emphasizing, convincing, demonstrating that Bar/Bat Mitzvah is just a new beginning — the first steps to continuing, maturing Jewish life.

Under ideal circumstances, we might call upon the home to offer support and modeling for our efforts. The home is, after all, the child's Temple; the parents, its architects. Again, ideally, we professionals are supposed to help with a little . . . decorating and remodeling. Obviously, it doesn't work that way. Many Jewish homes demonstrate little that is Jewish — no serious observance of Sabbath and holidays, no Jewish books or magazines to be found, little conversation about Jewish issues, etc. Many Jewish parents no longer have the knowledge to create a Jewish home even if they faithfully wanted to do so. And, in spite of the difficulties, without family involvement very little can be achieved. Our first priority then needs to be the regeneration of Jewish commitment in parents. To that end, we need to adopt a new family-oriented approach toward Jewish education.

The details of the "successful program" and how to go about accomplishing it is beyond the scope of this chapter, but I will discuss my own experience as a starter for others. The basic assumption is that we need children and families *together* in Jewish settings for as much time as possible — retreats, trips, frequent social interaction, and we need to turn Religious School into Jewish family time. In short, we need to make Religious Education into Family Education.

A Junior Congregation Program

Bar/Bat Mitzvah is a process that, to be "successful," begins before birth. Even the actual instruction should begin years before the ceremony, with attendance at an excellent Junior Congregation. I do not mean a program that runs for an hour or two on Saturday or Sunday, but an ongoing cluster of family programming of which a weekly or bi-weekly service is a part. Such programming might include the following: an enriching program of songs and stories; a Shabbat luncheon with appropriate blessings; and frequent trips, outings, and special holiday programs. The service itself should be conducted by the children, and an opportunity should be given to them to spend part of the morning in the adult service as well. The Junior Congregation could lead the concluding hymns, and an even younger group could come to the *bimah* for *Kiddush* and *Motzi* at the conclusion of the Shabbat service. If this is done each week, including *especially* on Bar/Bat Mitzvah Shabbatot, the children perceive that they are participating in a process of evolving stages. Sunday provides an excellent opportunity for families to have a briefer but well structured service, and to have breakfast together. Whatever components are appropriate to any particular synagogue's approach to Junior Congregation, the process should begin as early as possible, certainly by Grade 3.

Bar/Bat Mitvah Class

The importance of the group experience carries over into the actual Bar/Bat Mitzvah instruction, which may begin in Grade 5, but no later than Grade 6. The trick is to allow for individual differences within a group setting, and this can be done with an individual checklist of goals which allows each child to proceed at his/her own pace while the class establishes a group norm. It does not really matter whether a child accomplishes the class goals within two months or ten. What does matter is the conscientious commitment to *daily* practice and working to one's own capabilities. The discipline involved ensures the best results in the program and, more important, translates to other areas of life. The child learns that an hour of "cramming" once a week does not work, yet ten minutes or so each day leads to success. The habits learned in such a process might be as important as the mastery of the Hebrew text, because, in the process of becoming practicing Jews, children come to understand themselves and what they are really capable of accomplishing. I have worked with the near-deaf and mentally retarded, as well as with children far brighter than I. Intellectual ability, I have found, is a poor predictor of success. The quality of motivation which results in a commitment to daily preparation is a far more reliable indicator of how well children will do, and more important, how they will come to feel about themselves as individuals and as Jews.

Family Meetings

I conduct a meeting with families before our classwork begins. Attending this session is an absolute must for entering the program, because here we begin to work together, family and synagogue, toward our objectives. To that end, there are several things I stress at the outset which fall under the general categories of preparation, communication, and appropriateness. I urge that families that are going through this for the first time seek out other families for advice. I welcome questions and indicate a desire to help and to be available to them at any time. I urge families to come directly to me if there is any problem whatsoever. I have found the second worst thing in this process is for families to be silent when something is bothering them. The *worst* thing is for them to discuss their perceptions with others who are unable to help them. I am sure, however, that this phenomenon will be minimized if families believe that the professional truly cares, wants to listen, and has the interests of the family uppermost. I want parents to know that it is not the quantity of material that the youngster "performs" at the ceremony that concerns me, but the quality of the family's experience in getting to that point. This process also determines the degree of the child's desire to continue contact with the synagogue after it is no longer compulsory, and that is what this is all about.

In the child's presence, I speak to the parents about these and other matters, including such mundane things as making reservations for use of the kitchen. I urge the parents not to stretch beyond their means to celebrate this occasion. It is important for children to understand the dynamics of this event from the perspective of their parents. Thus, rather than compartmentalizing each segment of preparation of the Bar/Bat Mitzvah — such as next week's assignment, or including all the child's classmates in a children's party — we look at the entire effort together as one integrated entity which is to happen within a Jewish framework. At this time, I also give the children a special message:

> You are about to prepare for one of the greatest events in the life of a Jew — your Bar/Bat Mitzvah! You have probably been looking forward eagerly to the great day, and it *is* a wonderful experience. Of course, becoming a Bar/Bat Mitzvah means a lot more than just one memorable morning in the synagogue, and it means more than parties and gifts. Those things are all exciting, it's true. But a *real* Bar/Bat Mitzvah is something you *become* and *remain,* not for a day or a week, but for the rest of your life! The beautiful blessings and prayers you learn can be yours whenever you come to the synagogue. And, if you work hard, you will be able to chant any Haftarah for Shabbat or Yom Tov.
>
> But, even more important, real study can show you how to *live* as a Jew. We Jews, you know, believe in deeds, not in words. We believe that what is important is not what people *say,* but how they *live.* And we have a word for the *kind* of deed that is expected of the dedicated Jew. That word is *mitzvah.* For more than two thousand years, Jewish people have thought and written about what kinds of *mitzvot* God wants. We have sometimes found brand new answers to that question; we have also discovered new life and new wisdom in very old answers. You are now about to continue that search, that great adventure. In so doing, you are going to *become* a son or daughter of *mitzvah* — a Bar or Bat Mitzvah!

What is going to be expected of each of you now that you are becoming a Bar/Bat Mitzvah? Up to this time, you have had to prepare for tests and quizzes in school. Perhaps you worked on a more ambitious project or report that took even more preparation. But this is the first time that most of you will be learning a large amount of material over a long period of time. You may be wondering how you are going to accomplish all this, and it is natural for you to be a little bit nervous. But there's no reason to be. A few simple guidelines will get you started just right.

You may remember how difficult it once seemed to subtract, or to spell a hard word. Eventually, though, you learned and went on to more advanced skills. The same thing is true here. New exercises may seem difficult at first, but they will soon become old friends.

And you needn't worry about studying endlessly for hours and hours. In fact, you should probably not spend more than ten or twenty minutes a day. But you must work *every* day! That is the key to success. Don't skip a day, or you will probably skip two. Before you know it, you will have a lot of catching up to do. If you have ever saved up to buy something special, you know that the best way is to put a little away at regular intervals, not to promise yourself that you will someday "get around to it." A little work every day will add up to quite a bit in a week, and a substantial amount in a month. Therefore, do as Rabbi Shammai advised: "Set a fixed time for study." You will be astounded and very pleased at the results.

The Teaching Process

My class curriculum is threefold: cantillation, Musaf prayers, and review of general Judaica. Whatever the curricular demands of any particular program, the above principles will give the best chance for success. I would add only that a child should never be asked to do anything "cold." Anything assigned at home should be a review of material that has already been thoroughly introduced and drilled in class. In addition, the children are generally provided a tape recording of the assigned material. To give or not to give the tape seems to be a matter of principle in Bar/Bat Mitzvah instruction today. But I think we need to be guided by common sense and by a simple guideline: if you err, it should be on the side of creating less pressure for a child. I do require a candidate to chant the blessings before the Haftarah and ten lines of Haftarah text without a tape before embarking on the rest of the Haftarah. But, after that, if the student seems to need a tape to help with accents and phrasing, I do not think the future of Jewish education in our time will be compromised by making use of this useful tool. After all, a word with an *etnachta,* depending on the number of syllables in it and in the preceding word, may be sounded with as little as one note or as many as a half dozen or more. How is a twelve-year-old to know how to handle this? And what's wrong with making it easier? I believe that independence — which is what we're all after — will come faster the more students are exposed to proper accentuation which they can repeat again and again. On the other hand, if the student shows exceptional facility, he/she should probably be encouraged to work out such problems without a tape. (Additional remarks by Marshall Portnoy on teaching cantillation can be found in Chapter 19.)

I am aware that there is great concern about the fact that our students do not understand the meaning of the Hebrew text which they chant. I don't see this as an issue. The language of the Siddur and the Prophets is among the most difficult in any literary culture. I would challenge most laypersons to explain a Haftarah in translation, let alone in the original. I do believe it would be a good idea to teach, in the early Hebrew School years, 200 or so prayer words — as many as possible of which relate to a common conversational word: e.g., *atah, lechem, min, ha-aretz, z'man, hazeh,* etc. Famous phrases and key concepts in the Haftarot, Torah portions, and prayers we teach, such as *"Ronee v'simchi," "Ma navu al he-harim," "Higid l'cha Adonai mah tov,"* should also be taught. Understanding even the occasional word of a prayer or a Torah or Haftarah portion will add a great deal to the learning experience of the student.

Individual Instruction

Perhaps the most rewarding aspect of Bar/Bat Mitzvah is the individual work that follows the classroom experience. In general, the Haftarah should not require an inordinate amount of work if the preparation in cantillation has been adequate, and this should leave time for individual Bar/Bat Mitzvah projects. Most of my students elect to learn a Torah portion; some prefer to learn the *nusach* for the Shabbat Shacharit service or the Friday evening service. A few prefer to undertake literary research on the prophetic and biblical texts. Some naturally have more than they can handle in completing the required work. In any case, each child is challenged according to his/her needs and ability. Students may do as much or as little additional work as they wish. My approach is to inspire, to support, and to create an unpressured warm atmosphere, but at the same time to let students know that this is their ceremony, not mine. And this relates to the questions of responsibility discussed above, which are the essence of the Jewish concept of *mitzvah.*

Flexibility, sensitivity, and insight are crucial to this intensely interactive experience. I strongly encourage the presence of a parent at each individual session. Crucial information about the family's mode of operation and schedule constraints is imparted at these meetings. One child may need a set appointment each week; another works better when each appointment is set at the conclusion of the previous one.

The parents and the child — and the tutor — may be working within the same process with three different agendas. A father may be trying to relive his own Bar Mitzvah experience through his child. A mother may feel inadequate because she does not have the Hebrew skills to help her child at home. Including the parents in this process also leads to more of them wanting to acquire the skills to participate in the ceremony, perhaps by reading from the Torah, or even considering a course of study for themselves. The child may be conflicted because he/she would really like to read more *aliyot* from the Torah, but won't because his/her friends did not. If the tutor has little contact with the family, he or she will not be in a position to pick up on the verbal — and incredibly telling nonverbal — cues that families transmit. In addition, a family's circumstances change over the two years or more that the tutor is with them. If the tutor does not know what is going on, his/her effectiveness is greatly handicapped, and he/she may not be remembered as anything more than a tutor. And the best of tutors will probably not change the course of Jewish commitment in America. Personal connectedness is initially what leads anyone to participation, involvement, and eventual commitment. That is true for every sphere of life.

Particular sensitivity is necessary in dealing with the "broken" and "blended" families that comprise an ever greater percentage of those encountered in Bar/Bat Mitzvah teaching. Every story is different, but most will have one thing in common: their need for understanding, which is generally greater than in "original-unit" families. At least one spouse will probably be very verbal about that need. The principle I follow in dealing with these situations is one of full disclosure. If I have a transaction with one parent, the other is immediately informed about what happened. As this is somewhat cumbersome and can lead to misunderstanding, I insist as much as possible on seeing both parents together. I have also learned to include stepparents in the process, as long as this has been negotiated. In general, one can appeal to the parents for civilized behavior on the basis of what is best for the child's emotional well-being. In the case of a parent with overwhelming needs, it may be necessary to seek help from other professionals. These situations are difficult, to be sure, but your support can boost a child's self-esteem immeasurably. (For a further discussion of dealing with divorced families, see Chapter 48.)

Evaluation

How can we know how we are doing? In August of each year, I mail a survey to all families that have celebrated a Bar/Bat Mitzvah from the previous summer through June (see Appendix at the end of this chapter). Each year, the return rate exceeds 90%. And each year I learn something from it, especially about an area that needs attention.

There is one more question I think we owe it to ourselves and to our families to ask and answer honestly: "Why are you doing what you do?" If your answers have to do with love of children and the belief that this special process can be a pure delight, bonding family members to one another and to Judaism, then whatever the Cantor or other tutor does will not be far from the mark. I have enjoyed seeing the many new games, color-coded materials, computer techniques and graphics that are now being marketed for the teaching of B'nai Mitzvah students. I use some myself, and I believe that all of them are effective in the hands of a teacher who would have been effective anyway. This material can be wonderful, entertaining, and a great diversion. But the essence of our sacred calling is a transaction between people who are committed to the transmission of a heritage from one generation to the next.

Will we prepare a next generation which will see their own children celebrate Bar/Bat Mitzvah meaningfully? I fervently hope so. As professionals, we should count ourselves fortunate in being given the opportunity to fulfill the *mitzvah "v'shinantam l'vanecha."* Being Jewish in America presents us with great difficulties and great challenges. The Bar/Bat Mitzvah experience may be an extremely important avenue toward reclaiming many of our young people — along with their families — to an ongoing relationship with their Jewish heritage.

APPENDIX

Dear Parents,

This past year, your child celebrated a Bar/Bat Mitzvah in our congregation. In order to have the best program possible, I'm asking you to take a moment to let me know your general reactions to your child's and family's experience during this process. Please answer the following questions, and add any comments you like. Return this form to me in the envelope provided. Please do not include your name. These forms will be seen only by me; they are solely designed to help me do an effective job in working with our young people. Thanks so much for taking this time.

1. My child's experience in preparing for the Bar/Bat Mitzvah was generally:

   ☐ EXCELLENT ☐ GOOD ☐ FAIR ☐ POOR

2. The individual sessions with the Cantor were:

   ☐ VERY CONVENIENT ☐ MOSTLY CONVENIENT

   ☐ MOSTLY INCONVENIENT ☐ VERY INCONVENIENT

3. The individual sessions with the Cantor were:

   ☐ VERY POSITIVE ☐ MOSTLY POSITIVE

   ☐ MOSTLY NEGATIVE ☐ VERY NEGATIVE

4. In relation to my child's preparation and progress, the Cantor/tutor was:

   ☐ EXTREMELY INTERESTED ☐ MOSTLY INTERESTED

   ☐ MOSTLY DISINTERESTED ☐ EXTREMELY DISINTERESTED

5. My child was adequately prepared for the Bar/Bat Mitzvah:

   ☐ STRONGLY AGREE ☐ MOSTLY AGREE

   ☐ MOSTLY DISAGREE ☐ STRONGLY DISAGREE

Please add any comments you would like on scheduling, Bar/Bat Mitzvah class, ideas for the program, parent orientation, or anything you would like me to know.

Thanks so much.

(CANTOR/TUTOR'S NAME)

Chapter 3
Bar/Bat Mitzvah: A Window of Opportunity

Saul Wachs

During my thirteenth year, my family attended the Bar Mitzvah of a distant relative. What was special about the service was the fact that the Bar Mitzvah chanted the Musaf in addition to the Haftarah; in the mid-1940s, that was a bit unusual. My mother was impressed by the service and asked me if I would like to learn to chant the service for my upcoming Bar Mitzvah. I reacted positively to the idea.

With some trepidation, my mother approached Hazzan Joseph Mann, our Cantor at the West Philadelphia Jewish Community Center. He was a distinguished artist and Hazzan, but did not have any formal educational responsibilities within the congregation. To our delight, he reacted enthusiastically and said that he was prepared to teach me to lead the Musaf service on the day of my Bar Mitzvah. I later realized how much a sincere Cantor wants to transmit the liturgical tradition of which he/she is the guardian. Of course, the Rabbi had to agree, as did the members of the religious committee. Fortunately, the proposal was accepted and my studies began.

During the time that I studied, Hazzan Mann conceived of the idea of inviting other boys who were to celebrate their Bar Mitzvah ceremony during the 1944-45 academic year to act as a choir. Together, we learned selections of the Torah and Musaf liturgy. On the day of my Bar Mitzvah ceremony, I conducted the service with the other boys accompanying me as a choir. Subsequently, each of the boys would follow the same pattern, i.e., acting as Hazzan on the day of his Bar Mitzvah while the rest of us sang as accompanying choir.

Gradually, we were also encouraged to sing with Hazzan Mann on any Shabbat when there was no Bar Mitzvah ceremony. Thus, for a three-year period, I had the chance to sing with a great Cantor and, more important, to develop a close personal relationship with a warmhearted Jewish leader. I believe that that experience had a profound effect on my life. I still remember many of the melodies that we sang. I use them, occasionally, when I *daven* today. I also felt that special pleasure that comes from contributing to the community. I enjoyed the challenge of leading a service in the synagogue. I also enjoyed conducting services for Junior Congregation, and the combination of these two experiences was so positive that I decided to devote myself to Jewish communal service as a Hazzan and a Jewish educator. Although I ultimately made Jewish education my main professional career, I continue to maintain a lively interest in *hazzanut* and Jewish music. In fact, I have devoted myself in particular to the teaching of prayer, liturgy, and liturgical music.

My own experience is only one of many that I can cite. At a CAJE conference, several years ago, I had a discussion with David Alcot, a leading educator. When I probed the genesis of his career commitments, he spoke movingly of Hazzan Alan Michelson (z"l) of Congregation Adat Ari-El in southern California, in whose choir he had sung. David told me that at least nine people became Rabbis, Hazzanim, or Directors of Education because of the close relationships they developed with Cantor Michelson (a distinguished artist in his own right) through singing in his choir.

(Editor's Note: The Editor of this volume was herself a student of Cantor Michelson's. At a time when most avenues in the Conservative movement were closed to women, the door to Cantor Michelson's study was open to all. He was a nurturing teacher with a passion for handing on the tradition of *hazzanut,* a passion that was absorbed by many of his students through the years.)

I have heard wonderful children's choirs at Shabbat services at Congregations Adat Shalom and Shaare Zedek of suburban Detroit, to name just two that come to mind.

A few years ago, I was in the Agron Street Synagogue in Jerusalem for a Shabbat morning service. Hazzan Abraham Lubin led the service as a guest Hazzan, and a choir of children from Beth Torah in North Miami Beach sang. It made a profound impression on the entire congregation. In fact, Rabbi Yosef Green, spiritual leader of the congregation, did not deliver a formal *d'var Torah* that day, telling the worshipers that what we had all experienced together was sufficient to instruct and inspire us.

Recently, I spoke at Temple Sinai in Dresher, Pennsylvania for Shabbat. A choir trained by Hazzan Nathan Chaitovsky sang during the Musaf service. Once again, I was struck by the powerful effect of the experience upon the congregation and upon the children. In fact, that congregation has nurtured several future Rabbis, Cantors, Jewish educators, and lay leaders, many of whom, as children or teenagers, worked closely with Hazzan Chaitovsky. In another local congregation, Beth Sholom, Hazzan David Tillman has inspired large numbers of young people to sing and has taken many of them to choral festivals on local, regional, and even international levels. Hazzan Tillman is an active force at all levels of the educational program of the congregation.

I want to suggest from all of this, that the Bar/Bat Mitzvah experience offers us a "window of opportunity" through which we may reach the heart of the young person and create a memory that will have a lasting, beneficial effect. The Bar/Bat Mitzvah candidate is preparing for a presentation in which huge resources of time, energy, and money are often expended. If the relationship between the young person and the Cantor is close, trusting, and sensitive, and if that Cantor is also a skilled teacher, then the experience of Bar/Bat Mitzvah preparation can cement a deep intergenerational connection that will enrich the student throughout his/her life.

Moreover, if we can recreate the once prevalent practice of children's choirs or intergenerational choirs in which the young stand near the Cantor and observe, close up, fervent prayer, it is possible that we will develop an important new source of Cantors to serve the Jewish community in the future. I would suggest, based on informal research, that the percentage of Rabbis, Cantors, Jewish educators, and leading laity who, as children, sang in synagogue choirs and learned to conduct services is much higher than is ordinarily supposed. A great Cantor/Educator can be a powerful model who inspires the young person at an important stage of his/her development.

It has been said that "Jewish education is the process of creating memories," and these memories can be building blocks in a Jewish education that profoundly affects the young Jew. Of course, there are Cantors who are either unable or unwilling to work effectively with the young. This may stem from the fear (unwarranted, in my opinion) that intense involvement with the young will detract from the Cantor's artistic aspirations. It is also true that some Cantors, while musically or vocally gifted, do not have the native ability to work with the young. To force them to do so is to invite disaster. People are never too young to sense that the "teacher" is not happy to be teaching. In that situation, someone else should assume the responsibility of working with the young person. The important point is that the process of liturgical study should be a positive, personalized experience that simultaneously builds the self-esteem of the young person and leads that person to continued experiences of Jewish learning. This idea can only work if the Cantor is committed to its success.

In sum, I suggest the following:

1. Cantorial training should include professional training in working with the young. This should include skills in tutoring and some knowledge of counseling and developmental psychology in addition to experiences of choral conducting.
2. The Cantor should encourage young people to master liturgical skills. While this is an important component at all levels of Jewish education, it assumes special importance in connection with the Bar/Bat Mitzvah ceremony.
3. The development of choirs that sing with the Cantor in the synagogue should be made a high priority.

The Cantor can make a distinctive contribution to the nurturing of adolescent spirituality and Jewish identity. The young person, the family, the school, and the synagogue, all take the Bar/Bat Mitzvah ceremony seriously. It is therefore truly a window of opportunity during which we can teach important Jewish skills, shape attitudes, and build a personal relationship that will help to bind the heart of the young person to the Cantor and to the tradition that he/she embodies.

Chapter 4
Bar/Bat Mitzvah: Policies and Programs

Carol K. Ingall

Let's speak the unspeakable and be done with it. Bar/Bat Mitzvah is the bane of Jewish education. It is the tail that wags the dog, the lens through which a youngster's entire Jewish schooling is viewed. Curricula are reshaped to produce stellar performances on the pulpit. The child does admirably on the Bar/Bat Mitzvah day and the school is vindicated. A faltering, flustered showing or a truncated rendition are proof positive of the declining standards which riddle our schools. Having set Bar/Bat Mitzvah as the be-all and end-all of Jewish schooling, our clientele follow with the feet — ending their formal Jewish education at age thirteen.

Yet, it is the promise of the Bar or Bat Mitzvah that brings many of our parents to our doors. We can attribute the bulk of Religious School enrollment to the upcoming Bar or Bat Mitzvah. When the big day dawns, families are genuinely caught up in the magnitude of the event. Only the most jaded of us would claim that the source of the excitement lies in the festivities alone. Parents and professional educators wish for remarkably similar outcomes for the children involved. They want Jewish education to "take," for these kids to mature into committed Jewish adults, for reassurance that there will be yet another Jewish generation. In interviews with hundreds of B'nai Mitzvah, we hear again and again, "My Bar/Bat Mitzvah is the most important religious event of my life." It is up to us as professionals to harness all the excitement and positive Jewish energy that Bar/Bat Mitzvah generates and make it work for us.

Setting the Ground Rules

We can avoid all sorts of mishaps if we determine school policies at the outset and stick to them. Obviously, there will be exceptions, but make sure that the exceptions are the rarities.

There are a number of questions which have to be addressed by the Director of Education and synagogue staff before establishing a Bar/Bat Mitzvah policy:

1. Does one have to be a member to become a Bar or Bat Mitzvah at the synagogue?

   For most synagogues, the school is the primary means of recruiting members. In order to attend the school, a family must join the synagogue. Synagogue memberships are required not only because they produce revenue. Many educators argue that schooling without a synagogue component is bound to end in failure. However, there are a number of schools which allow non-synagogue members to join. These schools suggest that mandating synagogue membership is unfair, often producing economic hardship. They pride themselves on turning down no request for a Jewish education. In the case of community schools unconnected with a synagogue, Bar and Bat Mitzvah education is a rarity. The Bar/Bat Mitzvah instructor would have to train children for participation in a number of different synagogues. It is more practical for each child to be trained in the synagogue in which he/she will participate.

2. How many years of study in the school are necessary for a student to become a Bar/Bat Mitzvah?

   Schools differ widely from two years in many Reform congregations to five years in Conservative congregations.

3. What is the policy about transfer from a less rigorous school?

   The standard practice is to accept transfer credits at face value. If a student has difficulty in his or her new school, the Director of Education may want to consider having the child repeat a given year or offering the options of working with a tutor.

4. Can tutoring substitute for formal schooling?

   In many situations, tutoring is the only way a student will attain a religious education. As more and more Jewish children attend private schools (non-Jewish Day Schools) and attend school until late in the afternoon, more tutoring arrangements will have to be made. To assure standardization and communication, the school should hire the tutors and supervise the program. Students might attend Religious School on Sunday and pay a surcharge to the school for tutorial work. Tutoring may also be the best solution for children with learning disabilities and/or emotional problems. A student may have to be tutored for his or her entire Religious School career. An accommodation can be made so that the tutoring hours are fewer than the normal class hours — e.g., two hours of tutoring, rather than four hours of weekday classes. Holding out for obligatory attendance at Religious School is wise. Students should feel part of a community of learners.

5. Is there a policy regarding attendance at Shabbat services?

   If Bar/Bat Mitzvah is to become more than just a performance, attendance at services must be mandatory. A number of schools have settled on twice a month for the six months prior to the Bar or Bat Mitzvah. Others have made Shabbat service attendance as one of the many projects students must complete during their twelfth year. A student must attend one-third of the services during the year. Failure to comply means failure to complete the course of study. Attendance is taken by the Bar/Bat Mitzvah instructor who is also expected to attend services.

6. When will a child begin his or her Bar/Bat Mitzvah study?

   Most schools begin instruction the year before Bar or Bat Mitzvah. In my congregation's program (discussed below), students begin to work on projects in the late fall of the sixth grade.

7. What services will the school provide?

   Schools often provide an instructor to teach Haftarah trope and/or Torah trope. If a student is particularly able and opts to do more, a school should be prepared to assist him or her. A school should provide these services as part of its obligation to its students, rather than treating them as "extras" for which the parents are billed.

8. Will each Bar or Bat Mitzvah ceremony be the same?

   A school should determine a policy for exceptional children, on both sides of the spectrum. A student who cannot present a full Shabbat Haftarah should be given some options. He/she might prefer to have an *aliyah* and/or Torah reading on Monday, Thursday, or Rosh Chodesh. Learning disabled children might be given transliterations to help them get over the hurdle of the Hebrew language. (See Chapters 14, 15, and 16 for other approaches to working with this population.) Many children learn better through aural means. For them, the use of tapes and/or a piano might be more effective.

   Brighter children or more poised, musical children might want to do more. A Director of Education might insist on completion of a special Bar/Bat Mitzvah study program to enable a child to read the Torah, rather than just recite a Haftarah.

9. Will Bar/Bat Mitzvah be contingent upon a pledge to continue study?

   Many schools require promises that students continue for Confirmation or high school. Directors of Education who reject these pledges do so because they don't work. A recalcitrant child and/or an uncommitted family will not maintain their promise. Insisting upon a pledge encourages families to lie. It has been suggested that we bill parents for Confirmation during the Bar/Bat Mitzvah year. Whether that would have any effect (positive or negative) has not yet been ascertained.

10. What is the synagogue/school policy toward *kashrut,* if any?

    Synagogues that require *kashrut* pledges run the same risk as synagogues that demand study pledges. Both are unenforceable outside the synagogue. Each Director of Education must decide whether or not to attend the receptions to which he/she is invited.

Scheduling

Dealing with the bugaboo of dates can be a horror. Certain dates are desirable; others are not. It's easy to see which aren't. No Jewish children should be born during the months of January and February in the midwest. Such births necessitate, thirteen years later, their grandparents return from Florida mid-season. They also require steely-nerved parents who can withstand gnashing their teeth over the prospect of paralyzing storms. July and August dates are not popular either. This is due, in part, to the dismay of the professionals who discover their summers are not their own. Even if the *Klai Kodesh* were available, these summer dates would be problematic. Few children want to have a Bar or Bat Mitzvah ceremony without their peers.

The unpopular dates are easier to categorize than the popular ones. Is a December date a good one? "Yes," say those whose lives revolve around the academic calendar. "No," say those who spend every winter vacation in the sun. Labor Day weekend is ideal for those who want to make a gala weekend of the event. It is anathema to those who refuse to cut short their summers.

To avoid being caught in the date crossfire, set a policy and appoint a lay committee to administer it. Have the committee assign the dates, using strict guidelines. Such guidelines might be:

1. The date closest to the child's Hebrew or English birthdate takes precedence.
2. More flexibility with girls' dates than boys'. This is no vestigial sexism, but a reflection of *halachic* reality — girls may become B'not Mitzvah throughout the twelfth year; boys may not.
3. First come, first served.
4. No swapping of dates except through the intercession of the committee. You don't want to unleash a particularly predatory set of parents, intent on capturing a given date, on the unsuspecting holders of that date.
5. The option of a Bar or Bat Mitzvah any time the Torah is read. Not everyone wants a Shabbat morning Bar/Bat Mitzvah. Make sure this option is well-known. It may ease the burden on families who for financial, social, or personal reasons, shy away from a larger scale *simchah*.

Participation in the Service

Many Directors of Educations have based the child's participation in the service to the completion of a special course of study or project. These children, for example, read from the Torah and complete a Haftarah in a synagogue where the norm is doing a Haftarah only.

Work out a balance between honors for the Bar/Bat Mitzvah and for the congregation. If there is no congregation to speak of, the day can belong to the Bar or Bat Mitzvah. The family can assign all the honors, including, if the *Klai Kodesh* are willing, chanting the service and delivering a *d'var Torah.* If there is a core congregation who attends week after week, it would be unfair of the Bar/Bat Mitzvah family to whisk the service away. An arrangement can be made whereby several *aliyot* are reserved for the congregation, as are several liturgical pieces such as "*Adon Olam*" or "*Yigdal.*" A *Kiddush* could be provided for all.

A Bar/Bat Mitzvah committee of parents and interested laypeople could be useful in areas other than scheduling. Have the committee plan workshops for the parents of future B'nai Mitzvah. For example, let them share their expertise on invitations (setting up an array of different types — formal and informal, child-made and professionally printed, ones with Hebrew and without). Have the committee discuss planning, holding the hands of those first timers who can't possibly imagine how to go about setting up lists and interviewing caterers. Describe various kinds of receptions, lending encouragement to those resisting lavish affairs. The committee can run through the service with families, review the number of *aliyot* allotted to the family, and the "choreography" of the worship service. The committee, Director of Education, and/or clergy can utilize some workshop time to review the *brachot* with the parents. They can make copies of the Torah blessings and *Shehecheyanu* (or whatever will be recited in Hebrew) available for distribution to uncles and aunts, grandparents, and other relatives. Let them level with other parents about how much study time will be required of their children at home. Inform parents that they will often have to play the "heavy," making sure that their children rehearse their parts and complete their course work. Offering such a Bar/Bat Mitzvah workshop is a very real contribution the school can make to parents. (For another approach to having laypeople from the congregation involved with B'nai Mitzvah and their families, see Chapter 50.)

Creating a Special Study Program

An adolescent comes of age in Samoa, Africa, Asia — imagine any place that is remote, unspoiled by modern civilization. His or her puberty ritual might be making a canoe, hunting a ferocious beast, or fending for himself/herself in the wilderness. The rites reflect the values of the society in which he/she will be taking an adult part — values of physical strength, independence, and resourcefulness. Our tribal rites of Bar and Bat Mitzvah center on reading from our sacred books and public worship. They are a distillation of Jewish values, a statement of the centrality of study and prayer. To create an authentic preparation for Bar and Bat Mitzvah would require highlighting those values, not merely as rehearsals for the big event, but as ends in themselves.

Rabbi Burt Jacobson has created a novel study program which supplements formal school. Used in the "*Hey*" level and tested in both Reform and Conservative schools, *Crossing the River* was originally designed to be used in a one-on-one tutorial mode. This "apprenticeship program" relies heavily on values clarification. The Student's Values Book requires them to imagine themselves in hypothetical situations, examine their responses, and record them. For example, in a unit called, "Growing Up Jewish in America," students read a synopsis of American Judaism, quiz themselves, and then complete an interview, ostensibly written by an Israeli journalist, on the attitudes of a typical American teenager on his/her Bar/Bat Mitzvah. Jacobson's approach is very open and non-judgmental, presenting a number of styles of being Jewish. He draws heavily on the thinking of Franz Rosenzweig and the option of choosing *mitzvot.* It is one of the few programs which asks students to consider seriously the implications of joining the adult Jewish community. (For a more complete description of this curriculum, see Chapter 40.)

A.R.E. Publishing, Inc. has produced a mini-course called *Bar/Bat Mitzvah: A Family Education Unit.* This can be used outside the school setting by families who want to capitalize on the momentum of Bar and Bat Mitzvah to cement their Jewishness. The mini-course includes exercises on the meaning of Bar or Bat Mitzvah, of tradition, of *Matan Torah,* rites of passage, and Hebrew names. The authors offer topics for family research, presentations, and bibliographies. Projects for family learning include: the history of Bar and Bat Mitzvah, the order of the service, Torah reading, *tallit, tefillin, mitzvot,* and *kipah.*

An interesting program, developed in England by Rabbi Howard Cooper and Margaret Sassienie, stresses Bar/Bat Mitzvah in the broader context of a young person's general religious education. In the three trimester program, the ceremony/service is a part of a whole educational process which helps to integrate the student's Jewish development with his/her emerging adolescent development. Each student has his or her Bar/Bat Mitzvah ceremony as usual during the year. A group composed of those with a Bar or Bat Mitzvah that year remain together throughout the school year and also have a joint Bar/Bat Mitzvah at the conclusion of the program. Central to the program are the opportunities provided for the students to discover and experience for themselves as an individual, certain "adult responsibilities" (*mitzvot*) in three circles of Jewish life: the family, the congregation/community, the Jewish world.

A number of synagogues utilize a variation of the project format, such as the Thirteen Mitzvot programs or the Bar/Bat Mitzvah program at Temple Emanu-El, Providence, Rhode Island. In these programs there is no text other than a notebook or set of project cards. Students in the program complete projects, scouting style, at their own pace. Advisors check the projects over after they have been turned in, returning them with their comments to the students. The scope of these programs is determined by the number of projects required and the depth of the projects. In some schools students are involved in a choice of service projects within the Jewish community. Volunteering at a home for the aged or Jewish hospital is a commitment for the year prior to Bar and Bat

Mitzvah. In the Emanu-El program, students complete 33 projects, some experimental, such as attending weddings and funerals, some strictly cognitive, such as identifying the books of the Torah, the patriarchs and matriarchs. Whether based on a Torah, *avodah,* and *gemilut chasadim* framework, or synagogue, home, and community, all of the project programs hope to produce familiarity with the Jewish calendar, synagogue service, the local Jewish community, and the State of Israel. (For an overview of several Mitzvah Programs, see Unit IV.)

An ideal Bar or Bat Mitzvah program would utilize components of all the prototypes described above. It would also supplement the standard curriculum. Such a program would emphasize study and prayer, consistent with the Bar/Bat Mitzvah ceremony itself. As long as Bar/Bat Mitzvah is inevitable, our students will be fidgety teenagers with short attention spans and the feeling they have outgrown Religious School. The most successful Bar/Bat Mitzvah programs are tailored to these realities. They represent a clean break with the school. By utilizing mini-courses or projects, they avoid the tedium of a year-long course of study. By meeting at different times from the rest of the school such as Shabbat mornings before services, Shabbat afternoons, or during the week, they are different from Religious School. Ideally, the teacher/advisor is a new face, unconnected with the Religious School. Texts give way to brightly colored workbooks or file cards, requiring students to work individually or with their families.

An ideal program would ask students to consider seriously the implications of their Bar/Bat Mitzvah and to assume responsibility for their Jewish lives. Be it through the acceptance of ritual, synagogue observance, and/or community responsibility, we should utilize the year before Bar/Bat Mitzvah to begin to up the Jewish ante. Service projects, mastery of certain *tefillot,* building *sukkot,* and giving *mishloach manot* are within the reach of most of our youngsters.

Family experiences should be a part of any program. Trips to local Jewish landmarks, book discussions, study-prayer-meal combinations will bring out parents who are often reluctant to come to services. Investigation of names, working on family trees, and collecting oral history are likely to appeal to even the most blasé of parents. (For more on Family Education programs, see Unit VI.)

In preparing programs, include a number of crafts projects. Making "stained glass" windows, illuminating one's Haftarah, creating *mezuzot* and one's own personal Jewish art often appeal to those students who aren't comfortable in a reading-research setting. Baking *challot* and *hamentaschen,* preparing Shabbat meals will bring parent volunteers and interest to the program that the purely cognitive, no matter how well done, will rarely achieve.

No student should be shut out of such a program if he/she wants to be part of it. Requirements can be revised and tailored to a special student's needs. One of my most treasured mementos is a letter written in an awkward script from a severely learning disabled student:

> I was not able to attend Hebrew school, and I wanted to belong to the Temple, and I feel that by going to class on Saturdays with Mrs. Ingall I have learned a lot about my religion. I can learn my religion at home, but I like being a part of a class. I feel that becoming a Bat Mitzvah makes me glad and a part of my synagogue and makes me want to continue to learn and become a Jewish young lady that my parents and teachers can be proud of now and later. My parents are happy that I am going to be Bat Mitzvah because they helped me and worked very hard with me.

Completion of the program can be recognized by increasing the Bar/Bat Mitzvah's role in the service or by offering a tangible reward. Some synagogues award certificates or gifts or create special weekends for "graduates" of Bar/Bat Mitzvah programs. Some offer no incentive, knowing that the program will stand on its own merit — *Torah lishmah.*

If the program is a successful one, there is a greater likelihood of encouraging students to continue in high school programs or Confirmation programs. It is rare to pick up a student for a high school program who hasn't successfully completed a supplemental Bar/Bat Mitzvah program. Religious School must be presented to parents as a commitment through high school. If this expectation is not made early on, there will always be attrition after Bar and Bat Mitzvah. (For more on post-Bar and Bat Mitzvah education, see Chapters 44 and 45.)

The Bar/Bat Mitzvah year is a difficult one. Family seams become unraveled. Financial issues, parents' and children's concerns about performance, residual bitterness over divorces and family feuds can threaten to overshadow the religious significance of the event. Bar/Bat Mitzvah is not merely recognition of a child's birthday, but a family event. Through the creation of a thoughtful and challenging program, the Director of Education can make Bar or Bat Mitzvah even more significant to the child and his/her family.

Chapter 5
My Ideal Bar/Bat Mitzvah Program

Jeffrey Schein

Bar/Bat Mitzvah is a rite of passage. As in any rite of passage, drama and crisis inhere in the event. From an educator's point of view, a Bar/Bat Mitzvah ascending the *bimah* to read or chant from the Torah represents Jewish tradition's reenactment of its primary ritual of affirming Jewish adulthood. Because so many Jewish children successfully emerge from this trial as more assured and competent young adults, we can meaningfully speak of Bar/Bat Mitzvah as a Jewish success story.

Yet, the success is only partial. A rite of passage also implies that 1) we know where the person has come from and where he or she is going (i.e., we have defined what we mean by a young adult); and 2) that the community has provided a place for the young adult to exercise the privileges and responsibilities that pertain to young adult status.

In this regard, I am sharply critical of the efforts of the Jewish community around the B'nai Mitzvah process. I don't believe we program on the basis of what we know about the nature of young adulthood. A significant literature about early adolescence that informs the work of the best practitioners in the field of general education is often unexamined by Jewish educators. Nor have we faced up to the challenge of restructuring our schools and synagogues in a way that allows a Bar or Bat Mitzvah to play the role of young adult in a meaningful fashion.

I believe this is so despite enormous programmatic creativity on the part of Rabbis and Jewish educators, and the good intentions of parents and the community. We do not have today the "Bar/Bat Mitzvah factories" of our worst nightmares. But we do have a process that is driven by the institutional needs of a congregation to train X number of children, rather than to implement a Jewish vision of young adulthood.

In this chapter, I have intentionally erred on the side of rhetorical overstatement. I have tried to sketch out an "ideal" Bar/Bat Mitzvah program. Each element in the program has been "field-tested" in my many years of work as a Director of Education. My suggestion, however, that one can have a program that is "vision" rather than "institution" driven is pedagogic. I recognize the *chutzpah* in ignoring legitimate institutional needs, but I think colleagues will glean more from an "idealized" picture than from one anchored in institutional realities that are not their own.

Confessions of a Jewish Educator

I spent my first five years as a Jewish educator "mistreating" my 12 and 13-year-old students. Mistakenly, I treated them as if they were older teenagers. I took them through mini-courses on Jewish identity and values that assumed a focused sense of "I" that in truth is the fruit of a succesfully negotiated later adolescence (fifteen to eighteen-year-olds). I learned from the fine group of educators working at the Center for Early Adolescence at the University of North Carolina at Chapel Hill that I was not alone in this regard. Indeed, Joan Lipsitz, the Director of this Center, wrote *Growing Up Forgotten* in part because she found so many educators confusing these two stages of development.

Early and later adolescence are the flip sides of the same coin. In early adolescence, a "negative identity" paves the way for future positive identifications. Young teens know much better what they don't like than what they do like. Asking them to value Jewish values, as opposed (as I will argue later) to acting upon them, is a developmentally inappropriate activity. Would that we could be all powerful and could have the wonderful surge of affirmation that marks the growth of an older teen without the ridiculous, brooding negativity of the earlier years. But what we have is a developmental logic we need to understand better.

I have found it helpful to frame the challenge of working with the Bar/Bat Mitzvah age student in terms suggested by Dr. Norman Newberg of the University of Pennsylvania. Utilizing Erik Erikson's life cycle framework, Dr. Newberg suggests that each "crisis" (defined as a potential for growth) in the life cycle can be characterized by a seed statement that captures an individual's emerging sense of self at that stage of life.

The seed statement for an individual wrestling with the issue of industry versus inferiority (age span of 6-13 in Erikson's system) is "I am what I learn." Self-image at this age is very connected to intellectual achievement. Part of the power of the Bar/Bat Mitzvah ceremony is that it allows the young adult to demonstrate a cumulative intellectual mastery of aspects of Jewish tradition.

The seed statement for an individual trying to reconcile identity with identity diffusion (approximately ages 14-18) is "I am myself." Much of the psychic energy previously devoted to intellectual achievement is now transferred to social awareness. The web of relationships that confirm the value of the self becomes the focus of development.

Our B'nai Mitzvah students are in transition between these two stages of development. But the transition is just beginning. "Ideal" teaching and programming for the early adolescent, in my view, would be weighted about 80-20 in favor of learning that consolidates "I am what I learn." This kind of learning emphasizes the ability of the students to interpret what they formerly understood by rote and opens the door for meaningful participation in the adult community. The remaining 20% allows students to stretch beyond themselves to issues of Jewish identity and values that will be a major focus of their later Jewish growth. Because I originally inverted this formula and spent most of my time dealing with issues of Jewish values and identity and less with the consolidation of "I am what I learn," I believe the 12 and 13-year-olds I worked with during my first ten years as a Jewish educator arrived intuitively at the conclusion I have tried to lay out more discursively here: namely, I did not really understand who they were as young adolescents.

Prelude to a Program

In many ways, what I hope to develop for B'nai Mitzvah students are programmatic embodiments of this transition into Jewish young adulthood. I believe the activities described in the next section demonstrate a better sense of the proportionality between the seed statements of "I am what I learn" and "I am myself" than I had when I began my work with early adolescents. I have also looked for ways to intertwine the valuational, intellectual, and social dimensions of learning. So, for instance, the "Mikraot G'dolot" project described below begins as a Jewish/intellectual challenge as the student seeks to comment on a line from his or her Torah portion. But it incorporates a significant social element as other students become the *parshanim* and comment on his/her commentary. Similarly, the Reb Hayim dilemmas discussed below are essentially a tool for furthering moral development. Yet, moral development is clearly linked to social awareness in the dilemmas presented in the Reb Hayim format.

I assume that a young adolescent has a wonderfully fluid sense of "I" that is defined through relationships rather than an established sense of self. For each area of the programs, I try to focus on the relationship between past and future experience in the school, congregation, and community. I try to define a new task and status that comes with becoming a Bar/Bat Mitzvah. These tasks and experiences are most often "intergenerational." I believe that the reality of being a "young adult" in the Jewish community will only make sense to the early adolescent if he/she has significant contact with those who are "young" and those who are "adult."

The five programs described below do not constitute a full Bar/Bat Mitzvah program. Training for trope and other areas of ritual competence, for instance, are not described. Together, however, I hope they will give the reader a sample of the kind of programmatic thinking that weds Bar/Bat Mitzvah preparation with the insights about early adolescence already discussed.

In Relationship to Self: Reb Hayim (or Sally)

Reb Hayim is a project that credits Bar/Bat Mitzvah students with having achieved a degree of wisdom in their 12 or 13 years of living. The project asks students to give a response (*te'shuvah*) to a question (*sh'aylah*) posed by the teacher or another student. The project, besides having classical roots in the tradition of Responsa literature, also reminds us of the "Bintel Briefs" in the *Daily Forward*. Truth to tell, there is also a touch of Ann Landers in it.

These questions are most effective when they challenge the young teen's budding sense of loyalty to peers and community. According to Lawrence Kohlberg, the transition from a self to a group-oriented morality is occurring for many young adolescents. Questions that allow students to think about these conflicting claims facilitate their moral development. They also provide a chance to explore a wide range of Jewish subjects. The Reb Hayim exercises found in Appendix 1 deal with subjects as diverse as Pesach, God, and Valentine's Day. Formulated as open-ended requests for advice, Reb Hayim sessions ask students to substitute their own names for Reb Hayim or Sally and offer advice to the person posing the questions.

Teachers make the most out of this format when:

1. They first give all students a chance to write out their responses to the dilemma.
2. Students then have a chance to share their responses in class.
3. Teachers collect the Reb Hayim letters, study the responses, and then come back to students the following week with questions that require further analysis.

Perhaps more important than the surface learnings of the Reb Hayim format are the opportunities for driving home the message that a young adult is a moral/Jewish philosopher in the making. In the past, I have found it helpful to put in the hallway a permanent *chochmah* display of the most interesting responses to Reb Hayim dilemmas. The Reb Hayim responses can also be published as a journal of Responsa literature for the entire school. An interesting use of the format is to ask younger children in the school to submit Reb Hayim dilemmas to the Bar/Bat Mitzvah class (see Appendix 1 for examples).

In Relationship to Judaism: The Mikraot G'dolot Project

The "Mikraot G'dolot" project provides students with the opportunity to write commentary for the Torah portion of their Bar/Bat Mitzvah. The project was conceived as a replacement or supplement to the traditional Bar/Bat Mitzvah *d'var Torah*. Occasionally, these talks are brilliant. They may be meaningful in terms of the learning that goes into them even when the finished product is questionable. But most often, I would characterize these talks as fulfilling the three p's: pat, pretentious, and predictable.

Again, I believe this is largely because we have given B'nai Mitzvah students a task that is more appropriate for older adolescents. A 12 or 13-year-old is just beginning to engage in the kind of abstract reasoning that can make for a meaningful *d'var Torah*.

The project unfolds in the following way: Students are introduced to the notion of commentary and study the structure of a page of the "great commentary." They are then told that as a group they will work toward leaving their own *mikraot g'dolot* as a gift to the next year's Bar/Bat Mitzvah class and to the congregation as a whole. The commentary will include a page with a line from the Torah portion for each Bar/Bat Mitzvah student.

Students are then asked to find the single line from their Torah portion that is most interesting to them. They box that line in the center of an 8½" x 14" sheet of paper. Around the box they will enter the first piece of commentary: their own comment on what they think that line means. Each student's page then circulates around the class for comments by peers. Students are asked to sign their commentary Rabbi __________ (Sarah, Jack, etc.).

The second step in the process is to provide the students with some hermeneutical tools that might give them a deeper understanding of their line. Students are introduced to three metaphors for understanding the expansive nature of Torah commentary: the Torah as a puzzle, a mirror, and an old-new book. The puzzle aspect of Torah study points to the unanswered questions (pieces of the puzzle) found in the Torah text itself. The mirror metaphor helps the student see himself/herself in the characters of the Torah. The old-new book metaphor is designed to help students see the great perennial questions of human existence that are still with us today even though we dress them in different cultural garments than are found in the Torah.

Using the techniques of synectics (more literature about this technique is available from the Melton Center and in the volume *Models of Teaching* by Bruce Joyce, Marsha Weil, and Beverly Showers), students are asked to apply these metaphors to key sections of the Torah (e.g., the Joseph story, Cain and Abel, etc.). Students then return to their own Torah portions and try to apply these metaphors to their own portions. Students combine the responses of other students with their own expanded insights as they prepare to make their contribution to their *mikraot g'dolot*.

The art teacher then spends an hour teaching some basic techniques of calligraphy to the students who are then given as much as two hours to calligraph carefully their line of Torah onto a piece of parchment paper. They then place the parchment paper at the center of a large blue sheet of "commentary" and use pen or felt marker to record neatly the commentaries they have amassed about their line of Torah.

Their *mikraot g'dolot* is then placed on display for the congregation to see. Each Shabbat, it is turned to the page of the Bar/Bat Mitzvah of that week.

In Relationship to School, Peers, and Jewish Community: Mitzvah Honor Society and the Torah-Thon

B'nai Mitzvah students need to have a special niche within programs that encompass the whole school population. At Congregation Or Ami in Lafayette Hill, Pennsylvania, one of the most valuable parts of the educational program was a Mitzvah Honor Society. Each month a list of "Mitzvot of the Month" was circulated, and students were encouraged to perform a requisite number of *mitzvot* to become part of the Mitzvah Honor Society.

While this was generally a very successful program, the staff was perplexed by the utter lack of participation by junior high school students. The staff was able to turn this situation around for seventh and eighth graders when they began to fulfill the precept of *lishmoa oznecha l'mah ha-peh m'daber,* let our ears listen to what our mouths have said. There was nothing in our Mitzvah Honor Society that credited these students with being young adults. They were treated as generic *mitzvah-doers,* just as their younger brothers and sisters might have been. The staff felt that we had treated much of our own talk about the responsibilities of young adulthood as empty rhetoric.

Eventually, the staff evolved two unique forms of participation for our seventh and eighth graders. In seventh grade, students became responsible for compiling the list of monthly *mitzvot* for the Mitzvah Honor Society. Their own lack of knowledge about how such a list might be compiled was challenged. The process of "*mitzvah* scouting" became their own. They were responsible for developing the list and then presenting and explaining the list at school-wide assemblies.

After becoming a Bar/Bat Mitzvah, students took on a more intensive kind of responsibility. They were assigned the responsiblity of helping to move a younger grade of students along in their involvement in the Mitzvah Honor Society. They were responsible for charting each individual student's progress, developing skits or dramatizations to motivate performance of a particular *mitzvah* and, in some instances, for organizing such activities as *hamentaschen* baking so that their students could perform the *mitzvah* of *mishloach manot.*

In regard to *tzedakah,* a similar logic held. Many a teacher and Director of Education has taken note of the inverse *tzedakah* curve. Younger children seem to give much more generously to *tzedakah* than do Bar/Bat Mitzvah students. At Or Ami, this frustration led to creating a new Bar/Bat Mitzvah class tradition. Much as the "Mikraot G'dolot" project was a way of showcasing the group's Jewish intelligence, a Torah-Thon became the means for displaying the group's wedding of compassion with ritual skill in regard to Torah reading.

During the second half of the Bar/Bat Mitzvah year, students were taken through a process of *tzedakah* decision making. They would decide upon several key *tzedakah* organizations that they would like to support. They would then begin to find sponsors for a Torah-Thon held on or around Shavuot (in some instances as a *Tikkun Leil Shavuot*). Friends, family members, and community members would sponsor students for each line they would read from the Torah during the Torah-Thon. The students (usually a group of 20) were able to raise well over $1,000!

(Forms relating to the Mitzvah Honor Society and the Torah-Thon can be found in Appendix 2.)

In Relationship to Adults: Working with Senior Citizens

The enormous feeling of continuity (*dor l'dor*) that adults feel when they watch Torah scrolls being handed down from one generation to the next can be expanded upon for B'nai Mitzvah students by opportunities to work with senior adults. It is not infrequent that Religious School students will have made a visit to a Jewish nursing home for a holiday. But this periodic *mitzvah* can be given regularity by giving a Bar/Bat Mitzvah class the responsibility for leading Shabbat services at such an institution.

The very process of dividing these responsibilities fairly is a lesson in what it means to be part of a voluntary community that feels obligated to perform *mitzvot.* This is education for Jewish citizenship. The specific responsibilities for leading services can reinforce the skills students are developing as part of their own Bar/Bat Mitzvah preparation. If in addition the students can do oral histories of some of the individuals in the nursing home, they will have the important Jewish feeling that the gifts they give are not just for their own synagogue community, but also for the wider Jewish world.

Conclusion

In his chapter entitled "Jewish Education: Crisis and Vision" (in *Imagining the Jewish Future,* David Teutsch, ed., SUNY Press, 1992), Jonathan Woocher has remarked that what starts out looking like formal problems of pedagogy and Jewish education are often, upon analysis, problems about Judaism and the Jewish community. The prolonged adolescence that is a function of modernity challenges the Jewish community to come up with forms of apprenticeship that assure a Bar/Bat Mitzvah that he or she does indeed have a new status in the community. I am pessimistic about the power of Jewish schools to respond to this need in isolation. But working in concert with the congregations that sponsor them, Jewish schools can utilize the high energy surrounding the Bar/Bat Mitzvah to transform their communities as well as their education programs.

APPENDIX 1

Primary Level: Reb Hayim Dilemmas

EVERYDAY LIFE

Dear Reb Hayim,

1. Why do I have to go to Religious School?
2. My Mommy doesn't want me to play with Charlie because my mommy says Charlie's mommy doesn't like Jews. But I want to play with Charlie because he's the best skater on the street and I like to skate.
3. Do you have to be married to be pregnant?
4. I'd like to do more Jewish things in my home, but my parents aren't interested. What should I do?
5. Some kids get to learn about religion during schooltime; why do we have to use our free time to learn about Judaism?

JEWISH IDENTITY

Dear Reb Hayim,

1. Why do I need to learn Hebrew?
2. My parents want me to have a Bar Mitzvah. How do I tell them no?
3. Why are there Christmas specials on TV, but no Chanukah specials?
4. My friend Marie tells me I can believe in Jesus in my heart and not tell my parents. Marie is my best friend. What do I do?
5. What will happen to me if I eat pork?
6. Is it all right for me to make a Christmas stocking even though I'm Jewish?
7. My mom wants me to go to Shabbat services this week. My dad wants me to go play in the soccer game. What should I do?
8. My team has a picnic on Sunday. That's when we meet for Religious School class. What should I do?

HOLIDAYS

Dear Reb Hayim,

1. I have an important game on the High Holy Days. I'm the only kicker on the team. Should I disappoint myself as a Jew or disappoint my team? Could I leave in the middle of services to go play?
2. My teacher keeps telling me all this stuff when it's Sukkot or Tu B'Shevat time about how beautiful nature is. Then my friend's house gets knocked over by a mud slide. That doesn't sound very beautiful to me. What's so beautiful about nature then? Why does my teacher talk that way?

ELEMENTARY AND JUNIOR HIGH LEVELS: REB HAYIM DILEMMAS

ISRAEL

Dear Reb Hayim,

1. I'm an American Jew and I love being in America. Why do I have to study about Israel, and why do I have to say things like "next year in Jerusalem"? I don't ever want to live anywhere but here in America.
2. If the United States/Canada and Israel got into a war, which side would you fight for?

JEWISH HISTORY

Dear Reb Hayim,

1. Why is Jewish history important to us today?
2. Why is Jewish history so sad?
3. A friend of mine in Religious School says that if he lived during the Russian pogroms, he would have converted to Christianity. Would you have converted if you were alive then?

JEWISH ETHICS

Dear Reb Hayim,

1. My parents talk about how they are not going to pay the government taxes. It has something to do with "fake deductions." Is what my parents are doing wrong? Should I tell anyone?
2. Most people don't live by all the ideals we talk about at services in the synagogue. So why do we talk so much about them?
3. I'm saving my money to buy "Star Wars" cards. But at Religious School, they keep asking for money for *tzedakah*. What good will it do to give my money to people I'll never know?

APPENDIX 1 (Cont.)

PRAYER

Dear Reb Hayim,

1. I go to services on Friday night. They're long and boring. I don't feel like I'm praying. What does it feel like to really feel like you're praying?
2. Does God hear our prayers?
3. What language does God understand?
4. Can we use our own prayers rather than those in the Siddur?
5. I read a prayer that says that the Jews are chosen over all other peoples. What does this mean exactly? Is it true?

JEWISH IDENTITY

Dear Reb Hayim,

1. If I don't want to, why do I have to come to Religious School?
2. Is being Jewish really that important?
3. Can I just feel Jewish without learning so much about it?
4. At Religious School, I learn about Shabbat how to light the candles, say prayers and sing songs. But at home, my mom says we can't do it because my dad doesn't come home until late on Friday night. Do you see any way to solve this problem?
5. I hear that a Jew is anyone born of a Jewish mother. That sounds unfair to fathers. Don't they count, too? Also, what if a person becomes another religion? Are they still Jewish because they were born to a Jewish mother? Maybe when you're done answering these questions, you can answer one last one: Why is it important to know who is a Jew? It sounds important to me, but I just can't seem to put my finger on why.

UNBELIEVABLY COMPLEX — WHAT'S JEWISH LIFE ALL ABOUT, ANYWAY?

Finally, there is this new "Reb Hayim" category. Uncensored, it comes out as follows:

Dear Reb Hayim,

What should I do? I am 13 years old, a Bar Mitzvah. I go to Religious School to study Torah because:

1. My parents want me to, but they don't care what grades I get.
2. I don't have Jewish friends in my regular school and I like to be with Jewish kids my own age.
3. My Religious School teacher expects or wants me to use my class time for learning, not for socializing.
4. My teacher is good and prepares interesting lessons, but it is pretty hard to learn because most of us don't come to learn.
5. I want to learn because it sounds interesting.

Should I do

- What the kids want?
- What the teachers want?
- What my parents want?
- What I want?

Dear Reb Hayim,

I always find reading the Passover Haggadah very interesting. I know exactly how the Israelites must have felt. I'm a slave, too. I'm 13, but my parents won't let me make any of my own decisions. They still set a bedtime for me on school nights and I can't stay out past midnight on weekends. And they're always telling me what's right and wrong, as if I don't have a mind of my own!

My parents could teach Pharaoh a thing or two. How can I get them to give me more freedom? Sometime I'm going to write my own Haggadah all about being freed from "parental bondage."

Sincerely,
Edna Enslaved

Dear Reb Hayim,

I'm about to be Confirmed, but I may not be able to go through with it. Not because I don't want to. Here's the situation.

Right after Confirmation, we're moving to California. But our congregation here has a rule which says you cannot be Bar/Bat Mitzvah or Confirmed if you have financial obligations to the synagogue. A number of years ago, my father made a pledge to the synagogue to help with a new building. We still owe several hundred dollars, and that's hard to pay with the move coming up.

APPENDIX 1 (Cont.)

The Board of Directors has told my father that I cannot be Confirmed until the pledge is paid. Now my father is angry because he feels the Board of Directors is blackmailing him.

I haven't been a great student, but I've worked pretty hard since Bar Mitzvah to become a Confirmand. And now it looks like all that work is for nothing. Is it? I don't know if I should be angry at the Board of Directors or at my father. Who do you think is right in this situation? What should I do?

Sincerely,
Carl Confirmation (maybe?)

Dear Reb Hayim,

I am sixteen. The other day I bought my girlfriend a Valentine card. You've got to understand, Reb Hayim, that my girlfriend is Jewish. This is not a dilemma about dating or marrying non-Jews.

Anyway, here's what happened. First, my mother tells me that Valentine's Day is a very goofy holiday. She thinks it treats love as a goopy, sentimental thing. She keeps lecturing me that love is not just a good feeling, it's an attitude. It's caring and commitment, etc.

Then my father, the amateur historian, comes in. He tells me that I should have a Jewish conscience about this . . . that Valentine's Day is named after a fourth century Christian saint. This guy was great with kids, but he was a vicious anti-Semite. A peculiar kind of love, my father says. He tells me that I should have a Jewish conscience (whatever that means) about my actions.

Hey, Reb Hayim, I just wanted to give a little gift to my girlfriend. But now I am confused. What do you think? Should I take seriously this stuff about love being too mushy, and acting with a Jewish conscience? Should I send a Valentine card?

Sincerely yours,
Larry, Who Is Confused About Love

Dear Reb Hayim,

Don't get me wrong. *Matzah's* okay. It tastes all right. And I think it's important for Jews to eat *matzah* rather than bread during Passover.

But only in their own homes! Taking it to school is for the birds. (Actually, I wish I could feed it to the birds. It's awfully crumbly and messy.) Each year my non-Jewish friends ask me why I'm eating those funny crackers. Some even tease me about it.

I'm tired of explaining. Wouldn't it be okay if I just kept Passover in my home and didn't worry about it outside of my home?

Sincerely yours,
Manny Matzah

Dear Reb Hayim,

I want to go to my friend's Christmas party. They're going to sing a few Christmas carols, but I don't think it's any big deal. My parents tell me I shouldn't go. They say it's my decision, but I don't want them to be upset with me.

Please help me. Am I right about the Christmas carols being no big deal? Should I risk getting my parents upset with me because I'm going?

Please answer both these questions. I need good advice.

Signed,
Confused

Dear Reb Hayim,

The other day my mother had a friend over. She was not Jewish. She and my Mom were talking about religion. The friend said something that confused me.

She said that most of the Jewish people she knew were really good people (kind, honest, etc.). She asked my mom and me whether there was something about Judaism which helped Jews be good people. I couldn't answer that. I love being Jewish. Judaism has taught me how to pray, to appreciate the land of Israel, and to celebrate Jewish holidays in a beautiful way.

But what does any of that have to do with being a good person? I hope you have a better answer for my friend than I do.

Shalom,
Glad to be Jewish,
But Not Sure Why

APPENDIX 2

Mitavah Honor Society (December)

THIS SHEET SHOULD BE RETURNED TO THE SYNAGOGUE BY ____________________.

STUDENT'S NAME ____

B'NAI AVRAHAM (Keep Jewish tradition alive)	STUDENT'S SIGNATURE	PARENT'S SIGNATURE
1. Attending Chanukah family service on Friday, December _____.	____________________	____________________
2. Reading Chanukah story with family on one night of Chanukah. (Teacher will provide you with story if you don't have one.)	____________________	____________________
3. Teaching non-Jewish friend how to play *dreidle.*	____________________	____________________
4. Leading family in singing a Chanukah song while Chanukah lights are burning.	____________________	____________________
5. Taking a walk around neighborhood and see how many *chanukiot* you see glowing. This is even more fun if you do it with another family.	____________________	____________________

APPENDIX 2 (Cont.)

Mitzvah Honor Society (December)

THIS SHEET SHOULD BE RETURNED TO THE SYNAGOGUE BY ______________.

STUDENT'S NAME ______________________________

B'NAI NOAH (*Mitzvot* which make our world a better place)	STUDENT'S SIGNATURE	PARENT'S SIGNATURE
1. Bring can of food with you to Chanukah family service.	______________	______________
2. Write postcard to our Russian family, the Volvovskys.	______________	______________
3. Play *dreidle* one night with pennies and contribute all the winnings to *tzedakah.*	______________	______________

APPENDIX 2 (Cont.)

Mitzvah Honor Society (October and November)

THIS SHEET SHOULD BE RETURNED TO THE SYNAGOGUE BY ______________________.

STUDENT'S NAME ____

B'NAI AVRAHAM (Keep Jewish tradition alive)	STUDENT'S SIGNATURE	PARENT'S SIGNATURE
1. Participated in Simchat Torah celebration.	____________	____________
2. Contributed a Student's Eye View column to Rosh Chodesh (this will be explained to students).	____________	____________
3. Attended Family or Kabbalat Shabbat service in November.	____________	____________
4. Watched *An American Tail* or read *Mollie's Pilgrim* to prepare for Thanksgiving.	____________	____________
5. Wrote a special prayer of Thanksgiving and led family in *Hamotzi* on Thanksgiving evening.	____________	____________
6. Helped decorate *sukkah.*	____________	____________

APPENDIX 2 (Cont.)

Mitzvah Honor Society (October and November)

THIS SHEET SHOULD BE RETURNED TO THE SYNAGOGUE BY ______________________.

STUDENT'S NAME ____

B'NAI NOAH (*Mitzvot* which make our world a better place)	STUDENT'S SIGNATURE	PARENT'S SIGNATURE
1. Brought a can of food to Caring Is Sharing (collected both on Friday night for synagogue and on weekends for school).	____________________	____________________

APPENDIX 3

Torah Reading Sponsorship

NAME ____

TORAH-THON
(Benefits worthwhile charities — Jewish and non-Jewish)

KIND OF SPONSORSHIP:

$1 per line of Torah read (usually 10 lines read)
$18 (chai) General Sponsorship
Other ____

NAME OF SPONSOR	AMOUNT OF SPONSORSHIP	Tikkun Leil Shavuot Schedule
______________	______________	6:45 – to Roxborough Y
______________	______________	7:00 – Warm Ups
______________	______________	7:15 – Volleyball (7th vs. 8th, or staff vs. students)
______________	______________	7:45 – 15 minute free-throw contest
______________	______________	8:00 – Staff vs. student basketball
______________	______________	8:30 – 3 on 3 basketball
______________	______________	9:00 – 1 on 1 basketball
______________	______________	9:45 – Return to synagogue
______________	______________	10:00 – Begin Torah Reading
______________	______________	11:00 – Break; Figure Torah-thon earnings
______________	______________	12:15 – Video
______________	______________	12:30 – Laila Tov

Chapter 6
Personalizing Bar/Bat Mitzvah in a Large Congregation

Robin Eisenberg

BACKGROUND

One of the first conversations a family new to the synagogue has about our Bar/Bat Mitzvah program goes something like this: "I understand Temple Beth El is huge — how many children share a service?" My response: "Each child has his or her own service. We work with each child and family to fit their educational and spiritual needs to the service." Usually, this is followed by surprise and a moment of silence or a joyful, "How nice!"

Our congregation in Boca Raton was once predominately a retirement congregation with a small Religious School. Over the past twelve years, the enrollment has tripled, reaching nearly 600 students. Our Bar/Bat Mitzvah program serves 70-80 students each year. In order to accomplish this, we have a morning and Havdalah service every Shabbat for most of the year. We also offer families the option of Mondays or Thursdays. These are especially popular during vacation times. As a general rule, the Senior Rabbi participates in the morning service and the Assistant Rabbi in the Havdalah. Families may request the Rabbi not scheduled either in place of, or in addition, to the assigned Rabbi. This system works very well if a family feels a special relationship to a particular Rabbi. In most cases, when possible, these requests are granted.

The B'nai Mitzvah program at Temple Beth El consists of a series of well-organized experiences for the students and their families. Developed and implemented by a sub-committee of the Religious School, it is seen as the showcase of the congregation. This sub-committee has consistently reiterated the congregation's commitment to allowing each student to celebrate during an individual service and encouraging families to develop components of the service to suit their individual needs. The Director of Education is the senior staff person responsible for the program.

GOALS

In order to create a system which can accommodate 70-80 students each year, our goals are specific and realistic; yet, the implementation is flexible.

These goals are brought to fruition through a series of group and individual learning experiences for students and their families.

1. Students entering the Bar/Bat Mitzvah program shall be able to read the following prayers fluently prior to admission to B'nai Mitzvah class: *"Barchu," "Yotzer," "V'haeer," "Sh'ma," "V'ahavta," "Mee Chamochah," "Avot," "Gevurot," "Kedushah,"* blessings before and after Torah reading, blessings before and after Haftarah reading, Havdalah service.
2. Students shall complete the activities to be done in B'nai Mitzvah class prior to beginning private instruction.
3. Students shall be able to chant prayers listed in goal #1 prior to beginning B'nai Mitzvah class.
4. Students shall write a speech about the Torah portion and relate the portion to their lives.
5. Students shall write a speech about the Haftarah portion and relate the portion to their lives.
6. Students and their families shall choose a *tzedakah* project to do during the year preceding ceremony.
7. Parents shall attend all individual instruction sessions.
8. Students shall conduct the entire service in Hebrew and English at Bar or Bat Mitzvah.

IMPLEMENTATION

The Bar/Bat Mitzvah program utilizes both group and individual sessions.

Group Sessions

There are four group meetings for students and their parents. Each of these meetings gives information regarding our program and encourages families to adapt it to their needs.

Approximately 18 months prior to their service, families attend an introductory meeting. This meeting is conducted by the senior staff of the synagogue. This meeting brings together families celebrating Bar or Bat Mitzvah within a six-month period of time. Seated at round tables, families introduce themselves, then complete page 10 in *Bar and Bat Mitzvah: A Family Education Unit* (A.R.E. Publishing, Inc.). They then share their responses with the other families sitting at their table.

The major part of the meeting is spent on explaining the logistics of the Bar/Bat Mitzvah program. Each family is given a manual which outlines the history of Bar/Bat Mitzvah celebration at Temple Beth El, commitment to continue studies to Grade 10, as well as details such as fees, photography, and training schedule. We invite a number of families who have recently celebrated a Bar/Bat Mitzvah to describe ways that they made their services special.

One year prior to their service, students enter the B'nai Mitzvah class. On the first day of class, parents attend with their child. At this time, the nature of the class is explained to parents and children together. The class includes two components. The first component is a "chanting" class taught by the Cantors. In this part, each student has an assignment sheet listing all the possible prayers for their service. Students work in small groups and are tested on a regular basis. No one is forced to chant, but everyone is encouraged to do so, and most do.

The other part of the B'nai Mitzvah class is taught by the Assistant Rabbi. Each student is required to do 18 assignments. The Assistant Rabbi serves as a facilitator, resources with the student, and checks student work. The 18 assignments include such topics as developing outlines for speeches for Torah and Haftarah, researching meaning and uses of *tallit* and *kipah,* and doing a family history. Many of the 18 assignments relate directly to the student's worship service and to that student's life. Again, the individual student's interests and learning style are taken into account.

Approximately nine months prior to their service, parents and students have a meeting during which the service is simulated. This meeting provides an opportunity for families to see a typical service and begin to consider the options available to them. Some of these options include: the "standard" Temple Beth El service, a more "traditional" service, a creative service written by the family, a "standard" service with some creative readings, and any combination of the above. Involvement of siblings, grandparents, and other relatives and friends is discussed at this meeting. Again, the emphasis is on helping families make the service a special experience.

Approximately six months prior to the Bar or Bat Mitzvah, as the child begins private instruction, the family is invited to attend a support group. The support group is made up of those celebrating within a 6-8 week period of time. The Senior Rabbi conducts this special group. Some of the matters discussed include participation in a Bar/Bat Mitzvah service, creative approaches to the ceremony, and helping the child learn and feel good about studying. Families share ideas, hopes, and values within a supportive atmosphere.

Individual Sessions

Approximately one year prior to the Bar/Bat Mitzvah, each family meets individually with the Rabbi who will be conducting the service. This meeting allows families to work out details, speak about concerns, and get advice on how to handle this important family *simchah*. It also provides an opportunity for everyone to get to know the Rabbi better.

Students are involved in six months of private instruction. During this period, students move from instructor to instructor, studying privately with the Assistant Rabbi, a tutor, a Cantorial Associate, and the Cantor. Parents are strongly encouraged to sit in on all sessions. This eliminates many potential problems and surprises. The Director of Education monitors students via the weekly reports received from the four staff people, as well as through personal contact. In cases where more time is needed, the Director of Education will test the student to ascertain need.

Following is a description of the sequence of private instruction.

SEQUENCE OF PRIVATE INSTRUCTION

First Month (with Assistant Rabbi)

Discuss portion with child/parent. Work with child on Torah, Haftarah speeches. Use Torah portion outline from Bar/Bat Mitzvah class as a guide. Families are encouraged to read portions together and to reflect on their meaning.

Second Month (with tutor)

Review of prayers — reading them, then using melodies. A chart is provided so that students can see what to practice.

Third and Fourth Months (with Cantorial Associate)

Introduce Torah/Haftarah. Continue melodies of prayers.

Fifth and Sixth Months (with Cantor)

Continue work on Torah/Haftarah. Go over entire service in order during last four sessions. Read from Torah the last four weeks.

SEVEN WEEK REHEARSAL

The Director of Education conducts a rehearsal seven weeks prior to the ceremony. After this rehearsal, a report of the student's progress is sent to the Rabbi, the Cantor, and the Cantorial Associate. The report includes a listing of all material covered, an assessment of how the student is prepared, and an overview of what the student needs to work on between this rehearsal and the service. In some cases, the seven week rehearsal is deemed to be sufficient. However, most students require a second or third run-through to smooth out rough spots. In the rare case, a student may be seen by the Director of Education for the remaining seven weeks. The final rehearsal is held with the Rabbi the week of the service.

THE INDIVIDUAL SERVICE

Temple Beth El is a Reform congregation which uses the Siddur *Shaarei Tefillah (Gates of Prayer)*. The first four levels of Hebrew are geared to teaching decoding skills and then applying these skills to the prayers of the Shabbat evening, morning, and Havdalah services.

The students in our Hebrew program have 75 minutes of Hebrew each Sunday and attend a mid-week class for one hour and 30 minutes. Included in the mid-week class will be a brief chapel service in which students will practice what they are learning. The prayer book is the "lifetime tool of the Jew" and can function in a child's life. The emphasis in our program is the study of prayer book. Not only will students be able to sight-read in the prayer book, they will understand each prayer.

The expectation for a child who has gone through all four levels is to conduct the entire service in Hebrew and English, as well as read from the Torah and Haftarah. For students with special needs, this expectation is adjusted according to the individual circumstances. We have celebrated B'nai Mitzvah for children who are deaf, learning disabled, and mentally handicapped. Children in unique circumstances, such as twins or children living in foreign countries or other states, have been accommodated, and have been able to study for and celebrate an individualized ceremony. In each case, we have worked with the family to tailor a special service for the child.

Families are encouraged to share individual talents and interests in their service. Students, parents, and siblings have done so in many unique ways. These have included playing melodies on musical instruments, singing additional songs, and using creative writing skills for anything from a single new prayer to an entire service. Families have taken the message of Torah portions and made them part of their service. Some of these include: making a *tallit,* learning the rules of *kashrut,* and building a replica of the Temple in Jerusalem.

Another way families are encouraged to individualize the service is through *tzedakah* and *mitzvah* projects. Each child is expected to perform an act of *gemilut chasadim,* such as collecting food for the food bank, clothes and furniture for New Americans, and money for people with AIDS. Families may opt to share their service with a New American, create centerpieces out of non-perishable food, toys, or sporting goods to be donated later to a food bank or institution serving children, have guests bring food for the food bank, batik the *tallit* worn by the child, plant a tree in honor of each guest, etc. The variety of projects, the enthusiasm with which families approach this part of becoming a Bar/Bat Mitzvah, and the benefits to those less fortunate have made this a significant part of our program.

EVALUATION/CONCLUSION

The system described herein has evolved over the past ten years. During that time, we have grown from 20 B'nai Mitzvah students a year to over 70. The sheer number has demanded an efficient system; yet, we are able to maintain our priorities of family involvement and enabling each student to reach his/her potential.

The process has worked best for those who participate in all aspects as a family. When parents attend sessions, they understand the training and feel part of the system. All personnel have day and night sessions, during the week and weekends, to try to accommodate individual schedules.

Bar/Bat Mitzvah is seen as an affirmation of the Covenant with God and with the Jewish community. On his or her special day, the child stands with the family and together they reaffirm this. Bar/Bat Mitzvah takes on lasting significance for the family when they approach this life cycle event as an educational and spiritual experience for all members. The synagogue provides the opportunity for observance of Bar/Bat Mitzvah; the real work and significance of the ceremony evolves from the home and the family's individualization of the service and celebration.

Chapter 7
Solving Problems: The Religious Practices Committee

George M. Stern

The Rabbi and the Cantor of Temple Beth Torah in Upper Nyack, New York initiated a discussion of Bar/Bat Mitzvah practices and how they fit into the total ritual picture of the congregation at the synagogue. This had not been done for a number of years. The aim was to review the situation, assess it, and make recommendations for the future.

Description of the Present Program

At the present time, the Bar/Bat Mitzvah program takes top priority in the life of our synagogue. Its demands on the synagogue staff are many. It involves both the Rabbi and Cantor in preparation as well as in the service itself. An additional person is hired to rehearse the students and to review with the family their extensive participation in the service. The organist meets at least twice with each candidate. Of late, many families have also availed themselves of the services of a tutor, often a synagogue member (paid on a private basis). Apart from synagogue dues and building fund, the Bar/Bat Mitzvah fee is by far a member's greatest financial obligation to the synagogue.

It has come to be expected that Bar/Bat Mitzvah families will sponsor an Oneg Shabbat (which is a nice way to encourage them to share with the congregation). Students and families also participate in the Shabbat eve service, the student by singing, the parents at the time of the candle lighting and the student's "solo." It might be noted that more and more family members have been involved in the candle lighting recently.

There is no question but that many families join synagogues in order to afford their children the opportunity to become Bar/Bat Mitzvah. It is said that the type of service held at Temple Beth Torah and the involvement of the student in the service is sufficiently distinctive as to be one of the synagogue's assets in drawing new members (although, to our knowledge, no family has cited that as the primary reason for joining the congregation).

Extensive preparation is expected of the students. They lead most of the service, Hebrew and English, from prior to the "*Barchu*" up to the Torah Service. In theory, they have learned the Hebrew prayers in school. In fact, many require extensive review; some come to the Cantor largely unprepared to lead prayers.

Each student has about 22 fifteen minute lessons with the Cantor, who tutors prayers as well as Torah and Haftarah. Torah portions learned vary in length from three to five *aliyot* (9-15 verses, approximately); Haftarah portions comprise five to seven verses. Many students chant either the Haftarah or both Torah and Haftarah, learning the chant through rote memorization from a tape (the trope itself is not taught).

In addition, each student is expected to prepare a "project," which can consist of a talk on the Torah or Haftarah portions; a report on a *mitzvah* project performed; an art, music, or a variety of other project possibilities. As with the technical aspects of leading the service and reading or chanting Torah and Haftarah, the project results vary widely.

Lastly, in a very limited number of cases, entire families join in either writing a creative service or working on a family project in lieu of the regular project.

Analysis

The feelings generally created at the service are positive and uplifting. For both the family and the child, the service itself seems to be an emotional "high" that leaves a very positive Jewish feeling, crucial to Jewish identity building. The students demonstrate a competence in prayer which, whether the result of rote learning or not, is valuable for their future comfort in a synagogue setting. Certainly their ability to deal with the Hebrew is superior to that of many of their parents. Those who attend the service are often afforded a positive Shabbat worship experience, valuable in and of itself and as an antidote to the negative feelings so many report from previous worship experiences.

In part, the factors contributing to the program's success contribute as well to negative results. Concerns can be divided into two categories: effects on the students and effects on the congregation as a whole.

Over the years, and especially recently, we have noted an increasing emphasis on "quantity" and "performance." A program originally designed for flexibility to meet needs of individual students has become hardened in stone, especially in the minds of some families. We have, in short, lost some control over the program. Students are under increased pressure to "do" five *aliyot,* and pressure to chant has also increased. This frequently places the Cantor "between a rock and a hard place": either of being the "ogre" who must say "no," or jeopardizing the quality of what the student does in order to allow for quantity. He also finds that the push for quantity eliminates the possibility of friendly, personal contact with the students. There is time only for "work," no informal chatting, which can be very important in terms of developing a meaningful relationship that can have positive consequences beyond the Bar/Bat Mitzvah. The pressure on the student to "show off" by "doing more" also affects the time spent on the project, since in the minds of many parents, the rote memorization of the *aliyot* would seem to be more important than the creative possibilities the project affords. A discussion of "rote" versus "creative" learning is very much in order.

An often negative consequence of the multiplication of *aliyot* is the assigning of such an honor to those incapable of executing it competently, creating socially embarrassing and religiously offensive situations.

The custom of having students sing a solo Friday night forces non-singers or those who simply would prefer not to sing into an awkward situation of embarrassment and/or contention with family, while simultaneously often turning the congregation into passive listeners when they might be participants.

The expectation that students will lead most of the morning service means that it is not always led with careful attention to the words and meanings of the prayers. If prayers are important, then they should be led, and prayed, well. If they are not important, then they should be replaced with something more meaningful.

Because the service is known as a "Bar Mitzvah service," it is attended only by invited guests (and an occasional student carrying an attendance card, most often without parents). The atmosphere, therefore, while joyous, is often non-participatory. The lack of involved congregants discourages active participation by the guests, which in turn results in non-prayerful behavior, particularly, but not solely, on the part of teenagers.

Over all, the message given out by the Bar/Bat Mitzvah ceremony as it now stands is that it is a private event of no consequence to the general congregation/community, that Shabbat morning is not a time for regular worship, and that "performance," i.e., quantity, is what becoming a Bar/Bat Mitzvah is all about.

So much is made of the service that, no matter what we say to the contrary, it seems like a "culminating event" for our students and their families. We play into the oft-repeated contention that "I can make my child go to Religious School until the Bar/Bat Mitzvah, but after that it's up to him/her, because I wouldn't want him/her to be turned off to Judaism by forcing continued study." That contention, especially the reason, makes sense only if you believe that what occurs after the Bar/Bat Mitzvah is, indeed, of less importance. Our program in fact gives that message: just note the fee schedule and the amount of staff time taken up by the program, the failure to articulate similar expressions of the importance of Confirmation (through fees, by making it a gala event well attended by synagogue leaders, or other means), the failure to build up the Saturday morning service as a congregational experience.

The congregation's expectation that the Friday evening *Oneg* will be sponsored by the Bar/Bat Mitzvah families has led to a "counter-expectation," namely, that families have the "right" to do so. That eliminates some of the flexibility we might have in planning Shabbat eve experiences different from the "norm" (e.g., the scheduling of the 6:30 services on "better" dates and the developing of Shabbat experiences not conducive to a formal Oneg). The family's participation in the Friday night service also cuts down on the possibility of having other congregants participate without turning the service into a "circus" with constant movement to and from the *bimah*. Here, too, then, a message of "ownership" of the service is subtly given, though it is not as strong as the Saturday morning message.

Recommendations

The above critique required a great deal of thought and analysis before any recommendations for change could be considered. The Religious Practices Committee, from whom these recommendations would come, needed to engage in careful deliberations, taking into account the emotions involved, yet at the same time cognizant of the role Bar and Bat Mitzvah should play in encouraging appropriate religious practice by the congregation.

Following are the changes recommended by the Rabbi and the Cantor to the Religious Practices Committee. (For the letter which accompanied these recommendations, see Appendix 1.)

1. The Cantor's role as sole administrator of the entire Bar/Bat Mitzvah program must be reemphasized. He will make decisions regarding the number of verses of Torah (*aliyot*) to be read, the advisability of chanting, the need for "outside" tutoring. Doing "only" three *aliyot* will not be sufficient reason for such tutoring. The Cantor will undertake regular and specific communication with families so they are continually aware of their child's progress and "prognosis."
2. An analysis of the prayer component of the Religious School curriculum should be done with the Director of Education so as to see if there are any curricular reasons for the number of students who seem unfamiliar with the basic elements of the worship service. Consideration should be given to: the establishment of a pre-Bar/Bat Mitzvah "prayer class" to be led by the Cantor, the use of the "prayer tape" beginning in the fourth rather than in the sixth grade, the insistence that students will lead only those prayers which they can learn in school or on their own (to be checked by the Cantor), and the establishment of a required trope class for any student who wants to chant.
3. An increase in tutoring time to 20 minutes a week would afford a less harried lesson, more meaningful contact with the Cantor, and more chance for review. Such a recommendation should only be made after other issues are explored, since a decrease in pressure for quantity on the children might alleviate the need for more time with the Cantor.
4. Eliminate the requirement of singing a solo on Friday night or change it to involve either a musical piece or the reading of an English prayer.
5. Involve parent(s) and the Bar/Bat Mitzvah in the candle lighting and *Kiddush,* eliminating both the calling up of the father later in the service and the involvement of other children and relatives in the candle lighting. This will allow for more flexibility in involving others in the service and make it possible for students to opt not to do a solo. It is also in keeping with the Reform notion of gender equality in ritual.
6. Establish congregational "ownership" of the Friday evening service by making it clear that special events, including creative worship and 6:30 services, may occur any week. Bar/Bat Mitzvah families would be given notice of such happenings so that they could adjust their plans and help determine their own participation accordingly. (In some cases, they might be even more involved than usual, depending on what is planned and depending on their own comfort with services.) Families wishing to co-sponsor an Oneg at another time could be invited to do so. If the 6:30 service were regularized (e.g., the third Friday of every month), families with preferences might be accommodated where feasible.
7. Have the Rabbi read a part of the *sedra* on Saturday morning to bring the number of *aliyot* to five, if requested. That might relieve pressure on the children to read enough Torah for five *aliyot* themselves.
8. Reemphasize the importance of individual creativity by bolstering the Rabbi's involvement in the pro-

ject. The Rabbi will give to each student a topic on which to base an essay, requiring varying amounts of research and personal reflection (depending on student and portion). That essay will be the project, unless the student suggests another possibility deemed viable by Rabbi (or by the Cantor if it is to be a music project).

9. Reinforce regular worship as a *mitzvah* for all Jews by instituting worship service attendance requirement at all grade levels, Kindergarten through Grade 10. This recommendation can be instituted with the cooperation of the school. Possible suggestions for service attendance requirements each year: Grades K and 1: two services; Grades 2 and 3: four services; Grades 4, 5, and 6: six services; Grade 7: eight services (to be completed prior to Bar/Bat Mitzvah if during seventh grade); Grades 8, 9, 10: six services (for eighth graders whose Bar/Bat Mitzvah occurs during eighth grade, three of the six would have to be completed prior to the Bar/Bat Mitzvah). Attendance might be further encouraged by the institution of Shabbat dinners before or after services and the involvement of youngsters in Family Services. The latter would also require some coordination with the school.
10. Give a clear message that a Bar/Bat Mitzvah ceremony is part of regular Jewish liturgy (not an isolated event) to be led seriously and with an attention to ritual (not social) detail. Possibilities for getting that message across include:
    a. Alter the content of the Bar/Bat Mitzvah rehearsal to put more emphasis on proper English reading.
    b. Limit the quantity of the service led by the Bar/ Bat Mitzvah students(s). Assign to each two Hebrew prayers (to be read or sung) and two English prayers.
    c. In cases of double ceremonies, eliminate the repetition of the Haftarah blessing by having the first student to read Haftarah do the "before" blessing and the second the "after" blessing.
    d. Include students in Grade 7 and up in a section of the Shabbat morning service. One way the latter might be effected would be to have seventh graders come up as a group to lead the "*V'ahavta*" or a final song. Consideration should also be given to assigning an *aliyah* to a post-Bar/Bat Mitzvah student and/or an adult synagogue member. This will give at least the synagogue's teenagers a feeling that the service is "theirs," and perhaps help curtail inappropriate behavior. It will also give them a chance to turn in attendance cards.
11. Institute a required test of all those to do an *aliyah* prior to the service, with the clear understanding that the Rabbi or Cantor have the final say as to whether the blessings are to be done in Hebrew or English. No one will be called who is not at the synagogue early enough to be tested. Because this requirement puts the clergy in an awkward situation, families could be required to provide names and addresses of those receiving *aliyot* at least two weeks in advance. A note about appropriate recitation of the *aliyah* can be sent out over the Rabbi's signature, together with both Ashkenazic and Sephardic transliterations of the blessings for their review prior to meeting with the Rabbi or Cantor on the Shabbat of the Bar/Bat Mitzvah.
12. Establish a required course for parents that, in several lessons, would provide them with a background about Bar/Bat Mitzvah, an understanding of the service, and of Jewish concepts and terms (see Appendix 3). Such a course would re-emphasize the importance of the *mitzvah* of continual study and help put the Bar/Bat Mitzvah in perspective as part of Jewish life, not its ultimate goal.

The Committee: Study, Action, and Evaluation

The Religious Practices Committee met three times over a period of several months to discuss the original report and its recommendations. Members were also in contact with the Rabbi between meetings to speed up the decision making process. The Rabbi, Cantor, and eight committee members (three of whom were also synagogue board members) were at most of the meetings. The Director of Education was also consulted. It was felt that decisions should be made carefully, but also without undue delay.

Appendix 2 contains the results of the deliberations as approved by the Religious Practices Committee and by the Board of Trustees. The particular format of

Appendix 2 is the letter of explanation which was sent to all members of the congregation. Dissemination of the information was augmented by inclusion of procedures in the two-part parents class (Appendix 3) and by a review of changes as the Cantor met with each child and parents to begin studies.

Appendix 4 contains the schedule the Cantor uses to keep students on track and to help emphasize the importance of quality preparation of prayers and speech/project, as well as Torah and Haftarah portions.

On the whole, the new program was well received and has achieved many of its goals. Pressure for "quantity" over "quality" has been reduced. When the child prepares fewer than five *aliyot,* the Rabbi or Cantor are generally asked to augment what he/she does, as recommended. The Religious School undertook a careful review of its prayer curriculum, and has instituted changes which are beginning to bear fruit.

During the 1991-92 and 1992-93 school years, we experimented with a trope class offered to all students. For some students, the class worked well. For others, disinterest and/or lack of ability remain problems. The class is currently under review. If it is not required, we will have to decide whether or not to allow a child to chant simply by using tapes to learn the portion.

The two-part parent program was well received, but it has been decided to replace it with a Family Education program in the sixth grade, before the Bar/Bat Mitzvah frenzy begins. Parents and children will study together and separately during three two hour sessions, during regular Sunday School hours. They will learn (review) all the terms involved in the Bar/Bat Mitzvah preparation (Torah, Haftarah, *aliyah, parashah,* etc.), and discuss the perspective of the synagogue (and of Reform Judaism) that Bar/Bat Mitzvah is just one of many life cycle events (to be followed by Confirmation). Each child will receive a study guide to his/her Torah and Haftarah portions. Using the guides, families will be asked to respond to questions that will result in a creative understanding of the Torah and Haftarah material. The aim is to engage parents and children together in meaningful text study, and to point the way toward an appropriate and intelligent Bar/Bat Mitzvah speech/project.

Assigning an *aliyah* to a congregant has enabled us to celebrate some additional *simchahs* and to introduce B'nai Mitzvah to Confirmands, all of whom are expected to do an *aliyah* during the school year. (Thus, Confirmands serve as examples of students who have continued their studies.) We have not, however, noticed any significant increase in congregant attendance on Bar/Bat Mitzvah Sabbaths.

The establishment of service attendance targets by the Religious School has significantly increased attendance at monthly Family Services. We are now discussing ways to help families make the transition from Family Service to "regular" services, perhaps by giving service attendance credit for Family Services through the sixth grade only. Discomfort with service attendance requirements surfaces from time to time — for good reason — but overall, the increased exposure to services by more families has been deemed of value.

APPENDIX 1

December 8th

Dear Member of the Religious Practices Committee,

Enclosed is a copy of a report on the Bar/Bat Mitzvah program at Temple Beth Torah. The Report will serve as the basis for the major topic of our Religious Practices meeting on December 20.

The report contains an overview of the Bar/Bat Mitzvah program as currently implemented and a number of proposals for change. Some will seen innocuous to you; others may appear "radical." None is an idea not already done in other congregations. You will undoubtedly come up with other ideas, as well as cogent arguments for and against the recommendations made. In all cases, however, we would hope that you will keep in mind the major aims of the proposals, namely: (1) to rationalize the demands made on the students and (2) to help put the Bar/Bat Mitzvah in an appropriate perspective for families and for the entire congregation.

Throughout your private and public deliberations, it will be helpful if you can maintain an attitude of detachment, so that expectations resulting from years of inertia will not jeopardize the chance for meaningful change.

We thank you for your involvement in this important discussion and look forward to seeing you on the 20th.

Sincerely,

Rabbi George M. Stern
Cantor William S. Wood

APPENDIX 2

TO: The Members of Temple Beth Torah
FROM: The Religious Practices Committee
RE: Review of Bar/Bat Mitzvah Procedures

During the past year, the Religious Practices Committee undertook an extensive review of the Temple's Bar/ Bat Mitzvah program. Since the preparation for and celebration of the Bar/Bat Mitzvah ceremony is of utmost importance to many of our members, we wanted to be sure that we maximize the learning processes involved while at the same time minimizing undue pressure on our students. We want the entire experience to be positive, filled with educational and emotional growth. We also were cognizant of the subtle messages given out by everything that we do, so we also looked at all that we require and do from the standpoint of what Jewish and congregational messages are projected by the various aspects of our procedures.

On the whole, we realized how fortunate we are to have a program that works well and efficiently and produces not only knowledgeable students, but warm feelings for families and guests. Still, there is always room for change and improvement. The following represents a distillation of decisions made in many hours of deliberation.

First, a list of the items discussed in more detail below:

1. The Cantor is in charge of the program and will assign no new work within two weeks of the ceremony. [See Appendix 4 for the normal tutoring schedule.]
2. Prayer to be read or song to be sung Friday night.
3. Families involved in candles and *Kiddush* Friday night.
4. Rabbi or Cantor to read *aliyot* portions if necessary.
5. Non-family congregant to be called for first *aliyah.*
6. Rabbi to contact certain people with honors in advance.
7. Project to be strengthened with assistance of Rabbi.
8. Trope (chant) class requirement may be instituted.
9. Two-session class to be required for parents.
10. Service requirement (12) continuing as in the past.

Now, the details:

1. The Cantor remains in sole charge of the Bar/Bat Mitzvah process. While of course he consults with both students and parents, the ultimate decision as to both quantity of work prepared and acceptable quality rests with him. To avoid any possible misunderstandings as to what is expected and when, the Cantor will present to each prospective student/family a schedule of work due at the time the private lessons start (5-6 months prior to the ceremony). To avoid unnecessary pressure, the Committee reiterated its long-standing rule that *no new work will be assigned or accepted during the two weeks prior to the ceremony*. Work not started as of that time will not be assigned.
2. Since musical abilities of our students vary, it was felt that the Friday night requirement of leading a song is unfair. It has been changed to expect that the students will *either read a prayer or lead the congregation in singing,* whichever is deemed appropriate by the student and Cantor in consultation.
3. The immediate family of the Bar/Bat Mitzvah will participate in the candle blessings and *Kiddush* on Friday evening, with the parents sharing in the English and Hebrew of the candles and in the English introduction to the *Kiddush.* We are aware that we need to experiment with the aesthetics of having so many people gathered around the candles and will do so carefully.
4. For the most part, students prepare 3, 4, or 5 Torah *aliyot.* We insist that quality is more important than quantity. The honor of reading from our people's most ancient religious work must be accepted with seriousness and an eye toward perfection. It is not a matter of "no one will know if you make a mistake." While we encourage students to maximize the number of *aliyot* (to five), we wish to avoid pressuring the slower readers into doing more than they are

APPENDIX 2 (Cont.)

capable of accomplishing well. Therefore, the Rabbi or Cantor will gladly prepare one or two *aliyot* themselves, to a maximum of five per student, so that families can have the honor of calling relatives and friends for the *brachot* (blessings) without insisting that their children prepare more than ought to be asked of them.

5. It is important that the Temple convey the message that Saturday morning services are for the purposes of congregational prayer; they are not private sessions for Bar/Bat Mitzvah families. Therefore, we are going to reserve the first set of each child's *aliyah* blessings for a member of the congregation, to be chosen by the Committee and Rabbi. This might be a student who read the portion previously, a congregant celebrating a *simchah,* or such other person as might be chosen. However, in order not to reduce the number of *people* given the honor by each Bar/Bat Mitzvah family, we will allow the "doubling up" of a second *aliyah,* in addition to the one already allowed (if desired) for the parents. Assuming five *aliyot,* this will mean that two people can be called for both the second and fourth *aliyot,* instead of only for the latter. Families may wish to utilize this opportunity to double up people — one of whom is less familiar with the *aliyah* than the other — so that the more competent can project the *brachah* more forcefully. Please note that this change affects only the timing of who is called, not the total number of people given an honor by each family.
6. At least three weeks prior to the service, *the names and addresses of those being called for the oral aliyot and for hagbah and gelilah (raising and binding the scroll) are to be submitted to the Rabbi.* He will arrange to send them explanations of what they will be doing and, in the case of the *aliyot,* both Ashkenazic and Sephardic transliterations, so that they can practice what they are most familiar with and come prepared to do honor to themselves, the family, and the Torah. They will also have the option of reciting the prayers in English, should this be the only way to have the honor done appropriately. This should eliminate potentially embarrassing situations at services.
7. We consider the potential learning experience involved with the "project" to be of utmost importance. Rabbi Stern will therefore be meeting with the students more regularly to be more directive with them, steering them as part of the process towards a better understanding of their Torah and Haftarah portions. In order to assure that the project will be taken seriously and be done in a timely fashion, *the Cantor will insist that the project be well under way during the third month of lessons or no further work will be assigned.* [See Appendix 4 for full timetable.]
8. To reduce the amount of rote learning and increase the skills learned by our students, the Committee is seriously considering a requirement that students who wish to chant Torah and/or Haftarah first learn the "trope," the chant system, prior to using a music tape. That would enable them to chant any portion (just as their Hebrew classes enable them to read any portion), adding to their Jewish skills repertoire. It will also make learning the melody of their particular portion easier. Beginning this fall, the Religious School is making trope available as an elective for our older afternoon students. The course will be taught by the Cantor during school hours. We are hoping that it will be successful. If so, the Religious Practices Committee will work with the school to make the successful completion of the trope class a prerequisite for chanting Torah and Haftarah at the Bar/Bat Mitzvah ceremony. The imposition of this requirement will be made carefully and will be phased in so that no student wishing to chant will be denied the opportunity unless having first been given a chance to take the trope elective. All families involved will receive prior notification when this class becomes a requirement. Please note that our desire is to increase skills and make the preparation of a child's portions simpler in the long run.
9. To assist families in placing the Bar/Bat Mitzvah in appropriate Jewish perspective and to increase

APPENDIX 2 (Cont.)

their own Jewish awareness, Rabbi Stern is in the process of designing a *two-session "class" which will be required of Bar/Bat Mitzvah parents,* focusing on certain aspects of modern Jewish life and the role Bar/Bat Mitzvah plays in late twentieth-century Jewish living [see Appendix 3]. In order to make it possible for families to attend without difficulty, each session will be offered twice early in the year and twice later in the year. A third optional class may also be structured. During these classes, procedure booklets on the Bar/Bat Mitzvah at Temple Beth Torah will be made available as well.

10. The Religious School has instituted a program of expected service attendance at all levels of the school program. The Religious Practices Committee enthusiastically endorses the school's program. Meanwhile, the Committee will continue to expect its own requirement of 12 services (including at least three on Saturdays) to be attended by any student expecting to lead the service on the morning he/she becomes a Bar/Bat Mitzvah. Cards for that purpose will continue to be utilized, in addition to whatever procedures for attendance the school institutes for its own purposes. As in the past, students who do not complete the service requirement will read Torah and Haftarah, while the Rabbi and Cantor conduct the service. The Committee also continues to expect that parents will attend services with their children.

Implementation of the ten items is as follows: #1 and #10 are merely reiterations of old policy; #3 has been instituted already; #2, 4, 5, 6, and 7 will begin immediately following Simchat Torah (end of October); #8 will be phased in after a review of the school's trope class this winter; #9 is being developed by the Rabbi and will probably begin with sessions this winter for families contemplating mid to late 1990 ceremonies.

They will be notified well in advance of the required dates.

It is hoped that the above information will be useful to you and that you will agree that the Religious Practices Committee's work has resulted in an even more meaningful program than we have had up to now. If you have any questions, feel free to be in touch with a member of the Religious Practices Committee or the Rabbi or Cantor.

APPENDIX 3

Proposed Two Session Course for Pre-Bar/Bat Mitzvah Parents

Week One: The Bar/Bat Mitzvah

Experiential exercise: Jewish memories (positive and negative) from childhood; memories of Bar/Bat Mitzvah

Brief "history" of Bar/Bat Mitzvah ceremony, including its changing role in Reform

Quick review of Jewish life cycle ceremonies to see how Bar/Bat Mitzvah fits into a lifetime "Jewish system" and with emphasis on continuing education

Give out copies of "When A Child Comes of Age: A Practical Guide to the Bar/Bat Mitzvah at Temple Beth Torah."

Week Two: An Agenda for Jewish Teens and a Jewish Future

Interdating and intermarriage

Positive aspects of Jewish identity

Al Sheloshah Devarim: Torah, prayer, and good deeds in Jewish life

Note: In the year following the introduction of this course, a decision was made to "fold" it into a new sixth grade Family Education Program as part of the Religious School Curriculum. This will make it possible for students and parents to come together to review all of the terms and customs association with the Shabbat morning service (and thus with Bar and Bat Mitzvah). The stress will be on Bar/Bat Mitzvah as only one of many life cycle events, to be followed certainly by Confirmation. During part of the program, the Rabbi will work with parents alone and while the Cantor works with the students.

APPENDIX 4

Proposed Timetable for Bar/Bat Mitzvah Lessons

First Month – prayers as needed, read and/or sung; chanting of Torah blessings; project chosen.

Second Month – Haftarah portion read and its blessings chanted.

Third Month – If chanting, learn Haftarah melody; start Torah reading; choose reading or solo for Friday night.

By 3½ Months – Complete nine verses of Torah; complete project. If project is not completed, a timetable will be worked out with the Rabbi, who will simultaneously determine whether or not student can continue to add rote material with the Cantor. If project is completed, student can continue to learn more verses and/or chant the Torah.

By 4½ Months – All work completed. *No new work will be assigned as of two weeks prior to the ceremony.*

End of Fifth Month – The Ceremony!

NOTE: Students wishing to chant Haftarah and/or Torah will have to take the special trope class to be offered by the Cantor as part of the school program. This will not affect the schedule above in any way. It should be noted, however, that students who complete the trope class may be able to learn their Haftarah or Torah portions in chant from the outset (assuming a sufficiently high level of Hebrew proficiency).

Chapter 8

Setting Standards: The Bar/Bat Mitzvah Committee

Shoshana Silberman

At the request of the president of the Jewish Center of Princeton, New Jersey, a Committee was established to investigate the process of Bar/Bat Mitzvah preparation and celebration. Areas to be considered included: the Bar/Bat Mitzvah event in the context of a Shabbat morning congregational experience; the scheduling of large classes of B'nai Mitzvah; goals, expectations, and preparation of B'nai Mitzvah; and goals, preparation, and support of parents of B'nai Mitzvah. The Committee was comprised of eight laypeople, plus, ex-officio, the Rabbi, Cantor, Director of Education, Administrator, and two board members.

HOW THE COMMITTEE FUNCTIONED

The Committee met for four initial sessions. Each of the four areas outlined above was the topic for a meeting. The initial sessions were open forums for brainstorming and developing a consensus regarding each of the issues. Staff members were present at all of these sessions and were consulted for input. A summary of the conclusions reached for each of the four objectives was presented to the staff for review and for their suggestions. A final report was compiled and reviewed by the entire Committee. It contains suggestions and guidelines rather than hard and fast recommendations. Moreover, many of the ideas contained in this report require experimentation and ongoing evaluation before becoming standard practice.

CONCLUSIONS OF THE COMMITTEE

Overall Congregational Goals for Bar/Bat Mitzvah

The Committee reached the following general conclusions regarding the preparation and celebration of Bar/Bat Mitzvah at the Jewish Center.

- The preparation of B'nai Mitzvah and their families must begin as early as possible.

- An attempt should be made to keep the number of B'nai Mitzvah celebrated on Shabbat mornings to the current level (approximately 25 per year) so that there is an adequate number of Shabbat mornings during the year when other events and congregational experiences can be scheduled.

- More alternatives for participation in the service should be available to both parents and Bar/Bat Mitzvah students.

- Greater support needs to be available for parents and Bar/Bat Mitzvah students to enable them to have a more meaningful experience.

- The Bar/Bat Mitzvah event should be viewed as a springboard to strengthen the Jewish experience of the family and the student. Such a view mandates that the actual celebration day become an event in a continuum of Jewish education and participation. This continuum should be designed to build new peer relationships, to encourage community service, to encourage Torah study, to shape a philosophy of Judaism, and to strengthen the commitment of family members to each other and the family's commitment to the Jewish community.

The Bar/Bat Mitzvah Event and the Shabbat Morning Congregation

The committee welcomes the celebration of Bar/Bat Mitzvah during the context of the Shabbat morning congregational experience. Several ideas, however, were put forth to enhance the event.

1. Guests at Bar/Bat Mitzvah celebrations represent, at times, a different "congregation" from regular attendees. In order to make guests feel part of the congregation, we should experiment with the following practices and assess their impact:

   - Make greater use of the booklets which explain the service. Either put them out routinely when there is a Bar or Bat Mitzvah celebration or repeatedly encourage their use.

   - Ask the Rabbi and/or Cantor to explain the service at certain key moments (e.g., before *"Shochen Ad,"* before the Torah service, before the beginning of the Musaf service).

   - Distribute an attractive insert to be included in Bar/Bat Mitzvah invitations extending a welcome from the Jewish Center and explaining our policies concerning attire, *tallit,* and *kipah* use, our egalitarian *minhag,* and that we encourage participation in the service.

   - Make ushers available to assist guests. Perhaps these ushers could be drawn from other B'nai Mitzvah families.

   - Request that Bar/Bat Mitzvah parents inform their guests what to expect (e.g., babysitting, proper attire, length of service, etc.).

2. Parents of the Bar/Bat Mitzvah and other relatives may be encouraged to participate in the service, subject to the review of the Rabbi and Cantor. A wide selection of opportunities should be identified for them. For example, various blessings could be suggested to the parents — the three-fold priestly blessing, *"Birkat Shehecheyanu," "Birkat Shep'tarani,"* suggested readings in the Siddurim on the occasion of a Bar/Bat Mitzvah, *"V'taher Libenu,"* and *"Likrat Shabbat."*

   At the same time, parents should be advised that their participation ought to be pleasing not only to the family experience, but also sensitive to the experience of the congregation. For example, highly personal remarks by parents from the *bimah* should be deferred to a more private time, such as the party following the services. To help parents define the limits of their remarks, they could be asked to review their intentions with the staff prior to the service.

3. Students in the Bar/Bat Mitzvah class could be encouraged to participate in the Bar/Bat Mitzvah services of their classmates (see "Goals, Expectations, and Preparation of B'nai Mitzvah" below).

4. Parents should be educated on how to control photographers, caterers, and band members during the congregational *Kiddush.*

The Scheduling of Large Classes of B'nai Mitzvah

In the near future, a Bar/Bat Mitzvah class at the Jewish Center will exceed 30 students in a given year. The Committee felt strongly that to continue the current practice of scheduling all B'nai Mitzvah on Shabbat morning would be impractical. The solution of "doubling" B'nai Mitzvah was rejected (except when parents want to do it on a voluntary basis).

Therefore, the Committee recommended the following:

Becoming Bar/Bat Mitzvah may be celebrated any time the Torah is read as part of a worship service. In any one year, it would be desirable if approximately two thirds of the celebrations were held on Saturday mornings during the course of regular Shabbat services. The remaining celebrations (one third) would be held at alternative times, such as Shabbat Minchah/Ma'ariv; on Rosh Chodesh if it falls on a Sunday when Hebrew School is not in session; on the second day of Sukkot or Pesach; on the Mondays of civil holidays (Memorial Day, Presidents Day, Labor Day, or Martin Luther King Day); or on any Monday or Thursday that the synagogue can accommodate.

In order to obtain this distribution, a meeting might be held before the assignment of dates to explain the options to parents and solicit their preferences. No attempt should be made, however, to force parents to accept an alternative to a Shabbat morning Bar/Bat Mitzvah if that is their strong preference.

When a Bar/Bat Mitzvah is held at a time other than Shabbat morning, the Committee suggests the following:

- The Bar/Bat Mitzvah parents should be encouraged to be actively involved in the planning and/ or conducting of the service (with resources/ support provided by the Jewish Center staff).

- It is understood that either the Rabbi or Cantor (but not both) will officiate at the service.

- Guests are expected to dress in attire appropriate for a Jewish service.

- The goals and expectations of the student will be identical to those celebrating their Bar/Bat Mitzvah on Shabbat morning. The reciting of the Haftarah by a Bar/Bat Mitzvah at the following Shabbat morning service (if no other Bar/Bat Mitzvah is taking place) will be encouraged.

Goals, Expectations, and Preparation of B'nai Mitzvah

The Bar/Bat Mitzvah Committee would like the Bar/ Bat Mitzvah event to be viewed as a year of expectation and experience. That is, rather than focusing all of the attention upon the single day of the actual celebration, the entire "Zayin" year should be viewed as "the year of the Bar/Bat Mitzvah." The following ideas were suggested to structure this year of expectation:

1. There should be regular synagogue attendance during the year. In addition, the Bar/Bat Mitzvah candidate could be encouraged to participate in the service on a regular basis. This participation will help develop a feeling of belonging to a congregation and make the student comfortable in the service. Bar/Bat Mitzvah candidates can participate in Shabbat morning services in any way except reading the Torah or Haftarah. This includes leading the Preliminary Service, binding the Torah, reading the *"Ashrey,"* and *"Mizmor L'David"* when the Torah goes back to the Ark, or leading the Musaf service. In addition, we suggest a plan to institute a Family Shabbat Eve Service which will feature participation by Hebrew School students. Bar/Bat Mitzvah candidates should also be encouraged to attend and participate in a weekday morning service so that they may wear *tefillin* and a *tallit* for the first time.
2. The Bar/Bat Mitzvah student might be asked to do community service (13 hours will be recommended) during the 12 months preceding the celebration date. At the beginning of this time, the student would meet with a staff member assigned to administrate this program. The staff member would present options, explain procedures, and draw up a contract of commitment. The student could discuss this contract with his/her parent(s) and the contract would be signed by both student and parent(s). (For a discussion of similar Mitzvah Programs, see Unit IV.)
3. Post-Bar/Bat Mitzvah peer-to-peer tutoring should be encouraged. Students can help fellow students with chanting the text and prayers, as well as providing advice about the service. (See page 111 for mention of students as tutors.) Two arrangements for involving post-Bar/Bat Mitzvah students in tutoring are:
   - Assigning each candidate to a specific tutor. Arrangements can be made by the tutor and the candidate to meet at their mutual convenience, frequency to be determined by need.
   - Establishing a clinic staffed by three or four post-Bar/Bat Mitzvah students which will be available at some convenient time, perhaps before or after Sunday Religious School. According to their need, candidates will either be encouraged or assigned to go to the clinic where the staff will listen to them recite and offer them tutoring and advice.
4. The Rabbi should meet with each student for Torah study three months prior to the celebration. The meeting should be viewed as a discussion of the student's Torah portion for educational purposes. The student should come to the meeting with some understanding of the portion. Parents should be encouraged to participate in the discussion or in follow-up discussions. The student should be encouraged to write a short speech or *d'var Torah* about his/her portion.
5. Activities associated with the preparation of Bar/ Bat Mitzvah should have an earlier starting date. The Committee envisions a preparation program which will begin with the Cantor's Bar/Bat Mitzvah prep class during the semester before the celebration date. Six months before the event, a tutor will begin working with each student individually to ensure

fluent reading of the texts and blessings. Beginning three months before the event, the Cantor will complete the candidate's training in chanting the text, the blessings, and whatever parts of the service the student chooses to lead.

6. Each post-Bar/Bat Mitzvah student should be strongly encouraged to participate in services during the two years following the event, reading Torah or Haftarah or leading parts of the service.

Goals, Preparation, and Support for Parents of B'nai Mitzvah

The Committee felt that there should be an effort made toward developing a group spirit among B'nai Mitzvah parents. This might develop into a Havurah especially for them and their families. The Committee hopes that improved support for parents will lead to better preparation of both the parent and the student, as well as to a long-term commitment to Judaism. In order to facilitate the education of parents and to encourage the formation of support groups for them, the following programs are suggested:

1. A Shabbat dinner should be held for the students in the *"Dalet"* (fourth grade) year. During this evening, parents would participate in a session with a leader to encourage group interaction. Additional family programs should be scheduled for the other grades as well.
2. There should be two meetings with the parents held soon after the dates for B'nai Mitzvah are assigned. This would occur in the fall of the *"Vav"* (6th grade) year. The first, on a Sunday evening, would involve a potluck dinner. This dinner would be followed by a program enabling the parents to get acquainted with each other and with the Bar Mitzvah process, including the options available to the Bar/Bat Mitzvah family regarding participation in the service. The second meeting, held no more than a month afterward, would be a business meeting during which the regulations of Bar/Bat Mitzvah at the Jewish Center would be outlined.
3. Each Bar/Bat Mitzvah family will be encouraged to accept assignment of a trained volunteer from the congregation who will act as a support, mentor, and/or tutor for the family. This volunteer congregant could be a parent of a Bar/Bat Mitzvah from a previous year or a senior citizen. The objectives for these "mentors" is to build a stronger sense of a congregational community and to help the family through the preparation process. (For a description of a successful mentor program, see Chapter 50).
4. This Committee would like to see a parents' class offered on a regular basis. The Adult Education Committee and the staff might sponsor a three or four session series of seminars on the Bar/Bat Mitzvah. The purpose of this class would be to teach some of the prayers, to educate the parents about the structure of the liturgy, and to provide an open forum for discussion of the service and its celebration.
5. To put these proposals into practice will require another staff member, specifically to assist the Cantor in tutoring, to administrate the social service requirement, and to coordinate programs for parents as described in this report.

THE REPORT IN PRACTICE

Following the committee's report, the congregation voted to hire a part-time staff person to assist with our B'nai Mitzvah program. The person who was already teaching in the Religious School also became the Bar/Bat Mitzvah tutor. She now helps students with Hebrew reading and trope before their sessions with the Cantor. This extra practice has given our students much confidence and has also encouraged them to do more parts of the service and/or Torah readings for their Bar or Bat Mitzvah.

Instead of establishing a separate "clinic," a Bar/Bat Mitzvah Lab became part of the *"Zayin"* (7th grade) curriculum. This course (led by our new staff person) has included peer tutoring both in skills and emotional support. Also, as part of the *"Zayin"* program, the students now do several *tzedakah* projects as a class instead of individual service hours as first suggested. Involvement in such activities as feeding the homeless who are temporarily located at nearby motels, entertaining at a local nursing home, packaging *mishloach manot* for the elderly, or sending toys to new immigrant children in Israel has given the students both group spirit and a sense of spirituality about Jewish life.

Attractive booklets are placed on pews each Shabbat with announcements and explanations about our synagogue's customs. More adult courses addressed to those who are beginning their Jewish studies have also been initiated. Family programs have been added, making people feel more comfortable with each other and more comfortable in the synagogue.

CONCLUSION

The committee's report opened our hearts and minds to issues of inclusiveness and participation not only of Bar/Bat Mitzvah students and their families, but of *all our members*. I believe this process will guide us in focusing on other synagogue needs as well.

Chapter 9

Folk Judaism, Elite Judaism, and the Role of Bar Mitzvah in the Development of the Synagogue and Jewish School in America

Stuart Schoenfeld

Most scholars of Jewish life in North America discuss Bar and Bat Mitzvah only in passing. This is unfortunate because these commonly held, and typically very public, life cycle events are a major part of the North America Jewish experience.

Three different types of questions may be raised by research on Bar and Bat Mitzvah. First are those about social change and change in religious ritual. Bar Mitzvah and Bat Mitzvah have a history, and their modern history in particular is one of innovation and variation. A study of this historical development gives the opportunity to explore theories about modernization, assimilation, and secularization while at the same time illuminating a life cycle event which is part of the early adolescent experience of almost all North American Jews. A second set of questions is concerned with the meanings — overt and symbolic — conveyed in ritual ceremonies and celebrations. There are authoritatively defined meanings (see, e.g., Spiro, 1977) and some attempts at interpretation by psychologists (see, e.g., Arlow, 1982 [1951]), but very little ethnographic material using observations and interviews to discover what the rituals mean to those involved (see Weissler, 1986, for an example). A third set of questions addresses the relationship between Bar and Bat Mitzvah and the formal organizations of the Jewish community. Although scholars have not discussed it, "everybody" seems to know that most synagogues do not permit Bar or Bat Mitzvah without affiliation and a specified minimum of Jewish education. The examination of the origin of these requirements, their functions, and changes in them should contribute to a better understanding of the relationship between North American Jews and their community institutions.[1]

This chapter deals, in part, with the third set of questions. It is more historical than contemporary in its focus, calling attention to when and how minimum educational requirements became virtually unavoidable, the problems this strategy addressed, and some subsequent developments. The distinction between "folk" and "elite" religion is used to place the imposition of minimum requirements in context and to relate it to a broader framework for the interpretation of Jewish life in North America. The paper argues that there was, and to some extent continues to be, an elite-folk struggle over Bar and Bat Mitzvah, and that the compromise adopted in that struggle was decisive for the direction that Judaism in North America subsequently took.[2]

FOLK AND ELITE RELIGION

The contrast between elite and folk religion in Judaism comes from the work of Charles Liebman (1973)[3]. He describes elite religion as the symbols and rituals . . . and beliefs which the leaders acknowledge as legitimate. But more importantly, elite religion is also the religious organization itself, its hierarchical arrangements, the authority of the leaders and their sources of authority, and the rights and obligations of the followers to the organization and its leaders (1976:46).

Folk religion is described as a kind of subculture . . .

which the acknowledged leaders ignore or even condemn, but in which a majority of the members participate. . . . As far as the elite religion is concerned, folk religion is not a movement, but an error, or a set of errors, shared by many people (ibid).

Liebman cautions,

> It is a mistake to think of folk religion as necessarily more primitive than elite religion. While its ceremonies and sanctums evoke emotions and inchoate ideas associated with basic instincts and primitive emotions, it is also more flexible than elite religion. Hence it is also capable of developing ceremonial responses to contemporary needs which may be incorporated into the elite religion (ibid.:47).

FOLK JUDAISM AND BAR MITZVAH

There is scattered but abundant evidence to indicate that, in the period of mass migration at the turn of the century, standards of Jewish education were low, expectations were low, and teenaged boys who lived in conformity with the *mitzvot* were very rare. Nevertheless, the Bar Mitzvah was considered an important event, to be celebrated with a synagogue ceremony. The folk values gave higher — sometimes exclusive — priority to a successful performance than to understanding, even at the most basic level, or to behavioral commitment. As early at 1885, an elite critic of the religious practices of American Jews called Bar Mitzvah "the greatest of holidays among our Jewish brethren" and ironically described the conspicuous donation, the emphasis on the reception, the inflated cliché-filled speeches, and the boy's subsequent refusal to allow his tutor to teach him how to wear *tefillin* (Sarna, 1981:76).

An observer of a later phase of the period of mass immigration stressed the estrangement between the culturally foreign immigrants and their American-oriented sons, who, he writes,

> . . . gradually quit going to the synagogue, give up 'chaider' promptly when they are 13 years old, avoid the Yiddish theaters, seek the up-town places of amusement, dress in the latest American fashion, and have a keen eye for the right thing in neckties. They even refuse sometimes to be present at supper on Friday evenings. Thus, indeed, the sway of the old people is broken. (Hapgood, 1967:27; see also Feldstein, 1978:172)

Instead of being a ceremony acknowledging full participation of the adolescent in sacred rituals, Bar Mitzvah appears to have become a ritual of discontinuity, the last time the boy was obligated to present himself as a participant in his father's world. It became a ritual in which traditional commitments were affirmed and then ignored. For the parents — themselves rebellious children who had left their own parents — it appears that the ritual affirmation of religious continuity was emotionally important.

The increasing importance of Bar Mitzvah as a public ritual, combined with the inability of most North American Jewish boys to prepare a *drasha* — a learned commentary on a biblical text — led to the publication of books of Bar Mitzvah speeches which the boy could memorize. The first edition of what appears to be the first of these compilations appeared in 1907 and sold 10,000 copies (Engelman, 1951:36)[4]. These books continued to be published until at least 1954. (Wise, 1954)

Personal reports of Bar Mitzvah ceremonies in the early twentieth century recall differing experiences. Angoff (in Howe and Libo, 1979:122) writes of a simple Thursday morning ceremony and his delight at his mother's "great appreciation . . . [that h]er oldest son was now a full man in Israel." Marx recalls that he had a Bar Mitzvah ceremony "out of deference to Grandpa, who would have been bitterly hurt if his grandsons hadn't shown that much respect for their traditional faith" (1961:57). Levenson, on the other hand, remembers reading a speech "before a packed house of menfolk, womenfolk, and kinfolk" and realizing that the Jewish view of adult "rights" was that they were not only responsibilities, but "privileges, for which I had to be grateful" (1973:184).

The rise of the Bar Mitzvah as a major social event has not yet been studied. Rosenberg writes that in 1935 the Bar Mitzvah "affair," on Saturday night, with a catered meal and a band at a banquet hall "was just then beginning to become the rage in Flatbush"

(1984:18). Levitats, writing in 1949, noted that "the reception party or dinner and ball are usually elaborate and sumptuous" (1949:153). He further noted the wide circulation of a film made of the Bar Mitzvah celebration in Hollywood of Edward G. Robinson's son, and commented, "The child usually measures the success of the event by the value of the gifts he receives" (ibid.). Duker reported, at about the same period, the following:

> The commercial Bar Mitzvah ceremony . . . has evolved its own ritual, resembling closely the extravaganza of the wedding ceremony. There is the march, the bringing in of the Bar Mitzvah cake, the lighting of the thirteen candles, or of fourteen — one for luck — the use of the choir, the rendition, sometimes of "*Mein Yiddishe Momme*" by the Bar Mitzvah celebrant or of "*Dos Pintele Yid*" by an artist. So much importance is now being attached to this commercial hall ceremonial, that we have heard of cases where it has replaced the synagogue ritual completely, even eliminating the custom of calling up the Bar Mitzvah lad to the reading of the Torah. The Bar Mitzvah cake, usually in the form of a Torah scroll, is also an American innovation (1969:413).

ELITE JUDAISM AND BAR MITZVAH

This pattern of folk observance of the Bar Mitzvah was obviously distressing to those who participated in elite Judaism, whose values and personal futures were committed to raising the standards of Jewish education and creating a stable membership for American synagogues.

The institutional base of elite Judaism had lagged behind migration patterns. Although congregations were almost always established in new locations after the settlement of only a small number of Jews, elite Judaism requires, in addition, higher level study for those with whom religious authority will be shared and formal structures to interpret and standardize beliefs and practices of those congregations which acknowledge common authority. In America, elite Judaism took the organizational form of Rabbinic seminaries, Rabbinic associations, and federations of congregations. The national institutions of the Reform movement were established in the late nineteenth century, after several generations of German-Jewish immigration. The institutions of Conservative and Orthodox Judaism developed toward the end of the mass immigration of Eastern European Jews.

By the twenties, several competing elites were self-consciously fashioning somewhat different versions of American Judaism, adaptations of the religious community to the conditions of North American life. On the one hand, these adaptations had to speak to a new constituency of "American Jews," to provide them a way of thinking about themselves that harmonized their Jewish and American identities (see Eisen, 1983). On the other hand, American Judaism is voluntaristic, sustained by the affiliation and financial support of members. A number of studies (cited by Sherman, 1960:208-209) suggest that overall from the end of mass immigration until after World War II, far fewer than one-half of American Jewish families were synagogue members. Organized Jewish schools enrolled only a minority of school-aged children and many received tutoring only before their Bar Mitzvah.

The development of an American pattern of Bar Mitzvah observance combining lack of religious commitment with a big party was a continuing object of elite criticism. In 1930, a psychologist giving a series of lectures on Jewish parenting under the sponsorship of the Women's League for Conservative Judaism included a long critical section on Bar Mitzvah, which read in part:

> . . . The . . . celebrations do much to counteract whatever good the synagogue ritual may accomplish. . . . I have seen children brought from the inspiring and chastening atmosphere of the synagogue to fashionable hotels where a great banquet was prepared in utter defiance of the Sabbath or the Jewish dietary laws and involving an outlay which made the occasion one of vulgar display of parental wealth rather than of parental concern for the spiritual welfare of the child. . . . To make the party a real event vaudeville artists are sometimes engaged and one is privileged to enjoy the puerile vulgarisms of the variety theater capping the climax of a

> Bar Mitzvah ceremony. . . . (Kohn, 1932:30-31, passim).

A Rabbi, replying to a questionnaire item about whether his congregation conducted Bat Mitzvah, wrote, "The Bar Mitzvah ceremony is enough of a farce" (Silverman, 1932:330)[5].

BAR MITZVAH AND INSTITUTION BUILDING

One way of strengthening synagogues and synagogue schools and enforcing a higher level of adherence to elite norms was to use the folk expectation that Jewish boys would have a Bar Mitzvah ceremony as a basis for pressuring otherwise reluctant North American Jews to become more involved with the synagogue. A 1937 editorial in *Reconstructionist* on Confirmation and Bar Mitzvah included this succinct statement of strategy and tactics:

> In order that these rites may not represent merely the attainment of certain ages, but also the accomplishment of certain minimum education, it would be necessary for the national organizations, such as the United synagogue of America and the Union of American Hebrew Congregations, to set up for their respective constituents standard requirements for Bar Mitzvah and for Confirmation.

Another tactical variation was possible — setting standards through local boards of Jewish education. This local approach was implemented in Chicago in 1938 by a regulation binding congregations affiliated with the Board of Jewish Education to require all boys, prior to a Bar Mitzvah ceremony (1) A minimum of three years attendance at a daily Hebrew School of recognized standing, or (2) Evidence of the candidate's fitness to be determined by the Board of Jewish Education through examinations that will test the following: (a) Understanding of the Hebrew language equivalent to what is expected of pupils in affiliated schools who have studied for a period of three years. (b) Ability to read the prayers with a reasonable degree of fluency as well as the ability to follow the services as practiced in the adult synagogue. (c) Understanding of the customs and ceremonies of Jewish life. (d) Knowledge and understanding of the major events, personalities, and movements of Jewish history, and of the contemporary Jewish world with special emphasis on the positive and constructive phases of present-day Jewish life (quoted in Levitats, 1949:155).

National standards for Bar Mitzvah, Bat Mitzvah, and Confirmation were first implemented by the Conservative movement which included them in its "Statement of Objectives and Standards for the Congregational School" adopted in 1946. This document specified for Bar or Bat Mitzvah a minimum of three years enrollment in a congregational school meeting three times a week for six hours, and for Confirmation age of fifteen and five years enrollment.

The most detailed discussion of educational requirements for Bar Mitzvah appears in a pamphlet published in 1951 by The American Association for Jewish Education, written by its director of research and information, Uriah Zevi Engelman. This pamphlet gives more details about the imposition of minimum requirements in various localities and strongly endorses the practice. This pamphlet did not necessarily have a direct effect — the A.A.J.E. was and remains[6] a purely advisory body — but it is a significant document because it records and comments on how tendencies toward folk and elite Judaism interacted in the shaping of American Judaism. The pamphlet was an unusual one for the A.A.J.E. Its 18 previous pamphlets had dealt with such technical topics as directories, budgeting, salaries, enrollment, and the funding of Jewish education by local federations. This was its first publication on a Jewish ritual.

The pamphlet is introduced by Judah Pilch, the Executive Director of the Association, who sets out immediately the elite critique of folk laxity. "In the past several decades," Pilch wrote,

> Bar Mitzvah has come to be considered merely a rite, and preparation for Bar Mitzvah has tended to become preparation for the ceremony itself.. . . As a consequence, the education of the child was in all too many cases restricted to the narrow requirements of the rite. . . . Bar Mitzvah represents a powerful

motivation, a goal which children and their parents readily understand, and will work to attain.

Recognizing the value of this motivation, increasing numbers of Jewish educators and Rabbis have sought to direct Bar Mitzvah preparation from mere coaching for a performance, to education for living as American Jews. . . .

The pamphlet then gives a brief but scholarly history of Bar Mitzvah and its relationship to Jewish education, a historical sketch of Bar Mitzvah in America, and detailed results of a 1950 survey of minimum educational requirements for Bar Mitzvah.

Community Practices

One hundred and twelve communities participated in the survey. Fifty-one (45.5%) reported no minimum educational requirements for Bar Mitzvah. The remainder indicated that at least one congregation in the community made such requirements. Of the 112 communities responding to the survey, 107 had Jewish populations of less than 100,000. In communities of this size, minimum requirements were imposed by synagogues representing all branches of Judaism. For the five communities of over 100,000 no information was available beyond the fact that at least one congregation in each of these communities had educational requirements. The most common requirement in place was three years attendance, but some congregations required less and a few congregations required more. (As might be expected, Orthodox congregations required more and Reform less, with Conservative in the middle, but the differences between them — in numbers of years only, as number of hours were not reported — are not dramatic.) The number of communities in which Bat Mitzvahs were held was not given; where Bat Mitzvah was held, the educational requirements were the same for girls as boys.

Intercongregational Cooperation

Minimum requirements were more effective where they were jointly imposed by congregations acting as a cartel. Joint congregational action, usually through the local board of Jewish education, was taken to standardize minimum regulations in Cleveland (1942), Cincinnati (1944), Minneapolis (1947), Schenectady (1948), Indianapolis (1949), and Bridgeport (1950).

Community Bar Mitzvah Boards

Formal committees to "administer and enforce" communally adopted regulations were established in a number of larger communities. Chicago, which took the initiative in establishing minimum requirements, did so in 1938. It was followed by Philadelphia (1949), New Haven (1948), Los Angeles (1949), Miami (1950), and Boston (1950). The "smaller communities" of Akron and Syracuse set up Bar Mitzvah boards in 1944 and 1949, respectively.

National Action

The pamphlet reported in a section on "Bar Mitzvah educational requirements by national organizations" on regulations established by the New York Federation of Reform Synagogues in 1945 and the United Synagogue Commission on Jewish Education. The Reform regulations required two years school attendance, attainment of age thirteen, and "a definite understanding" of continuing attendance at Religious School until Confirmation. The Reform ceremony was to include reading from Hebrew sections of the *Union Prayer Book,* reciting the blessing over the Torah in Hebrew, chanting from the *parashah* in Hebrew in the congregations where laity normally did this, reading the blessings over the Haftarah in Hebrew, reading the Haftarah in either Hebrew or English and a prayer or talk which "should express the emotions and thoughts of the candidate himself." The United Synagogue Commission on Jewish Education requirements mentioned are those discussed previously in this paper.

Bar Mitzvah Certificates

Facsimiles of Bar Mitzvah certificates from New Haven and Syracuse were included in the pamphlet. These certificates were not worded to be records of a congregational ceremony, but spoke explicitly of education. The New Haven certificate spoke of "completion of the educational requirements for . . . Bar Mitzvah" and was signed by the president and director of the local board of Jewish education as well as the congregational president and Rabbi. The Syracuse certificate spoke of "study" making the boy "eligible for the ceremony of Bar Mitzvah" and was signed by the President of the Syracuse Rabbinical Council, the Director of the Board of Jewish Education, and the congregational Rabbi.

Local and national educational standards for Bar Mitzvah could set a climate of opinion, but the autonomy of each congregation and the differences between the branches of Judaism ensured continuing diversity and competition. For example, the Conservative movement's standard of six hours of school, three days a week meant, in effect, phasing out the Sunday School, which had been the most common Conservative congregational school. This change led some families to change their affiliation to Reform, or to Conservative and Orthodox congregations which did not adopt these standards (Kelman, 1975:74). At an experience-sharing session at the 1949 convention of the Rabbinical Assembly, the phasing out of the Sunday School in favor of the three day a week Hebrew School was discussed by a Rabbi from Youngstown, Ohio. In the first two years of this transition, about ninety families resigned from his congregation and joined the Reform Congregation "up the street, whose Rabbi campaigned on the platform, "Come to us and they will be just as good Jews" (Karp, 1983:226). Nevertheless, by 1959, 74% of Conservative congregations had phased out their Sunday schools (Wertheimer, 1984:128).

ELITE AND FOLK ACCOMMODATION

In the social science literature on Jewish life in the fifties and sixties, Bar and Bat Mitzvah are mentioned in passing. Gartner (1969)[7], Sklare (1972)[8], and Sklare and Greenblum (1979)[9] have the most to say.

The data gleaned from these studies indicate the importance of Bar (and later Bat) Mitzvah as a family event, as the goal of Jewish education, and as motivation for synagogue affiliation. However, these studies do not systematically pursue the implications of Bar/Bat Mitzvah as an organizing event shaping local and national patterns in family life, synagogues, and schools. These institutions were linked by the establishment of normally unavoidable educational prerequisites for Bar and Bat Mitzvah in a pattern which influenced subsequent developments.

It is not possible to argue strictly cause-and-effect in this pattern of development. The necessary scientific conditions for separating out the effects of variables are not present in a historical case study. It is simply argued that a discussion of the changes in Jewish education, synagogue affiliation, and family life which leaves out this educational requirement misses something important.

Changes in Jewish life in this period have been attributed to a reaction to the Holocaust, the psychological effects of the State of Israel, occupational mobility, geographic relocation from exclusively Jewish city neighborhoods to mixed neighborhoods in the suburbs, and the conventional expectation of religious affiliation within middle-class life (Glaser, 1972:119-123; Janowsky, 1964:133; Gans, 1958 and many others). Explanations based on these causes make the changes in educational and affiliation patterns appear to be consequences of a spontaneous consensus among Jews in the post-war period.

While there was undoubtedly much enthusiasm for synagogue-building and a heightened interest in Jewish education, it is easy to overestimate the degree to which all North American Jews took for granted affiliation with an expensive synagogue and a minimum of three or more years of Jewish education. In the sociological analysis of structural change, it has been firmly established for at least several decades (the widespread attention given to Dahrendorf, 1959 is commonly considered a turning point) that what appears to be structural adjustments of one part of a social system to changes in another part may also be analyzed as a pattern of tension between interest groups, conflict, and accommodation. Certain features of Jewish education, synagogue affiliation, and family life become more understandable if the imposition of minimum educational requirements for Bar (and by extension Bat) Mitzvah is seen as the outcome of a process of tension, conflict, and accommodation between "elite" and "folk" interest groups within Judaism.

The pattern of Jewish education in North America was substantially different before and after minimum educational requirements became widespread. First, the percentage of enrolled school-aged children approximately doubled. From the period of mass migration until World War II, from 25 to 30% of Jewish children aged 5-14 were enrolled in Jewish education each year. A study of enrollment between 1948 and 1958 showed an increase of 131.2%, raising the percentage of children 5-14 receiving Jewish education to between 40 and 45%. In 1962, it was estimated that of Jewish children 5-17, 53% were enrolled in Jewish education. Second, the setting of Jewish education changed. While in the prewar period congregational schools were common, a substantial percentage of students were enrolled in communally sponsored Talmud Torahs, tiny *chedarim,* secular Yiddish schools, or were privately tutored. By 1958, the congregational schools had become dominant, accounting for 88.5% of total enrollments.[10] Third, it appears that attendance expectations changed. A 1918 New York report found that more than half of the students "dropped out" of class without completing the year. A 1919 Chicago report estimated a drop-out rate of one-third. By the 1950s, with a Bar Mitzvah ceremony usually dependent on continuous enrollment for a number of years, the drop-out rate was much lower.[11]

Coerced enrollment in Jewish education, however, was rarely accompanied by a change in the home environment. Tension between what the school taught and what the family believed and practiced remained an institutionalized part of Jewish life, with many students having a school experience that has been referred to as "Siddur and yelling." Jewish educators, however, clearly preferred to have students under these circumstances than not to have them at all. Vastly increased numbers, the financial subsidies from synagogue dues, the apparent stability gained by integrating school and synagogue, and the investment in curriculum support by the Reform and Conservative movements made it possible to begin changing the concern over the quality of Jewish education from hand-wringing rhetoric to modest action.

The "normalization" of several years Jewish education prior to Bar Mitzvah may also have contributed to the increasing frequency of Bat Mitzvahs. If coeducation was normal in the public schools which most North American Jewish children attended, and if Jewish education was mandatory for boys, it became harder to accept the idea that Jewish education was unnecessary for girls, or that they should be denied being the center of attention in an impressive synagogue ceremony. Scattered reports indicate female enrollment (as a percentage of the total) gradually increasing from the period of mass migration to 1962 (as reported in Janowsky, 1964:136-7).

The monopolistic imposition of minimum educational requirements was associated with intergeneration changes in expectations of what constituted a proper synagogue. *Landsmenschaft* synagogues evolved into synagogue centers (often shifting from Orthodox to Conservative and relocating in the suburbs in the process) or aged with their founders. New architecturally dramatic synagogues, featuring educational wings, attractive social halls, and catering sized kitchens, made symbolic statements about collective economic and cultural mobility. For some Jews voluntary affiliation, with its attendant financial obligations, with these multi-functional impressive and expensive synagogues was a matter of personal feelings of obligation or pride. For others — at least a significant minority — it was a matter of necessity. If one's two children were to have a Bar or Bat Mitzvah at these synagogues, synagogue affiliation during the years that they were in Hebrew school was required.[12]

Assuming a family with two children spaced three years apart, coercive affiliation during the period of Jewish education usually meant about six years — from the time the older child turned ten until the younger child became 13. A 1967 Conservative movement survey of synagogue membership found that a son's completion of Bar Mitzvah or Hebrew School followed only death and geographic relocation as a reason given for disaffiliation (cited in Wertheimer, 1984:128)[13]. The period of mandatory affiliation could serve for some as a framework for the organization of new neighborhood social networks based on childrens' friendships, car pooling, and friendships developing from common organizational membership. From an institutional perspective, six years of mandatory but satisfying synagogue membership could sometimes lead to additional years of voluntary affiliation.

The setting of minimum educational requirements for Bar and Bat Mitzvah set a pattern for compromise between elite and folk. From the elite perspective, a Bar or Bat Mitzvah ceremony is not an important part of Jewish identity. Elite Judaism, of whatever branch, is committed to a Jewish way of life. Life cycle ceremonies have meaning only because they are integrated into this way of life, and others — such as Brit Milah — have a more important place in this way of life. For the elite, the importance attached to Bar Mitzvah, and later to Bat Mitzvah, in North American folk Judaism provided an opportunity to pursue elite goals. The religious elite used their control over the setting in which Bar and Bat Mitzvah ceremonies are held to require enrollment in Hebrew school. These enrollments helped stabilize congregational membership and provided a more stable financial and membership base.

While the elite have control over the setting and the ceremony, the laity have retained control over the celebration. The generally successful imposition of minimum educational requirements did not necessarily tame the vulgar excess about which secular as well as religious critics complained. A Reform Rabbi in the 1950s inveighed in colorful detail against circus, cowboy, and baseball "theme" Bar Mitzvahs (Herman, 1967). Rabbi Moshe Feinstein in 1959 published a *Responsum* condemning the American Bar Mitzvah celebration (quoted in Sherwin, 1973:53). In 1978 a Bar Mitzvah party at the Orange Bowl in Florida made the national press. However, the extent to which conspicuous consumption was ever the keynote of typical Bar Mitzvahs may be questioned; other, perhaps more important, themes can be identified. And, as the folkways of American Jews — a community still in transition — continue to change, the celebrations have changed, and new elements have been added to the synagogue ceremony.

DISCUSSION

The analysis in this paper raises additional theoretical and substantive questions which go beyond its scope. To what extent is it legitimate to speak of American Jews as a "folk"? What are the implications of the extensive political science literature on elites for an approach to the understanding of American Jews? When, how, and why does a practice stop being a folk custom and either disappear or become an elite prescription? Has the gap between elite and folk Judaism narrowed or widened, or has the quality of the relationship changed? Each of these questions requires an extended response.

It is possible, however, to remark briefly on two implications of the approach taken in this paper.

First, the attention to "folk" religion suggests that a somewhat different set of questions be asked in research about Jewish identification. The set of questions reported by Cohen (1983:55-57), to cite a well-known example, includes questions about *kashrut,* Sabbath candles, *mezuzot,* fasting on Yom Kippur, taking part in a Seder, attending services, synagogue membership, Jewish organization membership, non-sectarian organization membership, Jewish giving, non-Jewish giving, intermarriage, and Jewish friends. While the responses to these items are informative and valuable, the list is essentially eclectic and not theoretically structured.

For those questions which deal specifically with ritual observance, one starting point for a theoretically derived list could be the sacramental function of religion. In all cultures significant status passages are socially announced through rituals. In most cultures these rituals have a religious content — relating the passing from one status into another to theological teachings and folk beliefs about the meaning of life. Using this as a guide, it would be informative for studies of "Jewish identification" to also include questions about *bris,* Bar and Bat Mitzvah[14], weddings, and burials. Quantitative intergenerational data about these practices will give information about the extent to which this sacramental function of Judaism endures. Qualitative research will give some insight into the meaning of these events and the extent to which they are connected with other aspects of the lives of American Jews.

Second, this approach has implications for the debate over whether the American Jewish population identifies less with Jewish life with each generation, has developed a modest but stable identification with Jewish life or is becoming polarized (Cohen, 1983; Waxman, 1983; Silberman, 1985). Bar and Bat Mitzvah are major folk rituals of Jewish identification[15], usually requiring months of preparation on the part of the entire family. While data on the extent of Bar and Bat Mitzvah are not available, it does appear that even many families who are far removed from participation in Jewish life have these ceremonies. The content of Bar and Bat Mitzvah ceremonies varies from setting to setting, but their ubiquity indicates that they are seen as conventionally expected events in the Jewish life cycle. Data indicating a decline in the percentage of children having Bar and Bat Mitzvah ceremonies would indeed be an indication of declining Jewish identification. Data indicating the opposite would be an indication of stability. Qualitative data about different ways of celebrating Bar and Bat Mitzvah and the meaning of the event to those who participate would give some insight into the alternative paths along which Jewish identification may be developing.

NOTES

[1]These theoretical perspectives are discussed in more detail in Schoenfeld, 1985.

[2]Writing from Canada, the author is keenly aware of both substantial similarities and differences in Jewish life in the U.S. and Canada. As publications about Bar/Bat Mitzvah in Canada and their relationship to Jewish education are completely lacking, the analysis in this paper relies on American sources. Research is presently being conducted on the hypothesis that in this particular case the American and Canadian patterns are very similar.

[3]Liebman cites Bock (1966) as a source of this distinction. Mordecai Kaplan appears to be another, although uncited source. Kaplan (1967 [1934]) includes a chapter on "The Folk Aspect of the Jewish Religion" and one on "Jewish Folkways." Liebman elsewhere (1975) shows his awareness of Kaplan's thought and concludes that his approach to Judaism is widely shared beyond those who identify themselves as Reconstructionists.

[4]In comparison, Janowsky estimates that in 1908 only 100,000 students were receiving Jewish education, including those "receiving private instruction" (1964:130).

[5]In the Reform movement, the criticism is more complex because of the only partially successful attempt to replace Bar Mitzvah with Confirmation. At the first convention of the Central Conference of American Rabbis (1890), Dr. David Phillipson characterized Bar Mitzvah as "an antiquated, soulless ceremony with no meaning for us and our time" (1890:47), "one of the many religious forms which have lived their day and should disappear entirely . . ." (50). He criticized, however, the "abuses" which were now associated with Confirmation — "extravagance in the dress of the girls, . . . the vulgar display of presents in every home on Confirmation day, . . . grand and magnificent receptions, rivaling the splendor of wedding receptions." (57)

[6]Now reorganized as the Jewish Education Service of North America.

[7]Gartner observes that the rise of public education in the late nineteenth century led to a pattern of Reform Jewish education in supplementary Sunday schools; a typical three year program of education led to a graduating Confirmation ceremony for boys and girls around age 13. Some Reform congregations retained the Bar Mitzvah ceremony (1969:9-10). Later, the early twentieth century Talmud Torahs provided an ambitious program of Jewish education. However, most students attended only two or three years and parents demanded preparation for Bar Mitzvah, an event "despised by the pedagogues." The girls who attended were not preoccupied with Bar Mitzvah and made better pupils (ibid.:17). He also mentions the post-war establishment of prerequisites for "the still universally desired Bar Mitzvah" (ibid.:25). His collection of sources includes two Bar Mitzvah speeches — one from 1873 and one from 1931.

[8]Sklare's study of the Conservative movement notes that Bar Mitzvah and Confirmation ceremonies attracted attendance to otherwise sparsely attended services (1972:99), with Bar Mitzvah ceremonies as a main support of the Saturday morning service and Confirmation attracting attendance on Shavuot (ibid.:101). Higher requirements for Bar Mitzvah — at least three years Hebrew school — extending years of Sunday school by setting the age of Confirmation higher, and the encouragement of female education leading to Bat Mitzvah are mentioned as common; at the time of his study, the parental desire for a Bat Mitzvah ceremony was still small (ibid.:155). He reports the "widespread feeling among both parents and children that Bar Mitzvah and Confirmation are equivalent to graduation exercises," with virtually no classes held beyond them (ibid.:157).

[9]In 1957-8 Sklare and Greenblum studied a mid-west suburb with a growing Jewish minority. Some of their findings about Bar Mitzvah, Bat Mitzvah and Confirmation reflect the particular and unrepresentative makeup of the suburb. At the time of the study, the suburb had one Conservative congregation, with 27% of the affiliation of the study's respondents, and four Reform congregations, with 73% of the affiliation (1979:97-98). As might be expected, there was also an unusually high percentage of fourth generation Americans and of those of German-Jewish descent (ibid.:32-33). In families with at least one child age 10 or older, 95% enrolled their children in Sunday or Hebrew school. A smaller proportion of both mothers and fathers reported having had formal Jewish education themselves (ibid.:294), including those who received tutoring solely as Bar Mitzvah preparation (ibid.:295). The Saturday morning service at the Conservative congregation, and the largest Reform one were sustained by Bar Mitzvah ceremonies. The Conservative congregation also had a Tefillin club for recent Bar Mitzvahs and a Bat Mitzvah Club for girls. The congregation also had a Hebrew high school program with a small enrollment. The Reform congregations were differentiated by social status, style and choices among the practices then controversial within Reform. Controversial issues within Reform included the relative importance of Friday night, Saturday morning and Sunday morning services; the challenge of Bar and Bat Mitzvah to Confirmation; and the relationship of Sunday school to weekday Hebrew school. There is no specific statement about compulsory education before Bar and Bat Mitzvah. The only Jewish schools were congregational ones. Affiliation rates rose from 19% of families in the "preschool" years to 56% of families in the "early-school years" to 87% of families in the "peak-school" years (ibid.:181). Affiliation for the purpose of Bar/Bat Mitzvah and Confirmation was common. Some disaffiliation after these ceremonies is reported.

[10]This was of course to change with the gradual but steady shift to day schools, most of which were not directly linked to a congregation.

[11]The figures in the preceding paragraphs are taken from Janowsky, 1964:128-142.

[12]Bar and Bat Mitzvahs could still be held at the few synagogues which did not impose minimum educational requirements, but these synagogues were usually aging, old-fashioned, poor congregations in "the old neighborhood." *Simchahs* held in these settings in the 1950s appeared declasse'. For families in transition, who still had some connection to "the old neighborhood," a Thursday morning ceremony downtown and a Saturday morning ceremony uptown were sometimes held.

[13]Johnson (1978 [1974]:94) mentions a more recent case where a congregation retained only 10 percent of those families whose children reached Bar Mitzvah age.

[14]After the preparation of this paper, the author learned that questions about Bar Mitzvah have been included in some community surveys and that statistically interesting results are found in the 1985 Philadelphia data (Yancy:1985).

[15]The assimilation of Bar and Bat Mitzvah into civil Judaism is indicated by the practice of having adult Bar Mitzvahs as part of UJA tours of Israel.

REFERENCES

Arlow, Jacob. 1982 [1951]. "A Psychoanalytic Study of a Religious Initiation Rite: Bar Mitzvah." Pp. 187-217 in Mortimer Oslow, ed., *Judaism and Psychoanalysis*. New York: Ktav.

Angoff, Charles. 1979. Excerpt from "Memories of Boston," *Menorah Journal,* Autumn-Winter, 1962, reprinted in Irving Howe and Kenneth Libo, eds., *How We Lived,* New York: Richard Marek.

Bock, E. Wilbur. 1966. "Symbols in the Conflict: Official versus Folk Religion," *Journal for the Scientific Study of Religion* 5 (Spring):204-12.

Cohen, Steven M. 1983. *American Modernity and Jewish Identity*. New York: Tavistock.

"Confirmation and Bar Mitzvah." 1937. *The Reconstructionist* 3 (9, June 11):6-7.

Dahrendorf, Ralf. 1959. *Class and Class Conflict in Industrial Society*. Stanford: Stanford University Press.

Duker, Abraham G. 1969. "Emerging Culture Patterns in American Jewish Life," in Abraham J. Karp, ed., *The*

Jewish Experience in America, vol. 5: *At Home in America.* New York: Ktav.

Eisen, Arnold M. 1983. *The Chosen People in America: A Study in Jewish Religious Ideology.* Bloomington: University of Indiana Press.

Engelman, Uriah Zevi. 1951. *Educational Requirements for Bar Mitzvah.* New York: American Association for Jewish Education.

Feldstein, Stanley. 1978. *The Land That I Show You.* New York: Doubleday.

Gans, Herbert J. 1958. "The Origin and Growth of a Jewish Community in the Suburbs: A Study of the Jews of Park Forest." Pp. 205-248 in Marshall Sklare, ed., *The Jews: Social Patterns of an American Group.* New York: Free Press.

Gartner, Lloyd. 1969. (ed.) *Jewish Education in the United States.* New York: Teachers College, Columbia University.

Glazer, Nathan. 1972. *American Judaism.* Second edition, revised. Chicago: University of Chicago Press.

Hapgood, Hutchins. 1976. *The Spirit of the Ghetto.* New York: Schocken.

Herman, Erwin. 1967. "Bar Mitzvah a la Carte." Pp. 253-256 in Paul Kresh, ed., *The American Judaism Reader.* New York: Abelard Schuman.

Janowsky, Oscar I. 1964. "Jewish Education." Pp. 123-172 in Oscar I. Janowsky, ed. *The American Jew: A Reappraisal.* Philadelphia: Jewish Publication Society.

Johnson, George. 1978 [1974]. "Synagogue Survival Strategies in a Rootless Society: A Case Study." Pp. 77-95 in Jack Nusan Porter, ed., *The Sociology of American Jews: A Critical Anthology.* Washington, DC: University Press of America.

Kaplan, Mordecai M. 1967 [1934]. *Judaism as a Civilization: Toward a Reconstruction of American Jewish Life.* New York: Schocken.

Karp, Abraham J. 1983. "The Conservative Rabbi — 'Dissatisfied But Not Unhappy.'" *American Jewish Archives* 35:188-262.

Kelman, Wolfe. 1975. "The Synagogue in America." Pp. 69-89 in Jacob Neusner, ed., *Understanding American Judaism: Toward the Description of a Modern Religion. Volume I: The Rabbi and the Synagogue.* New York: Ktav.

Kohn, Jacob. 1932. *Modern Problems of Jewish Parents.* New York: Women's League of the United Synagogue.

Levenson, Sam. 1973. *In One Era and Out the Other.* New York: Simon and Schuster.

Levitats, Isaac. 1949. "Communal Regulation of Bar Mitzvah." *Jewish Social Studies* XI:153-162.

Liebman, Charles. 1973. *The Ambivalent American Jew.* Philadelphia: Jewish Publication Society.

______. 1975. "Reconstructionism in American Jewish Life." Pp. 219-246 in Jacob Neusner, ed., *Understanding American Judaism. Volume II: Sectors of American Judaism.* New York: Ktav.

Marx, Harpo. 1961. *Harpo Speaks.* (with Roland Barber) New York: Random House,

Rosenberg, Stuart. 1984. *The Real Jewish World: A Rabbi's Second Thoughts.* Toronto: Clarke-Irwin.

Sarna, Jonathan. 1981. trans. and ed. *People Walk on Their Heads: Moses Weinberger's Jews and Judaism in New York.* New York: Holmes and Meier.

Schoenfeld, Stuart. 1985. "Theoretical Approaches to the Study of Bar and Bat Mitzvah." Unpublished paper presented at the Ninth World Congress of Jewish Studies, Jerusalem.

Sherman, C. Bezalel. 1965. *The Jew Within American Society.* Detroit: Wayne State University Press.

Sherwin, Byron. 1973. "Bar-Mitzvah." *Judaism:* 53-65.

Silverman, Morris. 1932. "Report of Survey on Ritual." *Proceedings of the Rabbinical Assembly* 32:322-343.

Silberman, Charles E. 1985. *A Certain People: American Jews and Their Lives Today.* New York: Summit Books.

Sklare, Marshall. 1972. *Conservative Judaism: An American Religious Movement.* New York: Schocken.

Sklare, Marshall, and Joseph Greenblum. 1979. *Jewish Identity on the Suburban Frontier: A Study of Group Survival in the Open Society.* Chicago: University of Chicago Press.

Spiro, Jack. 1977. "The Educational Significance of the Bar Mitzvah Initiation." *Religious Education* 72(4):383-399.

United Synagogue of America, Commission on Education. 1946. "Statement on the Objectives and Standards for the Congregational School." *Conservative Judaism* 2(3):24-32.

Waxman, Chaim. 1983. *America's Jews in Transition.* Philadelphia: Temple University Press.

Weissler, Chava. 1986. "Coming of Age in the Havura Movement; Bar Mitzvah in the Havura Family." In Paul Hyman and Steven M. Cohen, eds., *The Evolving Jewish Family.* New York: Holmes and Meier: 200-217.

Wertheimer, Jack. 1984. "The Conservative Synagogue Revised." *American Jewish History* 73(2)118-132.

Wise, Judah. 1954. *On This Day: Brief Bar Mitzvah Addresses Based on the Portions of the Week.* New York: Bloch.

Yancey, William I. 1985. "Jews and Non-Jews in a Metropolitan Community: Results of Recent Research on Social Structure and Ethnic Identity in Philadelphia. Presented at the Association for Jewish Studies meetings, Boston.

(Originally published as Stuart Schoenfeld "Folk Judaism, Elite Judaism and the Role of Bar Mitzvah in the Development of the Synagogue and Jewish School in America." CONTEMPORARY JEWRY, the journal of the Association for the Social Scientific Study of Jewry, Vol. 9, pp. 67-85. Reprinted with permission.)

Unit II: Overview
The Tutor's Voice

A metaphor: Lines and lines of little children stand in the wings of a large stage, each holding a small Torah. They are all waiting their turn to walk out onto the stage and into your life. You, their tutor, are ready to greet them, and to open that Torah to them. As long as there are Jews, the procession never stops. And after all the possible permutations of Bar/Bat Mitzvah education have been tried and analyzed, from Family Education to Mitzvah Projects to improved Hebrew curriculum in the schools, the Bar/Bat Mitzvah experience ultimately depends on the one-on-one relationship between the tutor and the student.

To be a tutor is to experience a sense of great excitement and anticipation each time another child steps into your life ready to receive instruction in Torah. What Torah portion will you get to discuss? How musical will this child be? Will you have a good time learning together?

Of course, a tutor's ideal is not just to teach the mechanics, but to imbue each student with a love of Torah and of our Jewish heritage. It is hard to know how close we come to the ideal, especially since adolescents rarely give *any* indication of how much they have taken what they have learned to heart. But it is likely that the Bar or Bat Mitzvah tutor has more chance of making an impact on a child's attitude toward Judaism than nearly any other person in this formative period.

Statistical evidence given in the Introduction, the broad survey of B'nai Mitzvah educators, indicated that roughly 75% of the training of B'nai Mitzvah is entrusted to tutors. The questions posed there are, "Who are these tutors? What is their training?" Obviously, it is not possible to reach all the tutors presently working to find answers to these questions. But the tutor's voice has seldom if ever been heard, and certainly not in a book with a wide audience. This Unit is, therefore, an important first.

In Chapter 10, Cantor Helen Leneman offers her own tutoring suggestions, developed and refined through experience. Included are suggested "do's and don'ts" and extensive examples of diary accounts.

Chapter 11 consists of a "panel" of tutors, each of whom offers responses to a prepared list of questions. The individuals and their answers are real, of course, but they never did actually sit down together for such a panel. Instead, the tutors all responded in writing to the same questions, a rather Talmudic process.

In Chapter 12, Cantor Shira Belfer gives an overview of her tutoring methodology, which combines principles of music and Jewish and general education with personal intuition.

In Chapter 13, Ellen Goldenberg describes her job as a tutor and outlines her procedures for working with, and offering support to, each student.

Following these chapters are three chapters devoted to special needs children and to techniques and strategies for tutoring them.

In Chapter 14, Sara Rubinow Simon, a Covenant Award winner, makes a case for enabling every child to experience a Bar/Bat Mitzvah by adapting curriculum and the Bar/Bat Mitzvah ceremony itself.

In Chapter 15, Cantor Helen Leneman describes her experiences with three "special" children. Her account illustrates how working with these children offers great challenges and equally great rewards.

In Chapter 16, another "panel" of experts discuss the issues surrounding the tutoring of this population. Both concrete suggestions and illustrative anecdotal accounts are offered.

The chapters above reflect a cross section of approaches and attitudes regarding the tutoring process. They will give tutors new ideas and inspiration for their own work, as well as an opportunity to compare and contrast methods. Perhaps this book will serve as a catalyst for similar "panels" and other opportunities for sharing and brainstorming. A national network could be formed, which would help tutors explore and develop new techniques, as well as provide support.

Chapter 10
A Tutor Reflects

Cantor Helen Leneman

This chapter contains some thoughts concerning tutoring methods and the reasons behind them, plus extensive excerpts from the diaries kept by this author about a wide range of students. The hope here is to inspire other tutors to employ similar techniques and to encourage the keeping of diaries.

SEQUENCE OF TUTORING

At the initial meeting with the parent(s) and child, it is important to spell out what the final objectives are, as well as the steps that will be taken to achieve them. These will vary depending on the synagogue, of course. If the student will be learning trope, spend some time at this first meeting explaining the meaning and origins of trope. Provide trope materials and a tape, and start teaching then and there. This gives the student and parent(s) an idea of your approach, and will show you and the student how well matched your teaching/learning styles are. You can also evaluate the student's abilities, taking into account the nervousness of an initial encounter. After the lesson, set up a few appointments. I generally plan on 20 sessions with each student.

Lessons 1-3: Teach trope and Torah or Haftarah blessings. Make clear assignments for the student to prepare using his/her tape. By the third or fourth lesson, you will have a fair idea of the student's abilities and attitude toward lessons. Then type up a precise schedule (a sample format is reproduced in the Appendix at the end of this chapter), indicating date and material to be covered. You might use the format of a contract, which both student and parents must sign. A schedule (or a contract) will be taken very seriously and students are more likely to adhere to it.

Lessons 4-10: Teach the meaning of and the chant for the Torah or Haftarah portion (start with the larger assignment). Teach the blessings. By the tenth lesson, or roughly mid-way through the whole process, the student may not be on schedule. In some cases he/she is weeks ahead of it, in others, weeks behind. Be sure to build in a "cushion" of at least four weeks at the end if needed. At this point, you can type up a "revised schedule" which will have to be more strictly adhered to (see Appendix).

Lessons 11-20 (or beyond): Teach the meaning of and the chant for whichever portion has not yet been taught. When possible, teach a second trope system. If you have already taught the Torah trope, teach Haftarah trope now, or vice versa. Where required, help the student with his/her speech or *d'rash*, and teach the required prayers.

WHAT WORKS AND WHAT DOESN'T

Here are some suggestions and ideas for what works and what doesn't. First, the DON'T'S:

1. Don't fall into the trap of teaching *material* instead of *children*. If you are a musician, do not become obsessed with achieving note-perfect repetitions from every student.
2. While it is important to be organized, don't be obsessed with keeping every student on a very strict timetable. Each student must move at his/her own pace (with a little prodding from teacher and parents, of course).
3. Don't lose sight of long-term goals in favor of short-term objectives. Among those long-term goals are increased self-esteem and a positive sense of Jewish identity, along with skills mastery.
4. Never impose your views on students, but don't be shy about expressing them. Discussions about Torah portions can be real eye-openers for students. Try to stimulate students to think for themselves. Appreciate the ideas they come up with even as you help them put their ideas in perspective.

On the DO side:

1. Foster relationships, instead of trying to produce polished performances that will reflect well on you. That is an easy pitfall for any tutor, especially when that tutor is also the Cantor. Your goal is not to mold a child into a performer, but rather to give him or her a positive learning experience.
2. Determine the "personal best" of each individual student, and insist that he/she rise to that level. Musically, of course, this varies enormously. The term "tone-deaf" is bandied around too freely. Musically weak students who have had no experience singing and trying to reproduce tunes may sound tone-deaf initially. But with the right kind of training and encouragement, they can learn to approximate the trope tunes. It usually takes several sessions with a very unmusical child to determine what that child's personal best is. Once you see they are really making an effort, and certain trope melodies are way off the mark, simply adjust your ear and accept the fact that this may always be that particular student's rendition of the melody. Note this in your diary, so that in future lessons you will remember not to criticize the student for that rendition.
3. Use lesson time to explain how students can drill and tutor themselves (usually with the assistance of the tape) at home. Try not to correct trope or Hebrew mistakes during lessons; stop and ask them to correct themselves. One of the reasons for teaching the trope is to enable students to learn a Torah or Haftarah portion on their own, not only for the Bar/Bat Mitzvah, but for other occasions in the future.
4. Be demanding and understanding at the same time. Insist on students doing their best, and never back down from this. In the end, they will appreciate this seriousness, because it pushes them to achieve more than they otherwise would. And in the long run, such achievement is the most positive result, because of the great sense of accomplishment they derive from it.
5. Avoid rigidity. Be understanding about the stress in students' lives, the demanding schedules, the pull of extra-curricular activities, and the general difficulty of the age. Help them work out a reasonable schedule, and don't berate them for the occasional lapse. Work together toward a common goal: to do their very best, which means to be extremely well prepared.
6. At the outset, try to determine the student's attitude. Ask why he or she is preparing for Bar/Bat Mitzvah (e.g., because they want to, because their parents want them to, or for another reason). This information helps you to arrive at realistic expectations. Ask how they like school and how heavy their schedule is. Some children at this age are very forthcoming and talkative, while others are shy and reticent. Despite your best efforts, even after six months, some students will remain hard to approach.
7. Explain to all your students and their parents how much time and commitment it will take to accomplish the goal. Point out that it will require a given number of hours to master all the material. The number of hours varies with ability, of course, but it probably averages out to 100 hours. This can be done five hours a week for 20 weeks, or it can be bunched together at the beginning, middle, or end. The closer to the end these hours fall, of course, the higher the stress level. It would be rare for one to learn the material in fewer hours. This should be conveyed repeatedly. The printed schedule (see Appendix) lends structure and order to the process which reduces stress for both students and parents. Posting it on the refrigerator helps keep track of lesson dates and times and involves the whole family actively in the process.
8. To understand a student's attitude better, it is very helpful to *speak with the parents* — not only at the initial meeting, but by phone or personal contact every few weeks. It is important to gauge how much parental support there is when judging a student's progress. Usually one parent is more involved than the other, but there are many cases where they are both equally involved (or uninvolved). The degree of parental involvement and interest in their child's progress is probably the most important factor influencing that child's attitude. Unfortunately, it is a factor beyond our control.

Some knowledge of the student's personal life is useful as well. For example, students in a joint custody situation often have problems with losing or forgetting to bring material to lessons because they don't have duplicate copies at both parents' houses. As for the emotional impact of this situation, it varies a great deal, and assumptions should never be made. (For a more detailed discussion of this issue, see Chapter 48.)

9. When possible, try to begin B'nai Mitzvah training with a small group, rather than individually. Students enjoy learning the skills together with their friends or peers, and they usually continue to ask about each others' progress months after the private studies have begun. This is only possible, of course, when several students from one synagogue are working with the same tutor, or if the instructor is the Cantor or B'nai Mitzvah educator at that synagogue. Also, it will work only when the students get along socially, and when their abilities are more or less the same. You can determine this by the second lesson, and then you might decide whether to continue for a few more weeks as a group, or switch to private instruction.
10. To achieve these goals requires that the tutor enjoy teaching adolescents. If the tutoring is seen as a chore, it will also be a chore for the student. Teaching adolescents is the most challenging and potentially rewarding experience for anyone open to the challenge.

"DON'T EXPECT ANYTHING EXQUISITE . . ." NOTES FROM THE DIARIES OF A TUTOR

In my years of tutoring, I have begun to see a pattern of student "types": Type A who needs no prodding, who finds it all easy and is always ahead of schedule; Type B who starts falling behind because of lack of diligence rather than ability, and who needs constant urging; Type C who is weak in ability, but tries hard and still falls behind; and the most difficult, but rare, Type D who is doing this under duress, is sullen and resentful and constantly asks for shortcuts. This type is the greatest challenge and can also cause the greatest heartache. I will offer excerpts from my diary notes for students of each type.

Keeping a detailed diary is for me a crucial part of the teaching process, especially when the teaching load is large. The first year that I had more than 10 private students at a time ("in the pipeline" is a common expression), I came to depend on my diary to remind me at a glance where we had left off at the last lesson, what particular problems we had encountered, and what was assigned for this lesson. One piece of advice: anything negative that needs to be written about a student should be written in code or in another language. Curious eyes often rove, especially as the students are aware you are writing about them.

The title of this section is a direct quote from a student who, before chanting her portion, warned me, "Don't expect anything exquisite." But I *do* (as we should) — and so (therefore) I often get it.

I will discuss students from two different synagogues, because the course of study was so different in each. The Reform synagogue referred to in Part 1 (below) has very precise and extensive requirements: 21 verses of Torah, 10-15 of Haftarah, plus a 500 word speech about the Torah portion and a 300 word speech about the Haftarah. Students also learn a few Hebrew lines from the Torah Service. All of this is learned with an adult tutor chosen by the family from a list provided by the synagogue. This particular synagogue also allows the students, with their tutor's guidance, to choose the specific 21 verses of their *parashah* they wish to chant. The Conservative synagogue referred to in Part 2 below requires students to learn the full Haftarah, a minimum of the Maftir, and any prayers in the service they want to learn. The speech is entirely the Rabbi's domain in this particular synagogue. The Cantor tutors some of the students, but families are given a choice and may also use outside tutors recommended by the synagogue.

The sequence I follow in tutoring is different in these two situations because of the difference in the number of verses required for Torah or Haftarah. I begin with Torah trope for the Reform students in this group, and with Haftarah trope for the Conservative. Eventually, I will teach both, but I prefer to start with the largest part of the assignment. If a student falls far behind, in rare cases I might not be able to teach both trope systems, or I might teach only a few basic trope signs.

Part 1

At this particular Reform synagogue, which uses outside tutors to train its B'nai Mitzvah students, I have expressed a preference for particularly musical children, and that is what I have often received. First, some examples of two typical Type A students and their rates of progress; then a comparison of a Type B student and a Type C. (See above for an explanation of the types.) Some of these students began together in a group. Let's call the top Type A student Abby, the next one Alicia, the Type B student Bonnie and the Type C student Cathy. The first three lessons were group lessons. Here are excerpts from my diaries, followed by a discussion of important points.

Lesson #1

Abby: Very bright, assertive, musical.

Alicia: Very bright, quite musical.

Bonnie: The least musical, also shy.

Work done: 4 lines of Torah trope; tried to chant part of "*V'ahavta*" using trope.

Lesson #2

Abby: Listened to tape at home, learned all signs perfectly.

Alicia: Came very prepared. Chants some signs perfectly, others are shaky.

Bonnie: (Missed this class)

Lesson #3

Abby and Alicia: Know all trope signs. Also did "*V'ahavta*" using trope.

Bonnie: Only knows some signs. Initial impression regarding musicality was wrong; shyness inhibited her at first and she is very musical.

There seemed no need after this lesson to continue as a group, since two of the students had learned so much trope already. They both seemed ready and eager to start preparing their individual portions.

My procedure is as follows. The student first reads through the verses of an *aliyah*; then I ask what words he or she recognized (if any). I then translate the key words, pointing out roots and other words they may know based on that root. We may also discuss the biblical account and their reactions to it. After they can read it without mistakes, which can be the first time or the fourth or fifth, I have them chant a verse at a time, first using the trope names and only then the actual text. I follow this procedure from the first through the seventh *aliyah*, but the rate of learning differs widely between students. I record exactly what we did, and below those notes write what I plan to accomplish the following week. Here are notes on the two Type A students:

(Note: #1, #2, etc. refer to first, second *aliyah*; Haftarah blessing #1 is the blessing before the reading; Haftarah blessing #2 is the blessing after the reading.)

Individual Lesson #1

Abby: Reviewed trope — note perfect. We read, translated, tried to chant #1. Hard for her to put it all together so far. Also read, translated #2. Her Hebrew is weak, she is insecure.

Alicia: Knows all trope. We read, translated, chanted #1. Very slow because of problems with Hebrew, especially vowels.

Lesson #4

Abby: Has learned #1-3, but there are hesitant spots and accent errors. We read, translated, and chanted #4 — she practically knows it already! We also started #5.

Alicia: Has learned #1-2, but she is very hesitant, though correct. We read, translated, chanted #3; very slow, but basically correct.

Lesson #7

Abby: #2-5 (renumbered, formerly #1-4): all good! #6 good, but hesitant. We read, translated, chanted #7 — almost learned. She probably won't need a tape. We added verses, since she is so far ahead. Created a long first *aliyah*.

Alicia: #1-3 good, some hesitant spots. Can't do #4 yet; we drilled, and started #5. Needs more fluency.

Lesson #9

Abby: Torah from *Tikkun* (2nd time): #2-6 okay but got stuck a few times. Can't do #7 yet; we drilled one verse at a time, with vowels, then *Tikkun*. Worked on #1 (newest *aliyah*), only with vowels. She has never used the tape I made. Started Haftarah trope — she's so quick! Learned Haftarah blessing #1 on her own, from tape.

Alicia: Torah from *Tikkun* (1st time): #1-2 almost perfect; after that she needed cues. Taped all, it should help. Started Haftarah trope.

Lesson #12

Abby: Knows Haftarah trope. Haftarah blessing #2 almost learned. We read, translated, chanted 3 verses of Haftarah — she practically learned them. Torah *Tikkun*: still can't do #1. #2-7 mostly okay, stuck in spots.

Alicia: She is slipping. Torah *Tikkun* only #1-3. She hasn't progressed in several weeks. Was sick, also seems distracted. Said she practiced mostly with vowels; I showed her how to practice verse at a time, with/without vowels, on *Tikkun* sheet.

The twelfth lesson is roughly the midway point. A revised schedule had to be made up (prototypes of the original and revised versions can be compared in the Appendix to this chapter). At this point, a real disparity between these two students is visible. I was concerned enough about Alicia's backsliding to call her mother (her parents are divorced and her father lives out of state). She told me she has been under stress at work and that her daughter always "picks up" on these feelings. She said things are getting better and she will make sure Alicia catches up. This is a good example of how critical communication with parents is. Any time a student's mood, attitude, or work habits seem to shift, it is important to notify the parent. This must be done in a non-critical, non-judgmental way, however; the motivation for the call is concern, and the purpose is to get information that will aid in understanding the student.

Both girls started out with rather weak Hebrew skills. This weakness made learning the Torah without vowels very difficult and frustrating for Alicia. The reason it was easier for Abby was her phenomenal ear and musical memory. Basically, she only had to hear something once and she could repeat it perfectly. And once she did it, she never forgot it. Musically gifted children find learning trope a challenge they can easily meet, and don't realize how much of a struggle it is for those who are not so gifted. The ability to reproduce a tune and subsequently remember that tune, is a prerequisite for accurate chanting. Without this ability, the student will only approximate correct chanting. The only reason Abby had trouble with one particular *aliyah* was the nature of those verses, which had a great deal of confusing repetition.

Lesson #14

Abby: Torah *Tikkun* is all okay! She finds the way even if she misses a trope; it flows now. Chants 3 verses of Haftarah. We went on to next 3 (read, translate, chant — same method as Torah). Fantastic ability.

Alicia: Torah *Tikkun*: she worked hard! Learned #1-5. Some errors in #6-7; I had her mark her copy (the vowel side only). Has learned Haftarah trope well. She learned to chant 3 verses without tape. Said she doesn't *want* tape. Haftarah blessing #1 is still shaky, especially the Hebrew.

These girls both started their studies in September, but Abby's Bat Mitzvah date was in May, two months after Alicia's. She was so far ahead that by the eighteenth lesson, which was about two months before her date, we cut back to twice a month. I consider it unfortunate that a student as bright and highly musical as Abby had no outlet for this talent. Her synagogue had no interest in having B'nai Mitzvah sing or lead part of the service; I could not extend either her Torah or Haftarah portions because it would bend the rules. I prefer a system that lets students utilize their full potential.

Abby and I had many in-depth discussions about her speech, which dealt with the concept of holiness. She said she was an atheist and having trouble understanding the idea of "holiness" separate from God. She was probably surprised that I neither condemned nor criticized her views. Having respect for children of this age, who are just beginning to think abstractly about ideas and philosophies, is crucial. Abby's parents frequently sat in on these discussions, showing a high level of involvement. During the last few lessons, however, Abby said she felt her parents were so stressed out that they were "psyching" her. She hesitated in a few spots while chanting, and they seemed to be blowing this out of proportion. Abby's level of achievement was very high, but apparently her parents wanted total perfection. I calmed them down and Abby was grateful. Remaining neutral in such situations is a challenge that must be met!

In spite of the differing rates of learning, both girls had 23 lessons and mastered the required material, as all students eventually do. Alicia continued to have weekly lessons, and had to increase her personal study time greatly to make up for the weeks when she hardly progressed. But in the end, she learned everything and was poised, confident, and proud of her accomplishment.

Both of these girls, in spite of totally different home environments and personalities, were unusually mature and serious about their preparation. That, of course, made my work easy! But abilities are not as important a factor in progress as *attitude*. The next two students I will discuss were a Type B and a Type C in ability, but Type A for attitude. (Here are examples of these attitudes: If I make a correction and then ask a student to repeat the whole verse, "C" students will sigh, roll their eyes, and say incredulously, *"the whole thing?"* "B" students will simply say, "Okay," and do it. "A" students will do it without comment, and then ask if the second time was better.)

Bonnie started group lessons with Abby and Alicia; Cathy began her studies alone, later in the year.

Lesson #1

Bonnie: Knows only some trope. Has trouble with key changes. We read and translated #1 (not ready to chant).

Cathy: Has almost no musical memory. Serious problems reading Hebrew. Finding trope very hard!

Lesson #3

Bonnie: Chants #1 very weakly, but has the idea. We drilled a lot together. Read and translated #2. She enjoys the translating a lot. Has a lot of trouble musically with key changes; will need a tape soon.

Cathy: Studied a lot; learned much more of the trope. Started reading #1 — extremely weak reading, can't possibly chant. Will need tape soon. Said her father will help her with reading.

Lesson #6

Bonnie: She worked with the tape I made; #1 is much smoother now. #2-3 are still shaky. We read, translated, chanted #4-5, then I taped these.

Cathy: She almost learned #1, but it's very slow. I made a tape. We read, translated, chanted #2-3, and I taped.

Lesson #10

Bonnie: #1-4 good, except for key changes; #5 is still shaky. We drilled a lot, again; she isn't studying enough. #6-7 are still very weak. I taped them. She is getting behind!

Cathy: #1 and #2 are much more solid. #3 and #4 are better but there are many Hebrew errors, still. The Hebrew is really slowing her down. We went on to #5, and taped it.

At this point, these students had already fallen so far behind the original schedule that I needed to make revised copies for them. I always build in extra weeks as a "cushion," and in their cases I needed these weeks. Bonnie needed a total of 26 weeks, Cathy needed 29, to learn all the material.

What does not come across in the notes is that these two girls were both trying their very hardest. Mastering the material was a tremendous struggle for them both. Bonnie often came unprepared because she was simply overwhelmed with school work. But she truly wanted to excel, and was finally able to when winter break gave her more time for her preparation. Cathy worked diligently at her own pace, and made steady, if slow, progress. Once we established a regular routine of one *aliyah* per week (and later, three verses of Haftarah), which was what she could achieve, she became much more relaxed.

Both of these girls, though not strong musically, showed unusual interest in the meaning and background of their portions. They constantly asked questions. I had to remind myself that skills mastery is not the only goal. In some lessons we covered much less ground because I gave a lengthy explanation of the *Shalosh Regalim*, or discussed the reasons Moses was kept from entering the Promised Land. I realized after the lesson that what I left them with was probably far more important in the greater scheme of things than perfecting one trope sign.

Lesson #14

Bonnie: Torah from *Tikkun* (3rd time): #1-5 almost okay, but gets stuck in several spots. It hasn't "clicked in" yet, but will with time. We drilled #6-7 with/without vowels several times. It's getting there. We started Haftarah trope; she picked it up fast.

Cathy: Torah from *Tikkun* (2nd time): #1-4 almost okay, but too many Hebrew errors (same as when she does with vowels). We drilled #5-6 with/without vowels. #7 is still very weak with vowels.

Lesson #18

Bonnie: Torah from *Tikkun* all good — she worked hard! Haftarah: learned 5 verses but not well, full of trope/ Hebrew errors, very slow. We went on to the next 5, reading only.

Cathy: Torah from *Tikkun*: #1-5 almost okay, still errors. #6-7 not there yet, not even ready for *Tikkun*. The Hebrew is really holding her back. Haftarah trope (3rd time): probably knows enough of it. Learned Haftarah blessing #1 from tape. We read, translated, chanted 3 verses of Haftarah and taped.

Lesson #20

Bonnie: Haftarah: she worked on without tape, to prove something, but it is too hesitant, even if correct. I told her to use tape just for the flow. Torah from *Tikkun* almost learned, still gets stuck in spots. I had her mark those on vowel side. Haftarah blessings are both learned.

Cathy: Torah from *Tikkun*: can almost do all of it. Haftarah: learned 3 verses; shaky, but correct. We read, translated, chanted 3 more verses, and I taped. Having trouble with Haftarah blessing #2.

Lesson #22

Bonnie: She is a bit behind — has only 5 more weeks. Torah is good, Haftarah still weak. Still hasn't started speech, only outline.

Cathy: She still has over 2 months so is okay. Torah is okay, her best. Haftarah still has many Hebrew errors.

Lesson #26

Bonnie: This is the last lesson before our rehearsal. She couldn't learn the whole Haftarah; I advised her to cut the last few verses; she was very upset but agreed. She forgot the tune to the Haftarah blessing #1. Torah is fine. She is very stressed.

Cathy: Torah and Haftarah are fine (for her). We're working on speeches and reviewing blessings.

The last few weeks, Bonnie's mother called me several times with worries about Bonnie's speech. As in Abby's case, the standards she was setting seemed impossible. I felt Bonnie's speech was exceptional; she had shown a great deal of interest and initiative in the preparation, and it was unusually well written. There have been cases I suspected a parent's hand in the speech writing, but from the way Bonnie was able to discuss the ideas in the speech, it was clear she wrote it herself. Yet, her mother still didn't seem to feel it was Bonnie's best effort, and nothing I could say could change her mind. I reassured Bonnie that it was an excellent speech, and hoped that my opinion had enough weight to at least somewhat offset her mother's. Some parents need to learn the distinction between being positive and having overly high expectations. They need to focus on what their child *has* accomplished, not on what he/she *could* accomplish. Parental pressure did get to Bonnie, and she lost her place in the Torah reading during her Bat Mitzvah service. She eventually found it again, but it was surely an upsetting moment for her.

Cathy's parents, unlike many others, seemed happy with whatever she achieved from week to week. They never demanded more from her than she was capable of, and they seemed fully aware of how much that was. As a result, she probably had a more positive experience than children who may do better with their chanting or their speech.

Part 2

The students from this Conservative synagogue represented a much wider range of "types." They came with different backgrounds, abilities, and attitudes.

After several weeks, one of the students seemed to be working below potential. I called her mother, who told me the girl was actually terrified of me, afraid before each lesson that she would not be prepared enough to make me happy. I was glad to get this information, as it helped me to realize that I was not giving these students enough positive feedback. I started praising them more lavishly, for even the smallest improvement. Their attitudes and performance then took a sharp turn for the better. Letting some trope errors slide and just saying "good" will ultimately be more effective than constant corrections.

While a student is chanting, I circle their errors in my own Chumash in pencil. When these errors are later corrected, I erase the marks. I discovered that pointing this out to the student — "I'm so happy to be using the other end of the pencil today" — always brings a big smile of satisfaction, even to the most uncommunicative child. Often I don't even mark every single error in my book, and some weeks I mention only the most serious ones. The stress needs to be on positive feedback as much as possible.

I derived a tremendous sense of accomplishment from these students, because I was able to encourage them to stretch far beyond what they thought were their capabilities. At this synagogue students are offered an opportunity to accomplish the maximum of which they are capable.

One of them, who had started out a giggly and nervous child, stood on the *bimah* with poise and confidence, which came from her sense of accomplishment and pride. Her mother said the whole process of study with me brought about dramatic changes in her daughter's attitude to synagogue and Hebrew school. What sweeter words can a Cantor/tutor hope to hear?

The students discussed so far, in spite of the problems some of them presented, were still basically above average. The true challenge is the average or below-average student. Following are diary excerpts for four more students: two were Type C in ability, though Type A in attitude; I call them Carl and Chaim. Another, Claire, was a Type C in attitude, but probably much higher in ability. She had fewer months to prepare than most students do. She was working with a tutor for her Hebrew, along with me. The last, Dolly, was a Type D in both ability and attitude. Her lessons started about three months earlier than others, so that she could have some additional remedial Hebrew. She resisted lessons from the first, and after 15 lessons with me, abruptly switched to a different tutor. Dolly was in a joint custody situation, and her parents were not on speaking terms. Consequently, scheduled lessons were often missed, and materials were constantly lost or forgotten. I tried to reach out to her, but Dolly was a sullen child with a chip on her shoulder. Perhaps I could have been easier on her.

Lesson #1

Carl: Highly motivated, not musical at all. Did some Haftarah trope — very hard; no musical memory. Tried Haftarah blessing #1; weak Hebrew.

Chaim: Quiet, shy. Not musical, no musical memory; approximated tunes. Can't distinguish up from down. Tried some Haftarah trope; seems impossible.

Claire: (Started in group) Picks up melodies fast, but doesn't concentrate in a group. Very weak Hebrew. Can barely read Haftarah blessing #1; has obviously depended on tapes.

Dolly: Very weak musically and in Hebrew. Needs remedial Hebrew work. Will learn trope in English system (see Chapter 17 Appendix), because she can't even read names of the signs.

Lesson #4

Carl: Has sort of learned basic trope signs; may never be more accurate than this. Can't do some at all, will just approximate. Haftarah blessing #1 quite inaccurate, probably can't do better. It needs more flow; he needs to work more with the tape. Started Haftarah blessing #2; very slow reading. Said his mother will help him.

Chaim: He's very diligent. Much improvement in his chanting. Haftarah blessing #2 much better. Started taping Haftarah; will do 6 verses a week. It's a long portion, but his Hebrew background is strong, we've already read and translated most of the portion.

Claire: We're working on both Haftarah blessings. She resists reading the Hebrew, just wants to memorize from tapes. Can barely read, but when I chant, she can mimic perfectly. Started taping Haftarah since she refuses to learn it by trope signs.

Dolly: She didn't study *at all*. She lost all her sheets, forgot to bring her tape, was truculent and sullen. Still can't read Haftarah blessing #1, so how can she chant it?

Lesson #7

Carl: We started reading and translating Haftarah portion; can't chant yet. Will probably need a tape from the start. Has worked on reading Haftarah blessing #2 with his mother; great improvement! We started chanting it and I taped it.

Chaim: Has almost learned Haftarah blessing #1. Has learned to chant about half of Haftarah blessing #2. Hasn't really learned much Haftarah, only 2 verses. So far he's not studying enough. I gave him the talk about how many hours are needed.

Claire: Has learned about half of Haftarah blessing #2. We worked on some of it, but she really can't read it, is learning purely by rote. Started to read and translate Haftarah, but she refused to translate, said her other tutor does that. Won't try in trope, says she never learned it. She has learned about 4 Haftarah verses correctly, by rote, and from marks she made in the book. It's like teaching someone who never learned any trope — amazing, how she's resisting! I told her there was nothing for us to do together. Talked to mother, switched to alternate weeks.

Dolly: Couldn't learn Haftarah blessing #1 from tape, said it was too fast. No change in her trope; this must be it. Read 5 verses of Haftarah together; she is very nervous and insecure. Asked Rabbi about cutting portion; said it was too early to do that. She read some of Haftarah blessing #2; *very* hard for her!

Lesson #9

Carl: Haftarah blessing #2 is much improved. Starting to get the chant for 4 verses of Haftarah. Taped all Haftarah.

Chaim: Has learned Haftarah blessing #2 (his best). Can chant over half his Haftarah; just a few errors. I taped the rest.

Claire: 3 weeks since last lesson; she has done nothing. Asked me to re-tape Haftarah verses and Haftarah blessing #2, wasn't clear why. Was it too fast? Sort of learned 2 more verses of Haftarah, but many trope errors.

Dolly: Couldn't prepare for lesson because she didn't have the tape all week. Maybe she really can't do the Haftarah blessing #1 any better than this? I'll believe it the first time she really prepares for a lesson. Can't chant Haftarah blessing #2 at all. We talked about schedules — said she just has *no time* to study. I told her to give something up, she said she can't. I told her she won't make it at this rate, she said she knows. Her skills are so poor, but so are her study habits. When we repeat something often enough in the lesson, she can get it, but she never repeats it all week.

It became clear to me at this point that the students making the greatest progress were also getting the strongest support at home. Carl's mother helped him all week long with his Hebrew reading, and always wanted to know how he was doing. Chaim had the advantage of strong Hebrew skills. His musical abilities were better than I had initially thought. Like Carl, he needed hours and hours of work on his own to get something. Neither of these students could chant a verse well the first or second time, but there was amazing improvement from week to week.

I discussed Claire's attitude problem with her mother. She felt I should just do it Claire's way. She saw nothing wrong in rote learning, had no interest in trope or even in having Claire continue Hebrew school. With no parental support, I had no choice but to give in and let Claire learn in her way.

I also had a conference with Dolly's mother (her father remained totally uninvolved and made it clear that the Bat Mitzvah was only the mother's idea). She promised to get behind Dolly and make her study more, but she also admitted that Dolly was home alone a lot while she worked, or at her father's, where she rarely studied. She seemed committed to having Dolly learn something, but was not able to exert the control to see this through.

Lesson #12

Carl: Has really learned over half his Haftarah, and most of Haftarah blessing #2. We went on to the rest of the Haftarah. Also started Torah trope.

Chaim: Can do all of Haftarah, but there are trope errors. He marked in his copy. Started Torah trope; seems impossible for him, but now I know he'll get it on his own. Read and translated Maftir.

Claire: This is her last lesson before the rehearsal. The past few times I just let go, stopped correcting her errors. The goal became *fluency*, not accuracy. Hebrew is sloppy throughout (typical of rote learning). She never tried Maftir from *Tikkun* before the rehearsal; it is rushed and sloppy, but she did learn it fast. Haftarah errors were never corrected. Haftarah blessing #2 is rushed; she races, then stumbles.

Dolly: There's been improvement since my talk with her mother. She can sort of do about half of

Haftarah blessing #2. What is the bottom line? At least the Hebrew, including accents, must be right; the trope never will be. She eventually needs some flow. She can repeat phrases fine after me; at home she said she does it *with* tape; I suggested she try it another way. Unfortunately, her date has just been changed, so she has a new Haftarah portion now. She read through it, not too badly. I try to explain rules to make the Hebrew easier; she just doesn't care. She basically ignores me, sits at the edge of her seat, glances at the time constantly and then races out at the end.

Lesson #15

Carl: Haftarah is okay; could be more accurate and needs more fluency. Pushed him to sing through the verses, fewer pauses. He learned some Torah trope, the easier signs. Read and translated Maftir.

Chaim: He's confusing Torah and Haftarah trope. Can't do Maftir correctly yet. Reviewed Haftarah; mixing in Torah trope. I pointed out differences, numbers of notes, patterns. Read, translated, and chanted #7 (his mother's request).

Dolly: First half of Haftarah blessing #2 is probably as good as it will get (at least the Hebrew is correct). Barely reads the rest. Barely learned to chant 2 verses of Haftarah in 3 weeks. Should I just give up on trope altogether?

This was only the midway point for Carl, who had started early and ended up having 31 sessions with me. Chaim still had another 3 months, so he was also on schedule. He had a total of 25 lessons. Claire had become a Bat Mitzvah. She sped through her prayers and portions like a robot, and I felt frustrated that I had never been able to convince her or her mother that there was another, more gratifying way to learn skills and get in touch with one's Jewish identity.

Dolly at this point had another four months to study. But at the rate she was learning, I felt that an alarm needed to be sounded. After a long talk with her mother, it was decided that Dolly had to give something up in order to study more. In spite of my best efforts, the lack of communication with Dolly had led to a breakdown in communication with her mother as well. Because of scheduling problems, we never had an open discussion of all the issues. A week later, I got a message that all future lessons were cancelled. Dolly did become Bat Mitzvah (virtually everyone who starts down that path does make it to the end, one way or another). She found a teacher who didn't insist on trope, who simply made tapes for her to parrot. It was another rote-learned performance, very robot-like and musically as inaccurate as it had always been. She was never seen in Religious School again after that day.

Lesson #25

Carl: He has learned Maftir and #7; doesn't want more *aliyot*. Wants to learn "*Ashrei,*" which he never studied. I even translated it for him — he enjoys that! We will drill a few lines a week, and he will practice with his mother.

Chaim: He learned Maftir and #7. Wanted to do more prayers, but was too unmusical to be encouraged. Did learn "*Chatzi Kaddish.*" He still confuses the two trope systems, but can find his way out when he gets lost.

Carl mastered "*Ashrei,*" which was a great accomplishment with his weak Hebrew background. Once I accepted his unmusical chant, I was able to help him chant with greater fluency. The same was true for Chaim, with whom I also stressed fluency and flow. Both these students seemed to get a great deal from their time of study with me; they wrote me sincere thank-you notes after becoming B'nai Mitzvah. My goal is always to make study for B'nai Mitzvah a positive experience. When I fail, I always engage in a great deal of soul searching. What could I have done to make the experience more positive without lowering my standards? In some cases, it is simply a matter of the chemistry between teacher and student, or starting off on the right (or wrong) foot. By careful, critical analysis of diary notes, I learn important lessons which can be applied later to other students.

POSTCRIPT: A DAY IN THE LIFE OF A BAR/BAT MITZVAH TUTOR

There are some more personal, less purely technical aspects of tutoring that can also have an impact on the whole process. The most important of these is the location of the lessons: a synagogue office, the tutor's home, or the student's home. A child in his/her own environment will be much more relaxed and able to concentrate on the lesson. Pets, also, are a great ice breaker. I have even taught in a room containing two caged guinea pigs. The background noises during the taping of a Torah portion were a unique touch, and the shared laughter added a special warmth to my relationship with that student. For children who are themselves animal lovers, my own home is heaven. I have a very friendly dog and two cats!

Of course, the more common setting for lessons is a synagogue office. But if the possibility of teaching in a home presents itself, I would recommend it. Seeing students in their own environment lends another dimension to one's understanding of who they are; and when they see the teacher in his or her own home, this can bridge the distance between teacher and student.

CONCLUSION

It has been said that teachers can "touch the future." This is certainly true for B'nai Mitzvah tutors. By serving as role models, and by being consistently caring while demanding high standards, tutors can not only touch, but can *mold* the future — the next generation of Jews.

APPENDIX

Prototype Bar/Bat Mitzvah Schedule: Synagogue "S"

Name:
Maftir portion:
Haftarah:
Date:

LESSON #	DATE	MATERIAL
1	Nov. 16	Haftarah trope Haftarah blessing #1 (trope)
2	Nov. 23	Haftarah trope: Exercise sheet Haftarah blessing #1
3	Nov. 30	Haftarah trope Read Haftarah Haftarah blessing #2
4	Dec. 6	Chant Haftarah v. 1-3 Haftarah blessing #2: TAPE
5	Dec. 14	Chant Haftarah v. 4-6 Haftarah blessings
6	Dec. 21	Chant Haftarah v. 7-9 Tape v. 1-9 Haftarah blessings
7	Dec. 28	Chant Haftarah v. 10-12 Tape v. 10-12
8	Jan. 4	Chant v. 13-15, tape
9	Jan. 11	Chant v. 16-18, tape
10	Jan. 18	Chant v. 19-21, tape
11	Jan. 25	Chant v. 22-24, tape
12	Feb. 1	Chant v. 25-27, tape
13	Feb. 15	Chant v. 28, tape Review blessings

APPENDIX (Cont.)

14	Feb. 22	Chant Haftarah (all) Review blessings Start Torah trope
15	Mar. 1	Read Maftir Torah trope: Exercise sheet
16	Mar. 8	Torah trope Review Haftarah, blessings
17	Mar. 15	Chant Maftir Read #7
18	Mar. 22	Chant Maftir from *Tikkun* Chant #7
19	Apr. 5	Same
20	Apr. 12	Chant Maftir, #7 from *Tikkun* Review Haftarah, blessings
21	Apr. 19	Same
22	Apr. 26	Review all/Rehearse

APPENDIX (Cont.)

Prototype Bar/Bat Mitzvah Schedule: Temple "R"

Name:
Torah portion:
Chapters, verses:
Haftarah portion:
Chapters, verses:
Date:

LESSON #	DATE	MATERIAL
1	Jan. 24	Torah trope: Signs and Names
2	Jan. 31	Torah trope: Exercise sheet
3	Feb. 7	Same; and Torah Blessings
4	Feb. 14	Same; and read 1st *aliyah* (#1)
5	Feb. 21	Read #1, #2; Chant #1
6	Feb. 28	Chant #1, #2, read #3, #4
7	Mar. 7	Chant #1-3, read #4-6 Tape #1-4
8	Mar. 14	Chant #1-4, read #5-7 Tape #5
9	Mar. 21	Chant #1-5, read #6-7 Tape #6
10	Mar. 28	Chant #1-6, read #7 Tape #7
11	Apr. 4	Chant #1-2 from *Tikkun* Chant #3-7 with vowels
12	Apr. 11	Chant #1-4 from *Tikkun* Chant #5-7 with vowels Start Haftarah trope
13	Apr. 18	Chant all Torah from *Tikkun* Haftarah trope: Exercise sheet

APPENDIX (Cont.)

14	Apr. 25	Chant Torah *Tikkun* Haftarah blessing #1 with trope Exercise sheet
15	May 2	Haftarah blessing #1 Read Haftarah portion
16	May 9	Haftarah blessing #2: TAPE Read Haftarah portion Chant verses 1-3
17	May 16	Haftarah blessing #2 Chant verses 1-6 Tape verses 1-6
18	May 23	Haftarah blessings #1, 2 Chant verses 1-9 Tape verses 7-9
19	May 30	Chant verses 1-12 (all) Tape verses 10-12
20	June 6	Review Torah Chant all Haftarah Review Haftarah blessings
21	June 13	Start speeches, and review all
22	June 20	Work on speeches Learn Torah service
23	June 27	Work on speeches, Torah service
24	July 5	Review all/Rehearse in sanctuary

APPENDIX (Cont.)

Prototype *Revised* Bar/Bat Mitzvah Schedule: Temple "R"

10	Mar. 28	Chant #1-5, tape #5, read #6
11	Apr. 4	Chant #1-6, tape #6, read #7
12	Apr. 11	Chant #1-7, tape #7 Chant #1-2 from *Tikkun*
13	Apr. 18	Chant #1-4 *Tikkun* Chant #5-7 with vowels
14	Apr. 25	Chant #1-6 *Tikkun*, #7 with vowels
15	May 2	Chant all Torah *Tikkun* Read Haftarah
16	May 9	Same; and start Haftarah trope
17	May 16	Haftarah trope: Exercise sheet Read Haftarah
18	May 23	Haftarah blessing #1, with trope Read Haftarah Chant verses 1-3, and tape
19	May 30	Haftarah blessing #1 Blessing #2: tape Chant verses 1-6, tape 4-6
20	June 6	Chant verses 1-6, tape 7-9 Blessings #1, 2
21	June 13	Chant verses 1-9, tape 10-12 Blessings #1, 2 Review Torah
22	June 20	Chant verses 1-9 Review all Start speeches
23	June 27	Chant all Haftarah Review all Work on speeches
24	July 5	Same, and learn Torah service
25	July 12	Same
26	July 19	Final review/rehearsal

Chapter 11
"Panel": Discussion of B'nai Mitzvah Tutors

Participants:
Nathaniel Schudrich
Barbara Elish
Marsha Fensin
Saul Oresky
Ran and Hannah Anbar

QUESTION #1: What is your background: what training and preparation did you have for the job of tutoring B'nai Mitzvah students?

Nathaniel: My father was a Rabbi; I grew up in an observant Conservative home. When it was time for my Bar Mitzvah training, I went to the Cantor of our *shul*. But after three lessons, I was very confused. I had no idea what trope was. I kept seeing this wishbone (*etnachta*) and noticing it always sounded the same. When I asked the Cantor what those little signs were, he said it wasn't important. I went crying to my father, told him I was confused, and asked him to teach me. In about an hour he taught me all the trope marks, and in another hour I learned my whole Haftarah. Of course, I'd been hearing those tunes all my life, and I guess I was musical. I ended up *leyning* (chanting) the whole Torah portion. We took a long car trip that summer and I'd practice the portion in the back seat, and my father would correct my mistakes. I started *leyning* professionally and tutoring when I was 15. After college, I started teaching Judaic subjects at different Talmud Torahs and Jewish Day Schools.

Barbara: As a child, I had a pretty minimal Jewish education. Then when my oldest child started Hebrew School, I felt uncomfortable knowing so little, so I started taking adult education courses. Eventually this led to a Master's degree in Religious Education, which I received from H.U.C. in 1989. I am basically self-taught in Hebrew and in the reading of Torah commentaries. I attend Torah study sessions weekly at my synagogue, as wells as an Ulpan given by WIZO. I have also learned from the four CAJE conferences I've attended.

Marsha: I had a very traditional upbringing. I attended an Orthodox *shul* with my father, but of course I sat upstairs and was never allowed a Bat Mitzvah ceremony. I went to a Yiddish *cheder*. I have been involved with Jewish music for 20 years. I became a tutor out of necessity: there was a need at my synagogue, and since I was the one who sang, I was asked to teach. I went to a class and learned trope in order to teach it. I have been in my current position for seven years, and am currently pursuing Cantorial certification through H.U.C. and the American Conference of Cantors.

Saul: After my Bar Mitzvah, I continued reading Torah and Haftarah at weekly youth services. When I was 16, I began leading Junior Congregation services, which I did for about three years. Camp Ramah and Ramah seminar in Israel were also formative experiences. I was active in Hillel at the University of Maryland, and one year was Hazzan and Baal Koreh for Hillel's liberal High Holy Day services. I've been training B'nai Mitzvah students for different synagogues in this area for over 18 years.

Ran: I was born in Israel and moved to the United States with my parents when I was nine years old. I grew up in a "secular" Jewish home. After I became Bar Mitzvah, I did not return to a synagogue until my senior year in college. A wonderful Israeli Torah reader at this synagogue inspired me to learn cantillation skills during the summer between college and medical school. While at medical school, I attended an Orthodox synagogue regularly and learned many of my "synagogue skills." I began tutoring B'nai Mitzvah after I became an academic pediatrician because I very much enjoyed interacting with children over issues other than their health.

Hannah: I grew up as a member of Germantown Jewish Centre in Philadelphia at the time when reading Torah and tutoring Bar and Bat Mitzvah students was the "in" thing to do. When the Cantor, who was the program director, left us, my brother Jamie and I were asked to supervise the Bar/Bat Mitzvah training. We were both teenagers. I received a Doctorate in Educational Psychology and am again co-directing the Bar/ Bat Mitzvah program at Germantown.

QUESTION #2: What sequence do you follow in your tutoring? How many sessions/hours do you devote to trope, translation, Hebrew reading, speech, and general discussion?

Nathaniel: With a private student who reads Hebrew moderately well, I start six to seven months in advance. At the first session, I go over what Torah and Haftarah are, and the meaning of Bar/Bat Mitzvah. If there is time, I begin discussing trope, which I continue in the next session. I break down what trope marks are and what they do. I explain the purposes and also go over basic Hebrew reading skills if they need this. I don't get to the Haftarah portion itself until the student has mastered trope and can read the Hebrew with reasonable fluency. When we read through the portion, I point out key words. I always begin with Haftarah because that is the norm in Conservative synagogues.

Barbara: The children I tutor are those in need of remedial work who have been referred to me by the congregations's Cantor. Because I begin to work with these children only two months or less before they become Bar/Bat Mitzvah, I am limited in what I can help them accomplish. My job is to make students' Hebrew reading more fluent and to help them write *Divrei Torah.* Our synagogue does not teach trope; our students learn the melodies from cassette tapes. While I do not teach the children to chant, I do emphasize fluency of reading. I teach key words in the portion relating these to other words containing the same root that they know.

If I begin to work with a child more than two months before the Bar/Bat Mitzvah date, the student and I have lengthy discussions about the portion the child is preparing. Most of each hour long lesson is usually devoted to honing Hebrew reading skills. I teach students how to practice by repeating a problem word or phrase five times and then reading from the beginning of the verse or sentence in order to incorporate that word or phrase without hesitation. This is similar to the way one would learn to play a new piece on a musical instrument. The remainder of the lesson includes discussion on the background of the portions: what took place before, what will happen after, what the portion means "on the surface," and what relevance it has today. I also explain the order of the service and the meanings of the prayers. It has been an advantage to have taught many of these students in Hebrew class, as I have an idea of what they already know before we begin studying together one on one.

Marsha: Tutoring at our synagogue is a team effort. I personally see students a total of 12 times: these are half hour sessions held once a week for three months. In these sessions we work on 15-20 verses of Haftarah, doing some translating, and learning to chant. In addition to these sessions with me, though, students attend a six month B'nai Mitzvah class, and spend eight months translating and discussing their Torah portions one-on-one with the Rabbi.

Saul: Like most tutors, I start tutoring six to seven months ahead of the scheduled Bar/Bat Mitzvah date. I usually teach a total of 20 to 30 sessions. I can only generalize about the number of sessions devoted to trope, blessings, and the rest. Each student learns at his/her own pace and may learn one component, such as the blessings, faster than another component, such as singing the trope. I do proceed sequentially, however, from one task to the next. After a basic introductory lesson, I teach Haftarah trope and blessings, then the portion itself, the Torah service, followed by Torah trope and Maftir portion. Mixed into all these main tasks are practice in Hebrew reading, discussion of the portions, the student's own concerns and problems, and of course, far ranging discussions of related topics.

Ran: Most of our students begin their studies with us one year before they become B'nai Mitzvah. As members of our congregation have grown more enthusiastic about our program, some students have begun their studies half a year earlier. We begin by teaching the Haftarah blessings. As the blessing before the Haftarah includes Haftarah trope, we then launch into an explanation of the usefulness of trope. We do not teach trope as a separate entity from the text. Instead, our students master trope in a *"gestalt"* fashion as they learn to chant their portions. After completing their Haftarah, most of our students learn to read several *aliyot* from the Torah. Our most advanced students also learn to lead the Torah and Musaf services.

Hannah: At our home, Ran and I meet for an average of 25 one hour one-on-one sessions with each of our students. During this time, we spent approximately three hours on translation, three hours teaching trope related skills, six hours on Hebrew reading. In addition, about half of our time is spent engaged in general discussion. An additional critical element of our program involves utilizing teenage tutors as "mentors." These tutors meet on a weekly basis with our students in order to teach and reinforce our students' skills. If there is time, we will elaborate on this tutoring program later on.

QUESTION #3: Can you relate a personal experience with one particular student that stands out in your memory?

Barbara: I have found that on a one-to-one basis, most students are quite well behaved. I had one student who was not liked by his classroom teachers because he was never well behaved. I found him to be very pleasant, inquisitive, and extremely hard working. B'nai Mitzvah students, in general, realize the importance of the work they have been assigned and take it quite seriously. This boy did whatever I assigned. Like other students, about a month before his Bar Mitzvah date, he began to ask a lot of questions. It seemed that even with all the years that he (like others) had spent in Religious School, he didn't have a clear idea of what Torah and Haftarah are. This led to many interesting discussions. Also, like other students, he was quite concerned about what his *d'var Torah* was to include. From past experience, I was not surprised when he came up with some very perceptive thoughts about the relevance of his portions. After his final meeting with the Rabbi, just a week before his ceremony, he came out feeling he had really learned his material and was quite pleased that the Rabbi did not make even one correction in his *d'var Torah.*

Marsha: We handle the Bar/Bat Mitzvah year in a personal way, and because of this, the Rabbis and I develop a personal relationship with each student, which usually translates into a good relationship with the family. I had one student with a severe attention deficit problem, and had to break down our tutoring time to two sessions of 15 minutes each per week. I wish I could describe all the moving around we did during our sessions. We would change seats constantly in my office; go into other, empty offices; discuss sports, the redecorating of the synagogue, his siblings, or his parents. Eventually, I had to shorten the number of verses he chanted, but he chanted beautifully. That was largely because both his parents and I had that expectation of him.

Ran: The great joy gained from our program is in the interaction with B'nai Mitzvah students. Thus, I believe that the most effective way to teach is on an individual basis. Children at this age are usually very responsive to attention and direction. This is best illustrated by a former student of ours who was kicked out of Hebrew School at the age of 11 because of unruly behavior. When he was referred to us for his Bar Mitzvah education, our charge was, "See what you can do. Maybe he'll chant a few verses from his Haftarah." When this student first came to our home, his eyes were always cast downward and his face displayed sadness. After a few lessons, everything changed. We pointed out to this student that he had a beautiful voice. His musical memory was tremendous, and this more than compensated for his poor reading ability. As he acquired confidence, he was able to maintain eye contact and smile. He had a great time writing a speech about the war between Gog and Magog and about adversities he himself had faced. By the end of the process, he not only chanted his complete Haftarah, but also read most of the Torah *aliyot.* The key in helping his student was in identifying his strengths and using them as a foundation for his Bar Mitzvah experience. This key works for most students. It is up to the tutor to identify these strengths expeditiously .

QUESTION #4: What works, and what doesn't work? In your experience, what elements make a successful tutor?

Nathaniel: Teaching is a natural, simple thing to do: you present something, you take it slowly, you make it interesting. Jump around on the desk, if you have to! For the students, it's the daily practice that makes the difference. I have the students write down what time they practiced every day. What works best is teaching the child how to apply the trope marks to sentences or phrases, to work very slowly through the first few verses to teach them these techniques. And it's so crucial that the tutor be knowledgeable — about trope, Judaism, and Hebrew. Other key elements of success are patience and a positive attitude. I consider myself lucky to be tutoring; it's such a wonderful experience to work one-on-one. When students get frustrated, I stop and tell them about my own failures and difficulties in life.

Marsha: What works is positive reinforcement and a personal approach. What doesn't work is having low expectations and appealing to the lowest rather than the highest common denominator.

Barbara: Most of my experience has been positive, and I have come up with several reasons why this is so. Let me formulate them as rules:

1. Don't watch the clock. Treat students in such a way that they feel tutoring them is what you want to be doing at that moment. Children need to feel that when you are with them, nothing else is important to you. This also means being willing to spend a few extra minutes with them.
2. Relate the material being studied to a student's life whenever possible. Don't teach only abstract concepts without examples. You cannot teach children from a place that is higher than their level. Explain simply why words are read the way they are. If they understand why they are doing something, they're more likely to remember the word and generalize a rule to another case. For their Torah portions, these should be put into context with the portions before and after their own.
3. Obviously, you should really love children of this age. It is also important to *show* that you like them and enjoy working with them. Bar/Bat Mitzvah tutoring offers a wonderful opportunity for students to develop a good relationship with an adult, who is also a positive Jewish role model. Speak to them on a personal level and use whatever you learn about their lives in later sessions. For example, if you know a student has a big soccer game or a concert coming up, ask at the next lesson how the game or concert went.
4. Be enthusiastic about the material you're teaching. If *you* don't love it, you can't expect your students to take it seriously.
5. Explain clearly at the outset what exactly is expected of them. Always answer their questions. Be organized, so that you remember what was assigned to each student from week to week. This will give them a sense of security and confidence.

Saul: My experience as a B'nai Mitzvah tutor has been the greatest contributor to my perspective on the Jewish community, because there is something in the nature of Bar/Bat Mitzvah that reveals the strengths and weaknesses of Jewish families. I believe a tutor must, above all, be *flexible.* Try anything, try everything to get that student to want to learn that Haftarah, to come to *shul,* to become familiar with the service, to care about and try to understand what the portions are about. Use any means at your disposal:

keyboard, tape recorder, flash cards, humorous mnemonics to teach confusing Hebrew vowels or similar trope signs. It's a visual generation; get them to look up from the book periodically so that they can connect in another way. That is the crux: they have to *connect*. Humor is also crucial. If you cannot get your student to smile at least once in a while during a lesson, you are not doing your job. Also, if you're not spending at least five minutes of every lesson in open, informal, freewheeling conversation, you're really not communicating with the student. Of course, this is easier with some students than others, but it must always be part of the agenda. We must remember that teaching the blessings and Haftarah is the *means*, not the *end*. If Bar/Bat Mitzvah is not a positive experience, we failed. We have *not* failed if a student mispronounces from the *bimah* some of the Hebrew in the Haftarah — that may be the best that student can do, and if so, both you and your student have triumphed. If your student enjoyed the Bar/Bat Mitzvah service, as well as the party, did a creditable job with the Hebrew, and has come away with some Jewish knowledge and not just today's equivalent of a fountain pen to show for the experience, your system works.

QUESTION #5: From your vantage point as a tutor working for different synagogues, what areas do you see in need of improvement in the Religious School or B'nai Mitzvah programs? Do you have any practical ideas for implementing change in these areas?

Nathaniel: One of my own greatest frustrations is seeing incompetent tutors. Maybe there could be a tutor training program out there, to teach people how to teach. It's a shame, but many tutors really don't know what they're doing. For example, some tutors are not meticulous about Hebrew or accents, and some actually don't even know trope, but are teaching students to chant! There should certainly be cooperation between the Religious School and Bar/Bat Mitzvah program in a synagogue. The Religious School should teach basics of trope, or the prayers considered basic in that congregation. Religious Schools should try to coordinate with the Cantor to determine which prayers they should be teaching. What better way to teach Hebrew than through a prayer curriculum, anyway?

Barbara: A negative part of many B'nai Mitzvah preparation programs is the fact that the children have very little experience with the Rabbi. In most cases, they meet with the Rabbi once six months prior to their ceremony and then once again during the week prior to the service for a final rehearsal. B'nai Mitzvah preparation is a perfect opportunity to develop a relationship with the Rabbi that could be long lasting and could affect their future connection with Judaism. Developing a relationship with the clergy will help children feel an attachment to the synagogue. In my opinion, Mitzvah Programs and projects are another negative aspect of many Bar/Bat Mitzvah programs. Having children do projects that they cannot relate to or that are banal, or will not become part of their lives, is meaningless. When asked to break a bad habit, for example, children invariably will say that they will stop biting their nails or will be kinder to their siblings. Empty promises made in order to fill in a sheet are not kept.

(Editor's note: The most successful Mitzvah Programs are integrated into the seventh grade curriculum; for several examples, see Chapters 26, 27, and 28. On relationships with clergy, an area in need of more honest appraisal, refer to Chapters 2 and 3, which explore the relationship with the Cantor. No chapters exploring the relationship between student and Rabbi were submitted.)

Here are some very specific areas that need improvement, and suggestions for those improvements:

1. We need to *teach* children something, not just assign work. If they don't have reading skills, teach them reading skills! Teach them trope; the skill can be used for any portion and in this way we will be creating Torah readers, not just "single gig performers." Ideally, a trope class could be part of the seventh grade curriculum.
2. The tutor should be in communication with a student's teacher and/or Director of Education prior to the beginning of training, so the amount of time at a session can be predetermined, and the length of sessions can thus vary according to the needs of individual students.

3. Involve the parents more. Require that they attend a certain number of lessons. Have the family work together on any blessings that the parents will have to recite. Answer any questions they may have during those sessions. Give parents a list of times during which you will be available to answer any additional questions.
4. Ritual committees should become better versed in what Bar/Bat Mitzvah training is all about. They should understand that the congregation's Cantor is not necessarily the best one to tutor children. Often, Cantors would choose to delete this duty from their job description if given the opportunity. Instead of insisting on using Cantors for this job, it might be a good idea in many cases to hire a B'nai Mitzvah tutor who is more interested and better trained to teach.

(Editor's note: This idea was explored in the Introduction to this book, pages 3-5.)

Saul: I think the overall system itself must change to succeed with more of the students. It should become more encompassing. For example, the Religious School, to which B'nai Mitzvah instruction is either formally or informally connected, must do more. It must run, or at least be part of, a larger effort to educate families. When Judaism is a focus of the whole family, Bar/Bat Mitzvah is a natural event. The turnout and enthusiasm for "Family Involvement Days" sponsored by my own Religious School have demonstrated success in accomplishing this. In addition, post-B'nai Mitzvah involvement needs to strengthen those concepts and practices learned during the Bar/Bat Mitzvah process. What's more, it must be fun. If pre-B'nai Mitzvah students look forward to post-B'nai activities, they will see becoming Bar or Bat Mitzvah as a joyous milestone, not an annoying millstone.

(Editor's Note: See Unit VI for Family Education programs. See Unit VII for innovative post Bar/Bat Mitzvah curriculum suggestions. This is certainly a key area in need of more energy and focus.)

QUESTION #6: This question is for Ran and Hannah. Could you tell us now about the unique "mentor program" which you developed?

Ran: As our program grew, it became impossible for us to keep up with tutoring the large number of students ourselves. So the mentor program was born. With the help of our tutors, we can maintain that essential one-on-one relationship with our students. The tutors have mostly been recruited from among the students who have completed our program in the recent past. However, some of our best pre-B'nai Mitzvah students also serve as tutors. We have also recruited a few adults from the congregation to help. In fact, our current tutors range in age from 12 to 80!

At other synagogues, tutors are not individually matched with students. We feel, however, that it is important to do this. We make permanent assignments, also, with the expectation that this will enhance a sense of responsibility in both student and tutor. The tutor assignment takes place after the Bar/Bat Mitzvah Program Director has assessed the student's personality and abilities. A particularly strong student may be assigned to a weaker tutor whose main contribution to their student will be to provide an incentive to prepare their assignment on a regular basis. Weaker students are assigned to the strongest tutors, who have the ability and enthusiasm to provide intensive support throughout the year. Some of these tutors will telephone their student two or three times a week in order to facilitate their education. Conversely, quiet, shy students cannot be successfully matched with shy tutors. We have often matched students with poor musical skills and excellent Hebrew reading skills to tutors with good musical but poor Hebrew skills. This gives virtually any student who wants to be a tutor the chance to be one. The reason this system works, of course, is because of the close monitoring and supervision provided by the Bar/Bat Mitzvah Program Directors.

Hannah: Tutors are responsible for monitoring students' weekly progress as they learn their portions and blessings. Prior to completion of the session, both tutor and student check in with one of the Program Directors, who then suggests a goal for the coming week.

The Program Directors meet at their home with each student individually every two to four weeks. At these meetings, they assess the student's progress and individualize the student's experience. Students who are able to master the required material early are given the option of focusing on a variety of possible individual projects. Depending on their particular strengths and talents, these can include learning a special trope system, such as Purim trope, leading various parts of the Shabbat service, discussing Jewish ethics, drawing scenes from the Torah, or any other suitable project.

The "mentor" aspect of this program is enriched by the fact that students all meet with their tutors on Shabbat, and attend services together whenever possible. Tutors are strongly encouraged to attend services, while students are all required to attend. Lessons take place after services. (Lessons can be conducted without writing in a traditional synagogue.)

(Editor's Note: This aspect of the program is feasible only where the tutors are active members of the congregation whose children they tutor.)

As the tutoring program has grown, we have been confronted with an unanticipated problem which we are only too glad to have: tutoring has become an "in" activity. Even some less-than-stellar students have indicated that they wish to tutor. This has allowed us even greater flexibility in assignment of tutors. Our weakest students in the Bar/Bat Mitzvah program have been assigned two tutors: the primary tutor meets with them on Shabbat, while the secondary tutor is responsible for meeting with them during the week, at Hebrew School. The availability of so many tutors has also allowed us to accommodate students who wish to begin training at age 11. No tutor is usually responsible for more than one student. We should mention that tutors are not paid for their work; their "payment" is the respect of adult congregants and of their students.

Our tutors enjoy working one-on-one with students and continuing their involvement with the synagogue and Judaism. There is nothing that compares to teaching a single individual and seeing the fruit of your labor within a year. Tutors are rewarded by being invited to a twice yearly outing to a movie or ball game. In addition, at the end of the academic year, tutors are recognized at a Shabbat morning service, and given a commemorative award.

The success of this Bar/Bat Mitzvah program lies in the continued involvement of its graduates in our synagogue life. It is our hope that when our students continue their race into adulthood, they will retain much of what they have learned at Germantown, and that this knowledge and self-assurance will serve as a foundation for building the Jewish community of the next century.

EDITOR'S COMMENTS

Imparting knowledge and teaching skills to B'nai Mitzvah students will build their self-confidence and strengthen their positive Jewish identity. This is the common goal of all B'nai Mitzvah tutors. This panel discussion and the following chapters show a wide variety of approaches to realizing that goal; the level of commitment and creativity on the part of tutors is evident throughout.

Chapter 12
A Methodology for B'nai Mitzvah Tutoring

Shira Belfer

The methodology presented here has been honed over 20 years of tutoring B'nai Mitzvah students. It has been taught to a number of colleagues across the country through workshops at conferences, such as CAJE, as well as in private sessions. Feedback on the methodology from those who have used it, as well my own personal experience with over 400 students (adults and children) has enabled me to fine tune it.

This methodology is easy to use, combining principles of music education and of Jewish and general education with personal intuition and experience about how we think and feel under certain conditions.

To me, the Bar/Bat Mitzvah experience is the single most important experience in the life of today's young Jews. It colors their attitudes toward Jewishness for the rest of their lives. Therefore, it is crucial for the family, and in particular the student, that the Bar/Bat Mitzvah process be enjoyable, fulfilling, and rewarding.

TECHNICAL DETAILS

In this program, the teaching process is divided into six separate skill categories. Successful B'nai Mitzvah teaching involves the *merging of all of these skills*. The skills are: (1) Hebrew reading; (2) chanting/singing; (3) memory; (4) learning how to practice; (5) Understanding what we are doing, and how and why we are doing it; and (6) putting the previous five skills together *simultaneously*. Of these, I believe the most important skill by far is learning how to practice. Once the student knows how to practice in an enjoyable and non-tedious manner, he/she will henceforward be motivated to learn, and all of the other listed skills will either develop or improve as a result. As an added by-product, the "practice" methodology can be applied to learning just about anything, so it becomes even more valuable to students as a lifelong skill.

GETTING STARTED

Since there is an emotional component to this methodology, it is important to get off to a good start. To this end, the process begins with an initial meeting (orientation/evaluation) between the Cantor, the student, and his/her parents, one year to eight months before the Bar/Bat Mitzvah. If one parent is not living in the same household as the child, I ask both parents to be present at this initial meeting if they can. If that is not comfortable for the family, I meet with both parents at separate times and ask that the child be at one or both of those meetings.

I ask the student to read some Hebrew for me, and I ask the following questions: Do you know what "B.C.E." and "C.E." refer to? Do you know what a prophet is, and when the prophets lived? What do you think life was like in biblical times? Do you know why we read the text of the Torah and Haftarah out loud, or why we chant it, as opposed to just reading it?

In addition, I also discuss with student and parents what the Bar/Bat Mitzvah ceremony means to them. I explain my teaching methodology, what the synagogue community expects of the student, and how long the process takes (usually six months; the student has a half hour private lesson with me once a week and is expected to attend a B'nai Mitzvah class and at least two "dress rehearsals").

The meeting takes place with the parents present because it gives them an opportunity to observe their child's attitude, to ask any questions that they may have about the process, the teacher, and/or Judaism in general. It gives the child a fresh look at parental concerns and Jewish attitudes, and it gives the child a sense of what he/she will be involved in for the next few months.

After this meeting, students also become secure in the knowledge that their parents understand the process and are interested in it. Students also get to see the Cantor in a different light. Students can feel secure in the knowledge that they will have a great deal of individual attention from the Cantor and from their parents in the coming months. Hopefully, an open and trusting relationship with both Cantor and parents will develop.

SKILLS

Let us now address each of the skill categories outlined above in detail.

1. Hebrew Reading

(Note: *Always* use enlarged text for students (adults and children). It is easier to read, therefore easier to use for study. I have found that the use of an enlarged text often eliminates many reading "difficulties.")

The student must be able to read Hebrew in a relatively fluent manner in order to chant Torah or Haftarah. If the student is already a good Hebrew reader, then this is not a problem. However, general experience shows that most B'nai Mitzvah students are not. So, before doing anything else, I test the student to determine reading ability. I place in front of the student a large print version of the *brachah* before reading the Haftarah and ask him/her to read it out loud. Reading level is based on the reading speed, accuracy, and the ability of the student to translate.

Most students are simply *rusty*, as opposed to unable to read. They may have forgotten a letter or two or confuse certain letters. A series of mnemonics (such as "*koof* has a crutch") developed by me and a colleague, Roy Dolliner, is extremely helpful for students who need the remedial assistance. (I would be happy to share these mnemonics with anyone who is interested.) Once students have confidence that, contrary to what they may have been told by teachers or parents, they can indeed read, they usually come up with devices of their own to help them read with fluency. With the application of these techniques, all students' Hebrew reading ability increases dramatically within a few weeks. This is also an upward spiral in terms of the students' confidence and motivation.

2. Chanting/Singing

I consider singing to be one of the *least* important skills involved in this process. For the student who is musical and performance-oriented in the first place, the singing aspect is no problem. In the case of students who are not musical and/or are shy about singing out loud, their singing/musical ability usually improves on its own when their confidence increases through improvement of other skills.

Improving the musical ability of an individual student is not in the purview of the Bar/Bat Mitzvah process. Nor does the Cantor/tutor have the time to do so, since this is a complicated process if done properly. Therefore, I don't worry about a student's lack of musical ability. In addition, I always tell my students that what they "have" is just fine, and they should feel good and confident about using what they have. (For a discussion of the more technical aspects of teaching trope, see Chapter 21.) Parents, and adults in general, are usually much more concerned with the student's musical ability than is the student. When a student's lack of ability is pointed out to him or her, this does much more harm than good in terms of the student's overall ability and performance. Many Bar/Bat Mitzvah tutors, unfortunately, are overly concerned with the musical aspects of the training, and wonder constantly why they are not as successful as they would like to be. I believe that in their zeal for certain "good" musical sounds, they unconsciously undermine the confidence of the student.

3. Memory

Memory can be trained and increased. There are skills involved in increasing one's ability to retain knowledge in certain patterns and blocks, and this is necessary for anyone who wants to chant Torah. This methodology can be applied to any other area of knowledge.

I teach Torah reading *aliyot* in reverse order. In other words, first I teach the student Maftir, then the seventh *aliyah*, etc. In this way, the student learns a "chunk" of text rather than individual sentences. It is better when a Bar/Bat Mitzvah can read a "whole section" of Torah rather than "just a small part." Knowing they have mastered a lot of material will inspire confidence in students.

I have developed four memory rules for Torah and Haftarah reading. They are:

Rule #1: Any word, phrase, set of phrases, or whole sentence that is problematic will be forever remembered if it can be said correctly five times in a row while staring at the text. I have never known this rule to fail. For example: the word *"La'aluvat"* in the *brachah* after the Haftarah reading is a difficult word for most students. Have the student stare at the word and say *"la'aluvat"* five times. If he/she makes a mistake, start counting from one again. Once the student can say the word five times in a row correctly, have him or her read the entire phrase *"V'la'aluvat nefesh toshiah."* If the student has trouble with this, go through the process five times in the same manner as described, with the original word again first. The student will now do this with ease. Then add the phrase, using the same method as with the word. Then have the student read the entire sentence. The student will read with speed and accuracy.

Rule #2: Build memory skills as you would build blocks. The methodology used in learning the phrase described above is an example.

Rule #3: Whenever you practice, start with the very last sentence that you learned last time, and add the first sentence of the new material to it. Then move on to the rest of the new material that you want to learn. When the student practices using this rule, various memory blocks are connected, making the overall memory blocks larger. This is very good for remembering large passages of Torah reading.

Rule #4: Pay attention to details! For example,"va" as opposed to "v'" or "ba" as opposed to "b". These small differences make great differences in the meaning of the text.

Other technical details about memory training will become clear in the "Learning How To Practice" section which follows.

4. Learning How To Practice

Based on observations, I believe that B'nai Mitzvah material (including all Torah and Haftarah reading) can be learned best when studied for 45 minutes or less a day, MAXIMUM.

Of course, how that 45 minutes is used is crucial. In order to train the brain to concentrate, I start with a *very short* period of time, three times a day. On beginning, the student must find three separate five minute periods in the day to practice, only 15 minutes!

If the student is a morning person, then the first practice period should be in the morning before the student goes to school or work. Students who are not morning people should make the first practice session immediately when they come home from school — even before milk and cookies and shmoozing on the phone. The second period should be immediately after dinner (before doing anything else) and the third period immediately prior to falling asleep. (This means literally that the student is actually already in bed ready to turn out the lights as soon as the practice is finished.) Each five minute period is measured by setting a timer.

The student should use a visual aid to map out and keep track of practice times. (See the Bar/Bat Mitzvah Practice Record in the Appendix at the end of this chapter.) The purpose of the Practice Record is to help students know whether they have actually practiced three separate times during any given day, and to help the parents track practice sessions. As you can see on the chart, there is a place for parents to initial at the end of the week. I ask students and parents to agree on a place in the house where the practice chart will be accessible to both of them (e.g., the refrigerator, the room of the Bar/Bat Mitzvah, etc.). Each time the student practices, the chart is to be checked off in the appropriate box on the appropriate day; one check for each practice period of the day, so that there are three checks per day for the three practice periods. At the end of the week, the chart should have a continuous line of checks all the way across the page for that week with a parent's initials in the initial box. In joint custody cases, when the student lives in two different places, I send a practice chart to each house and ask the student to fill in both charts. This way the student shares the process with each parent, and both parents are continuously informed of their child's progress.

Students bring the chart to their lesson each time so that I can also see their progress and/or problems. I make it a point to tell my students that this chart is for them, not for me, since I will know whether and how much they have practiced within seconds of hearing them at their lesson. It is their job and their responsibility to practice; it is not their parents' responsibility. But their parents can help them *learn* to practice. This system is good for both parent and student because it helps to make both conscious of the child's growing independence.

Once the student is comfortable with five minutes three times per day (usually this takes two to three weeks), the student then increases one of the practice sessions to ten minutes, so that the daily practice sessions are now five, five, and ten minutes. It is important that each increase in time start with the practice session immediately prior to going to sleep. This is because the brain continues to learn as we sleep even though we have physically stopped practicing, and the best concentration conditioning takes place while we sleep. The following week, have the student increase time in one of the other daily practice sessions so that the sessions per day are now five, ten, and ten. Then the student should increase the third daily session so that per day the student practices three separate times of ten minutes each, for a daily total of one half hour.

After two to three months, depending on the student, have the student increase practice sessions to three times per day of fifteen minutes each, for a total of 45 minutes per day.

Unusually gifted students can train themselves to more than 45 minutes of practice time/concentration per day. But beware of the student who is convinced that he or she is capable of more. Practicing/focusing on any learning task for more than 45 minutes per day is not only useless, it actually encourages and enables the student to "learn in" mistakes. Such mistakes, once thoroughly learned with this method, can be corrected only by great effort. For this reason, I never tell my students that they can increase their own concentration/practice beyond the 45 minutes per day. I then check carefully for mistakes, and caution the student strongly about the pitfalls involved in increasing time.

Once students reach the half hour per day of practice time, they no longer really need to fill in the practice record since they have learned how to practice every day and feel comfortable with it. However, I still require them to continue to fill it out so that they and their parents can have an ongoing "testimonial" to mark the development of their skills, and so that parents can stay informed of their child's progress.

Practicing in this way is easy! There is no one who cannot find a five, ten or fifteen minute block of time three times during a day. Such short periods ensure that the student will be focused when studying, and mistakes will be lessened. Also, within any one block of practice time, boredom is minimized.

In virtually all cases, students see their skill levels increase steadily. With this comes an upward spiraling of confidence in themselves. The more confidence, the faster and better this methodology continues to work. And, the better the students do, the more confidence and success the teacher feels. So this methodology also rewards the teacher.

5. Understanding What We Are Doing, How, and Why

It is essential that the student understand what he/she will do, why, and how. Many B'nai Mitzvah tutors do not take the time to explain methodology and/or text to their students. Not doing so actually slows down the learning process and the ability of the student to accomplish great things. I have found that explanation greatly increases the student's confidence in the teacher and in themselves. If students understand the "scene" in the Torah or Haftarah reading, then it is easier for them to understand what they are doing in terms of reading phrases or sentences, and why certain trope marks are used and the patterns in which they appear. Students should be encouraged to look for and pick out words in the text that they already know, and facts about the stories from the Bible that they remember learning in Religious School. Students should always be given credit by the teacher for knowing a lot! After all, they have spent at least eight years in secular school and at least some time in Religious School by the age of 13, and I have never found a student who hasn't retained something from all that previous education.

In most congregational settings, it is probably the Rabbi who spends time with the student on the actual meaning of the text and the Torah and Haftarah portions. The Cantor usually covers the "technical" parts of the process (relating to the actual "performance"). However, the Cantor/tutor can and should give the student a general overview of the material in the beginning, and, from time to time, point out words that the student might know in the text and the trope patterns that go with these words. The student's speech is usually discussed and developed with the Rabbi, and the actual delivery of the speech is "polished" by both the Rabbi and the Cantor in the "dress rehearsals."

If you as the teacher are in the position of developing the speech or *d'var Torah* yourself, and do not feel qualified for this job, be sure to seek help from those who know this material in depth, so that you can intelligently discuss it with your students.

Contact with both the Rabbi and the Cantor is essential for the student to be comfortable in the synagogue, and I believe that the amount of contact and kinds of attention that the student receives from all of the clergy at the time of the Bar/Bat Mitzvah preparation is of paramount importance to the student's present and future attitude toward Jewish life. (For more comments on Cantor/student relations, see Chapters 2 and 3.)

6. Putting All of the Skills Together

Putting together the five skills discussed above is the most important and difficult part of the methodology. Begin with encouragement and patience. Be sensitive to the student at hand. Make it clear that you believe the student can definitely accomplish what is expected of him/her. (Obviously, different students should have different realistic expectations and goals. These should be thoroughly discussed with parents and the Jewish professionals involved in advance of the beginning of the process, and on an ongoing basis during the process.)

The process is fun! The students should enjoy all aspects of their Bar/Bat Mitzvah preparation. Encourage students to give feedback to the Cantor/tutor and parents at all times about how they are feeling during the teaching process. If the student is not enjoying the process, it is the teacher's responsibility to find out why and to make changes. The student is involved in the B'nai Mitzvah process because those around him/her love Judaism and want to pass it on to future generations. The teacher loves what he/she does, and hopes that the student will love it, too, and will want to continue Jewish learning after Bar/Bat Mitzvah.

Pursuant to maintaining high standards for all students, the following may be of interest:

TEACHER GUIDELINES

1. Do not ask a student to do something that you would not do yourself, either in learning or practicing.
2. Say what you mean, and mean what you say. Do things in the manner in which you would like your students to do them. Maintain the same high standards for yourself that you expect from your students.
3. If you yourself need to learn a Torah or Haftarah portion, use this same methodology yourself so that you know what you're talking about and your students will believe in you.
4. Don't keep your students waiting for a lesson. If on occasion you are late, apologize for making them wait.
5. Show respect for your students; encourage them to ask questions.
6. Show respect for parents of B'nai Mitzvah students. Most parents are genuinely interested in their child, their child's progress, and the "Jewishness" of the Bar/Bat Mitzvah experience, even if they don't outwardly show it.
7. Be sensitive as to how you present yourself to your students and their parents. As a role model, you can have a positive or negative influence.
8. Praise your students often. Positive encouragement does wonders.
9. Communicate with your students and their parents. Make sure parents know how their children are doing; communicate both verbally and in writing to avoid later confusion.
10. Be prepared in advance for your students; do for them what you said you would do, when you said you would do it. This is especially true with regard to the preparation of tapes.
11. Have fun in the process!

EVALUATING

The student should be critiqued by the teacher at every lesson on an ongoing basis. This might be something as simple as saying, "You had a fine lesson, you're doing well," or "You need to do better next time," or "We should be moving at a faster pace, but your reading has improved." Praise the student at least as much as you criticize, as positive reinforcement increases the student's ability to do better.

Parents should be included in the evaluation process. Send them a written evaluation at least twice during the process — near the beginning, in the middle, and if possible, at the end. The beginning evaluation is a simple assessment of the student's ability and what he/she will probably be able to accomplish. The middle evaluation is how the student is doing, and what you have accomplished so far. The final evaluation should reflect what has been accomplished, and the teacher's pride and joy in working with the student. Written evaluation records are very important when you encounter "problem" students and parents. They avoid confusion on everybody's part. And note, it is much more important to tell students and their parents when they are doing well than when they are doing poorly.

Evaluation of the teacher usually takes place on an informal basis, and often has more to do with whether or not the teacher is liked by students than it does with teaching skills. Parents also evaluate teachers. They are quick to complain or to praise the teacher to friends or through letters to the synagogue board or the Director of Education.

Evaluation of the program should take place at least once a year. It should be noted whether the actual program is meeting the stated goals of the community for B'nai Mitzvah, and whether there are generally positive feelings about the program. A written survey/ evaluation of the program should be solicited from the current group of families (one from children, one from parents, one from adult students), and those evaluations should be reviewed by the clergy and the synagogue board. The evaluation form should be simple, direct, and easy to complete.

CONCLUSION

This methodology builds confidence and motivation in both teacher and student. It is my hope that by sharing these ideas, I have made it possible for many more teachers and students to enjoy that experience. When both students and teachers enjoy the B'nai Mitzvah preparation process, we are building a community of positive, committed, and joyful young Jewish adults.

APPENDIX

Bar/Bat Mitzvah Practice Record

Signature	Week of:	Sun			Mon			Tue			Wed			Thu			Fri			Sat		
	10/23	✓	✓	✓	✓	✓	✓	✓	✓	✓	✓	✓	✓	✓	✓	✓	✓	✓	✓	✓	✓	✓
	/ /																					
	/ /																					
	/ /																					
	/ /																					
	/ /																					
	/ /																					
	/ /																					
	/ /																					
	/ /																					
	/ /																					
	/ /																					
	/ /																					
	/ /																					
	/ /																					
	/ /																					
	/ /																					
	/ /																					
	/ /																					
	/ /																					
	/ /																					
	/ /																					
	/ /																					
	/ /																					
	/ /																					
	/ /																					
	/ /																					
	/ /																					
	/ /																					
	/ /																					
	/ /																					
	/ /																					
	/ /																					
	/ /																					
	/ /																					
	/ /																					
	/ /																					
	/ /																					
	/ /																					

Chapter 13

The Job of Tutoring B'nai Mitzvah

Ellen Goldenberg

My job as tutor is to train the students to chant a selection from a Torah portion, the length of which is determined by the capability of the individual student. The average number of verses studied is 15-18, thus providing the family with six *aliyot*. In addition, Haftarah is studied, and again the number of verses is determined by the student's ability. Preference is given to learning more of the Torah portion after a minimum number of verses (usually 7-10) of Haftarah is learned. The student is expected to lead the bulk of the service in Hebrew and English, and if there are any gaps in the student's skills in *tefilah*, it is the tutor's responsibility to bring the student up to par. The student's primary goal, however, is Torah and Haftarah.

Because the parents are paying for the tutor, and every child is required to have a private tutor, it is imperative that the number of tutor hours be kept at a reasonable level. It becomes the tutor's job to motivate the student to respond to instruction and achieve the greatest level of skill in the most efficient manner. In other congregations in our area, the synagogue pays for the tutors. After many discussions with tutors who work under both systems, most agree that when the tutor is paid directly by the parent, the parent is more likely to keep track of their child's progress. On the other hand, a student whose skills are far behind, or who has learning problems, sometimes does not get as much extra time as he/she could because the parent may balk at paying for the lessons, or even feel inconvenienced at having to transport the child to the tutor.

Although I work as a tutor for a synagogue, I am not strictly speaking a staff member. There are advantages and disadvantages in this. The advantages of this arrangement are: (1) I can work individually with students in my home; (2) I do not need to report to a supervisor on students' progress; (3) I am able to give individual attention to each family and can share perpectives with them on the Bar/Bat Mitzvah as being more than a worship service and a party; 4) I can offer flexibility in scheduling, with no need for turning in lesson plans, getting substitutes, etc.

The disadvantages are: (1) I am not paid as a teacher, which provides me with no benefits, and with an income that varies with the number of B'nai Mitzvah scheduled; (2) The fee, a very moderate one, is set by the the synagogue and cannot be altered. Still, parents sometimes balk at paying for the tutor; (3) Since the Rabbi doesn't become involved in planning the service until about four weeks before the date, parents rely on the tutor for all kinds of support beyond just teaching.

Most students will have 10-12 hours of instruction with a tutor. This could be in one hour sessions or in shorter lessons, depending on the student's needs. In general, I try to see each student for one hour each week for the first four weeks. This gets them into a regular practicing routine, and enables them to learn the most commonly used trope marks most efficiently. If a student's reading level causes him/her to struggle, some of the time during these initial four weeks is dedicated to review of decoding strategies, such as rules of the *shva* pronunciation, accent changes, delineating vowels from trope marks, etc.

Part of the experience of one-on-one tutoring is enabling the student to understand the selected verses of his/her Torah portion. In preparation for writing the speech, some time is spent discussing the background of the portion: what came before it, why is this included in the Torah (especially in the case of *halachah* or rituals). The purpose of this dialogue is to help the student to be comfortable with preparing a speech and to enable him/her to see the relevance of the theme to his/her own life. In addition, the Haftarah portion is discussed to show the connection with the Torah portion, even if the connection is made to verses not chosen for that student's particular reading.

The ultimate goal is not for students to show how much they have mastered, but to approach Bar/Bat Mitzvah as confident, literate Jews. It is important that parents not view Bar/Bat Mitzvah as a competition of one child over another, but that they understand that the goals set for each child are definitely an individual matter.

At the beginning session with each student, I map out the task at hand. After introducing them to their Torah section, I unroll a mini-Torah and show them that their goal is to be able to chant the assigned verses well enough so that they will be able to read from the Torah, which has only the letters, without vowels or trope. I explain that I have never let a student get up and make a fool of himself/herself, that whatever they would accomplish would take hard work, that ultimately they would feel very proud of what they accomplish. There is no average number of verses or prayers to top, no goal set in stone. For the children of this congregation (who have only learned to decode the *alef bet* since fourth grade, and whose Hebrew studies amounted to barely two or three hours per week), feeling secure in the task at hand has as much to do with their accomplishments as having the fluent skills that some others have. In fact, students from this synagogue do more at their Bar/Bat Mitzvah service than students who have gone through more time-intensive programs elsewhere.

Outlining a time frame for the student and family makes the learning process more even. Since students start studying six months before the Bar/Bat Mitzvah (it seems like a lifetime away to them), it is important to have a date set on which you will stop adding new material. This is usually about six weeks before the date of the Bar/Bat Mitzvah, which incidentally coincides with the date invitations are usually sent out. It is reassuring for the student and family to know at this point that they really know everything they need to as they approach the post office. By this time, the student should be able to chant the Torah portion confidently and be able to make the transition from the Torah booklet to the *Tikkun* page. Most of the Haftarah should be under control and any extraneous details, such as smoothing out prayers, finishing the speech, typing it in large type so that it is readable, can be easily achieved and are also under control. Sometimes, when a Bar/Bat Mitzvah is scheduled early in September and the student will be away for all or part of the summer, this has to be adjusted.

About three weeks before the "dress rehearsal" with the Rabbi, I go through the entire service in order with the student. I give the student some of the following reassuring hints at this time:

- You never have to read more than three Hebrew words at a time. Phrasing is very important to reading fluently. (Sometimes I draw vertical lines to delineate the small groups.)

- Always read at the pace which is the slowest you need in the prayer. Nobody will ever say that you sound unsure, even at the slowest pace, if you don't speed up on the final *brachah*.

- Speak slowly and clearly. If you are reading a responsive prayer (such as "*Ashrei*") and do it fast (to get it over with), nobody will do the responsive lines and you will end up doing the whole thing yourself.

Some additional hints for tutors:

- Spend a lot of time on the first prayer the student will do. Being confident on the first prayer is really important, as students should know they will not be nervous about this prayer.

- Encourage students to point to each word as they read (even English) or chant. Most students do much better this way, as it slows them down and keeps their tempo even.

- Since the prayer after chanting the Haftarah is usually the last thing a student does except reading the speech, write words of encouragement and congratulations on this page in the booklet. The student can basically relax and know he/she has "made it" even before the final "Amen."

Because tutoring takes place in a relaxed, informal setting, the students' family politics, frequently a source of stress for them, often need to be resolved with reassurance from the tutor. Often I feel like a psychologist, listening to and reflecting on students' concerns about all the peripheral "stuff" which may be distracting them from their studies. In homes where neither parent is fluent at reading Hebrew, both parents and children may feel helpless or inadequate. Many times, a parent or grandparent has requested to take the last 15 minutes of a session so that they, too, can brush up on their *brachot*.

In other ways, family politics frequently set the tone for the success of the student. Some situations with which my students have had to cope include divorced families, blended families, Jewish parents who can't read Hebrew, non-Jewish parents who may or may not be supportive, either philosophically or financially. In one case, a child, whose parents had joint custody and were both Jewish, had to contend with the fact that each parent wanted the child to have the Bat Mitzvah at a different synagogue. One was a Conservative synagogue at which a girl chanted a Haftarah at a Friday night service. The other was a Reform synagogue where a child chanted Torah and lead the service. This child did indeed have a Bat Mitzvah celebration in each parent's community. One took place on the Shabbat following her thirteenth birthday, the other later in the year.

In making Bar/Bat Mitzvah celebrations a positive experience for different kinds of students and their families, the most important factor for being a good tutor, aside from trope and Hebrew literacy, is that of offering support to the child. For most teens, self-confidence is like a shell for a very fragile being. Presenting themselves in front of a large group is a challenge which can be frightening and awesome. For parents, too, competing with their peers on a social level can be like a rite of passage to becoming an adult role model for their Bar/Bat Mitzvah child. If we as private tutors see Bar/Bat Mitzvah as a stressful family event, then our job is to focus the child on his/her part: learning the required materials.

Although I am a private tutor, I am bound by the philosophy and *modus operandi* of the synagogue. Here, the Rabbi assigns the student to a tutor after the student is screened by him for reading ability, learning style, and special interests, such as music. He guides the student's choice of verses to be learned and then turns the job of Bar/Bat Mitzvah preparation over to the tutor. Occasionally, the Rabbi will meet with the student if there is a problem, but for the most part, he does not meet formally with the student or the family until one month before the actual ceremony. I prepare the parents for that meeting by telling them what to expect and what information they will need to know (such as the student's Hebrew name and the names of all the *aliyot*, Torah dresser, Ark openers, etc.). Students are often shocked when I tell them that this is their last lesson, and they often request to schedule another lesson after the full rehearsal with the Rabbi. That extra lesson, I have found, is almost always cancelled.

The most frequent comment I have heard from parents is that they felt the synagogue staff, especially the Rabbi, should have had more communication with the family during the whole process. Realizing that the Rabbi is a busy person, I would strongly advocate temporary Havurah-type groups in which parents can share their feelings and concerns.

Finally, it is imperative, from my perspective, that the tutor actually attend the student's Bar/Bat Mitzvah ceremony. I recall that the first few times I tutored and did not receive an invitation, I actually felt uncomfortable attending the service. It was only after some words of wisdom from a colleague that I realized that the invitation in the mail was not an indication of gratitude, and that it was important to the student to have the security of the teacher's presence. I now preface my first session with all students by actually writing the date of their Bar/Bat Mitzvah on my personal calendar in their presence and assuring them that I will try my best to attend. If it turns out that I have a conflict, I make sure to tell the student in advance and call with some last minute support. I rarely attend a reception unless the parents are personal family friends, but I always stay at the Oneg long enough to give positive feedback to the student and family.

Being a B'nai Mitzvah tutor is more than a job. Tutors can have an impact on both their students and the students' families that will have a ripple effect extending far beyond the ceremony itself. The successful tutor can transmit new and meaningful ways of being Jewish.

Chapter 14
Children with Special Learning Needs

Sara Rubinow Simon

Significant changes have taken place in communities across North America in recent years. It is no longer unacceptable to be "different." In fact, it is common for people to strive to be unique and innovative. In the religious world also, there are new opportunities to be creative and distinctive during the worship service. With this greater latitude comes the chance for different modes and levels of involvement requiring varying skill levels so that individuals who may have been excluded in the past are able to take part in religious services in many different ways.

Driven by federal legislation in the past 20 years mandating equal access and an appropriate education for all, there has been a heightened awareness of individual differences and also of the existence of people with previously untapped ability. The ensuing emphasis on the field of special education has intensified the challenge to find the methodology and the setting that will enable each person to achieve his or her full potential. Special education, rather than being esoteric and only within the domain of certified special education professionals, is essentially good education because it considers the strengths and weaknesses of the individual learner and the teaching style of the instructor, as well as the content material to be mastered.

The impact of special education has also been felt within the Jewish community. With this new perspective, it becomes incumbent upon the Jewish community to ensure that every Jew be given the opportunity to receive an appropriate Jewish education, including a chance to celebrate the Bar/Bat Mitzvah milestone. Congregations have increasingly become more flexible regarding what they consider appropriate public affirmation of the attainment of adult status. There are now very few instances in which synagogues refuse to allow a person with special needs to participate (to the best of his or her ability) in congregational programs and services. Modern Rabbinic Responsa are reinterpreting traditional practices in light of new information regarding the ability of people with special needs to function effectively in society. Technological and attitudinal advances have helped sensitize us to our responsibility to view each person as a unique individual.

In the past, parents of children with special needs, frustrated by the absence of a suitable synagogue school situation, either hired a private tutor or gave up the hope that their children would be able to receive a religious education. Occasionally, a small class would meet for a short time, and then disband through lack of support and direction. Happily, Jewish communities in growing numbers have established community based trans-ideological programs. Such programs are usually funded by their local federations for those children with more severe disabilities who cannot effectively be taught within the context of their own congregational religious school.

As the stigma of having special needs disappears, synagogue religious schools are finding it increasingly easy to obtain data from parents that helps them to identify and accommodate students who have a broader range of learning styles and special learning needs (see the Appendix for a sample Religious School registration form). Further, with the assistance of their central agency for Jewish education, teachers are acquiring the requisite skills to individualize instructional strategies and materials. Through the Special Needs Department of the Board of Jewish Education of Greater Washington, for example, supplementary schools can receive on-site observations. Through such observations, teachers are helped to adapt teaching methodology and materials to dovetail with strategies utilized in the students' secular schools. They also receive assistance with diagnostic/prescriptive Hebrew programs, training in classroom and behavior management techniques, Bar/Bat Mitzvah preparation through pairing with selected tutors, and liaison with the congregation to plan appropriate synagogue participation.

In communities without a central agency for Jewish education, the public schools and university special education departments can provide assistance in "packaging" lessons by applying general guidelines that can be adapted to any learning situation.

It is strongly recommended that youngsters with special learning needs be part of an ongoing religious education program for as many years as the regular program, albeit with appropriate modifications in curriculum and behavioral objectives. Within this framework, the Bar/Bat Mitzvah is then only one facet of preparing to lead a rich Jewish life rather than the single focus. Goals are geared to a suitable cognitive level, guided by a Jewish literacy checklist, so that there will be familiarity with the elements of the Jewish home, Shabbat, the Jewish holiday and life cycles, basic prayers and blessings in Hebrew and/or English, the synagogue, the Jewish community, Bible heroes, *mitzvot* and Jewish values, Israel, etc. It is possible to adapt the curriculum to fit the special learning profile so that maximum mastery can be achieved in each area. In this way, the youngster will have a chance to acquire the tools necessary to function competently in the Jewish mainstream.

When approaching Bar/Bat Mitzvah preparation, it is important to consider the youngster's wishes and expectations as well as the family's so that there can be cooperative planning and support.

Can the family feel comfortable with the outcome should there be unplanned glitches? Does the family regularly attend services so that the youngster feels at home in the synagogue and has absorbed parts of the service by "osmosis" or by living through siblings' B'nai Mitzvah? Can he/she stand up in front of a large number of people, particularly strangers? Will he/she have the chance to use the skills acquired again in the future?

Selection of the date and time of the Bar/Bat Mitzvah must take into account the youngster's ability to sit through a longer or shorter service in the main sanctuary or in the chapel. Would a Rosh Chodesh or a Monday or Thursday morning service be more suitable than Shabbat? Can he/she participate alone, or is it preferable to have somebody by the child's side to prompt or accompany him/her? Can he/she learn a Haftarah? A Torah portion? Chant or read either? Deliver a speech or message? Lead an English prayer? Lead a Hebrew prayer? Read or recite by rote? Perform non-verbal roles such as opening or closing the Ark? Wrapping the Torah? Holding the *Kiddush* cup? Saying "Amen"? These are merely some examples of options; there are others to consider.

It is all too common to assume that children with special learning needs cannot master the Hebrew portion of the service, yet there is no necessary correlation between Hebrew and English reading ability. If a youngster can read English, there is a good chance that he or she can also learn to read Hebrew on some level, although it may be time and labor intensive. Even if only minimal decoding ability is achieved, there is great delight in being able to identify letters or words in any Siddur or Hebrew book. By learning the geography or layout of the page, the familiar elements can be located. There are lists of high frequency words that can be used for whole word recognition similar to the Dolch lists used in English reading. It is possible for someone who has been labeled as being dyslexic to learn to read Hebrew fluently and accurately. It is therefore important to make a serious attempt at helping the student learn to read, utilizing a variety of approaches and materials and providing adequate drill time. Transliteration, rather than being a help, is limited to a single selection and cannot be transferred. If transliteration must be used, it is advisable to dictate the Hebrew passage and have the youngster write it down in English characters the way he/she hears and processes it so that the child can read it back according to his/her own notation system. Chanting also helps to bind the Hebrew into a structure than can be retained more easily.

Unfortunately, children with special needs can still be "handicapped" by the attitudes of others. These "others" are, in some cases, their own parents. Even parents who have come to terms with their child's limitations in the secular world may have a particularly hard time as the Bar/Bat Mitzvah period approaches. Some parents, as well as psychologists and Jewish educators, think that they are being kind to these young people by not "burdening" them with all the extra lessons, expectations, and tensions involved in Bar/Bat Mitzvah preparation. But it is not a burden! The Bar/Bat Mitzvah ceremony and celebration can be the most normalizing and memorable milestone these youngsters can have. In the same way, the joy of adults with special needs who become Bar/Bat Mitzvah at a later age attests to the tremendous power of this event. These adults never had the chance to celebrate becoming Bar/Bat Mitzvah when they were teenagers because it was not acceptable that the process be made available to them at that time. It is hoped that there will be fewer such delays in future years because attitudes in the Jewish community have changed.

Approaching each Bar/Bat Mitzvah student as a unique individual, whether or not special learning needs have been identified, greatly increases the chances of success and achievement. Educators must be aware of different teaching and learning styles. They must be eclectic and pragmatic, flexible, make educated guesses, and be ready to try many different methodologies to find what works for each child. Success is a magical motivator. The potential exists. This is the message of special education!

APPENDIX

Religious School Registration Form

Student's Name: ____
(Last) (First) (Middle) (Hebrew name)

Street Address: ____

City: ______________________ State: __________ Zip Code: __________

Home Telephone Number: (____) ______________ Date of Birth: ______________

Secular School: ______________________________ Grade: __________

Mother's Name: ______________________ Hebrew Name: ______________

Street Address: ____

City: ______________________ State: __________ Zip Code: __________

Telephone Numbers: Daytime: (____) ______________ Evenings: (____) ______________

Father's Name: ______________________ Hebrew Name: ______________

Street Address: ____

City: ______________________ State: __________ Zip Code: __________

Telephone Numbers: Daytime: (____) ______________ Evenings: (____) ______________

In Case of Emergency: ______________________ (____) ______________ ______________
Name Telephone Number Relationship

Are there any problems of which the school needs to be aware? __________ Please comment on the reverse side of this form. The information will remain confidential.

__ Health problems: allergies, e.g., foods, bee stings; hearing or visual problems; frequent need to use bathroom; nosebleeds; chronic illnesses; etc.

__ Learning problems: in reading, writing, comprehension, organization, speech/language, attention, memory, etc.

__ I/We would like an appointment with the Director of Education to discuss further the information on this form.

Parent's Signature: ______________________________ Date: ______________

EMERGENCY INFORMATION:

In case of emergency, do you give your permission to the Director of Education, Rabbi, or teacher, to call your doctor or to take your child to the hospital to receive appropriate emergency treatment?

__ Yes __ No Your Signature ______________________________

Doctor's Name: ______________________ Telephone Number: (____) ______________
Dentist's Name: ______________________ Telephone Number: (____) ______________

Chapter 15
Three Special Children

Cantor Helen Leneman

One who denies a child knowledge of our religious heritage steals the child's inheritance.

(Sanhedrin 91b)

It has been estimated that 10-15% of any school population has learning difficulties requiring special education. These special needs children have a variety of physical or emotional disabilities. But often they are more "handicapped" by the attitudes of others than by their own actual limits.

Although I have no special training in working with special needs children, I have tutored several of them in my role as Cantor. In most cases, the parents helped me provide an enriching experience for their child. But I have also tutored some whose learning difficulties I was not made aware of until very late in the course of study.

I am going to discuss three such special needs children who stand out in bold relief against the hundreds of other children I have tutored over the years. I did not have the assistance of their public school teachers or special private tutors, though obviously such assistance would have benefited both me and the children. Their difficulties were not discussed with candor by the parents, and I was left basically to my own devices in their training. I am convinced in retrospect that all three children were capable of achieving more than they actually did. It is vitally important to work as a team with the parents and with special learning needs experts outside the synagogue, those who know the student's strengths and weaknesses and special learning styles. The tutor will be able to use his or her time with the student far more efficiently if given this knowledge from the outset.

The first two children (whom I will call Amanda and Beth) were both very slow learners, at least two years behind their grade level. In addition, Amanda was mildly retarded and Beth had severe dyslexia and other reading problems. The third child (whom I will call Karen) was believed to suffer from fetal alcohol syndrome. She was emotionally delayed, subject to severe mood swings and occasional tantrums. What all three girls shared was a certain sweetness and innocence rarely found in the mainstream adolescent. In addition, all three had phenomenal musical abilities. They were obviously "auditory learners," and all three had pleasant and accurate soprano voices. Because of these abilities, they worked well with a trained musician and singer.

None of these girls had attended Hebrew School regularly because no provisions were available for them, and their parents felt they would be ridiculed. (This was several years ago; there are many more opportunities available now than there were at that time.) Mainstreaming in the synagogue's Hebrew School probably would have benefited them. Only Amanda attended synagogue regularly, and she had learned to sing several prayers from hearing them often. No other tutor was working with Amanda or Beth on Hebrew or Jewish studies. I was chosen to train them for their B'not Mitzvah because I was the Cantor at their synagogue. They had both also sung in the Junior Choir with my encouragement. Karen had studied rudimentary Hebrew in a special program, and was always eager to look into my Chumash and point to letters she recognized. Yet, in all three cases, I was asked to teach using transliterated Hebrew. The idea of chanting had not occurred to the families. When I explained that it would simplify the learning process, and that it would be particularly meaningful to their children because it was what all the other children did, they were pleased to go along.

I typed up the *aliyot*, indicated by *Aliyah* #1, #2, etc., a total of between 9 and 14 verses, in large print with the words broken down by dashes into syllables. The children could not understand all of my transliterations, so I eventually let them write out the sounds the way *they* heard them. In hindsight, it would have been preferable to let them do that from the start, if not actually to work with Hebrew.

The method was the same for all three: I chanted a phrase and let them repeat it after me. (In one case, I sat at the piano and played the tunes. That did not seem to affect the ease or speed at which this student learned compared to the others.) We then went on to the next phrase. Near the end of the lesson, after repeating two or three phrases many times, I taped those phrases. Typically these children forgot very quickly, and the repetition seemed endless. It takes tremendous patience to work with such children. But the look on their faces when they could chant a whole phrase was the greatest payoff a teacher can get. It is a look of sheer joy and amazement, the look of a child who has always been at the bottom of the educational heap and has never expected to achieve anything. I initially attempted hour-long sessions, but this was an unreasonable length of time to hold their attention. Eventually I switched to 45 minute or even half hour sessions. I began almost a year before the Bat Mitzvah date with Amanda and Beth, but only seven months early with Karen.

The main advantage Karen had was her ability to retain large chunks of material once they were mastered. She rarely went over the verses during the week, yet was able to chant up to ten verses perfectly week after week. But after she had known these ten verses for many weeks, she resisted learning any more. She felt she had worked hard enough and had reached her limit. I regret not spending the remaining months we had left teaching her some more Hebrew, because it obviously meant a lot to her to know even a few letters. Instead, we repeated the few prayers she had learned by rote with another tutor, and she practiced giving her speech. This was the hardest part of the process for Karen, so afraid was she of being ridiculed. Her parents had helped her write the speech and as a result, there were words she could neither pronounce nor understand. It would probably have been preferable to let Karen write something very simple but from her heart. This is true for all children, but particularly for those with special needs. They are rarely given a chance to express themselves, certainly not in public. Giving them the opportunity to do so makes them feel they have something worthwhile to say, and they know people will be listening. This can be a tremendous boost to their self-esteem, which all adolescents need. Special needs children need extra large doses of it.

Both Amanda and Beth rarely mastered more than one verse per lesson, and often forgot that by the next week. Yet, we worked for a full year and in that time, all the material was mastered. In addition to self-respect, they gained some understanding of Torah and of their particular portions. Again, in retrospect, I regret not being able to teach them even rudimentary Hebrew. Their parents were convinced it would be utterly beyond them, and lacking assurance to oppose that judgment, I gave in. I am encouraged by educators such as Sara Rubinow Simon, who insist any child can learn at least some Hebrew and thus achieve a special connection to the Torah and Siddur (see Chapter 14).

The qualities that make a tutor of mainstream children successful are essentially the same for special needs children. Patience, always a necessary ingredient, is needed one hundredfold when working with these children. The ability truly to care for the students, to nurture and support them every step of the way, is also needed. Constant positive reinforcement, and an avoidance of pressure, are other essentials needed in extra large doses. So, too, is having realistic expectations — neither too high nor too low. Discovering each child's personal best is very difficult with special needs children. The assessment will be more accurate if made by the tutor working in tandem with the child's other teachers. The general expectations of special needs children — both their own and others — tend to be low. When greater demands are made, they can usually rise to the occasion. The will to succeed, to be like the other children in Hebrew School, can be powerful enough to overcome many barriers that have previously seemed insurmountable.

The extraordinary demands made on the tutor will ultimately lead to extraordinary rewards. I was told by the parents of all three children I tutored that their Bat Mitzvah ceremony was a life changing event. For the children, it was their first time standing alone and showing off in public what they had learned. It was also life changing for the parents, the extended family and the whole congregation, as possibly the first realization of just how much these children are capable of accomplishing. With patience and persistence, I had helped them reach heights that gave them a strength and self-confidence they had never had before.

Both Amanda and Beth wrote touching, heartfelt speeches. And all three girls stood up on the *bimah* with incredible dignity and pride. Amanda had a stooped posture. Yet, on the day she became a Bat Mitzvah, her back and neck straightened and she seemed to have grown inches in stature. Beth was always so soft-spoken it was difficult to hear her. Yet, when she stood at the Torah, her clear voice rang out confidently. Karen was often sullen and withdrawn, and it was a chore to make her smile. On her Bat Mitzvah day, the smile on her face seemed to glow from deep within. All three girls had emerged from a private shell, a place where they had hidden for most of their lives. They were not hiding now.

Chapter 16
"Panel": Tutoring Special Needs Children

Participants:
Shira Belfer
Jennifer Solle
Zev Halpern
Ellen Goldenberg

QUESTION #1: What is your background? What training and preparation did you have for the job of tutoring B'nai Mitzvah students with special learning needs?

Jennifer: I attended Talmud Torah of Minneapolis, where I was also a tutor for students who were behind. On Shabbat mornings, I received B'nai Mitzvah training, which included learning Torah and Haftarah trope and prayers at my own synagogue. In ninth grade, I became involved in the synagogue's tutoring program. Later I began tutoring students privately, which I have continued to do.

I got my B.A. in Elementary Education and am working on my Masters in Special Education. I have just started a pilot program at a Reform congregation for special needs students who have been turned down or suspended from other Hebrew School programs.

Zev: After completing a Yeshiva education, I received my B.A. and Master of Education in Human Development and Counseling from the University of Maryland Institute for Child Study. I have been actively involved in instructing a diverse variety of special needs children for Bar/Bat Mitzvah since 1975. I am now a Certified Clinical Mental Health Counselor, Certified Employee Assistance Professional, and Certified Addiction Specialist, and am president of an employee assistance/managed behavioral health care firm located in Rockville, Maryland.

Shira: I began to teach B'nai Mitzvah students at age 15, having learned trope and the chanting of Torah and Haftarah from Rabbi Hillel Hyman (z"l), who always cautioned his students to pay attention to details. I earned Bachelor degrees in Music Performance and Music Education at Syracuse University. This program had a special emphasis on behavior modification techniques used as educational tools. I am a graduate of the Cantorial School of Hebrew Union College-Jewish Institute of Religion in New York and I am currently Cantor at Congregation Beth Shalom in Mahopac, New York.

Ellen: I majored in voice and piano at Ithaca College and earned a Bachelor of Science degree in Music Education. Afterward, I taught music in public school for several years. Then I started teaching fifth grade Hebrew school at a Reform congregation and began tutoring B'nai Mitzvah students. I am currently one of three tutors working for a mid-size Reform congregation in Rochester, New York.

QUESTION #2: What sequence do you follow in your tutoring? How many session/hours, if any, do you devote to trope, translation, Hebrew reading, speech, and general discussions?

Shira: In large measure, the methodology I described in Chapters 12 and 21 (which should be used in conjunction with one another) was developed because of special students and special cases. I have worked with the following types of special children, using this methodology very successfully: emotionally disturbed (abused, autistic, hyperactive); developmentally disabled (what some people refer to as "retarded"); physically disabled (deaf, blind).

I treat special children essentially the same way I treat mainstream children, with encouragement and positive reinforcement. I use the *same* methodology with the following considerations:

1. What special devices does the child need to function (medication, physical devices, etc.)?
2. I allocate approximately twice the time in the B'nai Mitzvah preparation process.
3. I usually try to modify the service (or specifically the parts that the Bat/Bat Mitzvah will do) as necessary, so the student will shine and have a feeling of accomplishment.

Ellen: Dealing with learning disabled students presents certain challenges which require extreme patience and creative teaching methods. Frequently I use visualization for students whose aural memory or processing frustrates them. For instance, demonstrating the trope sequence of *darga tevir* as a "musical roller coaster" with a visual (color coded, of course) has helped. *Etnachta* becomes "over the hill." Students whose visual processing is deficient seem to be confused by the vowels and trope, and frequently need to have the text enlarged.

Jennifer: Because most of my students have had special learning needs, I conduct my tutoring sessions in an individualized manner based on the student's own strengths, weaknesses, and needs. I work with most of my students for about one year prior to their Bat/Bat Mitzvah date. The content of the service varies according to the student's synagogue affiliation, background knowledge, and what the parents want. How much material I teach varies enormously: some learn both Torah and Haftarah trope; others learn neither. Some learn the English translations of their portions; others do not. Most students learn some prayers, but the number of prayers varies a great deal.

I color code the "families" of trope and teach one "family" or color at a time. For musically inclined students, this whole process usually takes 6-8 weeks of one hour weekly sessions. For those with auditory processing and discrimination problems, it can take 12 or more weeks. I have some of these students just memorize the tune of the portion chanted, rather than memorizing each of the Torah note's appearance and sound. Of course, in the long run, this is not beneficial, but under time constraints, sometimes it is necessary. Students learn to read their Torah or Haftarah portions and to chant prayers concurrent with learning trope.

QUESTION #3: Can you relate a personal experience with one particular student that stands out in your memory?

Shira: Approximately 15 years ago, I received a call from parents who had been referred to me as a "possible solution" to their child's difficulties. (I will call him David.) They wished their special child (age nine and a half) could have a Bar Mitzvah when he turned thirteen. He had a brain dysfunction which made it extremely difficult for him to focus on any one task for longer than about one minute. As a result, he was not able to learn to read, and he was emotionally disabled. (Others made fun of him all the time, and because he had originally been wrongly diagnosed by school officials as hyperactive, he had lost four years of opportunity for special education.) His parents had discovered, when he was about five, that when certain kinds of music were played, he would suddenly focus and remember exactly what he had heard. At the time that I was called, he was under the care of a psychiatrist and a neurological team which had suggested that music might possibly be the vehicle for getting him to read and learn. Since his parents were committed Jews, they wished that their son could be called to the Torah as a Bar Mitzvah, and they hoped that he would be able to perform at least some small part of Jewish ritual to mark the occasion.

Because of my training in Behavior Modification Technique, and also because of my genuine curiosity as to whether or not it would be possible to teach this child, we decided to embark on an experiment. Using the music of the *brachot* before and after the Torah reading and the Haftarah trope as the vehicle, I decided to try to increase David's ability to focus and concentrate for intervals of five minutes at a time.

We began meeting three times per week at five minutes per time. I sang the sounds (melody) of the Haftarah trope to him in the general patterns with which the trope sounds occur. He instantly remembered the sounds and sang them back to me perfectly. We actually did this for three minutes the first session, and for the full five minutes in the other two sessions. He enjoyed the music, and was hungry for more at the end of the five minutes, but we stopped exactly at the end of the five minutes. I recorded the patterns of trope that I had sung, and handed him a sheet on which the trope marks and their names were written according to the patterns that were sung on that tape (please refer to Chapter 21 for a graphic representation of this). On the days that we did not meet, his parents played the tape and showed him the trope pattern sheet for five minutes each day. At the end of three weeks, nine five minute sessions, he was able to sing a pattern of trope sounds and identify which line on the sheet matched that pattern.

We continued to meet three times per week, increasing the meeting time by one minute each week for four weeks, until we were meeting three times per week for ten minutes at a time. After he could focus for ten minutes, we decided to increase the time of each meeting to twelve and fifteen minutes per time. Soon, David was able to focus on his Bar Mitzvah material for fifteen minutes three times per week with me, and on the days that I did not see him, fifteen minutes per day with one or the other of his parents. Using music/song as the medium, I taught him the letters of the Hebrew alphabet, and at the end of one year, *he could read Hebrew*.

Going into the second year, we decided to increase concentration time in seven minute intervals. By the time we reached the end of the second year, David was able to concentrate on the task at hand for 40 minutes per session. Eventually, we were able to increase his concentration level to one hour per session. Needless to say, once he was able to focus for an hour at a time, he was able to master all the skills required for him to have a Bar Mitzvah ceremony. It was the Torah trope teaching method described in Chapters 12 and 21 of this book that most helped him to focus; he said this himself later on. Ultimately, he chanted three verses from the Torah, and an entire Haftarah with the *brachot*. In addition to participating in a Bar Mitzvah ceremony, David's progress made medical history. He improved in all subject areas, and was able to master all that he needed to catch up to his peers in public school. He was even able to go to college. David and his parents wrote to me that it was his Bar Mitzvah that was the turning point of his life.

I also had two other experiences that stand out for me. I successfully tutored two blind students. With the assistance of the Jewish Braille Institute, I was able to have the students work with texts that had been transliterated into Braille. Again, using the same methodology described above, these students were able to participate in the most important Jewish experience of their lives.

Ellen: Sometimes we may not realize that for a student with deficient visual processing, the "aids" of vowels and trope marks are actually hindrances. Josh was a student who, after studying six verses of Torah for five months, was relieved to see "all those confusing little dots" disappear from his visual field when he was presented with the *Tikkun* page. The next week he learned three more verses!

Jennifer: Kevin had been labeled "learning disabled" and was convinced he was a failure in everything, especially Hebrew. He was a wonderful child, but needed to realize that everyone has his/her own strengths and limits. I began tutoring him one year prior to his date. He learned to chant his Maftir from me and with the help a tape. He learned a few notes, but it was very difficult for him to remember the names and the sounds. However, he enjoyed learning from a tape and headphones. He used the same technique to learn the blessings before and after the Torah, and a few other prayers. He, his parents, and I were all pleased with his progress. Then, the Rabbi stepped in.

Although the Director of Education had told me at the outset that Kevin's disability would be taken into consideration, she apparently had not convinced the Rabbi. The Rabbi informed us (six months into the process) that Kevin did not need to read his Maftir, but that, in order to have his Bar Mitzvah service, he needed to read his Haftarah (which was very long), as well as the blessings before and after the Haftarah. And "by the way," the Rabbi added, "his reading of the Maftir isn't very good and the prayers still need work." Kevin was once again convinced he was a failure. After three months of struggling with his

Haftarah and blessings, his parents and I agreed that, in light of his learning disability, it would be acceptable if he chanted two thirds of his Haftarah.

The Rabbi didn't show up at the first scheduled meeting. At the next meeting, he told Kevin again he was doing it all wrong, could not use transliteration (this for a student who could barely read English), and still needed a lot of work in order to have his Bar Mitzvah ceremony in three months. Also, he would make no exceptions for him, even if he did have a learning disability.

Kevin's parents and I felt we had no choice but to go ahead anyhow and do what we had to do for the Bar Mitzvah. The week before his Bar Mitzvah date, Kevin had learned the Haftarah blessings, and two thirds of the Haftarah, with a lot of ego boosting and self-esteem building. He stood on the *bimah* and did his service wonderfully. The Rabbi was not pleased that Kevin didn't do all of the Haftarah. But Kevin was now a Bar Mitzvah, and he knew that he could accomplish anything and succeed.

QUESTION #4: What works, and what doesn't work? In your experience, what elements make a successful tutor of special needs children?

Zev: From my years of working with many special needs children, I devised this list of suggestions:

1. All parts of the service should be introduced at the first or second lesson, so the child can see the total picture. This can apply to a child whose goal is to chant three lines or to one who will chant the entire portion. Then fragmented sections should be taught. This method is known as "visual chunking"; the size of the chunks is entirely dependent on the particular child.

   The point is not to overwhelm the student, but rather to let him/her know what you are going to try to accomplish together. This is the time to communicate that you are going to help the child "do the best he or she can." This works with all students. Provide motivation by explaining the rewards they will receive (social and tangible) for their effort. This can be extremely meaningful to the child and can provide fuel for extraordinary perseverance on the part of a special needs student.

2. Positive reinforcement in the form of relationship building, important in working with any children, is crucial with special needs children. Some tutors who work with groups of these children together have found it helps to use a "universal positive reinforcer," for example, clapping, handshake, high five, pat on back, verbal and facial excitement, or anything positive that works for the group or for a particular child. This method can also be used one-on-one. The main point is that positive reactions can never be too extreme — one should "light up like a pinball machine" every time the student makes the smallest progress.

3. As reinforcement outside lessons, the tutor can include little messages on the tape that the student works from at home, such as "Good luck," "Work hard," or "See you next week." These are both a way of staying "close" to the student and a reminder of the continuity of the whole process. How students practice at home is crucial. Enlist the help of the parents. With the parents present, model the type of homework/practice sessions you would like to see. Make sure the rewards for practice and study are perceived and received at the student's level of understanding.

4. As the date of the Bat/Bat Mitzvah approaches, take the student to the synagogue where the ceremony will take place to see other children's Bar/Bat Mitzvah services. Point out the different parts of the service as they occur. Seek out the Rabbi and Cantor to introduce the special needs child to them. While this can sometimes be a frustrating experience, attitudes are changing, and we need to be active agents of change. Obtain permission to provide the child with a *bimah* tour. I've seen magical things occur when a special needs child opens the Ark and experiences the tangible reward that holding and touching a Torah can provide.

5. Run through the service several times in the sanctuary. Go through the steps of the service repeatedly. Continue to ask if there is anything the student does not understand. Often the sequence can be very confusing; be very explicit about the

cues for different parts of the service. For example, "When the Rabbi and Cantor approach the Ark, go with them; when they take out the Torah and face the congregation, that is when you start singing the *Sh'ma*." The student may find it helpful to write these cues into the prayer book. Make every attempt to enlist the support of the Rabbi and Cantor to work out specialized cues.

Jennifer: A tutor is not just a tutor. He/she is an advocate for the student when discussing the Bar/Bat Mitzvah with the parents, Rabbi, and/or Cantor. He/she is a detective trying to discover what learning style best meets the needs of the student, and how to teach all the Hebrew material using the most suitable method and a variety of materials. The tutor is a self-esteem builder for the student. A good tutor will teach with a sense of humor and a bagful of patience.

QUESTION #5: From your vantage point as a tutor working for different synagogues, what is in need of improvement in the Religious School or in Bar/Bat Mitzvah programs?

Zev: I feel that Religious Schools and Bar/Bat Mitzvah programs could and should both be doing more to involve the parents as co-participants in the instructional goals and objectives. Adults and children think very differently about the reasons for having a Bar/Bat Mitzvah ceremony. This is a developmental issue and must be addressed to build Religious School curricula with clear goals and objectives.

Jennifer: Every child is an individual and learns in an individual manner. This is especially true for Hebrew. Rabbis, Cantors, and other Jewish professionals must realize this and eliminate the notion of Bar/Bat Mitzvah "factories." Jewish educators should make necessary exceptions for children with special needs, and should be understanding of those students and their families.

Editor's Comments

Everyone should be entitled to a Jewish education, whether in Hebrew school or in chanting from the Torah for a Bar/Bat Mitzvah. All students, especially special needs students, should have a Bar or Bat Mitzvah ceremony. It gives them a goal to work toward, and a tremendous sense of accomplishment that will sustain them for years to come.

The accounts in this and the previous two chapters have illustrated that the enormous challenges of teaching special needs children are more than amply compensated by the tremendous rewards. The process of preparing for Bar/Bat Mitzvah, and the ceremony itself can show these children what they are capable of achieving when given the chance. This realization can change their lives.

Unit III: Teaching Trope

Overview

Trope is an important link in the centuries-long chain of Jewish tradition. Trope melodies may be as old as the Temples in Jerusalem. They certainly echoed in the *cheders* of Eastern Europe. And still today, the sweet sound of an adolescent voice chanting ancient texts is linked in our Jewish consciousness with boys or girls entering spiritual adulthood. Chanting Torah and Haftarah lends beauty and rich color to their ceremonies of passage.

Particularly in this modern, high tech age, learning an ancient skill has deep resonance. Far from the evening news, MTV, and shopping malls, the hours spent mastering this skill and applying it to texts written in another millennium transport the child of today into a timeless place.

Learning trope is a unique challenge to all children, a challenge with ramifications that transcend this specific study. Learning trope takes discipline, commitment, and focus — qualities necessary for success in all learning. It is also safe to say that a student's musical skills will improve during the course of trope study.

In Chapter 17, Cantor Helen Leneman discusses the hows, whys, and whens of teaching trope. Her discussion covers issues involving the instructor, the students, the course itself, and methodologies. Exercise sheets are included. The advantages and disadvantages of a variety of available options are presented.

Chapter 18 is a "panel" discussion including four experienced trope teachers from diverse backgrounds. Although their methods and philosophies differ greatly, all offer cogent explanations for their methods along with concrete suggestions for implementing them. Readers can select what best suits their own situation.

In Chapter 19, Cantor Marshall Portnoy explains and illustrates key functions of cantillation as a grammatical system. He feels the basic functions of trope can be explained in ways that will be clear, as well as fun and challenging for students.

Linda Hirschhorn believes in challenging her students to "stretch." In Chapter 20, she describes a demanding method of trope instruction that can be used for both class and private instruction. She herself does both and is thus in a position to reinforce what was learned in class with each individual student.

In Chapter 21, Cantor Shira Belfer explains her step-by-step method of teaching trope. She outlines a sample lesson, explaining how a Torah portion can be taught from the start utilizing the *Tikkun*, once trope has been mastered.

The *Computer Tutor System*, used by hundreds of schools, synagogues and individuals, was created by Benjamin and Shira Levy. In Chapter 22, they explain how the computer can be an aid in learning Torah and Haftarah portions. Its advantages are flexibility (in terms of musical pitch and speed) and added motivation for today's computer-literate children.

In Chapter 23, the concluding chapter of this Unit, Cantor Helen Leneman provides extensive reviews of the most widely used materials for teaching and learning trope.

Chapter 17
Teaching Trope: The Hows, Whys, and Whens

Helen Leneman

There are many factors to consider when either adding trope to the curriculum or expanding a program in which learning trope may play but a small part. Four areas will be discussed here: the instructor, the student, the course of study, and the methodology.

The Instructor

In many synagogues, the dearth of qualified instructors is a frequently cited reason for not teaching trope. There are several requirements for a successful trope instructor:

1. The instructor should be musical. This does not necessarily imply musical training or even the ability to read music (though that certainly helps), but the instructor should be able to chant accurately and to hear if students are repeating notes correctly. He/she should also have a pleasant voice, to make the course of study more enjoyable and to give the students a good sound to emulate. A definite plus would be the ability to sing in several ranges, so that each student can hear the trope in pitches that he/she can repeat.
2. In addition to musicality and a pleasing voice, a good understanding of the whole trope system is very important. This includes theory, history, and development, as well as the intricacies of the trope language itself. Many trope instructors studied with one mentor, who may have taught only the rudiments. That knowledge may be adequate for a student, but not for a teacher. Within the trope system, just as in a foreign language, there are numerous exceptions, substitutions, and rules. B'nai Mitzvah students do not need to know all of these aspects, but their instructor does, as does the person who trains trope tutors. If the course of study is brief and does not delve into the complexities of trope, the instructor will be inadequately prepared to teach trope correctly. If the instructor learned trope by rote, that is how the students will learn it. Those who learned trope at one of the professional schools, such as Hebrew Union College-Jewish Institute of Religion or Jewish Theological Seminary, are required to spend at least a year studying trope, and obviously have the background to teach it.

   Some instructors are largely self-taught. There are several very thorough books available on the subject of trope (see Chapter 23), so that a highly motivated and musically talented person could probably gain enough understanding from a lengthy course of self-study to become a successful teacher.
3. The trope instructor should work well with adolescents. Trope, because it involves singing, is impacted directly by the physical changes taking place in the adolescent. Boys are dealing with changing voices. Girls, too, want to sound older and will tend to "belt" over their natural high voices. There is a likelihood for far greater embarrassment and self-consciousness in singing than in purely academic areas. The teacher must know how to deal with these stressful emotions in a group setting. Laughter can sometimes ease the tension, as long as it is *with* a student and not *at* him or her. Some teachers might work well with adolescents one-on-one, but the issue of peer pressure is much more evident in a classroom setting. Trope classes should not be offered in Religious School unless there is an instructor who is highly sensitive to adolescent psychology and who knows how to praise all students equally while also keeping the momentum of the class.

4. A good background in Hebrew and Judaica is important. Trope marks will eventually be applied to biblical texts (Torah and Haftarah) as part of the course of study. Teaching content requires a thorough knowledge of Hebrew. Accent and pronunciation problems arise repeatedly when Hebrew is chanted, and the teacher must be able to explain and solve these problems for the students. In addition to this direct application of trope to text, questions may arise during a trope lesson that are unrelated to trope. Having a student's respect is crucial to the success of the teacher in any subject, and being able to answer most questions that arise can bolster this respect immeasurably.

The Student

Trope can be taught privately or to a class. A majority of congregations teach it both ways. Issues involved in private tutoring are covered in Unit II. Classes can be started in fifth, sixth, or seventh grade. Factors of maturity and motivation should be considered when making this choice. A reluctance to sing in front of peers will be more prevalent in the older group. However, the motivation increases greatly as the actual Bar/Bat Mitzvah date approaches. Before seventh grade, the event still seems too distant. For that reason, it is advisable to offer only an "Introduction to Trope" class, without the requirement or expectation that the students will study or remember the material between classes.

When teaching trope to seventh graders as a class, there are positive and negative aspects. The major advantage is the peer support that results from the students' understanding that they are "all in this together." Knowing that they are all responsible for the same material will make them feel less alone, less apprehensive or intimidated.

Class size is critical. If there are more than ten students, trying to hear each student individually becomes a very time-consuming process. In the long run, this is simply not effective. The other students grow restless while waiting for their turn, often creating discipline problems. The teacher can ask small groups of students to chant together, but then it is impossible to gauge the skill level of any given student.

Even in small classes, there are inherent difficulties. The level of musicality varies enormously among students. Those who have the most trouble hearing and repeating musical phrases will need a much greater amount of time to drill. This can become boring for the students who have no trouble with the musical aspect. And since accomplishment in this area is so dependent on innate ability or prior musical experience, students who may be putting forth the greatest effort may still get the poorest results. This inequity can be glaring in a classroom setting, and for that reason the instructor must be extra sensitive here. On the other hand, a well managed class can provide valuable support for all class members.

If there is no alternative to a large seventh grade class, one solution is to divide the class into groups or pairs. Students who have mastered a few trope marks can be paired with those having difficulties. The "student tutors" work one-on-one with the slower students, either in the back of the room (if it is a large space) or in another room. Both students will be eager to show results, so they will be motivated to work hard. This arrangement can only work with a mature group, and it must be handled with great tact. The less musical students must not be made to feel inferior. Emphasize repeatedly that just as some of us are good at sports and others at math, some of us find singing easier than others. The instructor might explain the concept of a "personal best," so that students will not wonder why an obviously weak rendition from one student may earn the same praise as a perfect rendition from another.

The Course of Study

There are many possible components of a trope course. Factors to be considered when choosing these components include the following:

1. Will this be private instruction or a class?
2. How many sessions will there be, and of what length?
3. Will the course include Torah trope, Haftarah trope, or both?

The ultimate goal or objective of the course will determine the answers. The goal for the student will be a combination of the following, from most to least common:

1. To learn enough trope to chant Torah and/or Haftarah at the Bar/Bat Mitzvah ceremony.
2. To learn trope for its own sake, as a Jewish life skill.
3. To become a tutor for the synagogue.
4. To become a Torah reader for the congregation.
5. To read Haftarah again at various times throughout the year.

Depending on the goal, the instructor, and other factors, the following are all possible components of a trope course. (Several examples of courses can be found in the books discussed in Chapter 23.)

1. Basic introduction to trope: its background, origins, and purposes.
2. A packet for students consisting of several pages of trope phrases (no text), with and without the names of the trope marks, for learning and drilling purposes.
3. A tape of the trope corresponding to the packet. (See Appendix 1 for examples of items #2 and #3.)
4. Pages of musical notation of the trope signs.
5. Samples of different texts of Torah and/or Haftarah with trope.
6. Various games for reinforcement. (See Appendix 2 for one example.)

Advantages and disadvantages of some of these elements will be discussed in the next section.

Methodology

There are numerous pragmatic and philosophical differences in the way trope instruction is approached. There is no right or wrong way, as long as the students master trope in a reasonable length of time and have some understanding of the system. Many exercise sheets, games, text examples, and other materials have been based on published texts, reworked, and treated as original packets for so many years now, that the original sources have been forgotten. In spite of the preponderance of certain methods, trope defies standardization because the melodic renditions are never exactly the same. The "Lithuanian" and the "Binder" trope systems may be frequently heard, but even these common systems are not always chanted precisely. Renditions common to the west coast are often unknown on the east coast, and vice versa. For this reason, no musical notations have been included in this book. The exercise sheets and games may be used with any melodic system.

There are several options in teaching trope, whether privately or to a class (see below), that show the greatest variability from synagogue to synagogue.

1. The order in which the trope marks are taught

   There are two views governing this choice: (1) it is better to start with the most common, easiest marks and (2) it is better to start with the rarer and more difficult ones. Starting with the easiest groups — *mercha-tipcha, mapach-pashta* — gives students a sense of accomplishment in mastering something quickly. If texts are used near the beginning of the course, these simple trope marks can be easily applied. Marks learned at the beginning of the course will be reinforced for many weeks and will, therefore, be the strongest ones. Since they are the most frequently used, this will give the student a good anchor. The disadvantage of teaching these easier groups first is the time factor. If time is limited, there is a risk that the more difficult marks — *pazer, tlishot* — which are harder to master, will not be well learned.

   The advantage of teaching the difficult trope marks first is allotting enough time for students to learn them. The other plus is the psychology of "getting them out of the way." But there is a danger of spending too much time trying to master these, and too little on the basic, more frequently used marks. It can also be daunting, especially for the less musical students, to start off the course with complex tunes like the *pazer.*

   Whichever order is ultimately chosen, the most important rule is to stick to a timetable. Any trope mark that is not learned well can be drilled and reinforced later on.

2. The use or non-use of musical notation

   Musical notation is an enormous boon to students who read music. They can learn any trope mark directly from the music, either by singing it (if they sight-sing) or playing it on the piano at home. Some tutors believe that even non-readers can benefit from musical notation because they can relate to the dots of music going up or down on the page.

   Some synagogues have produced their own adaptations of musical notation by writing the words of the trope with the syllables rising or falling on the line according to the musical line.

This form of notation also indicates how many notes are given to a single syllable, much as musical notation would.

No one method is effective for every student. There are students who read music, but find it easier to master trope without the written music. Some students will relate instantly to the alternate method described above, while for others it will be a source of more confusion. Using musical notation in a classroom setting obviously puts those who do not read music at a disadvantage, and has the potential of alienating and frustrating them. Including music sheets as part of the course material can make these students feel they are missing some essential knowledge. It is preferable to include music sheets as an optional choice, if at all, without putting any stress on this option.

Since actual melodies differ from congregation to congregation, musical notation is not transferable. Teaching trope without music transmits the idea that it is a flexible system, not a rigid one. After all, trope did not have its beginnings in musical notation. Too much stress on musical precision takes away some of the beauty of improvisation. The dual purpose of trope is expressiveness and punctuation. This should not be forgotten.

3. When to begin using trope

Applying trope to biblical text is the skill that any course is ultimately aiming for. How soon this should be attempted depends mainly on the Hebrew reading level of the students, although musical skill should also be considered. Putting words to music is a difficult skill to start with, and if either the words or the music are a hurdle for the student, that doubles the difficulty.

If the first applied text is identical in syllables and accentuation to the trope words themselves, this can be very reinforcing for the students. For example, *mercha-tipcha* is the same as *va-yach Moshe* in accents and numbers of syllables. But there are few such instances. When one syllable words, words accented on the first syllable, multi-syllable words, hyphenated words, or single words with two trope signs, must be sung to trope melodies, this is a skill in itself. It entails adapting the tune learned with one accent and note pattern — that of the trope name itself — to an entirely different pattern of accents and notes. Very few students can do this correctly at first sight. It is the most difficult skill of all, and the most time consuming to master. It makes no sense to attempt it unless the trope melodies and the text are well learned first. Since this is a lengthy process, it makes more sense in most cases to save it for the private lessons, when the students learn their own individual portions phrase by phrase.

A trope course the goal of which is to train future tutors or Torah/Haftarah readers will be much longer than a normal introductory course. In such a course, time should be spent studying all the variables in applying trope to a text. This skill is necessary for true mastery of trope.

4. The use of an instructional tape

Many synagogues do not provide tapes to B'nai Mitzvah students because they believe students will not use them anyway, or they will practice incorrectly. The hope is that students will drill enough in the course of a lesson to retain the melodies. However, this places a lot of pressure on the instructor to ensure that all the students have mastered whatever trope marks were taught in the lesson. Another reason for not providing tapes is to avoid the kind of musical rigidity discussed above. Students may feel they must learn to repeat each tune note-perfect as per the tape.

Just as LP records were used in B'nai Mitzvah training long before portable cassette players become commonplace, so one day the use of tapes may be completely overshadowed by the advent of computer disks. Learning trope by computer is the most recent development in Bar/Bat Mitzvah education, and is discussed more fully in Chapter 22.

In spite of some disagreement, the large majority of synagogues do provide trope tapes. There is much greater disagreement on the taping of individual portions. Synagogues in which trope is not taught at all routinely provide each student with a tape of his or her Torah and/or Haftarah portion. Learning a portion this way is a rote procedure. Tutors often do not know trope themselves, and when unsure of the correctness of a student's rendition will simply play back the tape. Since this chapter is concerned with teaching trope as a system, such a procedure need not be discussed.

Synagogues are divided on whether to provide an individual tape in addition to the trope tape. If done properly, this can be viewed as a reinforcement of the learning of trope. Very few students have studied enough trope or Hebrew to master a portion in the few months they have without daily reinforcement. Even with private lessons, those who are weak Hebrew readers or are unmusical will not be able to improve from lesson to lesson because they will not be able to correct their reading or their tunes. They may actually be reinforcing their errors. For this reason, providing tapes of the portions after the student has learned trope and can read the portion with some fluency should not be labeled rote learning. It enables students to hear verses as they should sound and thus gives them a model and a goal.

It is preferable in many cases to tape during the lesson a verse or a small section at a time. At the lesson, the student will work on each new section using his/her understanding of trope. Once it is done correctly at the lesson, a tape will provide important reinforcement for the following week of study.

5. Teaching trope with flash cards vs. in phrases

Trope flash cards have become a popular teaching device. They are useful for learning the names of the trope marks. However, trope is a system of phrases, not individual sounds. The names of the marks are never used without their corresponding melody, and since learning the melody is more crucial than learning the name, they should never be separated. To link the word *mercha* indelibly with the tune to which it is sung is the goal of trope instruction. If a student calls *ytiv* by another name, but sings the right tune, he/she should not be criticized.

Since trope marks are divided according to their function, either standing alone as "independents" or always linked to another mark as "dependents" (there are many variations on this terminology), it is useful to teach them this way. Students should be taught from the start that there is a rhyme and reason to all this. No trope mark appears accidentally. Trope is a form of punctuation and expression. If this is explained, chanting will be easier because it will make more sense. For example, a few verses can be chanted in English utilizing trope melodies, to clarify the function of trope. (See Chapter 19 for an example.)

Dependent signs such as *mercha* and *munach* never appear outside a phrase, so having students try to sing one of these from a flash card does not accomplish anything. Only usable and meaningful skills should be taught. *Mercha* should be taught right from the start together with *tipcha*, whether this is done with flash cards or simply from a sheet with boxes representing missing Hebrew words (several examples can be found in Appendix 1). Other grouped signs, such as *mapach-pashta* or *kadma-v'azlah*, should all be taught as phrases. If flash cards or overhead projections are seen as more effective teaching devices, they should be adapted to a correct grouping of the trope marks. Once the most common groupings have been learned, different combinations can also be introduced (see Appendix 1). The one aspect of trope that will never be used again is the names of the marks, except in those rare instances where the Bar/Bat Mitzvah student is expected to become a tutor. Therefore, no undue stress should be laid on learning these names. Mastery of the tunes and the way they normally appear in biblical texts is the final goal of trope instruction.

6. Teaching trope names in Hebrew or transliteration

The names of the trope signs are usually taught using Hebrew letters. The exception is whenever musical notation is used. Since it is a skill seemingly unique to Israelis to be able to read music from left to right simultaneously with the Hebrew syllabified left to right, no B'nai Mitzvah students are ever asked to duplicate this mind-boggling skill. Therefore, when musical notation is provided, the names of the trope marks are transliterated. (This also makes it easier for students with weak Hebrew skills to learn the trope names.) Transliteration in general is an ill-advised method of learning a language, however, and for those students who have depended on that method in the past, learning trope this way simply reinforces that dependency. Having eventually to master many verses of Torah and Haftarah in Hebrew without this crutch is a far more difficult job for these students. It might be advisable just to insist on the trope names being learned from the Hebrew letters exclusively, prior to transliteration with musical notation.

A unique alternative to both of these is the system devised by Cantor William Sharlin. Since the Aramaic-Hebrew terms for the trope marks refer to either their shape or their tune, Cantor Sharlin decided that native English speakers would not relate to them in this way. But since they were originally named in such a way to ease the learning process, he rewrote them in English to produce the same results. The great advantage to his system is that it is fun for students. Also, they do learn trope more quickly because relating the names directly to the shapes and sounds aids the learning process. They also do not have the additional step of mastering the more difficult Aramaic-Hebrew terms. It is an ideal system for students with Hebrew deficiencies. Its main disadvantage, and the reason it will probably not be widely adopted, is its very uniqueness. *Mercha-tipcha* is a universal system, very rooted in tradition and used everywhere. Students who learn it for their Bar/Bat Mitzvah might years later become tutors while studying in college in another state, and they will still use the same terms. One solution is to teach *both* systems. The Sharlin method (reproduced in Appendix 3) can be used to learn the trope tunes, and later in the course of study, *mercha-tipcha* can be taught.

7. Including technical explanations, such as rules and exceptions

   Including technical explanations in a trope course is likely to turn students off. There are numerous rules and exceptions in the trope system, but it is usually more effective to explain these when they are encountered in the course of learning a portion. "Learn by doing" is often the best method for teaching a multi-faceted skill such as trope. The exception to this is when training B'nai Mitzvah students who are expected to become tutors in their own right. Training such students would be like training adult tutors, and some recommended books for such a course are discussed in Chapter 23.

Conclusion

It is my hope that through the suggestions in this and the following chapters, synagogues that did not know how and where to start teaching trope will derive not only inspiration, but also the wherewithal to begin implementing a program that includes trope in its curriculum.

APPENDIX 1

Trope Tape: Table of Contents

I. TORAH TROPE: "Signs and Names"

II. TORAH TROPE: "Trope Exercise Sheet"

III. HAFTARAH TROPE: "Signs and Names"

IV. HAFTARAH TROPE: "Trope Exercise Sheet"

V. HAFTARAH BLESSING (with trope)
[Not reproduced here; widely available]

APPENDIX 1 (Cont.)

Trope Signs and Names

1. מַרְכָ֥א טִפְּחָ֖א מֻנַּ֣ח אֶתְנַחְתָּ֑א

2. מַרְכָ֥א טִפְּחָ֖א סוֹף־פָּסֽוּק׃

3. קַדְמָ֨א מַהְפַּ֤ך פַּשְׁטָא֙ מֻנַּ֣ח זָקֵף־קָטֹ֔ן

4. מֻנַּ֣ח|מֻנַּ֣ח רְבִ֗יעִי קַדְמָ֨א וְאַזְלָ֜א

5. אַזְלָא־גֵּ֜רֵשׁ גֵּרְשַׁ֞יִם דַּרְגָּ֧א תְּבִ֛יר

6. יְ֚תִיב פָּזֵ֡ר זָקֵף־גָּד֕וֹל

7. מֻנַּ֣ח זַרְקָא֮ מֻנַּ֣ח סֶגּוֹל֒

8. תְּ֠לִישָׁא־קְטַנָּה֩ תְּ֠לִישָׁא־גְדוֹלָה

9. מַרְכָ֥א טִפְּחָ֖א סוֹף־פָּסֽוּק׃

APPENDIX 1 (Cont.)

Trope Exercise Sheet

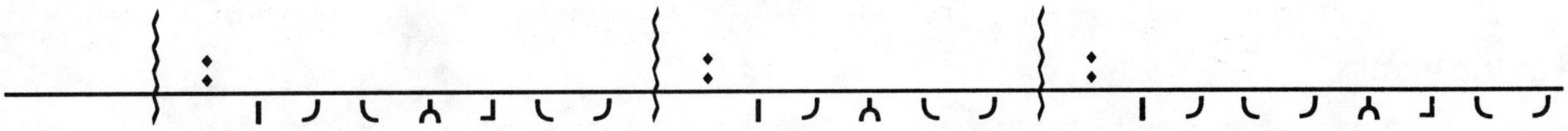

.1

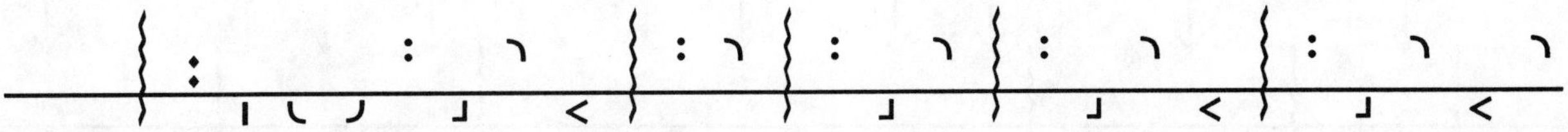

.2

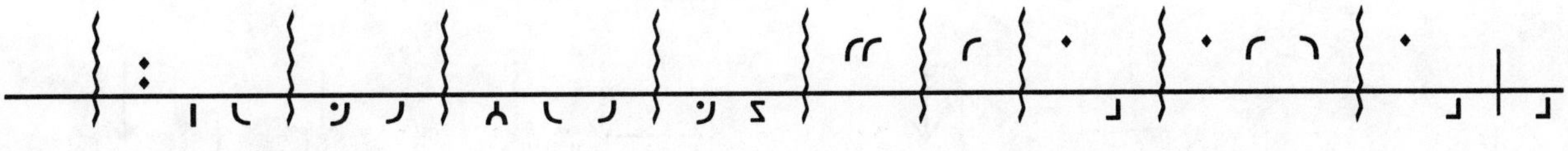

.3

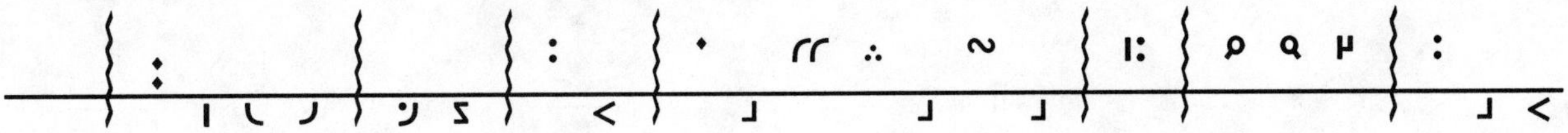

.4

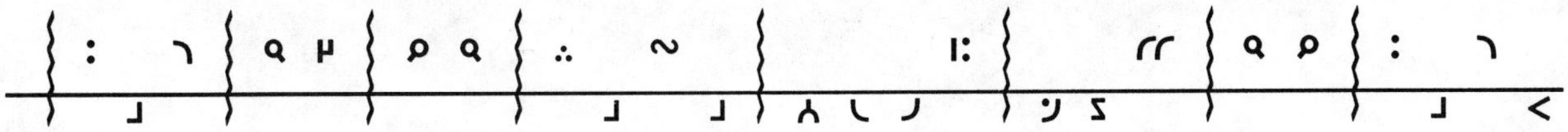

.5

Concluding Exercise

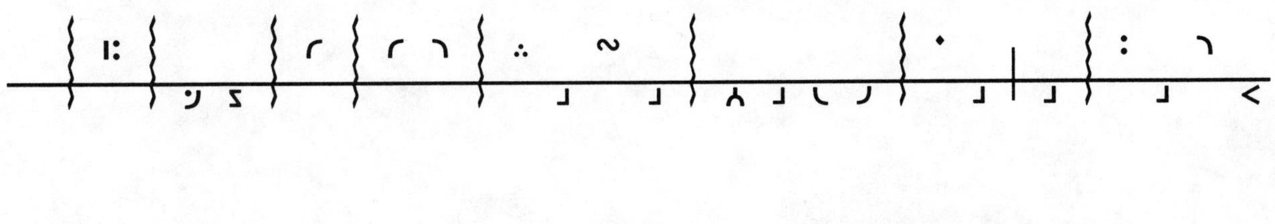

APPENDIX 2

Trope Phrase Completion Game

Fill in the blanks.

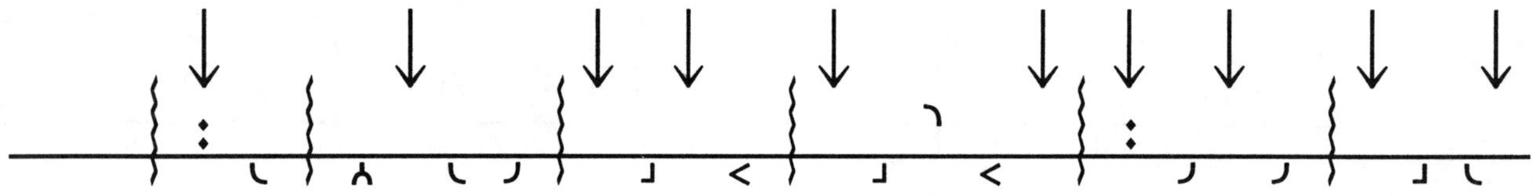

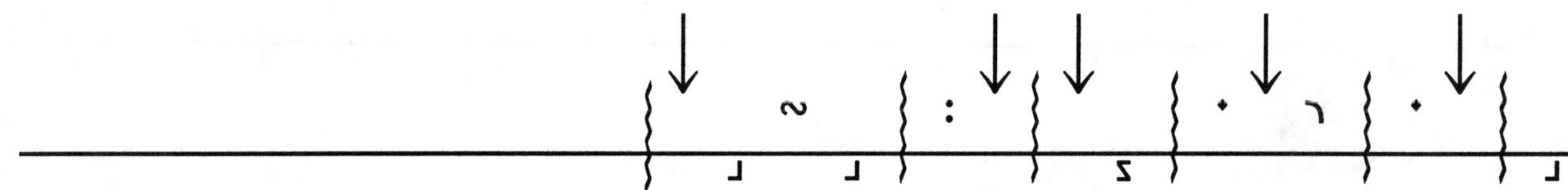

APPENDIX 3

English Trope Names

(Created by Cantor William Sharlin)

*1. open parenthesis

2. closed parenthesis

*3. right angle (Note: melody depends on the sign that follows)

4. upside-down wishbone

5. vertical line

6. pre-apostrophe

*7. bird's beak

8. apostrophe (Note: always appears over last letter)

9. vertical eyes

*10. backwards Z

11. open eye

APPENDIX 3 (Cont.)

12. eyelashes

13. black diamond

14. upper parenthesis

15. right lollipop

16. left lollipop

17. pre-beak <

18. backwards 4

19. eyes and line

20. sideways S ∾

21. tri-dot ∴

•These are "conjunctives" and never stand alone; they are always the first part of a melodic pattern.

Chapter 18
"Panel": Strategies for Teaching Trope

Participants:
Ellen Goldenberg
Marsha Fensin
Neil Newman
Nathaniel Schudrich

QUESTION #1: Do you teach trope privately or to a class? And how do you begin the course of study?

Ellen: I teach trope exclusively as a private tutor. The uniqueness of my approach is that I teach Torah and Haftarah trope at the same time. In the first lesson, I begin with Torah trope, teaching *mercha-tipcha*, the *etnachta* group, and *sof pasuk* variations. I emphasize the fact that the last part of each group is the deciding factor as to which group the trope mark belongs. This is especially important when explaining combinations which contain *munach* and *mercha* with other signs. Most students have already learned to chant the "*V'ahavta*" in class. When I was teaching fifth grade, I was the one who taught this prayer, so students all learned it with the correct trope melody. Assuming they learned the "*V'ahavta*" according to trope, they have some ear for the modality of Torah trope. I frequently refer back to the Siddur to demonstrate trope groups, and reassure students that this is not as overwhelming a task as they might think.

To create a transition between Torah and Haftarah trope, I conduct a brief review of one or more prayers from the Siddur or hold a short discussion about the meaning of the verses studied. The remainder of the first lesson is devoted to Haftarah trope. We go over the first Haftarah blessing, which they have previously learned in class. Once I am sure there are no inconsistencies in the melody they learned, I add the trope markings and color code all of the *mapach-pashta-munach-katon* groups in the blessing. This way, the student is already comfortable with the melody of the most difficult and varied Haftarah trope sequences. We spend much time arranging trope flashcards, trying to master various sequences of this group, especially those that are found in the blessing.

Marsha: I used to teach a semester course on Haftarah trope, but I now do only individual tutoring. When I taught the class, we began by studying the background of Haftarah: students learned the origins of trope and got a list of all the prophetic readings corresponding to each *parashah* of the year. When I began the actual teaching of trope, I always started by teaching the Haftarah blessing, for which students had both the musical notation and the trope marks. The course delved into the function of each trope, and included various games and quizzes to reinforce recognition of the trope marks. My course also included a complete vocabulary list, containing all words of the *brachot* with their roots and definitions.

Neil: Our curriculum includes a full Unit on *T'amim* (trope marks). It begins with an introduction, in which we refer the students back to the "*Vayomer*" paragraph of the "*Sh'ma*" which they have just learned, and points out that they have already had a chance to hear what Torah cantillation sounds like. We also point out that the "*Vayomer*" paragraph will be a handy reference, if they learned it well, should they get "stuck" later on, since it uses many of the melodic phrases that are found in Torah cantillation. The first three sentences of "*Vayomer*," we further point out, contain individual notes and even full phrases that the students will begin learning in class in the coming weeks. So the first class begins with the students practicing those phrases, first by reading them with the correct accents (by noting where the trope mark is placed) and then singing them. Each student has a "buddy" in class, and at this time the students pair off and practice singing these three phrases. *Then* the word and concept of *ta'am* and *t'amim* are introduced and explained.

QUESTION #2: What is the next stage in your course? Do you move directly to text, or continue drilling trope?

Nathaniel: I teach individual students exclusively. I find it takes about three or four weeks of lessons for them to have a grasp of trope, and that's when we start looking at the Haftarah. I don't start using text with trope until the student can chant trope relatively fluently. I find it's too fragmented to teach the text along with each trope phrase. You need the tools before you can use them. Also, before I move on to Torah trope, I try to teach prayers to the student for a few weeks, to give them a break between the two. I also tell them not to even look at Haftarah trope while they're learning Torah trope.

Ellen: In the first lesson, after isolating the trope groups for the first three verses of a student's Torah portion, I have them study the entire three verses with their study tape for the next week. Sufficient examples of variations of the trope groups taught so far are usually found in two or three verses.

I do the same with the first verses of the Haftarah. In general, the student isolates the trope groups just learned in the first few verses of Haftarah, but is only asked to review the Haftarah blessings and one or two verses of Haftarah.

For subsequent lessons, the order in which other trope groups are introduced in the Torah portion depends mainly on which trope marks are most frequently used in that particular portion. In the second and third lessons, the *munach revii* or *darga tevir* groups might be isolated, and any other group or mark which comes more than once or twice in the student's portion. Each time, we go back to the beginning of the portion to color code new combinations. Remember, the student has learned these phrases by rote for two weeks, and is now integrating the color coded trope signs with a tune that is already familiar. As progress is being made in the Haftarah verse by verse, more of the Haftarah trope melodies become familiar — each group is isolated by color, sound, and reference to the original Haftarah blessing. The student is encouraged to begin each study session of Haftarah with the blessing. This sets the mood for the new tonality.

As is consistent with the philosophy of the congregation, the emphasis is definitely placed on the mastery of a quantity of Torah over Haftarah. In another two weeks, a bridge is made between trope signs of the *mapach* group in Torah and Haftarah.

Marsha: I apply the trope to the text right away, so that students can get used to seeing the trope marks repeat over and over again. I constantly emphasize to them how simple it all is. I make a tape of their portion, and we learn the system along with the text. When I taught the semester course, I used the phrase by phrase method. I explained that learning trope by phrases helps them to sound as if they actually understand what they are chanting. We also discuss how trope delineates a verse grammatically. Of course, I present this material according to their ability to understand these concepts.

Neil: I explain to students that their job is to learn the trope marks and their names, and to be able to sing each *ta'am*, or note, on pitch. I tell them that everyone is born with different levels of musical talent and skill, but that often a person can make up for little talent in singing with hard work and effort. I then explain that since these notes were originally organized in phrases for the most part, it is best to learn them that way. I then introduce the *mercha-tipcha-munach-etnachta* phrase. They practice it in several variations, and drill phrases with their "buddy." Then I immediately introduce the "really hard part" of learning this system: applying it to actual Bible text. I present several Bible phrases with all the trope variations and combinations they have just learned.

I continue in this manner through all the trope marks, and provide a packet of trope drills and a corresponding tape.

QUESTION #3: Do you utilize musical notation to teach trope?

Marsha: In the semester course, I provided musical notation of the trope marks, as well as the *brachot*. When I do individual tutoring, I give students the music, but they don't have time to use it as much as in a class situation. If they have had music lessons of some kind, they might pick it up and play with it at home. But in actuality this seldom happens.

Neil: My course does utilize musical notation. It is printed alongside each trope group and all its variations.

Nathaniel: I don't use musical notation to teach trope. I suppose it would be a good idea, but it's just never been my approach.

QUESTION #4: Do you have any special methods or aids to help students learn trope?

Ellen: I find that it is helpful for students to use colored pencils to color code and delineate trope groups. This gives them an extra visual cue.

Marsha: Students learning trope obviously mimic the sound of the teacher's voice. We have an unusual situation in that one of our Rabbis loves to sing, but isn't very good at it. I encourage him, though, because he provides a wonderful role model for students who themselves are not the best singers. My philosophy is that everyone, musical or not, can chant a Haftarah. I try to provide an encouraging atmosphere for the "tone deaf" students, and they usually rise to the occasion.

Nathaniel: First of all, I always explain the two parts to every trope, the "introductory" note and the main melody. Then I can explain how these two parts appear in words. I sit down with the words in front of me and demonstrate that idea by singing some words and pointing out the two parts of the melody as I do so. I may even do this with English words to clarify.

To emphasize trope phrases, I will put little lines in the text, dividing the phrases. Often I'll ask students to sit with a pencil and mark off the phrases themselves. I have them mark their own mistakes, too.

To get students with singing problems to expand their vocal range, I have them sing an "ah" vowel while they glide their voice over many tones. Each week I have them go higher, until eventually they realize what their range actually is.

Conclusion

There are as many variables in methods of teaching trope as there are teachers. There is no right or wrong way to do it, but there are distinct teaching and learning styles. If students are well matched with tutors, both will thrive; otherwise, each will struggle. We can hope that teachers and tutors will continue to adapt and find new ways to help their students reach their goal and, ideally, to continue beyond.

Chapter 19
Cantillation

Marshall Portnoy

Cantillation, to me, is far more than the accentuation of the Tanach; it's a way of thinking. What other system can convey the meaning of a sentence beyond the shadow of a doubt, give you a pleasant way of conveying that meaning to a congregation, and even tell you what syllable to stress?

Cantillation, to me, is a commitment to the words of Tanach — that they be conveyed in such a way that they cannot be misunderstood. So, the first question I ask a group of students is: "What causes a public speaker to be misunderstood?" The group gives all possible answers: mumbling, mispronunciation, misphrasing, and misaccenting (e.g., does "project" mean a task or to show something on a screen? Does "perfect" mean flawless, or to make something flawless?). I dwell a lot on misphrasing — that meaning is both *effected* and *affected* by pausing, for example:

We dislike class clowns. Like you, we find them disturbing.

We dislike class clowns like you. We find them disturbing.

Once the students understand the reason for cantillation, I review some of the history behind it. I ask them to learn such terms as *chieronomy*, *ta'am*, and *neume*, which is the proper word for trope. I don't insist they master these terms. I do insist, however, that students understand the *purposes* of the *t'amim* (pausal power, accenting, and musical declamation), and how the *t'amim* achieve this by location of the sign on the word and in other ways.

I teach combinations of the trope melodies, most common first, least common last. I apply the trope to text immediately, but I do it first with English sentences (read right to left) that the children make up, such as:

(It-was-closed. alas) (to-the-store went) (Michael and Samantha)

(tomorrow," come-back "Let's) (said, Michael)

(it-was-open. they-returned and-when) (with-him; agreed Samantha)

The students are taught to notice that the trope marks generally fall above or below the first available letter in the accented syllable, and that they appropriately divide the sentence into its meaningful components. I give out all the aids I can — notated music, fast, slow, and medium speed tapes. I want to make it as easy and as much fun for the students as possible. I encourage them to make flash cards for themselves, so that they can practice writing the signs and recognizing them instantly.

Since pausal power is the most significant purpose of cantillation, I try to get the students to perceive the hierarchical relationship among the trope marks. It is important that students differentiate between those signs that continue a thought (like *mercha*) and those that stop a thought (like *etnachta* or *tevir*). Actually, the students intuit these relationships very quickly, and are soon ready to recognize the families of trope marks that comprise our cantillation system.

Since this is not difficult for the students, I have never understood why some teachers fail to differentiate between the *pashta*, a disjunctive trope, and the *kadma*, a conjunctive. To initiate the blessing before the Haftarah with the "*Baruch*" sung as a *pashta* is to miss the point. The words do not mean "Blessed — You are the Lord our God," but "Blessed are You, Lord our God." A *pashta* can and often does complete a phrase, but a *kadma* never can; a *kadma* always leads us to a next trope. Some teachers are worried that their students cannot learn about pre-positives and post-positives. Believe me, not only do they learn it easily, but they find it fun, like solving a crossword puzzle. I teach them the following rules:

1. If it's a *pashta*, it falls over the last letter of the word.
2. If it's a *kadma*, it falls over the first letter of the accented syllable; thus, it almost never falls over a word's last letter. When it does, you'll notice that it's notated a little to the right of the final letter.

Now for the complicated part: since we've learned that the trope falls on the accented syllable, I explain that if a *pashta* word is not accented on the last syllable, there is a secondary *pashta* on the accented syllable to show where to stress the word.

I believe all students are musical enough to distinguish between the highs and lows required by the cantillation. Of course, not all children can learn all the trope marks and melodies and the basic concepts governing their interaction. We make appropriate demands on each student as common sense and compassion dictate. Thus, one student may be asked to prepare two verses in a week without a tape, while another may be hard pressed to prepare four words in trope with the aid of a drill tape. (I sing on the drill tape and the student repeats. He/she then sings along with that repetition at home.)

Do what works best, while helping to create a situation in which the student feels good about himself/herself. If what you're doing doesn't work, you can always try something else. But if the student isn't happy, nothing will work. Trust, mutual respect, and a warm genuine personal transaction are more important to the student, and to you, than all the trope systems in the world. With this approach, you may wind up teaching more about cantillation than you ever thought possible.

Chapter 20
On Teaching Trope

Linda Hirschhorn

As a teacher, I work from two main premises. First, students are capable of far more than they imagine themselves to be, and it is therefore the teacher's duty to challenge the students to stretch beyond themselves. Second, it is often good to start with the most difficult material first.

This second assumption may sound strange, but in the case of Torah and Haftarah chanting, I have found it to be particularly true. For the student who has mastered the system of Torah chanting successfully, Haftarah chanting comes as a relief, and requires only minimal instruction time. Students who have cut their teeth first on Haftarah, on the other hand, will feel daunted by how much more they will be required to do to get a handle on Torah chanting.

Having explained my motivation, let me go on to my methodology. There is only a slight difference between giving lessons to a private student or teaching a class. I will describe my methods for both situations. The size of the class does not affect the methodology. Currently my class consists of five students; last year's class had 15. The class meets twice a week for two hours. The first requirement of all my students is that they be able to read Hebrew with reasonable fluency. Those students who cannot read well enough are required to get additional tutoring. For the first two months of class, we study Torah trope once a week during the last 45 minutes of class. I hand out four pages of musically notated trope marks. I do not use a tape. Even the person who has never seen a piece of music in his or her life can still recognize shapes that are higher or lower than each other. This helps fix the shape of each melody in the student's mind. The process of studying from the music in class helps the student learn to refer independently to the music when studying alone.

I first teach *mercha-tipcha-munach-etnachta* and variations of the *sof pasuk* sequence. I explain the concept of the changing melodies of some signs depending on the sign that follows it (for example, in the case of a *mercha* preceding a *sof pasuk*.) Sometimes I tell the joke about the person on the bus who wants to get off at Broadway and doesn't know where the stop is. He asks his fellow passenger, who says "Just watch me and get off one stop before I do."

With private students, I immediately apply the trope just learned to a text. In a class, however, it is not an efficient use of time to have each student experiment with his/her knowledge of beginning trope phrases, so we skip that step for now.

In the second trope lesson, I go on to the *mapach-pashta-munach-katon* family. When these melodies feel comfortable, we practice going back to a *tipcha* from *pashta-katon*. One of the benefits of using musical notation is that you can point out the relationship of ending notes to beginning notes; for example, the last note of the *katon* or *etnachta* is the starting note of the *tipcha*. This helps ground them in correct key relationship. If you assume what I call the "stretch principle," even unmusical students will learn to chant in their own fashion. It may not be as pretty as we might like, but it will nonetheless be an approximation of the correct tunes.

The second lesson continues with the *kadma* family and *gershayim*. With *kadma*, it is necessary to explain that a sign can look identical to another sign (*pashta* in this case), but depending on what follows or precedes it, or its placement on the word, it goes by a different name and melody.

Each lesson begins with a review of the preceding pages. The third and fourth lessons cover *munach revii*, *darga tevir*, and the *tlishot*. Since these are a little trickier melodically, constant repetition is very helpful. The last two lessons include *zarka*, *zakef gadol*, and *ytiv*. I take a couple of weeks for review. You can use any games or gimmicks you want. One example might be a card divided into 20 squares. Each square shows one of the trope marks (with or without its name). You sing a word with a trope melody, and the students put a marker on the correct trope. A series of four in a row of correct trope marks is "Bingo."

Three months into the class, I teach the Haftarah blessings. The melody of the blessings sets the groundwork for learning the Haftarah trope. If the students are all becoming B'nai Mitzvah around the same time of year, I will teach them the new trope sounds as a class; otherwise they will learn them in individual sessions. At this point, they are thoroughly familiar with the names of the trope marks, the sequences in which they regularly appear, and how to apply a trope melody to a word. It takes no more than two lessons for them to learn the Haftarah melodies, particularly since these melodies are familiar from the blessing they have already learned. I deviate from my "no tape" principle here. For students who confuse the two melodies, I will make a tape of the Haftarah trope, which they can listen to while they follow the musical notation.

After the trope classes are completed, I start individual lessons. At the beginning of the year, students receive a booklet with their Torah and Haftarah portions. By the time they start their individual lessons, they have already read their portion in English. They have been asked to choose a section of 20-30 verses that they found most interesting or with which they disagreed most strongly, on which they would like to develop their *drash*. These are the verses they will learn to chant. I provide no tapes. If they can develop the skill of figuring out the melody for each word, they will remember it better and will be able to use it beyond their Bar/Bat Mitzvah date. Most important, they will feel really great about themselves for having mastered something so terribly difficult.

In the first individual lesson, I explain how the accents work. I explain that the change in melody of the trope comes on the part of the word under (or over) which the trope appears. I explain other rules as we encounter them: for example, the double *pashta* over a word, when to use a *kadma,* how to sing a *mercha-pashta*, and others. If the first few verses of a student's portion look particularly difficult, I might start with an easier section, such as one with many *mercha-tipcha* combinations. After these explanations, I immediately go to text and demonstrate the application of these melodies. Then I have the student try chanting a few words by himself/herself. Within a very short time, students are able to do four words this way. I have them practice several times until it begins to roll smoothly off their tongues. At that point, we shift to the "Torah" side of the page (no vowels or trope), and to their amazement they can still chant the four words they have just practiced. Thus, from the very beginning, I demystify the whole notion that it's so very difficult to read from the Torah because there are no dots, trope marks, or punctuation. This half hour lesson should cover at least one full verse from both sides of the page. The assignment is to prepare that verse from the "Torah" side for the following week. Students should get better and better, and eventually should be able to get a handle on an *aliyah* of three or four verses in two weeks at most. Of course, some portions are more difficult and longer than others and will take more time.

With this method, students learn their seven *aliyot* plus Maftir in about three or four months. Naturally, there are always differences between students. Some will go much slower, others will want to stop after three *aliyot* and Maftir (this is the minimum requirement). The teacher/tutor has to be the judge in each case. They will all have learned trope skills, in any case.

Some students chant all of the Haftarah, while others choose to do only a part. The latter students read the portion beforehand and select what appeals to them. If very pressed for time, you can teach them only the trope melodies that appear in the section they have selected. The primary goal, skill in the system itself, has already been achieved. Most students need only two to three more weeks to chant the Haftarah smoothly.

My total teaching time comes to about six months per student based on a half hour lesson per week, with occasional extra long lessons as needed. At the end of our time together, the students and I feel great about the process and the results.

Chapter 21
Strategies for Teaching Trope

Shira Belfer

As I discussed previously (see Chapter 12), I consider singing to be one of the least important skills involved in the B'nai Mitzvah training process. For the musical student, the singing aspect is no problem. I do often find, however, that even musical students have trouble on occasion moving from one trope to another. It is useful in these cases to point out the musical interval from the last note of the last trope to the first note of the next trope. Usually, once students hear this interval, they have no trouble. For example: moving from *kadma* to *mapach* in Haftarah trope, the "*ma*" of *mapach* starts on the same note as the "*ma*" of *kadma*.

Students may also have trouble remembering the pattern of a trope mark or how many notes to sing, or they will miss notes in the middle of a "long" trope mark, such a *pazer*. In this case, I find it useful to have students draw an actual graphic pattern for themselves of the notes as I sing them, next to the trope marks with which they are having trouble. (This is *not* the same as looking directly at notes themselves, which most people find quite confusing.)

Example: *kadma v'azlah*:

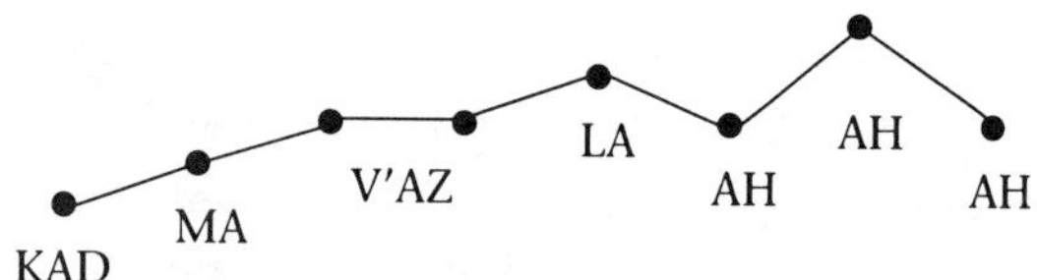

Some students may have difficulty "hearing" certain notes or trope melodies. I do not worry about whether the sounds that these students produce are particularly musical. I am only concerned with whether the sounds that are produced approach the *pattern* of the sounds of the appropriate trope for that particular word or sentence.

I insist that my students learn the trope sounds for both Torah and Haftarah, and the names of the trope marks themselves. I teach the music aurally, and do not provide the musical notes unless someone specifically asks for them. I have found that for most people looking at a page full of notes is confusing. I believe that it is easier to learn the trope "alphabet" itself than any other symbols. Colors, a popular trope teaching device, teach the student only how to identify colors and not sets of words or trope marks; they are also completely useless afterward. As I tell my students, our ancestors learned to read Torah and Haftarah with trope. So, if it was all they needed, it should be all we need. The tropes and their phrasing patterns also aid in retention of this material.

I prefer to teach trope in a class setting initially. (I realize it is not possible to arrange for a class in many congregations due to time considerations.) All B'nai Mitzvah students at my congregation take a class (30-40 minutes once a week) during the six month preparation period before the Bar/Bat Mitzvah. In this class, I teach all *brachot* for Torah and Haftarah; basic prayers; reading, singing, and understanding why and when we do these prayers, and what they mean. I then work with students on an individual basis on the trope melodies and these prayers when they have their private lessons.

Using the methodology described in Chapter 16 and this chapter (either with or without the B'nai Mitzvah class), it usually takes a student one week to learn the names of all of the trope marks, and two weeks to master the musical sounds for Haftarah trope. Usually, it takes two to three weeks to master the sounds for Torah trope. I teach Haftarah trope first, because in my experience, it is easier for the student to learn it first. Also, not all students read the Torah for Bar/Bat Mitzvah, whereas virtually all of my students chant some or all of the Haftarah. I use the blessing before the Haftarah to teach Haftarah trope. Trope marks are applied to the text immediately for both Torah and Haftarah. This way the students learn two things simultaneously: the blessing itself and the trope, both the names and the musical renditions. For Torah reading, both melody and words are applied immediately to each phrase on the "Torah" side of the *Tikkun*. In other words, the students read from the side with no vowels or trope markings *immediately* as they learn the reading in phrases. This is quite different from the way most teachers teach Torah reading.

I do use cassette tapes to help students learn both musical sounds and reading. Things are recorded both at the lesson and beforehand, such as particular sets of phrases, trope melodies, and patterns of trope marks, problematic words and phrases, and the student's Torah and Haftarah portion. Students use the tape at home for practice only and never during the lesson. I caution my students not to rely on a tape, and to learn how to decipher the trope themselves. Once students have confidence in knowing the trope marks, very few of them actually want to learn with a tape; they try to do it on their own. I encourage this, unless they are making too many mistakes. In that case, I urge them to work with the tape, and to pay more attention to details when working on their own.

Here is a sample lesson to teach Torah reading: Using a photocopied page from the *Tikkun*, I have the student *read* the first phrase of the first verse out loud *according to the phrases from the trope*. Then the student immediately transfers to the "Torah" side (the left-hand column, with no vowel or trope markings) and *reads* only the words of that phrase from the "Torah" side. Then we transfer back to the right-hand side. The student *sings* the trope for that phrase, then the trope (*melody*) *simultaneously* with the words. Next, we transfer back to the "Torah" side. The student sings the words and melody *only for that phrase from the "Torah" side*. I then congratulate the student on just having "read his/her first words from the Torah. This is very important for the continuing motivation of the student in a daunting process.

Now we go back to right-hand side. We proceed with the next phrase, and follow the same methodology as above. As soon as the student can sing the second phrase correctly from the "Torah" side, sing the first two phrases together *from that side*.

We proceed with each phrase as above until the student can chant one entire verse from the "Torah" side. Then we go back to the right-hand side and start the process over for the next verse. We continue this same process in phrases for all verses that need to be learned. I do not have the student learn more than four long verses of Torah at one lesson. Three verses per lesson is an ideal number.

For Haftarah, I follow the same methodology in terms of learning by phrase. Because there is no transfer involved (Haftarah is only rarely chanted from a scroll), the student can learn up to six verses per lesson. More than that will only produce mistakes and hamper the learning process.

Conclusion

This method makes learning trope easy for any student. Students also understand what they are learning and why, thus facilitating the learning process. Constant positive feedback creates an ideal learning environment, and ultimately this is reflected in the end result — the ceremony itself. At that ceremony, students can proudly utilize their knowledge as they take their place as adult Jews, chanting from the Torah and Haftarah before their congregation.

Chapter 22
Trope by Computer

Shira Levy and Benjamin Levy

Lev Software was founded in 1988 with the goal of creating useful computer programs for people of all ages who are interested in Hebrew and Jewish education. Our first computer program, *Haftutor,* was developed after research showed a need for such among teachers and Bar/Bat Mitzvah students. *Haftutor* was well received in Israel by users and critics alike. In 1989, five new programs were added to comprise what is now known as the *Computer Tutor System.* This System has found its way into hundreds of homes and synagogues in America.

Unique to the *Computer Tutor System* is the ability to merge Hebrew text with customized melodies, so that each synagogue can have selected material on disk available to congregants for home use and in the classroom. The System can adapt to any trope specification, so that individual traditions are preserved.

Description of the *Computer Tutor System*

The System includes three main pieces of hardware:

1. An IBM compatible, personal (laptop) computer with graphics, 640 KB memory, and disk drives (preferably with a mouse).
2. A computer projection panel which connects to the computer and dynamically reproduces the image on a large wall or silver screen.
3. A portable overhead projector with 300 watt halogen bulbs.

The System consists of three main software programs:

1. *Haftutor* – The complete set of 54 weekly Haftarah portions from the Prophets and 27 special portions chanted on holidays.
2. *Torah Tutor* – The entire Torah complete with all trope.
3. *Tefila Tutor* – 30 *tefilot* customized to a particular *nusach* determined and provided by the Cantor or music director.

The three software programs are identical to each other in operation. Once the user learns how to use one, they can all be used. It is so easy that one does not need any previous computer experience and does not have to make any hardware modifications whatsoever.

Program Description

The program starts with two scrolls opening up. Introductory text teaches the user how to use the program. The user presses a key and gets a menu (see Appendix 1).

The user makes a menu selection and gets a screen with four lines of Hebrew complete with trope and vowels. The cursor appears in the shape of a *yad* which points to each syllable as the melody is played through the speaker. Keyboard function keys instruct the program to sound the notes one syllable at a time or continuously (with or without transliteration). Tempo may be speeded up or slowed down. Pitch may be raised or lowered in a two-octave range (see Appendix 2).

Aid in Hebrew skills

All of the programs in the System hone Hebrew skills for adequate Bar/Bat Mitzvah preparation. The main computer screen display is always in large Hebrew letters with vowels and trope markings (where appropriate). With the use of the mouse, students can "click" on a Hebrew letter and discover the name of that letter. The student can remove or insert vowels and trope with one keystroke. Reading Hebrew without vowels presents a challenge to most non-Hebrew speakers, but these programs offer the easiest and most effective medium of practicing. Transliteration for each and every syllable is also just a keystroke away. Unlike printed transliteration, the student cannot "fake it" by reading the transliteration below or to the side of the Hebrew. The computer will show one syllable at a time so the student can crack difficult or yet unfamiliar sounds. With the optional "Hebrew Talker," not only is the syllable shown on the screen, it is correctly pronounced by a voice box as well.

Aid in Liturgy and Trope Skills

The *Computer Tutor System* helps to motivate teachers for liturgy and trope skills. Trope skills are easy for anyone who can carry a simple tune. The trope programs (*Trope Tutor, Haftutor, Torah Tutor*) link the connection between words and melody. A trope can sound different depending on how many syllables there are in the word(s) to which it is connected (see Appendix 3).

The student controls the tempo of the melody, and actually plays one syllable at a time. Very quickly, one can put words and melody together. The program's ability to regulate the musical key to suit a particular vocal range is a unique feature not possible with tapes or video.

Parental Involvement

The System helps get parents actively involved with their child's progress in the preparation process. Parents whose Hebrew skills are "sketchy" can spot check their child's Hebrew reading by stopping and transliterating a word together. Or, they can follow the *yad* as the text is read or chanted. In this way, they always know where the student is reading. Adults can use the blessings included in the System to brush up for an *aliyah*.

Evaluation

How do these programs compare with other teaching tools? The computer is a compelling device, fast and versatile. Using it as a teaching tool makes as much if not more sense than using a cassette tape recording or even a prerecorded video of a Bar Mitzvah ceremony. For those who believe in using only printed materials, the computer can do that, too — as many pages and as many times as desired.

Some have asked, "Why replace the cassette tape recording?" Another question might be asked, however: "Why did the cassette replace the use of the reel-to-reel?" And before that, "Why did the reel-to-reel replace the use of the vinyl record?" In a few years, when a new and superior invention comes along, people may ask, "Why did "x" replace the computer in Bar/Bat Mitzvah preparation?"

Synagogue Use of Computer Program

The System described herein is designed for synagogues of any size or denomination. It has three main advantages:

1. It is affordable and cost effective (the Bible never needs updating). You can spread the investment over 10 years and more. By selling individual copies to parents, synagogues even make money.
2. The programs all concentrate on Hebrew skills which are at the core of Jewish education.
3. The programs can be tailored to suit any text or melody.

The Rabbi of a congregation in Minnesota (800 families) has her students using the *Computer Tutor System* on a network of seven computers equipped with earphones. She says her students especially enjoy being challenged by the speed of the programs, making it as fast as possible and trying to keep up.

Aid to Professional Staff

With the *Trope Tutor* program customized to the Cantor's *nusach*, a trope standard is established. Future tutors will use the established trope and continue the synagogue's traditions. Customizing (merging text and melody) is done in three phases:

1. The Cantor writes the music out in standard music notation, and fully vocalized Hebrew text.
2. Lev Software personnel transcribe the above to computer files.
3. Specific Haftarah and Torah verses assigned to the student, plus the blessings and liturgy, are made into a personalized diskette which the individual student can take home.

Rabbis who have not learned trope as part of their initial training can teach themselves using the *Computer Tutor System*. Cantors or tutors who use the computer to drill Hebrew and trope skills have more time to work on content with their students. The program adds structure to the lesson, as the screen printouts provide periodic checkpoints of progress. A Cantor who has a computer set up in his/her office can then add exciting music software to help with other musical duties.

Although many teachers are hesitant at first (since computers are still new to them), the *Computer Tutor System* is so easy to operate and student reactions are so positive that all are soon won over. Using the System saves time and creates a better learning environment for everyone.

Conclusion

It is evident that computer technology will be with us well into the twenty-first century. Students of today are already using computers in every aspect of their secular education. Jewish education now begins to catch up, using the *Computer Tutor System.*

For the last 25 years, Bar/Bat Mitzvah training methods have often centered around memorizing from a prerecorded tape produced by a Cantor or tutor. The System changes the focus from memorizing someone else's performance to improving on Hebrew and trope reading skills. Students can build on these skills for years to come. The wide acceptance and praise of the *Computer Tutor System* makes it a viable option for any Bar/Bat Mitzvah teacher with an eye to the future.

(For information on Lev Software, write P.O. Box 17832, Plantation, FL 33318.)

APPENDIX 1

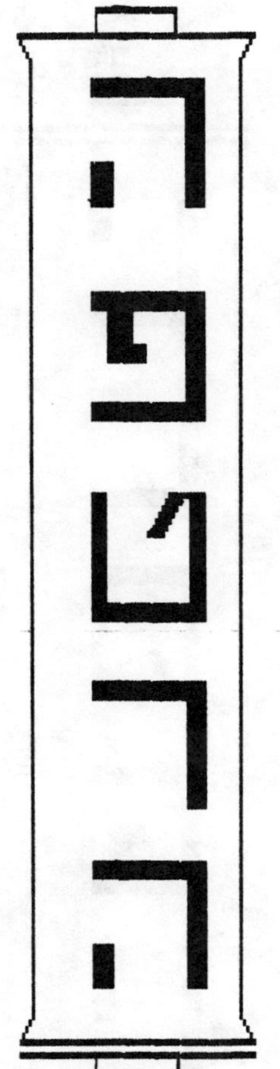

Your Name

H A F T U T O R

Produced by: LEV Software

1-800-776-6538

Haftara Number ?

01 - BERESHITH
02 - BRACHA BEFORE HAFTARA
03 - BRACHA AFTER HAFTARA
04 - BRACHA BEFORE TORAH
05 - BRACHA AFTER TORAH

ENTER

HELP F10

EXIT ESC

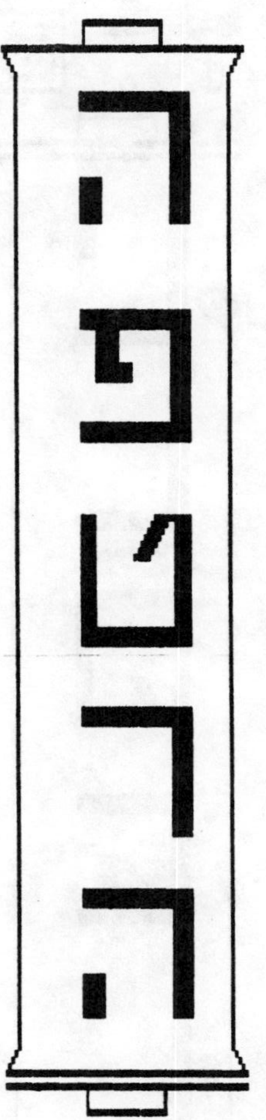

APPENDIX 2

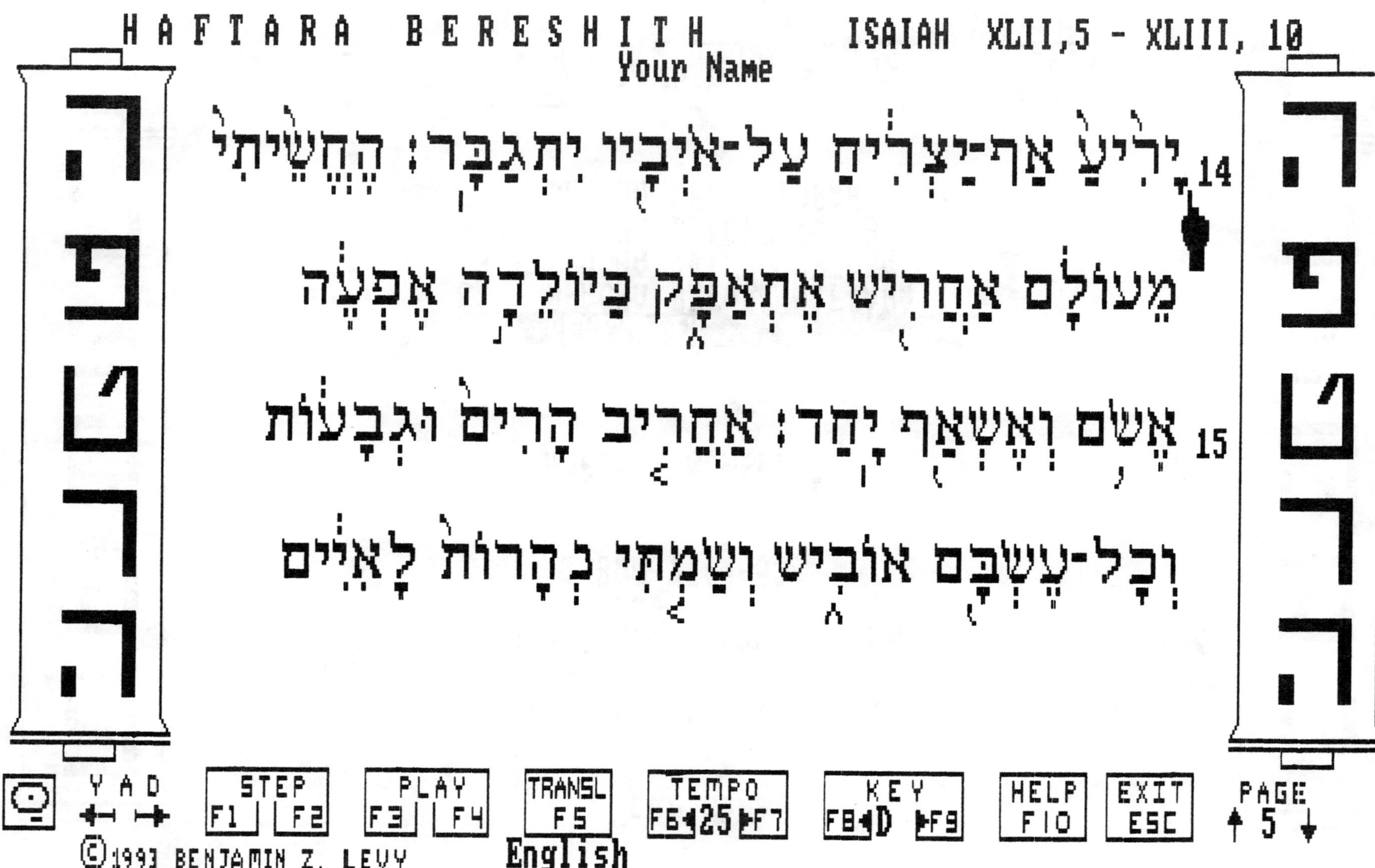
HAFTARA BERESHITH
ISAIAH XLII,5 - XLIII, 10
Your Name
הפטרה
14 יָרִיעַ אַף־יַצְרִיחַ עַל־אֹיְבָיו יִתְגַּבָּר׃ הֶחֱשֵׁיתִי
מֵעוֹלָם אַחֲרִישׁ אֶתְאַפָּק כַּיּוֹלֵדָה אֶפְעֶה
15 אֶשֹּׁם וְאֶשְׁאַף יָחַד׃ אַחֲרִיב הָרִים וּגְבָעוֹת
וְכָל־עֶשְׂבָּם אוֹבִישׁ וְשַׂמְתִּי נְהָרוֹת לָאִיִּים
YAD
STEP
F1 F2
PLAY
F3 F4
TRANSL
F5
English
TEMPO
F6 25 F7
KEY
F8 D F9
HELP
F10
EXIT
ESC
PAGE
5
© 1993 BENJAMIN Z. LEVY

APPENDIX 3

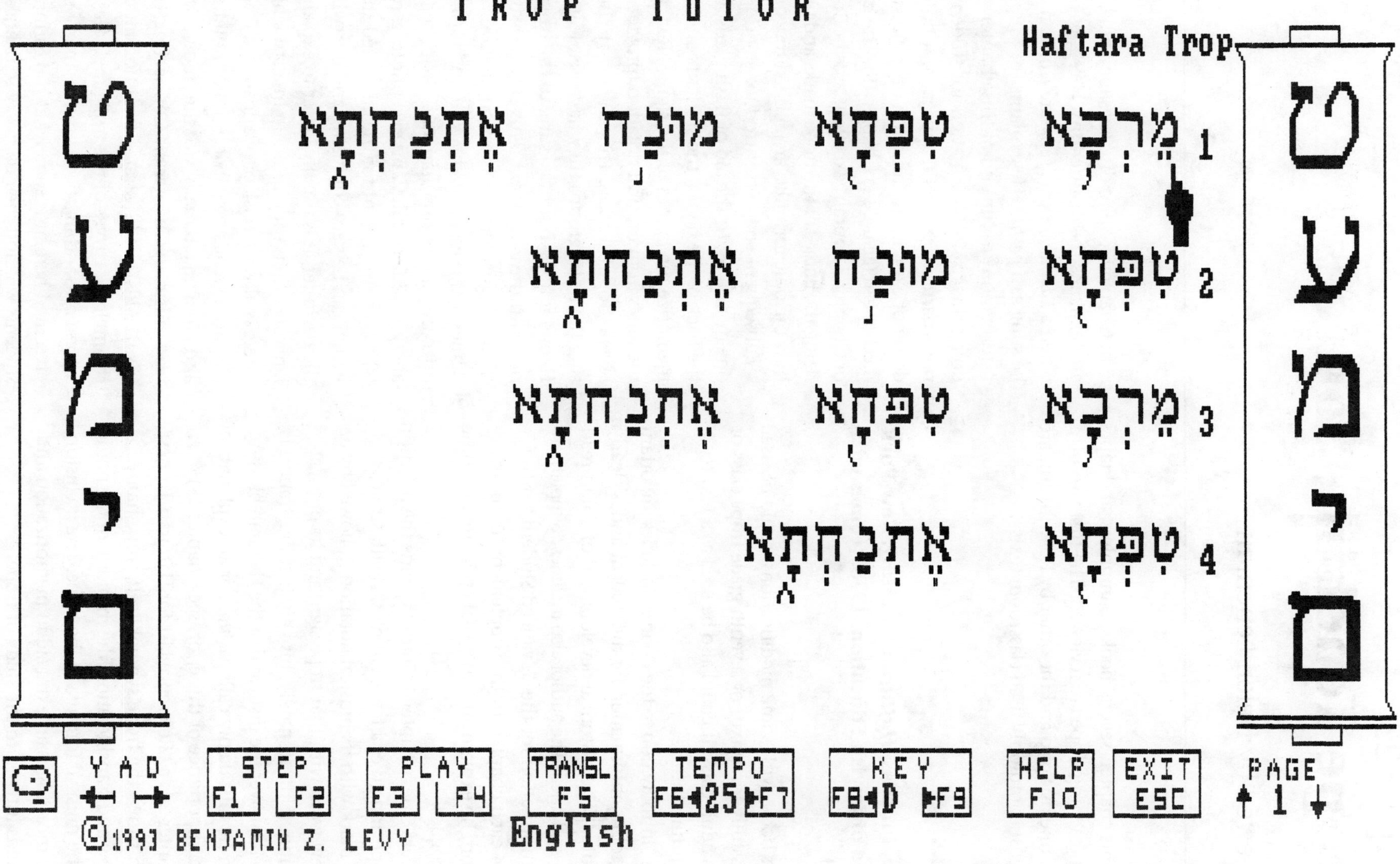
TROP TUTOR
Haftara Trop
טעמים
1 מרכא טפחא מונח אתנחתא
2 טפחא מונח אתנחתא
3 מרכא טפחא אתנחתא
4 טפחא אתנחתא
טעמים
YAD
STEP F1 F2
PLAY F3 F4
TRANSL F5
TEMPO F6 25 F7
KEY F8 D F9
HELP F10
EXIT ESC
PAGE 1
©1993 BENJAMIN Z. LEVY
English

Chapter 23
Trope Teaching Sources

Reviewed by Helen Leneman

In this chapter, several books, pamphlets, and tapes about teaching trope are reviewed. The first two of these, one by Spiro and the other by Rosenbaum, are the most commonly used classroom texts.

BOOKS

Spiro, Pinchas. *Haftarah Chanting*. New York: Board of Jewish Education, 1978. (comes with tape)

This book, with some modifications, could be used successfully for a sixth or seventh grade trope class or for an adult class. It could also be used as a text to train future tutors.

The "Introduction to the Course" includes important background information for the student and is clearly presented. The historical development of Torah reading is explained. The author also includes "Supplementary Information for the Advanced Student" at the end of each chapter. In the supplement to this introduction, he explains the triennial cycle used in some synagogues.

In Part One, Chapter 1, Spiro explains the function of trope and gives a few examples. He illustrates a trope mark with its musical notation, followed by a Hebrew word with that trope sign, and its musical notation. (Unfortunately, his very first illustration is of a *kadma* over the first word of the Haftarah blessing which he mistakenly calls *pashta*. For an explanation of the importance of this error, see Chapter 19).

Chapter 2 is a "Reference List for Haftarah Tropes" which shows the trope symbol itself, trope name in Hebrew and transliteration, the meaning of the name, and the musical formula of the trope. The inclusion of the meaning is an extra aid in memorization and also adds interest to the study of trope.

In Chapter 3, Spiro discusses look-alike trope marks and explains the distinctions. He states here that when a *kadma* appears separate from an *azla*, it is to be sung as a *pashta*. He explains (in "Supplementary Information" at the end of this chapter) that he is doing this to simplify matters for students, but this is not a particularly useful approach. It unfortunately does not explain the function of trope as a phrasing mechanism (again, see Chapter 19). The last two pages of Chapter 3 contain excellent aids both for memorizing the names of the trope marks and understanding how melodic formulas are applied to words.

Subsequent chapters introduce the trope phrases one by one. With the aid of flash cards (included in the back of the book), the students are to try to memorize the names of the signs. Next, they learn the tunes from musical notation (provided), and drill several trope exercises. They then try to isolate and to sing the trope groups they have just learned in Haftarah texts, but have sung to the trope words and not with the actual text. This sequence is logical, but there is a great deal of stress on memorizing the trope names first. Most students will find it easier to memorize the names simultaneously with the tunes. Spiro also gives many rules and exceptions throughout, which are important for the advanced student, but which can be very confusing and overwhelming for the beginner. It is usually better to explain these rules later on, when they come up in a student's portion. There is always a risk of overload in a trope course.

Spiro depends heavily on music notation, but he also offers an alternative for the student who does not read music. In Chapter 8, "Connecting Tones and Visual Aids," he illustrates a method for delineating the melodic curves of the trope melodies. The idea is a good one and has been used by many teachers. As presented here, it is somewhat too formulaic. Most students will find their own way to delineate melodies, and what works best for them is what they design themselves.

Applying trope to words is not done until Part Two, when students presumably have a good grasp of trope. Before text is introduced, some basic rules of Hebrew accentuation are explained in a very clear and straightforward manner. Following that explanation, numerous examples are given of how to apply different trope melodies to words of two, three, or more syllables and with different accents. The idea is a good one, but it might be preferable to let the students start experimenting with trope and text, and bring up the examples when they arise. In any case, hundreds of phrases are given with trope marks for students to try out. No musical notation is given, so the students would need supervision to ensure they are chanting these phrases correctly. Parts Three and Four offer pages of trope exercises with words, followed by three sample Haftarah portions for the student to try out.

Part Five contains the Torah and Haftarah blessings. In the Haftarah blessing, Spiro unfortunately took the liberty of altering all the *pashtas* to look like *kadmas*; not a single one appears in its proper place over the last letter of the word! This is sure to bring up questions from the student who will encounter this blessing printed correctly in many other texts. This should therefore be kept in mind by the instructor.

Part Six is a "Supplement for the Junior Torah Reader" and introduces the trope, including explanations, musical notation, and drills in the same manner as Haftarah trope was taught, but in a condensed fashion. Suggestions on how to prepare a Torah reading are given, along with musical notation for High Holy Day and *Megillat Esther* trope. This is all very useful material for the advanced and self-motivated student. Even such a student, though, would probably need a Cantor or tutor to assist him or her from time to time.

With some modifications by the teacher, this book is a very thorough and clear approach that can be used successfully for either classroom or individual instruction.

Rosenbaum, Samuel. *A Guide to Haftarah Chanting*. New York: Ktav Publishing House, Inc., 1973. (comes with tape)

The philosophy behind Rosenbaum's approach is that the whole cannot be understood without first analyzing each component part. His book has been widely used and misused, in the form of photocopied pages that have been circulated and taken out of context. His approach is quite different from Spiro's, because he focuses even more on learning the trope names without music. He also stresses learning trope *words* over *phrases*.

The Introduction, "So You'd Like To Chant a Haftarah?" is an excellent, interesting explanation of the development of trope, written to be understood by a twelve-year-old without being condescending. Unit One proceeds with a page devoted to each trope mark: the rules that govern it, and ten Hebrew phrases in which the student is to isolate that one trope mark and pronounce the word correctly. This approach initially avoids both the phrasing and musical aspects of trope. After the trope marks for one phrase are learned, students are asked to isolate and mark individual trope marks for full Haftarah portions (printed in the book).

Rosenbaum also discusses the content of these portions, which is a good way of incorporating important material that also gives a context for the study of Haftarah trope. Only after this is done for several portions does the author discuss the fact that the signs just learned make up a group. He then proceeds in the same way through all the trope marks. (Incidentally, he explains the *pashta* exactly as Spiro does, without qualifying the explanation as an oversimplification. It is a pity, as Marshall Portnoy notes in Chapter 19, that these educators underestimate the ability of students to grasp the difference between the function of a *kadma* and a *pashta*.)

Rosenbaum's book does not introduce the actual *singing* of trope until Unit Two, 50 pages into the course. This approach totally separates the two skills of word and tune memorization. The introduction to

"The Trope Tunes" is again very well written and will be interesting to the twelve-year-old, as well as to adults.

The approach to learning the tunes is the same as learning the words: the tune for each trope is learned separately, and then the groups are put together. Musical notation is also used. Rules and exceptions are sprinkled throughout as they arise. *Kadmas* are treated throughout as *pashtas* unless followed by an *azla*. If text study were included, the discrepancies of phrasing would immediately pinpoint this error. This book, however, is designed to be a technical manual for learning trope. The sad reality is that time constraints and a dearth of teachers with deep understanding of texts precludes inclusion of a more ideal, multifaceted approach.

Unit Three includes the Torah and Haftarah blessings with their musical notation, as in Spiro. However, some of the wording in Rosenbaum's introductory remarks is not gender sensitive (e.g., that *brachot* "make a man aware of his dependence on God," that "a number of men are honored with an *aliyah*," and the honor of chanting a Haftarah is "usually given to . . . any competent man of the congregation").

Five complete Haftarah portions are included in large print in the back of the book. The first few phrases of each are marked off in boxes, and the student is advised to follow that example and mark the entire text that way. This is an excellent exercise, although it should surely be checked by a teacher. This stress on phrasing, however, was not evident earlier in the book.

If a teacher wishes to use Rosenbaum's book, but does not agree with the method of analyzing parts before looking at the whole picture, the book can be used in a variety of ways. It is a rich collection of textual examples and interesting, well presented information.

PAMPHLETS

The following pamphlets, one by Neumann, and the other by Gellis and Gribetz, are also of interest.

Neumann, Richard. *The Roots of Biblical Chants.* New York: Board of Jewish Education, 1982.

This slim pamphlet contains a brief, interesting introduction to the historical development of trope. The author discusses the evolution of Torah chant and its influence on Western music, with musical examples.

The most fascinating aspect of this booklet is its illustrations of several hand signs, which were the origin of the trope symbols as we know them today. The illustrations of hands forming the signs against a black background are clear and will be of interest to any student of trope. Also included in the pamphlet is a list of the Torah trope marks, including the meaning of the words and musical notation. A similar list of Haftarah trope marks is also included. This booklet provides a bibliography for the serious student of trope, and is aimed more at adults than children.

Gellis, Maurice, and Gribetz, Dennis. *The Glory of Torah Reading.* Jersey City, NJ: M.P. Press, 1982.

Gellis and Gribetz wrote their pamphlet based on over 50 years of experience each as a *ba'al koreh* (professional Torah reader). This is not a booklet for the novice, but would serve as an excellent reference guide for the fine points and esoterica of Torah trope.

The first part of the booklet explains essential rules of Hebrew grammar, because the authors feel it is the lack of this kind of knowledge that mars so much of Torah reading today. They then discuss each trope mark and the rules that govern it. They are very precise and always discuss grammatical rules alongside trope rules, making this a difficult text for someone not well versed in advanced Hebrew. Their belief is that such a person should not be reading Torah. They also mix in Torah commentaries in their explanations of some exceptional trope and grammar cases. There is no musical notation provided.

Trope instructors who have encountered a *shalshelet* and wondered how many times it appears in the Torah, and under what circumstances, will find the answer here. Inquisitive students have asked their tutors the meaning of the *pay* or *samech* printed after certain paragraphs in their *Chumash*; the answer can be found here. In short, this is an excellent booklet for the tutor or Torah reader interested in refining his or her skills, but would not be useful as a book for a course.

Rosenberg, Yitzchok Mordechai. *T'aamim Lakorim*. New York: Chadish Press, 1981. (comes with tape)

In his "Introduction to the Teacher," Rosenberg describes this spiral-bound publication as a "cantillation curriculum." One stated goal of the curriculum is to "help prepare tomorrow's Torah readers." The book contains complete texts for readings of frequently recited Torah and Haftarah portions, Megillot, High Holy Days, Rosh Chodesh, and others. Complete tapes of all Torah and Haftarah portions, along with all other readings for the year, are available from the Chadish Media catalogue. The two tapes reviewed here supplement this textbook.

Tape #1 starts with one verse samples of each trope system, in a very "cantorial" voice, with Ashkenazic pronunciation and using "*Hashem*" in place of "*Adonai*." Despite the assertion by the author that this book may be used by all schools, it is difficult to understand for whom this course is intended.

Unit I of the textbook is a basic introduction to cantillation, containing numerous generalities, historical notes, and explanations, all in no particular order or sequence. Exceptions and rules are presented in a disorganized fashion. The right-hand column on each fact-laden page contains questions designed for immediate recall of a fact just read. The "instructor" on the tape reads every page and then instructs the student to answer the questions. After a brief pause, he exclaims "Very good! Now let's go on." The tone can be described as patronizing, at best.

Unit 2 introduces all the trope marks, in their common groupings. The instructor on the tape sings and then reads through all the trope signs (with Ashkenazic pronunciation). Rules such as the *munach* having many different melodies are given without any explanation. A great deal of stress is placed on memorizing the names of the signs (similar to Rosenbaum's approach) and their placement over or under words. Numerous exercises are given to test this knowledge. The student is also asked to jump back and forth in the textbook. Without question, this course is designed for fluent Hebrew readers.

After each group of trope marks is taught, students are asked to do the following: draw the trope sign; write its name in Hebrew and English, and give its "title" (these are given along with the trope names); give its relation to other *t'amim*; write whether it appears over or under the word, and whether it connects or separates phrases. Some of this is valuable knowledge, but it is quite advanced for students at this level.

Unit 3 reviews the functions of trope and contains many lengthy exercises, challenging to the advanced student of trope. Some could be shortened or adapted for a less ambitious course. Throughout, there is undue stress on memorizing the trope words rather than learning to chant text correctly utilizing trope melodies.

Unit 4 contains musical notation for the following trope systems: Torah, Haftarah, Megillat Esther, Shalosh Regalim, Megillat Aycha, High Holy Days, Shirat Hayam, and Ten Commandments, all of which have their own unique trope melodies. This section would be very useful for Cantors and professional Torah readers. The tape includes musical renditions of all the trope systems.

Tape #2 includes chanting of all the portions mentioned above, done by different readers. Blessings are also included, using "*Hashem*" in place of "*Adonai*." The Haftarah blessing, after all the lengthy explanations of the functions and rules governing different trope marks, is chanted incorrectly, with the opening mark sung as a *pashta* rather than a *kadma* (see Chapter 19). Some of the special blessings (e.g., for the Megillot) are sung by a Cantor in a manner that is geared to performance more than instruction.

The first Torah reading is chanted phrase by phrase, initially in trope, then the text. This is a good pedagogical method, used by Rosenbaum and others. After a few phrases, the reader switches to straight text chanting.

As a sourcebook for texts and exercises, this book could serve as a valuable supplement to an organized and systematic trope course. The tapes, because of the tone of the instructor, the Hebrew pronunciation, and the quality of some of the singing, are of limited use to all but the Orthodox community.

OTHER MATERIALS

MitzvahVision Videotapes

MitzvahVision has produced two instructional videotapes designed as home study guides, to supplement and support the teacher's role in preparing the Bar/Bat Mitzvah student. The first tape is an overview of the blessings from a typical Bar/Bat Mitzvah ceremony. Included are the Blessing over the candles, the *"Kiddush," "Sh'ma,"* and *"V'ahavta,"* blessing over the *tallit*, Torah blessings, and Haftarah blessings. The melodies selected are the most traditional and most commonly chanted ones. This tape also includes an introduction to the trope system. Cantor David Serkin, the instructor on this tape, acknowledges that his system is based on Pinchas Spiro's.

There are 53 versions of the second tape. Each Maftir and Haftarah portion has been taped. The Maftir is shown first with vowels and trope marks, and then as it appears in the *Tikkun*. Cantor Serkin chants while the student follows a pointer which identifies the text on the screen. (This is similar to the method of learning by computer described in Chapter 22.)

The greatest advantage of learning with a videotape is the flexibility: students can pause, rewind, and easily find their place any time. The drawback to learning, or even supplementing lessons, with such a tape, is the lack of standardization of melodies in synagogues. If a student is studying trope and blessings at his/her Hebrew School, chances are the melodies on this tape will not be identical to the ones taught at his/her synagogue.

This tape would seem most valuable to students in Cantor Serkin's own congregation, or to communities with no qualified trope and *tefillah* instructors. Ambitious students in such communities who wish to learn these skills for Bar/Bat Mitzvah would undeniably be able to do so with these videotapes.

(For ordering information, contact MitzvahVision, P.O Box 1331, Mercer Island, WA 98040.)

Parashah Series: Chanting Your Torah and Haftarah Portions

Transcontinental Music Publications has recently issued audiocassettes designed to be used in conjunction with the UAHC Press booklets *Your Bar/Bat Mitzvah: Parasha and Haftarah*. Each cassette includes the Torah blessings and selections from the weekly Torah portion (12-20 verses) chanted on one side. The Haftarah blessings and the entire Haftarah are chanted on the reverse side.

To date, only the Book of Genesis is available. The additional books will be available on tape in the future.

The trope used for these tapes is Binder trope, taught at Hebrew Union College and fairly standard in Reform congregations that include trope instruction. Thus, the problem mentioned above of lack of standardization among synagogues is less of an issue for these tapes. However, the selection of only a number of verses from each *parashah* is random, and unless a student has been assigned those exact verses, the tapes are of no use.

The choice to tape complete Haftarah portions is an interesting one, since it is in Conservative congregations that complete Haftarah portions are chanted, while the large majority of Reform congregations do abridged Haftarah portions. No one at Transcontinental was available to comment on this choice.

These tapes begin with both Torah blessings and proceed with a selected number of verses from the weekly *parashah*, including the Maftir verses. In the tape heard, *Bereshit*, Chapter 1, verses 1-13 were chosen. The Cantor is Josee Wolff, who possesses a beautiful, clear voice. She pronounces the Hebrew very precisely and with great attention to correct accents. The only criticism might be that her voice is too high and classically trained to be a good model for students to copy. In addition, her tempo is very slow and deliberate, which would be useful only for the very early stages of studying a *parashah*. There is also an annoying echo on the tape.

Side 2 includes both Haftarah blessings (the second is the abbreviated version) and the full Haftarah. Some of the singing, especially the blessing after the

Haftarah, is too high in pitch for most children. They could, of course, take it down an octave, but that is not easy for everyone to do.

In spite of these reservations, I would not hesitate to recommend this series of tapes for the congregation teaching Binder trope and in need of auxiliary aids. The rendition is so concise and correct, that even tutors and other professionals in need of brushing up their skills might benefit from studying these tapes.

(For ordering information, contact Transcontinental Music Publications, 838 Fifth Ave., New York, NY 10021.)

OTHER BOOKS

The following books are not reviewed here because they are used mainly by schools for teaching trope to college level students. However, they are excellent reference works and belong in the library of any student or teacher of trope.

Binder, A.W. *Biblical Chant.* New York: Philosophical Library, 1959.

Rosowsky, Solomon. *Cantillation of the Bible.* New York: Reconstructionist Press, 1957.

Unit IV: Mitzvah Programs
Overview

The rationale behind any Mitzvah Program is that children learn best by doing, and this truth can be applied with optimum results to learning about *mitzvot.*

In Chapter 24, Cantor Helen Leneman describes the basic structure, goals, and implementation of a Mitzvah Program.

In Chapter 25, Rabbi Jeffrey Salkin offers many cogent and convincing reasons for including a *mitzvah* component in a Bar/Bat Mitzvah program, and also spells out ways of carrying out such a program.

In Chapter 26, Carol K. Ingall, one of the early initiators of the Mitzvah Program concept, explains in detail her original program, now published by the Melton Research Center.

In Chapter 27, Cantor Janice Roger describes the "B'Mitzvotav Program," a learning through doing program at her synagogue. This is a required program, but it offers a wide selection of both mandatory and optional activities to fill the requirements.

In Chapter 28, Marlene Myerson provides an overview of a creative program in a Canadian synagogue. This program actively engages both families and local community social service agencies.

It is hoped that the wide array of material in this Unit will provide a stimulus to congregations not presently offering a Mitzvah Program, to mix and match and thus create a program suited to the needs and available resources of their institutions.

Chapter 24
Components of a Mitzvah Program

Helen Leneman

Material for this chapter was contributed by: Melton Research Center, Jewish Theological Seminary of America, New York; Cantor Janice Roger, Indianapolis Hebrew Congregation; Marsha Fensin, Temple Sinai of Milwaukee, Wisconsin; Cantor Nancy Ginsberg, Wynnewood, Pennsylvania; Marlene Myerson, Temple Emanu-El of Willowdale, Ontario; Shoshana Glatzer in *Coming of Age as a Jew — Bar/Bat Mitzvah*, a publication of the Board of Jewish Education of Greater New York.

Definition of a Mitzvah Program

A Mitzvah Program is one that engages students in performing a number of *mitzvot*, usually in connection with a forthcoming Bar/Bat Mitzvah. This chapter will describe several such programs, as well as ways of carrying them out.

Options for a Mitzvah Program

Several different options exist for a Mitzvah Program:

1. It can be done in sixth or seventh grade.
2. It can be done as a one-on-one activity with a "coordinator," or as a class.
3. It can be voluntary or required.
4. It can be a separate program, or it can be incorporated into the Religious School curriculum.

The advantages and disadvantages of doing any type of program for B'nai Mitzvah in the sixth versus seventh grade are similar. Starting in sixth grade has the advantage of time on its side: there is a year or more to complete the program. This has the potential of being more meaningful and thorough than other programs. The disadvantage is also the time factor: the actual "event," the Bar/Bat Mitzvah ceremony, seems far off, and this can make it difficult to stimulate motivation.

The advantage of doing a Mitzvah Program in seventh grade is the involvement of the students, who have been gearing up for this year and eagerly accept special programs to mark it. Parents, also, will be more motivated and involved. The disadvantage is the fact that many students drop out of Religious School and therefore out of the Mitzvah Program after the Bar/Bat Mitzvah. It can also be difficult or impossible to complete the program prior to the Bar/Bat Mitzvah. This is a problem especially for those students becoming Bar/Bat Mitzvah early in the school year.

Mitzvah Programs can work both as classes and individualized activities. A class promotes bonding between the students involved in the Mitzvah Program, and also gives them all the same level of understanding of the *mitzvot* they study and perform during the year. The ideal would combine the two, as the original program at Temple Emanuel in Providence did (see Chapter 26 for a description of this Mitzvah Program, now published by The Melton Research Center as *Bar/Bat Mitzvah Curriculum — Hey Level*). Today, most synagogues do not have the time or resources to conduct such a comprehensive program, and generally choose to do it either as a private or a class activity.

Most Mitzvah Programs are part of the seventh grade curriculum. When students are recognized as capable of assuming adult behavior and are allowed the choice of whether or not to be involved in such a program, results may be more positive. Many synagogues are too unsure of their students' commitment to offer a Mitzvah Program as a choice. Yet, even when the course is required, an element of choice exists, as there are usually opportunities for choice within each category of *mitzvot*.

Other elements in most Mitzvah Programs that have their origin in the Melton Program are the "diary" and color coded cards. The diary is for the student to record impressions, responses, and personal reactions to doing the various *mitzvot* throughout the year.

Carol K. Ingall initiated the use of cards of different colors to differentiate the categories of *mitzvot.* These not only help the student see clearly the differences between categories, but they also give the course the character of a game, always appealing to students.

The categories of *mitzvot* in the Melton Program, designed to "stress the multi-faceted aspects of Jewish life," are (1) cognitive learning, (2) ritual experiences, (3) the synagogue, and (4) the Jewish people. In the Melton program, there are 33 *mitzvot* to be performed within those four areas. Today, most synagogues using a Mitzvah Program require 13 *mitzvot*, combining requirements with electives. Indianapolis Hebrew Congregation requires 26, with 13 of those required.

Most Mitzvah Programs are divided into Torah, Avodah/Worship, Gemilut Chasadim/Acts of Loving-kindness. Temple Sinai of Milwaukee divides *mitzvot* into Learning, Living, and Doing. Torah is also called Scholarship, and within this category, many synagogues provide a reading list. The Melton program even includes the library call numbers, an excellent aid for the student afraid to take that first step into research.

The area of ritual or worship experience includes both home and synagogue rituals. It is generally an area of action, contrasted with the stress on study in the first category. It also includes life cycle and holidays. The third category, loving deeds, is often combined with community. This eliminates the need for the Melton program's fourth category, peoplehood/history. Yet with the elimination of this category, many *mitzvot* are forced into categories that do not make sense. Examples will be found below. In the loving deeds category, some synagogues provide lists, including phone numbers and addresses, of places in the community that can be visited. This is another aid to the student having trouble self-starting.

Utilizing the original four categories, here are the elements most commonly found in Mitzvah Programs. All of these can either be designed as a class curriculum, done as individualized activities with the assistance of a coordinator, or a combination of both.

I. Torah/Scholarship
   A. Read/study/watch/attend and report on:
      1. A Jewish book or books (suggested reading lists should be provided).
      2. One or more televised educational programs with a Jewish theme.
      3. One or more articles in a Jewish magazine (possible addition: subscribe to a Jewish magazine).
      4. A Jewish subject (this should be more specific).
      5. A famous Jew (a list of suggestions should be provided).
      6. An historical Jewish event.
      7. A Jewish life cycle event (although this is not exactly in the right category, the fact that it is a study and report activity puts it here).
      8. Ads in a Jewish paper or magazine: how these differ from ones found in a non-Jewish publication.
      9. Articles of Jewish interest in the newspaper.
   B. Other possible activities (all include a written report):
      1. Write an essay on Bar/Bat Mitzvah (meaning, history, etc.).
      2. Attend Shabbat morning Torah study.
      3. Attend and complete the Cantor's trope class.
      4. Read your Torah portion and the portion before your own, and explain the connection between the two.
      5. Go to a Jewish camp and write about what made it special.
      6. Ask the Rabbi something you never understood.
      7. Submit written reactions to several of the Rabbi's sermons.
      8. Read your Haftarah portion in English and write about what you think it means. If you do a good job on this, you will read it at your Bar/Bat Mitzvah ceremony.

The Melton Program has cards with basic questions in the areas of religious philosophy, the Jewish calendar, Tanach, and Talmud which would be excellent starting points for a class curriculum. They might be difficult for many children to research and complete outside of class.

II. Ritual: Synagogue and Home

A. Attend this service/minimum number of services/write impressions of

1. Friday evening/Shabbat morning, with your family.
2. Shabbat service at another synagogue (possibly of a different affiliation than your own).
3. Shalosh Regalim services.
4. Life cycle event.

In addition to the above, singing in the Junior Choir or participating in a Junior Congregation also appear in this category. Some synagogues provide printed questions to guide the student in evaluating his/her experience of services. The Melton program has a card with questions about synagogue personnel, including the Rabbi, Cantor, *shamash*, *gabbai*, and others.

B. Describe or make/build and use these ritual objects:

1. The Ark and other ritual objects in the sanctuary.
2. Any ritual object: e.g., *Kiddush* cup, Havdalah candle.
3. A *sukkah*.

The Melton program has question cards on *tefillin* and *tallit*. Since these involve research, they are in the "scholarship" category, but they can also fit in the "ritual" category.

C. Perform these home rituals/describe feelings

1. Recite *Kiddush*/other blessings.
2. Light candles.

The Melton program has a "Shabbat at Home" card that includes a reading list, questions to discuss with parents, and the assignment to describe feelings about Shabbat in the home. Another card, "Living Jewishly," includes questions about Jewish ritual objects and Jewish books found in the home.

III. LOVING DEEDS/COMMUNITY

A. Make any of these contributions:

1. Food to a food drive.
2. Plant trees in Israel.
3. Money to Mazon or other charity. ("Explain your choice")
4. 13 hours of volunteer work in the community.
5. Old clothes or toys.
6. Leftover food from Bar/Bat Mitzvah party to shelter.
7. Portion of allowance/Bar/Bat Mitzvah money to charity.

Other suggested activities involving *tzedakah* consciousness are:

8. Visit a *tzedakah* organization; describe your impressions.
9. Write an elected official about an area of concern to you.
10. Participate in a fund-raiser.
11. Visit a home for the mentally or physically disabled.

B. Possible good deeds

1. Tutor another student.
2. Help a sick classmate.
3. Help an older neighbor with chores.
4. Assist the Rabbi or Cantor on hospital visits.
5. Make a *tzedakah* box; have your family contribute to it every Shabbat.

Although many of the activities described in this last category involve the community in some way, there are still other activities that more specifically relate to Jewish history and peoplehood. Understanding the concept of peoplehood is vital to a strong and positive Jewish identity, and this is a crucial age for forging this identity. By lumping some of these activities into other categories, Mitzvah Programs put most of the stress on "doing," without enough on the understanding of *Jewish* doing. For example, "doing a family history" shows up in various forms, usually in either the Torah or Community category. The purpose of doing such a history is for students to find out where *they* came from. It is neither an academic exercise nor a community activity. "Visiting Jewish sites" is another common activity. Though this involves going into the community, the goal is for students to understand their roots and history. With that general goal in mind, here are some proposed activities for a fourth category.

IV. HISTORY/PEOPLEHOOD

A. Interview and write about

1. An older person in the community.
2. A grandparent, about life when he/she was 13.
3. Any older relative.
4. Our family history.

The Melton program has a "Family History" card with many questions to guide students in their research. Other programs suggest making a family tree. One program suggests getting an Israeli or Russian Jewish pen pal.

B. Studying history

1. Visit Jewish sites and write your impressions.

This is the only common activity that fits into the "history" category, and it is usually done as a field trip. Further study of Jewish history is suggested in Melton cards on "Founders of Judaism," and on personalities in the medieval, modern, and contemporary periods, as well as in Israel. These topics are usually covered — or should be — in the Religious School curriculum. If they are included in a Mitzvah Program, the stress should be on "extra credit" work, such as additional reading and reports. It is still useful to include this category.

Conclusion

The world may well rest on the three pillars of Torah, Worship, and Good Deeds, but the structure of Jewish life is rooted to the ground by its history and peoplehood. Both those roots and the structure itself are greatly strengthened and enhanced by the addition of Mitzvah Programs to B'nai Mitzvah curricula. Children need to learn that "deed not creed" is more than a catchy phrase. By participating actively in a Mitzvah Program containing the components described in this chapter, they will learn for themselves that doing *mitzvot* is a way of life.

Chapter 25
Putting the Mitzvah Back in Bar and Bat Mitzvah

Jeffrey K. Salkin

MITZVAH: THE TORAH'S ACTIVE VOICE

Mitzvot teach us to sanctify life. They foster altruism and self-esteem, so crucial to the life of a young Jew. They can bring Jewish families closer to the Jewish people, to all people, and to God. Getting ready for Bar and Bat Mitzvah provides a perfect opportunity to bring *mitzvah* into our Jewish lives. The terms Bar and Bat Mitzvah must be understood once again as "old enough to do *mitzvot*."

Not each *mitzvah* will speak to every Jew. But each is sacred. So, too, is the idea that *what we do shapes who we are*, that the deed shapes the heart more than the heart shapes the deed. Most Jewish parents want their children to feel Jewish and to be somehow connected to the Jewish past and the Jewish future. Judaism teaches that only through the doing can there be a genuine, rooted, profound feeling of Jewishness.

A Jew's actions, then, create a Jewish world. Such actions have consequences. Perhaps the most powerful Jewish idea is *Kiddush HaShem*, adding to the holiness of God's reputation. In some contexts, *Kiddush HaShem* means martyrdom for the sake of Jewish identity and Jewish ideals. But its deeper meaning is that when Jews act admirably, when Jews act like *menschen*, their lives serve as living advertisements for God.

More than anything else, that is the goal of Bar and Bat Mitzvah, and that is the goal of all Jewish life.

TEN BASIC JEWISH VALUES AND MITZVOT THAT MAKE THEM REAL

The following is a list of basic Jewish values. Since Judaism lacks a catechism of values, any such list is highly selective. This list represents both ritual *mitzvot* and ethical *mitzvot*. Martin Buber would have dubbed them "the total inherited 'ought' of the group of which I am a part." Decades ago, the Jewish essayist Hayim Greenberg said, "A Jew who can name all the plants in Israel in Hebrew possesses one qualification for useful service in the State of Israel . . . but if he does not know to their deepest sounding such Hebrew expressions as *mitzvah, tzedakah, chesed, Kiddush HaShem* . . . he cannot carry a part in that choir that gives voice to the Jewish melody. These are the powers that build a Jewish personality." This list represents the Jewish tradition's best ways of building a Jewish personality and deepening human character.

Under each *mitzvah*, there is a list of projects that gives those *mitzvot* shape and meaning. At the conclusion of this chapter, the reader will find a listing of organizations and projects that can help families fulfill many of these *mitzvot*. Some of those *mitzvot* are for young people to do by themselves, and others will be appropriate for the entire family to do together. This is a way to start applying Jewish wisdom to everyday life.

Gemilut Chasadim: Acts of Loving-kindness

So powerful is *gemilut chasadim* that the Torah begins with it: God makes garments for Adam and Eve: and the Torah ends with it: God buries Moses. So powerful is *gemilut chasadim* that performing such acts of loving-kindness is the closest that humans can come to a genuine imitation of God. Parents and teachers might do some or all of the following:

Encourage their child to visit someone who has lost a loved one, fulfilling the *mitzvah* of *nichum avelim*, comforting mourners.

Encourage their child to visit or call on someone who is ill, fulfilling the *mitzvah* of *bikur cholim*, visiting the sick.

Encourage their child to learn magic, clowning, or balloon animal making to use in the pediatric ward of a hospital.

Arrange to have the leftover food from their celebration brought to a soup kitchen that feeds the homeless and the hungry. Arrange for a food barrel to be placed in their synagogue.

Just before Pesach, bring the leftover *chametz* from their home to a local food pantry. Organize others in their synagogue to do it as well.

Volunteer as a family at a soup kitchen for the homeless. Ask people to bring canned food to their Bar or Bat Mitzvah party for distribution to the homeless. A growing number of Jews are already doing this *mitzvah*.

Have the children collect food for the hungry on Halloween, rather than candy for the well fed.

Give three per cent of the cost of their Bar and Bat Mitzvah celebration to MAZON, The Jewish Hunger Fund.

Encourage their child to write to an elected official, expressing an opinion about an important social or political issue, fulfilling the *mitzvah* of *mishpat*, justice.

Use a Jewish idea in the letter.

As a family, participate in a clothing drive for the needy.

Tzedakah: Righteous Giving and Generosity

Some Jews say *tzedakah* is the highest *mitzvah*. It is translated as "charity" or "justice" or simply "giving." The exact translation hardly matters. *Tzedakah* is not what we give; it is what we owe as part of our Covenant with God. The practice of *tzedakah* transcends ritual practices. Proverbs says: "*Tzedakah* redeems from death." It can potentially save individuals from a physical death; it can also redeem the giver from an internal death of the soul.

Parents can choose one of the *tzedakah* projects at the end of this article and donate to it in honor of their child's becoming a Bar or Bat Mitzvah, or encourage the child to set aside a portion of his/her gift money. Some young people have even given away all their gift money. Several years ago, twins in California used all their gift money to help Cambodian boat people.

Families can set aside some *tzedakah* every Friday night before Shabbat. Use a family *pushke*, a *tzedakah* container. Decide as a family where the money should go. Decent, gracious, loving human beings are made, not born. This is the easiest, most hands-on, lowest-cost way of teaching the value of *tzedakah* to a child.

It is time for Jews to re-frame the old cliché that Bar and Bat Mitzvah is "when I become a man (or woman)." It should be "Bar and Bat Mitzvah is when I become a *mensch*."

Remember that money is not the only thing that can be given. So can time. Parents should set aside time each week for a socially redeeming purpose, and encourage their child to do the same.

Talmud Torah: The Study of Torah

Jewish learning can be extended beyond the words of the Hebrew texts. Jewish wisdom can enter our lives in many ways:

Read Jewish books together as a family.

Learn to sing Hebrew songs together.

Visit a Jewish museum as a family.

Hidur P'nei Zakeyn: Honoring the Elderly

The elderly are deserving of respect regardless of their accomplishments or status. Their stories are our history.

A child can call, write, or visit with an elderly relative or friend.

A child can deliver flowers to a nursing home before the start of Shabbat.

Zikaron: Memory

The Torah commands us no less than 169 times to remember. Perhaps there is mystical significance in 13 being the square root of 169. At the age of 13, Jewish children have a fairly extensive memory, one that is both tribal and individual. They remember Shabbat. They remember that Jews were slaves in Egypt. Jewish parents must remember to teach their children to remember. Following are ways they can do this:

Make sure their child knows his or her Hebrew name and the person for whom he or she was named. What special Jewish qualities did that person have that parents hoped their child would emulate?

Find out their family's name in "the old country."

Find out the name of the town that their family was from. Ask someone in the family who knows this, so that it becomes more than simply "some place in Russia." Look up the town in the *Encyclopaedia Judaica*. Learn something about the town and what it gave to the Jewish world. It gave something. Of this you can be sure. And that "something" must not die.

Collect clothing and food for needy immigrants. Tutor immigrants in English. Since we "were strangers in the land of Egypt," we should be sensitive to the needs of new immigrants, strangers to this country.

Shabbat

"More than Israel has kept the Sabbath, the Sabbath has kept Israel." Every Jewish life should have more than a small taste of Shabbat. The following will be a start toward a full Shabbat experience. Families can:

Have Shabbat dinners at their home. Recite together "*Hamotzi*," "*Kiddush*," and "*Birkat Hamazon*," the blessing after the meal. Invite friends to share in their Shabbat celebrations.

Encourage their child to learn to cook a traditional Shabbat or holiday dish.

Minimize, then discontinue, commercial transactions, such as business and shopping on Shabbat.

Attend synagogue services as a family.

Reserve a half hour on Saturday for study together as a family, either from *Pirke Avot*, the ethical sections of the Mishnah (which is found in most prayer books), or from the Torah portion of the week.

Tell a Jewish story on Shabbat.

End Shabbat with a Havdalah service.

Kedushat Halashon: The Sanctity of Speech

Most people assume that sanctity of speech means prayer. But sanctity of speech is much deeper than that. According to Joseph Telushkin, author of *Jewish Literacy*, the most widely-violated commandment in the Torah is Leviticus 19:16: "Do not go about as a talebearer among your people." *Kedushat Halashon* means that we teach our children to watch their mouths just as we teach them to watch their hands — that we teach them to avoid gossip, talebearing, rumormongering, and other acts of verbal violence, just as we teach them to avoid physical violence. In Hebrew, Jews call such prohibited speech *lashon ha-ra*, "the evil tongue." Negative statements about others are called *rechilut*. If modern Jews are truly serious about ethics being at the root of Jewish behavior, then this *mitzvah* surely calls out to us.

Kedushat Hazeman: The Holiness of Festivals and Sacred Seasons

To be a Jew is to feel a part of Judaism's entire festival calendar. To be a Jew is to go through the cycle of the seasons as a Jew. Families might do the following:

Participate in a Passover Seder. Families can include a recently-arrived Soviet Jew at the Seder. Ask their child to write a special reading to be used during the family celebration.

Ask their child to write a special prayer to use when the family lights the *chanukiah* at home.

Build a *sukkah* in their backyard. Decorate it. Have dinner in it, or, at least make *Hamotzi* and *Kiddush* in it. If the weather is warm, encourage their children to sleep in it overnight.

Have the entire family attend the Purim service dressed as characters from the *Megillah.*

Plant a tree in Israel each year on Tu B'Shevat, the New Year of trees.

Tza'ar Ba'alei Chayim: Preventing Cruelty to Animals

Judaism instructs that humans must treat animals with dignity. It teaches that animals cannot be subjected to wanton destruction and pain; that animals of unequal strength cannot be yoked together; that an animal collapsed under the burden of a load must be helped even if it belongs to an enemy. Judaism is even concerned about the psychological pain of animals. It advises that a mother bird must be sent away to spare her the pain of seeing the eggs being removed from her nest.

Families might become involved with an organization that deals with animal rights. They can give money to the local animal shelter or adopt a dog or cat.

They can refrain from wearing fur or leather goods.

Tikkun HaNefesh: The Repair of the Self

An important part of becoming Bar and Bat Mitzvah is growing as an individual. The ancient Rabbis believed that the ultimate goal of the *mitzvot* was nothing less than *l'tzaref haberiot*, refining the individual into better human material. We can encourage our children to:

Rid themselves of a bad habit.

Help patch up a bad relationship by establishing *shalom* with another person.

PLACES TO SEND TZEDAKAH MONEY

Soup Kitchens for the Homeless

Soup kitchens feed the poor and the homeless. Sometimes, they feed entire families. Donate leftovers from your B'nai Mitzvah celebrations. Consider how much smoked salmon and salad is thrown out on any Saturday afternoon after a Bar and Bat Mitzvah party, and then consider how many hungry people walk around the streets of even the poshest suburbs. It doesn't have to be that way. To find a local food bank, consult the "Social and Human Services" section of the Yellow Pages.

Some Notable Food Banks:

Mary Brennan Interfaith Nutrition Network (INN), 146-148 Front Street, Hempstead, NY 11550.

Long Island Cares, Inc., P.O. Box 1073, West Brentwood, NY 11717. Operates the Long Island Regional Food Bank which distributes huge quantities of donated food to soup kitchens and hunger organizations throughout Long Island.

Yad Ezra Kosher Food Pantry, 26641 Harding, Oak Park, MI 48237.

Rachel's Table, 633 Salisbury Street, Worcester, MA 01609. Picks up leftovers from *simchahs* and distributes it to the needy.

Hebrew Union College, Brookdale Center, 1 West 4th Street, New York, NY 10012. Attention: Dr. Lawrence Raphael, Dean of Administration. A one-night-a-week program to feed the homeless.

Passover Fund, B'nai B'rith Project Hope, c/o Len Elenowitz, 8801 Post Oak Road, Potomac, MD 20854. Delivers Passover packages to Washington-area Jews.

Local Soviet Jewry Committees

These groups often include the most caring, dynamic, altruistic members of the Jewish community. Call the local Jewish Federation or Jewish Community Center for information on locating the local Soviet Jewry committee, or contact the National Conference on Soviet Jewry, 1522 K Street, N.W., Suite 1100, Washington, DC 20005 for details about the nearest chapter.

Agencies that Help the Homebound Jewish Elderly

Many aged live in utter isolation, in bleak apartments with multiple locks on their doors. The condition in which they live is a scandal, and their numbers are larger than most people think. Agencies organized to help these individuals include:

Dorot, 171 West 85th Street, New York, NY 10025. Dorot means "generations" — generations of Jews together bringing light into lives that would have been otherwise darkened. Dorot operates a soup kitchen and distributes clothing to homebound elderly Jews.

Hatzilu, 44 East 89th Street, Brooklyn, NY 11236. Aids the Jewish poor and elderly of Brooklyn, Queens, and Long Island.

The Ark, 6450 North California Avenue, Chicago, IL 60645. Offers extensive services to poor Jews, including dental and medical care, employment counseling, a food pantry, and help in navigating the social service bureaucracy.

Sunday Jewish Food Program, Federation Homes, 156 Wintonbury Avenue, Bloomfield, CT 06002. Offers a Sunday kosher meal program to many Jews in the greater Hartford area.

Other Organizations that Do Worthy Things:

ARMDI: American Red Magen David for Israel, 888 Seventh Avenue, Suite 403, New York, NY 10106. The sole support arm in the United States for the Magen David, Israel's emergency medical and blood services organization.

American Jewish World Service, 15 West 26th Street, 9th floor, New York, NY 10010. Has become the Jewish response to suffering caused by famine, epidemic, or natural disaster. The group has managed projects in Africa, South America, Mexico, and the United States.

American Rabbinic Network for Ethiopian Jewry, 859 South Oakland Avenue, Pasadena, CA 91106. Thousands of Ethiopian Jews have emigrated to Israel, but many still remain in Ethiopia. ARNEJ keeps them in our consciousness through education and fund-raising.

Bet Tzedek, 145 South Fairfax Avenue, Suite #200, Los Angeles, CA 90036. Provides free legal work for poor Jews and non-Jews. Has produced a video, narrated by actress Bea Arthur, which portrays six examples of their work.

The Eldridge Street Project, 12 Eldridge Street, New York, NY 10002. Established to preserve and restore the Eldridge Street Synagogue, one of the most beautiful older synagogues of New York City. Also plans to establish a Jewish historic cultural district on the Lower East Side. Deserves *tzedakah* because it preserves a valuable piece of our past.

Jewish Foundation for Christian Rescuers/ADL, 823 United Nations Plaza, New York, NY 10017. Many Christians who saved Jews from the Nazis now live in poverty in the United States, Europe, and Israel. Jews must remember them; our history is incomplete without them. The foundation sustains them financially and emotionally, thus bearing witness to eternal gratitude.

God's Love We Deliver, 895 Amsterdam Avenue, New York, NY 10025. Prepares and delivers meals for people with AIDS.

Interns for Peace, 270 West 89th Street, New York, NY 10024. This apolitical organization trains workers to help Arabs and Jews develop common interests, hoping this will erode the walls of hatred.

North American Jewish Student's Appeal, 165 Pidgeon Hill Road, Huntington Station, NY 11746. Provides supplemental funds to several Jewish student groups on campuses around the country: the Bayit Project, which establishes Jewish residences on campus; the Progressive Zionist Caucus, which promotes pluralism in Israel; various Jewish student newspapers, seminars, and projects.

MAZON, 2940 Westwood Boulevard, Suite 7, Los Angeles, CA 90064. Asks Jews to send three percent of the cost of a *simchah* to MAZON so we can share our blessings with the needy. MAZON then makes allocations to hunger organizations around the country.

National Institute for Jewish Hospice, 8723 Alden Drive, Suite #652, Los Angeles, CA 90048. The only national Jewish organization providing non-hospital alternatives for the terminally ill, enabling people to die with appropriate care and with dignity.

The Jewish Braille Institute of America, 110 East 30th Street, New York, NY 10016. Provides books, tapes, special materials for summer camps, college and career counselling, and free *B'nai Mitzvah* training to blind and partially sighted Jewish adults. Improves the quality of Jewish life for the estimated 20,000 Jewish blind and 50,000 Jews who are severely visually impaired.

The New Israel Fund, 111 West 40th Street, Suite 2300, New York, NY 10018. Funds the following programs in Israel: Jewish/Arab relations; pluralism; civil rights and civil liberties; women's rights, especially rape crisis centers; and community action.

United Jewish Appeal – Federation of Jewish Philanthropies, 130 East 59th Street, New York, NY 10022. Most comprehensive Jewish charity in the world. Raises almost $750 million annually from American Jews to serve the worldwide needs of Jews. Jewish elderly on the Lower East side, Jewish farmers in the Galilee, Jews in Eastern Europe and in Moslem nations all benefit. Giving to the UJA is absolutely essential for every serious Jew's *tzedakah* plans.

Israel Bonds, 730 Broadway, 7th floor, New York, NY 10003 (or your local bond office. This and the UJA are the great international pillars of support for Israel. Israel's capital improvements and infrastructure are largely the result of the strong commitment to Israel Bonds by Jews all over the world. Not just *tzedakah* — it's an investment in Israel's future.

Simon Wiesenthal Center, 9760 West Pico Boulevard, Los Angeles, CA 90035. Has taken a leading role in discovering Nazis in hiding, as well as exposing modern hate groups. Ensures that Americans will remember the Holocaust.

Trevor's Campaign for the Homeless, 3415 Westchester Pike, Suite #201, Newtown Square, PA 19073. Trevor Ferrell, now an adult, began his "campaign" at the age of eleven. Includes a nightly food run, a shelter, housing for women and children, and day-care.

The National Yiddish Book Center, 48 Woodbridge St., South Hadley, MA 01075. Yiddish must survive, and more than in vulgar humor or small catchphrases. By finding, saving, and treasuring Yiddish books, the Book Center redeems a small part of the Jewish past.

Lifeline for the Old – Yad LaKashish, 14 Shivtei Yisrael Street, Jerusalem. Jerusalem's elderly create lovely handicrafts, *challah* covers, *tallitot*, toys, metal *mezuzot* cases, ceramic items, clothing, book binding. Also employs young and old handicapped individuals. Contributions can be sent to American Friends of Lifeline for the Old in Israel, c/o Florence Schiffman, 1500 Palisades Avenue., Fort Lee, NJ 07024.

Ziv Tzedakah Fund, Inc., c/o Bena Siegel, Treasurer, 11818 Trail Ridge Drive, Potomac, MD 20854. This is the independent *tzedakah* fund of Danny Siegel: poet, writer, and *mitzvah* impresario. He searches for and finds righteous people doing holy work and raises money for them.

Shelters for Battered Jewish Women

Such organizations as those that follow provide temporary shelter, counseling, and support services to Jewish women who are victims of domestic violence.

Rebbetzin Chana Weinberg, 398 Mt. Wilson Lane, Baltimore, MD 21208. Operates one of the few battered women's shelters for Jewish women in North America. Contributions should be made to Chana Weinberg Tzedakah Fund.

Shalva, 1610 West Highland, Chicago, IL 60660. Founded by Orthodox women who worked in a *mikvah* (ritual bath) and noticed scars on the women they were tending.

CONCLUSION

The idea of *mitzvah* is central to Jewish identity because it is the essence of the covenant made at Sinai. Bar/Bat Mitzvah offers an ideal opportunity to rekindle in B'nai Mitzvah and their families the sense of *mitzvah* as a holy obligation.

(This chapter was adapted from *Putting God on the Guest List: How To Reclaim the Spiritual Meaning of Your Child's Bar or Bat Mitzvah*, published by Jewish Lights Publishing, P.O. Box 237, Sunset Farm Offices, Route 4, Woodstock, Vermont 05091, (802) 457-4000, 160 pages, $21.95 hardcover, $14.95 paperback.)

Chapter 26

Enriching the Bar/Bat Mitzvah Experience with a Mitzvah Program

Carol K. Ingall

Introduction to Mitzvah Programs

Mitzvah Programs have become increasingly popular since the original such program was created in the late 1970s. Known as the Temple Emanu-El Program, it was a joint creation of Rabbi Joel Zaiman and this author, when we were both at Temple Emanu-El of Providence, Rhode Island. When I left Emanu-El, the program became the property of the Melton Research Center.

The initial impetus for creating such a program came from Rabbi Zaiman. An inventive Rabbi, he had developed PEP, the Parent Education Program, and felt strongly about involving parents in some way in their children's B'nai Mitzvah education. He created a curriculum based on questions and answers, and I created the "colored card" format.

The original program was created for the sixth grade year, seen as a "preparatory" year for B'nai Mitzvah. It was designed to be completed in a minimum of one year.

The chance for a child to work intensively with a coordinator is an advantage of making this a one-on-one program. The original program combined a weekly class with a weekly private session. The class was not mandatory; those students who could complete the program without attending the class were allowed to do so. In addition, there was an alternate program, a B'nai Mitzvah class, for those students who did not choose the Mitzvah Program. Today, in most places, the choice is between the Mitzvah Program and nothing. There needs to be a "safety net" to catch those children who do not do the Mitzvah Program.

I have always believed strongly in the importance of this being a voluntary program. As I wrote in my introduction to the Teacher's Guide (now published along with the student project cards by The Melton Research Center as *Bar/Bat Mitzvah Curriculum — Hey Level*), "The thrust of the program depends on its voluntary character . . . the decision is a commitment, and as such is invested with a far more compelling quality than a requirement." At Emanu-El, only a student who completed the program could read Torah at his/ her Bar/Bat Mitzvah ceremony. Therefore, the entire nature of the service was different for these students.

In the years since being at Emanu-El, I have adapted this Mitzvah Program on request for several synagogues. The great value of a Mitzvah Program is the opportunity it gives students to act like adult Jews in the community, for example, when they accompany clergy to *shiva* calls or to visit the sick. People in the community can see the future in these fresh faced children, and this has a very positive impact.

Preparation for Bar/Bat Mitzvah provides a wonderful window of opportunity. It is a chance for the whole family to become involved. For a Mitzvah Program to be successful, the teachers must take the students seriously; they must treat them with respect. The hope is that when they are treated as adults with new responsibilities, they will rise to the occasion.

The following portion of this chapter appeared originally under the title "On Becoming a Jewish Adult: Educating for Bar and Bat Mitzvah" in *Conservative Judaism*, Vol. III, No. 3, Spring 1976.

> My Hebrew name is Devorah and I was named after my great-grandfather whose name was David . . . . He came to America and saved money to send for his wife, two sons and a daughter. When he saved enough, my great-grandmother made contact with a man who took people to the port. She was afraid my

grandfather would make too much noise and someone would stop them . . . . She put him on the bottom of the carriage and stuffed his mouth with candy. My grandfather, great-uncle, great-aunt and great-grandmother came to America on the bottom of a boat because they were so poor . . . .

My favorite part of the service is the "*Amidah*" . . . . The reason why I like the "*Amidah*" is because the prayer is read silently instead of being read out loud. To me this seems more personal, more of myself. When a prayer is read silently, I can express my own personal thoughts and feelings. When prayers are being read with the entire congregation included, it reminds me of a form letter . . . .

As a firstborn, I attended a siyum for the firstborn on the morning of the first Seder. The firstborn is supposed to fast to associate himself with the firstborns in Egypt who were saved from the tenth plague. This helps us realize that we might have been there, and we were spared. We are supposed to fast, but the Rabbis thought of a way of getting out of it. When a Jew studies and prays and completes a section of the Talmud, it is a *mitzvah*, a cause for celebrating. Celebrating to all Jews means "food" . . . .

These comments on Jewish life were written by students engaged in a new venture, the Bar/Bat Mitzvah Program of Temple Emanu-El, in Providence, Rhode Island. The students, children of Emanu-El members, attend our Religious School or the local day school. Upon entering the sixth grade they and their parents were presented with the option of enrolling in a new and entirely voluntary educational experiment. They would still learn to chant the Haftarah with the Cantor; those who were interested and qualified would still learn to chant the Torah with our Ritual Director. But they would be participating in a new program of study designed to identify and highlight the fundamentals of adult Jewish life.

The program was developed by the Rabbis in response to requests by the Education Committee and the Bar/Bat Mitzvah Committee that the synagogue take seriously these rites of passage. The members of these committees, concerned parents themselves, had long believed that the Bar or Bat Mitzvah had to become more than a onetime performance. If it was to mark the entry into adult Jewish life, it required a new kind of education and preparation. In addition, many of these parents had been involved in our Parent Education Program (PEP) when their children began Religious School, and were therefore ready for intense involvement. We began by projecting a program, and then created its context. The purpose of the program would be to create a set of experiences which would introduce the would-be Bar or Bat Mitzvah to the adult Jewish world. We would reinforce the cognitive domain to which he or she had been introduced in formal schooling, singling out significant Jewish information and ideas. We would expose the student to ritual in order to experience Jewish living through the world of *mitzvot*. The synagogue was clearly important to us; we would try to encourage synagogue attendance and participation. Finally, we would emphasize the world of the Jewish people through the study of our leaders, institutions, and organizations throughout the ages.

We saw the program as an opportunity to introduce the students, at this most impressionable age, to positive Jewish ego models: to the coordinator, older teens, and community resource people who would be invited to participate in the program. Perhaps most important we would provide a relaxed learning experience, outside the framework of the Religious School, which would ignore differences in academic ability and school background, creating a sense of community within our synagogue family. Emanu-El's students come from four private schools and four public school systems; they have little or no contact with those students from Emanu-El families who attend the local day school. In this setting they could meet one another in a noncompetitive endeavor common to all of them.

The Bar or Bat Mitzvah ceremony would become much more meaningful if the entire family were involved in preparing for it. We would therefore design a program to include parents, whenever possible, in discussions at home and in the synagogue, in programs and field trips. Their involvement would emphasize to their children the importance of the event. Through their participation the parents themselves would learn and in so doing strengthen their dedication to Judaism.

Informal

The context was to be relaxed, individualized, personal. As coordinator, I saw the program as a proving ground for informal education. I would be a kind of *shadchan*, introducing students to books and to resource people, but the students would initiate the learning process. They would call upon me for assistance; I would meet with them when and where they needed help. There were obvious benefits for me: I would have all the advantages of formal teaching and none of the disadvantages — sharing ideas and experiences with no grades and no discipline problems. I felt, and still do feel, that I would have to establish an individual relationship with each child, which is what we promised the students and their parents when we described the program to them.

The response to the proposal was extraordinary; parents and students were excited. The first year we offered the program, 49 of our 51 students volunteered to participate. In our second year, 36 out of 37 students chose the program.

Each student receives a packet of color coded cards and a small notebook for record keeping. The cards fall into four general categories: cognitive learning (white), rituals and life cycle (blue), the synagogue (yellow), and the community (pink). Each student must complete the projects indicated on his/her 32 cards. Depending on his or her Bar or Bat Mitzvah date, each student has anywhere from 14 months to two years to complete the projects. Some sample cards are reproduced below:

Learning

A. Read about Bar/Bat Mitzvah in one of the following books, available in our synagogue library. You do not have to borrow the book. The selections are short enough to read in a brief sitting.
   1. Edidin, *Jewish Customs and Ceremonies*, pp. 55ff.
   2. Glustrom, *The Language of Judaism*, pp. 231ff.

B. Then discuss with your parents:
   1. Is Bar or Bat Mitzvah important? Why?
   2. How do you feel about your coming Bar/Bat Mitzvah?
   3. How do your parents feel?
   4. Many things happen when one becomes a Bar/Bat Mitzvah. There is the preparation, the party, the service, your part in the service, and your future as a Jew. How do you feel about each of these aspects of becoming a Bar/Bat Mitzvah?

Learning

Many times questions will occur to you concerning Jewish life and thought. The following list of reference books will help you answer these questions. For now, you will be provided with a list of questions to answer, which will enable you to familiarize yourself with these works of reference . . . .

We list 22 books, including encyclopedias, dictionaries, handbooks, yearbooks, concordances, and Siddurim. The list runs the gamut from Rabbinic classics such as Ginzberg's *Legends of the Jews* to Strassfeld's *The Jewish Catalog*. Some of the sample reference questions are:

1. Locate three places in the Tanach where the word "fangs" appears.
2. Give three explanations offered by the Rabbis for the phrase, "The voice of thy brother's blood crieth unto me from the ground" (Genesis 22:8-9).
3. In what U.S. city did Golda Meir grow up?

Ritual

Attend (preferably with parents) eight of the following events:

A. *Brit*
B. *Pidyon Haben* (redemption of firstborn son)
C. Wedding
D. Funeral (chapel and cemetery)
E. *Shiva*
F. Unveiling
G. *Yizkor* Service
H. Minchah (weekday afternoon) Service
I. Ma'ariv Service
J. Shacharit Service

Ritual

During the course of these two years, participate and/or perform the following *mitzvot*:

A. *Tashlich* (symbolic casting away of sins on Rosh Hashanah)
B. Building a *sukkah*
C. *Lulav* and *Etrog*
D. *Hakafah* on Simchat Torah
E. *Mishloach Manot* (exchanging edibles on Purim)
F. *Matanot l'Evyonim* (gifts to the poor on Purim)
G. *Se'udah Shlisheet* (third meal on Shabbat)
H. *Melaveh Malkah* (festivities at the conclusion of Shabbat)
I. *Sefirat Haomer*
J. *Bikur Cholim* (visiting the sick)
K. Burying *Shaymot* (sacred books)
L. *Likboa Mezuzah* (affixing a *mezuzah*)
M. Havdalah
N. *Hachnasat Orchim* (hospitality — toward an Israeli or Russian Jewish family)

Synagogue

Attend Shabbat services with your family. Try to follow the prayers carefully. Which prayer of that service was most meaningful to you? Quote the part that was most important to you. Discuss this with your parents.

Synagogue

Identify the following ritual objects in the synagogue and explain the significance of each:

A. *Aron Hakodesh*
B. *Parochet*
C. *Yad*
D. *Rimmonim*
E. *Keter*
F. *Ner Tamid*
G. Torah

Jewish People

Who in your opinion are the five outstanding Jews in the world at the present time?

Jewish People

You have a personal history. You did not come out of thin air.

A. What is your Hebrew name? Who are you named for? Write a sentence or two on why your parents named you after this person.
B. What is your last name? Does it have a story? Is it based on a place name, like Shapiro (named after Spier, a town in Germany)? Clue: look at maps of Eastern Europe in a Jewish history atlas. Do any of the towns sound like your name? Is your name based on an occupation (like Schneider, tailor in Yiddish)?
C. Your family has a history. Tell the story of how your ancestors came to America and established themselves here. Tell about your grandparents and their families.
D. While visiting the American Jewish Historical Society, check the immigration records, e.g., those of the National Council of Jewish Women. Does your name or that of any of your relatives appear? What do the records say?

As each project is completed the report is turned in to me. I read it, and if it is satisfactory, I record it and return it. No grades are given. The project is recorded twice, once in my record book and once in the student's notebook. The student's notebook resembles a bank book, and not unintentionally: we are telling him or her that the experiences and ideas contained in these projects are important — more than that, they are a kind of riches.

Shabbat Discussions

Since there are few eleven and twelve-year-olds sufficiently motivated to find their way around these projects on their own, we provide a variety of opportunities to complete the requirements. There is a Shabbat morning discussion group in which the students can share ideas and information that enable them to proceed on their own, with the help of the coordinator, community resource people, and synagogue staff. For example, the month of January was set aside for a discussion of Rhode Island's Jewish communal agencies, part of a larger project on Jewish organizations. Each Shabbat morning a different agency leader discussed the workings of his institution with the group. Each agency official received an abstract of the program and sample project cards as part of his invitation, and eagerly accepted. The executive director and president of the Jewish Federation, the director of the Jewish Community Center, and the director of the Jewish Family and Children's Service participated, and seemed to enjoy the experience. They claimed that our students asked better questions than many adult groups they had addressed. Their appearing was important to the students, for it confirmed the notion that the adult Jewish community cared about them.

In the course of preparing for a project on Torah the students met with two of Emanu-El's *ba'alei kriah*. Each explained how, when, and from whom he learned the trope, and gave a demonstration and an introductory lesson from Torah and *Tikkun*. One had learned the skill as a child from his grandfather, the other as an adult from his Rabbi. The students saw that adults were learners, too, and that learning for Jews was an ongoing, never ending activity.

After the recitation of Yizkor we used the discussion group for exchanges on what it means to remember the dead. We touched upon such important issues as the purpose of prayer, immortality, *Kiddush HaShem* and the survival of the Jewish people. One youngster wanted to know if he could recite *Kaddish* for the victims of a plane crash reported in the morning's newspaper. Another asked if he was being hypocritical in reciting "whom I affectionately recall" about a grandfather he never knew.

In theory, only those students who are interested in the program or discussion for a given morning attend; in fact, there is a substantial contingent that comes regardless of what is scheduled. Planning the discussion group for 9:00 a.m. Shabbat morning offers a fringe benefit: a built-in clientele for our Shabbat services which follow. Kids in the program are very visible Shabbat mornings during services; they sit together, many of them students who had never attended a service before.

Library Period

For the projects which require the use of the library, there is a Thursday afternoon library period offered. During this time the librarian and I help students individually — finding books, interpreting information, discussing Haftarot, or rehearsing prayers. This hour holds the program together; the library becomes a drop-in center, and students do drop in — anywhere from four to ten a week, sometimes singly, sometimes in pairs or with parents. For example, a student and her mother met with me to design a Bat Mitzvah invitation. Using a concordance, the three of us chose a verse based on the child's name to appear on the front of the invitation. It was a glorious learning experience: in a casual, informal manner we discussed verses associated with names, examined the role of Miriam in Tanach, and learned to use a concordance. On another Thursday, a student and I discovered her great-grandfather's name in a list of naturalization records from the Providence Country courthouse. I use this library hour to introduce students to Jewish books. A student who showed me a comic book based on the Golem legend left the library with Bellow's *Great Jewish Short Stories*, containing a more authentic version of the tale. One student who is studying Latin noticed *liber regum* in his Tanach, which led to a discussion of the Masoretic text and the differences between the Jewish and Christian canon. Another student, fascinated by Shabbetai Zevi, prompted a mini-lecture on manic-depressive psychosis. He left the library with a review of a book by Gershom Scholem. A third, interested in Jewish symbols, precipitated a search for the history of the *Magen David*. It ended with three of us reading *Encyclopaedia Judaica* — and all of us learning. Like the Shabbat morning discussion group, attendance is entirely voluntary. As the "big day" nears, approximately two to three months before the Bar or Bat Mitzvah, students come of their own accord each week to both sessions.

Workshops

We have also arranged workshops on Sunday and weekday afternoons. One of the most popular was in *mezuzah*-making, using plastic toothbrush holders and the talents of a local calligrapher. The 25 students who sweated and splotched their way through the *parshiyot* all agreed that they would never again take a *mezuzah* for granted. We have held *kashrut* workshops — small group meetings in the kitchens of students enrolled in the program. The host students and their mothers opened cabinets, displayed utensils and shopping lists to each group, explaining the how's and why's of keeping kosher.

Field Trips

We arranged a recent field trip to complete a project on New York Jewish landmarks. Fifty students and their families traveled by bus to New York to wander through the Lower East Side, visiting synagogues, museums, and other Jewish institutions. Here is a student's account of the expedition:

> On Sunday, December 28th, some members of the Bar/Bat Mitzvah group went on a trip to New York. The trip was a great success.
>
> We started out at seven o'clock and got to the Lower East Side at around eleven. Then the kids with parents went one way, and the kids without their parents went another with Mrs. Ingall.
>
> Both groups had excellent tours using walking maps of the area, came back to the bus and went to Temple Emanu-El (of New York, of course). It was really huge, but a little too "churchy" for many of us. We then went to the Jewish Museum, passing the Spanish-Portuguese Synagogue (Touro's sister synagogue) on the way. The museum was very hot and crowded, though the exhibits were good. Finally, we went to the Yeshiva University Museum. We got an excellent tour and most important, a great supper. Then came the worst part; to spoil it all, WE CAME HOME!!!

Students and parents alike benefited enormously from a trip to a local funeral home, done as part of a study of Jewish death and mourning practices — one of the projects in the program. The trip was preceded and followed by intensive discussion with the Rabbi and coordinator. At the funeral home, the directors answered questions coming from parents as well as students. A student reported his feelings:

> Everybody in the program thought it was a valuable experience. It still didn't answer all our questions about death. It exposed us to something we all are frightened about and gave us a chance to think about death and mourning when we are not personally involved. When that sad time should come, hopefully we will be better able to handle the situation, for fear of the unknown is our greatest fear.

Liaison

Since these opportunities are voluntary, it is necessary to provide a means of cohesion between the group, parents, the synagogue and myself. *Bat-Kol*, the monthly newsletter that is mailed to all those associated with the program, largely fulfills this requirement. It contains news items (who will become a Bat or Bar Mitzvah during the month), reprints of particularly witty or perceptive project reports, puzzles based on Jewish personalities, and a calendar of events for the month. An important event was a combined Tu B'Shevat party and *Melaveh Malkah*, when over a hundred people — students and their families — shared fellowship and opportunities to complete several projects (Minchah, *Se'udah Shlisheet*, Ma'ariv, Havdalah, and *Melaveh Malkah*). "Alumni" of the program, those students who had become B'nai Mitzvah, led the services. Students in the program provided the *Melaveh Malkah* entertainment as solo performers, in duets, or in family ensembles. As well as becoming another vehicle for informal education (there was a bilingual program), the party served to cement some of the cross-school friendships. One mother reported to me that her son, who had resisted her efforts to have him attend a Jewish camp, will do so this summer, requesting a particular camp where a friend whom he met in the program is going.

Functional Jews

The program is built on the premise that Bar/Bat Mitzvah is a beginning, not an end. As such it tries to introduce the student to the adult Jewish community, to teach him or her Jewish skills, to provide the opportunity to witness rites of passage, and to underscore that being a Jew means being a part of the Jewish people. Our goal is to make Jewish children "functional Jews," to use Leonard Fein's phrase — emphasizing the behavioral aspects of being a Jewish adult. All those who complete the program are invited to meet with members of Temple Emanu-El's Bar and Bat Mitzvah Committee, the Education Committee, and the Rabbis. Together they sit down and exchange ideas. The students chat about what they enjoyed most or found most difficult, the help they received from their families, and how they would improve the program. These meetings have proven very popular with both the adults and the students involved, serving to highlight the fundamental message of the program — "we think you are special because you take your Jewishness seriously . . . we need you . . . welcome you to our community."

(This chapter first appeared under the title "On Becoming a Jewish Adult" in *Conservative Judaism*.

Chapter 27
"B'Mitzvotav": A Learning-through-Doing Program

Janice Roger

It is a tradition that at the Bar Mitzvah ceremony of his son, a father says: "Blessed be the One who has relieved me of the responsibility for this (boy)."

It is difficult for us to imagine today's thirteen-year-old mature enough to take responsibility for the complexities of the Jewish tradition let alone his or her own life on a day-to-day basis. Rather, today we view Bar or Bat Mitzvah as life cycle event which marks transition in the life of the student. This is one of the reasons why the Indianapolis Hebrew Congregation created the "B'Mitzvotav Program."

The "B'Mitzvotav Program" is a requirement in our congregation for all Bar/Bat Mitzvah students. It supplements tutorial preparation by having the students "practice" the performance of *mitzvot.* It is our hope that each student will become aware of the following:

1. That the Bar/Bat Mitzvah service signifies a public announcement of one's recognition that Judaism is an integral part of his or her life.
2. That many *mitzvot* relate to daily life, not just to Jewish holy days or life cycle events.
3. That *mitzvot* become a frame of reference for living a Jewish life.

WHAT IS THE B'MITZVOTAV PROGRAM?

The "B'Mitzvotav Program" is a learning-through-doing program based on Rabbinic teachings. According to tradition, there are 613 *mitzvot* in the Torah. We learn from the verse in *Pirke Avot*: "The world rests on three things: on Torah, on worship, and on acts of loving-kindness." This program was created around these three categories of *mitzvot.* To help prepare students to become B'nai Mitzvah, each is asked to fulfill a total of 26 *mitzvot.* Of these, 13 are required of every student and 13 are chosen from a list of options. Each of the three categories — Torah (study), worship (*avodah*), and acts of loving-kindness (*gemilut chasadim*) — contains both required and elective *mitzvot.* Students are also encouraged to formulate additional ideas for elective *mitzvot.*

HOW THE PROGRAM WORKS

The "B'Mitzvotav Program" is designed to help prepare students for the increasing responsibilities they will assume as they enter Jewish adulthood. The Rabbis and Cantor explain the program and answer any questions students might have, but it is up to each Bar/Bat Mitzvah to fulfill the program's requirements. As each *mitzvah* is completed, the students sign and turn in the appropriate Mitzvah Card to the Cantor.

Some *mitzvot,* such as leading the congregation in prayer and reading or chanting of the Torah and Haftarah portions, can not be completed until the day of the Bar/Bat Mitzvah ceremony. All of the elective *mitzvot,* however, must be finished before that day. Each student sets a completion date with the Cantor. However, cards may be handed in during any appointment with the Cantor or Rabbis.

WHAT ARE THE MITZVOT TO BE FULFILLED?

The *mitzvot,* both required and elective, are listed in a booklet. Each child is asked to read through the book before his/her first meeting with the Cantor. The listing of the *mitzvot* is as follows:

The Mitzvah of Torah — Study

Required Activities

1. Attend Religious School and pledge to continue to study formally until Confirmation and informally for the rest of your life.

2. Attend the Bureau of Jewish Education for three or more years of Hebrew study (or the equivalent) before the date of your Bar/Bat Mitzvah.
3. Meet with the Rabbi and choose your Torah and Haftarah readings.
4. Study your Torah and Haftarah portions with your family and then with the Rabbi, and write introductions to your readings so the congregation will understand their message.
5. Meet with the Cantor to prepare your Torah and Haftarah portions and other participation in the Bar/Bat Mitzvah service.
6. Attend a Bar/Bat Mitzvah workshop.
7. Read and write a report on the book *Coming of Age* to be handed in to the Rabbi at the six week meeting.

Elective Activities (Choose 5)

1. Start a Jewish library. Add a Jewish book to your personal collection. Read it and then hand in a brief report.
2. Watch two programs of Jewish interest on television. Write a brief report on each one and submit it to the Cantor.
3. Subscribe to a Jewish magazine. Write brief reports on two articles.
4. Write a report on a Jewish subject that interests you.
5. Study about Jewish culture. Learn to play a piece of Jewish music or create a piece of Jewish artwork.
6. Attend one Saturday morning Torah study.
7. Write a report on a famous Jewish person.
8. Write a report on an important event in Jewish history.
9. Do a taped interview with a grandparent about Jewish life when he/she was 13 years of age.
10. Write a detailed report on the customs and traditions involved in a Jewish life cycle event.
11. Participate in and complete the Trope Class offered by the Cantor.

The Mitzvah of Avodah — Worship

Required Activities

1. Attend with your family three Shabbat evening and five Shabbat morning services.
2. Lead the congregation in *Kiddush* at Shabbat evening services the night before your Bar/Bat Mitzvah ceremony.
3. Lead the congregation in prayer the Shabbat morning of your Bar/Bat Mitzvah service.
4. Read or chant the Torah and Haftarah portions and their blessings before the congregation.
5. Write your own prayer, "On Becoming a Bar/Bat Mitzvah," to read before the Ark the morning you celebrate becoming Bar/Bat Mitzvah.

Elective Activities (Choose 3)

1. Light Shabbat candles every Friday evening for at least four consecutive weeks.
2. Lead your family in *Kiddush* every Friday evening for at least four consecutive weeks.
3. Recite the *"Sh'ma"* and *"V'ahavta"* in Hebrew and English every night before going to bed for two weeks.
4. Lead your family in *Hamotzi* before your main meal every day for two weeks.
5. Attend with your family any special service (e.g., festival services, Yizkor service) between now and your Bar/Bat Mitzvah ceremony.
6. Write a creative prayer for a sick friend or relative.
7. Participate as a member of "Cantor's Chanters."
8. Make and use a Jewish object such as a *mezuzah* case, Havdalah candle, *chanukiah*, *challah* cover.
9. Help build a *sukkah* at your or a friend's home.
10. Attend a life cycle event (*Brit Milah*, naming, wedding, funeral) and write a brief report.

The Mitzvah of Gemilut Chasadim — Acts of Loving-kindness

Required Activity

1. Volunteer 13 hours of your time at the Temple or in the community.

Elective Activities (Choose 5)

1. Make a contribution to one of the Temple Funds in honor of/in memory of someone.
2. Pledge a part of your gift money to the charity of your choice.
3. Clean out your closets and drawers and donate the old clothing to charity.

4. Support a local recycling project by bringing in at least one month's worth of your family's old newspapers, bottles, or cans to the appropriate drop-off center.
5. Read the daily paper for a week and determine the issues affecting our community and the world. Write to an elected official about an issue of concern either in the community, the country, or to the Jewish people.
6. Help a classmate who is ill. Bring homework, library books, messages between home and school.
7. Show hospitality. Invite a new classmate or neighbor over for a meal.
8. Write, call, or visit your grandparents. Send a card for their birthday, anniversary, etc.
9. Adopt an elderly person at Hooverwood or Park Regency. Send them cards or visit them regularly.
10. Prepare and donate a food package to a needy family.
11. Comfort a mourner by paying a visit or sending a card.
12. Help out your family, or talk with your parents to figure out a new chore or task that will indicate your growing responsibility and maturity.
13. Help an older adult who lives in your neighborhood by raking leaves, shoveling snow, or running an errand.

THE BAR/BAT MITZVAH WORKSHOP

Each Bar/Bat Mitzvah student, along with his/her parents, attends a Bar/Bat Mitzvah workshop. Approximately seven families meet with the Cantor and Assistant Rabbi. Families are invited according to the date of the Bar/Bat Mitzvah ceremony. The workshop includes study and discussion about the meaning and history of Bar/Bat Mitzvah, the place of *mitzvot* in Jewish life, what it means to become an adult, and a role play of the Bar/Bat Mitzvah ceremony.

The morning is structured as follows (times are approximate):

9:15 a.m. Introduction of families and schedule. Teach the song *"Al Sh'loshah D'varim."*

9:30 a.m. Youth/Adulthood: A Peer Group Activity. Mothers meet together, fathers meet together, and the Bar/Bat Mitzvah students meet together. Each person is asked to answer questions about the differences between childhood and adulthood. They share these answers with their peer group. Finally, the entire group reassembles and all share their answers.

9:50 a.m. Discussion of "life stages" using the time line of Samuel the Younger in *Pirke Avot* 5:25; also, a brief history of the Bar/Bat Mitzvah ceremony is given.

10:00 a.m. *Mitzvah* in Jewish Life. Participants brainstorm the range of *mitzvot* and discover that many of our ethical and moral behaviors, as well as our rituals, have their roots in the Torah.

10:30 a.m. Shabbat Morning Worship and *Kiddush*.

11:45 a.m. My Dear Child/Parent (Letters Home). In recognition of the fact that the meaning of Bar/Bat Mitzvah often gets lost in the whirl of activity that takes place the week before the event, we have the members of each family write letters, parent to child and child to parents. We encourage each writer to include his/her feelings about the receiver as well as feelings about the meaning of Bar/Bat Mitzvah. Each author addresses the letter which is mailed by the congregation about one week before the Bar/Bat Mitzvah service takes place.

12:15 p.m. Bar/Bat Mitzvah Role Play. A "scene" from the service is played out (mostly by students) so that they have some feeling for what will actually happen. Each person has a role; some are active while others are passive (e.g., the Bar Mitzvah is active, "Aunt Sadie" from Brooklyn is passive). Everyone is asked to observe what goes on. After the actual role play, there is a discussion about what has happened. This gives families an opportunity to ask questions about the service, allows the leaders to reassure families, and creates time for those with experience to share their insights.

12:45 p.m. Brit Mitzvah. A closing ceremony which includes the "*Shehecheyanu.*"

THE RESULTS

The "B'Mitzvotav Program" is a student-oriented program. B'nai Mitzvah who successfully complete it receive a certificate and two books at their Bar/Bat Mitzvah service: *Gates of Mitzvah* and *Gates of the Season* (both published by the Central Conference of American Rabbis).

Of the 35 students who celebrated becoming Bar/Bat Mitzvah in 1990-91, only two did not complete the program. Part of the success, of course, is constant urging by the Cantor and the child's parents. However, the program was designed so that its completion would not be " . . . too baffling for you, nor is it beyond reach" (Deuteronomy 30:11).

The "B'Mitzvotav Program" helps students make the transition to adulthood by teaching a more adult understanding of Judaism and our value system.

Chapter 28
Becoming a Bar/Bat Mitzvah through Mitzvot

Marlene Myerson

INTRODUCTION

Preparation for Bar/Bat Mitzvah provides Jewish educators with a unique opportunity to make an impact on students' lives as Jews. By requiring our B'nai Mitzvah students to learn their blessings and portions, and establishing a set schedule of study and practice with a tutor, we fulfill our responsibility to help them learn about and experience the benefits of hard work and conscientious effort. But, equally as important, this can serve as an occasion for our young people to experience, first hand, the power of the idea of *mitzvah.* By actively engaging B'nai Mitzvah students in the fulfillment of a wide variety of *mitzvot,* we can enable them to experience Jewish life in its deepest meaning. The real challenge for us as Jewish educators is to find ways to create meaningful links between the active doing of *mitzvot* and the Bar/Bat Mitzvah event itself.

The focus of this chapter will be to describe two successful Mitzvah Programs which can enhance Bar/Bat Mitzvah preparation and add a significant dimension to students' experience.

BAR/BAT MITZVAH FAMILY ORIENTATION PROGRAMS

The first step in launching a Bar/Bat Mitzvah program of *mitzvot* is gaining the enthusiastic support of students and their parents for the project, as well as their commitment to its success. Since families tend to be very excited about this life cycle event, they are generally very eager to become involved in anything related to it.

Issue an invitation to families to attend two Bar/Bat Mitzvah Family Orientation Programs to be held one week apart. (See sample letter in Figure 1.) These orientation meetings are held once a year in order to include all families who will be celebrating becoming Bar/Bat Mitzvah in the next calendar year.

Figure 1

Dear (Names of Parents and Child)

You and your family are about to embark on an important and exciting Jewish experience — preparation for becoming Bar (or Bat) Mitzvah!

In order to begin the Bar/Bat Mitzvah process for our (*year*) students, we will be holding two Orientation Evenings on (*date*) at (*time*) and on (*date*) at (*time*) in (*place*).

The first meeting will focus on the religious dimensions of Bar/Bat Mitzvah. The meaning of Bar/Bat Mitzvah, its history, ritual, and significance within our tradition will be examined. The uniqueness of the Bar/Bat Mitzvah experience within the context of (name of institution) will also be explored. We will consider ways in which we can make this experience truly meaningful for the entire family.

The second meeting will be devoted to the social service project which all B'nai Mitzvah are asked to undertake. It is our hope that, through this experience, the Bar/Bat Mitzvah students will develop an understanding of the ethical dimensions inherent in Jewish identity.

This evening will consist of an explanation and a discussion of the purpose of the project and a brief presentation by a representative of each of the participating social service agencies. Parents and B'nai Mitzvah will have the opportunity to chat with the agency representatives in order to determine the specific commitments, logistics, and mechanics involved in each of these programs.

Attendance at both of these Orientation Evenings is a requirement for all Bar/Bat Mitzvah students and their parents. I look forward to sharing these evenings with you as we initiate the Bar/Bat Mitzvah process for you and your family.

The First Orientation Meeting

Objectives

1. To understand the historical significance of Bar/Bat Mitzvah.
2. To understand the purpose of Bar/Bat Mitzvah as a life cycle event which stresses *mitzvot* and represents a significant milestone in Jewish education, *but not* graduation.
3. To introduce the "Gesher-13 Mitzvah-Pak."

Schedule

1. Welcome families.
2. Introduction: Brainstorm words related to Bar/Bat Mitzvah such as party, presents, tradition, *mitzvah.*
3. Brief review of history of Bar Mitzvah and Bat Mitzvah.
4. After a brief introduction, show the video *The Mitzvah Machine* (United Synagogue).
5. Discussion following video should focus on concepts of choice, responsibility, and privileges.

Sample Questions for Discussion

1. Why was Jeff so blasé about his Bar Mitzvah?
2. What does the word *mitzvah* mean?
3. Can the skills learned for the Bar/Bat Mitzvah ceremony ever be used again? How? When?
4. Can a Bar/Bat Mitzvah ceremony change someone? Is it meant to? Does the ceremony make one a Bar/Bat Mitzvah?
5. Why does the Rabbi say that one doesn't "have a Bar/Bat Mitzvah, one *becomes* a Bar/Bat Mitzvah"?
6. What is meant by the comment "Bar/Bat Mitzvah is just a beginning"?
7. Introduce "Gesher-13 Mitzvah-Pak."

GESHER-13 MITZVAH-PAK

The "Gesher-13 Mitzvah-Pak" consists of 20 colored cards, each one listing a *mitzvah* which can be performed by the Bar/Bat Mitzvah student, and a larger card which explains the "Gesher-13" program (Figure 2).

Figure 2

"Gesher-13" is our special Mitzvah Program for seventh graders. As you begin the process of becoming Bar/Bat Mitzvah, one of the most important aspects of the entire process is the opportunity to learn first hand how powerful the idea of *mitzvah* can be in your life as an individual and as a Jew. This is why the "Gesher-13 Mitzvah-Pak" has been created: to act as a bridge between your childhood and your adulthood, and to allow you the opportunity to experience doing a wide variety of *mitzvot,* and to experience Jewish life in its deepest meaning.

In the "Gesher-13 Mitzvah-Pak," there are two different categories of *mitzvot* for you to experience: Home and Community. The goal of the program is for you to perform *mitzvot* in each of these areas — a total of 13 in all. In this packet you will find activity cards which have to be signed by you and one of your parents as you fulfill the *mitzvah* described on that card. When each card is completed, bring it into the school office and place it into the "Gesher-13" envelope which has your name on it.

Gesher-13 Activity Cards

Each of the following *mitzvot* is printed on a 4" x 5" colored card:

Home

1. Light the Shabbat candles and recite the blessing for your family on a Friday night.
2. Recite the blessings for lighting the *chanukiah* with your family.
3. Interview a relative about his or her most memorable Jewish experience. Either tape record or write the interview out for your class.
4. Share a favorite family recipe with your class. Samples are mandatory!
5. Write an essay on what your Bar/Bat Mitzvah celebration means to you and your family, and why you are becoming a Bar/Bat Mitzvah (four paragraphs in length).
6. A name often reflects something about one's personal history. Find out the meaning of your Hebrew name and why your parents gave you this name.

7. Attend a Jewish life cycle ceremony (for example: *Brit Milah,* Bar/Bat Mitzvah, wedding, funeral, etc.). Describe the Jewish customs you observe. Ask your parents for help in understanding these ceremonies.
8. Trace your Jewish roots by designing a family tree, and prepare a report on your ancestors and their Jewish experiences. (For children in intermarried families, trace both the Jewish and non-Jewish roots.)
9. Recite the *Kiddush* for your family on a Friday evening.
10. Bake a *challah* and share it with your family on Shabbat.

Community

1. Visit the Jewish Home for the Aged. Interview an older person who was born in a foreign country. Write a report on his or her Jewish life and customs.
2. Prepare a basket of goodies (home-baked cookies, tiny jars of jam, candies) and deliver it to a friend as a *mishloach manot* gift for Purim.
3. Correspond with an Israeli pen pal.
4. Contribute food to a Pesach Food Drive.
5. Tutor another student from the Religious School. Help him or her improve his/her Hebrew skills.
6. Attend at least three Friday night Shabbat services during the year.
7. Attend a Shabbat service at another synagogue. Describe in writing what you most enjoyed about the service.
8. Remember our connections with the Jews in Israel by donating money to JNF to plant a tree.
9. In honor of your Bar/Bat Mitzvah, make a donation to MAZON.
10. Participate in the United Jewish Appeal Walk-a-thon.

Social Service Project

Providing students with the opportunity to participate in a social service project is one way of connecting the ethical dimension of Judaism to the Bar/Bat Mitzvah process.

The first step is to identify agencies in your community which would be willing to accept your students as volunteers. You may meet some initial resistance, based on the assumption that twelve-year-olds lack the maturity to make a useful contribution, but be persistent. If given the opportunity, these young people can and will prove that they are very capable.

Ideally, you should have a wide variety of agencies that serve diverse populations in different settings. This will allow students to select an agency that is appropriate for their particular needs or interests. In some settings, the students are utilized as helpers in group activities; in others, they work one-on-one with individuals. Some suggestions are: day care centers, senior citizen residences, hospitals, programs for physically and/or mentally disabled children, summer camps for disabled children, the Institute for the Blind, the Jewish Community Center, and Meals on Wheels (the delivery of hot meals to shut-ins).

Once the agencies have agreed to accept the B'nai Mitzvah as volunteers, ask for a representative of each agency who will act as the contact/liaison between the B'nai Mitzvah and the agency. Be sure to discuss with them your expectations of the student's involvement. A minimum of ten weekly visits of two hours in duration should be required. Sometimes, the agencies will have additional requirements, such as attendance at a volunteer training program or a longer time commitment as a volunteer. Clarifying these expectations from the beginning avoids misunderstandings later on.

Launching the Program: The Second Orientation Evening

The second Orientation Evening is devoted to the Social Service Project. It provides an opportunity for B'nai Mitzvah students and their parents to hear, first-hand, about the various agencies and to ask questions directly to the agency representatives.

Invite representatives from each of the agencies. Each student should receive a kit which has been prepared in advance and which contains the following:

1. A letter of explanation to the student about the project
2. A letter of explanation to the parents about the project
3. A list of Project requirements (Appendix 1)
4. A Project selection form (Appendix 2)

5. Ten diary sheets to be used to record the students' thoughts and feelings after each weekly visit (Appendix 3)

Objectives for the Orientation

1. To provide an overview of the purpose of the Social Service Project.
2. To review the expectations of the Social Service Project.
3. To give the B'nai Mitzvah and their families an opportunity to hear about each of the agencies.
4. To give the B'nai Mitzvah and their families an opportunity to talk to the agency representatives before selecting a project.

Schedule

1. Review the purpose of the Social Service Project.
2. Review the expectations of the Project.
3. Introduce the representatives of each of the agencies. Ask them to make a brief (3-5 minutes) presentation so as to give the students and their parents an overview of their agency and the kinds of activities volunteers would be expected to do there. (In subsequent years, you can invite post-Bar/Bat Mitzvah students to speak about their personal experiences within a particular agency.)
4. Ask everyone to move into another room where you have set up tables for each individual agency. Some agencies provide displays and/or pamphlets which you should request in advance.
5. The B'nai Mitzvah and their parents can walk around the room, talking to each of the agency representatives, asking questions, and gathering available literature.
6. Have a display of the project diaries of former B'nai Mitzvah. Families enjoy having the opportunity to browse through them.

Following this Orientation Evening, students will select the agency at which they wish to do their volunteer work. They are responsible for contacting the agency representative in order to arrange a starting date. The project selection form is then completed by the student and handed in to the School office.

Once the student has completed ten visits to the selected agency, an appointment is made with the Director of Education (or the Social Service Project Coordinator). The student is asked to bring the ten diary sheets to this meeting. The Director of Education and the student review the diary sheets and discuss the implications of the experience. Use the questions recommended under "Conclusion" (see below) as a guide. In this way, you can help the student gain valuable insights into his/her own unique abilities to make a difference in the world. Focus on the experience as an example of *tikkun olam,* improving the world. You can help the students identify qualities in themselves that they had to draw on during their volunteer work. As the students begin to recognize their own growth and development as a result of the Project, they will understand that the Project is both a giving and a receiving experience.

The Completed Diary

As the final step in this Social Service Project, it is important to have the students complete a diary scrapbook of their experiences. This will enable them to consider the significance of their volunteer work and its impact both on others and on themselves. Ask each student to purchase an attractive, hard cover album — a photo album with peel-up sheets is ideal. Provide each student with a series of guidelines for setting up the finished diary. A suggested format is as follows:

1. Introduction – Describe your project choice. Discuss your reasons for selecting this particular project.
2. Research – Do some research into the disability, handicap, or general characteristics of the people you are working with.
3. Diary – A separate entry for each time you visited the agency or individual. Include your activities, your thoughts and feelings at the time, etc.
4. Conclusions – Your thoughts and feelings about your project experience. In discussing this, try to answer the following 12 questions:
   What was the most satisfying aspect of your project?
   What was the most disappointing aspect of your project?
   What things did you learn about others?
   What things did you learn about yourself?
   How did you help others grow?
   How did others help you grow?

How have you changed as a result of this project?
How have others changed as a result of this project?
What was "Jewish" about this project?
What is the meaning of the word *mitzvah?*
What is the attitude of Judaism toward the doing of *mitzvot?*
How has your project helped you better understand what the ceremony of Bar/Bat Mitzvah is all about?

5. Pictures – One day, take some pictures of the people and activities that were an important part of your project.

Students should complete their diaries two weeks before their Bar/Bat Mitzvah ceremony and submit them to the Director of Education or to the Social Service Project Coordinator. Often the Rabbi will refer to the project during the Bar/Bat Mitzvah service and, perhaps, ask the Bar/Bat Mitzvah to read one of the diary entries or the conclusion to the congregation.

It is a good idea to keep these diaries and to put them on display at the next year's Project Orientation Evening. They should then be returned to students to be kept for posterity!

CONCLUSION

As our youngsters begin their Bar/Bat Mitzvah preparation, it is important to provide them with as many opportunities as possible to make that experience meaningful. The "Gesher-13 Mitzvah-Pak" and the Social Service Project are two excellent vehicles for teaching our B'nai Mitzvah the true meaning of the word *"mitzvah."*

APPENDIX 1

Project Requirements

1. You are responsible for choosing the agency with which you would like to work from the approved list of participating organizations.

2. You must make your choice and submit the enclosed project selection form by (date).

3. You are to make arrangements directly with the agency representatives regarding when, where, and what your project will involve.

4. You are required to visit your agency or individual at least ten times before your Bar/Bat Mitzvah service.

5. You should keep a diary in which you record your activities, thoughts, and feelings after each visit. Diary sheets are included in this folder.

6. As soon as you have completed your ten visits, contact (Name of Director of Education or Social Service Project Coordinator) to arrange an appointment.

7. After meeting with the Coordinator, you will compile your diary entries and all other pertinent information (see Guidelines for Your Project) into a neat and attractive format, such as a hardcover scrapbook, available at any book store.

8. The finished project scrapbook must be submitted to the school office at least two weeks before your Bar/Bat Mitzvah service.

APPENDIX 2

Bar/Bat Mitzvah Project Selection Form

STUDENT'S NAME ______________________________ GRADE ______

DATE OF BAR/BAT MITZVAH CEREMONY ______________________________

THE AGENCY I HAVE CHOSEN TO WORK WITH IS ______________________________

MY STARTING DATE IS ______________________________
(You should start at least six months before your Bar/Bat Mitzvah ceremony.)

I understand the purpose of the Bar/Bat Mitzvah project and will try, to the best of my ability, to fulfill the project requirements.

____
(Student's signature)

Submit this form to the school office by ______________________________ (date).

APPENDIX 3

Diary Entry Form

STUDENT'S NAME ______________________________ GRADE________

PLACE ______________________________ VISIT # ________

DATE ______________________________ TIME______________________________

1. Describe what you did during your visit today. Be specific. Be sure to describe how you felt about your experience today.

2. Describe one incident that made your experience today different from other days.

3. What was positive about today's experience?

4. What frustrations did you encounter? How do you plan to change things next time?

Unit V: Family Education
Overview

The term "family education" when used in reference to B'nai Mitzvah generally refers to any course of study done by B'nai Mitzvah students together with their parents. The two primary goals of such a course are: the imparting of knowledge to both students and parents (the cognitive area) and opening the lines of communication among family members (the affective area). The Bar/Bat Mitzvah year is the ideal time to create a sense of community among and between families, and between families and synagogues.

In Chapter 29, Cantor Helen Leneman describes the basic components of a Family Education program, along with a wide variety of options for such a program.

In Chapters 30, Emily Bank relates her experience in the creation and implementation of a Family Education program.

In Chapter 31, Rabbi David Lieb describes a Family Education program he started in the 1970s, when such programs were a rarity, and discusses how it has evolved since that time to become a meaningful part of every family's Bar/Bat Mitzvah experience.

In Chapter 32, Cantor Helen Leneman reviews *Windows*, an exciting curriculum by Vicky Kelman from the Melton Research Center. This is an innovative program allowing much flexibilty in its implementation.

In Chapter 33, Barry Lutz discusses a Family Education Shabbaton program which features participation of all B'nai Mitzvah families in a Shabbat service and a discussion of its meaning for their lives, as well as discussions of individual Torah portions.

In Chapter 34, Rabbi Ron Aigen outlines a three session Family Education workshop that includes numerous exercises on Jewish identity, understanding responsibility, the meaning of *mitzvah* and Bar/Bat Mitzvah, and exploration of traditional texts. The program has fostered a strong sense of community among B'nai Mitzvah and their families.

Chapter 35 is the description, by Roberta Goodman and Dr. Lois Zachary, of a Family Education program which expands the meaning of the Bar/Bat Mitzvah experience for families. The outline will enable the reader to replicate this program, which successfully combines the concerns and values of students, families, and the synagogue.

Parents and synagogues alike have a great deal to gain from intergenerational study in the year or years preceding Bar/Bat Mitzvah. It is hoped that any congregation not presently offering Family Education will be able to tailor one or more of these programs to its needs.

Chapter 29

Family Education: A Synthesis

Helen Leneman

Ideas from a number of contributors are included in this chapter. Some of these contributors expand on these ideas in a separate chapter in this Unit. These individuals are: Ron Aigen, Congregation Dorshei Emet, the Reconstructionist Synagogue of Montreal; Emily Bank, the Ivriah, Flint, Michigan; Allen Leider, Temple Anshe Sholom, Olympia Fields, Illinois; David Lieb, Temple Beth El, San Pedro, California; Barry Lutz, Temple Ahavat Shalom, Northridge, California; and Greg Yaroslow, Temple Emanu El, San Bernardino, California.

Family Education is generally offered to the entire group of sixth graders together with their parents. Sometimes, the parents and children are separated for some learning activities and then brought back together. How the courses are arranged depends not only on who is available to teach them, but how large a group is involved. Obviously, the techniques would vary accordingly. Some synagogues utilize congregants as teachers, while others depend on professional staff only.

Many synagogues choose to make family education an intense one day activity, often a Shabbaton and conducted after Saturday morning worship services. These may be held once or twice a year. In larger congregations opting to do this activity in seventh grade, the ideal is two Shabbatonim a year: one in fall, for families with a Bar/Bat Mitzvah between January and June, and one in spring, for B'nai Mitzvah between July and December. If the Shabbatonim are done for sixth graders, the month is less crucial. The families involved participate in some way in the Shabbat service. The Shabbaton can also begin the evening before with participation in services.

The most limiting factor in the Shabbaton format is time, but this is also the reason it is popular, because there is less commitment demanded of congregants' schedules. Another format is to offer from four to six sessions, usually of two hours duration, either Saturday or Sunday (just prior to services or Religious School), or on a weeknight. This format allows instructors to teach subjects in much greater depth, but regular attendance on the part of both parents and children cannot be assured. The program must be presented as an extremely attractive package, and some form of positive reinforcement should be built in. (Chapter 34 offers curriculum suggestions for a lengthier course.)

Two important elements of Family Education programs that are sometimes overlooked are good closure activities and follow-up activities. A thoughtful and complete evaluation form presented at the end of a course would serve both functions. It should include a list of every activity of the day, with space for comments and suggestions after each (see Appendix 2 of Chapter 31 and the Appendix for Chapter 33 for examples of such forms) .

A reunion later in the year could be an occasion for participants to review course material and compare present attitudes with those held earlier in the year. The option of such a follow-up could be presented to the parents in the evaluation form.

The usual order for a one day course, after introductory remarks and a brief history of Bar/Bat Mitzvah, is the following:

1. Lecture (possibly followed by a quiz) on topics related to Bar/Bat Mitzvah
2. Personal questions and discussion between parents and children about Bar/Bat Mitzvah
3. Conclusion: review, evaluation; possibly Havdalah ceremony

If the families are all expected to attend Shabbat services, these services can be used as an occasion to teach the meaning of prayers and of Shabbat. Sessions could be held prior to and just after services for this purpose. (Chapter 33 includes discussion of such a program.) Following is an overview of each of the three components listed above.

1. Lecture/Quiz

Subjects taught in the course of the day are the same as those that would be offered in a longer course. Since anything taught must be geared in some way to the Bar/Bat Mitzvah ceremony, the most common topics after the History of the Bar/Bat Mitzvah are:

Essential Vocabulary
Tanach: what it is; structure, interpretation
The meaning of your child's Torah/Haftarah portion; writing a *drash*
Trope: background, function
Learning the Torah Blessings
The Geography of the Siddur
Mitzvah Projects
The Jewish Calendar
Music of the Service

Teaching many facts and terms in a very short time span can be done in one of two ways: a lecture format followed immediately by a quiz/review session, or a quiz to be completed first and then discussed. (See Appendix at the end of this chapter for a sample quiz.)

To make the activity more fun, Allen Leider's "The Bar/Bat Mitzvah Family Education Program" (unpublished paper written at Hebrew Union College), proposes a game of *Jewperdy* (based on the game *Jeopardy*). For example, in the category of "Worship and Wardrobe" for $300, the answer is "prayer shawl"; for $500, "commanded to wear in '*V'ahavta.*'" Under "Torah people," for $200, "the title of 'Torah lifter.'" All the questions would have been discussed in a prior lecture, so it is designed as a test of instant recall. The only drawback to this game is the obvious advantage the more knowledgeable parents or children will have over the others.

Handing out a quiz for parents and children to complete together is less likely to embarrass or discourage less knowledgeable families, since these families can sit quietly and learn without being put on the spot. Multiple choice questions, such as those used by Temple Emanu El of San Bernardino, California, are a good format (see Appendix 2 for complete text of their test). Injecting humor as this test does by adding a silly choice to several questions will make this activity more fun.

A similar quiz appears in the excellent book *Coming of Age As a Jew — Bar/Bat Mitzvah* (Board of Jewish Education of Greater New York). This book is reviewed in Chapter 38.

2. Personal Discussion

To pave the way for intergenerational discussion, children and their parents might go into separate rooms and then reconvene after completing their own discussions. To start off the discussions, trigger questions are essential. These can be very broad or very specific. Some synagogues prefer to view and discuss a Bar/Bat Mitzvah related video to trigger a discussion about values (see the Bibliography at the end of this book for reviews of videos with Bar/Bat Mitzvah themes). Examples of discussion questions geared for pre-Bar/Bat Mitzvah students:

Discuss and list the six most important elements to you having to do with the Bar/Bat Mitzvah experience. Be honest! (Let them write out their answers anonymously to encourage complete honesty.)

Becoming a Bar/Bat Mitzvah often means becoming more independent and more responsible. How do you show you are ready for this? How do you think your parents feel about your growing up? What fears and concerns do you think they have?

Complete the following statements about your parents and your relationship with them:
I appreciate . . . demand . . . wonder . . . hope . . . need . . . should . . . will never . . . always . . .

Complete the following:
I want to become Bar/Bat Mitzvah because . . .
I think my parents want me to become Bar/Bat Mitzvah because . . .
The most important thing I can get from my Jewish education is . . .
Judaism is important (not important) to me because . . .

The following questions are geared for parents:
How do you deal with your child's developing need for independence? How can the synagogue help in this matter?

Complete the following:
I want my child to become Bar/Bat Mitzvah because . . .
I belong to the synagogue because . . .
Religion is important to me because . . .
What do you imagine this service means to your son or daughter?

In addition, parents might answer some of the same questions their children answered above (e.g., completing statements about their children that start with "I appreciate . . . demand . . . etc."). The separate groups of parents and children are asked to write down responses to these questions. When the whole group reconvenes, responses can be written on a blackboard and differences between children's and parent's responses can be discussed. If the group is too large, it can be divided up.

An issue that frequently comes up in such a discussion is the pressure children are feeling to "perform," and the lack of awareness on the part of parents that they are exerting this pressure. Professionals leading these discussions should make note of this problem and propose positive, constructive solutions. The ideal solution is, of course, to find meaning in the Bar/Bat Mitzvah, both in the preparation and the event itself.

There are also questions that can open a direct discussion between parents and children. These deal with the parents' own B'nai Mitzvah ceremonies. Some synagogues request that the parents bring along any Bar/Bat Mitzvah memorabilia they have, such as pictures, invitations, tape, or *tallit*, to the Shabbaton. The physical presence of these articles can be an aid in generating a true sharing session. Possible trigger questions for this session might be:

Describe your recollections of when you became Bar/Bat Mitzvah (if you did).

If you did not participate in a Bar/Bat Mitzvah ceremony, why not? And, if you were to do so now, what do you imagine you would need to learn in order for it to be a meaningful experience?

Where did your/your sibling's/your cousin's Bar/Bat Mitzvah take place? Who was there? How did you feel that day before, during, and after the ceremony? What else do you remember about the day?

Other questions not directly related to the Bar/Bat Mitzvah will help children grasp the concept that their parents were once actually 12 years old themselves:

When I was your age, my favorite music was . . . I was most interested in . . . things that were different . . . things that were the same . . .

3. Concluding Activities

For closure, a summary of the day's activities followed by a brief Havdalah service seems to be the norm. Evaluation forms might be handed out then or mailed several days later. (For examples of such forms, see Appendixes to Chapter 30 and 33.) If a follow-up activity is planned, that might be mentioned then. A more unusual, personal sharing activity for closure is proposed by Allen Leider. Participants gather in a circle (depending on group size, this might have to be two or more separate circles) and share responses to the following question: "Whom would you really like to invite to your Bar/Bat Mitzvah ceremony, and why? The person can be dead or alive, historical or fictitious." Responses from students and adults are likely to be vastly different, and can be an opportunity for both to see new facets of each other. This is also a chance for families to draw closer to one another. Of course, the success of such an unusual trigger question depends a great deal on the mood set during the entire day.

Family Education, whether it takes place in a single day or over a period of weeks and months, is a new and important element of B'nai Mitzvah education. Parents will gain more from the whole process when they are better educated about it. Their increased interest and awareness will set an important example for their children. And the hope is that studying and learning side-by-side will strengthen bonds that are too often frayed during this difficult time. Families, synagogues, and the entire Jewish community can all gain from strong Family Education programs.

APPENDIX

Sample Bar/Bat Mitzvah Quiz

1. Which of the following biblical personalities had a Bar Mitzvah ceremony?
   a. Moses
   b. Abraham
   c. King David
   d. All of the above
   e. None of the above

2. According to tradition, who is considered a Bar Mitzvah?
   a. any Jewish boy who reaches the age of 13 years and one day.
   b. Only a thirteen-year-old Jewish boy who can read Hebrew.
   c. Only a thirteen-year-old Jewish boy who can read from the Torah without vowels.
   d. Only a thirteen-year-old Jewish boy who can expound on a Talmudic argument.
   e. All of the above.

3. The Haftarah is:
   a. Half of the Torah portion
   b. A blessing for the Bar/Bat Mitzvah
   c. A reading from the Prophets
   d. A speech given in English, Yiddish, or Hebrew
   e. None of the above

4. The words "Bar Mitzvah" mean:
   a. Manhood
   b. Festival of good deeds
   c. Son of the commandment
   d. Thirteen-year-old

5. Which of the following practices have historically been associated with the Bar Mitzvah ceremony?
   a. Wearing of *tefillin*
   b. The father saying, "Blessed is the One who has relieved me of responsibility for this child"
   c. Expounding on the Rabbinical commentaries of the portion of the week
   d. All of the above
   e. None of the above

6. What is the significance of becoming a Bar Mitzvah?
   a. Having a party and getting presents
   b. Accepting responsibility for following the commandments of Judaism
   c. Proving that you can read Hebrew
   d. An end to Jewish studies

7. When did the first known Bat Mitzvah ceremony take place?
   a. 420-430
   b. 1810-1820
   c. 1920-1930
   d. 1940-1950

8. An *aliyah* is:
   a. Being asked to recite the "*Sh'ma*"
   b. A prayer for welcoming the Sabbath day
   c. Being called up to the *bimah* to recite the blessings before and after the reading of the Torah
   d. All of the above
   e. None of the above

9. Which of the following does NOT happen at a Bar/Bat Mitzvah ceremony in our synagogue?
   a. The child reads or chants a portion of the Torah and its blessings.
   b. The child gives a speech instructing the congregation based on the Torah portion of the week.
   c. The child puts on the *tefillin* at the service.
   d. The child chants or reads the Haftarah of the week and its blessings.
   e. The child chants a tractate from the Mishnah.

10. When can a Bar/Bat Mitzvah be held?
   a. On Shabbat morning
   b. On Shabbat afternoon
   c. On any holy day or festival morning
   d. On a Monday morning
   e. On a Tuesday morning
   f. On a Wednesday morning
   g. On a Thursday morning
   h. On a Sunday morning

Chapter 30

A Maiden Voyage into Family Education Programming

Emily Bank

The Ivriah of Flint, Michigan, where the Family Education program described in this chapter was created, is a combined supplementary school of two congregations, one Reform and one Conservative. Rabbi Paul Tuchman of Temple Beth El and Rabbi Paul Reis of Congregation Beth Israel were the co-directors and creators of this program.

Sixth and seventh grade B'nai Mitzvah training for the children of both congregations is done through the school, with students separated by congregation for Bar/Bat Mitzvah classes. Because our students are combined for the rest of their hours each week and throughout their years in the school, and because one of the goals of the Ivriah is that our students understand and appreciate the diversity of Judaism, it seemed very appropriate to have a Bar/Bat Mitzvah Family Education program for a combined group of our B'nai Mitzvah students. We chose to have this program during the spring semester for our sixth grade, pre-B'nai Mitzvah students and their families. We invited all interested family members, including siblings, grandparents, and others.

Our primary goal for this program was to enhance for each family the meaningfulness of their upcoming Bar/Bat Mitzvah through a shared cognitive family learning experience. Our secondary goal was to provide a setting in which children and parents could interact in a new and different way, as co-learners, and thereby engender increased respect and appreciation for each other on the affective level.

We made the decision to implement this program relatively late in the year, which created scheduling problems. Our program was team-taught by the Rabbis of each of our two congregations and by me. We offered six 90 minute sessions spread over a 2½ month period, which was less than we would have liked, but it was the best we could manage. The sessions were from one to four weeks apart and were held on different nights of the week. During any given session, we covered from one to three different topics. These were the six session topics:

1. Sedra Study – We decided that an important part of our program should be the exploration by each family of the *sedra* to be read or chanted at their child's Bar/Bat Mitzvah service. At the first session, each family was given an extensive amount of printed material on their *sedra*. Using this material, the family was to do research and then present this *sedra* to the rest of the group at the last class session. This could be done in the form of a report, a video, a skit, or any other way the family chose. All the audiovisual resources of the school were made available. During this first session, we discussed what we mean by "Hebrew Bible," Tanach, as well as different ideas about the origin and interpretation of the Torah —the literal and the liberal.
2. This session was made up of two parts, structure of the Torah and history of Bar/Bat Mitzvah.
   a. Structure of the Torah (continuation of Session 1) – For the structure of the Torah, we included related topics: the Hebrew and Greek names of the Five Books; the historical period of time covered by each book; what is a *sedra*, a Maftir, the Haftarah; when and why did reading of the Haftarah originate?
   b. History of Bar/Bat Mitzvah – We gave a brief historical overview of this life cycle event: thirteen as the age of legal Jewish adulthood, as established by Talmudic and Midrashic literature; first mention of a Bar Mitzvah, placing it around the fifteenth century in Europe; the

form the ceremony took at that time; how the form changed in the late Middle Ages; different customs observed in Sephardic and Ashkenazic congregations; the first Bat Mitzvah, held in 1922; the Bar/Bat Mitzvah ceremony as practiced today in Reform, Conservative, and Orthodox congregations; the concern about "conspicuous consumption" in Bar/Bat Mitzvah celebrations, both historically (as seen in "Sumptuary Laws" of the Middle Ages) and today.

3. Geography of the Siddur – This was an overview of the prayer books and Torah commentaries used in our two congregations. We reviewed the content and organization of these four volumes in the hope of helping our students become more comfortable with them and better able to use them as personal resources.
4. Shabbat Service — We dealt with the structure of the service, breaking it down into its component parts. We also discussed the differences between the Reform and Conservative services.
5. Jewish Calendar – We delved into its complexities and the differences between it and our civil calendar.
6. *Sedra* Presentation – At this last session, each family gave their presentation on their own *sedra*. Each presentation took about ten minutes and answered the following questions:
   What is the name of the *sedra*?
   In which book is it found?
   Where are we in time and place when the *sedra* begins?
   What is the story line?
   Is there a main character? if so, tell us about him/her.
   What is the message of the *sedra*; and what is its relevance for us today?

Evaluation

This evaluation is a composite of the assessment of the program staff, plus the results of a survey we gave to all participants at the end of the sixth session (see Appendix to this chapter). We were basically happy with this first attempt at a Bar/Bat Mitzvah Family Education program, and we believe our participants had a positive learning experience. The three of us who led the program learned much in terms of what worked and what did not, and how to do this better next time. Based on our experience, here is a list of suggestions for any synagogue attempting a similar program.

1. Provide refreshments – As inconsequential and petty as that may sound, both adults and children appreciated the refreshments and commented on how this enhanced the informality of the program.
2. Maintain an open, positive attitude – Such an attitude contributes to a very nice give and take atmosphere. We stated at the outset that we were all here to learn from and teach one another and to enjoy the experience.
3. Include family *sedra* presentations – Family presentations require a high level of participation and family interaction, as well as a high level of involvement of the B'nai Mitzvah students. Our participants particularly liked the concept.
4. Offer at least six sessions, and on a regular night – Scheduling must be done well in advance. If sessions are not on a regular night, participants will find the schedule confusing.
5. Deal in both cognitive and affective areas – Our program stressed only the cognitive area, and therefore we did not achieve our primary goal, to enhance the meaningfulness of each family's upcoming Bar/Bat Mitzvah. At such a program, students should learn a great deal of basic Judaism. But time should also be spent discussing with students and their families their needs, desires, hopes, fears, and dreams concerning their Bar/Bat Mitzvah. A discussion should be included on what families want their Bar/Bat Mitzvah ceremony to be like, what kinds of symbols come to mind when they think about Bar/Bat Mitzvah, and what they think is the most meaningful thing they associate with becoming a Bar or Bat Mitzvah. Discuss with them how to plan the family's participation in the service, and how to personalize the service. Discuss ways in which each family can make their child's Bar/Bat Mitzvah specific and meaningful to the family and reflective of their values and special interests within the parameters of Reform and Conservative Judaism.

6. Create a forum in which all aspects of Bar/Bat Mitzvah can be discussed – Discussion should include everything from invitations and who should receive them, to who should have *aliyot*, and what the party should be like. All of this can be done in a variety of interactive ways: break-out groups and case studies are only two. Inviting some post-B'nai Mitzvah students and parents to class to share their own Bar/Bat Mitzvah experiences would also be helpful and of interest.
7. Find the appropriate teaching level – Whenever both adults and children are in the same classroom, the question of which group to target arises. Often the interest shown and the questions asked by the adults will lead to a risk of having spirited adult discussions and teaching to their level the majority of the time. If this occurs, you risk losing the children. Adult discussions will usually be over the children's heads — possibly even over some of the *adults'* heads. Don't make overly optimistic assumptions about the prior knowledge of the participating adults.

   In most cases, it is probably best to aim Family Education programs at the children's level and try to put aside for another time any adult questions that would lead the group astray. Parents want to see their children actively involved and, given the unfortunate fact that many parents are not much more Jewishly knowledgeable than their children, it is usually possible to teach on a lower level without offending adults.
8. Avoid lecture-style teaching – An emphasis on learner-centered teaching will foster involvement and interaction, particularly from the B'nai Mitzvah students.
9. Include a *mitzvah* component – A Mitzvah Program component was lacking from our program, but we feel this to be a vital aspect and plan to include it next time. Such a component could be done on either an individual or family level, or even as an entire Family Education class. (See all the chapters in Unit IV for descriptions of various Mitzvah Programs.)

Conclusion

We were pleased with our program as a first attempt. We hope to build on the positive aspects of our experience and change and correct those areas with which we were dissatisfied. We hope that readers who are planning Bar/Bat Mitzvah Family Education Programs of their own will find this summary of our "maiden voyage" helpful.

APPENDIX

Evaluation Form

1. _____ I am a child
   _____ I am a parent

2. The concept of this program was to provide a shared learning experience for families that would help to make their upcoming Bar/Bat Mitzvah a meaningful event. Do you think that the concept of this program is a valid one? Should we have the program again for next year's sixth grade?

The following topics were covered during the six sessions:

Session Number	Topic
1	Tanach: What do we mean by Hebrew Bible? Origins of the Torah, literal and liberal interpretations
2	The history and significance of Bar/Bat Mitzvah; structure of the Torah: the Five Books; Hebrew and Greek names; divisions into *sedrot*; what is the Haftarah?
3	Comparison of Reform and Conservative liturgy
4	Structure of the service Geography of the Siddur Geography of the Commentaries
5	Nusach and trope Jewish calendar
6	*Sedra* presentations by families

3. Do you think we should delete any of these topics next year? If so, which ones, and why?

4. Would any of the topics have been of more value to you if they were taught differently? Which ones, and how?

APPENDIX (Cont.)

5. Were there topics that we didn't cover that you would like to have covered? What are they?

6. Did you find the research material given to you in the first session adequate or inadequate? Was it of interest to you?

7. Did you as a family work together on your *sedra* presentation, or did only certain individuals actually do most of the work? If only certain individuals, which ones? (Mom, Dad, child and Mom, etc.)

8. Do you think the program next year should include *sedra* presentations by the families?

9. If we have this program for sixth grade families next year, do you think participation should be required, or left optional as it was this year?

10. Based on your experience this year, in what ways would you change the program for next year?

11. Please make any other comments that you think will help us design a program for next year. We really want your input! Attach extra sheets if you need more room.

Name (optional): ______________________________

Chapter 31
B'nai Mitzvah Family Education

David S. Lieb

Those who work with Bar/Bat Mitzvah students and their families learn very quickly that the service and everything surrounding it is not simply an event in the life of the thirteen-year-old. In fact, this occasion is probably more emotionally significant and fraught with deeper religious meaning for the parents than it is for the child. There are many levels of meaning for the student as well, although they are not easily articulated or understood. In short, becoming Bar or Bat Mitzvah is a process that profoundly affects the lives and feelings of both generations in the immediate household and is therefore a prime focus for Family Education.

This particular program in Family Education for Bar/Bat Mitzvah began in the late 1970s at my congregation in California. It was very clear to me that students had little appreciation for what this moment in their lives meant to their parents. At the same time, the students were not always telling their parents what it was that they were experiencing as they prepared for the ceremony. Moreover, the particular generation of parents involved presented some unique problems with regard to basic Jewish education.

Many of the parents then — and now — were relative newcomers to liberal Judaism and progressive, liberal Jewish education. Many of the mothers had not become Bat Mitzvah and so had no information or experience whatsoever. Many were Jews-by-choice and they also had no referent. The fathers who had become Bar Mitzvah within traditional congregations had learned their material by rote, but because they were not steeped in "old world Judaism," the day had nowhere near the emotional impact on them that it had on their own parents. For all of these reasons and more, there was a basic information "underload" about the history, religious meaning, and protocol of Bar/Bat Mitzvah.

This program, then, was an attempt to accomplish two things: fill in the vacuum of information, and get parents and students to talk with one another about this moment in the life of their family. At that time, I was not aware of anyone else doing this kind of program, hence, many of the lessons and methods that I crafted were experimental — not only for this particular subject, but in the entire realm of Family Education.

Over the years, I have modified the class structure several times. I first began by teaching the materials to all of the students, together with their parents, in the quarter of the year prior to their ceremony. That has remained much the same. Initially, there were six evening sessions, then four. Now I either teach the four or we conduct the program as a Shabbaton (see Appendix for an outline).

The lesson materials have remained fairly constant over the years, although some particulars have changed. These changes, more often than not, were necessitated as some of these curricular pieces were integrated into our Religious School (e.g., the liturgy of the Shabbat service). I usually begin the program with some immediate experiences in cross-generational interchange. The best technique that I have found involves asking both parents and students to answer some pointed questions and then exchanging their written responses. The dialogue that follows within the family is often quite revealing and serves as a catalyst for much more discussion at home. The most interesting responses are elicited by questions such as, "What do you imagine this means to your parents/child?" and "What are your recollections of your own service?"

These opening dialogues will be followed with several cognitive lessons that always involve families working together. The subject matter of these lessons includes the history and meaning of Bar/Bat Mitzvah and anything related to the reading of the Torah — i.e., how we get Torah portions, authorship of Torah, Rabbinic divisions of the text, *aliyot*, Haftarah, etc.

Sometimes we get very practical: when we finish the work on Torah portions, we explain *drash* as a dialogue with the Torah and deal with how to write a *drash*. We discuss Jewish sumptuary laws and the appropriate limits for the *Seudat Mitzvah*. I hand out copies of several articles covering excessively lavish Bar/Bat Mitzvah "events," including that of TV star Fred Savage. These are ample commentary on the notion of excess and the reasons for sumptuary laws.

We often unroll the Torah and explain how it is put together. To clarify the dual purposes of prayer as praise and petition, we have participants role play a teenager asking Dad for the car. We discuss what sorts of things are appropriate to "petition" God for. We give out samples of "Parent's prayers" (from *Gates of Prayer*) to give parents a model from which to work.

Other lessons have been taught on the psychology of adolescence, the structure of the liturgy, and the traditional threesome of *mitzvot* associated with becoming Bar Mitzvah — *tallit, tefillin*, and *tzedakah*. In the context of our Reform synagogue, I often use these as a means for exploring the denominational differences in approach to the concept of "being commanded to do *mitzvot*." What does it mean for a liberal Jew to say that he or she is commanded to do anything? What is the source of that authority and power? Also, every student is required to perform an act of *tzedakah* in honor of becoming Bar or Bat Mitzvah and this, too, often becomes a matter for family discussion and decision making.

Families are required to do a great deal of homework together, especially in the area of Torah study and in understanding the Torah portion which leads to the student's speech.

One of the most valuable components of our time together has been the free-for-all question and answer period. I always begin each class with ten minutes of questions on any issue whatsoever — including photographers, bands, flowers, invitations, and caterers. I do not make recommendations, but since every class is a mixture of "veterans" and "rookies," they talk to each other. It is amazing how much better people do at the serious business of religious maturity if they get the ancillary stuff resolved and off their minds. The more serious questions, on the other hand, also give each generation a glimpse at what is truly on the mind of the other.

Interestingly, when I first proposed this class, some people were upset that it was to become a mandatory part of the Bar/Bar Mitzvah educational preparation. But it was so well accepted that after about five years of teaching the program, the Board of Trustees put into my contract that I *had* to teach Family Education for Bar/Bat Mitzvah!

As the congregation has grown older, the number of B'nai Mitzvah students and families has decreased. (I recently officiated at the Bat Mitzvah service of a student at whose mother's service I also officiated.) But the complexities of the family structure that necessitated the program remain. More and more of the parents involved are Jews-by-choice or non-Jews who have no experiential referent for being the parent of a Bar or Bat Mitzvah. In a recent year, 10 out of 17 students came from such families. An interesting component of this is that it is often the non-Jewish partner who is more interested in the child becoming Bar/Bat Mitzvah than the Jewish spouse. In these cases, the educational program has to confront the ambivalence of the Jewish partner and the inexperience of the non-Jew. Families are also increasingly pressed for time to study together — the simple act of scheduling these classes is often a nightmare. It remains important and challenging work.

Some years ago, the father of one of our students sat in the back of the room mumbling,"I'm going to kill Mr. Schwartz, I'm going to kill Mr. Schwartz." When I asked him who Mr. Schwartz was, he said that he had been his Bar Mitzvah tutor who had taught him everything by rote, and never explained anything in the way we were now doing. This man really felt cheated. At that moment, father and daughter gained a new understanding of how significant the Bar/Bat Mitzvah experience could — and should — be. This realization represents all I ever really wanted to achieve with this class. And I'm really grateful to Mr. Schwartz for making it possible.

APPENDIX

Family Bar/Bat Mitzvah Program

SESSION #	MATERIAL TO BE COVERED	ASSIGNMENTS
1	An intergenerational exchange The rules of the game What does this mean, and where did it come from? To be commanded	Read paper on History of Bar/Bat Mitzvah Torah portion summaries
2	*"Al HaTorah"*: Torah, Haftarah, and *aliyot* Writing a *drash*	The Haftarah connection Main idea of *drash* *Drash* outline
3	*"Al HaAvodah"*: The Jewish service The music of the service *Tzitzit*, *tefillin*, and Jewish identity	Parent's prayer
4	*"V'al Gemilut Chasadim"*: *Tzedakah* and Jewish responsibility The life of *mitzvah* Review and evaluations	Tzedakah
At every Session:	Any questions participants have Administrivia	

Chapter 32
Windows by Vicky Kelman

Reviewed by Helen Leneman

Windows is a welcome addition to published Family Education material. This excellent program was created by Vicky Kelman and published by the Melton Research Center for Jewish Education. It consists of an attractive set of four workbooks, along with a Leader's Guide. The program is designed for sixth or seventh graders and their families. At the center of each program is a "community experience" designed to last about two hours and to be conducted by a leader, at the synagogue, with family participation. In addition, there are activities to be done at home both before and after this group activity.

The four programs are independent of one another. The four titles of these programs and their themes are: *Becoming* (Bar/Bat Mitzvah), *Belonging* (Community), *Being* (Ethics), and *Believing* (God). This is a suggested order for a seventh grade class. However, they do not all have to covered, nor need they be covered in the same year or in any particular order.

The words of the Introduction to the Leader's Guide best express the genesis and goals of this program:

> A window is an opening in the wall of a building or the side of a vehicle which lets air and light in, permits those inside to look out and those outside to look in. *Windows*, this series of programs, is designed to provide windows on different aspects of Jewish tradition. They provide some light and some fresh air for thinking about four important issues: *becoming* a grown-up, *being* a good person, *believing* and having faith, and *belonging* to a community. Just as windows provide a way to look in and look out, *Windows* is designed to provide a guide for helping participants look into Jewish tradition and into themselves. Its family format also provides a window through which the generations can come to see each other more closely.

The author offers the following suggestions for implementing the program based on observations from the first year of its use. Sunday morning is the most frequently selected time for this program, although one congregation did it on a retreat. It is crucial to meet with all the facilitators about two weeks in advance of the actual program so as to clarify the purposes of the program and to share information about the families who will be attending. The facilitators in most cases have been a team of synagogue professionals. Other valuable suggestions are offered in the "Field Notes" enclosed with the Leader's Guide.

To give the reader a better idea of the material included in this program, a few excerpts from the four areas follow. In *Belonging*, the "At Home" exercise is a page of questions to be answered separately by children and parents. Questions include:

List three things you like to do alone, and explain why.

List three things that would be impossible to do without other people.

Why is the presence of other people necessary?

Families are encouraged to discuss their answers. This activity starts them thinking about the need for community. The family activity that takes place at the synagogue includes, among other activities, an excellent exercise: a simulated synagogue board meeting in which the board has to decide on the most important uses for a large sum of money that has been donated. Families break up into smaller groups and through discussion, prioritize a list of ten possible items. During this interesting activity, the participants think about what they want from their synagogue, and become aware, perhaps for the first time, of the range of activities in which their synagogue might be involved. The concluding section of *Belonging,* as of all four booklets, is an excellent collection of supplementary readings on the topic. These are geared for adults and will give deeper meaning to the subject.

In the booklet called *Becoming,* an interesting discussion question for the group is the suggestion to move Bar/Bat Mitzvah to age 16 or 18. Different ways of stimulating this discussion are suggested: for example, one way is to have parents and children separately list arguments for/against age 16 versus age 13. Another group activity for *Becoming* involves viewing the video "The Mitzvah Machine" (see review in the Bibliography at the end of this book) and stopping it at the midway point. Families are asked to collaborate and come up with their own ending; they then act it out for the group. The supplementary readings contain a wide range of writings on the significance of Bar/Bat Mitzvah.

The program entitled *Being* deals with some of the most difficult issues. At home, families discuss questions about laws: what are examples of good and bad laws, and what purpose do laws have in our lives? When the participants all come together, they begin with a general discussion of laws, of knowing right from wrong and acting on that knowledge. Discussion then proceeds to Jewish law, with an introduction to Mishnah and Talmud. This section requires thorough preparation and a knowledgeable leader. If done properly, it is an excellent way to make Talmud relevant and understandable on some level to parents and children. After all the group discussions and activities, an individual writing assignment is given: explain how *halachah,* Jewish law, is like a path.

Vicky Kelman suggests using the *Believing* booklet last, since it deals with the most abstract issues. Questions of creation, revelation, and redemption are introduced, although these words are not used. These issues are presented in the form of the three questions which all religions attempt to answer:

Is the world basically a good place?

What is the source of our knowledge about right and wrong?

What is the future of our human endeavors on this earth?

Students pose these questions at home to their parents and they share their answers. When families convene at the synagogue, they can choose one of these three questions, and they divide up accordingly. Extensive quotes from Torah, Midrash, and modern writings on all three questions are listed in the booklet. A variety of activities is suggested based on those quotes. For example, participants can choose which quote, out of a list of several, is most meaningful to them personally, and discuss that choice. There are endless possibilities with such a wealth of material. In addition, the supplementary readings include still more thought provoking writings, ranging from Midrash to modern commentaries.

These four slim volumes are aptly titled *Windows,* as they offer a wonderfully fresh and broad view of essential questions that are especially appropriate for family discussion during the Bar/Bat Mitzvah year. With the guidance of professional leaders, the rich and creative material presented can become an exciting learning experience for B'nai Mitzvah students and their families. Learning together in such a meaningful way is a primary goal of all Family Education. Synagogues can achieve this through the use of this Melton Program.

Chapter 33

A Bar and Bat Mitzvah Family Preparation Program

Barry Lutz

Overview

In keeping with our philosophy that all events in Jewish life are opportunities for learning, growth, and enrichment, both lay leaders and staff at Temple Ahavat Shalom in Northridge, California began to explore ways to enrich and broaden the "traditional" Bar and Bat Mitzvah training process. Experience had made it clear that to view the ceremony narrowly as only an event to mark a significant point in the life of the child was a very limiting view. Bar/Bat Mitzvah meetings often became counseling sessions for parents who did not know what to do, how to respond, how to relate to their teenager. Seventh grade teachers found that suddenly the parents of their students were much more interested in the structure and symbolism of the service than were their students. Bar/Bat Mitzvah tutors, as well as Rabbis, were spending a great deal of time teaching students and their parents about our tradition of commentary and interpretation as it related to the finding of personal meaning in a Torah text. There was a growing desire to find some way to use the Bar/Bat Mitzvah experience as a way to incorporate a student and his/her family into the community's "Mitzvah Network." Lastly, there was a need to put the ceremony and event in perspective. That is to say that Bar/Bat Mitzvah is an important step on the road to Jewish adulthood, but it is only a step. (The ceremony marking entry into adult Jewish life is Confirmation.) We wanted to give our families the opportunity to put Bar/Bat Mitzvah into perspective as regards the entire educational process.

A Shabbaton for Bar/Bat Mitzvah students and their parents was the outcome of conversations about ways in which we might best meet the needs being expressed by parents, students, and professionals.

Two *Shabbatonim* are held each year — one in the fall (generally in November), for families who have a Bar/Bat Mitzvah between January 1 and June 30, and one in the spring (April) for families who have a Bar/Bat Mitzvah between July 1 and December 31. (Editors Note: More traditional congregations might rather hold such a mini-retreat on a Sunday or vacation day.)

Administrative Details

It was clear from the outset that there was no interest in making the Shabbaton an administrative session. Therefore, a Bar/Bat Mitzvah Handbook is distributed to all students at the inception of their tutoring (26 weeks prior to the ceremony). This handbook contains service guidelines, requirements, honors sheets, etc.

The Shabbaton

The following is the schedule for the Shabbaton:

9:00 Arrival – Parents and students arrive. Coffee and Danish served. Participants receive packets containing nametags, the *parashah* for the date of their Bar/Bat Mitzvah, articles relating to Bar/Bat Mitzvah, pencil and paper.

9:15 Welcome – A general introduction to the day given by the Senior Rabbi.

9:30 Shabbat: Finding Meaning for Ourselves

Goal

- To get participants to focus upon the Shabbat service (liturgy, choreography, and symbolism) as a structure which allows the participant to focus upon those ideals and values that they most highly cherish.

Set-up

Room large enough for all participants to sit comfortably in chairs arranged in a semi-circle (concentric semi-circles for a large group).

Materials

Prayer books for participants
Paper, pencils (in each family's packet)
Large newsprint art pad (or butcher paper)
Markers
A wall or easel for the large newsprint or butcher paper.

Procedure

1. Leader asks participants to join in an exercise in guided imagery.
   Think about a vacation . . . Where are you going? . . . What are you doing? . . . How do you feel? . . . What are you thinking about? . . . What does your vacation do for you? . . . Now it's time to return . . . How do you feel? . . . How have you changed since you left? . . . How has your business, your personal life, been affected?
2. After participants have "returned" from this guided imagery, the discussion now focuses upon Shabbat: How is Shabbat like a vacation? How is it different? What are the added elements that bring additional meaning to Shabbat?
3. In order to follow up the discussion of additional meaning, each participant is then asked to think about and list on a piece of paper five things that they most highly cherish or value.
4. Once this is completed, the participants are asked to share their lists with the other members of their family.
5. The leader then begins a discussion with participants about when they take time to reflect upon these things, to make sure that they are directing their lives in such a way that they are pursuing these items that are so highly cherished. (Most of the items on the list will be non-tangible things, but are conceptual, such as peace, a loving family, etc.)
6. It is suggested that because of the nature of so many of these items, we rarely take the time to make sure that our lives reflect and are directed toward these values and goals. Shabbat is introduced as a weekly opportunity for such reflection and redirection.
7. It is noted by the leader that if we allow the words, the choreography, and the symbolism of the Shabbat service to touch us, we can find in them reflection of our ideals and values.
8. The leader asks the participants to open their prayer books to a prayer of the leader's choosing. (The "*V'ahavta*" is a good choice because there are a lot of possible themes and because it is well-known.) After reading the prayer, the leader asks the participants if they can find any of their listed ideals or values in this prayer.
9. The session closes with the leader asking the participants to pay special attention to the Shabbat service, looking particularly for those places where the themes they have expressed might be found.
10. Leader concludes with a final reading about Shabbat. (Use a passage from the Siddur or a poem or other reading that has particular significance to the reader.)

10:30 Shabbat Morning Service

(Note: It is important to bear in mind the structure, tradition, and understandings in your particular congregation. At Ahavat Shalom, the Shabbat service that is most widely attended is Friday evening. Saturday mornings tend to be limited more to relatives and friends of the Bar/ Bat Mitzvah family. The influx of 90 "strangers" can be a bit overwhelming. It is our practice, therefore, to notify that day's Bar/Bat Mitzvah family well in advance.)

12:00 *Kiddush* and Lunch: Service Review and Reflection

Goals

- To review the service with participants and find out where they found personal meaning in the service.
- To encourage participants to think about their own service with a mind-set concerned more about meaning than performance.
- To get participants to begin the process of reflection upon the role and importance of reli-

gious observance and spiritual experiences in their own lives.

Materials Needed

Lunch provided by the synagogue and served by a volunteer committee not participating in the Shabbaton.

Newsprint lists from pre-service session.

Description

This is a "working session" led by the Cantor. At this session, the service is reviewed using the responses generated at the pre-service session. With the Cantor facilitating, participants have the opportunity to comment on the service and what was particularly meaningful to them.

12:45 Finding Meaning in Your *Parashah*.

Goals

- To introduce participants to the tradition of commentary and interpretation.
- To help participants begin to find personal meaning in "their" *parashah* through the commentaries and their own understanding of the text.
- To "invest" the participants in the process of commentary and interpretation and explain their potential role in the Jewish textual tradition.
- To begin, in each family, a process of thinking about "their" *parashah* and its personal significance for them. (This, hopefully, will provide the foundation for the Bar/Bat Mitzvah's personal "message.")

Materials

The *parashah* for each family (provided in Shabbaton package)

Procedure

1. The leader (in our case the Assistant Rabbi) hands out a well known Torah passage. The passage is read together. The leader then asks for comments on the passage, asks if there are any questions concerning the text (and points some out if no one responds).
2. Next, as a conclusion to this introduction, the leader then shares some Rabbinic and modern commentaries on the passage.
3. Each family group is then asked to take their own *parashah* out of their package and to read it together. They are asked to try to understand it, to look for any issues that strike them, and to find something of personal significance in the passage.
4. As this is being done, a few facilitators circulate around the room helping families with this process. (In our case, the facilitators are the Senior and Assistant Rabbis, the Director of Education, and the Cantor.)
5. After 15 or 20 minutes the group comes back together and the leader asks for volunteers who would like to share their passage and the meaning that they found in it.
6. The leader wraps up the session by talking about the process of commentary and the personal opportunity each family has to participate in this process through their Bar/Bat Mitzvah message.
7. The leader reminds them that we have just started this process today and encourages the families to continue this discussion at home over the next several months. This discussion, about the *parashah* of the Bar/Bat Mitzvah — or about the weekly *parashah* — provides a rich opportunity for family discussion, learning, and growth.

1:45 Adults in Training

Goals

- To help both parents and Bar/Bat Mitzvah candidates gain some perspective on the nature of their changing relationships — which are also marked by this life cycle event.
- To encourage participation in the Confirmation program by relating the concerns of the parents to the many social and educational benefits of participation in the Confirmation program.

Materials

None

Procedure

1. The group is divided into two, with parents going to one room and students going to another.

(Depending upon the number of participants you may want to divide these groups even further.) Our Senior Rabbi likes to facilitate the student group, so we bring in another professional to work with the Director of Education in facilitating the parent group. This individual facilitator for the adult group is a counselor with specific training, experience, and interest in working with teenagers and their families.

2. The student group focuses on the following: Becoming independent and taking on more responsibility. One does not magically become an adult by turning 13. Bar/Bat Mitzvah marks the beginning of becoming an "adult in training." How does becoming more independent and responsible happen? How do you think your parents feel about this? Why? What fears and concerns do you think your parents have? How can you handle your needs sensitively? The focus here is on keeping lines of discussion open, trying to understand each other's feelings.
3. The parents' group focuses on the following: Common concerns, relationship issues, how to deal with them. How do you deal with your child's developing need for independence? How can the synagogue help you? (The role of youth groups, Confirmation, etc.) The adult conversation is rather free-flowing, depending on the topics of concern within the group.
5. At 2:45, the groups reconvene for a report on the issues discussed in the different groups and a wrap-up of the session.

3:00 The Mitzvah in Bar/Bat Mitzvah

Goals

- To involve families in any of a large spectrum of *mitzvah* projects.
- To emphasize that a major component of a full adult Jewish life is active concern, advocacy, and response to the needs of the community.

Materials

Mitzvah sign-up sheets

Procedure

1. The leader (in our case the Senior Rabbi), introduces the session by talking about active involvement in the community as a major component in a full adult Jewish life.
2. Participants are introduced to our Social Action Committee and Mitzvah Network. The roles of both committees are described. (The appropriate committees to involve in this session will vary from congregation to congregation.)
3. The chairs of these committees describe their community work.
4. *Mitzvah* sign-up sheets are handed out to each participant. They are filled out and returned to the chairpeople. (These sheets are later reviewed and individuals contacted in order to participate in various community projects.)

3:15 Wrap-up and Closure

Conclusion

In the week following the Shabbaton, an evaluation sheet is mailed to all participants (see Appendix). This evaluation gives us important feedback as we continue to update and upgrade.

APPENDIX

Sample Evaluation Form

1. Service Preparation: In this session we looked at those things we most value and suggested how the structure of Shabbat and prayer might help us to better reflect upon those things.

   Comments:

   Suggestions:

2. Service Review: In this session we attempted to look at some of the issues raised in the first session in light of the just attended Shabbat services.

   Comments:

   Suggestions:

3. Torah Interpretation: Each family reviewed their individual Torah portion and looked for "deeper" meanings and symbolisms in the text that might be meaningful to them.

   Comments:

   Suggestions:

4. "Adults in Training" . . . During this session, adults and teens discussed with group facilitators the issues surrounding the teenage years and growing up.

   Comments:

   Suggestions:

5. The Mitzvah in Bar/Bat Mitzvah: During this brief session, a representative of the Mitzvah Network shared some of the possibilities for community involvement. Participants had the opportunity to sign up for those activities in which they might be interested in participating.

   Comments:

   Suggestions:

6. Please give us your overall reaction and comments on the Shabbaton.

Chapter 34
A Family Workshop Program

Ron Aigen

The following three session family workshop is the last phase of the Pre-B'nai Mitzvah Program at Dorshei Emet of Montreal (see Chapter 37 for description). The goals of this workshop for the parents and children are:

1. To help clarify and strengthen their own sense of Jewish identity.
2. To explore the meaning of *mitzvah*.
3. To learn the history of the Bar/Bat Mitzvah ceremony.
4. To personalize their connection with this ritual.
5. To strengthen their ties to the synagogue community.

Session I

In the first session, parents and children together explore questions of Jewish identity. As an icebreaker, we begin with a Jewish Identity Inventory (see Appendix 1). We then view a video, *Forms of Jewish Expression*, produced by the World Zionist Organization, Department of Youth and Education. Following a brief discussion of the video, the parents and children divide into separate groups for "Dayenu," a values clarification exercise (see Appendix 2). The two groups then reconvene to share their conclusions. In a large group discussion, we try to arrive at one group consensus. We consider the following questions:

As we aim for consensus, does the list become larger or smaller?

What distinguishes items within the first line from those within the second?

Where does Bar/Bat Mitzvah fall within your definitions of Jewish identity?

What number value was it assigned?

Session II

The second session is devoted to the history of the ceremony as a rite of passage. We begin with a "Rites of Passage" worksheet from page 11 of the mini-course *Bar and Bat Mitzvah: A Family Education Unit* (A.R.E. Publishing, Inc.). Parents then share with their children memories of their own Bar/Bat Mitzvah ceremony or whatever they remember about being a teenager (see "When I Was Your Age," Appendix 3).

Following a brief presentation of the history of Bar/Bat Mitzvah, the families then discuss a *midrash* (*Genesis Rabbah* 63:8-10) which leads to an intergenerational discussion of parent-child responsibilities (see "The Limits of Responsibility," Appendix 4).

The parents and children then divide into separate peer groups to engage in two different tasks. The parents work on preparing a kind of ethical will that might be used as a Bar/Bat Mitzvah charge. To prepare for this exercise, they first engage in text study (see Appendix 5). The children complete a "Words of Wisdom" exercise in which they get to fantasize about how they would ideally envision their relationship with their parents (see Appendix 6).

Session III

In the third session, we explore the meaning of *mitzvah* and community. Again, we begin with a group exercise in which each participant fills out a "Mitzvah Inventory Checklist" (see Appendix 7). This generates a discussion about the distinction between ritual and ethical *mitzvot*. Which ones create community? Which create Jewish community? The parents and children then separate. Both do the same four-station exercise on the meaning of *mitzvah* and Bar/Bat Mitzvah. For this exercise, they must choose one of four corners which best represents where they feel they stand, then discuss with their group what this answer means and why they prefer it over the other choices.

Introduce the first round with the statement: To me, *mitzvot* are:

a. good deeds
b. commandments from God (through Bible and Talmud)
c. the links in the chain of Jewish tradition
d. the necessary tools for fixing up the world (*tikkun olam*)

Introduce the second round with the statement: To me, a Bar/Bat Mitzvah means:

a. the end of Jewish education
b. a big party, presents, expenses, etc.
c. a transition point marking the entry into the adult Jewish community
d. a new generation takes on responsibility for Jewish tradition

The two groups reconvene to compare their positions and share their opinions. We then view a video, *The Mitzvah Machine* (United Synagogue), which serves as a summary. (See the Bibliography at the end of this book for a review of this and other suitable films on the subject.)

The last part of the evening is reserved for making the personal connections, translating values into actions. We ask each of the families to take responsibility for planning one of the synagogue festival celebrations in the coming year. We then spend some time explaining the idea of the Bar/Bat Mitzvah project which forms the speech component of the ceremony.

Conclusion

Although not all the families attend all aspects of this program on a regular basis, the majority do. One of the great strengths of this workshop, from the perspective of the parents, is that it allows parents and children to discuss interpersonal issues which they might not otherwise discuss. Certainly, many people feel that they have gained a better understanding of the Bar/Bat Mitzvah ritual, as well as a stronger or clearer sense of Jewish identity. Most families also appreciate the emotional support which this provides at a time when many parents are feeling a little overwhelmed. This last objective, that of developing a stronger sense of community among the peer groups of B'nai Mitzvah and parents, is certainly one of the major outcomes of this program.

APPENDIX 1

Jewish Identity Inventory

1. I am a Jew born in (city & country) ______________________________
(How many generations has your family been in this country? If your parents were born in the same country, you are second generation.)

2. I am a Jew whose ancestors originally came from (city & country) ______________________________

3. I am a Jew whose Hebrew name is ______________________________
ben/bat ______________________________
My name means ______________________________
I was named after ______________________________

4. My best Jewish memory is ______________________________
____

5. My worst Jewish memory is ______________________________
____

6. When I think about being Jewish I feel ______________________________
____

7. My earliest synagogue memory is ______________________________
____

8. For me, belonging to this synagogue means ______________________________
____

9. To me, the Bar/Bat Mitzvah ceremony means ______________________________
____

10. My biggest worry about my own (my child's) upcoming Bar/Bat Mitzvah is ______________________________
____

11. My (my child's) Bar/Bat Mitzvah ceremony will be a success if ______________________________
____

Please use this additional space if required. Do not forget to indicate the number of the question which is being continued.

APPENDIX 2

Dayenu

Requirements of Jewish Identity Worksheet

Traditionally, Jewish identity has been defined as anyone born to a Jewish mother. Today, many Jews, including Reconstructionists, feel that the traditional definition is no longer adequate. The object of this exercise is for you to compose a list of the characteristics and/or behaviors that you feel are the minimal requirements for Jewish identity.

First, from the following list, rank the items in order of importance to your definition for recognizing someone as having a Jewish identity, placing the most important items first.

Then, go back and draw *one* line where you would say, "*Dayenu*" — this is enough for me to define who is a Jew. This is my minimal definition of Jewish identity.

Finally, draw a *double* line where you would say "*Dayenu*" — this will be enough to ensure a Jewish future.

Then, in groups of three or four, try to reach a consensus for what needs to be within the first and second lines.

_______ a. keeping a kosher home

_______ b. belonging to a synagogue

_______ c. learning Jewish history

_______ d. practicing Jewish holiday and home rituals

_______ e. having a Jewish wedding

_______ f. supporting Israel (from giving *tzedakah* to making aliyah)

_______ g. having a Bar/Bat mitzvah ceremony

_______ h. knowledge of Hebrew

_______ i. having a Jewish mother

_______ j. contributing to Jewish *tzedakah* causes

_______ k. believing in God

_______ l. having one Jewish parent, (mother or father) *and* raised as a Jew, i.e. with a Jewish education, participation in Jewish rites of passage, etc.

_______ m. acting with justice and integrity in personal and professional dealings

_______ n. going to synagogue on Rosh Hashanah and Yom Kippur

_______ o. ____
(your own choice)

APPENDIX 3

When I Was Your Age

Share with your child your recollections about the following kinds of memories (add whatever you like).

1. My Bar/Bat Mitzvah (for women who didn't have a Bat Mitzvah, their feelings of not having one, or memories of a brother's/cousin's Bar/Bat Mitzvah). Where did it take place? When? Who was there? How did you feel that day? What do you remember about preparations for the event?

2. When I was your age:

   My favorite music was . . .

   I was most interested in . . .

   Things that were different . . .

   Things that were the same . . .

APPENDIX 4

The Limits of Responsibility

Blessed is the One who has freed me from the responsibility of this child.

A. *Midrash Rabbah* to Genesis (Toledot) 63: 8-10

And the boys grew (Genesis 25:27). R. Phinehas said in R. Levi's name: They were like a myrtle and a wild rosebush growing side by side; when they attained to maturity, one yielded its fragrance and the other its thorns. So for thirteen years, both went to school and came home from school. After this age, one went to the house of study and the other to idolatrous shrines. R. Eleazar b. R. Simeon said: A man is responsible for his son until the age of thirteen; thereafter he must say, "Blessed is the One who has now freed me from the responsibility of this child."

B. Questions

1. How do you feel about this *midrash*?
2. What actually happens in this story?
3. What is the *midrash* telling us about formal education?
4. What is the *midrash* telling us about the influence of parents and families on children?
5. What does the *midrash* say about the limits of parents' responsibility for their children's behavior?
6. What is the *midrash* telling the children about their relationship to their parents?
7. What do you think is the main message of this *midrash*?

APPENDIX 5

Text Study

Jewish Values — Sources

TORAH

You shall be a blessing . . . and all the families of the earth shall bless themselves by you. (Genesis 12:2-3)

You shall not insult the deaf or place a stumbling block before the blind. You shall fear your God: I am the Lord. You shall not favor the poor or show deference to the rich; judge your neighbor fairly. Do not deal basely with your fellow. Do not stand idly by the blood of your neighbor: I am the Lord.

You shall not hate your kinsman in your heart. Reprove your neighbor but incur no guilt because of him. You shall not take vengeance or bear a grudge against your kinfolk. Love your neighbor as yourself: I am the Lord. (Leviticus 19:14-18)

Proclaim liberty throughout the land, to all the inhabitants thereof. (Leviticus 25:10)

Justice, justice you shall pursue . . . (Deuteronomy 16:20)

Choose life — if you and your offspring would live — by loving the Lord your God, heeding His commands, and holding fast to them. (Deuteronomy 30:19)

Be strong and of good courage . . . (Deuteronomy 31:6)

PIRKE AVOT: ETHICS OF THE FATHERS

(1:6) Joshua ben Perahyah said: Provide yourself with a teacher; get yourself a companion; and judge all men favorably.

(1:12) Hillel said: Be of the disciples of Aaron, loving peace and pursuing peace; be one who loves his fellow men and draws them near to the Torah.

(1:14) He used to say: If I am not for myself, who is for me? If I care only for myself, what am I? If not now, when?

(2:5) Hillel said: Do not keep aloof from the community; be not sure of yourself till the day of your death; do not judge your fellow man until you have been in his position; do not say anything which cannot be understood at once, in the hope that ultimately it will be understood; and do not say: "When I shall have leisure I shall study," for you may never have leisure.

(4:1-2) Ben Zoma said: Who is wise? He who learns from every man, as it is said: "From all my teachers I gained wisdom." Who is strong? He who subdues his (evil) impulse, as it is said: "He who is slow to anger is better than a strong man; he who rules his spirit is better than one who conquers a city." Who is rich? He who is content with his lot, as it is said: "When you eat of the toil of your hands, happy shall you be in this world; and it shall be well with you in the world to come." Who is honored? He who honors his fellowmen, as it is said: "Those who honor me (by honoring man, created in the image of God) I will honor, and those who despise me shall be lightly esteemed."

(4:3) Ben Azzai said: Do not despise any man, and do not consider anything as impossible; for there is not a man who has not his hour, and there is not a thing that has not its place.

(5:25) Ben Bag-Bag said: Study the Torah again and again, for everything is contained in it; constantly examine it, grow old and gray over it, and swerve not from it, for there is nothing more excellent than it.

APPENDIX 5 (Cont.)

TALMUD

These are the things of which a person enjoys the fruits in his own lifetime, and also tastes of eternity, namely: honoring father and mother, hospitality, practice of kindness, early attendance at the school-house morning and evening, hospitality to strangers, visiting the sick, dowry of the bride, attending the dead to the grave, devotion in prayer and making peace between fellow men, but the study of Torah exceeds them all. (Shabbat 127a)

After Moses, David came and reduced the six hundred thirteen commandments to eleven, as it is written: "Lord, who shall sojourn in Your tabernacle? Who shall dwell on Your holy mountain? He who walks blamelessly, and does what is right, and speaks truth in his heart, who does not slander with his tongue, and does no evil to his friend, nor takes up a reproach against his neighbor, in whose eyes a reprobate is despised, but honors those who fear the Lord, who swears to his own hurt and does not change, who does not put out his money at interest, and does not take a bribe against the innocent." (Psalms 15:1-5) Then Isaiah came and reduced the commandments to six, as it is written, "He who walks righteously and speaks uprightly, he who despises the gain of oppressions, who shakes his hands lest they hold a bribe, who stops his ears from hearing of bloodshed, and shuts his eyes from looking upon evil" (Isaiah 33:15). Then Micah came and reduced them to three, as it is written, "It has been told you, O man, what is good, and what the Lord requires of you: To do justice, to love mercy, and to walk humbly with your God" (Micah 6:8). Then Isaiah came again and reduced them to two: "Thus says the Lord: Keep justice and do righteousness" (Isaiah 56:1). Amos came and reduced them to one, as it is written, "Thus says the Lord to the House of Israel: Seek Me and live" (Amos 5:4). Habakkuk came and also reduced them to one, as it is written, "The righteous shall live by his faith" (Habakkuk 2:4). (Makkot 24a)

Rabbi Simlai expounded: The Torah begins with an act of loving-kindness and it ends with an act of loving-kindness. It begins with an act of loving-kindness, as it is written, "The Lord God made for Adam and for his wife garments of skin and clothed them" (Genesis 3:21). It ends with an act of lovingkindness, as it is written, "He (God) buried him (Moses) in the valley in the land of Moab" (Deuteronomy 34:6). (Sota 14a)

The Holy One, praised be He, loves three: Whoever does not become angry, whoever does not become drunk, and whoever does not stand on his rights. The Holy One, praised be He, hates three: Whoever says one thing with his mouth and another thing in his heart, whoever knows of evidence in favor of someone but does not testify, and whoever sees a disgraceful thing in someone and testifies against him alone (since a minimum of two witnesses is needed to bring about a formal conviction, one witness merely gives the defendant a bad reputation). (Pesahim 113b)

ETHICAL WILLS

Devote yourself to science and religion; habituate yourself to moral living, for "habit is master over all things." As the Arabian philosopher holds, there are two sciences, ethics and physics. Strive to excel in both.

Show respect to yourself, your household, and your children, by providing decent clothing, as far as your means allow; for it is unbecoming for any one, when not at work, to go shabbily dressed.

If the Creator has mightily displayed His love to you and me, so that Jew and Gentile have thus far honored you for my sake, endeavor henceforth so to add to your honor that they may respect you for your own self. This you can effect by good morals and by courteous behavior; by steady devotion to your studies and your profession.

Let your countenance shine upon the sons of men: tend their sick, and may your advice cure them. Though you take fees from the rich, heal the poor gratuitously; the Lord will requite you. Thereby shall you find favor and good understanding in the sight

APPENDIX 5 (Cont.)

of God and man. Thus you will win the respect of high and low among Jews and non-Jews, and your good name will go forth far and wide. You will rejoice your friends and make your foes envious. Examine your Hebrew books at every new moon, the Arabic volumes once in two months, and the bound codices once every quarter. Arrange your library in fair order, so as to avoid wearying yourself in searching for the book you need. Always know the case and chest where it should be.

Never refuse to lend books to anyone who has not means to purchase books for himself, but only act thus to those who can be trusted to return the volumes. Cover the bookcases with rugs of fine quality; and preserve them from dampness and mice, and from all manner of injury, for your books are your good treasure . . . .

Make it a fixed rule in your home to read the Scriptures and to peruse grammatical works on Sabbaths and festivals, also to read Proverbs and the Ben Mishle.

My son, honor your comrades, and seek opportunities to benefit them by your wisdom, in counsel and deed. (Judah Ibn Tibbon in a letter to his son Samuel, twelfth century)

Now that you are becoming a Bar/Bat Mitzvah, the values which I hope you will carry with you in your life are expressed as follows:

APPENDIX 6

Words of Wisdom

	Phrases I heard and like	Phrases that bugged me	Words I would have wanted to hear but never heard
About Friends			
About School			
About My Appearance			
About Being Jewish			
About Family			
About Solving Problems			
General			

APPENDIX 7

Mitzvah Inventory Checklist

On the following list of *mitzvot,* place a check mark next to those which you yourself value and would try to observe.

The *mitzvot* which I take seriously and try to do are:

1. ☐ Acknowledge God's unity.
2. ☐ Imitate God.
3. ☐ Recite the *Sh'ma* morning and evening.
4. ☐ Study Torah and teach it to others.
5. ☐ Fix a *mezuzah* on the door to your house.
6. ☐ Praise God with thanks after eating.
7. ☐ Not eat milk and meat together.
8. ☐ Rest on the Sabbath day.
9. ☐ Tell the story of the Exodus from Egypt.
10. ☐ Eat only *matzah* (no bread) during Pesach.
11. ☐ Circumcise your sons.
12. ☐ Not eat non-kosher food.
13. ☐ Honor one's vows and oaths.
14. ☐ Build a fence around your roof and remove potential hazards from your home.
15. ☐ Give *tzedakah* to the poor.
16. ☐ Lend to the poor without interest.
17. ☐ Return stolen property.
18. ☐ Ensure weights and measures are accurate.
19. ☐ Honor your parents.
20. ☐ Pay your workers on time.
21. ☐ Not perpetuate injustice or take bribes.
22. ☐ Not favor the poor in judgment.
23. ☐ Not steal.

After you have completed your checklist, answer the following questions:

1. How would you distinguish between numbers 1-12 and 13-23?

2. Would you consider some to be ritual *mitzvot* and some to be ethical?

3. Which help create community?

4. Which help create Jewish community?

Chapter 35

Facilitating the B'nai Mitzvah Experience through Family Education Programming

Roberta Louis Goodman and Lois J. Zachary

INTRODUCTION

Jewish educators and synagogue professionals have an opportunity to play an active role in helping the family set priorities and guide what meaning the family assigns to the Bar/Bat Mitzvah experience. Family Bar/Bat Mitzvah programming presents an opportunity for bringing parents and students together for community building and values transmission within the synagogue setting.

This chapter describes a family Bar/Bat Mitzvah program for sixth graders and their parents in a large (900 families) Conservative congregation in upstate New York.

BACKGROUND

This program stemmed from a previous program for seventh grade parents and students which had focused on the logistical aspects of Bar/Bat Mitzvah. Feedback had indicated that by the time the program occurred, families had already made many of the critical decisions regarding Bar/Bat Mitzvah. Furthermore, the focus of that program had become concentrated on the *Kiddush* arrangements, rather than on the religious, social, personal, and communal meanings of Bar and Bat Mitzvah to the families. Finally, the old program was too frontally oriented, *telling* the families rather than *stimulating interaction.*

For this new program, a lay leader in the congregation (who was also a professional adult educator) was identified by the staff as having useful skills and knowledge. She and the Director of Education worked together on a draft of the overall program, as well as on the details pertaining to two of the sessions. The Director of Education worked with the senior staff of the congregation to finalize the program outline and the details of the other sessions.

The program provided exposure to all the synagogue professionals involved in the Bar/Bat Mitzvah experience: Director of Education, Cantor, Rabbi, and Administrator. Families also had contact with the synagogue Youth Director and other community professionals, such as the director of the community Hebrew High School.

The program was held six months prior to the first sixth grader becoming a Bar or Bat Mitzvah. For some, the Bar or Bat Mitzvah ceremony was over a year away. For socialization reasons, it was thought to be important to work with all the members of a grade together. Children attending the community day school instead of the Religious School, but who were to become Bar/Bat Mitzvah at the congregation, were invited to attend these sessions along with their parents.

GOALS OF THE PROGRAM

The goals of the program were:

1. To prepare students and parents together both collectively and spiritually for the Bar/Bat Mitzvah experience.
2. To create a sense of community among parents and B'nai Mitzvah, families and synagogue, families and families, families and synagogue professionals.
3. To involve parents and students in the B'nai Mitzvah process by providing opportunities for participation "beyond the reception."
4. To present and discuss the role of *mitzvah, tefillah* (prayer), *tzedakah,* and responsibility in becoming a Bar/Bat Mitzvah.

5. To present the history of Bar/Bat Mitzvah, the structure and liturgy of the Shabbat morning service and Musaf, and the Haftarah cantillation.

OVERVIEW OF THE PROGRAM

The program consisted of a Preparation Session (held during Hebrew School with sixth grade students only) and three sessions (with parents and students together). The latter sessions were held on consecutive Sundays during regular Religious School hours. The focus of the three sessions was as follows: Preparation Session – Hearing the Student Voice (sixth graders only); Session #1 (with families) – The Bar/Bat Mitzvah Experience; Session #2 (with families) – Symbols, Rituals, and History surrounding Bar and Bat Mitzvah; and Session #3 (with families) – a potpourri of issues: *tzedakah*, what happens after Bar/Bat Mitzvah, and the nuts and bolts of sponsoring and arranging the *Kiddush*.

The preparation session and Session #1, "The Bar/ Bat Mitzvah Experience," fulfill goals 1 through 4 and are the focus of this chapter. Sessions #2 and #3 fulfill goal 5. These sessions represent the unique aspects of these family educational experiences and are the focus of this chapter. They were unique because they created an understanding of the Bar and Bat Mitzvah experience from the perspective of those involved in it, and then provided a forum for participants to examine the substantive issues and values surrounding the Bar and Bat Mitzvah experience. This approach expanded and enhanced the meaning of the Bar and Bat Mitzvah experience for the families.

Following is an outline of these two aspects of the program and the results of each.

Preparation Session — Hearing the Student Voice

This session was for students only and took place in Hebrew School. It consisted of classroom interviews of the sixth graders as a group to determine how they presently related to the Bar/Bat Mitzvah experience. What is their understanding of what is involved in becoming a Bar or Bat Mitzvah? What are their perceived needs, desires, hopes, fears, and dreams? (For a detailed description of this segment of the program, see Appendix 1.)

The interviews with the sixth graders elicited anticipated types of responses as well as some deep thoughts, feelings, concerns, and Jewish values. When asked, "What kind of symbol comes to mind when you think about your Bar or Bat Mitzvah?", these students described a range of symbols: "a big box, wrapped"; "*yarmulkes* where you put your name and the date of your Bar Mitzvah"; "a big cake"; "Torah"; "Temple"; and "Adulthood."

The students vocalized a concern for "not wanting to be embarrassed" or "screwing up," "making a lot of mistakes."

Several students spoke about the meaning of Bar or Bat Mitzvah as "being an adult." Upon further probing of what it means to be a Jewish adult, one student responded: "You're expected to do more mature things, you have more responsibility."

When asked what those responsibilities were, many students chimed in: "You wear a *tallit* when you go to services," "You get serious presents," "You have to observe holidays more than you used to; you have to fast."

The time spent with the facilitator was effective in getting the students to express their feelings and thoughts in their own terms. This process identified the major issues and concerns that they had related to Bar and Bat Mitzvah.

Session #1 consisted of three parts — the panel presentation, case study, and parents-only rap session. Each of these parts is described below.

Session #1, Part A – Panel Presentation

This panel consisted of parents and students who have already been through a Bar and Bat Mitzvah experience. The facilitator begins by asking the panelists to reflect upon the difficult questions and concerns that the sixth graders raised in the Preparation Session interview(s). Then the panel responds to further questions from parents and students.

In preparation for Session #1, Part A, the panel discussion, the tapes made by the sixth graders are transcribed. A list of quotations was made which captured the range of feelings, thoughts, concerns, and questions of the students. This was done question by question according to the Interview Guide. Repeating themes among the quotations were identified.

Panelists were informed of these repeating themes for them to think about prior to their presentation. Then a case study was developed.

The panel presentation provided an opportunity to hear how others cope with a family member becoming a Bar or Bat Mitzvah. It affirmed and acknowledged the families' experiences. The panel format allowed people to receive answers from "expert" or "experienced" peers.

Session #1, Part B – A Case Study

This case study (see Appendix 2 for the complete version) was developed based on the concerns of the sixth graders identified in the class interview(s). Using a case study about a typical Bar and Bat Mitzvah family, this step involves: (1) reading the case study; (2) dividing parents and students into five groups; (3) having each small group respond to one key aspect of the Bar and Bat Mitzvah experience — *tzedakah, aliyot, mitzvah*, celebration, and invitations; (4) reporting back to all the families; and (5) debriefing the exercise. (See Appendix 3 for discussion starters for each of these five groups.)

The small group work showed how the case study effectively incorporated the concerns of the students and parents and the values of the school and synagogue. The five small group discussions reflected a strong orientation to Jewish values.

The discussion on *mitzvah* centered on the role of responsibility in the Jewish community as the meaning of the *mitzvah* in Bar and Bat Mitzvah. Participants felt it was important to present the Bar or Bar Mitzvah event in the school in a meaningful way, keeping it in perspective, and balancing both the social and religious aspects. They felt that family participation was an essential element.

The group dealing with celebration voiced concerns about the practical matters surrounding the reception: where to have it, prices, what to do with out of towners, caterers and *kashrut*, how many relatives to invite, and so forth. Group members felt that the Bar or Bat Mitzvah should play a central role in planning the celebration and give input into every aspect. They produced a list of ways to include and involve the child in decision making.

A number of questions were raised by the children regarding invitations. Can one invite some friends and not others? Which friends should be invited? What does one do about unpopular relatives? They felt it was important to invite favorite teachers, best friends, and helpful synagogue professionals. The whole group expressed a concern about how to encourage out of town relatives to attend.

Some of the concerns that surfaced in regard to *aliyot* were: Can women go up to the *bimah* alone? What about widows? Singles? Girls? What if people can't read Hebrew? How many people can be asked to do *aliyot*? What about non-Hebrew reading *aliyot*? Must people who do *aliyot* be Jewish? What about doubling up on an *aliyah*?

It was agreed that *aliyot* were important as: a way to have friends or family share more immediately in the experience; a way to honor special people and make them feel important; a way to say thank you to people, especially when they come from great distances.

A number of approaches were suggested for assigning *aliyot*:

1. Ask who wants to have an *aliyah*.
2. Pick relatives close to the child first.
3. Essential *aliyot* were considered to be parents, grandparents, and siblings.
4. Pick individuals who know the most Hebrew, as some won't want to read Hebrew.
5. Consider relatives who will be hurt if they are not asked.

It was suggested that transliterations, tapes, and tutoring by the Bar or Bat Mitzvah be utilized as ways of easing discomfort about being called up to the Torah or pronouncing unfamiliar Hebrew words.

Session #1, Part C – Parents-Only Rap Session with the Director of Education

In the parent rap session, the Director of Education answered any questions about the issues raised, and discussed any needed action plans to implement or respond to the needs and desires identified through this process.

By the time the rap session for parents and the Director of Education takes place, the parents are primed to discuss the Bar and Bat Mitzvah experience.

They echoed the desire of the "*tzedakah* group" for a class Bar and Bat Mitzvah project and were willing to help coordinate and implement the effort.

Other issues came to the fore. Many vocalized their concern about including all the classmates at a child's Bar or Bat Mitzvah. The concerns included a need for sensitivity toward the one child who is left out, as well as the desire to create class cohesion and synagogue friendships. Some wanted to spend Shabbat attending services with their children.

The Director of Education presented a potential change in the curriculum for the seventh grade in the following year. This would involve a 40 minute *Parashat Hashavua* class for students to be followed by their attendance at the Shabbat services (with the congregation). This would be in lieu of one weekday afternoon Hebrew class or Sunday's class. The parents welcomed this change. They recognized that it would enable all the students to attend the various Bar/Bat Mitzvah ceremonies of their classmates throughout the year (even without a personal invitation).

It was clear that this parent rap session could not have taken place on the level that it did without the previous panel and case study. The two activities prepared participants to look at the significance of the Bar and Bat Mitzvah period in the life of their family. Families felt free to discuss their concerns about extravagant practices related to Bar and Bat Mitzvah. Further, parents got to know one another. They and their children advocated for community, kindness and consideration, *mitzvah*, holiness, and *tzedakah*. Families left the session ready to examine the issues further. They felt more able to make decisions about what they wanted from the Bar or Bat Mitzvah experience and to implement these ideas.

Sessions #2 and #3

The Preparation Session with the sixth graders and Session #1 with families prepared the group for Sessions #2 and #3.

Follow-up

All of these sessions were held in the spring of the sixth grade year, with follow-up during the seventh grade year so as to continue the dialogue between synagogue and families. A parent committee was established to assist in the implementation of the *tzedakah* program.

The program generated a variety of possible outgrowths for the Bar/Bat Mitzvah year and afterward: building Family Education curriculum around common concerns, creating Shabbat morning family *Parashat Hashavua* study sessions, and establishing a support and informational network for families going through the Bar or Bat Mitzvah life cycle experience.

Conclusion

This program accomplished and exceeded its goals.

1. It initiated a dialogue and educational process between synagogue and home.
2. It successfully caught people's attention and engendered their support for making Bar and Bat Mitzvah a Jewishly or spiritually meaningful Jewish experience.
3. It succeeded in building a sense of community and common purpose, and provided a format for discussion among the parents.
4. It modeled how and what parents and children could discuss in making decisions about Bar and Bat Mitzvah.
5. It informed parents and children about their choices and the expectations for involvement.
6. It answered the question, "What is Bar and Bat Mitzvah?"

This new approach proved successful in combining the needs, concerns, values, and desires of the three parties involved: the Bar and Bat Mitzvah students, their parents, and the synagogue. The synagogue fulfilled its responsibility for helping families derive more meaning from the Bar and Bat Mitzvah experience.

(This chapter is based on an article by Lois J. Zachary and Roberta L. Goodman, "A Learner-Centered Approach to Family Life Education Programming: The B'nai Mitzvah Experience," *Jewish Education*, Vol. 59, No. 1, Spring-Summer 1991.)

APPENDIX 1

Preparation Session with Sixth Grade Students – Hearing the Student Voice

This segment of the program needs to be done at least two weeks in advance of the first family session. A cassette recorder and blank tape are needed for this session.

Select an adult facilitator — either a synagogue professional or lay leader — who works well with this age group. That individual meets with the sixth graders in groups of eight to 15 during regular school hours for approximately 40 minutes. This can be done as a classroom activity, but the teacher needs to inform the students that this will happen.

With the students seated in a circle, the facilitator tells them that their discussion today is in preparation for the upcoming Family Education sessions. It is an opportunity for them to express their reactions to the Bar/Bat Mitzvah experience, especially those things they want to share with their parents but may or may not be comfortable telling them directly. The questions focus on their perceived needs, desires, hopes, fears, dreams, and sense of reality regarding the Bar/Bat Mitzvah experience.

Be certain to inform the students that this session will be tape recorded. The purpose of the tape recording is to assist the sharing of their responses anonymously with the parents and to enable the panel of teenagers and adults, who have been through the Bar/Bat Mitzvah experience, to address their concerns or reactions at the first family session. The tape will not be played back at the family session. Only a transcribed copy of the students' comments may be read by the facilitator.

After having the students introduce themselves, here are the Interview Guide Questions:

1. Visualizing Exercise

   Sit back and close your eyes . . . Breathe easily . . . Picture in your mind what you'd like your Bar and Bat Mitzvah event to be like . . . Get it nice and clear . . . Think about all the things that you'd like to have happen and what the day is going to be like . . . Focus . . . Get a really clear picture of how you would like your Bar and Bat Mitzvah day to be . . . Open your eyes . . . Describe your pictures.
2. What kind of symbol(s) comes to mind when you think about your Bar or Bat Mitzvah?
3. What is the best thing that could happen on your Bar/Bat Mitzvah day?
4. What is the worst thing that could happen? (Probe positively for items that make up the "worry list.")
5. Think about the very best Bar or Bat Mitzvah experience that you know about. What was the one thing that stood out for you that you would like to see/have happen at your own Bar/Bat Mitzvah service?
6. What is most meaningful to you about becoming a Bar/Bat Mitzvah?
7. Is there anything you would want your parents — or all parents — to know about Bar/Bat Mitzvah?
8. Is there anything more you want to know?
9. Are there any questions that come to mind that perhaps you don't want to raise in a big group that you would like to have answers to? topics?

The key to this session is getting the participation of all the students, helping them feel comfortable expressing their thoughts, concerns, and questions, and avoiding having the students say what they think the adult facilitator wants to hear rather than what they really want to say.

APPENDIX 2

The Case Study

PREPARING FOR THE CASE STUDY

The case study is a vehicle for facilitating interaction among the families around key values and concerns related to the Bar/Bat Mitzvah experience. Identify the concerns which the students presented in the taped group sessions. Incorporate the students' concerns with the known concerns of the parents, and the values and concerns of the Religious School and synagogue. Reactions to past Bar and Bat Mitzvah programs identified the following parental needs and desires: parents are interested in Bar and Bat Mitzvah and in their children; they want to know about the logistics of Bar/Bat Mitzvah preparation — who does what, when,and where. The priorities of the Religious School and synagogue are reflected in the goals of the program. They include such things as: stressing the *mitzvah* in the Bar/Bat Mitzvah process, retaining a sense of holiness or sacredness throughout the entire experience, having families see the Bar/Bat Mitzvah as a community experience, helping families sort through their values and priorities, giving families a way of communicating and planning with one another.

Here is the case study that was developed for this program based on the concerns of one group:

Case Study

Billy Segal's Bar Mitzvah service is scheduled for May. (His father had the same Haftarah portion that Billy is going to chant for his Bar Mitzvah.) Billy's sister, Patti, became a Bat Mitzvah two years ago.

Billy has a large family. Among them are five aunts and eight uncles (some of whom are "into baseball"). Two of his mother's sisters are divorced and one of his father's brothers is separated from his wife. His cousins range in age from 4 to 23 years old. He has three grandparents and a great-grandmother. Billy's family lights Friday night candles as often as possible. They observe Chanukah, Passover, and the High Holy Days. None of the family is really comfortable with Hebrew. They perform holiday customs and rituals as best they can. All of them, however, enjoy being together celebrating as a family.

The Los Angeles Segal family relatives have told Grandma that they are not planning on coming to Billy's Bar Mitzvah celebration because they came east several years ago.

Billy is a sports fiend. He loves to watch and participate in sports. In the winter, he also skis.

Billy has "coasted through Hebrew." He "doesn't much like languages in general" and "Hebrew is particularly boring." He is looking forward to becoming Bar Mitzvah, because of the presents, being with his friends, and "having Hebrew School over at last."

Billy has a great sense of humor. For the most part, he doesn't take school too seriously, but does fairly well grade-wise. He has lots of friends and is a little nervous about his Bar Mitzvah day — he doesn't want to make a mistake during the service or look foolish and have his friends "mock him out." He hopes that his younger brother won't make faces at him during the ceremony to make him laugh.

Billy would like "to party" with his friends to celebrate his Bar Mitzvah day. He wants a party like his friend Jon's with "lots of music and great entertainment." He hopes that his friends will have an "awesome" time, too. He is concerned about having to limit the number of friends he can invite. His family is large and there is a limit to what his family can afford and/or wants to spend.

APPENDIX 3

Discussion Starters

Following are the discussion starters for the five groups based on the case study.

Mitzvah Group

What is the meaning of *mitzvah* in Bar Mitzvah?
What are some of the ways to keep the meaning of *mitzvah* in Bar/Bat Mitzvah?
How can Billy and his family build *mitzvah* into their celebration of Billy's special day?

Aliyot Group

What are the concerns in your group about *aliyot*?
What is the importance of *aliyot*?
Since there are so many family members, the Segal family is having difficulty figuring out how to assign *aliyot*. What help can you give them?
There are members of the Segal family who are nervous about being called up to the Torah. They are uncomfortable reciting the Hebrew. What can be done to make them feel more comfortable?

Tzedakah Group

What are your group's concerns about *tzedakah*?
How do you do *tzedakah*?
What are some of the ways that Billy could do *tzedakah*?
What role, if any, would his family play?

Invitations Group

List your group's concerns about invitations.
What advice would you give Billy about how to decide whom to invite to the ceremony and/or celebration?
What can Billy's family do to encourage the out of town relatives to attend?

Celebration Group

List the concerns the group members have about the Bar/Bat Mitzvah reception.
What are the choices open to Billy and the Segal family? What kind of celebration would be appropriate? Who? Where? When? Other options?
What role(s) can Billy play in planning the celebration?
What advice could you give Billy about putting together a guest list? Can Billy invite some of his friends and not others? Can Billy invite some of his Religious School classmates and not others?

Unit VI: Curricular and Extra-curricular Material

Overview

The notion that the curriculum for the seventh grade should be designated as a Bar/Bat Mitzvah Curriculum is not universally shared. A distinction should be made between a Bar/Bat Mitzvah curriculum and a curriculum designed for B'nai Mitzvah students. The first implies a curriculum focused exclusively on material relating to the Bar/Bat Mitzvah ceremony; the second is a broader concept implying the inclusion of all material germane to this age group and in particular to the year of the Bar/Bat Mitzvah. Some educators fear that too much emphasis will promote the idea that this is the culminating year of Jewish education, rather than just another guidepost along the path. Yet, this is an important transitional year, and an exceptional opportunity to help children gain understanding of and perspective about the Bar/Bat Mitzvah, about themselves, and about Judaism. This can be arrived at through an interesting and multi-faceted curriculum.

In Chapter 36, Cantor Helen Leneman offers a description of a Bar/Bat Mitzvah curriculum that she originated, along with some suggestions on how to go about designing such a curriculum.

In Chapter 37, Rabbi Ron Aigen describes an unusual, multi-faceted sixth grade curriculum (which could be easily adapted for seventh grade), which includes several field trips in conjunction with lessons on *tzedakah*, and weekly sessions devoted to current Jewish concerns.

In Chapter 38, Cantor Helen Leneman reviews the publication *Coming of Age as a Jew — Bar/Bat Mitzvah* by Shoshana Glatzer. This is a flexible and encompassing curriculum that can be used in a variety of possible ways and succeeds on both the cognitive and affective levels.

Chapter 39 is a report by Rabbi Allan Tuffs and Cantor Helen Leneman on "Living Mitzvot," a program originated by Rabbi Tuffs and designed to be the *mitzvah* component of a seventh grade curriculum. The program includes class discussions and outside work.

Chapter 40 is a review by Cantor Helen Leneman of Rabbi Burt Jacobson's unusual Bar/Bat Mitzvah program, *Crossing the River*. This ambitious, innovative work stresses genuine teacher-student dialogue, and the creative approach it models allows students to explore ideas in a non-judgmental atmosphere.

The next two chapters of the Unit describe retreat programs, an optional addition to the Bar/Bat Mitzvah curriculum that many synagogues have found appealing and rewarding to students and teachers alike.

In Chapter 41, Julie Vanek describes how much can be learned in the relaxed, enjoyable setting of a retreat. In addition, a sense of group solidarity can be fostered among students as they learn.

In Chapter 42, Cantor Helen Leneman reviews *Seven Weekends That Make a Difference* by Rabbi Philip Warmflash and Craig Taubman. The opening chapters are an excellent introduction to the concept of retreats, and they outline suggested schedules for a three day retreat, organizational tips, and ideas for possible weekend themes. Of the seven retreats contained in the book, two are especially appropriate for B'nai Mitzvah students.

In Chapter 43, Risa Gruberger describes a mini-course which she originated about writing a *drash*.

The programs in these chapters, all of which have been used successfully, are described in detail to make it easy for readers to replicate them. Where pertinent, information on how to obtain those programs is included. When these and other new curricula attain wider circulation, educators will have the tools to create new programs of their own.

Chapter 36
Designing a B'nai Mitzvah Curriculum

Helen Leneman

This chapter has two parts: a discussion of basic factors to consider when creating a B'nai Mitzvah curriculum and a description of a curriculum designed and used successfully by the author of this chapter. All the curricula discussed and outlined here can be customized to fit the needs of any class. All can be mixed and matched to suit both teachers and students.

BASIC FACTORS TO CONSIDER

Among the factors to consider when designing a Bar/Bat Mitzvah curriculum are: number of sessions, the teacher, the background of students, working as a team, the opening session, and the course itself.

Number of Sessions

A B'nai Mitzvah curriculum can be designed to run parallel to, in addition to, or instead of a "regular" seventh grade curriculum. "Regular" here means subjects not particularly oriented toward B'nai Mitzvah, such as values or history. A mini-curriculum of just three, or seven, or ten sessions, will encompass less than a full year curriculum of about 32 sessions. Yet, a great deal of material can be included in those few sessions; quality counts more than quantity. If the seventh grade class is large, it can be divided according to Bar/Bat Mitzvah dates. In this case, there might be two or three groups a year, allowing ten sessions per group. This must be decided upon before a curriculum is designed.

The Teacher

Working with seventh graders is a special skill. These children are often rebellious, and they are always full of questions and challenges. A teacher who is threatened by such behavior should not teach this grade! It takes very secure and open individuals whose own beliefs are firmly grounded to succeed in working with this age group. Failing to find such teachers means that the curriculum should be more conventional and should avoid too many values-oriented topics. Teachers should be evaluated as to where their strengths and interests lie, and should be placed accordingly. When a curriculum is being planned, the teachers should be involved in the process.

Background of Students

If, prior to the seventh grade, the school has not adequately covered basics such as Hebrew and prayers, then these need to be included in the curriculum. If, at the other extreme, the class is largely composed of day school students, then basics can be put aside in favor of other subject matter. One does not preclude the other, in any case. Both basics and more demanding subjects can be taught in the same curriculum. There is room for creativity at every level. For example, values can be taught through the study of Torah or prayers — and vice-versa. Prayers and Torah can also be taught on many different levels.

Working as a Team

If the main goal of a Bar/Bat Mitzvah program is skills mastery, it should be up to the school to instill deeper understanding of the Bar/Bat Mitzvah process, of Torah and Haftarah portions and their meaning, etc. Conversely, if skills are taught in the Religious School, more time will be spent on meaningful discussion about Torah and Haftarah portions during private tutorials. Unfortunately, in many congregations there is little communication between the Religious School and the individuals who run the B'nai Mitzvah program, usually the Cantor/Rabbi and tutor. In the ideal situation, the Director of Education and those involved in the team will decide who is responsible for teaching certain prayers, trope, Torah and Haftarah blessings, etc. At the very least, the goals and objectives for a B'nai Mitzvah class should be clearly understood by those directing the B'nai Mitzvah program, so that the program and school complement each other and clarify the entire learning process for students and teachers alike.

Once these practical considerations have been addressed, the subject matter of the course can be considered.

The Opening Session

The introductory lesson is crucial because it sets the tone for the rest of the year. The goal of this lesson is to get to know the students and for them to get to know each other. Following are some ideas for introductory lessons. Begin with a brief discussion of the curriculum, and then a discussion of the history and meaning of Bar/Bat Mitzvah. This can be done as a lecture, a question-and-answer session, or with handouts of printed questionnaires that test students' knowledge. Then move into more personal questions, such as: Why are you preparing to become a Bar/Bat Mitzvah? Was it your choice or your parents'? Explain. What are you most looking forward to? What are you most nervous about?

These and similar questions are often used in Family Education programs. The dual purpose of the questions is to get students in touch with their own feelings about the upcoming event, and to give teachers a better understanding of their students' attitudes.

If the teacher does not know the students at all, a list of more personal questions can be distributed for the students to return the next week with the promise of confidentiality. Questions might include: My favorite subject in school is . . . When I'm not in school, I like to . . . Something about my family . . . Something Jewish I like to do . . . Something about being Jewish that confuses me is . . . Something about Judaism I want to know more about is . . . The thing I liked best about Hebrew School last year was . . . This year in Hebrew School I hope to learn about . . . To me, the synagogue is . . . I think my parents send me to Hebrew School because . . .

The answers to some of these questions might even lead the teacher to restructure some of the lessons to respond to the students' remarks. At this opening session, a "class covenant" can also be discussed and distributed (see Chapter 40).

For this opening session, an interesting motivational activity was submitted by Nancy Messinger (Auerbach Central Agency for Jewish Education, Philadelphia). The teacher puts a series of numbers on the blackboard: 3, 4, 7, 8, 13, 40, 49, and challenges the students to find a relationship to something Jewish in each number. The teacher writes the students' answers on the board, providing answers when the students cannot. Then all the numbers except 13 are erased, and this is the opening for a discussion of the significance of this age and of becoming Bar/Bat Mitzvah.

The Course Itself

The subject matter for the course depends on many of the variables discussed above, but there is some agreement on the following as a part of basic curriculum: history of Bar/Bat Mitzvah; meaning of responsibility, both Jewish and in general; Torah and Haftarah blessings; order and structure of the service; meaning of *mitzvah* (usually involves projects).

In addition to these, depending on the amount of time available, many other topics can be covered: Bible, *Parashat Hashavua*, study of Prophets, life cycle events, holidays, history, Holocaust, Ritual objects/symbols, ethics/values. How many of these can be included depends on the curriculum already covered in previous grades. Many subjects, like holidays,for example, can be treated in a different, more challenging way in higher grades.

As an important closure exercise, the final session should be with post-Bar and Bat Mitzvah students who field questions from the class. This can be done as a panel if a large group is involved. Here are some suggested questions: What was the best/worst part of your Bar/Bat Mitzvah? Would you like to do it again? What would you do differently? Do you feel different in any way now? Have you taken on any new roles? What were you most worried or anxious about before the event? Was that part as bad as you had feared? Did you know what your Torah/Haftarah portions were about? Was that important to you? Were the services meaningful? How? If they were not, what would you do to make them more meaningful? What did you feel and think about during the ceremony? What did you learn about yourself and about Judaism in preparing for your Bar/Bat Mitzvah ceremony? What advice would you like to share with these students?

A MODEL CURRICULUM

Following is a description of a curriculum used by this author for a unique class. The synagogue was unaffiliated, and its Religious School was in only its third year of existence (previously, children had the option of attending a local Conservative school three times a week). Some of the children in the seventh grade class had been attending that Hebrew School, while others had attended an "alternative" school that provided few basics. Still others had attended no school at all. Most of the children did not know each other. This was the first time that a B'nai Mitzvah class had been taught. There were 16 students of varied backgrounds and levels of Jewish knowledge.

The curriculum evolved as the year progressed, but three subjects were decided on at the outset, to be linked by certain themes: prayer, Torah, and holidays. A central component, and the top priority, was a discussion of each child's individual Torah and Haftarah portion, and the opportunity for all students to chant their portions for the class as the date of their ceremony drew close. Class met for two hours on Sunday morning. The focus of each lesson depended on the imminence of either a holiday or a Bar/Bat Mitzvah. When neither was imminent, more time was devoted to the prayer curriculum; otherwise Torah and holidays took precedence. The variety and the lack of rigid structure worked well both for me and the class. I utilized available curricular material for the prayer and Torah units, but created an original unit for the High Holy Days. Details on sources for materials can be found in the Bibliography at the end of this book.

Topic I: Prayer

References:

Amudei Tfillah Series — Based on a unit by Beatrice Minkove (z"l):

Blake, Toby, and Sarah M. Siegman. *Kiddush*. Baltimore: Board of Jewish Education, 1986.

______. *V'Ahavta*. Baltimore: Board of Jewish Education, 1985.

Beiner, Irvin, and Sarah M. Siegman. *Aleinu*. Baltimore: Board of Jewish Education, 1986.

Glaser, Rachel; Toby Blake; and Sarah M. Siegman. *Brachot HaHaftarah*. Baltimore: Board of Jewish Education, 1987.

Lasday, Jeffrey, and Sarah M. Siegman. *Shema*. Baltimore: Board of Jewish Education, 1986.

(There are seven more booiks in this series.)

Fields, Harvey. *Bechol Levavcha*. (New York: UAHC Press, 1976).

The first 20 minutes of class were devoted to *davening* Shacharit. I would focus on one prayer, explain the basic ideas and vocabulary, then drill it with the class. Some prayers were mastered in one or two weeks, while longer ones took months. This method seemed cursory and superficial, so I searched for more interesting approaches. A successful prayer curriculum should combine skill, understanding, and relevance, and I had been unable to find a book that stressed all three. At the local BJE, I found the very useful set of books called *Amudei Tfillah*. Five of these are listed above. Each book contains: background and guidelines for the teacher, key concepts and words, excellent bibliographical material, and four lesson plans. The lessons are divided according to the key concepts, which in turn are linked to particular verses of any given prayer. The books contain student activity sheets which may be photocopied. Since no books need be purchased for the students, this is a strong plus for the budget conscious synagogue.

Each lesson is constructed as follows: concept, teacher's/students' objectives, materials needed by the teacher/students, advance preparation, and estimated teaching time.

The lesson itself is spelled out in terms of motivation, transition, development, and reinforcement. The strength of this curriculum is that it teaches and reinforces the Hebrew of the prayers, contains drills to reinforce the translation of the key Hebrew phrases, and also includes excellent thought-questions and exercises to stimulate discussion. Lessons are completely spelled out step-by-step, making this curriculum suitable for the less experienced or inventive teacher. For the more creative teacher, there is room for variation. This curriculum meets the challenge of making prayer relevant to children of this age.

Bechol Levavcha, though a popular text, was not the primary text for this particular class, but before teaching any prayer, I referred to it for valuable insights and ideas. It can certainly be used as either a primary or a supplementary text for a unit on prayer.

Topic II: Torah/Haftarah

References

Loeb, Sorel Goldberg, and Barbara Binder Kadden. *Teaching Torah*. Denver: A.R.E. Publishing, Inc., 1984.

A Torah Commentary for Our Times. Vol. I, *Genesis*, 1990, Vol. II, *Exodus and Leviticus*. New York: UAHC Press, 1991.

Kaplan, Louis. *An Outline and Interpretation of the Weekly Sidrot*. Baltimore: Board of Jewish Education, reprinted 1988.

Reich, Leo; Rachel Glaser; and Sarah Siegman. *Tree of Life Torah Curriculum*. Baltimore: Board of Jewish Education, 1989.

Beiner, Stan. *Sedra Scenes*. Denver: A.R.E. Publishing, Inc., 1982.

Beiner, Stan. *Bible Scenes*. Denver: A.R.E. Publishing, Inc., 1988.

Keeping Posted. Vol. XXVI, No. 4. New York: UAHC Press.

Journey through Judaism. New York: UAHC Press, 1991.

Studying the intricacies of Torah is much like plunging into unfamiliar narrow streets: it helps to start off with a total picture of the city, gained by looking at a map or standing on high ground. For this reason, I began by handing out photocopied time lines and lists of the yearly *parashiyot*, together with *Chumashim* and Jewish calendars. Students often have a skewed understanding of historical time; it helps to see in one place the key dates of 1700 B.C.E. for Abraham, 1000 B.C.E. for David, 586 B.C.E. and 70 C.E. for the Destruction of the Temples in Jerusalem, and 1492 C.E. for the Expulsion from Spain. Once the order of the Five Books was learned, students could find their own Torah and Haftarah portions listed on the Jewish calendars, as well as where these portions fit into the yearly cycle. This broader understanding is very helpful before delving into individual portions. I utilized both *Chumashim* and calendars in teaching holidays as well.

For an overview of Torah and Tanach, to supplement photocopied time lines and lists, *Etz Chaim* devotes one lesson to an introduction of the Five Books. In addition to the imparting of facts, this lesson is linked to the concept of a tree of life. A Poster Kit is included and this adds welcome visual stimulation to the lesson.

Students will be more inclined to show an interest in learning Torah if they see the connection to their own Bar/Bat Mitzvah portion immediately. This was why I handed out Jewish calendars in which they could find their portion listed on the Shabbat of their ceremony. I had a list of all Bar/Bat Mitzvah dates at the start of the school year and designed my lessons accordingly. Two or three weeks before every student's ceremony, I introduced his/her portion in class. In some cases this entailed introducing a book of the Torah as well. I focused on certain relevant ideas, preferably in the precise section from which they were reading (although this was not always possible). The most helpful text for this exercise is *Teaching Torah* which gives concise synopses of each portion and then focuses on several concepts found in the portion. The strength of this text is the relevance of the questions it provides. For example, in *Vayetze*, in discussing the priestly garments, questions are asked about forms of dress in general. The teacher might ask such questions as: "How do you feel when you are dressed up? For what occasions do you get dressed up?" While students relate to questions of this sort, the teacher needs to guard against trivializing the Torah's message. He/she can guide the students back to Torah, connecting its message to their own lives.

A Torah Commentary for Our Times provides an important link between the Torah text and students' interpretations: *midrash* and commentaries are delved into extensively. Students can gain an understanding of how commentators throughout the centuries have grappled with the meaning of the Torah text, and can find validation in searching for their own answers today. There are also excellent questions at the end of each *parashah*.

A completely different approach is found in *An Outline and Interpretation of the Weekly Sedroth*. These two volumes contain a detailed analysis, in outline form, of each *parashah*. General notes are presented before each book of the Tanach. Then a central idea is suggested for each *parashah*; and the entire *parashah* is presented in outline form with a great deal of interesting commentary for each verse. No discussion questions are included, but the creative teacher could extract many from the wealth of information provided. The approach is traditional. The commentary seems dated, no doubt due to the fact the book was originally published in 1948 and recently reprinted with no changes. Five Student Workbooks, the *Humosh Sedrah Course*, also written in the 40s, accompany the above two volumes. These volumes list the key Hebrew words of every *parashah* with their translation, followed by translating exercises and questions about the *parashah*. These could be used in class, for homework, or as quizzes. The level of Hebrew skill required probably restricts the use of this set to day schools and to supplementary schools with a heavy Hebrew emphasis.

While discussing key ideas in a student's *parashah*, the students had *Chumashim* at their desks. We did "*Chumash* searches" to see who could find a book, chapter, and verse first. I might point out a key phrase in Hebrew or English and ask the first student who found it to read it aloud. In this way all students gained some familiarity and ease with the *Chumash*.

After the *parashah* was thoroughly analyzed and discussed, I moved on to the accompanying Haftarah portion. A very good curriculum for exploring the Prophets is the aforementioned *Etz Chaim*. It contains excellent lesson plans on prophets in general, the connection between the Haftarah and Torah readings, and several individual portions (Deborah, Elijah, Isaiah, Jeremiah). *Keeping Posted*, Vol. XXVI, No. 4 is an excellent issue devoted to Prophets. (In general, this publication is full of innovative ideas on many subjects, and I regularly search the index and order issues on any subject I plan to teach.) *Journey through Judaism* is a compilation of the best of many years of *Keeping Posted*.

As a kind of reward after the thorough and serious discussion of the Torah and Haftarah portions, I often utilized the plays in *Sedra Scenes* and *Bible Scenes* which offer humorous, but true to the text, skits based on the Torah and Haftarah portions. This gave students a chance to act out parts, and most of them enjoyed this.

The week before a student's Bar/Bat Mitzvah ceremony, he/she got up in front of the class, introduced the portion to be read, then chanted the *brachot* and the Torah and Haftarah portions for the class. Students all followed along in their *Chumash*. There was no problem keeping the class quiet for these sessions — they all knew their turn would come, too! After each recitation, a brief "party" was held. (Parents were given the dates of their child's recitation at the start of the year, and they were asked to provide a snack for the whole class.) This became a sort of pre-celebration party, and for some children this rite of passage in front of their peers was a greater challenge than the ceremony on the *bimah*. It was also an important bonding activity for the whole class.

Topic III: Holidays

References:

Strassfeld, Michael. *The Jewish Holidays*. New York: Harper & Row, 1985.

Schauss, Hayyim. *The Jewish Festivals*. New York: Schocken, 1962.

Keeping Posted, miscellaneous issues. New York: UAHC Press.

Zwerin, Raymond A. *The Jewish Calendar*. Denver: A.R.E. Publishing, Inc., 1975.

A Yom Kippur Kit, including Kol Nidre cassette program with companion Listening Guide. Montreal: Limud Publications, 1974.

Since the High Holy Days fall near the beginning of the school year when the whole issue of time and seasons is uppermost on students' minds, I linked these holidays with the concept of time during the first lesson of the year. My long-term goal for the year was for the students to "plug in" to the Jewish calendar and for this connection to enhance a sense of Jewish identity. The subject matter of holidays is not directly connected to B'nai Mitzvah education. But many students in this class had never learned about their holidays and traditions. Even for a seventh grade class that has had the usual three to five years of Religious School behind them, holidays should be discussed and treated in some new and creative way every year.

Utilizing ideas from the references listed above for this unit, I wrote a Holiday unit covering the High Holy Days and Shalosh Regalim. For later holidays, such as Shavuot, Purim, and Pesach, I found *The Jewish Holidays* to contain the most interesting and unusual approach. In addition, the series of anthologies (published by the Jewish Publication Society) contains a wealth of information as well as stories and poems in a volume for each of the holidays. Often a story based on a holiday theme, when well read, can not only hold the attention of a class, but can also teach more about the feeling a holiday evokes than any amount of lecturing or quizzes.

Here are some of the themes and ideas I tried to impart in my four lesson Holiday Unit:

> We operate on a different time frame inside the synagogue (i.e., the festival calendar rather than the secular one).
>
> Rosh Hashanah is a time-based holiday.
>
> Biblical references are to the shofar, not Rosh Hashanah.
>
> The difference between individual atonement and having a priest atone for us.
>
> The High Holy Day theme of God as Ruler.
>
> The history and meaning of *"Kol Nidre."*
>
> We can write our own *"Al Chet."*
>
> Differences between biblical, agricultural, and historical festivals.

In addition to discussions and readings, there were sessions devoted to *Chumash* searching. The class found references to the shofar, to Yom Kippur, to Sukkot, etc. This was another way of making them more comfortable with the *Chumash* months before they began to chant their portions for each other. It also imparted the idea of how many of our customs and holidays originated in the Bible. The concept of time, of *antiquity*, is a difficult one for children. But reading about holidays they celebrate today in an ancient book will help to imbue them with feelings of continuity and identity with our people. If we can cultivate these feelings in our seventh graders, the primary goal of a "B'nai Mitzvah curriculum" has been met.

CONCLUSION

This is but one example of a B'nai Mitzvah curriculum. Hopefully, educators will be inspired by the ideas in this and other chapters in this Unit to create and/or expand their present seventh grade curricula.

Chapter 37

The Dorshei Emet Pre-Bar/Bat Mitzvah Program

Ron Aigen

GUIDELINES FOR THE PROGRAM

Since the majority of our families send their children to one of the many local Jewish day schools (which is the norm in Montreal), our synagogue had never felt the need for creating its own afternoon school. This meant we had little or no contact, educational or otherwise, with the children or their families before the Bar/Bat Mitzvah (notwithstanding the synagogue's policy of a two year membership requirement prior to that event). We therefore established guidelines on Bar/Bat Mitzvah which in turn gave rise to our pre-Bar/Bat Mitzvah Program.

Because "community" is central to our congregation's concept of Jewish identity, we set participation in the life of the community as our primary criterion for becoming a Bar/Bat Mitzvah in this synagogue. Our guidelines therefore set out the following objectives:

> We want our B'nai Mitzvah to acquire the skills of leading the Shabbat and holiday home rituals.
>
> We want our B'nai Mitzvah to be able to participate in the Shabbat morning service of our synagogue;
>
> We want our B'nai Mitzvah to develop some understanding of the Reconstructionist approach to Judaism, specifically with regard to prayer, Torah, and holidays.
>
> We want our B'nai Mitzvah to see how Judaism extends beyond the home and synagogue into the larger Jewish community.

In setting out to actualize these goals, we had to devise a program which would not be repetitious for the day school students. Yet, we had to take into account the abilities of non-day school students as well. In order to accomplish this, we made the prerequisite for entering the program good reading knowledge of Hebrew. Therefore, virtually all of the non-day school students have received some tutorial or afternoon school experience.

OVERVIEW OF THE PROGRAM

A program was created in which Grade 6 students (in the year prior to the actual tutoring for learning the Maftir and Haftarah) would meet over 18 weeks on a weekly basis for a one and a half hour session with the Rabbi. In the fall semester, the emphasis is on learning the melodies of the Shabbat morning service and Shabbat home rituals, as well as studying the topics of *tzedakah* and *gemilut chasadim.* Each child is given a cassette of the entire Shabbat morning service and Erev Shabbat home ritual, and encouraged to listen to it at home. About 10 to 15 minutes of meeting time is devoted to singing the melodies together. For those in day schools, we use this opportunity to compare the Reconstructionist version of prayers with those they learned in school by rote. This usually gives rise to spontaneous discussions of theology, e.g., what do we believe about chosenness, revival of the dead, the messianic concept, the concept of God. The pre-B'nai Mitzvah group, together with their families, is also expected to attend Shabbat morning services once a month. Slowly, the group takes on larger responsibility for leading parts of the service.

Part I (8 sessions)

The curriculum for *tzedakah* and *gemilut chasadim* follows the workbook *Tzedakah, Gemilut Chasadim and Ahavah* (A.R.E. Publishing, Inc.). In addition, we visit the local Federation building, the Cummings House, which houses virtually all the Montreal Jewish community institutions. Our tour includes a visit to the Educational Resource Centre for an audiovisual presentation of the structure and function of the Federation-CJA, a visit to the Golden Age Center, the Jewish Public Library, the Jewish Immigrant Aid Society, and the Federation offices. This tour comes toward the end of the unit on *tzedakah* to show how the Montreal Jewish community puts into practice what the students have been learning.

The final session of this first unit is held just prior to Chanukah, and the group, together with parents, participates in the synagogue's Chanukah Basket Project. We receive a list of needy Jewish poor from Baron de Hirsch, the community social welfare agency. We then pack and deliver food bags, including Chanukah candles and *gelt*, to the 200 families on the list. The children and parents participate together in the packing on the regularly scheduled weeknight pre-B'nai Mitzvah group meeting. Most return together with other synagogue members on the following Sunday morning for deliveries. This is generally one of the highlights of the program. This year, following the packing, we viewed and discussed a video on Jewish poverty in Montreal produced by the Federation-CJA.

Part II (9 sessions)

The second half of the program takes on a different format. The weekly sessions are devoted to topics of current Jewish concern through games, videos, guest speakers, and tours. The goal of this unit is to broaden the definition of what constitutes "Jewish" concerns for us today.

Two sessions are devoted to the Holocaust; one is the learning experience *Gestapo* (A.R.E. Publishing, Inc.). This is a very effective means of making a more personal connection with the facts that they have already learned in day school. For the non-day school student, it is a good introduction. This session is followed by a visit to the Montreal Holocaust Memorial Centre.

For an Israel-oriented session, we have a representative of Maccabi Canada show a video of the Maccabi Games. In preparation for this session we discuss Jewish texts on bodily health.

For a session on media and Jewish values, we view a National Film Board video *The Bronswick Affair,* which satirizes the ability of TV to brainwash. We then discuss the significance of Deuteronomy 13:2-4. Other topics in this unit have included nuclear war, prejudice, scribal arts, and *tefillin*, and the Havdalah ceremony. (See Appendix I for a complete outline of each session.)

During this semester, the students work at home in *hevruta* pairs on one of the *gemilut chasadim* projects in the A.R.E. workbook. These projects are then presented at a Friday night dinner for the families of this group.

The last part of the Pre-B'nai Mitzvah Program is a three part family workshop, attended by parents and child together. (For a description of this workshop, see Chapter 34.)

CONCLUSION

This program gives meaning to *becoming B'nai Mitzvah*, as it involves students in both community projects and in leading Shabbat services. The most important learning can take place outside classroom walls; this program utilizes the potential for such learning.

(Editor's note: Although designed as a sixth grade curriculum, this could be used successfully with seventh grade and called a B'nai Mitzvah program.)

APPENDIX I

Pre B'nai Mitzvah Group

Outline of Part I

Tuesday Evenings, 6:30 - 8:00 p.m.

MELODIES

Each week new melodies will be introduced;
They should be practiced at home with a prepared cassette and Siddur. Each student will need to purchase the cassette and a Reconstructionist Siddur.

PROGRAM

The program outline suggested below may be changed to accommodate special events.

1. October 8
   "Hineh Mah Tov"
   "Mah Tovu" (P. 72)
   "Adon Olam" (P. 200)

October 8
Introduction
"The Individual"

2. October 15
   "Candle lighting"
   "Shalom Aleichem"
   Kiddush for Erev Shabbat
   "Aleinu" (P. 194)

October 15
"Putting Values into Action"

TIKKUN OLAM
The reason the world needs fixing; The role of the Jew as fixer — *mitzvot* as tools.
Pp. 4-11 in workbook

3. October 22
   "V'haer einenu" (P. 116)
   "Avot" (P. 126)

October 22
"Expressing Our Individuality"
KAVOD/BUSHAH
honor/shame
Pp. 12-15 in workbook

4. October 29
   "El Adon" (P. 108)
   "Mi Kamocha" (P. 124)
   "Tzur Yisrael" (P. 124)

October 29
"Each in Our Own Special Way"
TZEDAKAH
Rambam's ladder
Pp. 16-21 in workbook

5. November 5
   "Sh'ma" (P. 120)
   "Yigdal" (P. 202)

November 5
"Every Person is Unique/Be Yourself"
MONEY MAGIC
(bring a calculator)
Pp. 25-33, 39 in workbook

APPENDIX 1 (Cont.)

6. November 12

November 12
Federation Tour 6:30-7:45 p.m.
meet at the Cummings Building,
5151 Cote St. Catherine (in lobby)

7. November 19
Birkat Hamazon
"*Yismechu*" (P. 130)
"*V'shamru*" (P. 136)

November 19
"The 'I' in Another/Yours or Mine"
GEMILUT CHASADIM
Deeds of Loving-kindness
Pp. 42-47 in workbook

MAZON and WORLD HUNGER

8. November 26

November 26
"Chanukah Baskets"
(Parents are included on this evening)

FAMILY SHABBATOT
All Pre-B'nai Mitzvah will be given parts in Shabbat services on October 19th, November 16th, December 7th, 1991, January 18th, February 15th, March 7th, April 18th, May 2nd and Shavuot/Sunday, June 7th. Please be on time — we begin at 10 A.M.

APPENDIX 1 (Cont.)

Pre B'nai Mitzvah Group

Outline of Part II

Tuesday Evenings, 6:30 - 8:00 p.m.

MELODIES	PROGRAM
Each week new melodies will be introduced. They should be practiced at home with a prepared cassette and Siddur.	The program outline suggested below may be changed to accommodate special events.
1. January 7 *"Mi Chamocha"* (P. 124) *"Tzur Yisrael"* (P. 124) *"Birkat HaMazon"* *"Yismechu"* (P. 130) *"V'shamru"* *"Sim Shalom"* (P. 136)	January 7 Being God-like Pp. 50-53 in workbook Review *Gemilut Chasadim* projects
2. January 14	January 14 *Gestapo: A Learning Experience about the Holocaust* (A.R.E.)
3. January 21	January 21 Visit to Holocaust Memorial Center. Meet at Cummings Building, 5151 Cote St. Catherine Rd. at 6:15 (in lobby). All parent(s) requested to attend.
4. January 28	January 28 Maccabia – Bodily Health, Fitness & Judaism Israel video
5. February 4	February 4 Debate: Does believing in God make a difference?
6. February 11	February 11 Media and Jewish Values (Video)
7. February 18 Bring *tefillin* Torah service Blessings for *aliyah*	February 18 Jewish Scribal Arts *Tefillin* and Making a Torah Film and workshop: *For Out of Zion* (United Synagogue)

8. February 25

February 25
Training for Religious and Racial Tolerance
Esther 3:8
Films: *Carols' Mirror* and *Walker* (both National Film Board of Canada)

9. March 3

March 3
Meeting with teenage Russian Jews

10. March 10
Havdalah

March 10
Jewish Games Night

FAMILY SHABBATOT

All Pre-B'nai Mitzvah and their families are asked to arrive by 10 a.m. on the following dates which are the appointed Shabbatot for group attendance:

January 18th
February 15th
March 7th
April 18th
May 2nd
Sunday, June 7th – Shavuot

Chapter 38
Coming of Age as a Jew — Bar/Bat Mitzvah by Shoshana Glatzer

Reviewed by Helen Leneman

Coming of Age as a Jew — Bar/Bat Mitzvah, written and edited by Shoshana Glatzer in collaboration with Ellen Singer, Susan Shulman-Tesel, and Lifsa Schachter (Board of Jewish Education of Greater New York) is now widely known and used with sixth graders in the Greater New York area. It is designed to supplement a Bar/Bat Mitzvah curriculum in Religious Schools. I recommend it, however, as a standard text for Bar/Bat Mitzvah classes. It is a very flexible curriculum that can be done with a class, with or without parents, with small and large groups. It fulfills many of the requirements outlined in Chapter 36.

The curriculum contains strategies to appeal to both the emotions and to the intellect of adolescent students. The goal is for students to come to understand that Bar/Bat Mitzvah is not a single day in their lives, but rather a transition to a new status in the Jewish community. There is an attempt to develop a new process, reflecting the uniqueness of American Jews. In concrete terms, the aim is for students to:

View the ceremony of becoming a Bar/Bat Mitzvah as a transition to Jewish adulthood and to a lifetime pursuit of learning.

Explore the idea that performance of *mitzvot* is a Jewish way of concretizing values.

Be encouraged to see themselves as part of the broader community expanding from their immediate families to *K'lal Israel.*

Learn to identify some of the privileges and responsibilities of Jewish adulthood.

Explore the meaning of the ritual in each phase in the life cycle of the Jew.

Experience one of the most important Jewish values: learning Torah.

The curriculum consists of a Teacher's Guide and a Student Workbook. Special attention is paid to the parent/student relationship through family homework assignments and projects. There are 17 lessons, divided into three basic units: Introduction, Transition, Living as a Bar/Bat Mitzvah.

At the end of Lesson 1, students are asked to interview one or both of their parents about that parent's Bar/Bat Mitzvah experience. They bring back the results of those interviews. The Teacher's Guide recommends several questions for the teachers to put to the students.

This exercise opens up the discussion of the meaning to both the parents and the children of becoming Bar/Bat Mitzvah. They may learn things about each other they never knew. And in sharing these interview results with the whole class, the students can all learn of the variety of possible Bar/Bat Mitzvah experiences.

Lesson 2 includes reprints of several Bar/Bat Mitzvah stories and book excerpts from different eras and countries. For example, "A Boston Bar Mitzvah" by Charles Angoff, "The First Bat Mitzvah in a Synagogue" by Judith Kaplan Eisenstein, and excerpts from *What Really Happened to the Bar Mitzvah Class of 5722?* by Michael Medved all appear here, followed by suggested discussion questions. The great diversity of experiences written about in these literary selections is sure to surprise many students.

The next few lessons focus on the students' stage of life — neither children nor adults, they are in transition. In one exercise, there is a chart of activities that includes such activities as: babysit for a one-year-old child, drive a car, light Chanukah candles, fast on Yom Kippur, ride a bicycle on the street, cook a meal. Students are asked to write the youngest age at which a child can do each activity unassisted. In a second column, their parents answer the same question.

In another lesson, students are asked how often they experience certain feelings (e.g., upset, lonely, angry, excited about growing up, embarrassed about the way I look, etc.).

Closing this section is a brief discussion of puberty and physical changes.

The text then turns to *mitzvot.* After the concept of *mitzvot* is briefly explained, there is a list of several *mitzvot* which the students classify, and possible motivations for performing them: to become part of the Jewish people, to become better human beings, to make the world a better place.

The next lesson progresses to contrasting *mitzvot* between people with those between people and God. A further classification is introduced: personal, family, and community *mitzvot.* All of these are presented in charts, lists, or other visually accessible forms for students to fill in. The interactive nature of this lesson is effective in keeping students actively involved.

Next, a *mitzvah* project is introduced. Students are asked to choose three activities in each of three categories: Torah, *avodah, gemilut chasadim.* The basic ideas here are similar to those of the standard Mitzvah Program (see Chapter 24). But being introduced in this way, after a logical progression through seven lessons, puts the performing of *mitzvot* in a context few other such programs achieve.

The next few lessons introduce the concept of symbols. Then Jewish symbols are introduced, and categories for these are explored (e.g., those which involve the action of eating, drinking, or wearing; or those which might involve children or adults, men or women).

After this section, three lessons are devoted to *tefillin.* Moving stories related to *tefillin* are included, such as "On the Wings of the Dove" by David Weiss, which illustrates the deep connection between *tefillin* and Jewish identity.

Following these chapters, *tallit* and *mezuzah* are explored. To introduce the *tallit,* the Teacher's Guide suggests several questions about *uniforms* leading to the notion of the *tallit* as a uniform.

The next chapters discuss the Torah service and its order in detail. The book is sensitive to the variety of ideologies, and included, among others, are the Reconstructionist versions of several prayers. An excellent "Torah Reading Service Questionnaire" is included. It covers all the basic material with humor, and if students do not know the answers, they will learn them from the teacher's explanations. Following is an example of a question from this questionnaire:

Why is the Torah read in the synagogue every Monday, Thursday, and Friday?

a. Why not?
b. So that three days will not pass without a Jew hearing the Torah read.
c. Because there is no basketball practice on Mondays and Thursdays.

Following this section, there is a discussion of public ceremonies. Examples given are weddings, graduation exercises, the naturalization ceremony, and a Little League Baseball Award ceremony. Students must answer questions specific to these ceremonies about the goals, necessary preparation, order of events, and other aspects. Then they relate this information to their own Bar/Bat Mitzvah ceremony. In so doing, they gain new insight into both its structure and meaning. This is one more example of the excellent approach of this curriculum. It takes students from where they are, using their knowledge of secular customs to deepen their understanding of parallel Jewish customs.

The next chapters discuss the importance of Hebrew names and encourage students to explore the origins of their own Hebrew names. There is an extensive glossary of Jewish life cycle terms, followed by a format for a board game and a crossword puzzle, all designed to reinforce the vocabulary studied. Questions provided for the board game could also be used for an oral quiz session. For the closing chapter, there are lessons in *Parashat Shmot* and *Parashat Korach* and their Haftarot, which also include a summary and review of all life cycle ceremonies. The last section contains Torah study guides for the whole family for ten *parashiyot* and their Haftarot.

Editor's Comments

When I used this curriculum, the children remained interested and stimulated throughout the course and emerged with a much better idea of what the whole Bar/Bat Mitzvah process is supposed to be about. The curriculum is encompassing and is bound to result in better educated and more interested young Jews.

Chapter 39
"Living Mitzvot": An Experiential Approach to B'nai Mitzvah Instruction

Allan C. Tuffs and Helen Leneman

While others have based their religious identity on creedal formulas, we Jews have tended to base our religious identity on adherence to a certain way of life. Whereas others have taught their children catechisms — formulations of theological principles — we Jews have taught our children *mitzvot* — commandments by which to live. At times in our history we have argued among ourselves about the origins of these commandments and how they should be fulfilled. However, most observant Jews, Reform, Conservative, and Orthodox, would agree that the performance of *mitzvot* is an essential part of Jewish life. Most would agree that God is revealed on earth through people performing righteous deeds.

If the concept of *mitzvah* is still vibrant and alive in our time, it follows that Jews are called upon to do certain things as individuals and as a community. There are, however, those who believe that, except in matters of ethical and moral behavior, God does not command us to do anything. For them, ritual practices, such as the dietary laws and the lighting of Shabbat candles, have become little more than folkways that can be embraced or discarded at the discretion of the individual. For them, the problem of how to choose what rituals to observe is relatively easy — one simply observes those ritual practices that he or she finds personally meaningful and disregards the rest. Others of us can not grant such sweeping authority to the individual in ritual matters. Believing that ritual practices are as much a part of religious life as moral and ethical deeds, we walk a middle ground between absolute "personal autonomy" and "God's commanding presence" in these matters. The question for Jewish educators who take this latter position is, how do we instill in our students a responsiveness to God's commanding presence and at the same time respect their uniqueness as individual human beings?

"Living Mitzvot" is a response to this dilemma. It is designed to be the *mitzvah* component of a well-rounded seventh grade curriculum. In addition to 20 minutes or more devoted weekly to "Living Mitzvot," the curriculum includes the following:

1. Torah study: The Torah portion of the week is studied in each session.
2. Hebrew: A Hebrew booklet with 20 lessons is given to the students, who are responsible for completing the work at home. The booklet is designed to review and reinforce the first four years of the Hebrew program and to help the student in translating the Torah. All work is checked in class, and the Rabbi makes himself available at all times on a "Hebrew Hotline" to help the student with problems.
3. Milon: This is part of the ongoing Hebrew curriculum. Students start a Hebrew dictionary in their second year and continue adding to it throughout their years in Hebrew School. In the seventh grade they add words from the weekly Torah portion to this *milon*.

The obvious strength of this program is the independence students are given in completing Hebrew assignments, their own *milon* and the "practicums" contained in the "Living Mitzvot." They can feel they have both the support and the respect of the staff. They are expected to be self-motivated, and children this age will rise to expectations that are challenging.

"Living Mitzvot" grew out of the work of Rabbi Allan Tuffs with approximately 250 B'nai Mitzvah students at Congregation Emanu-El B'ne Jeshurun in Milwaukee,

Wisconsin between 1982 and 1987. Early in his Rabbinic career, he could not find a curriculum that took personal observance seriously from a liberal Jewish perspective. In the curricula that he did find, seldom if ever was a student required actually to fulfill any *mitzvot.* Most curricula rightly pointed out that the word "*mitzvah*" did not mean "good deed," but "commandment," and yet did not command the student to do anything at all. Using this method of teaching *mitzvot,* B'nai Mitzvah students studied Jewish tradition in much the same way as an anthropologist would study an exotic culture at an academic arm's length. There is an old saying: "Tell me and I will forget. Show me and I will remember. Let me do and I will learn." If ever there was an educational endeavor in which that saying resonates with authenticity, it is in the teaching of our children the *mitzvot* of Jewish life. If we are going to teach them to live Jewishly, we must give them the experience of doing so. We must also give them a way of making decisions with regard to choosing how to observe *mitzvot.*

"Living Mitzvot" was created with these issues in mind. To date, it has been used by approximately 100 Reform and Conservative congregations in the U.S. and Canada. In some cases, "Living Mitzvot" is taught one-on-one during the individual tutorials that most students have in preparation for their Bar/Bat Mitzvah service. However, it is more effectively used in a group setting such as Hebrew School, in which class discussion can occur. The methodology of presenting the material is fairly simple. "Living Mitzvot" is comprised of 18 chapters divided into six units:

Unit I, "On Becoming a Bar/Bat Mitzvah," contains three chapters dealing with the meaning of the ceremony, of growing up and celebrating.

Unit II, "Torah — the Tree of Life," has two chapters on understanding the Torah and its meanings.

Unit III, "The Importance of Worship," is the largest section, with seven chapters covering prayer, Shabbat, and home observance.

Unit IV, "Deeds of Jewish Life," has three chapters distinguishing different kinds of *tzedakah.*

Unit V, "The Jewish People," discusses in two chapters the concepts of diversity and *K'lal Yisrael.*

The last unit and chapter, "Making Decisions as a Jewish Adult," brings all of these ideas and concepts together.

The classifications of the *mitzvot* into Torah, *avodah,* and *gemilut chasadim,* are the standards for any Mitzvah Program (see Chapter 24). Most Mitzvah Programs are designed to be done independently by the students with help from an advisor. This program includes class discussions and outside work (completion of each practicum). The advantages of a class Mitzvah Program are the peer support it provides, and the chance to hold discussions that will clarify the reasons for performing *mitzvot* in general.

At the beginning of each chapter, the teacher leads a discussion on a particular *mitzvah,* and students are often called upon to read. Usually no more than a half hour of class time is required per chapter. Students are then required to experiment with that *mitzvah* at home during the next week. In most chapters, students are asked to keep a log of their feelings and observations while fulfilling that particular *mitzvah.* At the beginning of the next class, the contents of those logs are discussed.

Unit I starts with discussions of age, helping the students understand the meaning of their "in-between" age. It contains good discussion questions for class, as well as some to be done at home with their parents. Chapter 3 includes a story that has become popular as a "values trigger," extracted from Herbert Tarr's book *Heaven Help Us* (New York: Bantam Books/ Random House). It is an outlandish example of the skewed values too often present in the Bar/Bat Mitzvah ceremony and party. Good discussion questions follow, such as: List the presents you would like to receive that in some way would reflect your adult status in Judaism; list other presents you might like to receive just because they may be enjoyable to you. These are answered at home, then discussed in class. It is very likely that the answers of one student might give other students new ideas, and in this way, they can learn from each other and not only from the teacher.

Unit II explains in very clear terms the distinction between *pshat* (simple meaning) and *drash* (interpretation). There is no overview of the Torah, such as a time line or list of the yearly readings, but this could be provided as supplementary material. The discussion of authorship of the Torah is an interesting one. The question "How can the Torah still be God's holy word if human beings had something to do with writing it?" is posed, along with "How do you believe God communicates with people?" Discussions of these questions and where they lead depends on the teacher, of course. Here, as always, the teacher must be open-minded and non-judgmental. Students may never have thought about these questions and the task here is to stimulate them to come up with their own ideas. There is no right or wrong answer. The practicum for the *pshat* section is for the students to answer simple factual questions about their own Torah portions.

The *drash* section explains very clearly the reason for writing a *drash*. One example is included, the well-known story of the Tower of Babel. Following the English text are several examples of *midrash* based on the story; these were reproduced from *Torah: A Modern Commentary* by Plaut (UAHC Press). After discussion of the different interpretations, students are asked several questions to stimulate them to come up with their own *drash*, for example, "What could a teacher learn from this story? An architect? The leader of a nation?" For the practicum, the students are asked to write a short interpretation of their own Torah portions.

The scope of this lesson could be expanded by using the two texts recommended in Chapter 36, *Teaching Torah* (A.R.E. Publishing, Inc.) and *A Torah Commentary for Our Times* (UAHC Press).

Unit III, Chapters 6-8 all deal with prayer. Chapter 6 requires students to say the "*Sh'ma*" every evening and morning and to pray about something that is important to them. For the practicum, they are asked to keep a record of what time of day they prayed, the contents of their personal prayers, and their level of *kavanah* (concentration). One of the questions discussed at the next class is whether their concentration improved during the week. The real question, of course, is: "Is prayer an acquired skill?"

Chapter 7 explains ritual by comparing it to a "well-worn path that can lead us closer to God." *Tallit, tefillin*, and *kipah* are briefly discussed, then *tefillin* are put on in class. Most Reform synagogues do not either expect or support the wearing of *tefillin*, and there has been opposition from some parents for this part of the class. But children should have a right to understand and experience even those aspects of their tradition that have been largely rejected. This is the same rationale for encouraging students to experiment with *kashrut*. These symbols can be introduced in a non-dogmatic fashion and there is certainly value in young Jews knowing the meaning and history of a 2000-year-old custom like laying *tefillin*.

Chapter 8 discusses the meaning of the *minyan* and distinguishes between private and public prayer. For the practicum, students fill out a log about services they attended, and answer the question: "How was praying in the synagogue different from praying at home?" These are difficult concepts, and dealing with them as a class should be very helpful for many children. There will always be some students who are more spiritual than others and can stimulate those who might have never thought along these lines. Chapters 9 and 10 deal with Shabbat. As in other sections of this text, the first discussion is philosophical and the second more technical. This is the rationale of the whole course: the most effective learning takes place through doing. The lofty meaning and goals of Shabbat are laid out, and then the means of attaining those goals is described. Many important concepts are synthesized into a few clear sentences without oversimplifying. Chapter 10 closes with this sentence: "One of the greatest challenges facing modern Jews is to find ways to make Shabbat a unique and spiritual day."

The practicum then challenges the students to do exactly that:

"Think of five activities you might not do in order to make Shabbat special. Also think of five things you might do (excluding Shabbat rituals such as *Kiddush*) that would help you to experience Shabbat."

In Chapter 11, the basic laws of *kashrut* are studied. The complete list of permitted and forbidden foods (taken from Leviticus 11:1-23) is included. Four rationales for observing the dietary laws are discussed, including health, compassion for living things, self-discipline, and identification with the Jewish people. Students are then required to keep "kosher style" and to recite *Hamotzi* before every meal for one week. The contents of their logs are shared at the beginning of the next class.

These and many other exercises appear in most Mitzvah Programs. The difference in this case is the context: students are seeing the observance of *kashrut* as a form of Jewish home observance, not an illogical custom observed only by Orthodox and Conservative Jews. They learn the background, traditions, and a variety of motivations for keeping kosher. If they choose to reject *kashrut*, they will do so after understanding, and not through ignorance.

The last chapter of this Unit deals with the Jewish home. Students are told that "Each of us must create a Jewish environment at home where we spend the most time." An interesting discussion question is included: the process of chemical osmosis is described, and students are asked if there is a lesson in it for Jewish survival. The practicum is to write an account of items in the student's home that identify it as Jewish. This lesson must be taught with an awareness of the potentially awkward position of the student who can find few of those items, to ensure that student will not be upset with his/her parents or with the school. The hope is that children will lead their parents to keeping a more Jewish home, but there could be resistance to this idea. This lesson must be taught with great care not to create guilt feelings. The teacher must stress the positive and not judge the child of uninvolved parents.

In Unit IV, "Deeds of Jewish Life," there is an attempt to distinguish between *tzedakah*, *gemilut chasadim*, and *tikkun olam*. In other curricula, these are considered as different reasons for doing *tzedakah*, or different categories of *tzedakah*. The ladder designed by Maimonides is given. This is always a good discussion trigger, but has usually been used frequently prior to the seventh grade. An extensive Talmudic quote is given in chapter 13, which has been found to be too difficult for most seventh graders. Other material should be used to explain the meaning of *tzedakah*.

Gemilut chasadim and *tikkun olam* are clearly explained and illustrated. Students will understand from the discussions that even the smallest act of charity is important. The practicums involve carrying out good deeds in all three categories.

Unit V, "The Jewish People," opens with a brief discussion of diversity. The differences between Ashkenazic and Sephardic Jews are just touched on. This topic is usually of great interest to students, particularly if their own family origins can be brought into the discussion. The curriculum could be expanded to include additional readings and discussions on this topic.

The branches of Judaism are not discussed at all; students are given a home assignment to prepare an oral report on one branch, and issues of *Keeping Posted* are recommended for research. There is much curricular material available on this topic, and the course could be expanded here as well, allotting classroom time on this subject in addition to assigning oral reports. The next chapter briefly discusses *K'lal Yisrael*, our concern for Jews everywhere in the world. Students might find it an interesting assignment to write a report on exotic Jews of different parts of the world, such as the Jews of India or Morocco. Because Soviet Jews and Ethiopian Jews have been the chief focus for so long, students may get the idea all Jews outside the United States are oppressed and in need of aid. Help students learn in addition the many interesting and joyous ways there are of being Jewish in the world. This is an important lesson for a Bar/Bat Mitzvah to internalize.

Chapter 18, the final chapter, is called "Making Decisions as a Jewish Adult." Now that students have not only studied certain *mitzvot*, but have also experienced doing them, they are required to make decisions about their personal commitment to living a Jewish life. The concept of being "free and commanded" at the same time is discussed. It is explained that to make intelligent choices, it is necessary to know not only the *mitzvot*, but to know yourself. To that end, students are required to complete a series of incomplete sentences that describe themselves as individuals. Examples of these incomplete sentences are: I consider my best quality to be . . . I consider my worst quality to be . . . My most prized possession is . . . I would be willing to die for . . . Students are also required to complete an additional set of incomplete statements including: I will refrain from doing the following things on Shabbat . . . I will support the following charities . . . I will work for the survival of the State of Israel by . . .

This second set of statements forms a personal pledge to live a life of *mitzvot*. Students are encouraged to review this personal pledge from time to time, and to update it so as to reflect their current understanding of their relationship to God and Judaism. There is an implicit assumption in this exercise that our personal autonomy extends to choices concerning how to fulfill *mitzvot*, but it does not allow us totally to disregard them. While none of us is able to keep all of the *mitzvot*, we should develop for ourselves a regimen of observances that includes the study of Torah, the worship of God, and the performance of moral and ethical deeds.

Our B'nai mitzvah students are full of energy and enthusiasm. They are anything but passive learners. Any attempt to awaken within their souls a passion for Jewish living must include not only their minds, but their entire beings as well. One cannot learn *mitzvot* by simply learning about them. One can only learn *mitzvot* by doing them. Becoming a Bar/Bat Mitzvah is as much about living as about learning, and "Living Mitzvot" effectively teaches Jewish ways of doing both.

(For information on "Living Mitzvot," contact Rabbi Allan Tuffs, Temple Shalom, 2901 Edgely Rd., Levittown, PA 19057.)

Chapter 40
Crossing the River: A Bar/Bat Mitzvah Apprenticeship Program by Burt Jacobson

Reviewed by Helen Leneman

Crossing the River is an original and imaginative set of materials. It is comprised of a student text, a student workbook, and a Teacher's Guide. It is unique in that it gives students many opportunities to think and to develop their own ideas. A class based on these materials would be highly interactive and involving.

The text is divided into six parts and contains a total of 36 chapters. Each part builds upon the last, so it would probably not work well to use only sections of the whole.

Rabbi Jacobson enumerates many goals for this program, among which are:

> To make Bar/Bat Mitzvah an inward as well as an outer process, helping youngsters make their transition from childhood to adulthood.
>
> To help youngsters develop a relationship with the ethical and religious *mitzvot* of the tradition, and to decide how they want to make the *mitzvot* a part of their lives.
>
> To introduce children to a number of accessible adult Jewish role models in the course of the year in order to help them understand the different ways people express Jewish values.
>
> To offer children opportunities to learn through doing as well as through studying.

The author goes on to enumerate an excellent list of general rules for teachers of Bar/Bat Mitzvah students, among which are:

> Do not patronize, preach, talk down to, or in any way try to impose your own values on your students.
>
> Really listen and hear what your students are saying; respect their opinions even when you disagree with them.
>
> Build trust between yourself and individual students, and foster trust between classmates.
>
> Encourage students to be open and honest about their feelings, ideas, and values.
>
> Be honest and open about your own feelings, ideas, and values without judging those of your students.
>
> Challenge students to probe deeper when they have not thought sufficiently about an issue; to this end, formulate exciting and challenging discussion questions.
>
> Remember that one of your central functions is to convey the beauty and depth of the tradition. This will happen best when you yourself are involved and concerned with this tradition.
>
> Approach the tradition in a non-dogmatic fashion. In practice this means viewing the tradition as the probings and wrestlings of great men and women with deep and important issues. These people can lend us their thinking when we study their words.

In keeping with the principles of mutual respect and affection between teachers and students, Rabbi Jacobson proposes that a "learning covenant" be developed with the class and signed by both the teacher and the students. It is suggested that this covenant be read aloud in class (and emended, if need be) whenever problems arise.

Some of the elements that usually find their way into these covenants have to do with mutual respect, classroom procedures, the consequences of misbehavior, respect, activities to be engaged in by teacher and students outside of class, attitudes of students and teachers toward each other, the means for staying on task, completion of homework, etc.

The Table of Contents in the Teacher's Guide lists several goals for each unit in a column alongside the list of units and chapters. This is an excellent idea, as it ensures that the teacher will keep on track by referring back constantly to this list.

Each of the six parts of the book is called a "journey"; these journeys are toward Adulthood, Jewishness, God, Jewish Tradition, Becoming a Good Person, and Becoming a Religious Jew. A format for teaching the 36 lessons in 30 weeks is also given.

In the Introduction to the program, Rabbi Jacobson explains his use of "crossing the river" as a metaphor. He opens with a "Let's pretend" story, to catch the students' attention. He describes a backpacking trip during which the hikers have reached a wide, rushing river. There are several choices: turn back, swim and risk drowning, or build a boat to get across. He then moves on to important river crossings in Jewish history, and from there, to the connection:

> One of the rivers that every person needs to cross is the river that divides childhood and adulthood. It takes time, skill, patience, and faith to learn how to get across this river . . . This book is about how young Jews, like you, can make the journey from childhood to adulthood.
>
> The approach of this book is not to tell you that there is one way of being a good Jewish person. Rather, it tries to introduce you to Jewish ideas, values and attitudes to help *you* begin to think about the kind of Jewish person you would like to be.
>
> When the Jewish people crossed the Reed Sea, they experienced a joyous feeling of freedom . . . They were happy because there was no Pharaoh around anymore to tell them what to do. But when the singing and dancing were over, the Jewish people had to begin their new life . . . At Mt. Sinai they learned that if they wanted to be *free*, they had to accept *responsibility*, so they would learn how to use their freedom in good rather than bad ways.

At this point, students are asked about the journeys and "crossings" in their lives.

Next, the meaning and concept of *mitzvot* are discussed, and the Rabbi points out that the students are already practicing many *mitzvot* in their lives, even though they don't know it. He calls the program the "Apprenticeship Program," because it gives students a chance to "test out" several *mitzvot* in their lives. The *mitzvah* project for the year is to complete one *mitzvah* in each of three categories; students report to the teacher monthly on their progress. The categories are the standard ones of Torah, *avodah, gemilut chasadim* (here called "Becoming a More Knowledgeable Jew," "Becoming a Better Person," and "Becoming a More Religious Person"). As in *Coming of Age as a Jew — Bar/Bat Mitzvah* and the program "Living Mitzvot" (see Chapters 38 and 39 respectively), the strength of including a Mitzvah Project within a complete course is the deeper contextual meaning this lends the *mitzvot.*

The general format of the book is the following: for most chapters, students first answer some thought questions in their workbook. Several pages of reading on the topic follow, interspersed with more and more questions. In theory, by the end of the lesson, the student will have more understanding of the questions posed at the beginning, and should be able to give a more informed answer.

In most curricula dealing with adulthood, children are asked questions about their fears of taking on new responsibilities. Here the approach is different. In the unit "Journey Toward Adulthood," children are helped to appreciate who they are *now*. The following paragraph captures the essence of this approach, and it is followed by provocative questions (see example below) that drive the message home.

> Children have certain wonderful qualities, such as curiosity, excitement, playfulness, honesty, and sensitivity. Many people lose some of these qualities as they grow up, because the responsibilities of adulthood

> become very difficult for them to carry out . . . There is such a thing as being *too responsible*. Sometimes adults feel that life is very serious. They dedicate almost all their time to work; they don't relax and have much fun.

The question that follows this quote is: Which qualities of childhood do you think are valuable and important for adults to have in their lives?

Other questions relating to childhood/adulthood are: What kind of person do I want to become as an adult? What do I want to do with my life? How can I become the kind of person I want to become?

The last chapter in this unit explains rites of passage in general and in the context of Bar/Bat Mitzvah. To help students clarify in their own minds what Bar/Bat Mitzvah means to them personally, 13 quotes are spread out across two pages and students are asked to choose the views with which they agree and which make the most sense. The following examples will give the flavor of these quotes:

> It's okay. I'm not sure I want to do it, but my parents want me to, and I want to make them happy.

> My parents don't care one way or the other actually. But I really want to do it. My best friend did it and she really liked it.

> It's showing my connection with my people and my ancestors. It's saying I want to carry on the traditions and ideals of my people.

For a change of pace, a new activity is then introduced: "You are on Israeli TV," a simulated television interview. The purported subject of the television show is "Bar/Bat Mitzvah Today," and the interviewer is going to explore the meaning of Bar/Bat Mitzvah with different twelve-year-olds. There are some excellent questions, designed to make the child really think about the whole process. "Camera shot" instructions are printed next to the interview questions, to give it the look of a real script. Students could relate well to this exercise if it is done successfully with a video camera.

The next unit, The "Journey Toward Jewishness" begins with explanations of what makes being Jewish special and different, by describing the Jewish people as a large family.

An excellent device is used to discuss the different ways of being Jewish. A visiting college student from China interviews two Jews to learn about Judaism. The answers given by the two (one Orthodox, one secular) are so different that the college student cannot understand how both individuals can be called Jews.

After the above exercise, students are asked to explore their own views of being Jewish. The device is the same as that used for exploring the meaning of Bar/Bat Mitzvah: students are asked to choose from among several quotes those which are closest to their own thinking. The quotes cover the whole spectrum of belief systems. This type of exercise can be very affirming, since it may be the first time some children see their own ideas printed on a page. But the key to this approach is for the teacher to remain truly non-judgmental without even attempting to sneak in his/her own values. This may be too much to ask of any teacher. But, if a teacher truly respects the students' feelings, expressing his/her own ideas can be beneficial, and can increase mutual trust.

Concluding this unit, there is an excellent short history of the development of the different movements in Judaism, followed by another "Interview" exercise, with the topic "What does being Jewish mean to you?"

The next unit, the "Journey Toward God," could be problematical for some children. Theirs is a very rebellious age, and favorite targets for their rebellion are religious beliefs and God in particular. Twelve-year-olds are not certain of anything in their lives, including the existence of God. Many (in my experience) proclaim themselves atheists or agnostics. Yet, this book seems to presuppose that the students all believe in God. The question "Why do you believe that God exists?" is an example of this weighted approach. Rabbi Jacobson offers different reasons to believe and different ways of believing, which is excellent, but he does not seem to grant permission to doubt. Doubts and disbelief would have to be dealt with in the classroom, in any case, but this text does not give the teacher tools for dealing with it. In a series of questions in the workbook, listing several answers for "Who/What/Where is God?" there is a space for "I don't know," but never for "I don't believe." Would the doubting child have the courage to put forth his or her doubts? Or would the absence of that option from the printed page make him or her afraid to speak openly? Rabbi Jacobson himself is aware of the shortcomings of this section and plans to revise it in the next edition.

The next unit, the "Journey Toward Jewish Tradition," opens with a fascinating exercise: students are told to imagine they are lost in the desert with a large group of friends. They finally find an oasis and enough food to sustain them. What should they do next? They realize help may never come. The parallel to the Jews in the Sinai desert is obvious. Students are asked to answer several practical and ethical questions that our ancestors also had to answer. They then compare their answers to the answers given in the Torah.

This exercise leads into the subsequent chapters of the unit, which discuss authorship of the Torah, the purposes of the laws in the Torah, different approaches to the *mitzvot*, the relationship of Bar/Bat Mitzvah to *mitzvot*, and the study of Torah and Talmud. There is an excellent brief introduction to Talmud which includes examples and offers very clear and relevant reasons for studying it.

The unit on "Becoming a Good Person" begins with a discussion of "being good to yourself." This is not always discussed as a *mitzvah* and is crucial, especially for this age group so prone to low self-esteem. The text also discusses self-respect and respect for one's body which is a needed value, especially for young people, who are bombarded with messages about drugs, smoking, and drinking.

The subsequent chapters of this unit include discussions of being good to others, caring for people who need help, and other standard ethical *mitzvot*. More unusual topics are helping children learn to tell others when their feelings are hurt, and learning to forgive and make peace.

The last chapter of the unit deals with family relationships. It begins with parents' responsibilities to their children (usually the reverse is discussed first), to help children see the side they don't often see. The *mitzvah* of honoring parents is presented with *specifics*, such as:

> Doing special things for your parents even when you are not asked to.
>
> Not doing/saying things that embarrass or hurt your parents.
>
> Caring for your parents when they get old.
>
> Going out of your way to treat your parents with more respect than anyone else.

These and other *mitzvot* are listed on a chart, and students can check one of three boxes next to each: "Do very well," "Need to improve," "Very difficult." This is a good and specific exercise designed to help children get in touch with their family relationships.

The text explains the meaning of "manipulation" and compares it to "negotiation," which it suggests is preferable. The value of communication in relationships is discussed. There are personal questions in the workbook designed to help students improve their relationships; these do not have to be shared with the class.

There is a risk that some parents might consider some of these questions to be meddling in the personal life of their child. But what other safe environment do these students have to air their grievances, hurts, and general problems with their families? It would perhaps be best if this section were taught by the Rabbi, not only because of the Rabbi's expertise and training, but also because of the role the Rabbi plays in the congregation's life. A respected and loved teacher, however, who has created a climate of trust in the classroom and has skills in interpersonal relationships could also accomplish much with this part of the course.

The last unit, the "Journey Toward Becoming a Religious Jew" is the longest, with 11 chapters. Topics covered include Shabbat, festivals and holidays, prayer, and *kashrut*. The discussion of Shabbat is geared both to observant and non-observant students and families, and is written to make increased observance very appealing. The workbook gives students many choices about what they can do to work toward this increased observance. Shabbat activities and terminology are also listed. The section could be helped by a less sexist reading about a traditional family Shabbat dinner.

For each holiday, including the High Holy Days, the special practices and customs associated with that holiday are listed. Students can check off one or more of the following for each practice: I've done this, I've never done this, I'd like to try this, I do this each year, I'd like to do it this year.

Exploring prayer is a challenge with this age group. Many students who have not established a way of relating to God find prayer irrelevant. It is interesting that of the 12 reasons to pray listed in the text, several do not include God; for example, "Prayer helps us feel good about life," "Prayer gives us the feeling that our small lives are part of something greater." Students check off one of the following for each statement about prayer: Very important, I agree, I don't agree, I don't know. This excellent and non-judgmental exercise will help students think about prayer in new ways. The same approach is used for *kashrut.*

The closing pages of the workbook are a "Student Evaluation." Students are asked if they liked *Crossing the River,* why or why not, what they learned from it, how difficult it was, and if they changed in any way because of it.

The last chapter lists the 43 *mitzvot* studied in this course, with references to text and workbook pages. The idea of choice and making a covenant is discussed. Students are told that although they had no choice about entering a covenant, since they were born Jewish, they do have a choice in how they relate to it. They can stop after becoming Bar/Bat Mitzvah, or they can say they want to go on and make their relation with God, the Torah, and the *mitzvot* stronger and deeper throughout their lives. *Crossing the River* features a fresh and unusual approach. Students who complete it will probably be more inclined to make this commitment.

(Copies of this curriculum are available for $50 for the two volumes from: Rabbi Burt Jacobson, c/o Mandy Bratt-Argent, P.O. Box 104, Canyon, CA 94516.)

Chapter 41
A Bar/Bat Mitzvah Retreat Program

Julie Vanek

This program was originally created by Rabbi David Whiman, Temple Shalom, Newton, Massachusetts, based on a program designed by Lois Edelstein, Director of Education, Temple Isaiah, Lexington, Massachusetts. The program was revised by Julie Vanek, Temple Educator, Temple Shalom, Newton, Massachusetts, the author of this chapter. (Editor's Note: As it is outlined, this program involves writing, the showing of a movie, sports, etc. Many congregations would find it more appropriate to hold this on a Sunday or a vacation day.)

BACKGROUND

In the spring of the sixth grade, all of the students who will become Bar/Bat Mitzvah during the following year at Temple Shalom of Newton go away together for a weekend retreat. The weekend is enjoyable and fun, but the purpose of the retreat is to get a lot of work accomplished. The retreat is designed to allow the staff to do some intensive training, convey the essential meaning of Bar/Bat Mitzvah, build a sense of group solidarity among the students, and to accomplish all of this in a relaxed and enjoyable setting.

Over the years, we have made use of various retreat facilities for this program. The cost of the entire weekend, including transportation, lodging, meals, staff, and materials, is covered through part of the Bar/Bat Mitzvah fee assessed by the synagogue. The cost of the weekend obviously depends on the retreat facilities available and how much they charge per person.

GOALS

The goals of the retreat are as follows:

1. To explain the difference between having a Bar/Bat Mitzvah and becoming a Bar/Bat Mitzvah.
2. To explore the role that the following play in the Bar/Bat Mitzvah service: the Bar/Bat Mitzvah, the Torah, Jewish tradition.
3. To distribute Torah and Haftarah portions and begin to get a sense of what they are about.
4. To practice melodies for the various blessings and prayers of the Bar/Bat Mitzvah service.
5. To explore the structure of the Torah and the Prophets sections of the Bible.
6. To explore the *mitzvah* part of becoming a Bar/Bat Mitzvah.

IMPLEMENTATION

The weekend is divided into seven study sessions ranging from an hour to two hours in length. The study sessions are interspersed with Shabbat services, sports, fun evening programs, and a little bit of free time. At first glance, the schedule is a bit daunting, but it works very well for one main reason: everything throughout the weekend is done in team competition.

Prior to the weekend, the students are divided into teams of 8-12, depending on the size of the class. We strive for an even mix of leadership potential, intellect, and singing ability on each team. Everything we do on the weekend is scored for team points: making team posters, chanting, answering trivia questions, playing softball, quizzes, etc. The team competition element keeps the students focused during the study sessions and solid team spirit sets the tone for the weekend. In previous years, small prizes were awarded at the end of the weekend to the top scoring teams. In recent years, we eliminated that aspect without any detriment to the competition.

Each team requires one staff person who is comfortable with the material being practiced and taught on the retreat. There needs to be at least one program leader who is not associated with a team to run the group parts of the program and to score teams on their various activities. In addition, we take along one high school student per team to serve as junior staff. They work with their teams in all activities and help run our evening programs as well as provide extra coverage on the bus, during meals, bedtime, and free time. The staff is briefed prior to the weekend as to the content of the program, expectations, and anything in particular they should watch for among the students.

A description of the goals and content for the seven sessions follows:

Session I – 75 minutes (can be broken into two segments)

Introductions/Team Assignments

Goals:

1. To introduce the staff on the retreat.
2. To explain the purpose of the weekend.
3. To get to know other team members and to develop team spirit.

Once everyone is settled in the program space, introductions are made, rules are explained, and the purpose of the weekend is detailed. The students are divided into their teams for the first time, and the staff leaders for each team take over the program. At Temple Shalom, the Religious School and the Hebrew School run in double sessions, which means that there are a good number of sixth graders who meet each other for the first time on this retreat. In teams, name games are played to get the students acquainted with one another. Individual name tags are made (mostly for the benefit of the staff). Each team is then asked to decide on a team name and to design a poster displaying that name. At the end of this session, posters are scored for creativity, Jewishness, teamwork, etc.

Session II – 1 hour

Bar/Bat Mitzvah: The Torah and You

Goals:

1. To express feelings surrounding Bar/Bat Mitzvah.
2. To define the term Bar/Bat Mitzvah.
3. To explore the meaning of *mitzvah* and responsibility.
4. To establish that at a Bar/Bat Mitzvah ceremony, both the Torah and the person are being celebrated.

This session follows Kabbalat Shabbat services and is one of the few sessions that is not conducted with the students sitting in teams. Each student is given a handout on which they are asked to respond to four questions concerning the importance of Bar/Bat Mitzvah to them and to their family, what they worry about most with regard to their Bar/Bat Mitzvah, and what they will be ready to do at their Bar/Bat Mitzvah. After they have written down their answers, they are asked to find someone they do not know very well and share their responses.

The book *Mitzvah* by Jacob Neusner is introduced at this point in the weekend and the students are asked to read pp. 1-11. We have written a study guide to facilitate the students' comprehension of the material. The study guide is discussed in the large group when everyone has completed it. The material that relates to goals 2-4 above is reinforced. After the discussion, questions can be asked about the material with points given out for correct answers.

We conclude our first evening with a Jewish trivia game played in teams and scored accordingly.

Session III – 90 minutes

Understanding the Torah

Goals:

1. To explore how a Torah is made, how it is read through the year, and how it is divided into books and *sedrot*.
2. To become proficient at finding one's way through the Torah when given chapter and verse.
3. To explain how weekly Torah portions get their names and to be able to locate the *sedra* in which a given passage of Torah falls.

Session III is the morning activity following Shabbat morning services and Torah reading. The session begins with the showing of the movie *For Out of Zion* (Ergo Media Inc.) which details how a Torah is made and read in the synagogue. The students are told to take notes during the movie, as there is an oral quiz for team points following.

Using a variety of visual aids, key vocabulary (verse, chapter, *sedra*, *parashah*, *Parashat Hashavua*, Torah portion) is defined and worked with. Students are asked to hunt through the Torah finding page numbers for the book, chapter, and verse given. Some of that is done individually on worksheets and some of it is done orally as a race for team points.

Following Session III, students engage in a sports activity. After lunch, we spend about an hour doing another activity — sing down, Jewish charades, etc.

Session IV – 30 minutes
Torah Portions
Goals:

1. To practice and perfect chanting of Torah blessings.
2. For each student to identify his/her Torah reading and identify the *sedra* from which it is taken.
3. For each student to read and summarize his/her Torah reading.

A brief review of the morning's material is a good way to begin this session. Teams are then sent off to practice the chanting of the Torah blessings (the students have already learned these in Hebrew class). They are scored in teams on how well they chant.

At the beginning of the weekend, each student is given a folder of materials used throughout the retreat. This folder also contains a copy of their Torah and Haftarah portions in Hebrew and English, as well as synopses of the portions. At this point, each student reads through his/her Torah materials and writes a brief summary of his/her portion. This part requires a lot of individual attention on the part of the staff.

Session V – 45 minutes
Understanding the Haftarah
Goals:

1. To explain Haftarah and the connection between Torah and Haftarah readings.
2. To become proficient in finding one's way through Prophets.
3. To practice and perfect Haftarah blessings.
4. For each student to read and summarize his/her Haftarah reading.

Session IV flows right into Session V, allowing for adjustments to be made if Session IV runs over. We usually do not finish the Haftarah material in Session V, but use Session VI to catch up on whatever we left out earlier in the day.

Visual aids are used to explain Haftarah, Prophets, and the connection between Torah and Haftarah readings. Teams practice the Haftarah blessings and are scored for points. (We usually have them practice only one blessing at a time, as these are more difficult than the Torah blessings.) We play some more speed races through the Prophets section of the Bible this time. Finally, each student reads the English translation of his/her Haftarah portion and summarizes it in writing. Again, the students need individual help to understand their portions.

Following another activity (we play our own rendition of *Jewish Pictionary*) and some free time, we gather as a group for Quiz #1. This is a written quiz with approximately ten questions on the material studied up to this point in the weekend. Our questions can be answered with one or two words or, in the case of a definition, with a sentence. We usually ask a silly extra credit question for fun. These quizzes are corrected by the staff and the individual scores are averaged by team for the team score. The quizzes are destroyed and thrown out so as to prevent team members ganging up on someone who did not score well.

While the quizzes are being scored, the students prepare for Havdalah with a staff member. This is often the first Havdalah experience that the students have had, so the symbolism is explained and the prayers practiced.

Just before dinner, the answers to the quiz are gone over orally in the large group and the team points are awarded. We do Havdalah after dinner, before Session VI begins.

Session VI – 90 minutes
Understanding the Haftarah (continued)

This session builds in extra time to finish anything that we could not complete earlier in the day, go over something that was difficult for the students, and/or to do something creative in teams for points.

Depending on the mood of the group, we will often begin this session by asking the teams to choose a Jewish song and interpret it for the group creatively. We let them brainstorm, develop, and practice their idea without much adult intervention. This activity gets the students moving around and doing something active before finishing up work on their Haftarah portions.

After the work is completed for the evening, we hold a relay race team competition — blowing a ping-pong ball across the floor, blowing up a balloon and sitting on it until it pops, etc. This is scored for team points.

Session VII – 2 hours
Mitzvah and B'mitzvotav
Goals:

1. To explain and define the concept of *mitzvah.*
2. To differentiate between "having a Bar/Bat Mitzvah" and "becoming a Bar/Bat Mitzvah."
3. To introduce *"B'mitzvotav": A Bar/Bat Mitzvah Program for Jewish Learning, Living and Doing,* created by Rabbi Jeffrey Sirkman, Larchmont Temple, Larchmont, New York. (Although the titles are the same, this program is not related to that described in Chapter 27.)

This session begins early on Sunday morning after two nights of very little sleep for the students and, most probably, for the staff as well. Since we do have work to be accomplished during this session, we plan to do something beforehand that will wake everybody up. This could be a round of trivia questions for team points, another chance to chant one of the Haftarah blessings in teams, some loud singing, etc.

The students are asked to read pages 11-20 in *Mitzvah* and to complete the study guide. We discuss the content, using examples from the book, focusing on responsibilities, being commanded to do something, and ordinary versus holy acts.

We then show the video, *The Mitzvah Machine* (United Synagogue). There are many different points that can be discussed and the video does come with a discussion guide. However, we choose to concentrate on the concept that one *becomes* a Bar/Bat Mitzvah as opposed to *having* a Bar/Bat Mitzvah. One of the ways we talk about becoming a Bar/Bat Mitzvah is by taking on responsibilities.

That then leads into an explanation of the "B'mitzvotav Program" (see Goal #3 above), which enables the students to formulate their own package of "Jewish doing" through the performance of *mitzvot.* The program is quite extensive so we take this opportunity to go through the different sections explaining, clarifying, and giving examples of how the program is to be completed.

One of the "B'mitzvotav Program" requirements is attending this weekend retreat. To fulfill that requirement, we ask the students to record their thoughts and impressions of the experience.

At the conclusion of this session, we give Quiz #2. This one is a little longer than the first one (about 15 questions) and covers material from the entire weekend. The quizzes are scored while the participants clean up and get ready to leave. We have an early lunch at camp, go over the answers to the quiz, award the final points, and board the bus for home by noon.

EVALUATION AND RESULTS

The students write candidly about the weekend in response to our request as part of their "B'mitzvotav Program." We collect these and read them as informal evaluations. The staff on the retreat (which includes the Director of Education, the Assistant Rabbi, the current teachers, and often one or more of the future seventh grade teachers) look carefully at the quizzes and take note of which concepts need to be reinforced.

In the four years that I have been running this retreat, there has only been the most positive feedback from students, parents, and staff. The students return with a strong sense of what becoming Bar/Bat Mitzvah entails, and they are inspired to begin the process.

FOLLOW-UP

Following the retreat, a letter is mailed to the parents describing the activities of the weekend in detail and explaining about the "B'mitzvotav Program." The piece that the students wrote on their impressions of the retreat is mailed home with the letter with the instructions to add it as the first entry in the "B'mitzvotav" diary.

The parents of these students are also invited to a meeting shortly after the retreat to begin the process for the parents. We run the parents through some of the activities adapted from the retreat, notably the handout with the questions about the importance of Bar/Bat Mitzvah to their family, a rating exercise on the important aspects of the Bar/Bat Mitzvah, and the showing of *The Mitzvah Machine.*

The folders which the students use on the retreat and in which they write their summaries of their Torah and Haftarah portions are collected at the end of the retreat and returned to the students when they begin their Bar/Bat Mitzvah tutoring. The materials from the weekend help the students in their preparation and guide them in their writing of an introduction to their Torah or Haftarah portion.

The "B'mitzvotav" folders are given to the students on the Sunday morning of the retreat. The students are encouraged to discuss them with their families as soon as possible. The students are monitored on their "B'mitzvotav" progress during their seventh grade year by their Hebrew teachers.

When our students become B'nai Mitzvah, many of them recall the retreat experience as a highlight of their preparation. They feel they came away from that weekend with an understanding and appreciation of the meaning and process of becoming B'nai Mitzvah on many different levels. A retreat format lends itself in an ideal fashion to the transmittal of such understanding. For this reason, those who desire to inject new life into their present Bar/Bat Mitzvah programs would do well to explore the possibility of adding a retreat component.

Chapter 42
Seven Weekends that Make a Difference by Philip Warmflash and Craig Taubman

Reviewed by Helen Leneman

The book entitled *Seven Weekends that Make a Difference* was published by the Los Angeles Hebrew High School. It contains excellent suggestions and ideas for putting together a retreat, and many innovative and interesting lesson plans. Of the seven topics, two are appropriate for students of Bar/Bat Mitzvah age; the others are more appropriate for eighth grade or higher.

The two introductory chapters are an excellent introduction to the concept of retreats. The authors credit many of their ideas to *Six Kallot: Retreats for Jewish Settings* by Shirley Barish (A.R.E. Publishing, Inc., now out of print). Their goal in writing this book was to help educators by sharing "seven tested, successful weekend retreats," and to encourage others to include retreats as part of synagogue programming. They explain the many reasons for doing weekend retreats: friendship, living Judaism, becoming a group, having time to explore new ideas, and seeing teachers and advisors as accessible role models.

Each unit in the book contains the following sections:

Goals
Settings
Super Sundays: an alternative, when a full weekend is not possible
Classrooms: using one of the programs as a mini-unit
Quotes: suggested uses for the many quotes included in the book
Pre-Kallah activities
Tefillot: prayers that fit in with the weekend's theme
Pe'ulot Erev: evening activities
Coming to terms: including new vocabulary words in the weekend Student Kallah Booklet

While a schedule for each retreat is also included, the authors stress the importance of flexibility. Here are their suggested schedules for a Friday night, Saturday, and Sunday retreat:

Friday

A. Arrival, time to get settled
B. Snack time, introductory program
C. Kabbalat Shabbat service, including explanations and student participation
D. Shabbat dinner, with singing and blessings
E. Free time
F. *Sichah* #1 (a discussion or educational group activity)
G. Social evening program
H. Oneg Shabbat, Closing Circle activity
I. Quiet time: possible story or other activity in bunk
J. Staff meeting: the weekend is not only for the children; there should be a special Oneg/party for the staff as well

Saturday

A. Breakfast, explanation of day's programs
B. *Tefillot*, including Torah reading
C. Free time
D. Lunch
E. *Sichah* #2
F. Structured group programs, i.e., hikes, sports, music, and dance
G. *Sichah* #3
H. Dinner, including story and singing
I. Havdalah

J. Evening program
K. Closing circle

Sunday

A. *Tefillot*
B. Breakfast
C. *Sichah* #4: closure discussion, summing up the weekend
D. Cleanup, should involve everyone
E. Closing circle and evaluation

In their step-by-step outline, the authors detail every possible question and angle that should be covered by the organizers of the retreat, including the following: finding the location; sending out a letter; organizing the staff; determining the attendance; arranging the program (themes, sessions, activities); assigning responsibility for discipline and administration; leading services — creative ways of leading prayer to stimulate and interest the students; organizing meals creatively — some original ideas, such as including family recipes cooked by the students themselves; providing clothing lists; involving students; fostering group building; arranging for group pictures; preparing evaluation forms, both for students and staff; and doing necessary follow-ups.

The seven topics suggested as retreat themes are:
The Jewish Family
Mitzvot
Judaism and Christianity
God Wrestling
American Judaism: Making a Difference
Mirrors: "Encounter Group"
Judaism and Sexuality

The first two are appropriate for Bar/Bat Mitzvah age students and older. The next two are more suited to students in eighth grade and higher, and the last three are geared to the high school level. All of these topics are presented in a format that could easily be adapted to a classroom setting or a one day workshop, and the presentation of all topics is equally strong and original.

The goals of the first program, "The Jewish Family," are for the student to be able to:

Define what a Jewish family is.
Understand the traditional role of the family in Jewish history.
Discuss personal feelings regarding their own families.
Help peers deal with issues and problems in their families.

The weekend is designed to encourage students to open up to one another. It can also be adapted as a day or weekend Family Education program. Several elements that appear here can be found in other Family Education programs, such as doing family interviews and family trees.

The first *Sichah* utilizes handout questionnaires. The use of two questionnaires, one for the child and one for the parents, is common in Family Education programs. However, here students are asked to answer these questions for themselves *and* as they imagine their parents would answer. Examples of the questions are: My favorite Jewish family time is . . . , Judaism is important/unimportant to our family because . . .

Other *Sichot* for this program include: studying sources that deal with the sociology of the Jewish family; a "family survival problem solving" session with students working in small groups; playing *Mishpacha Feud*, modeled after the game show *Family Feud*; and an imaginative closure activity, in which students write a letter to their unborn child. These letters can be returned to the students at the end of the year, at the time of their Bar/Bat Mitzvah, or before Rosh Hashanah.

The goals for the students in the "Mitzvot" program are:

- To learn and do as many mitzvot as possible during the weekend.
- To explore reasons for doing mitzvot.
- To understand that learning and practicing mitzvot are part of an ongoing process.
- To develop a contract to incorporate three new mitzvot into their lives and learn one quote which they feel is important for the understanding of mitzvot.

Before the first *Sicha*, students are given a brief Mitzvah pretest, in which they are asked, among other questions, to define *mitzvah*, to say how many *mitzvot* there are, what areas of life they cover, where we find the *mitzvot*.

The first *Sichah* focuses on *lashon hara*. Students do exercises and read sources dealing with this subject. Then they are challenged to avoid *lashon hara* throughout the weekend and to encourage their friends to do the same.

In the second *Sichah*, students play a "game without rules," which helps them understand the necessity for rules in society. There is an excellent discussion guide to help the leader steer the discussion. Another session focuses on the different approaches to *mitzvot* by the various Jewish denominations. Quotes are presented and students are asked to choose and discuss which quotes make the most sense to them.

There are many other activities, all of which feature an excellent balance between the cognitive and affective. While imparting knowledge, the activities also help students understand the importance of performing *mitzvot* in their own lives. The program is non-judgmental and gives students permission to express their feelings, while also guiding them toward a clear objective. This objective is not only to have them perform more *mitzvot*, but to *want* to do so and to understand why it is so important. The closure activity is the filling out of a contract, in which students promise to incorporate new *mitzvot* into their lives in the coming months.

The other five programs in this book are equally fine, but this is not the place to review them, since they are appropriate for older students. They would, however, provide excellent material for an eighth grade or Confirmation class retreat. In addition to the retreat programs, *Seven Weekends that Make a Difference* also contains a wealth of material in several appendixes. There is an excellent bibliography, a list of games, numerous original approaches to teaching prayer, and an extensive "weekend vocabulary" list.

For those seeking new and innovative approaches to crucial subjects for the classroom or for weekend retreats, this book is an important resource.

(For information, contact: Rabbi Philip Warmflash, Jewish Federation Council of Greater Los Angeles, 6505 Wilshire Blvd., Suite 414, Los Angeles, CA 90048.)

Chapter 43

A Mini-course on Writing a Drash

Risa Gruberger

INTRODUCTION

One of the many concerns of the Bar/Bat Mitzvah student is the speech. Who will write it? What shall I say? Will it be ready in time? To a twelve-year-old, the idea of giving a sermon which analyzes and hypothesizes about Torah and Haftarah can be daunting. Usually, the student creates his speech one-on-one with his tutor, the Rabbi, or the Director of Education. Sometimes speeches are written by the parents of the Bar/Bat Mitzvah. One unique possibility is to organize a mini-course to assist students in creating their speeches with their peers, in a relaxed, comfortable setting. This chapter provides a model of one such course.

WHY A MINI-COURSE?

Often, when an adolescent is asked to contemplate intellectual ideas in the company of an authority figure, the student is intimidated. He or she may respond by acting out or clamming up. In the group, however, where young people are able to exchange ideas freely with peers, and in a suitable environment, defenses disappear and students can make great strides in discovering their identity.

Developmentally, a twelve-year-old is entering into the realm of "formal operational thought." Psychologists describe this process as the ability to think abstractly. Studying Torah, as described in this mode, allows teenagers to find creative solutions outside the boundaries of conventional problem solving. Applying Bible stories to modern-day events provides an opportunity for students to explore and share their abstract ideas and personal values. Thus, a group approach to the *drash* fulfills a need for "intellectual play."

On the completion of the mini-course, a student may or may not have created a final draft of his/her speech. The goal is to produce at least a summary which demonstrates an understanding of the portion, how it relates to his/her life, and the lesson(s) to be learned from the Bible.

Successful B'nai Mitzvah programs focus on the adolescent's "ownership" of the experience. This is achieved when the teen finds personal or social meaning in the process, as well as in the event. This mini-course creates an atmosphere in which both personal and social meaning are realized.

Following is an overview of the group investigation process.

THE GROUP INVESTIGATION MODEL

In addition to Bible study, the group investigation model also reinforces the art of group dynamics. The mini-course is designed around this model of teaching, which combines characteristics of democracy with the process of academic inquiry. According to Herbert Thelen, who originated this model, the classroom is similar to the larger society; it has a culture and a social order. Its members care about the standards and expectations and the way of life that develops there. In group investigation, students are exposed to three basic ingredients: inquiry, knowledge, and the dynamics of the learning group. Each of these is described briefly below.

Inquiry

Reaction is stimulated by confrontation of a problem — something that puzzles the participants. In this case, the problem is the meaning of the Torah or Haftarah portion — gaining an understanding of a theme, story, or specific happening. For example, in the portion Noah, a possible inquiry is: Why was Noah called a "righteous man"? What made him more righteous than others? How is it possible that all humanity was corrupt except for one man? During inquiry, the student must add an awareness of self and a desire for personal meaning. In this example the student would question himself: "Am I a righteous person?"

In addition, the student must assume two roles, the participant and the observer, as he/she simultaneously inquires into the problem and observes himself/herself as an inquirer. Because inquiry is a social process, the many viewpoints and questions that emerge also stimulate students' interest in the problem.

Knowledge

Knowledge is the goal of inquiry. It is the process of "trying on" various ways of looking at experience. This learning involves emotions. Challenges are addressed in the process of knowledge. Views should be raised by both the facilitator and the students. For example, in the case of Noah, the facilitator might share the interpretation found in the Tanchuma:

> We are told of Noah he was "Righteous in his generation, but not in others." To what may this be compared? If a man places a silver coin among copper coins, then the silver appears attractive. So Noah appeared righteous in the generation of the flood.

The student shares characteristics of a righteous person in our generation. Continued investigation could lead to the question: Would a person who is considered righteous in our generation have been considered so in a past generation? In a future generation?

The facilitator must present the student with commentaries on the portions being investigated. The group will react to Rabbinic responses, as well as to each others' ideas. Individual reactions will vary. By engaging in group discussion, students become aware of different points of view.

Dynamics of the Learning Group

A "teachable group" is a prerequisite for any productive investigation. The group should not exceed 15 students. This is large enough for diverse reactions and small enough for individual participation. Given any group of adolescents, commonality of values will be present, allowing for comfortable communication and similar ways of working. The facilitator is also guaranteed enough differences to generate alternative reactions.

(Note: This mini-course is meant for students who are one year or less away from their Bar/Bat Mitzvah. It should not be introduced as the first group learning experience for the class. The element of trust will be present only if the culture of the class as a group has already been established.)

THE MINI-COURSE

Objectives

- Students will write a summary or outline about their Torah or Haftarah portions. The summary or outline will be the basis for the Bar/Bat Mitzvah speech.
- Students will participate in a group investigation process which will strengthen social skills.
- Students will enhance their knowledge of Bible.
- Parents will be relieved of the stress of speech writing.

The Role of the Facilitator

The facilitator should begin the mini-course with an orientation to group dynamics. During this orientation, the facilitator should introduce and have students practice the following:

1. The art of constructive criticism (see Appendix for guidelines)
2. Utilization of positive feedback
3. Listening skills
4. Group, not self involvement
5. Patience

In addition to expertise in group dynamics and familiarity with the group investigation model, the facilitator should have previous experience with Bible study and the ability to prepare commentary on each portion prior to the lesson. He/she serves as an academic counselor, bringing to the group both information and experience. As each student reports back to the class, the facilitator provides the group with questions to provoke creative thinking. For example, a student might be having difficulty locating a topic of interest related to his/her portion. After a summary of the portion has been delivered, the facilitator might ask each student to complete the following sentence: To me, the moral of the story is . . . As they respond to trigger sentences, students begin to explore their own ideas.

The facilitator initiates and maintains the scheduling for class presentations. At the end of each class session, it is a good idea to update the schedule, reminding students when their summaries or rewrites are due.

The facilitator has two main tasks: (1) to facilitate the discussions and (2) to schedule the class in such a way as to maintain the flow of the discussions, enabling each student an opportunity to be the focus for discussion.

As soon as possible, the facilitator should determine a date for each student's presentation to the class. Schedule those with the earliest Bar/Bat Mitzvah dates first. Generally, two or three students can present during each session, depending, of course, on the time allotted for the mini-course.

The Course Itself

Introduce the class with the following set induction: Parents, teachers, and Rabbis give lectures all the time. In a way, they are giving little speeches. What lecture/speech do you remember most from any of these people or someone else (perhaps a friend or a sibling)? Why do you remember that particular one? How did the person speak to you? What made you listen? What was the lesson/message/moral that you learned?

Make the transition to the investigation of the *drash* by saying: Together, we will study Torah in a way that will assist you in creating memorable speeches — "lectures" to be remembered.

Explain the word "*drasha*" — to search or investigate: The purpose of the *drash* (sermon or speech) is clear: to interpret the Torah and to provide the listeners with its application in their lives. Its origins are not so clear. We do know that by the end of the Second Temple period, sermons were a well established custom both in Palestine and in the Diaspora. Your task in this mini-course is to create a *drash* — an interpretation of your Torah or Haftarah portion — in your own words. (Remind students as they begin to look into the Torah, they need always to remember their task — to investigate.)

Ask students to generate a list, on the chalk board, of characteristics of an investigator, e.g., someone who listens, someone who asks a lot of questions, someone who is resourceful.

These characteristics will be a constant reminder to the students of their task.

For the main activity, begin by giving each student a guide to Torah study. The same guide should be used for every student's investigation. (Obviously, the outline will vary from synagogue to synagogue, depending on ideology.) Here is a suggestion for such a guide:

A Guide to Torah Study

Step 1: First identify the story, theme, or subject found in the Torah or Haftarah you wish to interpret.

Step 2: Ask challenging questions about the section.

Step 3: Having asked the questions, try to answer them and apply answers to the lives of your classmates.

Step 4: Conclude with a summary and a statement meant to inspire the listeners to "take to heart" the message of the Torah or Haftarah interpretation.

Along with the outline, provide each student with a translation of his/her Torah and Haftarah portion. In order of calendar dates, starting with the child with the earliest Bar/Bat Mitzvah date, each student becomes the focus for a roundtable discussion of his/her portion.

Allow students two weeks to prepare for Step 1. On the given date, the student should come to class prepared to share with the class his/her synopsis. The first step is a summary of the portion in the student's words. As an example, Daniel's portion is *Bo* from the book of Exodus, Chapters 10:1-13:16. Before Daniel begins his presentation, remind the other students to take out their guidelines for constructive feedback (see Appendix). Daniel begins by reading his summary. The role of the group is to listen carefully and provide feedback to him.

Daniel's First Draft

Here is Daniel's first draft:

> The beginning of my portion talks about the plague of locusts after Pharaoh refuses to let the Israelites go. It goes on to tell about the invasion of the locusts all across the land of Egypt. Then it is explained of the devastation and of Pharaoh's plea for forgiveness. After that, God lifted all the locusts off of Pharaoh's land and pushed them into the Sea of Reeds.
>
> Toward the middle of my portion, God tells Moses to hold his arm out to the sky and that a thick darkness will cover the land. Moses held out his arm and the thick darkness covered Egypt for three days.
>
> Then, at the end, my portion describes Pharaoh telling Moses that they may go, but that they must leave behind their flocks and his herds. The conclusion of my portion occurs before the real ending of this story. The very last sentence says that Pharaoh wouldn't let the Israelites go, right before the tenth plague.
>
> My portion is from *Bo*, which means "come in." The portion talks about the Israelites leaving Egypt. *Bo* comes from the book of Exodus.

When Daniel finishes, the facilitator asks for general questions concerning content. If necessary, explain points not understood or underscore the setting and time frame by reviewing the previous portion. All of the students are then asked to share what they think the theme of Daniel's portion is. Sometimes the word "theme" is unclear. Another approach is to ask students to share what they think the moral of the story is or the main idea. During the discussion, regularly remind the group of its role.

Some examples of student responses are:

> Plagues.
>
> God's punishment.
>
> Kindness — acceptable behavior ends with good results.
>
> Egyptians underestimating the power of God.
>
> Logical punishments. I mean, did the punishment of plagues fit the Egyptians' crime of enslaving the Jews? I think it did — darker hearts resulted in the plague of darkness.
>
> What goes around comes around.
>
> Faith in God.

The facilitator might then ask: "What does it mean to you to have faith in God?" Possible responses are:

> You just believe in God, even though you don't have to know exactly who or what God is.
>
> Having faith in God means if you believe in God, God will believe in you.
>
> You have to be a good person, try and do *mitzvot*.
>
> How about the *mitzvah* of treating your neighbor as you would like to be treated? The Egyptians did not follow that *mitzvah*. People should be treated equally.
>
> I think the theme is the misuse of power. Pharaoh thought he was God.
>
> History repeats itself. We have all sorts of plagues today like cancer and AIDS.

During this first discussion, Daniel takes notes, recording all of his classmates' ideas. These notes can assist him as he continues to refine his *drash*.

After this round is completed, Daniel is given two to three weeks to incorporate ideas his classmates gave that interested him into Step 2 of the Guide for Torah Study (asking challenging questions about the portion).

If the mini-course is meeting weekly, it is reasonable to allow two weeks (or more when needed) for each of the steps. As the student progresses through the guide, he/she continues to check in with the group for suggestions, feedback, and further investigation. (Daniel stays in class for the summaries by other students. This is a give and take procedure. Other students have just shared their ideas with Daniel; he must do the same for them.)

When Daniel shares his new additions, he will have completed Steps 1 and 2. (Some students are motivated to move on to Step 3, which is fine.) Some possible new additions to Daniel's *drash* might be:

> In my Torah portion, the last four plagues are the topic. The plague of locusts is discussed. Then the darkness plague is focused on. Next it is explained that Pharaoh would let the Israelites go on a condition, a condition which Moses didn't agree with. My portion ends before the Pharaoh had let the Israelites go.
>
> This portion really relates to our times and to us. It shows how history tends to repeat itself. For example, locusts came across the land of Egypt, causing devastation. We can say that very severe diseases have come across our land that are also causing devastation. Right now, cancer, AIDS, and many other diseases plague our country.
>
> During the ninth plague, darkness came across Egypt, covering it like a blanket. The Torah actually says, "a thick darkness came across Egypt, a darkness that could be touched." We could compare this to the problem of smog. We caused it, just as Pharaoh caused the darkness. It is covering us in the same way that God made the darkness cover Egypt.
>
> As you can see, my portion can be interpreted many different ways. It is very interesting how history repeats itself. My portion is proof.

At this point, the facilitator engages the group in a discussion which focuses on Step 3 (answering the questions and applying the answers to our lives today). The facilitator encourages students to discover how the portion relates to their lives. Some possible student responses:

> That was really good. I like how he relates different parts to what we are faced with today.
>
> The middle and end are clear, but I think you should be specific in the first paragraph, when you describe the plagues.

Here the facilitator might introduce this thought: Daniel, reread the first paragraph. Okay, what was the condition you speak about? Right . . . Moses would not agree to leave behind the flocks and herd. What other plague is introduced here? Right . . . Moses warns the Pharaoh that God will triumph with the slaying the first born of Egypt.

More student responses:

> I like the way he used the phrase `History repeats itself' more than once. It is clear that this is the theme.
>
> The *drash* is organized very well.
>
> I think a question to ponder at the end might be effective.

The facilitator resumes: Let's look at some questions together for a moment. How do you feel about history repeating itself? What are the implications for the future of the Jewish people? Thousand of years have passed since this story in the Torah. Has our world changed?

The students continue:

> Maybe God will be here for us to cure AIDS, like God was there for the Jews to take them out of slavery.
>
> There is so much war and destruction in the Torah. If history repeats itself, I think we are in trouble.
>
> It was a two-way street in Egypt, just like it is in the world we live in today. God didn't just let the people go. They first had to believe in God. God won't just wipe out smog. It's also up to us to try to fix our environment.

During the discussion that follows, Daniel again records all responses. At this point, he is on his own to complete his *drash* adding a summary statement. (It is acceptable to give class time to students for working on their rewrites, but don't do so when another student is presenting.) On average, students are motivated to complete the *drash* within a few weeks of the final discussion. If needed, assign the student a completion date. Flexibility with time is important. Each student is an individual.

After the final revision, the *drash* can easily be incorporated into the Bar Mitzvah speech.

CONCLUSION

There are, of course, other elements of a Bar or Bat Mitzvah speech. For example, a speech might include mention of the Bar or Bat Mitzvah's relationship with the community, family, and attitudes toward *tzedakah*, and *tikkun olam*. Some synagogue leaders encourage students to share their aspirations for the future. Often speeches include acknowledgement of appreciation for mentors, teachers, family, or friends. Since the focus of this mini-course is the *drash*, these additional elements can be developed one-on-one with Rabbis, educators, parents, or tutors. If time permits, however, these elements would make an excellent addition to the mini-course.

A mini-course such as the one described here will help students problem solve in order to understand and personalize Torah. In the company of friends, they can develop the speeches for their Bar/Bat Mitzvah in a relaxed fashion. They will derive satisfaction from the fact that the well thought out speech each creates will make an impact on those with whom they share them. In addition, students will learn to develop trust within a group setting, discover and practice constructive criticism, and gain an appreciation for a give and take format of communication. Finally, students will find that the skills they learn in this course are valuable tools that can be utilized at home and in school throughout their lives.

REFERENCES

Fields, Harvey J. *Bechol Levavcha With All Your Heart, Part Two*. New York: UAHC Press, 1978.

Joyce, Bruce; Marsha Weil; and Beverly Showers. *Models of Teaching*. Boston: Allyn and Bacon, 1992.

Loeb, Sorel Goldberg, and Barbara Binder Kadden. *Teaching Torah: A Treasury of Insights and Activities*. Denver: A.R.E. Publishing, Inc., 1984.

Russ, Ian. *The Psycho-social Tasks and Opportunities of Bar/Bat Mitzvah*. In *Bar/Bat Mitzvah Education: A Sourcebook*. Helen Leneman, ed. Denver: A.R.E. Publishing, Inc., 1993.

Salkin, Jeffrey K. *Putting God on the Guest List: How To Reclaim the Spiritual Meaning of Your Child's Bar or Bat Mitzvah*. Woodstock, VT: Jewish Lights Publishing, 1992.

Thelen, Herbert. *Education and the Human Quest*. New York: Harper & Row, Publishers, Inc., 1960.

APPENDIX

Guidelines for Constructive Feedback

1. Always begin your response with a positive comment.

2. Listen to each student's entire presentation before reacting.

3. There are many possible interpretations of Torah. Don't hesitate to offer yours, but do so in a constructive way.

4. Before you speak, think about what you would like to hear someone say about *your* work.

5. Be courteous. Give the presenter your attention at all times.

6. Your questions are important. They help further the creative process.

7. When something seems unclear to you, ask for clarification (for example, "I don't understand what you mean," "What I heard you say was . . . ").

8. Giving positive feedback to another ensures that you will be treated courteously when it is your turn.

Unit VII: Post-B'nai Mitzvah Programs

Overview

Something should change in the relationship of the student to the synagogue after the Bar/Bat Mitzvah ceremony. If nothing changes, "coming of age" is a meaningless phrase. Many congregations simply lessen the time commitment to Jewish study, giving the opposite message from what they want to say. It is also important not to just duplicate the Hebrew School experience of the early years. Classes for teens must be new and uniquely different from other educational programs in which students have been involved. An effective program must be flexible and creative in both subject matter and time requirements. Such programs can go a long way toward preventing the educational disengagement of teens and fostering adult Jewish literacy.

The two chapters in this Unit are by educators who created and implemented very successful post-Bar/Bat Mitzvah classes.

In Chapter 45 by Susan Protter and Chapter 46 by Rabbi Paul Sidlofsky, the authors provide detailed descriptions of their innovative programs, each very different from the other in scope and approach. Included in both chapters are goals, implementation, and lists of

suggested class topics. Chapter 44 also includes weekly formats, yearly programs, and Appendixes with core curriculum ideas and four detailed lesson plans.

The enthusiastic descriptions by these two educators should inspire many Religious Schools to add new post-Bar/Bat Mitzvah programs or improve on existing ones. When such programs are instituted, we will be paying more than lip service to the notion that Bar/Bat Mitzvah is a beginning, not an end.

Chapter 44
Post-Bar/Bat Mitzvah Education

Susan Protter

INTRODUCTION

Keeping supplemental Hebrew School students connected and committed to formal Jewish education becomes more of a challenge once they enter their teen years. Many excellent afternoon programs manage to provide B'nai Mitzvah students with an original and challenging educational experience only to end up seeing those teenagers disengage from synagogue education after their Bar/Bat Mitzvah ceremony. Motivating teens to continue to develop and mature as Jews is advantageous not only for Jewish education, but for the future of the Jewish community as well. Even synagogues with outstanding attendance at youth groups, camps, and other activities do not always see the success of these informal activities carry over to their post-Bar/Bat Mitzvah programs. It is crucial that we develop post-Bar/Bat Mitzvah programs which retain students and offer a positive experience for this age group.

Educators, Rabbis, Cantors, parents, and teens recognize that the dedication, commitment, and energy it takes to complete B'nai Mitzvah training can escalate to the overwhelming. The Bar/Bat Mitzvah as a life cycle event has become an integral and essential component in keeping all family members connected and committed to the Jewish community and to ritual. Although many families do not continue the intensity of their connection to the community after the Bar/Bat Mitzvah celebration, I do not believe that they completely abandon involvement either. Therefore, minimizing this life cycle event could give our children a mixed message, for we cannot teach Jewish history, language, self-esteem, and identity while simultaneously playing down the ritual events that enable Judaism to be experienced in our hearts and souls. Ritual events, especially B'nai Mitzvah, are at the core of what families need to stay connected to our heritage.

In order to offset family and teen post-Bar/Bat Mitzvah disengagement, we first must understand and accept the unique needs of teens after age thirteen — the nuances of the developmental, intellectual, emotional, and social progression of this age group. Then we can create Jewish educational programs that celebrate their special needs. I believe that the successful post B'nai Mitzvah program is one which inspires teens to take ownership of their own continuing Jewish education. However, because formulas for such post-B'nai Mitzvah programs require rethinking, we tend to continue to use both the afternoon Hebrew school and components of the secular school as models for our supplemental Jewish high schools. But our teenagers do not need or want a duplication (no matter how excellent) or continuation of their early Hebrew school experience, hence the tendency to drop out.

Disengagement from childhood lifestyle and family-directed events is an essential developmental passage that teens need to navigate. Part of this disengagement from pre-adolescent life includes the questioning of and desire to abandon formalized religion. The world of Hebrew School and Bar/Bat Mitzvah is the "stuff" of childhood and of adult expectations. To abandon this world seems logical, necessary, and justified to the new teenager. Therefore, I believe that Jewish educational programs for teens must be new and uniquely different from the other educational experiences in their lives. Teenagers can then develop their Jewish identities and intellectual understanding of Jewish ethics, values, and history as it relates to their present state of emotional change and flux.

The following is an overview of one successful teen program. Although this was done in a small school, it can be replicated in larger communities either for one synagogue or as part of a community high school.

PROGRAM BACKGROUND

This two-hour, once-a-week evening Judaica program was started in 1987 after parents and teens felt frustrated and dissatisfied with their post B'nai Mitzvah program. This 500 family Conservative synagogue maintained a very successful, yet traditional-style after school Hebrew program. The B'nai Mitzvah class is directed by the synagogue's Cantor, who is responsible for curriculum content and Bar/Bat Mitzvah preparation. The attendance and completion rate of this program was excellent and both students and parents felt positive about their pre-high school experience.

Our present program evolved over the past several years. Each year, our goals and objectives became more specific and better implemented. Parent and board support enabled our High School to blossom. In 1991, 100% of last year's B'nai Mitzvah class enrolled. The program is offered to grades 8-12: the majority of students are in eighth, ninth, and tenth grades. The teens are Confirmed at the end of the tenth grade.

GOALS

This school has very specific goals and a clear ideology. The primary objective of this program is to motivate teenagers to act in a Jewishly ethical and "*menschlichkeit*" way. The program inspires post-Bar/Bat Mitzvah students to take an active, positive, participatory role in their continued Jewish education. The objective is that the teenager become intrinsically motivated to attend classes. Students are expected to practice articulating their own opinions in a more developed and mature style. The goal is to build Jewish leadership and have the teens recognize that contributing to and participating in the Jewish community is a priority now and in the future. We believe that during the post-Bar/Bat Mitzvah years, the development of the teenager's Jewish ethical and moral identity must be nurtured. The *process* of learning takes precedence over the product. The teenager is pushed to develop his/her own ethical code based on Jewish source guidelines, and to appreciate the Jewish aspect inherent in most contemporary teen challenges. The school becomes a safe haven for the turmoil and chaos of adolescence and the synagogue the place to go for community, understanding, and information. The teen feels secure that confidentiality will be maintained and trust develops between teen and synagogue.

It is logical that if teenagers experience the three to five years post-Bar/Bat Mitzvah as exciting, valuable, interesting, and responsive to their needs and life experiences, they will be much more likely to reconnect with the Jewish community in college or thereafter. Since many of our social and ethical decisions are formed during the teen years, the goal of this high school Judaica program is to set the process of value formation in motion so that teens emerge from adolescence with the ethical aspects of their Jewish identity well articulated and secure.

ASSUMPTIONS AND ORGANIZATION

Regarding post-B'nai Mitzvah education, the following is invariably true: Teenagers are over-programmed and have little time to devote to their Jewish education; they can be a demanding population difficult to motivate, inspire, and keep interested. They are extremely self-critical, and this attitude colors their relationships and expectation of others (i.e., resulting in the teenager being highly critical and unforgiving of both people and programs).

Teens are a tough audience because their expectations are often unrealistic. They tend to dismiss something as "boring" before giving any effort to "get into" the subject by engaging in discussion. So how do we implement program goals?

To begin with, the following is essential: (1) Teachers who understand, respect, and enjoy teens, and who can be creative in both curriculum development and teaching methodology; and (2) A high school Judaica program separate and different from the supplementary school and B'nai Mitzvah program in terms of staff, curriculum content, social atmosphere, classroom environment, teaching style, and parental involvement.

Our staff does not use the "frontal approach" to teaching which calls for students to focus attention on the teacher. The frontal approach is used so often in Hebrew and secular schools because it enables large size classes to cover material in a time and teacher controlled fashion. But our high school program is not time bound, nor is there a pre-set, essential curriculum. Even though we have a Confirmation service in the tenth grade year, we purposely do not gear a whole year's curriculum to prepare for that event. The event is minimized so that the process can be maximized.

Our teachers employ a discussion-oriented, hands-on, experiential methodology. Classes are kept small so that discussion groups can be more intimate and informal. Teachers participate in classroom experiences with the teens; for example, if art is being done, teachers do it, too. If role plays are used, teachers are actors with students. During debates and discussion, teachers participate and share opinions. This method enables teens to see adults as role models, and it helps relationships form between students and teachers.

The successful development of relationships is a key factor in the teenagers' continuing involvement. Trusting, individualized, close, respectful, motivating relationships must develop between these students and their teachers. Our students stay enrolled in the program because they feel connected, needed, and respected by the staff. This point cannot be over-emphasized.

The teachers work together (with supervision from the director and Rabbi) to create and/or choose materials that will be appreciated by and relevant to teenagers today. Topics for study respond to the changing emotional and intellectual needs of the teenager, e.g., issues such as trust, communication, compromise, use of the telephone, choices in friends, curfew, use of the car, and interdating. These are issues which parents and teens negotiate on a daily basis.

In addition to these ongoing points of family conflict, teenagers also face social challenges that are more serious in nature and scope than any previous generation has had to face: divorce, the creation of blended families, changing sexual morals of society, the computer technology revolution, and the increasing demands for academic achievement. Finally, there are choices and decisions which today's teenager faces that can ultimately mean life or death: alcohol and drug abuse, the changing nature of drug experimentation, the impact and influence of the media (in both the recording and video fields) that describe and reflect the increasingly violent nature of our world, and the AIDS crisis. The AIDS epidemic has impacted teenagers by making them the next emerging risk group for contracting this deadly illness. Teens must develop a mature and intact value system early on in adolescence in order to navigate their way successfully through a sea of challenges.

An effective post-B'nai Mitzvah program will focus attention on all of these issues.

Starting with the contemporary issue, the Judaic content of the curriculum is then blended into the secular issue. This prioritizing does not contradict or compromise the overall goals of our program. On the contrary, the fact that we have realized that teens want to talk issues first and Jewishness second is another key factor in the school's appeal. The following is our program formula and format in summary form.

THE FORMAT

All aspects of this program's content are implemented concurrently. The main ingredient in the program formula is a distinctly separate high school department with its own administrator and teachers. The program's administrator also serves as the lead teacher. This allows an experienced teacher/primary curriculum designer to role model for the other staff members. The administrator "team-teaches" throughout the year with one or more staff members, including the Rabbi. This enables the administrator to observe the teaching styles of the other staff and to see first-hand how they relate to teens. Teaching team-style sparks creativity between teachers and makes for an exciting presentation of lessons for the teens.

The department is generously funded in both salaries and programming fees. In schools where there is a limited budget but a strong commitment to innovative programming, other creative funding solutions must be explored. These could include: locating interested synagogue members to underwrite one or two special program events per year, researching community businesses that might want to "adopt a teen program" and sponsor an event, an annual fund-raising drive to create a "special events treasure chest." Donors can be listed on a synagogue honor roll thanking them for their support. Each contributor could receive a certificate of merit that reads: "I am a role model for Jewish teens." These types of ideas build community involvement and can help nurture educational programs that might not have existed without this support.

The curriculum created by the program administrator has teacher/Rabbi input. Classroom atmosphere is relaxed and informal. The learning environment borrows techniques from the Jewish camp and youth group/rap group model. The teaching style does not duplicate methods used in the B'nai Mitzvah elementary program. Every lesson uses "hands-on" experiential teaching technique to encourage student participation. The program relies heavily on role play, sociodrama, arts and crafts, values clarification exercises, "New Games," debates and discussion, and media presentations.

Active participation in all *tzedakah* endeavors is expected from every teacher and student. This assists students in developing a *menschlichkeit* attitude and connects them to their surrounding community. All classes have mixed ages. This fosters leadership and role modeling and teaches patience, tolerance, and listening skills, while challenging students to learn from each other's experiences. Parents participate and are supportive and positive about staff, curriculum, and the learning environment.

The program calls for one weekday evening per week for two hours, 32 weeks per year. The year is divided into three trimesters. Here is an example of the breakdown of the weekly two hour session.

Weekly Format

First 15 minutes: Community meeting ("Any New News")

All teens and teachers participate in an animated, open-ended sharing session. Students are encouraged to speak in front of a large group in a personal and candid manner. The meeting builds a feeling of *hevruta* with the school community. It sets a social, relaxed mood to the evening. The meeting also has the added bonus of encouraging students to be on time. However, if they are late, no class content has been missed.

Next 45 minutes: Core Class

All teens, all grades take the same core subject class. The class is team taught by two or more teachers. Students start the lesson as one whole group and are then broken up into smaller discussion groups, each led by a teacher or older teen. These small groups are different week to week, enabling all students to get to know each other. Curriculum content in core areas focuses on the contemporary nature of Bible, spirituality, Jewish history, Jewish family, and other issues. (See Appendix 1.)

Next 15 minutes: Socializing Break/Recess

A snack is provided for the teens by the synagogue. Teachers and students socialize together during break. Teens are encouraged to bring music (audiotapes) and anything else they would like to share. Holiday foods are provided by parents throughout year. A relaxed break encourages teens to make social relationships with each other and when teens feel connected to friends, they want to attend the program.

Next 45 minutes: Elective Class

Elective classes use an inter-age, small size discussion format (10-15 students). Students choose which class they would like to take. Electives stress current event issues, sexuality, drug prevention, and arts and crafts. Classes are taught by one teacher. (See Appendix 2.)

Yearly Programs

Ongoing: *Tzedakah*

Teens create and choose *tzedakah* endeavors to do throughout the year. Past programs have included: the auction of teen-designed *mezuzot*, a canned food drive, and the creation of a quilt for donation to a new hospital. Suggested Resource: *Gym Shoes and Irises* by Danny Siegel (Spring Valley, NY: Town House Press, 1982).

3 or 4 per year: Parent/Teen Workshops

Family education can be exciting and relevant for both parents and teens. Workshops help enrich the ongoing weekly program and give parents an excellent window into what their teenager's concerns and challenges are. Parents join teens for a two hour program that addresses a topic relevant to both. (See Appendix 3.)

3 per year: Teen-Only Workshops
In place of core time, a contemporary topic is explored in more depth. Examples have included: AIDS prevention workshop using an ABC video *In the Shadow of Love*, a Purim play and discussion seminar especially designed for teens, a debate program on capital punishment created and taught by a fellow student.

1 Friday evening: Confirmation Shabbat
Service is led by all tenth grade students. Teens write and perform original poems, stories, skits, and art. Teens who are Confirmed may participate in the local B.J.E. organized summer trip to Israel.

Ongoing: Merge Program
Our high school occasionally joins together with teens (and parents) from another local synagogue. Teens can broaden their social networking, and the combined resources of both congregations coming together provide for guest speakers and additional programs.

Contemporary Topics for Grades 8-12

Core Class Topics
- Being Jewish in a Non-Jewish World
- The Power To Lead
- Why be Good?
- Jewish Heroes & Heroines
- In God's Image: Jewish Spirituality
- In the Beginning: A Contemporary Look at Genesis
- Let Freedom Reign: A Contemporary Look at Exodus
- The Holocaust: History and Ethical Lessons

Elective Class Topics
- Biblical Conflicts and Choices
- Jewish Symbols in Art
- Behind the Headlines
- Intermarriage: The Challenge, Our Response
- Jewish Bioethics
- A Look into Judaism and Christianity
- The Jewish Response to Substance Abuse
- Cult Prevention
- Peer Counseling from a Jewish Perspective
- Torn Between Two Lovers: Interdating in the American Cinema
- Teen Life on Hester Street
- Separate but Equal: Kosher Cooking
- To Lie or not To Lie . . . That is the Question
- Jewish Women Then and Now
- Sexuality from a Jewish Standpoint

Teen-Only Workshop Topics
- A Shushan Affair: A Modern Look at Purim
- The Dilemma of Capital Punishment
- Tu B'Shevat: The Theology of Ecology
- *In the Shadow of Love*: AIDS Education
- Leadership Training for Teacher's Aide Positions

Parent/Teen Workshop Topics
- Teen Stress and Its Relationship to Contemporary Values
- Israel: Land of Conflicts/Land of Choices
- Creating Jewish Memories
- The Times They Are a-Changing: Generational Differences
- Interdating
- AIDS and the Jewish Teen
- Building Blocks for the Survival of Judaism
- Trust and Communication
- I'll Meet You in the Middle: How To Compromise Together
- What is the Meaning of Success?

CONCLUSION

The future of Jewish cultural knowledge, spirituality, and community commitment rests on our efforts as teachers to motivate and educate all ages and stages of Jewish children and adults.

The collective voice of the Jewish teen community deserves our attention, direction, and commitment. It is our task as professional educators to nurture and listen carefully to our teens on their journey toward adulthood. Their success on this journey will ensure a better future for all of us.

APPENDIX 1

Core Curriculum Topics, Ideas, and Resources

(Editor's Note: These course descriptions, minus the references, are passed out to students. Teachers receive both course descriptions and references.)

Being Jewish in a Non-Jewish World

What do you do when the SAT is on the morning your sister will become a Bat Mitzvah? What do you say when your history teacher says that Israel violates the human rights of Palestinians? As American Jews in a non-Jewish world, we confront problems like these all the time. In order to understand how to deal with moral dilemmas, we need to know what "being Jewish" is really all about. In this class, we'll look at Jewish traditions, texts, and ethics and discuss how to cope with the issues we face in our daily lives.

Primary Resources:

Prager Janice, and Arlene Lepoff. *Why Be Different?* West Orange, NJ: Behrman House, Inc., 1986.

Movies: *Hester Street, Crossing Delancy.*

The Power To Lead

What makes some people effective leaders? What qualities make for positive/negative leadership? This course is designed to explore power, authority, leadership, and Jewish political traditions through studying important biblical figures, historical leaders, and contemporary figures. Students will explore important concepts and values of our biblical and historical tradition in a way that helps them relate these experiences to their own lives today.

Primary Resources:

Hirshberg, Naomi; Joan Kaye; Naomi Towvim. *The Power to Lead.* Boston: Bureau of Jewish Education of Greater Boston, 1986.

Epstein, Jill G. *Jewish Heroes: A Curriculum Guide for High School of Famous Jewish Personalities: What Is a Hero?* Unpublished manuscript. Contact author at Kehilat Shalom, 9915 Apple Ridge Road, Gaithersburg, MD 20879.

The Jewish Family

Students are invited to discover the uniqueness of the Jewish family. Class activities will include tracing our own family histories, using biblical portraits to study contemporary issues within the family and investigating current media examples of Jewish individuals and family.

Primary Resources:

Altschuler, Joanne, and Paulette Benson. *The Jewish Family: Past, Present and Future* Denver: A.R.E. Publishing, Inc., 1979.

Kurzweil, Arthur. *My Generations: A Course in Jewish History.* West Orange, NJ: Behrman House, Inc., 1983.

In God's Image

This class will cover a range of concepts from how students view their self-image, personal concepts of right and wrong, issues of good/evil, understanding the history of how people viewed God. Students will develop a deeper understanding of their beliefs in God and how Judaism can nurture personal concepts of self.

Primary Resources:

Bissell, Sherry. *God: The Eternal Challenge.* Denver: A.R.E Publishing, Inc., 1980.

Kaye, Joan S.; Jan Rabinowitch; and Naomi F. Towvim. *Why Be Good: Sensitivities and Ethics in Rabbinic Literature.* Boston: Bureau of Jewish Education of Greater Boston, 1985.

Kerdeman, Deborah, and Lawrence Kushner. *The Invisible Chariot.* Denver: A.R.E. Publishing, Inc., 1986.

APPENDIX 2

Four Suggested Lesson Plans

Lesson Plan #1 (45 minute class)

Contemporary Teen Topic: Conflicts and making difficult choices
Jewish Component: Biblical figures who have had to confront conflict and make choices

Introduction: What is conflict? Conflict is a part of all of the relationships we have with other people. Even "good" relationships have conflicts. Conflicts occur when human differences and uniqueness meet. What is a conflict for you may not be a conflict for somebody else. We all make choices about resolving conflicts. Sometimes we get help from others to help solve a conflict.

Do: Give out paper/pens. Quickly jot down your last conflict. Who was it with (a friend, parent, teacher)? What was the conflict? Did you seek help to resolve it? Do you see any common themes in these conflicts (i.e., disagreement, anger, frustration, truth, interpretation, hostility, justice?)

Choose three students (two girls as the prostitutes, one boy as King Solomon) Read aloud: "The case of the two women" (I Kings 3:16-28). In *The Prophets*, page 23, color code the three roles to make it easy to read aloud.

Discuss: What is the major conflict this story points out? Why do you think the one woman lies about the dead baby? Why do you think King Solomon first tries to cut the child in two? Would he have really gone ahead and "solved" the problem in such a way? Why did he try to do this? What emotions are primary in this conflict? What might have happened if these women attempted to solve it on their own? Do you agree with the solution? Did the "real mother" get the child? Was the decision "just"?

Resource used:

The Prophets: Nevi'im. Philadelphia: Jewish Publication Society of America, 1978.

APPENDIX 2 (Cont.)

Lesson Plan #2 (45 minute class)

Contemporary Teen Issue: Favoritism in the Family
Jewish Component: Biblical parents and their children where there is favoritism in the family

Family Jealousy: When Parents and Siblings Clash

Do you feel that your parents ever play favorites in your family? Are there times when your brother or sister is treated more fairly than you? When? When was the last time you felt overlooked in your family? (give examples) What does jealousy feel like? What other emotions are hidden within jealousy? (i.e., anger, irrationality, frustration, hurt, feeling cheated, overlooked, favoritism)? What does it mean to "play favorites"? Who else "plays favorites" (teachers, friends, etc.)?

When jealousy and its emotions take over: Here is the story of Joseph and how he incurs the jealousy and hatred of his brothers and resentment of his father. Let's act it out and look for which emotions and issues are contained in the story.

Choose teens for the following parts:

Characters for Genesis 37:1-36 (*The Torah* (Jewish Publication Society, page 67-69)
Narrator
Joseph (prop needed: colorful coat)
Father (called Jacob or Israel)
A man in the fields
Reuben
Judah
a few brothers (2-5 teens)

Story will be color coded and read aloud in play form.

Discussion:
What happened here? What did the dream mean? Why did it upset the father? Why did the father "berate" him? Why are the brothers so jealous? Do they have a "right" to be so angry? Are they irrational? Why do you think Reuben wants to protect Joseph? Why do the brothers upset the father by making him believe Joseph is dead? What could this family have done differently?

Resources used:
The Torah. Philadelphia: Jewish Publication Society of America, 1978.

APPENDIX 2 (Cont.)

Lesson Plan #3 (45 minute class)

Contemporary Teen Issue: Being a Good Person
Jewish Component: Ethical Monotheism

On the board, write: Ethical Monotheism. What words/concepts are there? Let's break it down.

Mono = one
theism/theology = brief in God, religion
ethics = right/wrong, good /evil, morals
ethical Monotheism = (read: *Why Be Different*, page 5)

Give out the following (typed on separate sheet)

Personal Goodness Assessment Sheet

The last really "good" thing I did was

The last "not so good" thing I did was

On the following scale, put a star where you fit.

/__________/____________/______________/___________________/____________

beyond bad	pretty bad	pretty good	exceptionally good	perfectly good

Put a circle where most of your friends fit.
Put a square for your parents.
Put a rectangle for your teachers.
The best/nicest thing I ever saw anybody do was . . .

Share the results! Highlight the whole area of how we define good. Who's to say what is good? If God demands that all people be good — what definition of "good" do we use? Are "good" and "ethical" the same?

APPENDIX 2 (Cont.)

Lesson Plan #4 (45 minutes)

Contemporary Teen Issue: Being Stereotyped
Developing our Belief System

Jewish Component: The Middle Way: Moses Maimonides

Moses Maimonides: "Finding Good in the Middle Way"

The "On the Fence" game:

Place a long piece of colored ribbon down the middle of the room. That's the "middle of the road." Read from a list of "ethical dilemmas." Have the kids move toward the choice/belief they hold.

Example: All Arabs are dishonest. (Yes/ No)
American teens are self-centered.
Chinese kids do better in school.
You should wait to have sex until after marriage.
You should choose a profession that makes money over one that does not.
(Make up about ten more similar sentences.)

Talk about the "gray" areas in statements like these. What other issues come into play? Even in a blanket stereotypical statement there can be some truth. "All Jewish girls are Japs," "Jews are all rich," etc. How do these things start? Introduce Moses Maimonides and his ideas of "Finding a Middle Way." Is there an "answer" between two extremes? ("Why Be Good" in Leaders Edition, *Keeping Posted*, Vol. XXXIV, No. 2, November 1988, UAHC Press, pages 4-5.)

Discuss: Do they feel they hold stereotypes? Why? Why not? What about the opinions of family and friends.

APPENDIX 3

Successful Parent/Teen Workshops

I. PREPARATION

A. **Topic:** Choose a topic that is contemporary, relevant, and controversial for both parents and teens. Design choice surveys to give to parents and teens to help zero in on interesting topics.

B. **Goals:** Write down your specific goals for the workshop. Ask yourself: What is interesting about this topic? Who would be an appropriate speaker? What do you want for the parents and teens to come away with? Imagine the issues that might come up for this topic.

C. **Agenda:** Prepare an agenda for the workshop. How exactly will your goals be implemented? Choose activities that inspire participation. Write down all needed materials for implementing the program. Meet with any guest speakers to become familiar with their teaching/presentation style. Confirm in writing exactly what is expected from the speaker.

D. **Teen Involvement:** Involve the teens. Get their help and advice. Have them design a publicity flyer. Ask them for role play ideas/dilemmas. Pre-choose teen actors to put on a "trigger" play.

II. IMPLEMENTATION

A. **Introduction:** Begin each program with a "safe" introduction/overview process. Start the participation process. Call on both parents and teens to contribute ideas.

B. **Discussion Groups:** Never put teens in the same small discussion group with their parents. Remind the teens ahead of time that they will be with other people's parents. Grouping in this way facilitates candor and cuts down on embarrassment. It enables each generation to listen to and hear each other's opinions. Each small discussion group should have a staff member acting as timekeeper/moderator. Have each group choose a reporter/recorder who will take notes on the process of the group, and will then report during large group time. The reporter's job is to record *how* the group came to its decisions: if there was argument or agreement; what range of opinions there was.

C. **Role Playing:** When doing role plays, make sure every card calls for both parent and teen "actors." Identify your teens who are comfortable with this process and distribute them among each group. Parents tend to "warm up" when they see that the teenagers are relaxed and enjoy role plays.

D. **Concluding:** Have enough time for all reporter/recorders to share the small group experience with all the workshop participants. Ask others in the small groups to add their opinions. Do not open it up for discussion or debate until all small groups have reported their findings. The leader will end the program by briefly summarizing the common ideas and opinions that were raised. Allow for anyone to share a final concluding personal comment about the evening.

E. **Evaluation:** Give out evaluation forms and pencils. Collect the filled in forms; give participants the option of mailing them in later. Invite everyone to stay for coffee and desserts.

Chapter 45
Life After Bar/Bat Mitzvah: The "Chai" Program

Paul Sidlofsky

Background

How do we retain students following Bar/Bat Mitzvah? That is the question. That is the problem. That is the challenge. The issue, however, is not only retention, but keeping their minds and their interest engaged as well. Confirmation is important, but we must look at the process leading to it, rather than just the end product itself. Today's teenager is busier than ever. More time is demanded by high school studies and extracurricular activities. A successful program must therefore be creative and flexible, both in its subject matter and in its time requirements.

One of my first challenges as a Rabbi/Educator was to bring new life to a post-Bar/Bat Mitzvah program, which had been in a steady decline. The synagogue had always prided itself in its program of continuing education, and had actually insisted that the students approaching Bar/Bat Mitzvah sign a pledge, promising to continue on to Confirmation. Clearly, such an approach was no longer productive.

With this in mind, plans were begun to restructure the existing program. The School Committee had already voted, during the previous year, to move classes for grades 8 through 10 from Sunday mornings to Tuesday evenings. Unfortunately, my hunch about such a move proved accurate. Attendance began at a higher rate, but as the school year progressed, it rapidly dwindled. This was in direct proportion to the amount of work and extracurricular activities in which our students were involved. A change of class date could not solve the problem. If anything, committing to weekday evenings was more difficult than doing so on Sunday mornings. It was back to square one. It was obvious that a major change, beyond simply moving the class date, was needed.

Goals

Major change and the creation of a quality program cannot occur overnight. I decided to spend the rest of the school year planning for a totally new program. A committee of teachers, students, and parents was formed to create the new curriculum. The following were the goals:

1. The creation of a unique program, clearly distinct from that of the pre-Bar/Bat Mitzvah curriculum.
2. The design of a flexible yet structured time schedule, which would suit the students' busy life-styles.
3. Emphasis on choice in subject matter for each student, within a pre-designated framework.
4. The formation of strong one-on-one relationships between students and staff.
5. The awareness of each student that Jewish life extends beyond the school, the synagogue, and even the Jewish community itself, and can be an on-going aspect of one's entire life.
6. The realization by each student that Jewish education and Jewish life do not end with Confirmation.

Implementation of the "Chai" Program

Curriculum

The curriculum for the "Chai" Program is simple yet creative, flexible yet well structured. It is designed for ninth and tenth grades (eighth grade has a separate introductory program, which is briefly described below). During both years, all students design individualized programs, choosing a number of options, each of which is worth a certain number of credits. A student must earn 18 credits (*chai*) during each year in order to complete the program. The following options are available:

1. Community Service Work – Individually or in pairs, students volunteer at various Jewish and/or general institutions. The experience is very rewarding and provides valuable training for students when looking for jobs in the future. Our program allows credit for a minimum of five and a maximum of 15 hours of Community Service Work, with two credits given for every five hours. Prime examples of institutions visited are: the local senior citizens' home, local food kitchens, and various organizations serving children.

2. Assistant Teaching – This is a chance to work for one hour a week with younger students as an assistant to an experienced teacher. Most students in the "Chai" Program opt to work with younger classes on Sunday mornings. Some, however, feel comfortable working in Hebrew classes, or even taking a small group of students on their own for portions of the class time.

   This option has many advantages. First, it is very popular among the "Chai" students. They earn credit while having fun working with younger children. Second, it is very educational. Teaching is the best way to learn, not only about teaching itself, but also about the subject matter, even when that is at an introductory level. Third, with increasing school enrollment, combined with an ever tightening budget, assistant teachers help ease the burden on the classroom teachers. More individual attention can be given to students without hiring extra staff. Finally, younger students respond well to the older ones, and also get the message that one can stay involved beyond Bar/Bat Mitzvah.

   Again, "Chai" students can opt for between five and 15 hours of teaching, with two credits being given for each five hours.

3. Youth Group – Students earn credit while having fun and making new friends. The concept is rather radical, but anyone who has been involved in youth groups will attest to its success in integrating social activities with a strong Jewish context. This option is a way for students to have positive Jewish experiences, and realize that there are ways to stay involved in the synagogue beyond tenth grade. We ask that students attend all educational programs, and at least one regional event.

   There is one caveat concerning this option. Students must have a genuine interest in the youth group in order to join. If they do so purely (or mostly) for the credits, they are likely to be a negative influence on other youth group members, who truly are committed.

   Should a student show genuine interest and attend programs regularly (determined by the Director of Education in consultation with the Youth Group Advisor), three credits are given for the entire year. Partial credit is not recommended, unless there are extenuating circumstances (sickness, starting the entire program late, etc.).

4. Retreat – Students participate in a weekend at a local camp. Families pay a fee to supplement the school budget allocation. Students share in creative services, study sessions, group dynamics activities, meals, and more. Free time is given to enjoy the camp setting and to encourage group cohesion. A movie is shown Saturday evening. Throughout the retreat, students are asked to keep a personal journal, recording thoughts and impressions. About four entries are made over the two days.

   There is no doubt that this is one of the most successful aspects of the "Chai" Program, both socially and educationally. It is greatly enjoyed by students and staff (Director of Education and teachers) alike. Because of its success and group format, we strongly encourage this option by offering six credits for the retreat.

5. Service Attendance – Though not a popular option, this is chosen by students on occasion. It provides an alternative for students with busy schedules, helps teach about the service, encourages involvement in the synagogue community, and gives the clear message that worship is an important aspect of Jewish life. Credit is given only for services attended at our synagogue and on Shabbat. (Since students generally attend High Holy Day services, no credit is given.) Three credits are given for six services, with a maximum of six credits being given.

6. Independent Study – This is a chance for students to explore virtually any Jewish topic of interest in detail, at their own pace (within one school year). Projects are not to overlap heavily with any topics

already covered in the "Chai" Program, but can expand on them should the student show special interest. They can take many forms (writing, music, art, etc.), as long as serious learning is demonstrated. Students work alone or with a partner, guided by the Director of Education and/or an advisor, who will also evaluate the projects. Topics and outlines must be submitted and approved prior to beginning work, in order to avoid later misunderstandings. Two credits are given for each five hours work. Between two and six credits are allowed.

7. Seminars – Seminars provide a wonderful selection of topics which are of interest to high school students. These sessions are about three hours in length, held in the late morning/early afternoon on Sundays, about five times per year. They take place in the homes of students, which make a comfortable and informal learning environment. The host families are asked to provide lunch for the group and always are happy to do so. In our program, a topic is discussed once only (other schools may want to expand this). Often, students are given material in advance, to read before the seminar. Each seminar is worth three credits.

   We choose seminar topics in the following manner: In the spring, a list of about a dozen topics is given to all students entering the program in the fall of that year. They are asked to indicate which topics are of interest. From that list, we choose the most popular and offer them. The seminars are planned and led by one or more of the program advisors, in conjunction with the Director of Education.

   The following topics have been offered in each of the past two years:

   Jewish Views on Relationships and Sexuality – Issues such as AIDS, abortion, gender roles, and the body are discussed. Students explore their own personal views, as well as studying classical Jewish texts and modern Jewish thinkers. Reading, discussion, and role play are among the techniques used.

   Jewish Views on Medical and Legal Ethics – Volunteer doctors and lawyers from the congregation help stimulate discussion on areas such as genetic engineering, AIDS, abortion, and euthanasia. Prior reading is required.

   Jewish Cooking – This seminar is not only experiential, but most educational as well. Origins of Jewish foods, holiday customs, and laws of *kashrut* are among the topics discussed extensively while preparing and then eating traditional Jewish foods.

   Anti-Semitism – Prejudice in general is discussed as a lead-in to this topic. Past events, including the Holocaust, are examined, with emphasis on current trends, national and local. Unfortunately, there always has been an abundance of reading material concerning past and current events.

   Holocaust – In this session, students take an historical look at this important event in modern Jewish history. How could it have happened? Is it a unique event? Could it happen again? Why is there evil? These are among the questions explored through discussion, reading, and video.

   Other seminar topics suggested, but not yet offered, are: Being Jewish in a Non-Jewish World, Jewish Music/Dance, Conversational Hebrew, Israel, Famous Jewish Personalities, etc.

8. Journal – This area is compulsory for all students, and is worth two credits for the year. Each student is required to make at least ten substantial entries during the year, which are responses to their Jewish identity. Program advisors will look at and discuss entries with each student.

9. Miscellaneous – One wonderful aspect of the "Chai" Program curriculum is its ability to incorporate programs in the community which become known to us over the course of the year. Students may receive credit, if approved, for some of these programs. Examples have included special lectures, movies, concerts, and other cultural events with Jewish themes.

Certain requirements are made of each student in addition to the eighteen credit option choices:

Group Meetings – Three times a year (September, January, May), all students with their parents get together for a one hour meeting, together with advisors and the Director of Education. Meetings are used to plan and evaluate various aspects of the program. Often, excellent suggestions for improvement arise from these meetings, and group cohesion is enhanced.

Office Hours – Once a month, for an hour on Sunday mornings, each advisor is available at the synagogue for a compulsory meeting with each individual student. The meeting is brief, but important for maintaining personal contact. The advisor and student review the past month's accomplishments, discuss journal entries, and plan for the coming month and beyond. The calendar/newsletter for the upcoming month is given out at this time.

Phone Contact – At least once a month, in addition to the office hours, advisors call each student to touch base concerning past, current and upcoming aspects of the individual's curriculum and the program as a whole.

Sessions with Rabbi(s) – In the Confirmation year (tenth grade) only, all students have a series of short classes with the Rabbi(s) on topics chosen by one or both parties. Classes take place Sunday mornings, about 6-12 times per year.

Confirmation Service and Rehearsals – All tenth grade students are required to prepare and participate in the Confirmation Service, which takes place on Erev Shavuot. A traditional service framework is used, and each student receives a part. In addition, each student is encouraged to prepare at least one creative piece for the service. These can be in the form of writing, music, art, dance, or any other appropriate medium.

Students put together their own service, led by a student-selected committee and chairperson. The committee is responsible for student preparation and attendance at rehearsals.

Each year at the service, the students present a gift of their own choosing to the synagogue.

Graduation Service and Dinner – On the Shabbat evening prior to Shavuot, a special graduation dinner and service is held for the Confirmation and post-Confirmation (twelfth grade) graduates and their families. All graduating students are required to attend.

Advisors

Though previously mentioned above, special note should be made about the program advisors. We have a unique concept in staffing. Rather than classroom teachers, one advisor is hired for each 8-12 students. The role of the advisor is twofold: (1) to help ensure that, despite the limitless flexibility of the "Chai" Program curriculum, each student is able to create, carry out, and evaluate an organized, viable, and individualized program, and to stay focused on his/her goals at all times; and (2) to serve as a mentor, along with the Director of Education, for each student, on both a professional and personal level.

Advisors are hired based on their knowledge of subject matter and ability/experience in working with/relating to high school students. Each advisor attends retreats, maintains ongoing contact with each of his/her assigned students, leads seminars, is present at all meetings, and helps in the ongoing planning and evaluation of all aspects of the "Chai" Program. Advisors are directly responsible to the Director of Education with whom they are expected to maintain contact on a regular basis.

Eighth Grade Program

Although a separate curriculum from the ninth and tenth grade "Chai" Program, the eighth grade program merits mention, as it forms an important bridge between Bar/Bat Mitzvah and the "Chai" Program. It serves to keep students involved after Bar/Bat Mitzvah and to introduce them to the 18 credit concept. It familiarizes them with and excites them about having a flexible and less demanding schedule, with interesting topics.

The eighth grade program has become very popular due to its interesting content and simplicity. Each student chooses one option from each of the following three categories in order to complete the year. Each category (1,2, or 3) is worth six credits.

1. a. Weekend Retreat
   b. Independent Study (12 hours)

2. a. Holocaust Class (12 Sundays, spread throughout the year, 10:00-11:00 A.M.)
   b. Jewish Community Class (12 hours total, including visits to local Jewish institutions and guest speakers)

3. a. Assistant Teaching (12 hours, 1 hour per week)
   b. Community Service Work (12 hours total)
   c. Service Attendance (10 services)
   d. Half each of two of the above
   e. Half of a, b, or c, plus student choir (for students who have already been in the choir)
   f. A category not already chosen from sections 1 or 2 above

Each student has some degree of choice, but this is limited. Later, in the "Chai" Program, they may choose freely from all options. Here, however, each student is required to spend a good percentage of the time in a classroom situation and/or with the group as a whole (clearly, the retreat is a popular option when paired with Independent Study).

The eighth grade has one teacher who participates in the retreat (including planning), teaches the classes, and helps monitor the progress of the students' choice(s) from category 3.

Evaluation of the Program

The "Chai" Program has a built-in method of evaluation. Ongoing contact among students, parents, advisors, and the Director of Education takes place in the form of phone calls, office hours, group sessions, seminars, retreats, meetings, and more. At each of these times, individual and group needs are discussed and acted upon. The programmatic structure leaves much room for flexibility, so that changes, additions, and deletions can be made. As a result, all participants feel a great sense of comfort with and ownership of this program.

Results

The current Confirmation Class, whose members had continued after Bar/Bat Mitzvah before this new program was implemented, consists of eight students. Now, after one year, the current post-Bar/Bat Mitzvah class (eighth grade) has 26 students. This will increase the "Chai Program" from approximately 20 this year to almost 40 next year. Clearly, the numbers indicate success.

Quantity, however, is important only if accompanied by quality. Two years ago, as few as two or three students would show up in each of the ninth and tenth grade classes. Now, one hundred percent of the students in the program complete their work with little pressure from parents or advisors (though at times, it is necessary), and last year, virtually the entire Confirmation Class completed more than 18 credits (with one student completing 25). Students seem motivated to do the work, and appear happy with the curriculum. Seminars generate excellent discussions, retreats form great bonds, community service opens the eyes of these privileged students, and assistant teaching brings out a side of these teenagers rarely seen at all, let alone in a Religious School setting.

Discipline problems have become virtually eliminated because of the individualized nature of the program and the treatment of all students as young adults in terms of both personal interaction and curriculum.

In the "Chai" Program, teenagers come to see that Jewish life can be enjoyable and relevant to their needs, that there is a Jewish world beyond the Religious School/classroom, and a world beyond the synagogue which can be compatible with Jewish values. They meet interesting and committed Jewish adults, often on a one-to-one basis, and therefore see that Judaism and Jewish education are not only for children. They complete their formal Religious School training not only satisfied with what they have accomplished and learned, but aware of and interested in continuing their Jewish learning and involvement. And, of course, students one or two years behind them hear of this and become more motivated to follow their lead.

In these and in so many other ways, "Chai" has truly meant new life for our post-Bar/Bat Mitzvah students.

Unit VIII: Social and Psychological Aspects
Overview

Adolescence is an in-between time of life. Adolescents are seeking independence and an identity of their own. They are torn between a longing for the continuity of childhood and a need to break away from childishness.

In Chapter 46, psychologist Dr. Ian Russ gives an explanation of how both the child's and the family's preparation for and enactment of the Bar/Bat Mitzvah ceremony can be seen as a symbolic passage from the psychosocial tasks of pre-adolescence to those of adolescence. He explains how the Bar/Bat Mitzvah can facilitate that passage.

In Chapter 47, Rabbi Sandy Eisenberg Sasso offers suggestions for using B'nai Mitzvah training as an occasion to explore emotional and family issues. Growing up as a Jew, she asserts, should be connected with growing up as an individual. This chapter will give the reader some ideas of how to integrate these.

In Chapter 48, Sally Weber, a social worker, outlines a model program that addresses the needs of the changing Jewish family. She also suggests ways that Jewish Family Service professionals can provide expertise to synagogue staffs.

In Chapter 49, Dr. Stuart Schoenfeld analyzes how the notion of increased autonomy for the Bar or Bat Mitzvah (as part of the movement into adolescence) is reflected both within and outside of the synagogue. The sociological aspects of invitation lists, the party, and the candlelighting ceremony are all discussed. These social aspects that parallel the ritual events are, he maintains, all part of the rite of passage.

In Chapter 50, the final chapter of this Unit and of the book, Sally Shafton describes a program that involves lay "counselors" working with each Bar/Bat Mitzvah family.

A careful reading of the chapters in this final Unit will bring the reader greater understanding of the psychosocial needs of the adolescent, particularly in the context of Bar and Bat Mitzvah. Here we return to the crucial element in all Bar/Bat Mitzvah education: the children themselves. While there is no doubt that new programs, methods, and curricula are important factors in revitalizing and strengthening current Bar/Bat Mitzvah programs, of major import must be our understanding of the needs of the students for whom all these programs are designed.

Chapter 46
The Psychosocial Tasks and Opportunities of Bar/Bat Mitzvah

Ian Russ

The social and cultural environment of Jewish Europe in the 1300s in which the ritual of Bar Mitzvah first sprang, produced children who, at age 13, had to be "adults." Children today, however, are more likely to be protected and sheltered from adulthood years longer. At puberty, contemporary adolescents are neither engaged to be married nor actively involved in apprenticeships. Therefore, the ritual of Bar/Bat Mitzvah is no longer a puberty rite of entrance into the adult world. Yet, it can still be an important transitional Jewish ceremony.

Rituals are an "essential link between the developing ego and the ethos of the community" (Erikson, 1982, p. 58). Rituals usually occur at predictable times and offer stability during times of transition. Their primary goal is to connect the individual with the community. In addition, rituals become a standard way for families and communities to transmit values to the next generation. The mastery of the formulas of rituals (in the case of Bar/Bat Mitzvah, these are the ceremonies of prayers, Torah, and Haftarah) can promote the growth of independence and self-esteem within the fabric and texture of community life.

However, when meaning is removed from a ceremony, the ritual devolves into ritualism — a habitual, empty act without the power to connect the individual to his or her culture and values. Yet, the act of doing even empty acts/ritual may still serve to maintain a certain kind of stability within the community, or the myth of stability. The spirit and excitement of the ritual are gone, but the practice continues in fear that the community or individual will disintegrate without it. One can observe this ritualism when watching assimilated families grapple with the words of the *Kaddish* at the grave-side. They know that saying *Kaddish* somehow binds the community, the deceased, and the remaining family together. Yet, as the family struggles with meaningless sounds read from a transliteration, the act rings hollow and the sense of obligation feels burdensome. And as we watch, feeling the pain of the ritual now turned to ritualism, we fear even more that the loss of this ancient recitation will bespeak the demise of a united community, even if this unity is only a myth.

Bar/Bat Mitzvah has this same downside potential. The child and the family and the community can either unite in a passionate, unifying celebration of community values and individual growth, or they can stand on the precipice prevented from falling by the skimpy guardrail of antiquated and meaningless behavior. Prevention of the second possibility requires that the preparation for Bar/Bat Mitzvah, as well as the ceremony itself, respond to the developmental needs of the child, the family, and the community.

This chapter will examine the psychological and social tasks of the pubescent child and the inherent opportunities the preparation and enactment of the Bar/Bat Mitzvah offer to master these tasks. The Bar/Bat Mitzvah preparation and ceremony bridge preadolescence and adolescence. Consequently, psychosocial tasks from both of these developmental stages will be addressed. The term "psychosocial" will be used extensively to connote the inseparability of psychological tasks and the social environment in which they must be mastered.

THE PSYCHOSOCIAL TASKS OF PREADOLESCENCE

Industry

The elementary school child has several tasks to master, primary among them to balance the feelings of industriousness and inferiority. Industry is the ability to make a plan, enact it, complete it, and review it (Erikson, 1963). When a child successfully completes and reviews a project, he or she is left with a sense of industriousness and competence. Feeling competent, the child is enabled to cooperate with others in group activities (Erikson, 1964). Homework and project-oriented assignments in school offer the child the opportunity for planning, completing, and reviewing his or her work which, in turn, leads to a sense of mastery. Positive self-esteem grows as the child realizes his or her ability to complete tasks successfully. Accomplishment energizes the child to initiate greater endeavors. Pride is developed as the child shows his or her completed work to trusted adults and parents. Parental and adult praise encourages independence and individuality while reinforcing social ties (Briggs, 1975).

Meaning and purpose develop as a person is able to blend his or her ideas with a goal and to act on them. The family and synagogue assist this process in setting the goal of Bar/Bat Mitzvah and, where possible, negotiating with the child the specific responsibilities to be undertaken. Will the child lead the whole service? Will he or she read seven *aliyot* from the Torah or only Maftir? Conflicts that arise need to be seen as opportunities for problem solving and not win or lose battles between adults and child. In the end, the Bar/Bat Mitzvah must own the ceremony. This can best occur if he or she is included in the planning and is listened to when expressing heartfelt feelings, even when they conflict with the wishes or expectations of the adults. After all, if the ceremony is symbolic of entering an early stage of adulthood, then the social skills of problem solving — expressing one's ideas and listening carefully to others — may legitimately be a part of the process.

Each child must be assessed individually and realistically by the parents and synagogue in order to assure the greatest opportunity for mastery and success. A child with learning disabilities requires a selection of material appropriate to his or her skills. Expectations and assignments must allow for success during each step of preparation. And bright and enthusiastic students should be allowed to bite off as big a chunk as they want, with the proviso that they can cut back if need be.

A difficult situation arises when the adults feel that the child does not want to work to his or her potential. Should this child be required to take on what the adults presume he or she is capable of, or should the child be able to minimize the task? The most productive response requires negotiation and problem solving. Remember, even if less is mastered, Jewish identity will be more positively influenced by the sense of success and ownership of the ritual than if the child experiences the preparation and ceremony as an arbitrary requirement imposed entirely from without by adults.

Other conflicts will be easier to resolve the more the child views the experience as his or her own. It becomes easier to resist the tugs and pulls of friends who want to have fun when Hebrew School or studying is required. This is not to say that parents and teachers shouldn't encourage a child to stretch and grow. In the end, the children also need a sense that they accomplished a worthwhile task, and that their preparation and work truly brought them to a new place.

Risks of Inferiority and Inertia

When a child is unable to complete tasks successfully or does not receive encouragement and praise from adults for doing so, he or she runs the risk of feeling inadequate and inferior. Over time, these feelings may lead to discouragement and isolation (Erikson, 1963). The child's feeling of inferiority often decreases the desire to work cooperatively with others. In the extreme, inadequacy and inferiority can lead to inertia, a lack of desire to move or initiate activity (Erikson, 1982).

For the twelve-year-old, the idea of leading a congregation in prayer, singing in front of an audience, reading a language which the child only in part understands (in front of many who might understand), and giving a speech/sermon which expresses personal ideas to a group of adults and peers can be overwhelming. If this sense of feeling overwhelmed persists, it can lead to feelings of inferiority resulting in the child's giving up. Preparation might best be broken down to "bite size" pieces which can be mastered, and then acknowledged and praised.

Balance of Industry and Inferiority

A healthy balance of industry and inferiority leads to a sense of competence and healthy self-esteem in a socially meaningful environment (Erikson, 1964). The preparation and completion of the Bar/Bat Mitzvah is an opportunity for mastery and self-esteem. Within the confines of family and community values, the young adolescent has the opportunity to set a goal (the Bar/Bat Mitzvah ceremony), make a plan (the commitment to study and attend Hebrew School), enact that plan (the learning), and complete it during the ceremony. Feedback and evaluation are offered throughout, as is encouragement. Praise and adulation are offered within the ceremony, by the giving of presents and by celebrating at a party.

THE PSYCHOSOCIAL TASKS OF ADOLESCENCE

Storm and Stress

Adolescence is an in-between time of life. Not yet having attained the obligations and responsibilities of adulthood, the adolescent often attempts to distance himself/herself from the perceived stigma of childhood. Stanley Hall (1904) described the adolescent's self-felt dilemma and consequent inconsistent behavior as "*sturm und drang*" (storm and stress), a period of extreme turmoil and crisis. In the 1960s, further research (Coleman, 1961) reinforced this idea, as adolescence was thought to be a culture unto itself — there being a "generation gap" between teens and adults.

Current research, however, gives a clear indication that for most youth there is little rebellion against parental authority (Bandura, 1972), and that on major issues of morality, political and religious beliefs, and sexual attitudes, the divergence of opinion between adolescents and their parents is minimal (Douvan and Adelson, 1966; Fogelman, 1976; Rutter, et al., 1976). Most adolescents record that they do not experience storm and stress, but rather some anxiety as they seek independence and search for their own identity. It appears that most people experience adolescence as part of the continuity of growth from childhood to adulthood.

While preparing for and completing the Bar/Bat Mitzvah ritual is at times stressful, it allows children to connect to twelve and thirteen-year-olds from previous Jewish generations and those yet to be born, and to share a common experience with Jews throughout the world. Sharing a family and community value binds the child with these social groupings and thereby continues a unique system for teaching and learning values.

A positive Jewish identity cannot be realized unless values and Jewish history are learned in the process of preparation. The child cannot magically be transformed into a connecting link in the lineage of Jewish values unless he or she learns and experiences those values. Also, the Bar/Bat Mitzvah will be denied the accomplishment and success that maximizes self-esteem if he or she has not mastered both text and history as well as the psychosocial tasks. In other words, if the Bar/Bat Mitzvah ceremony has already declined to a state of ritualism within the community and family, then the child will have difficulty finding meaning in the identity of being a "son or daughter of the commandments." Meaning will largely be determined by the value, both Judaically and developmentally, that this ritual has to the community and family.

Identity

The young teenager must develop a cohesive identity — balancing the demands of society with inner strivings and dreams. Group membership is important for the growing teen. The group's ideals and identity are important in helping to create an internal sense of wholeness (Erikson, 1980). Healthy identity implies a sense of certainty and anticipation of achievement with clear boundaries between one's self and others.

Bar/Bat Mitzvah is an opportunity for the adolescent to balance inner wishes with the demands of the family and community. The ritual is a community expectation. While most twelve and thirteen-year-olds initially desire a Bar/Bat Mitzvah ceremony, conflicts tend to arise during the preparation when other interests and wishes take precedence for the youth. A desire to be with friends, hang out at the mall, or participate in sports can often conflict with Hebrew classes and study. The adults must unite to create a safe environment that promotes the adolescent's self and peer relationships, minimizes conflicts, and fosters the adolescent's ability to negotiate his or her world. Successful negotiation of the inner strivings and outside pressures determines, in part, the success of forming a whole and cohesive self identity.

Role Confusion and Negative Identity

The opposite pole, identity confusion (Erikson, 1963, 1980), tugs at the teenager to meld into the surroundings and abandon any sense of distinction. This can result in uneven industriousness where some interests are pursued to excess, while other activities are abandoned totally, leaving character development unbalanced as the teenager seeks group identification over personal satisfaction. If the adolescent's loyalty to the group forsakes the development of an internal independent identity, there is a risk for difficulty in forming secure intimate relationships in adulthood. In more extreme situations, a negative identity develops. When this occurs, the teenager values everything outside of his or her domain while disliking everything in immediate reach. "Life and strength seem to exist only where one is not, while decay and danger threaten wherever one happens to be" (Erikson, 1980, p. 140).

For some children, Bar/Bat Mitzvah may not be appropriate if they cannot find any personal or social meaning in the event. In these cases, it may be better to put the event aside until it is meaningful. Psychotherapists have heard the alienation from Judaism symbolized by a patient's resentment of the empty and seemingly arbitrary requirements of a Bar or Bat Mitzvah which took him/her away from friends and more welcome activities. Their Jewish identity is a negative one, with satisfaction and excitement experienced only outside of Jewish activity.

It is not easy to recommend the possibility of postponing or even foregoing a Bar/Bat Mitzvah. Such a decision requires soul-searching and discussion with the child, the parents, the teachers, the Rabbi and/or the Cantor. An essential part of the soul-searching must include wondering what has gone wrong in this family or community that a child would not identify with a core ritual and value of modern Jewish life. The family and community must wonder whether it has given messages to the child that negate the values of tradition and observance, or whether other psychodynamic problems exist in the family. If the child is deviating from the family, it is important for the child to know the parents' feelings and to feel (perhaps) discomfort for deviating from parents' wishes; however, this must be balanced with the parents honoring the child's wishes and identity as well. A healthy environment is one that meets the developmental needs of the child and honors his or her evolving identity, even as it attempts to shape it.

Balancing Identity and Group Demands

The teen years are a period when the individual tries on various social values and beliefs (Coleman, 1980). Two categories of social phenomenon contribute to this process (Elder, 1968). The first is the increasing demands and expectations that society places upon the adolescent; one's role remains the same, but there are new demands for independence and performance. Or, entirely new roles develop. With these new roles come the inherent conflicts of multiple roles. The adolescent must master the simultaneous role conflicts of being a son or daughter to one's parents, a student at school and home, a boyfriend or girlfriend, a peer group member (Thomas, 1968), and a Bar/Bat Mitzvah. Demands from these different roles can create conflict and anxiety.

When an adolescent's identity balances self-esteem with group demands, he or she develops a healthy sense of fidelity, "the ability to sustain loyalties freely pledged in spite of the inevitable contradictions of value systems" (Erikson, 1964, p. 125). Fidelity and loyalty become the backbone of identity and lay the foundation to appreciate law and one's responsibilities within a legal system. Only one who is loyal can bind himself or herself legally or decide freely to deviate.

Clearly, pledging one's loyalty to Judaism and the Jewish community is at the center of the Bar/Bat Mitzvah ritual, a ceremony commemorating the child-cum-adult's entrance into the brotherhood and sisterhood of *mitzvah* observers. Just at the moment in which the neophyte adult gains the capacity to appreciate the need and complexity of law in society, Judaism requires adherence and loyalty to that law and structure. The choice is the individual's, yet the community and family assert their pressure to mold the adolescent's choice. The community asks the child to enter adulthood by asserting his or her fidelity to the past, present, and future of the Jewish people.

Freely choosing membership in the Jewish community increases the variety of roles and social demands confronting the teenager. He or she is still a member of a nuclear family, a student, a friend to his or her friends, and now a Bar/Bat Mitzvah. The internal demands for performance and loyalty and the external responsibilities can be enormous and often conflicting. Parents and teachers need to assist the child in negotiating these conflicts, choosing carefully when they will intervene and when they will encourage the budding teen to resolve the conflict himself/herself. Ultimately, the teenager must freely commit to being a member of the Jewish community. This is also true of the teen's commitment to peer groups, family, and career goals. Inherent in each commitment is conflict with the others. Anxiety is inevitable.

The healthy identity is flexible in its loyalties, understanding that conflicts can be negotiated and inevitable disappointments can be overcome. Growth is found in the opportunity to recognize and resolve these conflicts. Doing so, the teenager achieves a sense of self-mastery which leads to a unity of self, an identity.

Parents and educators must be careful to focus on the overall sense of growth and invest in the child's power to choose, rather than fight about any one particular choice. There will be times, for example, when a twelve-year-old will want to play with friends instead of studying, or attend a sports activity instead of Hebrew School. As difficult as it is from the adult's point of view, energy must be spent to help the child invest in the proper choices, balancing their conflicting obligations and wishes. At times, parents will have to intervene and impose a decision that is in accord with their values. However, if parental intervention regularly ignores the self-perceived obligations and wishes of the child, then the youth can feel unable to make healthy choices at a later date. The child may have difficulty clarifying his or her boundaries with family and peers.

Peer pressure to blend into the crowd is often greater for the adolescent than family pressures. At times, peer pressure can even overwhelm the individual's striving for a separate and distinct identity. The teenager's struggle to maintain a separate identity in the face of competing social pressures is expressed in the paraphrasing of a saying attributed to Mark Twain: "Maturity is reached when one can do what he or she wants to do, even if his or her parents [or friends] want him to do it." This level of maturity, of freely pledged loyalties, can only be reached when adults invest in helping children to make their own decisions, and to be clear about who they are in relation to others. The pubescent adolescent is in the midst of this struggle. When one reaches the early twenties, there should be enough practice and self-confidence in choosing one's loyalties that a person can commit to a mate.

Dependence and Independence

The teenager begins to loosen the ties to his or her parents. Of course, this is complicated as the pain of relinquishing one's parents often results in teenagers feeling needy and choosing behaviors that seem regressive. Many youths experience internal conflict as they depend upon their peers for emotional support and stability to break the ties with their parents. At times, the teenager experiences conflict because in order to establish his or her independence, he or she must submit to needing help from others.

The tasks of learning Hebrew, trope, the specifics of Torah and Haftarah chanting, and writing a brief speech/sermon is a true confrontation of the desire for independence and the need for dependence. Teenagers often vacillate between appreciating and resenting the needing of others to complete their tasks, just as they can alternately feel pride and abandonment in their independence. Teenagers often become fearful that "too much independence" could result in no longer being taken care of. Of course, this alternates with their declarations of independence and of not needing help from anyone. The preparation for the Bar/Bat Mitzvah offers a profound lesson in balancing these aspects of growth. The youth is encouraged to be as independent as he or she can manage, even though it is necessary to return to the teacher for information and skill refinement.

This independence, culminated by the child leading the congregation in prayer, is also the beginning of the resolution of one's separation from parents. To stand alone in front of an assembly of adults and peers is a profound statement of independence. The adolescent communicates to his parents that he or she chose a goal, worked to complete it, and now has mastered its intricacies. To give a speech/sermon expressing personal ideas about the text gives evidence to the community of beginning analytic thinking and the ability to prepare adequately. The congregation is present to witness and applaud the success. Leading the congregation in prayer enables the Bar/Bat Mitzvah to shed symbolically the stigma of childhood because what he or she did was not a child's task.

After the ceremony, it is important that the community offer and encourage the child to return and lead the congregation in prayer and other events. Some congregations do this by encouraging post-Bar/Bat Mitzvah teens to chant from the Torah or lead sections of the service on Shabbat and holidays. Some communities develop extensive programs for teens to become student teachers, junior counselors, day care aides, and so on. These opportunities are important as they increase the meaning of the Bar/Bat Mitzvah, even after the event.

Adolescent Cognition

Cognitive skills are a major factor in the teenager's development. Formal operational thought (Inhelder and Piaget, 1958) allows the young teenager to think abstractly. Suddenly, idealism is possible, and fantasy takes on a new role. The adolescent is not yet burdened with the internalization of what society says is possible and impossible. The newly found ability for abstract thinking, without the firm internalization of society's belief restrictions, allows many teenagers to find creative solutions outside the boundaries of conventional problem solving. Abstract thinking also allows the teen to greatly expand his or her vocabulary and develop a sense of satire and sarcasm. Metaphor becomes an important tool for the adolescent to express ideas and experiment with new beliefs.

The material for all students must be stimulating and incorporate their newly discovered (if somewhat uneven) abstract thinking and idealism. Students must be allowed the autonomy to "play" with the material. This ranges from applying ancient stories and lessons to modern day events (even if the connection seems to stretch credulity) to seeing how fast a particular *tefilah* can be recited. The goal here is to play with ideas, the stories, the words, and even the sounds. Play for the child is perhaps the primary way he or she makes an idea or value his or her own. Intellectual play for the budding adolescent is found in wit, satire, plays on words, placing ideas and events in peculiar juxtapositions, and thinking up problems and solutions they are sure no one before them ever considered.

As the child begins to assimilate these pieces and plays with them, he or she may also begin to alter them. Melodies may take on an individualized style, words may be accented out of context, or comments under the breath may be inserted. These signs need to be embraced. They indicate that the Bar/Bat Mitzvah has taken ownership of the ceremony (or at least is in the process of doing so).

BAR/BAT MITZVAH, THE PARTY, AND PSYCHOSOCIAL DEVELOPMENT

And now values and psychosocial development must confront the Bar/Bat Mitzvah party. It cannot be denied that the "party" has become inextricably tied to the Jewish ritual. For some, the party is bigger and societally more important than the religious rituals. Many are the editorials that decry the "paganism" and extravagance of these celebrations, and justly so. However, the parent of an almost thirteen-year-old does not have the luxury of handling the philosophical issues of parties and their overgrown importance. The developmental issue of the party's function is the same as other aspects of the Bar/Bat Mitzvah, requiring the following questions to be asked: For whom is the party? And how does it express or respond to the needs of the child within his or her social world? This social world includes the family and community and, most importantly, the child's peers. To have a ceremony which celebrates the teenager's entrance into the religious community as a junior partner, and not to acknowledge the child's entrance into adolescence and the primacy of friends and peer group loyalty, is unbalanced and unfair. The communities that families live in help determine the grandness of the party. Parties need to celebrate the child, youthfulness, mastery, growth, friendship, family, and community, and therefore need to be within the social boundaries of the community.

Early adolescence is an age when the child is constantly checking his or her "all rightness" by measuring his or her sameness and difference from friends. The correctness of one's individuality is constantly checked against the styles, behaviors, and habits of his or her friends. To be the odd person out is the cause of enormous embarrassment. Consequently, the party must be within community standards as well as the standards and economic feasibility of the family. If parents or the child feel that they want something more modest (or extravagant) than community standards, these issues must be discussed and resolved.

To arrive at Bar/Bat Mitzvah time and then decide that the community social standards are not to the family's liking, is too late. This does not mean, however, that families must simply capitulate to the crowd. It does mean that any deviance should be looked at seriously, and families must explore the consequences of these changes. It is often the fantasies of the parents that create expensive extravaganzas which lose sight of the needs and even the wishes of the child. The appropriate psychosocial needs of the child should be the focus of this process.

CONCLUSION

Industriousness, inferiority, self-esteem, loyalty, separateness, continuity, dependence, and independence all lie on a continuum. Growth is not measured in absolute terms of success and failure, but needs to be viewed as progress along this continuum. What's more, growth is uneven since the child and family will also be confronted with feelings of failure, being overwhelmed, inertia, conflict, poor resolutions of conflict, and more. The Bar/Bat Mitzvah is an opportunity to help the budding teenager form a bridge from the perceived stigma of childhood to the excitement of abstract thinking, a new quality of friendships and loyalty, increased separation from parents, and an appreciation for law and responsibility (including those laws and commandments known as *mitzvot*) within the context of Jewish family and community values.

BIBLIOGRAPHY

Aichorn, A. *Wayward Youth.* New York: Viking Press, 1935.

Bandura, A. "The Stormy Decade: Fact or Fiction?" In D. Rogers (ed.), *Issues in Adolescent Psychology* (2nd ed.). New York: Appleton-Century-Croft, 1972.

Briggs, D.C. *Your Child's Self-Esteem.* Garden City, NY: Dolphin, 1975.

Coleman, J.D. *The Nature of Adolescence.* New York: Methuen, 1980.

Coleman, J.S. *The Adolescent Society.* New York: Free Press, 1961.

Douvan, E., and J. Adelson. *The Adolescent Experience.* New York: John Wiley, 1966.

Elder, G.H. "Adolescent Socialization and Development." In E. Borgatta and W. Lambert (eds.), *Handbook of Personality Theory and Research.* Chicago: Rand McNally, 1968.

_____. "Adolescence in the Life Cycle: An Introduction." In S.E. Dragstin and G.H. Elder (eds.), *Adolescence in the Life Cycle.* New York: John Wiley, 1975.

Erikson, E.H. *Childhood and Society.* (2nd ed.). New York: W.W. Norton, 1936.

_____. *Insight and Responsibility.* New York: W.W. Norton, 1964.

_____. *Identity and the Life Cycle.* New York: W.W. Norton, 1980.

_____. *The Life Cycle Completed: A Review.* New York: W.W. Norton, 1982.

Fogelman, K. *Britain's Sixteen-Year-Olds.* London: National Children's Bureau, 1976.

Hall, G.S. *Adolescence* (*Vols. I and II*). Englewood Cliffs, NJ: Prentice Hall, 1904.

Inhelder, B., and J. Piaget. *The Growth of Logical Thinking*: New York: Basic Books, 1958.

Rutter, Graham, Chadwick, and Yule. "Adolescent Turmoil: Fact or Fiction?" *Journal of Child Psychology and Psychiatry* 17, 35-56, 1976.

Thomas, E.J. "Role Theory, Personality and the Individual." In E.F. Borgatta and W. Lambert (eds.), *Handbook of Personality Theory and Research.* Chicago: Rand McNally, 1968.

Chapter 47
Growing Up: Expanding Our Bar and Bat Mitzvah Horizons

Sandy Eisenberg Sasso

The many Jewish rituals that accompany birth, marriage, and death reflect our attitudes toward life and death. In these cases, ceremony and symbol teach about meaning, but make no educational demands on the ritual participant. Bar or Bat Mitzvah is the only Jewish life cycle ritual that involves teachers and a formal educational process. To become a Bar or Bat Mitzvah, an individual is required to be educated Jewishly. Rabbis and teachers make the process meaningful by how and what they teach.

Most Bar and Bat Mitzvah programs focus on synagogue skills, Hebrew language, and chanting — and forget the powerful transition of the life cycle through which the child is passing. The person standing before the congregation, dressed in adult religious and secular attire, is really a little boy or girl with braces and sweating palms that threaten to betray a facade of sophisticated control.

The outer mask of calm responsibility and competence represents a deeper reality within the emerging adolescent. He or she is beginning to change, physically and emotionally. Poised at adulthood's portal is a boy or girl yearning for the continuity of childhood and the abandon of youth, as well as for the break with childishness and the independence of maturity.

B'nai Mitzvah curricula rarely acknowledge this ambivalence. The synagogue ought to remain connected to the whole child. Hebrew language, chanting, *tallit* and *tefillin*, Judaica knowledge and skills are vital for a growing Jewish mind. Yet, children who are for the first time wrapping their arms in *tefillin* are also using deodorant for the first time. Those who are choosing an appropriate *tallit* may also be choosing, with great interest, the correct size bra. Hormones are doing cartwheels inside the bodies of boys and girls. Voice changes, menstruation, and wet dreams are transforming cherub-like faces into portraits of men and women — while we teach only prayer, Torah and Haftarah reading, and chanting proficiency.

Beyond Desperation

Intellectual challenge and skill acquisition are vital. Uncertain that they can accomplish anything well in the adult world, B'nai Mitzvah take great personal pride in displaying Hebrew competence and adult liturgical leadership. They connect with the religious heritage of the Jewish people and gain the basic knowledge needed to take part in the adult Jewish worship community.

Yet, the daily miracle of growth that is taking place both inside and outside is often ignored. Despite the fact that the children we are teaching have just grown six inches in one year, started voluntary mixed seating in the classrooms, and are spending more and more time checking their appearance in the mirror, we rarely acknowledge this process as teachers, except perhaps with a sigh of despair. How difficult it is to teach this age!

But there can be more. We at Beth-El Zedeck have developed programs that connect growing up as a Jew to growing up. Our B'nai Mitzvah curriculum includes Hebrew language and a variety of skill sessions about *tallit* and *tefillin*, chanting, and liturgy. This chapter, however, will focus on those aspects that deal with the physical and emotional growth of the child.

Turning the Hearts of Parents to their Children

Every child in the seventh grade spends a morning in a special session designed (in cooperation with Planned Parenthood) to improve communication between parents and children. Boys come with their fathers (or other significant males in the family); girls with their mothers (or other significant females). The main purpose is to explore the emotional and social changes of growing up, though some attention is also given to reviewing physical changes. Parents are encouraged to recall when they were adolescents, and children are asked to imagine what they may be like as young adults. Other exercises ask parents to solve dilemmas as though they were youngsters, and ask the children to solve similar problems acting as adults. Parents and children learn to understand each other better.

Evaluations are overwhelmingly positive. "It was a wonderful chance to communicate with my son." "I loved being able to talk to my Dad and have him talk to me." "I liked the chance to get closer to my Mom. I feel I am closer now, with your help."

A session is then held with a brief trigger film on the hormonal and sexual changes during puberty and adolescence. Every participant is encouraged to write down questions anonymously. The questions are pulled at random from a box and discussed openly and honestly.

The message to the children is clear: *the Religious School cares about your growing*. The synagogue recognizes that you will now be able to have an *aliyah* and wants to prepare you for that. But it also realizes that your bodies will be able to make babies and wants to help prepare you to make responsible choices.

If we teach our children to talk Torah but not how to talk to their parents, we have failed. We must teach that Jewish skills are also skills for living, that what is of deepest personal concern is also of prime Jewish concern.

Letting Go

The family seminar is another aspect of our program. For a series of five or six weeks, a small group of parents and B'nai Mitzvah meet with the Rabbi. The sessions are informal and the agenda is varied. Of course, time is spent on gaining a better understanding of the Torah and in planning a group *tzedakah* project. But sessions are also spent on talking about growing up.

Parents are asked, "How do you want to treat your son/daughter as a thirteen-year old Bar/Bat Mitzvah? What freedoms should he/she have, what responsibilities? Do you have any worries?" B'nai Mitzvah are asked, "How do you want to be treated as a thirteen-year old Bar/Bat Mitzvah? What freedoms do you want? What responsibilities will you accept? Do you have any worries?"

The sharing of responses is enlightening for parents and children. Avenues for communication are opened.

During a portion of the seminar, students and parents discuss what is gained in becoming an adult, what must be put aside as one matures, and what part of being a child need not be lost. Parents' fear of loss of control in their child's life, and the young people's fear of expectations being set too high are typical issues that arise during this sharing session.

One seminar session explores with the B'nai Mitzvah how they can better learn to respect themselves and others. Adolescents need a chance to talk about the positive and negative aspects of peer pressure, about self-esteem, and how they allow themselves to be pushed around by others. They need to talk about the fear and embarrassment they have in standing up for what is not popular and for people who are different. They need to hear what their parents' and teachers' Jewish heritage has to say about being a *mensch*.

The Time Is Ripe

Teaching our children how to make *brachot* and to chant the Haftarah is important. But if we only teach them to *make* blessings and not to *be* a blessing, then we have failed them, as well as the meaning of Bar or Bat Mitzvah.

Our Bar/Bat Mitzvah programs need to be a celebration of both physical growth and spiritual maturation. Becoming Bar or Bat Mitzvah will have deeper impact if growing up as a Jew can be connected with growing up.

(Originally published in RECONSTRUCTIONIST, Vol. LIV, No. 6, April/May 1989. Reprinted by permission.)

Chapter 48
Celebration and Negotiation: How To Keep the Divorce Battle off the Bimah

Sally Weber

A few years ago, the B'nai Mitzvah counselor at one of our larger synagogues anguished: "I don't know what I'm going to do. Almost half of the children up for Bar/Bat Mitzvah this year come from divorced families. Every time I meet with a parent to discuss the ceremony, it becomes a battleground. All the issues that didn't get finished in the divorce get played out in my office. The child gets trapped in the middle. I get trapped there, too. It's a crisis-a-week, and it's the child and the *simchah* which get lost."

One of the most significant findings of the 1990 National Jewish Population Study was that the Jewish family which we once considered normative — two born-Jewish parents in a first marriage with two children — represented a scant 17% of our families. Nearly half of the marriages now occurring will end in divorce. The rate of remarriage is relatively high, so our children are increasingly growing up in households with multiple parents, multiple siblings, multiple grandparents. Perhaps it is time to stop thinking of our families as "normative" or "non-normative," and to simply think of them as diverse.

In response to such conditions, the synagogue staff, in conjunction with Jewish Family Service, began looking at ways the synagogue might address the needs of the changing Jewish family. It became clear that these needs must be addressed as issues and not as problems, lest we find ourselves institutionally and communally in a state of constantly responding to crises. Our goal was to use "problem solving" approaches rather than "crisis intervention" as a mechanism for working with Jewish families going through major life cycle events.

The program was piloted by Valley Beth Shalom, a large Conservative congregation in the Los Angeles area. Called "Celebration and Negotiation," it is based on the assumption that if families are provided with practical models for approaching the major issues and decisions of the Bar/Bat Mitzvah preparation period, they will be able to negotiate those issues instead of letting the issues cloud the celebration. A further assumption is that, although there may well continue to be areas of profound dispute, these areas will be limited and "containable." They will therefore be more amenable to resolution or, at least, less explosive.

THE PROGRAM

This program has two primary components: (1) educating and sensitizing staff and congregants to the issues of divorced and remarried families approaching major Jewish life cycle celebrations, and (2) hands-on problem solving workshops and discussions for families preparing for those celebrations. Unlike many synagogue programs which begin with a social/educational approach leading to the Jewish involvement of a family, this program starts with Jewish involvement and teaches skills both to enhance that celebration and to strengthen family life.

Components of the program are:

1. A major Shabbat program during which the Rabbi delivers a sermon on the changing nature of the Jewish family in general, and the "Celebration and Negotiation" program in particular.
2. Staff development sessions with Rabbinic, education, and youth staff on the implications of the National Jewish Population Study and how it

relates to the synagogue population targeted by this program.

3. Workshop series with target families to help discuss concerns and develop new formats for celebration which fit family circumstances.
4. Workshops for congregants on the changing Jewish family, to sensitize the congregation to issues of our new family models.
5. Individual families will counsel with the Rabbinic staff when issues beyond the scope of this program arise. Issues of finances will certainly come up in these sessions.
6. In addition, we have developed a manual of new models for ritual celebration dealing with such issues as: "What will the invitation say?" "Who will be on the *bimah*, and with whom?" "Do I have a family table at the reception?" and more.

Who Will Attend

(Note: Families invited to this program will also participate in the regular family Bar/Bat Mitzvah orientation programs normally offered by the synagogue.)

This program is offered two times a year. It consists of three sessions for families with Bar/Bat Mitzvah dates of 8-12 months away. This assumes that:

1. Families are assigned their Bar/Bat Mitzvah dates at least 18 months in advance of the *simchah*.
2. School and/or synagogue registrations indicate which families are divorced and/or remarried; or
3. Synagogue staff knows the congregation well enough to have this information readily available.

The Rabbi sends letters to the targeted families, inviting them to attend three special parent/child sessions. There is a follow-up to this invitation from the Director of Education or B'nai Mitzvah staff. Emphasis is placed upon the importance of having both parents attend this program. The facilitator, a social worker, is available to talk with families in advance of the program regarding questions, concerns, or simply the logistics of everyone coming together.

When one parent or parental family lives out of the area, it is important to work with the participating family on ways of keeping that parent included in the process. The first method will be group problem-solving: it is quite likely that other participants in the program have either already had this experience or have friends or family members who have been through this. They may well have creative suggestions about how to proceed. Again, this helps normalize a non-traditional living situation for the Bar/Bat Mitzvah child. We will also encourage phone calls after the sessions to share what has been discussed, working long-distance on the "Consensus and Concern" journal (discussed below), or simple letter writing between child and parent. The social work staff can meet with families to discuss particular issues which arise in these situations and develop a plan which will work best for everyone concerned.

Again, there may be families for whom the pain of divorce was so intense that these approaches to communication are impossible — families who simply cannot talk to one another. There are also families in which a child has had two Bar/Bat Mitzvah ceremonies and two receptions, because of the parents' inability to come together on any common ground. It is crucial for us to know who these families are and to work with them individually, to ease the way as much as possible within our own congregational system. Social workers and Rabbinic staff must be particularly sensitive to these issues and available to these families.

Family Workshops

Following is a brief summary of the "Celebration and Negotiation" family workshops. Discussion techniques are being shared in order to indicate the variety of ways in which family issues can be discussed. Ultimately the following should be accomplished:

1. Families articulate their areas of consensus regarding the *simchah*, as well as their areas of concern. It is important to point out that these areas may well be different for each family — one family may have easily decided upon the wording of the invitation, but be very tense about who receives *aliyot*. Another may be very clear about the *aliyot*, but tense about the *tallit* presentation. The mere act of sharing areas of consensus and concern begins the task of providing viable models for celebration. Families are asked to create a "Concern and Consensus" journal in which they record issues they agree upon and issues which will require some degree of negotiation. This provides a working

tool for breaking issues into more manageable parts. Also, families can return to the journal at the end of the program to see where they have reached additional areas of consensus or to record possible models of negotiation which might lead to later consensus. For many families, journal entries will highlight their personal trail of successes in negotiating new models of communication.

2. Areas of decision making will be delineated, including the wording of invitations, how *aliyot* and *bimah* honors will be determined, and who will make what presentations to the Bar/Bat Mitzvah child. Decisions regarding the reception will also be discussed, including issues of seating, who is invited, who introduces whom, etc. Many of these issues are benign, some may seem banal, but all are crucial to include in order to assure families that there is no such thing as a stupid question and there is nothing obvious about how things should be handled. Again, any issue which can be negotiated comfortably clears the way for a greater possibility of negotiation around more difficult issues.
3. Issues of who pays for what are not discussed. Rather, frameworks are suggested within which those discussions can occur, emphasizing that these issues are best placed in the arena of adult discourse so as not to put the child in the middle. Rabbinic and social work staff will be available to meet individually with families for whom financial issues are a major problem.

A variety of discussion formats can be used in this program. For example, adults and children will write separate responses to "What Bar/Bat Mitzvah means to me," "What I am most looking forward to," and "What concerns me the most." The facilitator collects these responses and shares some of them. For parent responses, the facilitator asks the teens, "How many of you think your parent wrote this?" For teen responses, he/she asks the same of the parents. This exercise is an extremely effective family communication starter. Children will invariably be startled by a parent's response and comment, "Why didn't you know that was mine?" or "How could you think I'd write that?" Parental reactions are usually similar. Equally important, this exercise highlights common themes, as many similar issues and feelings will be repeated by different families. The facilitator lists key issues on the blackboard and uses these as part of the program's agenda. Thus, the curriculum is individualized for each series.

We also have parents meet with parents and students meet with students to share mutual concerns and mutual suggestions. Information from these sessions is then shared with the group as a whole. This encourages open communication and the sharing of common issues and concerns; in some instances, it can result in suggestions for resolution. We also have parents meet with children other than their own for some of the discussions. Sometimes it is easier to hear issues and concerns from someone else's child!

Specific problem solving techniques include keeping a "Concern and Consensus" journal, brainstorming, and the recommendations of solution by the staff. Using examples from families who have already been through the Bar/Bat Mitzvah experience, we present what worked for other families and how it might be adapted to fit the particular situations of these program participants. This is a very important part of the program.

Staff Training

The Rabbinic, educational, and youth staff have several sessions on the implications of the National Jewish Population Study and how that relates to the synagogue population targeted by this program. Personnel who work directly with Bar/Bat Mitzvah students, including part-time tutors, must also be involved in this training.

Divorces and remarriages are not secrets. Nor are they new to our experiences. However, in reality, synagogue membership tends to reflect Noah's ark — couples enter in pairs, either at the point of marriage or at the point of parenthood. It is more unusual (although not unknown) for a single parent to join a synagogue without a previous connection with that institution. Moreover, because of the financial stress experienced by divorcing families, we are more likely to lose one or both divorced households within two years after divorce unless we commit ourselves to active outreach to those families.

In addition, a remarried family presents (as they generally should) as "the" family. Unless there is reason to respond otherwise, our staff members do not necessarily have a relationship with those parents and family members not in the immediate picture. However, when Bar/Bat Mitzvah planning approaches, grandparents, aunts, uncles, new wives, new husbands, and new siblings suddenly spring forth, leaving us to figure out what the extended family really looks like. We do not always have much time to reflect on how to work toward the inclusion of complex family segments in what seems like a straightforward religious celebration.

Most synagogue schools by now use registration forms that obtain information regarding marital status of all parents, addresses other than primary residence, phone numbers, and custodial arrangements. Most schools have grappled, more or less successfully, with issues such as how to include both custodial parents in teacher conferences, and how to assure that both parents are notified of school events. In fewer instances, schools have explored ways of keeping non-custodial parents involved in their child's Religious School education, either through special events for students who spend weekends with non-custodial parents or through school newsletters sent to custodial and non-custodial parents alike. However, week in and week out, we rarely need to deal directly with the extended families (i.e., grandparents, new spouses, new siblings). How do we suddenly incorporate all those family members into our celebrations, or do we? A friend once joked that she had to show a videotape of extended family members at another *simchah* to her son in order to help him recognize people who would be at his Bar Mitzvah. It wasn't such a joke; in fact, it was a creative way of introducing a child to the sudden appearance of a new extended family.

We need to provide staff with a functional understanding of the widening definition of "normative." They need to know what Jewish families today look like. They also need to know what their own school population looks like. Teachers and Rabbinic staff often assume "old norms." While knowing that changes are occurring in the Jewish family, they still assume that those changes are happening "out there" and not within their own institutions.

If we continue to assume that two parent, never divorced families are the norm and anything else is an aberration, then each time a divorced/remarried family appears, we will be forced to reinvent the wheel. That is, each family is handled individually, often on a crisis basis. We need to help our teachers generalize from these family experiences, to begin "normalizing" the experience of these family structures in order to help deal with their issues supportively and directly.

Next, our teachers need to know that the issue of divorce and remarriage is not a secret to our children. And while this situation may be more or less painful to them, it is also a fact of life and a factor in their lives. Teachers need to speak in a forthright manner to children. In discussing an upcoming Bar/Bat Mitzvah, the teacher needs to say, "I know some of you have more than one family. Your families may have some special issues about how to involve people in your *simchah*. The synagogue will be here to help with that." Thus, children from more complex family circles can immediately feel included in congregational life. This also helps open the door for other children to share models of what happened at their family *simchah*. Positive or negative, their sharing will provide a baseline of openness and discussion which will help keep them connected to the synagogue regardless of family make-up.

Congregational Sensitivity

The training of the congregation occurs on many levels. First, there is the implied or explicit message from the pulpit. While supporting the centrality of the two parent family, we also need to find pulpit language which addresses the status and issues of alternative family structures. Descriptions such as "broken families" and "intact families" must be reconsidered. Can a family be "intact" with a strong, functioning, caring single parent? Of course. Is the only "mending" which can occur after divorce a remarriage? Of course not. Yet, we use words which create the aura of failure, of victims, then decry the self-fulfilling prophecy we have created when children and their parents become isolated and alienated in our synagogue communities. Surely this issue is worthy of a Shabbat sermon.

Equally worthy is the assistance which can be given from the pulpit in helping generalize and "normalize" these family situations. There are some who would argue that to do so is to encourage the breakup of the

Jewish family. In our program, we would argue the opposite: that this kind of recognition helps strengthen the core Jewish family values, whatever the composition of the household at any given moment.

Planning the Simchah

This program operates under the assumption that by dealing with problem areas directly and with sensitivity in a group setting, we can help even those in the most complex family structures to work together for the benefit of the child. Of course, there are situations which are not comfortably resolved in such a setting. And there are families for whom the conflict of divorce has been so painful that any issue will provoke a battle. However, it is our assumption that, by providing an arena for family discussions and for the creation and sharing of functional models of celebrations, these famiies will be in a better position to negotiate those issues which are more complex or more volatile. Lessening the areas of contention can strengthen a family's ability to problem solve in those more difficult arenas.

One of the areas of contention has to do with the wording on invitations. This is not as simple a matter as it would at first appear to be. Wording reflects personal status and family configuration. Each family will have its own set of issues. Providing models of how other families have dealt with this will be an important first step in demonstrating both acceptance and problem solving. Ideally, a workshop leader or Bar/Bat Mitzvah counselor should have a scrapbook of invitations available to show families in order to share both the wording and the overall beauty of the Bar/Bat Mitzvah invitation. A very brief example regarding the wording of invitations follows.

1. An invitation from the Bar/Bat Mitzvah child:

With great pleasure my family and I
Are delighted to invite you to join in our simchah as
I lead the congregation in prayer and
am called to the Torah as a Bat Mitzvah.

Sarah Cohen

2. An invitation from the parents, when both have remarried:

We are delighted to invite you to share
with our families this joyous occasion when
our daughter
Sarah Cohen
will be called to the Torah as a Bat Mitzvah.

Judy and Paul Schwartz
George and Denise Cohen

(Notice that in this example, the Bat Mitzvah girl's parents' names come first.)

3. An invitation from parents when there has not been a remarriage, or when a decision has been made not to list the names of new spouses:

We invite you to share in our happiness
when our daughter
Sarah Michelle
is called to the Torah as a Bat Mitzvah.

Judy Cohen and George Cohen

4. An invitation from parents when one has remarried:

We invite you to share in our happiness
when our daughter
Sarah Michelle
is called to the Torah as a Bat Mitzvah.

Judy Cohen
George and Denise Cohen

A second brief example concerns presenting the *tallit.* This is potentially the most moving and the most painful moment for divorced parents. At this time, parents share not only the *tallit,* but also memories of the family's beginnings. For some families, it becomes a "this is your life," for others, a moment of sharing the hopes and dreams of the past 13 years. For some families, it is a moment of sharing an oral "ethical will." In most instances, mother and father make the *tallit* presentation together. However, there are also times when parents who are not divorced make statements to their children separately. A case in point: After laboring for nine months to make a *tallit* for my older daughter, I realized that I had woven my presentation to her into the threads of the *tallit*. My husband and I decided that I would present the *tallit* at the beginning of the service; he would share his thoughts as a proud Dad later in the service. It fit comfortably into the morning and, indeed, we used the same format for our younger daughter's Bat Mitzvah ceremony. Some people were surprised that we hadn't made a joint presentation. For us, it fit very comfortably into our family style and into the purpose of the morning. The important thing was the openness of the Rabbi to letting us choose, within reason, the best way for us to convey our pride and joy at our daughter's Jewish coming of age.

I share the above example because it is important that families know from the onset that there is rarely only one way to accomplish something, that even those traditions which appear to be etched in stone are, in fact, traditions and not *halachah*. (It is also crucial that the B'nai Mitzvah staff be sensitive to and supportive of this point of view.)

The first question, of course, is whether or not the parents want to make a joint presentation. If the answer is yes, it's settled. However, there may be complicating factors — "Yes, but you can't bring your new husband up with you" is a key complication! For some families, the pain of divorce is so intense that it is not possible to stand before the child and present a *tallit* which, for them, may expose the failed dreams of the family rather than the celebration of the child's achievements as a person. There are other complications: A father who wishes to present his son with his own father's *tallit* and a mother who wants to present the *tallit* she purchased for her child on her first visit to Israel.

There is no list of solutions which can be provided for these situations. However, there are several ways in which this subject can be approached in a group setting:

1. Sharing and listing solutions which other families have already agreed upon may offer alternatives which some families had not yet considered. It also provides the opportunity to discuss what goes into this kind of decision making. For example, it may be a time to help the parents refocus on the one thing they still have in common: namely, their child. It provides an opportunity to acknowledge the pain of failed dreams, but also to support the dream which survived: that their child would grow to Jewish maturity.
2. Sharing and listing obstacles to solution-finding is more touchy, as it is much more personal. However, for families willing to engage in this process, it is an opportunity to objectify somewhat very emotional issues. Such discussions must be held on a voluntary basis, i.e., "Is there anyone who would be comfortable sharing what stands in the way of working out this situation?" The group facilitator then has the opportunity to rephrase the issue and even to comment, "Yes, that's a problem many families have." This comment in itself helps normalize what feels like an abnormal and isolated family dilemma.

During this discussion, it is important for the facilitator to know the boundaries of what the synagogue will and won't do, e.g., is it possible for parents to make separate presentations? Never offer possibilities unless they are, in fact, possible. It is also important for the facilitator, upon hearing an unusual but seemingly appropriate request, to say, "I think that's an excellent thought. I don't know if it's possible, but I will discuss it with the Rabbi and get back to you."

Taking an extreme example of the family with two *tallitot* to present (a true example) is it possible to present both *tallitot* using one for leading the service and one for reading the Torah? Yes, it's a forced compromise, awkward at best, but it can be turned into something positive, rather than adversarial. The presentation can go as follows: "Sarah, we have a major dilemma today — several *tallitot*! Dad and I have struggled long and hard on what to do, for here we have a *tallit* which represents the continuity of your family history and another which represents the freshness of your moving into the world as an independent Jewish adult. One *tallit* belonged to your grandfather, your father's father. The second was purchased by your Mom, especially for you, on her first trip to Israel. We offer both of them to you today — one to wear as you recite the words of prayer which all Jews read on Shabbat, the other to wear as you read your Torah portion, the part of today's service which is distinctive and unique to your Bat Mitzvah."

One of the purposes of providing the above discussion is to posit ways in which the facilitator can encourage solution-finding. It should be obvious, at this point, that this is not a program which staff members can walk into without a great deal of forethought and planning. Many of the models which can be shared as part of the healing process are models which they themselves will bring to the sessions.

There are many more examples of problem solving by families involved in this program. Central, however, are not the individual success stories, but the attitude, the openness on the part of the synagogue and its staff, to the reality of the changing Jewish family and all of its complexities.

CONCLUSION

We cannot ask family members to put their feelings of anger, frustration, and sorrow aside. But we can ask them to let us help them reframe their issues, refocus on new possibilities, and work together in the very limited sphere of this crucial life passage. By responding to this situation through a Jewish family program such as this, the synagogue enters into the complexity of the changing family as a supportive and compassionate partner.

Chapter 49
The Significance of the Social Aspects of Bar/Bat Mitzvah

Stuart Schoenfeld

The ritual of Bar Mitzvah was added to Jewish practice fairly late (Millgram, 1971) and until recently was only one of the many ways Jews sacralized the passage of time through the year and through life. In the modern period, as Jews have discarded many of the ways they have used to make time, place, and behavior sacred, Bar Mitzvah has been retained, and a parallel Bat Mitzvah ceremony has been initiated. This early adolescent ritual occasion has become one of the crucial times during which Jews construct the interconnections between synagogue, Jewish school, family, and individual biography.

This chapter reports one part of a research project which has explored the modern meaning of the Bar/Bat Mitzvah.[1] Methodologically, the research has been influenced by the assumption that one must study more than the formal norms for the ritual; one must study its enactment. This implies studying the organizational norms in particular settings, the process of preparing which the family goes through, and the social events which celebrate the ritual event.

All aspects of this study have been framed by a similar set of theoretical issues. The broadest question concerns the impact of modern social change on religion in general and Judaism in particular. Within this broad problematic, the research has been heavily influenced by the position of Thomas Luckmann on religious change and modernization (1967). Luckmann argued that the formal source of authority in modern society lies within the individual. Rather than simply accept and live by a received tradition, the individual in modern society acts as a consumer of many unintegrated systems of meaning, autonomously assembling a more or less personal product.

This thesis about modern religion and individualism gives a particular twist to the distinction used by Liebman in the study of Judaism (1973) and by other scholars — albeit in somewhat different ways — between elite and folk religion. When the emphasis of authority was thought to lie primarily on the side of tradition, the religious elite, who are responsible for conserving and adapting the sacred tradition, were able to claim the legitimacy to define religious belief and practice and to channel change within a process which they could usually control. The imminent authority of folk beliefs and practices, which emerge from the needs of daily life, could, however, never be ignored. In traditional Judaism the religious elite would sometimes campaign vigorously against folk beliefs and practices which they found subversive, but they would also accommodate others into their view of what was permissible, or deal with deviant beliefs and practices simply by overlooking them.

The relationship between elite and folk changes in modern times, when the emphasis of authority shifts from the elite conservers of tradition to the individual. It becomes possible, and frequent, for individual adherents to use the resources of the tradition, along with other resources, to create their own personal systems of beliefs and practices. Some individuals do this more self-consciously than others; the personal systems created also vary in their sophistication and coherence. Bar and Bat Mitzvah is one of those times, a socially structured, regularly occurring time, when the synagogue, the Jewish school, the Jewish family and the early adolescent confront each other over the relative weight of institutional authority versus individual autonomy, when the question of just what it is that people are doing when they think and act as Jews is addressed.

Consequently, each part of the research project on Bar/Bat Mitzvah addresses a different dimension of a common theme — the need for the people involved to somehow address the tension between the Judaism which is conserved and transmitted by the institution, and the Judaism which is the personal product of each family.[2] While the study acknowledges the traditional rhetoric of Bar/Bat Mitzvah as a rite of passage marking the transition to adult responsibility, it also acknowledges that this rhetoric is far from an accurate description of what the event means to the participants. The reality of being a thirteen-year-old Jewish child and of being Jewish parents in late twentieth century North America is far more complex than the ritual rhetoric. In a period when the substantive content of Jewish identity is in doubt and in which the transmission of Jewish identity from one generation to the next is in doubt, Bar and Bat Mitzvah perforce acquire many of the characteristics of rituals of identification, occasions where the child and family are not accepting a clear version of Jewish identity but socially constructing (or reconstructing) their own versions of it.

This chapter examines some aspects of the meaning of Bar/Bat Mitzvah to the family as expressed in the social events which surround the ritual. It is in these settings that families and B'nai Mitzvah have the freedom to write scripts or adapt social conventions to express their understanding of the encounter between the tradition the ritual identifies them with and the other things they have chosen to make important in their lives. Specifically, this chapter discusses whom it is important to have present at which social events, and what the family is communicating to those present through what they say and do.

The primary source of data is a set of interviews in the Spring of 1989 with 20 families who were soon to have a Bar/Bat Mitzvah celebration or who had recently had one at a large Reform temple. Interviews lasted about one hour and covered other topics in addition to the social events.[3] In addition, six interviews were held with temple staff involved with Bar/Bat Mitzvah. Since every congregation, even those within the same movement, has its own particular history, customs, and attitudes, the findings on Bar/Bat mitzvah celebration among families at this temple cannot be taken as "typical" of all congregations, even of Reform ones. They do, however, have the advantage of being based on systematic research, and not relying on the impressions of Bar/Bat Mitzvah celebrations which may be formed by newspaper accounts, explanations offered by religious authorities, or gossip.

"WE INVITE YOU TO CELEBRATE . . ." GATHERING TOGETHER SOCIAL NETWORKS

The formal rhetoric of Bar/Bat Mitzvah is that of incorporation into the Jewish community. This is symbolically achieved at the religious ritual, with the synagogue "community" representing the Jewish community and with gestures of solidarity with Jews outside the synagogue community — inscriptions into the *sefer* Bar/Bat Mitzvah in Israel, the designation of gifts to a Jewish institution — acknowledged before the congregation.

The celebrations, in contrast, involve membership in specific social networks. This may be initially seen by noting those people who are at the synagogue but not at the celebrations. Most weeks there is more than one Bar/Bat Mitzvah; three on one morning is quite common. After services, the families split into different groups for their celebrations. They jointly sponsor a simple congregational *Kiddush*, but rarely themselves attend. The congregational *Kiddush* is attended by those who are at services but are not invited to a Bar/Bat Mitzvah luncheon.

The children, most of whom have been enrolled in the congregational school for at least three years, do not, as a rule, invite congregational school classmates to their Bar/Bat Mitzvah. They will do so only if there is another connection, such as being in the same public school class. While the temple may be the setting for symbolic identification with a community, the cohort of children going through religious school together is not a social group which celebrates together.

The congregational Rabbis and Cantor only receive Bar/Bat Mitzvah invitations if they have had a personal relationship to the family or child. With a Bar/Bat Mitzvah service almost every week, and several on many weeks, an expectation in the congregation that one of the Rabbis or the Cantor would be normally included in the formal invitations and associated celebrations would oblige the Rabbis and Cantor to devote most weekends to Bar/Bat Mitzvah parties. Consequently, invitations are sent only when there is a special relationship. Religious school teachers, Hebrew school teachers, and the Bar/Bat Mitzvah tutors are also normally invited only on those occasions when they have an unusual relationship with the family or child. An expectation of their routine presence would also involve them in extensive social obligations. Sometimes teachers and tutors who receive an invitation will attend the service, but decline the invitation to the social events. Other times, teachers and tutors will acknowledge the courtesy, but decline the invitation to attend either the service or the reception.

The members of the family compile a basic guest list for the major social event, but they also choose from within this list to invite people to the other events which are typically held over the course of the weekend. The basic invitation list is composed of a larger number of people on the parent's list and a list of friends compiled by the Bar/Bat Mitzvah. Guest lists in the study ranged from 60 to over 300 people.

The Parents' List

In planning the social events around the Bar/Bat Mitzvah, most parents take the entire weekend as their frame of reference. Almost every family will have friends and relatives from out of town attending. Bar/Bat Mitzvah weekends are often reunions of people who do not ordinarily see each other. There is a felt social obligation to invite out of town guests to more intimate social gatherings before or after the main reception. The Bar/Bat Mitzvah weekend is also an intense emotional experience for the family, one to be shared with those who are emotionally close, whether physically distant or not. The smaller social gatherings of the Friday night dinner, the Sunday brunch or the informal Sunday at home are part of conventional practice, attended by far fewer than those who are invited to the main reception. Those attending these smaller gatherings may be out of town guests, an intimate circle of close friends and relatives, or a mixture of the two.

The major social events described by families in the study varied in time and location. Some were luncheons immediately after services; others were held on Saturday or Sunday evening. Luncheons were held at the temple social hall, but more frequently at hotel restaurants. Evening affairs were held at hotel restaurants, private clubs and at home.

A professional in the Jewish community recalled that some fifteen years ago, when her children were on the Bar/Bat Mitzvah "circuit," the typical pattern was a catered luncheon and an evening open house. Some families in the study followed this pattern; others hosted both a luncheon and a dinner dance. When there are two major social events, the guest lists often differ. Everyone is invited to lunch. Fewer people, but usually all the friends of the Bar/Bat Mitzvah, may be invited to the dinner dance. The move toward two major social events indicates a more elaborate style of celebration. Beyond the difference in scale, there is a difference in tone. Luncheons, even when they include dancing, are more sober, while the dinner dances are more flashy and exciting.

Parents with large local extended families had the largest guest lists. A number of these parents constructed the guest list according to how budget size for the catered affair could accommodate extended families — "uncles, aunts, and first cousins of each parent, with children of first cousins included only if budget allowed." Five first cousins for each parent would produce ten invitations; their children would add almost twenty more guests. At $65 per person, children of first cousins add $1,300 to the cost of the catered affair. Consequently, some families did not invite children of first cousins. When this logic is used, the B'nai Mitzvah are given the message that extended family at the degree of "second cousins" (children of parents' cousins) are not part of the group with whom the parents expect their children to socialize, even though second cousins are the same age cohort as the Bar or Bat Mitzvah.

It was more common, however, for parents to express an alternative criterion for inviting relatives. The alternative criterion is "We invite those people who are important in the life of our child. The relatives that we see socially and who know our child are the ones we want to have share the occasion with us. The others, regardless of degree of relationship, will have to understand and not be offended."

A similar criterion was also expressed by a number of parents about inviting their friends. "The friends we invite to the Bar/Bat Mitzvah celebration are those friends that are part of our child's life." One father, whose income level would have allowed a very large guest list, put it this way. "If you want to pay off a social obligation to your accountant, have a party, but don't invite him to your child's Bar Mitzvah celebration. We don't want people to feel obligated to give presents to a child they don't know or for our child to see a room of unfamiliar faces. It's his party."

The B'nai Mitzvah's Lists

The numerical range on the children's guest lists was remarkable. Some invited only a few close friends. Others invited 40 to 60 friends. In some cases the 40 to 60 was an edited version of a somewhat longer list. The number of children's friends invited was, of course, related to the scale of the social event. The larger number in total, the more child's friends could be accommodated.

There were, however, other aspects to the number of friends invited than simply scale. Some children at the temple were enrolled in one of two Jewish day schools. The schools encourage children to invite all their classmates and this was in fact very common. Some children also had diverse social networks. They wanted to include in their celebration friends from public school, the neighborhood, summer camp, sports teams, dance classes, and children of friends of the family.

The children's lists, like those of the parents, include those with whom they are more or less intimate. Sometimes other children are invited because it is not polite to leave them out. For example, all the Jewish children in the public school or day school class may be invited even though there may not be any emotional closeness. As well, it is possible for parents who are concerned about their child's social contacts to encourage the child to extend his/her list. On the other hand, some of the children are genuinely gregarious. Their lists are made up of individuals that they know from their social networks. During one interview, a child began discussing with her parents the large number of friends she had invited. As she complained about having to lower the number on her list, she gave several examples, by name, of friends who had been excluded, with particulars about having just been out with them or over to their houses.

Non-Jewish friends, from public school or the neighborhood, are frequently invited. Their presence can be a source of stress to the Bar/Bat Mitzvah. One child, with few Jewish friends, told her parents that she'd heard non-Jewish classmates making jokes about the Bar/Bat Mitzvah service and asked if she could invite her non-Jewish friends only to the reception. The parents checked with the parents of another child in the same class who had invited non-Jewish friends. The classmate's parents confirmed the parents' opinion that the child and the non-Jewish friends had considered the presence of non-Jewish friends at the service to be positive. Consequently, the child was reassured and the non-Jewish friends about whom there was an issue were invited to both the temple service and the party.

Invitations to children's friends, as for parents, follow the norm of reciprocity. Children who invite many friends are themselves likely to receive many invitations. In one family, the parents, when asked whether their child had been invited to other Bar or Bat Mitzvah parties, replied with a laugh, "She's booked well into the next century." They continued, "This has been going on since September [the interview was conducted in April]. She thinks that what you normally do on a weekend is to go to a Bar or Bat Mitzvah. There's rarely a week off."

This is not a universal pattern, but it is common. The year of Bar/Bat Mitzvah is for many a year of party dresses and suits, of learning and practicing social skills, of fitting into the social cliques which teenagers seem to need as part of their strategy of coping with the many uncertainties and insecurities of adolescence. Among staff of Jewish day schools, there is concern about those cases where the recommendation to invite classmates is only partially followed and a few unpopular children in the class are routinely excluded. Sometimes parents will give children a specific number of friends they can invite or ask them to reduce a long invitation list. In one case, parents insisted that the child's initial list of 90 friends be reduced to 60.

ASPECTS OF VERBAL AND SYMBOLIC COMMUNICATION AT THE MAIN SOCIAL EVENT

There are differences between each enactment of the synagogue ritual. Even more so, the social events differ one from the other. There are, however, among the families in the study, a number of aspects of the social events which are variations within a conventional pattern of celebration. Adults and adolescents were often separated. A poster-sized picture of the Bar/Bat Mitzvah was sometimes on display. Speeches were usually given by members of the family, followed by a candlelighting ceremony at the conclusion of the meal. Videotaping the social event was very common.

Separation of Adults and Adolescents

At the large formal receptions, there is often a physical separation of adults and adolescents. While at some receptions, the friends of the Bar/Bat Mitzvah will be served dinner in the same room as the adults, at many others a separate room is set aside for the kids so that they may party in their own style. There may be their own music, and food which is more suited to their tastes. There is certainly a more relaxed atmosphere, as the adolescents are not subject to the scrutiny of adults and need not abide by adult norms of polite behavior. The B'nai Mitzvah move back and forth from the adult space to the adolescent space. They prefer — based on what they say about what they do — to be with their peers.

Adults and adolescents may be completely separated. It is common to have a separate kids' party, with lower per capita cost than a formal reception. The luncheon may include adults and close friends, with a party for the child's friends in the evening instead of a formal dinner dance. Alternatively, a party for the child's friends may be held on a weekend after the Bar/Bat Mitzvah service. The focus of the Bar/Bat Mitzvah weekend itself is kept on the family — the group the child is coming from. The party for the child's friends is usually the last in the sequence of social events — a structural indication of the group the child is being incorporated into.

A Poster-sized Picture of the Bar/Bat Mitzvah

As the guests enter the reception, they may find on display a life-sized photograph of the Bar or Bat Mitzvah. The poster is informal, showing the child dressed for some preferred leisure time activity, for example, in a sports uniform. Guests will pause to write and sign well-wishes in the margins surrounding the photograph. The poster becomes a memento, suitable for hanging in the child's room next to the posters of teen television stars, musicians, and sports heros.

This poster may be contrasted to an older, but still used, photographic memento, the dignified photo of the child in synagogue clothes, wearing a *tallit* and perhaps holding a prayer book, on display in the family living room. The pious photo in the living room is an iconographic representation of the child's incorporation into family and tradition. The poster in the bedroom expresses the child's identification with the adolescent culture of his/her peers. In this culture, mass media provide role models, albeit often highly stereotyped ones, which the child, in the company of adolescent peers, uses as an important resource in the process of constructing his/her sense of self. The poster on the bedroom wall, next to pop culture posters, puts a heroic image of the child right up there with his/her role models. Another type of photographic record, the videotape, will be discussed below.

Speeches

Most, but not all events include a sibling as master of ceremonies, a speech by one or both parents and a speech by the Bar/Bat Mitzvah. The contents of these speeches are conventional. They mingle bits of biography, jokes about the family, and expressions of love and pride. The conventional form is adapted by each speaker. Sometimes the adaptation of the conventional form is very effectively done. One father, who was in a "blended household" — two parents with previous marriages and children from both marriages living together — began by saying, "Sheila and I are a precocious couple. We've been married five years and have a thirteen-year-old son." He was adapting a conventional form — the making of a joke at the beginning of the parental speech — and using it to get across an important message. The first thing he wanted assembled guests to hear was, "As far as my wife and I are concerned, this boy is not hers or mine, but ours." Other examples could be given of speeches which clearly celebrate the good feelings the members of the family have about each other, and of speeches which are more reserved.

Candle Lighting

The candlelighting ceremony — a twentieth century American invention — is very common. The Bar/Bat

Mitzvah stands with a lit taper at a table with 13 other candles. Guests, sometimes singly but usually several at a time, are called up to light the candles. Special things may be said about each person or group so honored. The band may play different music for each person or group as they go up. At the conclusion the Bar/Bat Mitzvah, usually with the help of his/her immediate family, blows out the candles. The band then strikes up "Happy Birthday" and the Bar Mitzvah cake is cut and served.

This secular ritual incorporates many things. It honors members of the extended family by giving them a secular version of an *"aliyah."* At the temple service the Bar/Bat Mitzvah is called up for the honor of reading the Torah. Usually only two other *aliyot* will be reserved for members of the Bar/Bat Mitzvah's family. At the candle lighting ceremony many more people can be called up. The parallel to having an *aliyah* is even more pronounced when the candles surround a Bar/Bat Mitzvah cake which has been made in the shape of a Torah scroll. Candle lighting is also a reminder of two common Jewish home observances, lighting Sabbath candles and Chanukah candles, and it incorporates the practice of lighting birthday candles. It may be important to note, however, that nothing sacred goes on in this ritual. There are no blessings, no references to Jewish beliefs or practices. The exclusion of religion symbolizes that while the family's Jewish identity has a religious dimension, it has a purely social dimension as well.

Videotaping

The videotape of the Bar/Bat Mitzvah is the current stage in a process that began with photo albums and home movies. The convention to memorialize family events with photographic records is very well established. As Sontag writes:

> Memorializing the achievements of individuals considered as members of families . . . is the earliest popular use of photographs. . . . Through photographs, each family constructs a portrait-chronicle of itself — a portable kit of images that bears witness to its connectedness. . . . Photography becomes a rite of family life just when, in the industrializing countries of Europe and America, the very institution of the family starts undergoing radical surgery. As that claustrophobic unit, the nuclear family, was being carved out of a much larger family aggregate, photography came along to memorialize, to restate symbolically, the imperiled continuity and vanishing extendedness of family life. These ghostly traces, photographs, supply the token presence of dispersed relatives. A family's photograph album is generally about the extended family — and, often, is all that remains of it (1977:8).

Entering the temple foyer, one sees a large permanent sign strictly forbidding taking pictures of any kind during the services. It is understandable that photography during the service is seen as disruptive.[4] It is nevertheless ironic that as a consequence, the videotape record which is a basic resource for remembering the event contains scenes of the social event, with little acknowledgement of the synagogue ritual.

The videotapes are done by professionals, friends, or members of the family. There are some conventional structures. A composite gives an idea of what the videotapes contain. A shot of the invitation identifies the content. A montage of shots of child from birth to his/her Bar/Bat Mitzvah establishes a developmental context. This montage will include shots of the Bar/Bat Mitzvah with members of the immediate family, doing activities the child enjoys. As the montage is made from stills, a song which the child chooses as appropriate for the time of his/her Bar/Bat Mitzvah celebration is used for the sound track. The montage ends with the Bar/Bat Mitzvah in synagogue dress. The video then records the arrival of guests and follows the sequence of events at the party. All guests are included, some as they arrive, all as the photographer goes from table to table. As they are taped, guests may be in a continuing conversation, but they often pause to put their good wishes and congratulations on record. At the conclusion, the tape may have a freeze-frame or fade of the Bar/Bat Mitzvah smiling.

Almost all families videotaped. One mother, approaching a second *simchah*, whose own mother had died since the first, said, "I feel strongly about the videotaping . . . . In 20-25 years from now, we'll be able to look at people who are no longer with us . . . ." One father who videotapes as a hobby has taped the three previous ones and will be taping this one. This family has developed its own routine. The Friday night before the next Bar/Bat Mitzvah, they watch the videos from the previous ones. He has made sure to include the B'nai Mitzvah's friends as well as family, and these friends are also invited to the viewing.

VARIATIONS: CELEBRATIONS WITHOUT SOCIAL RITUALS, UNUSUALLY ELABORATE SOCIAL EVENTS, AND TOURS OF ISRAEL

The aspects of the celebration discussed above are not found in all families, but they are sufficiently common to be part of a conventional pattern. This conventional pattern falls within what anthropologists would refer to as folk custom and also within the category of folk religion. As "folk" elaborations of a ritual occasion, the social celebrations of Bar and Bat Mitzvah are responses to the immediate life experiences of the families.

Before interpreting the conventional pattern of celebration, some variations — celebrations with little social ritual, unusually elaborate social events and tours of Israel — will be noted. The variations are of interest in themselves, but they also help understand conventional practice. Families were aware of celebrating unconventionally. The interviews indicated both reasons for these families being uncomfortable with conventional practice and the things they found attractive about the variations they chose.

Parties with Little Social Ritual

Some families hold major receptions without speeches or candlelighting or other gestures which express or interpret the meaning of the event to the family. Open houses do not lend themselves to formal activities in which all the guests are assembled together. Families may also choose to minimize or avoid social rituals at receptions in social halls. The absence of social rituals has different meanings according to context.

In one family, the parents and children were knowledgeable and active Reform Jews and a family who enjoyed spending time in each others' company. An informal open house was for them a time to relax among friends who knew them in these ways. They felt that social rituals expressing family solidarity and some kind of vague connection to Jewish tradition were, for them, unnecessary.

In a few other families the decision to celebrate without social rituals at parties in social halls indicated discomfort with the integration of Judaism into the life of the family. In the case of one family in which the parents were divorced and each remarried, one parent had married a non-Jewish spouse and maintained no connection with Judaism. Both parents, however, felt it was important to be present at their child's reception. A joint luncheon was held, but without any social rituals. In another case, a party without these social rituals of Jewish family and Jewish identity was held for a child with mostly non-Jewish friends. In other cases, families with strong social identities as Jews who, for various reasons, felt estranged from the personnel at the temple or the Judaism practiced there, placed their emphases on "just having a good time."

Bar/Bat Mitzvah Tours of Israel

Several families in the study celebrated Bar/Bat Mitzvah in Israel, either in combination with a synagogue ceremony in North America or by itself.

One family spoke about synagogue participation as important in the lives of the older generation, but not in theirs. They expressed strong feelings of Jewish identity based on the centrality of Jewish survival in Israel after the Holocaust, feelings which have personal meaning because they have many Israeli relatives. While enrolled in religious school, the Bar Mitzvah boy frequently missed class because he was away with the family. He was not looking forward to his Bar Mitzvah as a particularly important event. Nor were the parents looking forward to "another black tie dinner." The parents arranged a joint Bar/Bat Mitzvah tour with other relatives. The religious relatives were proud of the ceremony in Israel. The Bar Mitzvah became a family reunion with numerous Israeli relatives. Wherever they went through Israel, the B'nai Mitzvah received warm individual welcomes. The family returned with feelings of excitement and pride.

Another family with many local relatives decided on a Bar Mitzvah tour for their youngest child. In order to incorporate relatives in the event, a ceremony was first held in the temple. The large number of guests were invited to a buffet *Kiddush* rather than a formal dinner. Each guest was given a certificate marking a tree to be planted in the Bar Mitzvah's honor. As well, a party was held for friends of the Bar Mitzvah.

The Bar/Bat Mitzvah tour of Israel has become a common pattern, which requires a separate analysis.[5] Again, the way the opportunity is used by individual families is what is most important. It can be a way of expressing more authentic feelings of peoplehood and shared fate as an alternative to a ceremony which is primarily religious and ritualistic in emphasis. Or it can be a way of avoiding doing the same thing over again with a younger child, or a way of connecting with Israeli relatives, or an opportunity to meet the family goal of a trip to Israel. Travel agents and travel writers promote tours as less expensive than weekends with catered affairs, but this promotion doesn't take into consideration that many families will do something in North America as well, and that tours themselves can vary widely in cost. For unaffiliated families, who are not in the data from this study, a trip can be a way of having a Bar/Bat Mitzvah without meeting the educational and affiliation requirements which synagogues normally impose.

Exceptional Extravagance

Just as Bar/Bat Mitzvah celebrations varied in the number of guests invited, they varied in style. In general, as would be expected, the wealthier families had larger, more elaborate receptions. None of the families had what they considered to be an excessively extravagant reception, and to label any as such would be inappropriately judgmental.

Families were aware, though, of the common criticism of Bar/Bat Mitzvah receptions as examples of conspicuous consumption. This criticism may be found — among other places — in learned journals,[6] newspaper advice columns,[7] guidebooks for Bar/Bat Mitzvah planning,[8] in reports of notorious receptions in the media,[9] in the jokes about Bar/Bat Mitzvah and in stories which pass from person to person. Such widespread disapproval of excessive celebrations serves as a marker of the limits of what is conventionally approved. That the criticism continues, generation after generation, indicates that the criticism has been ineffective in controlling the behavior.[10]

Families in the study expressed their awareness of the criticism of excessively extravagant celebrations and often expressed agreement with it. For some families the social pressure to have a large, costly reception was a major concern. They explained that they felt they had to celebrate on a larger scale than they preferred in order to do what other members of the family did or to have an "event" similar to those their children were invited to. They discussed people they knew who had spent more than they anticipated, or realized, or felt that they could afford.

The issue of taste was separate, and was a concern among some families for whom money was a minor issue. Receptions showed bad taste when the concern with planning an elaborate party had displaced the religious or familiar emphasis of the event. "Theme" parties — where the atmosphere of the reception is set by decorations and activities drawn from athletics, pop music, plays, or movies — have been criticized as being in poor taste.[11] They are thought to indicate that the Jewish dimension of the Bar/Bat Mitzvah has so little meaning to the family that something else has to be introduced as a focus of attention. Theme parties were not held by the families in this study (although they are common in other cities), but party consultants were occasionally used to plan an exciting, memorable event. While it is conceivable that party consultants may be sensitive to the religious and familial importance of celebrating Bar/Bat Mitzvah, they do make their living by promoting other kinds of values.

THE TRANSITION TO ADOLESCENCE

There is a significant transition marked by the celebration of Bar/Bat Mitzvah, but it is one which the rhetoric drawn from tradition can, at best, acknowledge only obliquely. A *mitzvah* is literally a commandment. The oldest liturgical expression of Bar Mitzvah is the prayer "*Baruch Sheptarani*" — "Blessed be He who has freed me from the responsibility for this child" (Hertz, 1948:491) — which the father recites after being called to the Torah on the day his son becomes Bar Mitzvah. In this rite of passage (Van

Gennep, 1960; Turner, 1972, 1985), the boy is separated from the father's responsibility and is recognized as personally responsible for living by traditional sacred norms. In times of greater cultural stability, this was not a major event. Children were expected to behave according to sacred norms as soon as they were capable.

This understanding of Bar Mitzvah as a recognition of movement toward personal religious responsibility remains within contemporary Orthodoxy (Schoenfeld and Davids, 1988; Fishbane, 1988), along with the prayer "*Baruch Sheptarani.*" It is also found in the literature of the Conservative movement, in which *halachah* — as contemporarily interpreted by the movement — remains in theory binding. Jacob Neusner, for example, a prolific and influential scholar, has written a book for Bar/Bat Mitzvah age students in which he emphasizes that the transition is one in which the child becomes commanded (1981). Within the Reform movement, the formal rhetoric becomes one of "responsibility" rather than commandment. Responsibilities are less specific than commandments and give more leeway for individual judgment. Nevertheless, they still orient the individual toward obligations to the "Jewish community."

It is clear to all concerned in all the movements within Judaism that neither the ritual nor the social events pass the Bar/Bat Mitzvah from the world of childhood to the world of adults. The B'nai Mitzvah are not expected to feel that the weight of the commandments has suddenly descended on their shoulders or that they have undertaken new Jewish obligations. Instead, the real transition is one of leaving behind obligations from family and synagogue and moving into increased individual autonomy.

For some of the children, increased autonomy is associated with the choice to remain involved in Jewish activities by participating in the Confirmation program, continuing on in Jewish day schools, or participating in Jewish youth groups. For others, increased autonomy is associated with a radical decrease in the hours spent in formal Jewish settings. For all the children, the increase in individual choice is understood as part of the movement into adolescence. If we take as the frame of reference the entire sequence of events, social as well as ritual, we see that they constitute an extended rite of passage in which the child is symbolically launched from the sheltering world of family and community into an uncertain future which he/she will face in the company of peers.

The two sets of guest lists, the parents' and the child's, define the social networks — extended family and peers — that the child is growing out of and moving into. The parents' network and the child's may be jointly present at some social events, but they separate themselves into different parts of the same place. As the B'nai Mitzvah move back and forth from one to another, they go from people who are acknowledging that they have begun to move away to those who are welcoming them in. The formal representatives of Jewish tradition — Rabbi, Cantor, teachers, and tutor — are rarely invited to the social events. They have been important in getting the family to this point, but the rite of passage agenda to which the social events respond involves them only marginally.

The guest list specifies those to whom the events are addressed. The guests are more than witnesses. They give gifts, make complimentary remarks, and share a good time. Their approving participation assures the family that what they are going through is proper and that they have done it correctly. The montage of the child's development at the beginning of the videotapes, the speeches by family members and the photographs of the child on display are the family's way of summing up, of noting the accomplishments so far, of expressing pride in the child as "the product" of the family. The candle lighting ceremony provides an opportunity for many people who relate to the B'nai Mitzvah and their families in different ways to be symbolically joined by participating in a common ritual. The sequence in which people are called up at the candle lighting ceremony usually expresses the child's movement from extended family to peers. The first candles are usually lit by grandparents; the last, by friends.

The sequence of social events itself also shows this pattern of movement. In the sequence which follows the conventional pattern, the child moves from family settings through mixed ones and ends up in the company of peers. The Friday night which precedes the ceremony is family oriented. Both parents' guests and child's guests are present at the Saturday morning service, but it is primarily an adult activity. The teenage guests may feel less obligation to participate than their adult counterparts. Before and after the Bar/Bat Mitzvah goes through his/her part of the ceremony, peers who are present sometimes absent themselves from the sanctuary and socialize on the temple steps or in the halls. The receptions which follow the service are mixed, but the Bar/Bat Mitzvah will be found primarily among his/her guests. Where there is a separate kids' party, it is almost always the last in the sequence of celebrations.

Neither the synagogue ritual nor the social events make the transition happen. The child is in the process of entering adolescence, entering a period of life in which he/she must learn to rely less on parents and more on self and peers. The rite of passage, which consists of the sequence of social and ritual events, is a staged acknowledgement of the transition.

Excessively extravagant celebrations can make the child's successful transition to adolescence more difficult, and that is one of the reasons they meet with social disapproval. Parents can become so involved in the details of an elaborate party that they neglect the emotional issues that Bar/Bat Mitzvah raises for the child. As well, excessively elaborate celebrations upset the balance between the reciprocal dramatic themes of responsible parenthood and the child's successful maturation. When parents go "all out," the massive display of parental power usurps attention to which the child is entitled and belittles the transformation the child is going through.

LIVING WITH JEWISH AMBIVALENCE

Liebman introduces the contrast between "folk" and "elite" religion (1973) in order to help explore his theme of Jewish ambivalence. Most North American Jews — or perhaps most modern Jews, or even most modern individuals who attempt to somehow integrate traditions into their lives — find themselves simultaneously attracted to a traditional culture which has given dignity and meaning to the lives of their forebears and a contemporary culture based on the promise of personal fulfillment through individual autonomy. The folk religious practices of most modern Jews express this ambivalence, and it is particularly pronounced in the celebration of Bar/Bat Mitzvah.

In the Bar/Bat Mitzvah celebrations, the parents are making a presentation of self (Goffman, 1959). The parents present themselves as able to spend what those in their social circle spend, and to do so in what they consider good taste — the standards of which many vary from refined to exciting. They are also presenting themselves to their extended family and to their child. Their presentations communicate awareness of ambivalence about how to be Jewish in an open society, but they also communicate that it is possible to live with the ambivalence.

It is significant that while the social events are very "Jewish," there is very little overt religious content. The social events dramatize a strategy of living with ambivalence about Jewish identity — defining it as a social identity as well as, or instead of, a religious one. Jewish identity is presented as a way of locating oneself through family, friends, and subcultural style. Similarly, families who choose to celebrate with a trip to Israel are indicating to their children a strategy of identifying with a national as well as a religious heritage.

Through staging this sequence of ritual and social events, parents are communicating how they have come to terms with the role of Jewish identity in their lives. They have chosen, as autonomous individuals, what to include and what to exclude. Their choices may or may not be well thought out. The parents may or may not be able to articulate the reasons behind the role they have made for Jewish identity in their lives. Yet they have made the choice to identify as Jews. The Bar/Bat Mitzvah celebration is a dramatization to their children that they expect them to make that choice also. They're telling the child that it's important not to lose touch with his/her heritage.

Parents were aware that they could not predict the choices their children will make. In some families one sensed relief that the family had gotten this far in the process of living as a unit without losing their past. This is seen in answers to the question about what parents wanted their children to get from Jewish education. The most common answer was "Jewish history — to know where he/she came from." This past-oriented answer is very different from "to learn rules to live by" or "to learn to be a part of the community." The message the parents are giving seems to be, "We don't know what's going to become of you. We have chosen in some important ways to be like our parents and in some important ways to be unlike them. You will make the same choices, but we want you to know that being Jewish is in some way important to us and we hope it will be important to you." This attitude is also seen in the pleasure parents took in those cases where there was a possibility that the child would not have a Bar/Bat Mitzvah service and the child decided to have one.

This is a long way from becoming, with Bar/Bat Mitzvah, personally responsible for fulfilling commandments, or even a responsible member of the community. Commandments have their source in external authority. Replacing the rhetoric of commandments with the rhetoric of responsibility openly begs the question — responsible to whom or what? With adolescence, Jewish teenagers are moving away from the external authority of parents and tradition. They are entering an extended period in which they will make their individual choices. Bar/Bat Mitzvah marks their passage, not into participation as responsible members of the Jewish community, but into a socially structured, virtually inevitable period of uncertainty.

Sklare noted some years ago that the style of celebrating Bar/Bat Mitzvah borrows from Jewish wedding celebrations. He suggested that an elaboration of Bar/Bat Mitzvah celebrations along the lines of wedding parties serves the purpose of communicating to the child the importance of a future endogamous marriage (1971:195). If that is their latent function, they are ineffective, as Bar/Bat Mitzvah parties have, if anything, become more elaborate while the rate of Jewish exogamy has gone up and up.

Bar/Bat Mitzvah celebrations may be less rehearsals for Jewish weddings than substitutes for them. Marriage has traditionally been the real rite of passage into full participation in the Jewish community. The blessing on the birth of a child is for a future of "Torah, *chuppah*, and good deeds." Torah and good deeds are not ritual occasions, but *chuppah* — which means both the bridal canopy and the marriage ceremony — is. The Jewish community was traditionally composed of households. Children became full participants in the community when they married and established their own households. As well, marriage traditionally goes with the intention to have children, which Rabbis always mention as the very first commandment in the Bible. Raising Jewish children is a fundamental Jewish obligation, one which ensures the survival of the Jewish people.

The age of first marriage among Jews is now later than a generation ago. The chance of a child having a non-Jewish marriage is also much greater. In some families Jewish continuity is more precarious than others, but no family has guarantees and everybody knows it. The social dramatization of Jewish continuity has, to some extent, shifted down from the wedding to the Bar/Bat Mitzvah. At the time of entry into adolescent uncertainty, the ritual and social events of Bar/Bat Mitzvah are occasions for looking back and looking forward. The continuity of Jewish life across the generations is not assured, but it is at least dramatized as a value and a promise.

In understanding contemporary Jewish life, then, it is important to see Bar/Bat Mitzvah ceremonies not only as authorities explain their religious significance and not only as the critics of conspicuous consumption portray them. Bar/Bat Mitzvah ceremonies are events in which the formal rituals intersect with the personal agendas brought to them. They have meaning in the way they are enacted by the child and his/her family. Like other forms of folk religion, Bar/Bat Mitzvah celebrations address immediate issues in the lives of those involved. They ease the transition into adolescence for the child, provide a social as well as religious understanding of Jewish identity, and allow the parents to express their ambivalence.

RITUAL OCCASIONS AND EMOTIONAL EXPRESSION

There is yet something else. The transcripts and tapes of the interviews have an emotional tone which an analysis restricted to overt content may obscure. The discussion of Bar/Bat Mitzvah in the families in this study reflected deep feelings and important emotional issues, which this article can only explore in a preliminary way.

Ritual occasions are supposed to be socially structured occasions which take us out of the profane world and focus our attention on what is really valuable. Participants in the ritual may take the opportunity to speak out about the feelings and the values evoked by the occasion, or their feelings may be expressed indirectly through the way in which they are involved in the enactment of the event. Rites of passage can be particularly powerful in evoking emotional responses because they address the profoundly mysterious issues of birth, transformation, and death. While the transition into adolescence is, unlike puberty, socially constructed, it still has the power to evoke powerful feelings in the parents as well as the children. It is a time at which feelings about the changes in the relationship between parents and children come to the fore.

The feelings that parents and children have for each other are complex. Bar/Bat Mitzvah is often an occasion on which parents reflect on their own personal histories and the lives they have made for themselves, times at which they feel the need to come to terms with what they are passing on — not just as Jews but as people — from one generation to another. Through the range of social events that have been elaborated around the synagogue ritual, parents get the chance to express to their growing children the complexity of their love and concern in a way which is very public, but at the same time very personal.

NOTES

[1]Previous papers have dealt with the general social history of Bar and Bat Mitzvah (Schoenfeld, 1984), the way in which Bar and Bat Mitzvah became closely tied to Jewish education through the imposition of the requirement of a specified number of years of Jewish education at congregational schools in the 1940s and 1950s (Schoenfeld, 1988a), recent innovations in Jewish education related to Bar/Bat Mitzvah preparation (Schoenfeld, 1987), the way in which the celebration of Bar/Bat Mitzvah is integrated into the functioning of an observant Orthodox congregation (Schoenfeld and Davids, 1988b), the experience of a woman who arranged a Bat Mitzvah at age 24 (Schoenfeld, 1988c), the experience of a group of 18 women who participated in a group adult Bat Mitzvah at the Reform temple where the interviews were carried out (Schoenfeld, 1989), and the meanings which are associated with Bar Mitzvah in selected pieces of Jewish literature (Schoenfeld, 1988c).

[2]In this perspective, Bar/Bat Mitzvahs may be interpreted as what Meyerhoff (1977) called "definitional ceremonies."

[3]The interviews covered information about the parents' backgrounds, their reasons for affiliation with the Reform movement and this temple in particular, their Jewish observances, feelings about different aspects of Jewish identity, the child's experience at Religious School and in Hebrew instruction, what the difficult issues were in planning the Bar or Bat Mitzvah and the social side of the celebration.

[4]See Sontag (1977) for a discussion of how the act of making an event an object of a photographic record confuses the experience of it by overlaying the roles of coparticipants in an immediately meaningful structured activity with the inconsistent roles of observer and performer. Communal worship is in any case difficult enough. The photographer is an observer rather than a participant. The presence of an observer encourages participants to define the event as one for the record rather than for itself.

[5]See E. Cohen (1979) for a useful perspective on the interpretation of tourism.

[6]Spero, 1988.

[7]e.g., "Miss Manners," 1989.

[8]Lewit and Epstein, 1982.

[9]See, e.g., Feiler (1989) and Schulweis (1988).

[10]A full analysis of excessive extravagance at social affairs requires a separate paper.

[11]See, e.g., Herman, 1967.

[12]See Davis (1988) for detailed analyses along these lines.

REFERENCES

Cohen, E. (1979). "A Phenomenology of Tourist Experiences," *Sociology* 13: 179-201.

Davis, Judith. (1988). "Mazel Tov: The Bar Mitzvah as a Multigenerational Ritual of change and Continuity." In E. Imber-Black, J. Roberts and R.A. Whiting (eds.). *Rituals in Families and Family Therapies*, pp. 177-208. Norton.

Eliade, Mircea. (1975). *Rites and Symbols of Initiation.* New York: Harper and Row.

Feiler, Alan. (1989). "Is the Bar Mitzvah Reception Out of Control?" *Baltimore Jewish Times*. February 26, pp. 48-53.

Fishbane, Simcha. (1987). "Contemporary Bar Mitzvah Rituals in Modern Orthodoxy," *Religion and Culture*, Vol. 2, No. 1, Fall.

Goffman, Erving. (1959). *The Presentation of Self in Everyday Life*. New York: Doubleday.

Herman, Erwin L. (1967). "Bar Mitzvah a la Carte." In *The American Judaism Reader*, ed. Paul Kresh, pp. 253-256. New York: Abelard-Shuman.

Hertz, Joseph H. (1948). *The Authorized Daily Prayer Book*, revised edition. New York: Bloch.

Lewit, Jane, and Ellen Robinson Epstein. (1982). *The Bar/Bat Mitzvah Planbook*. New York: Stein and Day.

Liebman, Charles. (1973). *The Ambivalent American Jew*. Philadelphia: Jewish Publication Society.

Luckmann, Thomas. (1967). *The Invisible Religion*. New York: Macmillan.

Millgram, Abraham. (1971). *Jewish Worship*. Philadelphia: Jewish Publication Society.

"Miss Manners," *Baltimore Sun*, April 23, 1989, Sect. F, p.4.

Myerhoff, Barbara. (1977). *Number Our Days*. New York: Simon and Schuster.

Neusner, Jacob. (1981). *Mitzvah*. Chappaqua, NY: Rossel Books.

Schoenfeld, Stuart. (1984). "Changing Patterns of North American Bar Mitzvah: Towards a History and Sociological Analysis." Paper presented at the meetings of the Canadian Sociology and Anthropology Association, Guelph, Ontario.

Schoenfeld, Stuart. (1987). "Ritual Performance, Curriculum Design and Jewish Identity: Towards a Perspective on Contemporary Innovations in Bar/Bat Mitzvah Education." Paper presented at the meetings of the Association for Jewish Studies, Boston, December, 1987.

Schoenfeld, Stuart. (1988a). "Folk Religion, Elite Religion and the Role of Bar Mitzvah in the Development of the Synagogue and Jewish School in America." *Contemporary Jewry* 9 (1988): 57-85.

Schoenfeld, Stuart. (1988b). "Integration into the Group and Sacred Uniqueness: An Analysis of Adult Bar Mitzvah." In *Persistence and Flexibility: Anthropological Perspectives on the American Jewish Experience*, ed. Walter Zenner, pp. 117-135. Albany: State University of New York Press.

Schoenfeld, Stuart. (1988c). "Bar Mitzvah Stories: A Study in the Use of Literature as an Entre into Issues of Modern Jewish Identity." Unpublished manuscript.

Schoenfeld, Stuart. (1989). "Ritual and Role Transition: Adult Bat Mitzvah as a Successful Rite of Passage." Paper presented at the Conference on Research in Jewish Education, June, Chicago.

Schoenfeld, Stuart, and Leo Davids. (1988). "Practical and Symbolic Social Cohesion in the Bar Mitzvah Practices of an Orthodox Congregation." Unpublished manuscript.

Schulweis, Harold. (1988). "An Embarrassment of Riches." *Baltimore Jewish Times*, February 26, pp. 54, 76-79, 108.

Sklare, Marshall. (1971). *America's Jews*. New York: Random House.

Sontag, Susan. (1977). *On Photography*. New York: Farrar, Straus and Giroux.

Spero, Aryeh, "'Conspicuous Consumption' at Jewish Functions." *Judaism* 37 (1/145): 103-110.

Turner, Victor. (1972). *Dramas, Fields and Metaphors: Symbolic Action in Human Society*. Ithaca, NY: Cornell University Press.

Turner, Victor. (1985). "Are There Universals of Performance in Myth, Ritual and Drama?" In his *On the Edge of the Bush: Anthropology as Experience*, ed. Edith Turner. Tucson: University of Arizona Press.

Van Gennep, Arnold. (1960 [1909]). *The Rites of Passage*. Chicago: University of Chicago Press.

(Originally published in *Essays in the Social Scientific Study of Judaism and Jewish Society*, edited by Jack N. Lightstone. Montreal: Department of Religion, Concordia University, 1990. Reprinted by permission.)

Chapter 50
Para-Rabbinic and B'nai Mitzvah Counseling Program

Sally Shafton

"There are paralegals and paramedics, why not para-Rabbinics?" This question posed by Rabbi Harold Schulweis of Valley Beth Shalom Synagogue in Encino, California, led in 1978-1979 to the creation of just such a program. Not only would educated laypeople be of assistance to the Rabbi in his various tasks, they would also be enabled and empowered to reach out in a personal way to the families of the congregation. Our heritage, Rabbi Schulweis felt, was not getting to the average Jew. Perhaps laypeople could become a fresh source of creative, educational energy.

The question posed by Rabbi Schulweis resulted in a long term mutual commitment by the Rabbi who was deeply involved in creating, teaching, recruiting and follow-up in the program, and by the laypeople. The latter committed to two years of study (one night a week) and three years of service. Study included examinations, papers, role playing, field trips, outside speakers, and much discussion. At the completion of the course, each participant chose an area of specialization: Death and Dying, Life Cycle Events, Adoption, Adolescence, Divorce, or B'nai Mitzvah Counseling, which is the subject of this chapter.

GOALS

A main goal of the B'nai Mitzvah Counseling Program is to redirect the focus of the event from undue emphasis on celebration to ritual and learning. The role of the Counselors is to introduce content into the child's study of the *parashah* and Haftarah that relates to his/her life today. The program is still evolving, but its longevity is a measure of its success. Families have come to look forward to the first call from their Counselor, and the relationship between Counselor and family becomes very personal and supportive.

IMPLEMENTATION

The program personnel consists of a Coordinator and Counselors, each with an important function. The Coordinator's job is administration and ongoing education. The Coordinator can make or break the program; laypeople are solely responsible for its administration. Presently, Valley Beth Shalom is using 18 "units" of Counselors (singles and couples) working with families. With approximately 1,700 families in the congregation and two B'nai Mitzvah each Shabbat, each Counselor sees some six to eight families per year. There are ongoing educational sessions throughout the year for the Counselors; ongoing recruitment for new Counselors is also necessary. This is done primarily through referrals from the Rabbis or school administrator, and very often families going through the process later become Counselors themselves. There is a major orientation for new Counselors each year, and two or three meetings during the year to evaluate the work being done. In these evaluations, role playing and discussion are important. An example of role playing might be a Counselor meeting with a family whose child is hostile about the Bar/Bat Mitzvah experience. Another might be a Counselor encountering a hostile (or amicable) divorce situation. Unfortunately, the statistics of an average year of B'nai Mitzvah families indicate that a significant number involve divorce. (For a program geared to the needs of divorced families, see Chapter 48.)

Counselors make it very clear to everyone involved, particularly in a hostile divorce situation, that they are not therapists. They stress the possibility of setting aside differences during this event, so that the memory bank of this family will be enriched. However, if there are problems with which a Counselor cannot cope, the family is referred to the Rabbis, or to the para-Professional Counseling Center.

All family members are asked to be present at the first meeting with the Counselor, and in 90% of the cases, both parents do attend. The main value of the counseling program in the early meetings is to uncover problems that might have been overlooked by a busy school administration. The Counselor's task is to gain the confidence of this family, and to see what changes might have occurred since school enrollment five years previously. Any problems or special needs that the family may have at this time are brought to the attention of the Rabbis and staff.

The school has three meetings per year with the B'nai Mitzvah families. At the first meeting a booklet called *B'nai Mitzvah Guidelines* is distributed. This booklet contains a full description of the counseling program, and the families are told that they will be called soon by their own personal Counselor. One Counselor attends this meeting to be introduced and to say a few words about the program.

Meanwhile, the school office gives the Coordinator the whole year's list of dates, families, and pertinent data, and the Coordinator makes assignments. Shortly after the meeting, the family receives a card from the Coordinator, listing the name and phone number of their Counselor and preparing them for his/her call. The Counselor follows this card up with a call, making the first contact. (Since Valley Beth Shalom has a sizeable Iranian and Russian population, Farsi and Russian speaking volunteers are available to join Counselors at the home meeting.)

THE COUNSELOR'S JOB

The Counselor's first phone call can be very informative and telling (very often providing information that is different from the registration data in the school office). If there is a separation or divorce, both parents are called. If a family appears disinterested in meeting with Counselors, no one insists. However, Counselors do explain that even if this is their third child going through the process, it is different for each, and each child deserves his/her own special time and attention in and around this important event. If they still seem disinterested, Counselors offer to send an outline of the child's *parashah* or Haftarah in simple, understandable English. The hope is that parents will discuss it with their child, to show the child that there is more than mechanical learning involved in this experience.

The clues about a family that can be gleaned from this first phone call are varied and important. For example, in one first phone call the Counselor learned that a separated mother was involved with Jews for Jesus, and that she took her son to those services each time he was with her. In another first call, it was learned that the family was not at all comfortable with the family with whom they had been paired. The first phone call can reveal relationships within the family. When a mother says that her husband is "Mr. Religious," or a father says that his wife is interested, but has no confidence in her Judaic background, Counselors must have their antennae up. With information gleaned from that first call, Counselors knock on the front door, knowing a bit about the family (families) with whom they will interact for the next nine months.

In advance of this meeting, the families receive a copy of the outline of their *parashah* or Haftarah, usually from *Outline for the Parasha* by Louis L. Kaplan, and from *Guide to Sidrot and Haftarot* by Rabbi Arthur A. Chiel. The Counselor has already digested the meaning of the portion, picked at least two concepts for discussion, and come up with questions that will motivate family discussion. (A further discussion on possible *parashah* and Haftarah development will be addressed later.)

The home meeting takes place with the two families who are sharing the Shabbat day. Though these families may never have met before, suddenly their lives intertwine. The initial phone call informs the Counselor of the families' orientations in terms of observance and background. Not unusually, the families share little in terms of background, yet their commonality must be stressed and their diversity be shown as a strength. Any personal problems are left to be handled privately. The hope for the first home meeting is that all concerned get to know and feel comfortable with one another. Meeting in the home of one of the families is most conducive to creating the desired atmosphere, and in most cases, families are quick to volunteer their home.

After the introductory chat, the first discussion point is the meaning of a rite of passage: the first day in kindergarten, driving for the first time, school graduations, and marriage are all brought up. The attainment of manhood/womanhood in other cultures is discussed. Immediately after that, the Jewish backgrounds of all the participants and their grandparents are explored. It is fascinating to see how often children learn things about their parents' backgrounds that they simply had never had time to talk about before. Some B'nai Mitzvah have been shocked to learn that their parents had lived through anti-Semitic experiences, or that their mothers had not been able to become a Bat Mitzvah. The experiences of their grandparents and parents are then compared to what they are about to experience.

AGENDA FOR HOME MEETINGS

The "Agenda for Home Meetings" may be found in the Appendix at the end of this chapter. The discussion that follows will cover only those points in the Agenda that are not self-explanatory.

Bar/Bat Mitzvah Religious Service (Appendix, Section II)

The discussion begins after distributing the following cards to the families. These cards are a choreography of the worship service from beginning to end. Helpful and informative suggestions on each card describe the involvement of all the participants. Here are three of the twelve cards.

P'TICHAT ARON

1. Make sure that you have a *kipah* (head covering).
2. Those over 13 years should wear a *tallit* (prayer shawl).
3. The Rabbi will announce the opening of the Ark. Walk up to the doors of the Ark with your prayer book. Open one side of the Ark.
4. Stand at the side of the door and join in the prayers.
5. When designated to do so, close the door of the Ark.
6. Return to your seat.

FIRST ALIYAH
(Torah Blessing)

Please do the following:

1. Make sure that you have a *kipah.*
2. Make sure that you have a *tallit.*
3. Walk up to the right side of the Cantor's podium.
4. Touch the Torah with the fringes of the *tallit,* kiss them and recite:

Barchu Et Adonai Hamvorach
Congregation will answer:
Baruch Adonai Hamvorach L'olam Va'ed.
Baruch Adonai Hamvorach L'olam Va'ed.
Baruch Atah Adonai Eloheynu
Melech Ha'olam Asher Bachar Banu Mikol
Ha'amim V'natan Lanu Et Torato. Baruch
Adonai Noteyn Hatorah.

5. Wait for the reader to finish, touch the Torah with the *tallit,* kiss, recite:

Baruch Atah Adonai Eloheynu Melech Ha'olam
Asher Natan Lanu Torat Emet V'chaye Olam
Nata Betocheynu. Baruch Atah Adonai Noteyn
Hatorah.

6. Move to the left side of the podium and remain for the next reading.
7. After that reading, return to your seat.

RETURNING THE TORAH TO THE ARK

Please do the following:

1. Make sure that you have a *kipah* (head covering).
2. Make sure that you are wearing a *tallit* (prayer shawl).
3. At the end of the Torah service, there is a procession with the Torah.
4. When the Ark is opened, take the Torah from the Cantor and place it in the empty spot in the Ark.
5. At the end of the prayer *Etz Hayim,* return to your seat.

These cards are the size of playing cards. *Aliyot* and honors are described separately on each card so that the family can send a separate card to participants. If Aunt Bessie from Omaha is doing the second *aliyah,* she will receive that card, describing her participation in detail. She can now be an educated participant on the day of the Bar/Bat Mitzvah service.

Parents' Tallit Presentation (Appendix, Section IIA)

Here the Counselor guides the parents to the *parashah* or Haftarah for ideas on which to base their brief presentation. *Pirke Avot* or other applicable literature is a suggested source. Counselors offer to help with this, if families wish, as one of the goals is to make these statements meaningful, and to avoid personal rambling in an unprepared statement.

Aliyot for Family, Friends (Appendix, Section IIB)

The student is encouraged to record the *aliyah* blessing on a tape. This is sent along with the *aliyah* card to Aunt Sadie in Oklahoma City, so that when she comes to the *bimah* with Uncle Max they will be prepared. When relatives see that the child takes this experience seriously enough to send a tape and card, they will be inspired to prepare seriously themselves.

Aliyot for Family, Friends (Appendix, Section IIC)

The most stimulating and motivating part of the visit is the discussion of the *parashah* and/or Haftarah. The main thrust here, unlike any other coverage that the child gets with teachers or tutors, is the application of the meaning of these portions to the life of the family today. Hopefully, this discussion will be a stimulus for speech ideas for the student.

The following is an example of a *parashah* discussion based on *Vaera*, Exodus 6:2-9:35. Moses is instructed to go once again with Aaron to Pharaoh to request that his people may leave Egypt to worship God as they wish. Moses is very discouraged, as Pharaoh's "heart is hardened," and it seems futile to Moses to go on. There is further discussion in the *parashah* on the responsibility we have when we have a heritage given to us, as is the case when the land of Canaan is to be the heritage of the Israelites. The theme here to discuss with the family is the need for patience. God tells Moses to have faith and patience. Was there a time when the Bar/Bat Mitzvah wished he/she had more patience? We point out that even Moses, one of the great leaders of the Jewish people, was constantly striving to improve his behavior, in this case by developing more patience. We discuss that even great people must work at maturing, and that we are not alone when we fail ourselves or our families from time to time. We discuss God's advice to Moses that if he could develop patience, he would most likely win out over Pharaoh. Developing patience, then, in our own lives could serve us well in many areas — a lesson learned by getting better acquainted with the characteristics of Moses.

As we get to know Moses better, we learn what it is like for him to go against one whose "heart is hardened." How do we deal in life today with one who has "a hardened heart"? Or, how do we keep our own hearts from "hardening"? We talk here about free will, about having control over our own behavior. Pharaoh chose to behave in an evil way, but we can choose to behave in a way that is rewarding for ourselves and those around us. How do we deal with a classmate we do not like without "hardening our own hearts"? Can we use patience and control and by doing so, look forward to an improved relationship with that classmate? We go on to look at the responsibility we have as Jews to protect our heritage, as Moses had to do. What are some of the things we can do to "protect a heritage"?

This discussion can make the *parashah* come alive for the family. It can lead to understanding and appreciation for the ongoing relevance of our tradition. It can also be the kernel of the speech that the student will compose at a later date. Counselors are available to do speech brainstorming with the student as time goes on.

It should be noted here that Counselors use their own style in designing these home meetings. *Parashah* and Haftarah discussions will vary based on the theme and direction that the individual Counselor chooses to use. The agenda is only a guideline; variation is inevitable.

Attending Shabbat Services Together Prior to Bar/Bat Mitzvah (Appendix, Section IID)

Together (or one at a time, depending on availability) the two families join the Counselor at Shabbat services. There, the Counselor quietly helps families observe the choreography and synagogue skills they need to develop by the time of their big event. The

Counselor points out things which might have gone unnoticed otherwise, and generally helps the families become more comfortable in the synagogue.

Tzedakah (Appendix, Section III)

Tzedakah is an important part of the consciousness raising Counselors do. A part of this discussion can focus on "B'nai Mitzvah Centerpieces" other than flowers: e.g., books purchased with the assistance of the librarian can be softened by balloons or greens and, after the event, be given to the library or to a children's hospital. Similarly, food baskets can later be taken to a shelter for the homeless, or sports objects, art objects, or small dolls as centerpieces can be given to a children's home. The day after the Bar/Bat Mitzvah ceremony can be made significant by giving to the community in some way.

Reception (Appendix, Section IV)

The discussion surrounding the reception can be a very productive one. The goal is to make the celebration appropriate, to discourage extravaganzas and theme parties. The favored approach is to reflect with the family on a glitzy, inappropriate reception which took place recently in the community. Appropriate activities for a celebration are suggested, such as reciting the proper *brachot*, Israeli folk dancing and singing, storytelling, etc. The celebratory aspects of the day are not downplayed; the objective is celebration within an appropriate framework. At the home visit, a packet of instructional sheets, and sample invitations are left with the family. The packet includes copies of all the *brachot* and a listing of available communal and congregational services with phone numbers. Also included are several sample Bar/Bat Mitzvah explanation sheets, which may be included in the invitation if the family wishes. This sheet, often adapted by the family, describes the meaning and content of the service. It is a nice way to educate both non-Jewish guests and less knowledgeable Jewish guests, who are usually anxious to learn more.

EVALUATION

One indicator of success for the counseling relationship is the continued involvement of children and families. A significant goal is to see an increased percentage of those with ongoing identification. So far, about 45-50% of our families continue their commitment. Children attend USY, Camp Ramah, Brandeis Camp Alonim, Young Judea, First Step Hebrew High School, or others. And there is particular pride when the B'nai Mitzvah families themselves go on to become Counselors. Another sign of success is when a Counselor is late in making the first call to a family; the school office often gets a call from that family asking, "Where is my Counselor? They haven't called yet." Such concern speaks for itself.

Counselors are asked to submit evaluation forms to the school office concerning every family with whom they are working. There are comments on everything from the very first phone call through the family visits. Often, this evaluation form brings to light a situation that might have otherwise gone undiscovered, and the particular needs of the family can be better served by the teachers, Rabbis, or Director of Education.

This entire program can be revised to suit the needs, the staffing, and the characteristics of almost any congregation. The major key to the success of the program is the commitment of the Rabbi to teaching and engendering in the trainees a positive attitude so that they will become valued assistants. For the Counselors, other than being of service to the Rabbi, there is value derived from the significant education received, as well as the personal bonding that occurs among the participants.

Many Counselors come from minimal Judaic backgrounds and must grow into their roles. Being non-professionals (imagine, Jewish role models who are non-professionals!) offers greater potential for rapport with some families — especially those wherein the congregant would be too inhibited to ask questions of the Rabbis. It is much easier to admit a lack of knowledge to a lay person.

During this uniquely personal learning experience, families learn in their own homes, receive needed educational and moral support, become more competent and confident, and ultimately displace some of the stress of the occasion by focusing on the richness of this special Jewish experience.

The program is always evolving and changing, based on experience and new needs. The major flaw of the program is lack of time on the part of all participants, the malady of our times. Basically, there is one home meeting, lasting from two to two and a half hours, depending on the children's attention span. If a family requests further meetings with the Counselor, these can be arranged. However, most of the further contact after the home meeting takes place on the phone. Much greater impact could be made if there were at least three face-to-face meetings with the families. The dilemma is that improving and expanding the program risks destroying it. As it is now, only 10% of the families accept the invitation to attend services together. The demands on the Counselors' time are also heavy, and they, of course, live with the same time demands that the families do.

One of the great strengths of this program is the feeling of gratification engendered as para-Rabbinics and client families become like extended family. What joy there is to go to *shul* and meet up again with former students, now grown, who have gone on to college, or to marriage, etc.! Such a bond makes everyone involved feel more a part of the synagogue.

The impact of this program on the extravaganza reception has unfortunately not been felt. There is much work to do, and whether or not this trend will be reversed completely is open to question. However, many in-roads have been made in changing offensive and ostentatious customs. When the inappropriateness of a glitzy reception is discussed in the presence of the child, often there is more impact on the child than on the parents. Planting the seed is of vital importance.

The B'nai Mitzvah Counseling Program works at changing the perception that a child of 13 automatically goes through a process called Bar/Bat Mitzvah without familial and emotional involvement. The program affirms that this is not only a child's task, it is also a very special time in the history of a Jewish family. It affirms to families that their Jewish community cares about them, and that the strength congregants can gain from one another is deep and lasting. Together, Counselors and families participating in this program are building a stronger congregational community. It is hoped that as other congregations adopt and adapt such a program, a stronger American Jewish community will result.

APPENDIX

Bar/Bat Mitzvah Agenda for Home Meetings

(A Guide for Discussions)

I. Family Participation

A. Jewish backgrounds of parents, grandparents
B. Feelings about Jewish education and observance
C. Compare experience of parents' Bar/Bat Mitzvah to present experience.
D. Importance of total family involvement.
  1. Meaning of Bar/Bat Mitzvah to:
    a. Bar/Bat Mitzvah
    b. Parents and grandparents
    c. Siblings
E. Minyan (Thursday or Monday week before)
  1. Purpose of attendance; who attends
  2. Bring *tefillin*
  3. Sponsorship of breakfast — charge varies according to number attending
F. Kiddush following service (or Oneg Shabbat after Friday night Bat Mitzvah)
  1. Sisterhood will contact family six months before Bar/Bat Mitzvah date.

II. Bar/Bat Mitzvah Religious Service

A. Parents' *Tallit* Presentation
  1. Stress importance of 1-2 minutes in length.
  2. Tie remarks to tradition, *parashah*, Haftarah, literature
  3. Balance between personal feelings and religious aspect.

B. *Aliyot* for Family, Friends
  1. Each family gets 3, plus Bar/Bat Mitzvah child; Total of 8.
  2. Give copies of *aliyah* cards or sheets that describe service.
  3. Notify *aliyah* honorees in advance and make sure they know what is involved.
  4. Suggestions for *Aliyot* guests:
    a. Men to wear *tallit* and *yarmulke*
    b. Women to wear a head covering.
    c. Step to right of *Ba'al Kriah* for blessings.
    e. Touch fringe of *tallit* to Torah and kiss fringe.
  5. Grandparents and other older relatives should get special consideration.
  6. Give siblings a part in the service.
    a. If older, sibling(s) can be given an *aliyah* or read a portion of the Torah.
    b. If younger, can help open the Ark.

C. *Parashah* and Haftarah Discussion
  1. Review Kaplan Outline — can mail in advance or bring copies to meeting. Briefly discuss contents at meeting, including contemporary application.
  2. Study Aids
    a. Synagogue Library
    b. *Tikkun* — section provided by instructor
    c. Shilo Publishing, provides series which contains Maftir, Haftarah, and their accompanying blessings — booklet, book, record, or cassette.
    d. Shilo Publishing — second series includes the Maftir plus additional articles on the Torah, Ten Commandments, Prophets, and discussion of the week's Haftarah. Phone: (212) 925-3468
    e. Union of American Hebrew Congregations (UAHC) — Torah and Haftarah portions with cantillation and appropriate blessings; pamphlets include Jewish history, commentaries, *midrash* and contemporary applications to modern Jewish life. Phone: (212) 249-0100.
    f. Davka Corp — Hebrew and Judaic software; can order Torah and Haftarah portions as well as blessings. Phone (800) 621-8227.
    g. Lev Software — special program "Haftutor" includes selected Haftarah portion and blessings (vowels disappear and reappear) transliterate Hebrew in English and

APPENDIX (Cont.)

Russian. (See Chapter 22 for a full description.)

3. Tips on Child's Speech Preparation
   a. Child should be confident he/she understands so message will be clear to listeners.
   b. Permissible to have some adult help for organization and length.
   c. Parents can discuss ideas with child and help review and polish presentation.
4. When Meeting with the Rabbi Before the Ceremony:
   a. Parents should provide Rabbi with background material about the child and family.
   b. Outline the child's interests and accomplishments.
   c. Include information about special relatives who have traveled great distances to attend.
5. If Child or Parent Chooses To Make a Personal Prayer
   a. Prayer should reflect the thoughts of the child and parents.
   b. Prayer can be selected rather than written by child or parents.
   c. Suggestions:
      (1) Express feeling of gratitude upon reaching this milestone in life.
      (2) Child may ask for God's blessings on family and teachers for having guided and prepared him/her for this occasion.
      (3) May express aspirations for child's future as well as hopes for the welfare of the Jewish people.
      (4) Child may pledge to continue studying and remain devoted to the ideals of his/her faith.

D. Attending Shabbat Services Prior to Bar/Bat Mitzvah
   1. Stress importance of attendance.
      a. Will learn order of service.
      b. Will feel more at ease at own Bar/Bat Mitzvah
   2. Ask whether they would like Counselor to accompany them to services.
   3. Video cassette available from synagogue library — 20 minute Torah service.

E. Traditional Ritual Items
   1. Head Coverings — traditional sign of respect for God.
      a. Men — *yarmulkes*
      b. Women — *yarmulkes* or lace covering if going to *bimah.*
   2. *Tallit*
      a. Reminder to observe all of God's commandments.
      b. Selecting — Jewish religious supply shop, synagogue gift shop, purchase in Israel; could match father's. Make sure child likes it.
   3. *Tefillin*
      a. Symbolic reminder of our relationship to God.
      b. Mentioned 4 times in the Torah, once in the "*Sh'ma*"; central in all of Jewish prayer.
      c. Same root as Hebrew word for prayer, *tefillah.*
      d. Symbolic reminder of the entire Torah.
      e. Use begins at the age of religious responsibility, the Bar/Bat Mitzvah.

III. *Tzedakah*

A. Guests' Alternatives
   1. In lieu of present for child, make a charitable contribution in the child's name.
      a. Charity of one's choosing is appropriate.
      b. Suggested institutions and organizations that support the Jewish community:
         (1) United Jewish Appeal
         (2) Synagogue and auxiliaries
         (3) Jewish camps
         (4) Rabbinical schools
         (5) University of Judaism
         (6) Organizations which provide rehabilitation training

B. Parents
   1. Could give a percent of cost of the *simchah* to:

APPENDIX (Cont.)

a. MAZON
b. Operation Exodus
c. Jewish National Fund
d. UJWF
e. Charity of choice

2. Can reduce some anticipated expenditure such as flowers, food, and allocate savings as a donation.

C. Bar/Bat Mitzvah Child

1. Is influenced by adult models, especially parents, giving to charity.
2. Should be encouraged to contribute some of gift money to charity of choice.
   a. Important to begin practice of *tzedakah* as responsible Jewish adult.

IV. Reception (*Seudat Mitzvah*)

A. Simchah Service or dairy luncheon (contact name and phone #)

B. Luncheon or dinner (non-dairy) (contact name and phone #)

C. Invitations

1. Allow sufficient time — begin selecting or designing about 6 months before.
2. Invitations set the tone for the occasion.
3. Save previous Bar/Bat Mitzvah invitations to serve as models and source of ideas.
4. Have RSVP return envelopes addressed to the child.
5. Out-of-town invitations should be mailed 8 weeks in advance (travel arrangements); send local invitations about 6 weeks in advance.
6. To get exact count, may have to make follow-up calls to those who have not replied.
7. If parents are separated or divorced, basic invitation can be worded the same; difference is that the parents may want to list their names on two different lines on bottom of invitation.

D. Centerpieces

1. Suggest reusable, functional centerpieces for possible donations after the occasion.
   a. Could reflect season of the year or a Jewish holiday that is near:
      (1) Fall/Sukkot — individual baskets with fruits of the season
      (2) Chanukah — simple *chanukiah* at each table
   b. Assortment of books that are subsequently given to guests or donated to library or charitable organization
   c. Sports equipment, music, or toys with items donated to organizations
   d. Floral centerpieces — can be sent to hospitals or Home for Aged
2. A footed cake plate can be used as centerpiece with colorful display of assorted desserts.

E. Ways to Enhance *Seudat Mitzvah*

1. Havdalah (for Saturday evening) — give copy of service
2. *Hamotzi* and *Birkat Hamazon* — give copies
3. Music and Singing
   a. If on Shabbat at the synagogue, know what is appropriate and work out the details.
   b. Maintain a Jewish aspect, such as Israeli dancing.
   c. Group singing — provide song sheets with words in Hebrew/Yiddish and with transliteration.
4. Child can give a *d'var Torah* or Bar/Bat Mitzvah speech — experiencing the ceremony; words of thanks to family, teacher, guests.
5. Parents expressing public words of greeting to their guests and their joy on this *simchah*.

V. Other Topics to Discuss

A. Continuing Jewish education; participation in USY

B. Taking pictures; availability of videotape (call name and phone #)

C. Advise family to read "B'nai Mitzvah Guidelines," given to each Bar/Bat Mitzvah — booklet with valuable information.

APPENDIX (Cont.)

D. Thank-you notes
1. Suggest sending notes to Sisterhood, Men's Club, and USY for gifts.
2. Address people correctly — name should be written in proper form and spelled correctly.
3. Be specific about the gift — mimeographed note or "thank you for the gift" unacceptable.
4. Thank-you notes should be sent within a few weeks.
5. Parents should help the child keep in mind that gifts are a subordinate part of the total Bar/Bat
Mitzvah experience.

E. Tips for success: A few days before the *simchah*, the child should be reminded to:
1. Follow the service with an open Siddur or *Chumash*, participating in prayers and songs when not leading them.
2. Not wave or signal friends and family from the *bimah*.
3. Be prepared to shake hands with the Rabbi(s), Cantor, teacher, those presenting gifts, participants (*aliyot*) and officers on the *bimah*.

F. Guests
1. Out-of-towners
   a. Lodging — home hospitality or hotel reservations; provide list describing accommodations and proximity to synagogue
   b. Local host family
   c. Provide maps, directions, and schedules for the weekend.
2. Explaining the service to those unfamiliar with the synagogue and its customs
   a. Briefly describe the service in terms of Shacharit, Torah reading, *d'var Torah*, and Musaf
3. Identify those guests that are Shomer Shabbat and make appropriate accommodations.
4. Identify practices at the synagogue that the guests should know about
   a. Can women guests wear pantsuits?
   b. Would someone using pay phone offend members of the congregation?
   c. Would smoking on the Shabbat cause heads to turn?
   d. Cameras and tapes not to be used during the service.

G. Contact List – provide list of services offered by the congregation to B'nai Mitzvah families.

VI. Notes to Counselors

A. After your meeting with the families, it is important that you send your B'nai Mitzvah Counselor Report to the Religious School office to complete the student's file. These reports are of invaluable assistance to the Rabbis and the office for subsequent discussions with the families. If the family does not care to participate, send a report form anyway, stating under "Other comments" the reason they did not wish to meet, and the date of contact. This will ensure that there will be a record in the child's file that the family has been contacted.

B. If you find at your meeting that there are pressing problems in the family (such as divorce, ill health) that could affect the Bar/Bat Mitzvah, contact (Rabbi or the school office) immediately.

Bibliography

BOOKS AND CURRICULAR MATERIALS

Alper, Janice. *Learning Together: A Family Education Sourcebook*. Denver: A.R.E. Publishing, Inc., 1987.

Altschuler, Joanne, and Paulette Benson. *The Jewish Family: Past, Present, Future*. Denver: A.R.E. Publishing, Inc., 1979.

Amudei Tfillah Series (This series is based on a unit by Beatrice Minkove [z"l]. There are seven other titles not listed here.)

Blake, Toby, and Sarah M. Siegman. *Kiddush*. Baltimore: Board of Jewish Education, 1986.

______. *V'Ahavta*. Baltimore: Board of Jewish Education, 1985.

Beiner, Irvin, and Sarah M. Siegman. *Aleinu*. Baltimore: Board of Jewish Education, 1986.

Glaser, Rachel; Toby Blake; and Sarah M. Siegman. *Brachot HaHaftarah*. Baltimore: Board of Jewish Education, 1987.

Lasday, Jeffrey, and Sarah M. Siegman. *Shema*. Baltimore: Board of Jewish Education, 1986.

Beiner, Stan, *Bible Scenes*. Denver: A.R.E. Publishing, Inc., 1988.

_______. *Sedra Scenes*. Denver: A.R.E. Publishing, Inc., 1982.

Bennett, Alan, ed., *Journey through Judaism: The Best of Keeping Posted*. New York: UAHC Press, 1991.

Davis, Judith. "Mazel Tov: The Bar Mitzvah as a Multigenerational Ritual of Change and Continuity." In Evan Imber-Black; J. Roberts; and R.A. Whiting, eds., *Rituals in Families and Family Therapies*. New York: W.W. Norton, 1988.

Fields, Harvey. *Bechol Levavcha*. New York: Union of American Hebrew Congregations Press, 1975.

_______. *A Torah Commentary for Our Times*. New York: UAHC Press; Volume I, *Genesis*, 1990; Volume II, *Exodus and Leviticus*, 1991.

Gellis, Maurice, and Dennis Gribetz. *The Glory of Torah Reading*. Jersey City, NJ: M.P. Press, 1982.

Glatzer, Shoshana; with Ellen Singer; Susan Shulman-Tesel; Lifsa Schachter. *Coming of Age as a Jew — Bar/Bat Mitzvah*. New York: Board of Jewish Education, 1989.

Hirshberg, Naomi; Joan Kaye; and Naomi Towvim. *The Power To Lead*. Boston: Bureau of Jewish Education, 1986.

Hyman, Paula, and Steven M. Cohen, eds., *The Jewish Family: Myths and Reality*. New York: Holmes and Meier, 1986.

Kaplan, Louis. *An Outline and Interpretation of the Weekly Sidrot*. Baltimore: Board of Jewish Education, 1988.

Kaye, Joan S.; Jan Rabinowitch; and Naomi F. Towvim. *Why Be Good: Sensitivities and Ethics in Rabbinic Literature*. Boston: Bureau of Jewish Education, 1985.

Liebman, Charles. *The Ambivalent American Jew*. Philadelphia: Jewish Publication Society, 1973.

Loeb, Sorel Goldberg, and Barbara Binder Kadden. *Teaching Torah: Insights and Activities*. Denver: A.R.E. Publishing, Inc., 1984.

Marcus, Audrey Friedman, et al. *A Family Education Unit on Bar and Bat Mitzvah*. Denver: A.R.E. Publishing, Inc., 1977.

Neumann, Richard. *The Roots of Biblical Chants*. New York: Board of Jewish Education, 1982.

Neusner, Jacob. *Mitzvah*. Chappaqua, NY: Rossel Books, 1981.

Prager, Janice, and Arlene Lepoff. *Why Be Different?* West Orange, NJ: Behrman House, Inc., 1986.

Reich, Leo; Rachel Glaser; and Sarah Siegman. *Tree of Life Torah Curriculum*. Baltimore: Board of Jewish Education, 1989.

Rosenbaum, Samuel. *A Guide to Haftarah Chanting*. New York: Ktav Publishing House, Inc., 1973. (comes with tape)

Rosowsky, Salomon. *Cantillation of the Bible*. New York: Jewish Reconstructionist Foundation, 1957.

Salkin, Jeffrey K. *Putting God on the Guest List: How To Reclaim The Spiritual Meaning of Your Child's Bar or Bat Mitzvah*. Woodstock, VT: Jewish Lights Publishing, 1992.

Schauss, Hayyim, *The Jewish Festivals*. New York: Schocken Books, 1962.

Schoenfeld, Stuart. "Theoretical Approaches to the Study of Bar and Bat Mitzvah," Proceedings of the Ninth World Congress of Jewish Studies, Division D, volume II:119-128.

Siegel, Danny. *Gym Shoes and Irises*. Spring Valley, NY: Town House Press, 1987.

Singer, R. Aaron. "The Rabbi as an Educator of Youth." In Proceedings of the Rabbinical Assembly 29: 101-110, 1965.

Sklare, Marshall, and Joseph Greenblum. *Jewish Identity on the Suburban Frontier*. (2nd edition) Chicago: University of Chicago Press, 1979.

Spiro, Pinchas. *Haftarah Chanting*. New York: Board of Jewish Education, 1978. (comes with tape)

Strassfield, Michael. *The Jewish Holidays*. New York: Harper and Row, 1985.

VIDEOS WITH BAR/BAT MITZVAH THEMES

*** Highly recommended
** Recommended with reservations
* Not recommended

Most adults and children today relate more to film than either to lectures or written material. For that reason, a well made film shown at the appropriate time during a Family Education course is a welcome inclusion.

Any of the following films would be good discussion triggers for a Family Education program. They are also widely used in Religious Schools. Whatever the setting, the discussion leader should preview the film ahead of time and write out questions to ask the group before and after viewing the film.

The Mitzvah Machine (United Synagogue of America, 1988, 10 minutes)

This is probably the most popular video in this category and is the most often used in Family Education programs. The excellent and detailed Discussion Leader's Guide points out that this is a "trigger" film and that it does not delve into the complex topics introduced. Such follow-up is up to the discussion leader; supplementary materials are also recommended.

The film itself has a certain charm. It is animated, and the story is about a boy bored with his Bar Mitzvah preparation, who builds a robot to "perform" in his place. The basic message is that one *becomes* a Bar Mitzvah rather than *having* a Bar Mitzvah; and human beings, unlike robots, have free choice.

There is no subtlety in the way the message is presented. The successful use of this video depends largely on the discussion leader. The Guide suggests two sets of procedures for viewing the video, depending on the target group. A very long and thorough list of questions is also provided, along with a Bibliography.

A Secret Space (Board of Jewish Education of Greater New York, 1977, 80 minutes)

The length of this well acted film makes it somewhat impractical for use in a day-long Family Education program. The story is of a Jewish boy with no Jewish education who, by chance, finds a very "alternative" congregation (more nearly a Havurah) and gets interested in Judaism. He begins studying Hebrew and general Judaica with the Rabbi and the congregants, and begins attending services every week. His parents are totally secular, almost self-hating Jews. They are appalled at their son's new involvement and do not even want to attend his small Bar Mitzvah ceremony.

The weakness of this film, which may be too controversial to use in most settings, is that the whole milieu seems completely 1970s and thus is too dated to be useful today. The parents are almost caricatures of wealthy, self-centered, materialistic, and obnoxious Jews. Nonetheless, this film would certainly stimulate an interesting discussion. In its favor, it avoids preachiness or obvious messages.

The Journey (Board of Jewish Education of Greater New York, 1985, 34 minutes)

This is a very touching story of a young Russian boy and an American Jewish engineer who meet by chance during World War II in Leningrad. The boy's mother asks the American to share his knowledge of Judaism with her son as the man and boy embark on a train voyage together. Unfortunately, the man has had virtually no Jewish education and the boy, who has absorbed his Communist education, is a confirmed atheist with no interest in Judaism or any religion.

The relationship between Jewish education and Jewish identity is explored in this film and is sure to stimulate discussion of this issue. There is a moving surprise ending and a beautiful music soundtrack throughout.

The Discovery (The Jewish Theological Seminary, 1989, 60 minutes)

This video of a boy confused about his upcoming Bar Mitzvah is very popular because "Paul" (Josh Saviano) of television's "Wonder Years," is its star. It has a very slick, made-for-television appearance, including a cloying soundtrack. Some of the dialogue sounds extremely stilted; the Rabbi talks as if he is reading right from a textbook.

While this film might be a good discussion trigger on identity, it is hard to believe children of today would buy its message the way it is packaged here.

Birthday Boy (March 18, 1989 episode of Wonder Years, available from Board of Jewish Education of Greater New York, 25 minutes)

This episode deals with the Bar Mitzvah of Kevin's friend Paul, and Kevin's ambivalent reactions to the event.

On the school bus, Paul brags about his upcoming Bar Mitzvah, and how it will make him a man. Older boys insist "You're not a man till you lose your virginity." Paul's friends are not impressed when Paul says he will be standing up before a big crowd giving a speech and reading prayers. However, the party, the live band, the 100 presents, and the anticipated cash receive more interest. This reaction from peers will resonate for young people preparing to become B'nai Mitzvah today.

During dinner at Paul's house, Paul's grandfather regales the family with stories of his poverty-stricken childhood and the chicken he received as a Bar Mitzvah gift. The family members have heard this story a thousand times; they roll their eyes, but Kevin is enthralled. From his grandfather Paul receives the Siddur which his grandfather had given him. Paul, visibly moved, is a fine role model for Jewish students, and the scene could stimulate a discussion of generational differences in the ways to celebrate a Bar/Bat Mitzvah.

Later, Kevin attempts to find an identity of his own. When he asks his mother where his grandfather came from, she says only, "From Newark." Kevin then tries to bond with his non-verbal father by helping him work on the family car. Kevin feels that all he needs is recognition to tell him that he is growing up; if he could get that, who needs a rite of passage?

Kevin becomes so jealous of Paul's upcoming Bar Mitzvah (which is to take place on Kevin's own birthday) that he decides to boycott it. In the end, his friendship wins out and he shows up just in time for Paul's *aliyah.* Kevin enjoys the Bar Mitzvah and the party, and even feels "like it was my Bar Mitzvah, too." In some way, he also undergoes a rite of passage. Never preachy, the video lends itself to a discussion among students (and their families) on peer pressure, positive Jewish identity, and generation gap, as well as the broader issues of friendship and the need for self-identity.

The Outside Chance of Maximilian Glick (Southgate Entertainment, 1988, 95 min., available at many video stores)

In a small town north of Winnipeg in the 1960s, Max is preparing both for his upcoming Bar Mitzvah and for a piano competition. His piano teacher pairs him with Celia, a Polish Catholic girl. When Max becomes attached to Celia, his parents forbid him to see her.

When the town's Rabbi dies, a new Rabbi takes over — a Lubavicher, much to the embarrassment of the town's Jews, who prefer to keep a low profile. An interesting relationship develops between Max and the new Rabbi.

The main theme of the film is prejudice and stereotypes. Max rebels against his parents' small town prejudices. They claim, "Prejudice in Jews isn't negative; we are just preserving a heritage." He tells his family he will not go through with his Bar Mitzvah unless he can also play in the piano competition with Celia. They do not accept his ultimatum. Max gives up everything he loves until a twist in the plot makes him realize it is up to him to give his life meaning.

Max is an excellent role model, though perhaps so exceptional that some teenagers will have trouble relating to him. Urban youngsters may also have difficulty understanding the small town mentality of the Jews. The film is witty and insightful and offers an honest treatment of certain Jewish attitudes and values. It will stimulate discussion of crucial issues and would be a fine film to recommend to families who want to explore Jewish themes on their own.

Contributors

RABBI RON AIGEN was ordained by the Reconstructionist Rabbinical College. Since 1976, he has been the spiritual leader of Congregation Dorshei Emet, the Reconstructionist Synagogue of Montreal, where he continues to develop his Pre-Bar/Bat Mitzvah program. He is a graduate of SUNY Binghamton with a B.S. in psychology, and holds an M.A. in Community Psychology from Temple University. He is co-editor of *Community and the Individual Jew* (R.R.C. Press, 1986) and editor of *Hadesh Yameinu: A Siddur for Shabbat and Festivals* (1993).

RAN ANBAR has directed the Bar/Bat Mitzvah program with his wife at Germantown Jewish Centre in Philadelphia since 1990. He was born in Israel and moved to the United States with his family when he was nine years old. His full-time profession is as an academic pediatrician at Hahnemann University Hospital in Philadelphia.

HANNAH ANBAR directs the Bar/Bat Mitzvah program at Germantown Jewish Centre in Philadelphia with her husband. She grew up as a member of that congregation and, as a teenager, ran this same program. She is a full-time mother and has a Doctorate in Educational Psychology.

EMILY BANK holds a B.A. and M.A. in Elementary Education from the University of Michigan. She has many years of teaching experience both in secular and Jewish schools and has been the Director of the Ivriah, the Jewish Religious School of Flint, Michigan, since 1985. She has been teaching B'nai Mitzvah classes there since 1984.

CANTOR SHIRA BELFER is the Cantor of Congregation Beth Shalom in Mahopac, New York. The daughter of a pianist/music teacher, and of a Cantor who teaches *hazzanut* at the Theological Seminary and at the Hebrew Union College-Jewish Institute of Religion in New York, Cantor Belfer earned Bachelor degrees in Music Performance and Music Education at Syracuse University. She has been teaching B'nai Mitzvah students since the age of fifteen. She is a graduate of the School of Sacred Music of HUC-JIR.

DR. SHERRY H. BLUMBERG, Assistant Professor of Jewish Education at Hebrew Union College-Jewish Institute of Religion in New York, has a doctorate from the Rhea Hirsch School of HUC-JIR in Los Angeles. She has been a teacher in several congregations and was Director of Education at B'nai Israel in Sacramento and Temple Israel in Long Beach, California. Her publications include: *God the Eternal Challenge* and *Death, Burial & Mourning in the Jewish Tradition* (A.R.E.), the Teacher's Guide for *Rooftop Secrets* for UAHC Press, and a number of articles in books and journals.

ROBIN EISENBERG received her B.S. degree in Education and a Masters Ed. in Counseling. She has been Director of Education at Temple Beth El in Boca Raton, Florida since 1980. A recent President of the National Association of Temple Educators (NATE), she earned the title of Reform Jewish Educator (R.J.E.) through that organization. She has written numerous articles for *Compass, Pedagogic Reporter, NATE News,* and other publications.

BARBARA ELISH received her Master's degree in Religious Education from Hebrew Union College-Jewish Institute of Religion in New York in 1989. She was a Religious School teacher for nine years, a resource room director, family educator, and private B'nai Mitzvah tutor at Central Sunagogue of Nassau County in Rockville Centre, New York. She is currently the Director of Education at the Jewish Community Center of White Plains in White Plains, New York, where she oversees the B'nai Mitzvah preparation program. She has written articles for *Pedagogic Reporter, Jewish Education,* and CAJE *Bikurim.*

CANTOR MARSHA FENSIN is Cantor of Congregation B'nai Emunah, Tulsa, Oklahoma. She was Music Director of Congregation Sinai, Milwaukee, Wisconsin for eight years. She has been involved in Jewish music and education for over 20 years, and has worked with B'nai Mitzvah students, both tutoring and developing courses. She belongs to the Women Cantors' Network, the Wisconsin Jewish Music Council, Chicago Cantors' Association, and the American Conference of Cantors.

SHOSHANA GLATZER is founder and Director of the Teachers Center of the Board of Jewish Education of Greater New York. She holds a B.A. in Bible and an M.A. in Jewish Education from the Jewish Theological Seminary, and is currently pursuing her doctoral studies in curriculum and teaching. The author of *Coming of Age as a Jew — Bar/Bat Mitzvah* and many teacher guides and student workbooks, she is well known as a leader of teacher training workshops and for her work in curriculum development.

ELLEN GOLDENBERG majored in voice and piano at Ithaca College and earned a Bachelor of Science degree in Music Education. She taught music in public school for several years before she began teaching fifth grade Hebrew School at a Reform congregation and then began tutoring B'nai Mitzvah students. She is currently one of three tutors working for Temple Sinai, a mid-size Reform congregation in Rochester, New York. In addition, she is the Head Teacher of the Temple Beth El Nursery School and serves as Chairperson of the Midrasha High School for Judaic Studies in Rochester.

ROBERTA LOUIS GOODMAN received her Masters in Jewish Education from Hebrew Union College in 1981. She has planned and implemented many Bar/Bat Mitzvah and Family Education programs in congregations throughout North America. She specializes in Faith Development and Adult Education. A Field Researcher for the Council for Initiatives in Jewish Education, she is coauthor of *Head Start on Holidays: Jewish Programs for Preschoolers and Parents* (A.R.E.).

RISA GRUBERGER received her Master of Arts in Education from the University of Judaism. Assistant Director of Education at Shir Chadash in Woodland Hills, California, she was an Instructor at the University of Judaism Summer Institute in 1992, leading a 30-hour intensive seminar called "The Wonder Year: Successful Bar and Bat Mitzvah Programming."

ZEV HALPERN, after completing a Yeshiva education, received his B.A. and Masters of Education in Human Development and Counseling from the University of Maryland's Institute for Child Study. He has been actively involved in Bar/Bat Mitzvah education, specifically with special needs children, since 1975. He is licensed as a Certified Clinical Mental Heath Counselor, Certified Employee Assistance Professional, Certified Addiction Specialist, and Board Certified Professional Counselor. He is the founder and president of OPT Associates, Inc., an employee assistance/managed behavioral health care firm located in Rockville, Maryland.

LINDA HIRSCHHORN attended the Yeshiva Rabbi Moses Soloveichik in New York for her elementary school education. She spent years in the Habonim youth movement and lived in Israel for two years. Linda is currently the Bar/Bat Mitzvah teacher at Temple Beth Sholom in San Leandro, California, as well as their Cantorial soloist. She frequently serves as "guest Cantor" at other congregations around the country. Linda has produced four albums of original music and a songbook of rounds, *Gather Round: Songs of Celebration and Renewal* (Tara Publications).

CAROL K. INGALL has been involved in Jewish education since the 1960s, as a teacher and administrator. She is a consultant for the Melton Research Center, the Council for Initiatives in Jewish Education, and the Education Department of the United Synagogue of Conservative Judaism. She is teaching at the School of Education at Boston University where she is a doctoral candidate in moral education.

RABBI BURT JACOBSON was ordained by the Jewish Theological Seminary in 1966. He helped found the Jewish Renewal Movement, "Havurat Shalom," in Boston in 1968. He wrote *Teaching the Traditional Liturgy* for the Melton Institute, and contributed to *The First Jewish Catalog*. He is coeditor of a new *Siddur* to be published by P'nai Or Religious Fellowship for the Jewish Renewal Movement. He is the founding Rabbi of Kehilla Community Synagogue in Berkeley, California and has been involved in B'nai Mitzvah education since the mid-1970s.

BENJAMIN LEVY formed Lev Software soon after meeting his wife, Shira, in Israel in 1988. He was born in New York and raised in Israel. Along with a music degree, he has a degree in computers.

SHIRA LEVY is a partner in Lev Software with her husband, Benjamin. She was born in Israel and raised in New York. In addition to her degree in music, she has a degree in communications.

RABBI DAVID S. LIEB received a degree in Philosophy from the University of Illinois, and was ordained at Hebrew Union College-Jewish Institute of Religion in Cincinnati in 1969. He has been the spiritual leader of Temple Beth El and Center in San Pedro, California since 1971. He is the author of several published articles. Within his congregation, he has devoted special attention to new Family Education programs and adult Jewish studies.

BARRY LUTZ has served as Director of Education at Temple Ahavat Shalom in Northridge, California since 1984. He is a graduate of the Rhea Hirsch School of Education at HUC-JIR in Los Angeles, where he currently serves as a clinical faculty member. He is a board member of NATE and was assistant chair of the CAJE Conference held at the University of Southern California in 1992. He is very active in Family Education.

MARLENE MYERSON is the Director of Education at Temple Emanu-El in Willowdale, Ontario, Canada. She holds a Bachelors Degree in Jewish Studies and a Masters in Education from the University of Toronto, as well as the title of Reform Jewish Educator. She is on the Board of Directors of NATE and is actively involved in the Toronto Reform Educators' Council and the Canadian Council for Reform Judaism.

CANTOR DR. NEIL NEWMAN, Cantor at Beth El Synagogue in St. Louis Park since 1980, is a graduate of Temple University, Gratz College, and HUC-JIR in New York, where he received his Bachelor of Sacred Music and M.R.E. He concluded a Doctorate in Educational Administration and Supervision at Syracuse University in 1979. A member of the Cantors Assembly as well as the American Conference of Cantors, he has performed with the Syracuse Symphony Orchestra and Vocal Ensemble and the Minnesota Center Chorale in St. Joseph, Minnesota. In 1990, Dr. Newman completed a text for learning the skill of reading Torah, *Ta'amei Hamikrah/Torah Reading*.

SAUL ORESKY has a B.S. degree in Journalism from the University of Maryland. He served as *Hazzan* and *Ba'al Koreh* at Hillel while a student there. He has been training B'nai Mitzvah students for almost two decades, working for several different congregations throughout the greater Washington D.C. area. He currently chairs the Religious Committee at Mishkan Torah in Greenbelt, Maryland.

CANTOR MARSHALL A. PORTNOY has served Congregation Adath Jeshurun in Louisville, Kentucky since 1971. This congregation has received the Solomon Schechter Award in Music on nine occasions. He is the author of two books on Jewish music and dozens of articles on Jewish and secular topics. He graduated from Yale University, and holds the degree of *Hazzan* from the Cantors Institute of the Jewish Theological Seminary. He is a member of both the Cantors Assembly and the American Conference of Cantors.

SUSAN PROTTER is the administrator, lead teacher, and curriculum designer for Temple Beth Jacob's Jewish High School in Redwood City, California. She has a degree in sociology and is a credentialed teacher. Having worked with teens and college age students for many years, she is also the founder and director of G.A.L.I.T. (Guidance and Leadership in Training), a Jewish community leadership program for eighth and ninth graders in Palo Alto, California. In addition, she conducts workshops on teens and Jewish education for the Bureau of Jewish Education in San Francisco and other Bay Area agencies.

CANTOR JANICE ROGER has served as Cantor of the Indianapolis Hebrew Congregation since she completed her studies at the School of Sacred Music of Hebrew Union College-Jewish Institute of Religion in New York in 1979. She graduated from the High School of Jewish Studies in Chicago and also studied at the Spertus College of Judaica. In addition to her Cantorial duties, she is a Vice President of the American Conference of Cantors, has performed and presented workshops at CAJE conferences, and is a reviewer of books and recordings for the *National Jewish Post and Opinion.*

DR. IAN RUSS is the Saul E. White Visiting Professor in the Department of Psychology at the University of Judaism in Los Angeles. He is also a member of the faculty of the National College of Juvenile and Family Law, where he lectures judges and prosecutors on issues of child development and psychology as they affect child testimony, and on the social and psychological effects of child abuse. He completed his baccalaureate in Hebrew Language at UCLA and holds a Masters in Human Development from Pacific Oaks College in Pasadena, California. He received his doctorate in Social-Clinical Psychology from the Wright Institute in Los Angeles. He is licensed as a Family and Child Therapist.

RABBI JEFFREY K. SALKIN is the Rabbi of Central Synagogue of Nassau County, Rockville Centre, New York. A prolific author of scholarly and popular articles, he holds a Doctor of Ministry degree from Princeton Theological Seminary, where he wrote his dissertation on the problems of Bar and Bat Mitzvah in American Judaism. He is the author of *Putting God on the Guest List: How To Re-claim the Spiritual Meaning of Your Child's Bar or Bat Mitzvah* (Jewish Lights Publishing).

RABBI SANDY EISENBERG SASSO was the first woman ordained from the Reconstructionist Rabbinical College, in 1974. She and her husband, Dennis, are the first practicing Rabbinical couple in world Jewish history. They are Rabbis together of Congregation Beth-El Zedeck in Indianapolis. She received her B.A. Magna Cum Laude and her M.A. from Temple University. She is a Past President of the Reconstructionist Rabbinical Association. She has lectured nationally and internationally, and is the author of various articles on women and religion, as well as a children's book, *God's Paintbrush* (Jewish Lights Publishing).

DR. JEFFREY SCHEIN received his Rabbinic ordination from the Reconstructionist Rabbinical College and his doctoral degree in education from Temple University. He is currently Associate Professor of Jewish Education at the Cleveland College of Jewish Studies, as well as Education Consultant and Director of Special Projects for the Reconstructionist movement. His writings include *Creative Jewish Education* and *Tithadesh: Initiating Renewal and Reflection in Jewish Education*, both published by the Reconstructionist Press. He also serves as the national chair of the CAJE moral education network.

PROFESSOR STUART SCHOENFELD is on the faculty of the Department of Sociology, Glendon College, York University in Toronto. He is an active member of the Research Network in Jewish Education. He has published widely on the sociology and social psychology of Bar/Bat Mitzvah and on a variety of other topics in contemporary Jewish life.

NATHANIEL SCHUDRICH is "*Hazzan Sheni*" (Assistant Cantor), *Ba'al Koreh*, and Ritual Director at B'nai Israel in Rockville, Maryland. He has been a professional Torah reader and tutor since 1977 and has also taught Judaic subjects at several Talmud Torahs and Jewish Day Schools.

SALLY SHAFTON is a Para-Rabbinic at Valley Beth Shalom Synagogue in Encino, California. A perennial student in Hebrew and Jewish studies at the University of Judaism, she is a member of the Council of Jewish Life of the Jewish Federation Council of Los Angeles.

RABBI PAUL SIDLOFSKY was ordained at Leo Baeck College in London, England. During his years of training there, he served in several congregations in England and Canada. He went on to receive his Masters in Jewish Education from the Rhea Hirsch School of HUC-JIR in Los Angeles. A recent recipient of the title R.J.E., he served as Assistant Rabbi/Director of Education at Temple Emanu-El in Marblehead, Massachusetts and presently holds this title at Temple Shalom in Chevy Chase, Maryland.

DR. SHOSHANA SILBERMAN is the author of *A Family Haggadah, The Whole Megillah (Almost!)* (Kar-Ben Copies, Inc.) and *Tiku Shofar*, a Mahzor for students and families (United Synagogue Commission on Jewish Education). Presently, she is the Educational Director of the Jewish Center of Princeton, New Jersey. She has been involved in Jewish education as a teacher, principal, workshop leader, and curriculum writer. She received a B.S. from Columbia University and a B.H.L. from Gratz College. She also holds an M.S.T. from the University of Chicago and an Ed.D. from Temple University.

SARA RUBINOW SIMON earned a B.A. in Zoology from Barnard College, an M.A. in Education from American University, and an M.A. in Special Education from Fordham University. She is a doctoral candidate in Education Administration at American University. A specialist in Jewish special education, she was the founding Chairperson of the CAJE Task Force on Special Needs. She currently serves as Director of the Special Needs Department at the Board of Jewish Education of Greater Washington. She was the recipient of the 1991 Covenant Foundation Award.

JENNIFER SOLLE received a B.A. in Elementary Education and an M.A. in Special Education from University of St. Thomas. For her thesis, she created a curriculum for teaching Hebrew to special needs students. She is currently employed by the Learning Disabilities Association in Minneapolis as a teacher/evaluator, and hopes to teach in a Jewish Day School full time working with special needs students. She started a pilot program, at a Reform congregation, aimed at special needs students who have been turned down or expelled from other Hebrew School programs.

RABBI GEORGE STERN has been Rabbi of Temple Beth Torah in Upper Nyack, New York since 1972. He was ordained at HUC-JIR in New York in 1974, with a specialization in History. He graduated Phi Beta Kappa from Princeton University in 1969. He serves on the Commission on Synagogue Music of the Reform movement and has just completed a term as Chair of the Family Life Committee of the Central Conference of American Rabbis. He also serves as Adjunct Professor and Campus Rabbi at St. Thomas Aquinas College in Sparkhill, New York.

CRAIG TAUBMAN is a song writer whose career has run the gamut from pop, rock, religious, and commercials to children's musicals. He is the founding director of "Yad B'Yad," a teen performing arts program based in Los Angeles. The talented group of 30 children perform under his artistic direction. Craig was recently signed by Disney Records.

RABBI ALLAN COOPERMAN TUFFS has been spiritual leader of Temple Shalom in Levittown, Pennsylvania since 1989. He was born in British Columbia and was ordained by the Hebrew Union College-Jewish Institute of Religion. He served congregations in Wisconsin and Florida before his present position. He is currently a graduate fellow at the Graduate Theological Foundation.

JULIE VANEK is the Temple Educator at Temple Shalom of Newton in Newton, Massachusetts. She has a Masters in Jewish Education and Jewish Communal Service from Hebrew Union College-Jewish Institute of Religion. She has also earned the R.J.E. title. She served as President of the Boston Area Reform Temple Educators and is currently a board member of NATE. She received the Emanuel Gamoran Curriculum Award from NATE in 1989.

SAUL P. WACHS is Rosaline B. Feinstein Professor of Education and Chairperson of the Education Department of Gratz College. He is the author of numerous publications in the area of Jewish education and liturgy. Since 1972, Dr. Wachs has conducted High Holy Day services at Kehillath Israel Congregation of Brookline, Massachusetts. He has recorded cassettes of synagogue chant, as well as a cassette of prayers for children with special learning needs. Dr. Wachs has taught prayer to children and adults on five continents.

RABBI PHILIP WARMFLASH is Director of the Youth Department of the Jewish Federation Council in Los Angeles. He is also an instructor on the Continuing Education faculty of the University of Judaism. Prior to his arrival at the Federation, he was the Principal of the Los Angeles Hebrew High School. He has written several textbooks. He received his B.A. in Near Eastern and Judaic Studies from Brandeis University, his Masters and Rabbinic ordination from the Jewish Theological Seminary.

SALLY WEBER, LCSW, is a Regional Director of Adult and Children's Services of Jewish Family Service of Los Angeles. A licensed clinical social worker, she is a faculty member of the Hebrew Union College School of Jewish Communal Service and of the Whizin Institute of the University of Judaism. In addition, she serves as a faculty member for the Rabbinic Retreat program of the Jewish Theological Seminary and as a program consultant for other communal and educational organizations.

LOIS J. ZACHARY, Ed.D., is an educator with a private consultant practice specializing in adult development and learning. The focus of her work is the application of adult development and learning theory to a variety of related practice areas and settings, both formal and informal. Her publications include a long list of articles, monographs, and books on leadership development, adult development and learning, and adult Jewish education.